ALAN MOORE:

PORTRAIT OF AN EXTRAORDINARY GENTLEMAN

Alan Moore: Portrait of an Extraordinary Gentleman

First published in the UK by
abiogenesis press
P O Box 2065, LEIGH-ON-SEA, SS9 2WH, England
fax +44 (0)1702 475480
e-mail: gary@millidge.com
web site: www.millidge.com

American agent:
Top Shelf Productions, PO Box 1282, Marietta, GA 30061-1282, USA
fax: +1 770 427-6395
e-mail: staros@bellsouth.net
web site: www.topshelfcomix.com

The Italian language edition of this book is published by
Black Velvet Editrice, Via A. del Verrocchio 4, 40138 Bologna, Italy
e-mail: o.martini@libero.it

100% of all publisher's net profits and all creators' royalties from proceeds of this book are to be donated to the following charities in aid of Alzheimer's disease.

Alzheimer's Disease International
45/46 Lower Marsh, London SE1 7RG
fax: +44 (0)20 7401 7351
e-mail: e.rimmer@alz.co.uk
web site: www.alz.co.uk

AIMA - The Italian Association for Alzheimer's Disease
Ripa di Porta Ticinese, 21
20143 Milano, Italy
tel.: +39 02 89406254
toll free number: +39 800 371332
fax: +39 02 89404192
e-mail: segreterianazionale@alzheimer-aima.it, aimanaz@tin.it
web site: www.alzheimer-aima.it

Printed in Canada
by Quebecor Printing
8000 Blaise-Pascal Avenue, Montreal, Quebec, H1E 2S7, Canada

First printing MAY 2003
ISBN: 0 946790 06 X

ALAN MOORE:
PORTRAIT OF AN EXTRAORDINARY GENTLEMAN

Edited by **smoky man** and **Gary Spencer Millidge**

with assistance from **Omar Martini**

Conceived by **smoky man**
Book design and production by **Gary Spencer Millidge**
Cover photograph by **Piet Corr**
Introduction by **Terry Gilliam**

abio**genesis** press

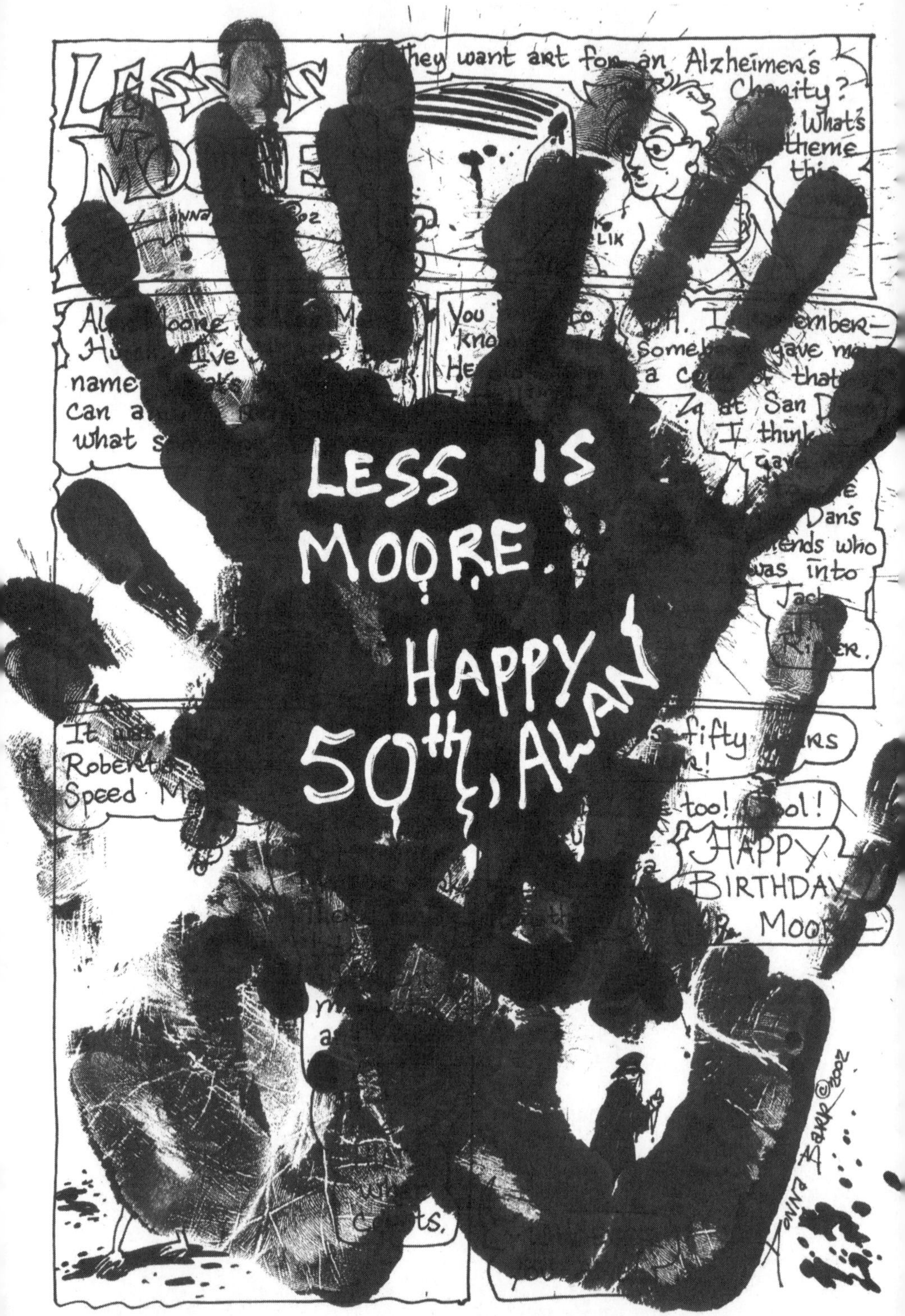
LESS IS MOORE.
HAPPY 50th, ALAN
They want art for an Alzheimer's Charity?
HAPPY BIRTHDAY
Donna Barr ©2002

PREFACE TO THE ENGLISH LANGUAGE EDITION

GARY SPENCER MILLIDGE

Born in London, Millidge is writer and illustrator of his self-published **Strangehaven** *comic book series, and also dabbles in music from time to time. He was once in a band called 'The' Watchmen.*

Text © 2003 Gary Spencer Millidge.

When smoky man approached me for an interview at the Bristol Comics Festival in 2002, I had no suspicion that our initial meeting would lead to this book that you now hold in your hands just a year or so later.

After giving smoky an interview for his web site Ultrazine over the following months, and collaborating with him on a translated excerpt from my Strangehaven comic book series (also for Ultrazine), he approached me for a contribution for his Alan Moore tribute section of the web site.

Of course I agreed – Alan being someone whose work I have always very much admired - but with my usual proviso, "as soon as I get the time." Without missing a beat, smoky asked me if I would be prepared to allow publication of my piece in a printed version of the web site contents as a 50th birthday celebration for Mr. Moore.

Well, yes, as a matter of fact, I replied, I was intending to write and illustrate a short comic strip biography of Alan Moore as part of a series of comic biographies I was planning for some time in the future. Could that be of use?

Smoky expressed his enthusiasm for my idea and, soon afterwards, asked me to contribute the cover for the book (an idea which later fell by the wayside); and then, he offered me the opportunity to publish an English-language edition of the project. Hmmm, come to think of it, I said, I could probably enlist the aid of a few other pals and acquaintances that may contribute some other interesting things.

Before I knew it, I was co-publishing and co-editing this mammoth tribute to probably the most well-respected and influential writer in the history of comics.

The project blossomed almost overnight from my vague notion of a 32-page pamphlet to this 352-page monster book you hold before you. Perhaps I underestimated the pulling power that the name Alan Moore holds amongst his peers; or rather, I underestimated the ability that myself and my two collaborators, smoky man and Omar Martini possessed of attracting such a diversity and quantity of high-quality contributions to the book.

Therefore I don't claim to be the most appropriate person to be either publishing this book or writing a biography of the great man - I have found myself in this position by circumstance – but I hope that it stands as a worthy effort nonetheless.

Alan is a private man, who does not often venture beyond his hometown of Northampton. Surprisingly little is know about him, considering his stature within the Industry.

We have endeavoured to go beyond the myth and shed a little light on Alan and his works, by building a composite portrait made up from the many varied contributions kindly donated here - from his closest collaborators and friends to top professionals across the world, some who have never met him, but who have been influenced by his life's work.

I have been fortunate enough to meet Alan several times, the first time way back in the early '80s at the legendary Westminster comic marts and more recently at his home in Northampton. On every occasion he's been the most friendly, charming and unpretentious man you could imagine, not bad for someone just this side of godhood.

During the production of the book, the news broke that Alan had announced his decision to retire – or at least, retire from mainstream comics work – at the age of 50. We hope that this book serves as a fitting tribute to the genius that is Alan Moore.

• Gary Spencer Millidge
Leigh-on-Sea, April 2003

DONNA BARR

Left: *Barr is the award-winning author of* **The Desert Peach** *and* **Stinz***, drawing since 1954, writing since 1963, published since 1986, publishing since 1996. www.stinz.com. Illustration ©2003 Donna Barr.*

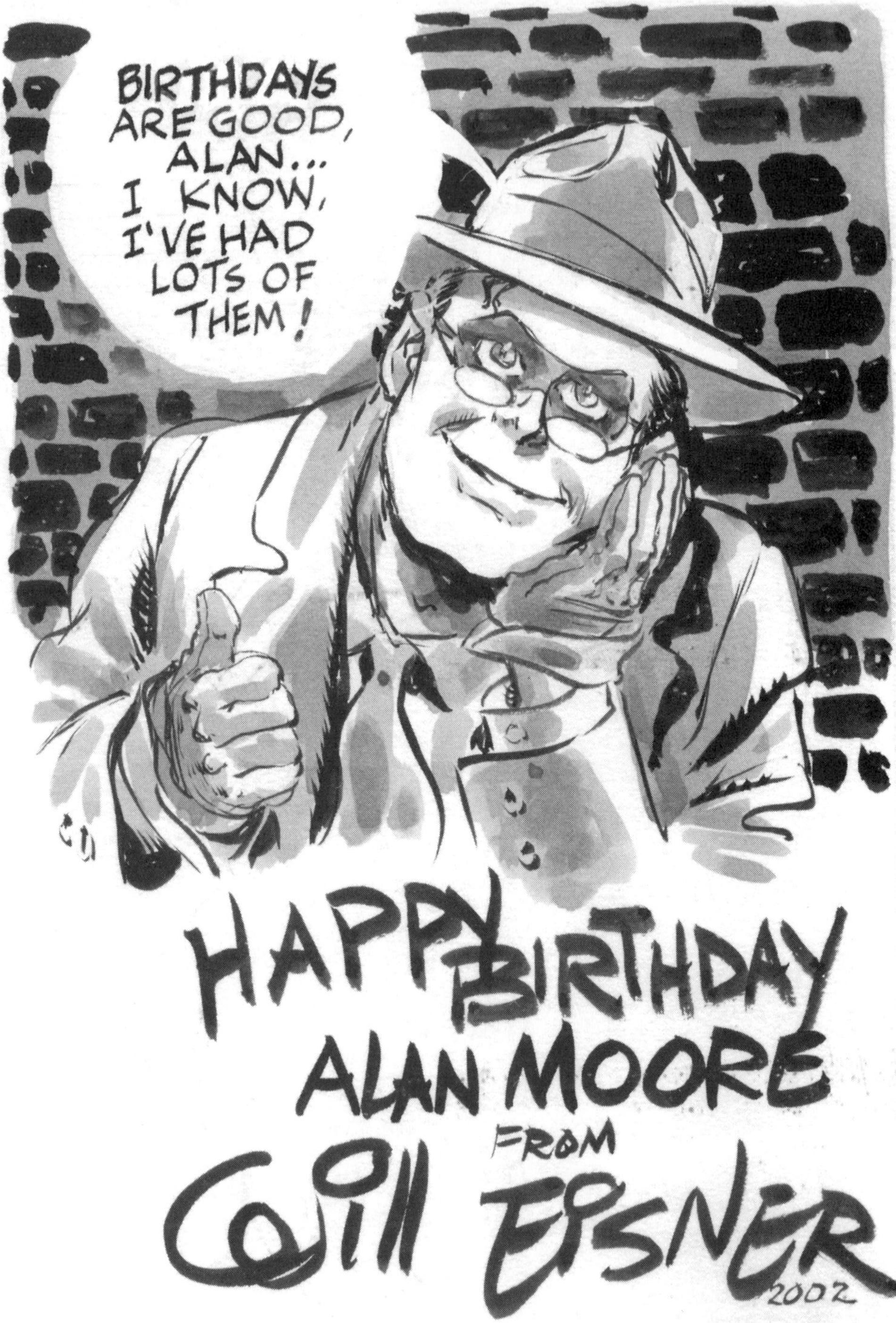
BIRTHDAYS ARE GOOD, ALAN... I KNOW, I'VE HAD LOTS OF THEM!
HAPPY BIRTHDAY ALAN MOORE FROM Will Eisner
2002

EDITOR'S FOREWORD

SMOKY MAN

smoky man is the creator of **Ultrazine.org,** *the popular Italian non-profit comics webmagazine with a special section devoted to Alan Moore. In 2002 he co-edited the expanded Italian edition of the* **Pocket Essential: Alan Moore** *book published by Black Velvet Editrice and contributed to the book* **Carta Canta**.

This book endeavours to be a devoted and well-deserved homage to the genius of Alan Moore, one of the greatest writers and most important figures in comics history.
A gift - an appreciated one, we hope - for the 50th birthday of this extraordinary gentleman who gave us all those masterpieces which we know well during his long career. And we are sure we'll see many more from him in the future.

This book which is a choral, blaring, polyphonic "Happy Birthday" composed of anecdotes, short essays, illustrations, comics and much more, contributed by creators from all over the world. They sketch a multi-faceted portrait both human and professional of the Man from Northampton.

I would like to think to this volume as a small fragment of memory relating to the history of contemporary comics. So I find a particular resonance to the charity mission of this project in aid to fight against Alzheimer's, the terrible disease that erases memories.

Memory is important, even within the small world of comics.

As the book's editor, an honour beyond my own merits, my first acknowledgement, together with a resonant and huge "Happy Birthday", goes to Alan Moore, of course. Without him none of the things you are going to read would have been possible.
Special thanks to my friends and publishers Gary Millidge and Omar Martini and to all the authors and collaborators who have enthusiastically contributed, making this book a reality.

Good reading.

• **smoky man**
Ultrazine.org

WILL EISNER

Left:*After revolutionising sequential art with his creation of* **The Spirit** *in the 1940s, Eisner went on to invent the graphic novel and become one of the most influential comics creators in history. He is still creating new work today. www.willeisner.com*

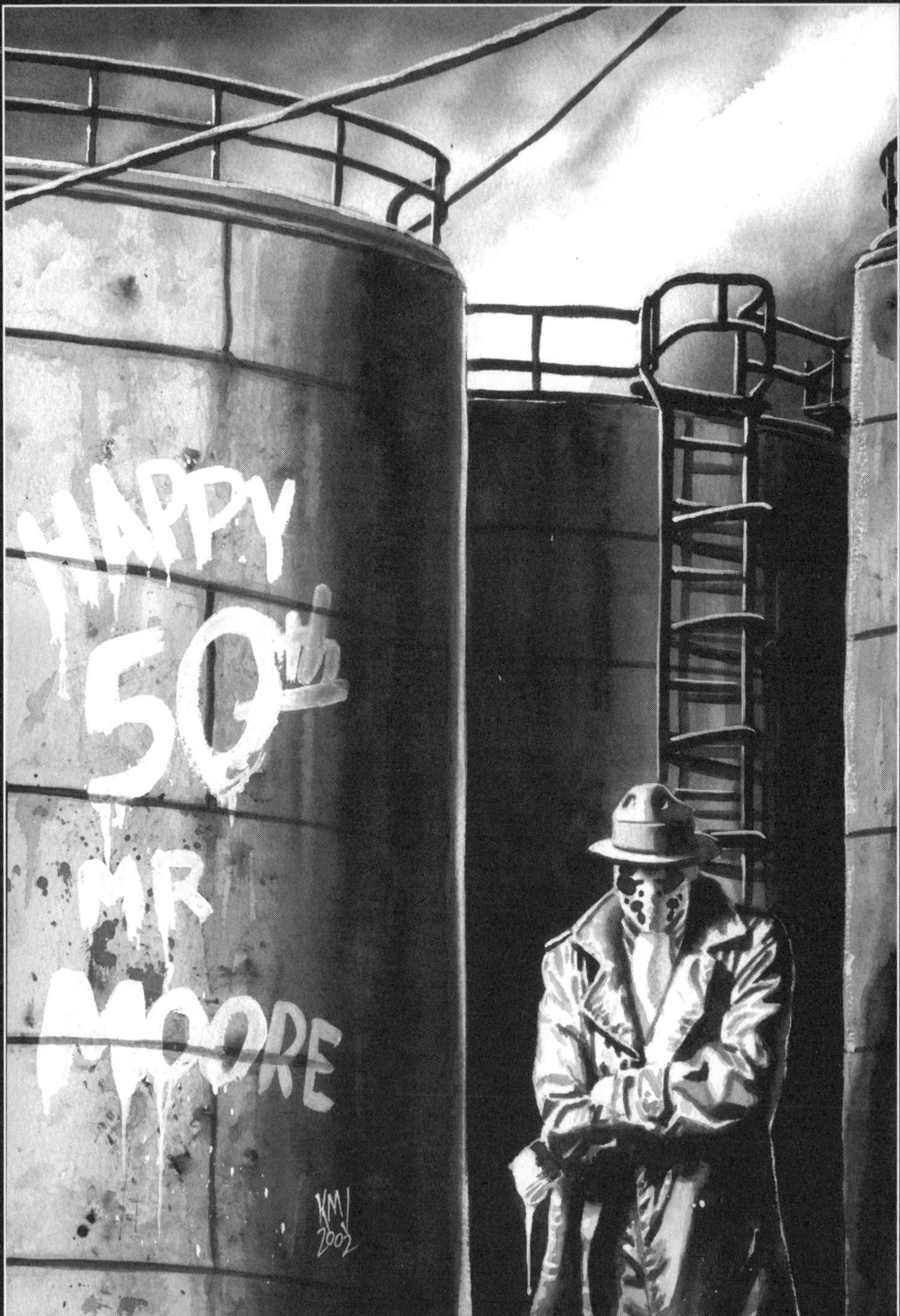
HAPPY
50th
MR
MOORE
KM
2002

INTRODUCTION

TERRY GILLIAM

Terry Gilliam is the internationally acclaimed film director of Brazil, 12 Monkeys and The Fisher King and is famously a former member of Monty Python's Flying Circus.
Text ©2003 Terry Gilliam .

God I am so tired of people asking me what is happening with the film version of Watchmen, "When are you going to do it?" "Have you got the money?" "Who's going to play Rorschach?" "We've read that you've written a new script."

No. I don't have the money, No, I haven't written a new script. No, I'm not going to do the film. Ever. Now go away and leave me alone!!!

This nightmare began back in 1988 or 89 when Joel Silver, the producer of Die Hard, Lethal Weapon, The Matrix, suggested that we make a film of the Watchmen. "The what?" I said. He thrust a fat hardback comic book in my hand and said read. I read. I loved.

But, how to make a film of a masterpiece? Always a problem. So far, no one has made a good version of War and Peace, and to me Watchmen is the W and P of comics...sorry, graphic novels.

I sat down with Charles McKeown, my writing partner on Baron Munchausen and Brazil, to squeeze out a script. Time passed. Frustration increased. How do you condense this monster book into a 2 - 2½ hour film? What goes? What stays? Therein lies the problem. I talked to Alan Moore. He didn't know how to do it. He seemed relieved that I had taken on the responsibility of fucking up his work rather than leaving it to him. I suggested perhaps a 5 part mini series would be better. I still believe that.

With every bit of narrative tightening, we were losing character detail...and without their neuroses and complex relationships the characters were becoming more like normal run-of-the-mill-quirky-super-heroes. There wasn't time to tell all their stories. The Comedian was reduced to someone who dies at the beginning. That's all, just a convenient corpse to kick off the action. None of this was satisfying to me. I wasn't happy with our results.

By now, actors were fluttering around Watchmen like crazed moths beating at a dirty street lamp. Robin Williams was keen to play Rorschach. Was that Richard Gere knocking on the door? The pressure on me was building. Thank god, Joel solved the problem. He failed to convince the studios to hand over enough money to make the film. Brilliant! I was saved! And, perhaps, Watchmen as well!

Certain works should be left alone...in their original form. Everything does not have to become a movie. Hitchhikers Guide to the Galaxy was always best in it's original manifestation... a radio show.

So, forget about the movie. Let your imagination animate the characters. Do your own sound effects. Your own camera moves. Dave Gibbons' artwork is perfect. From my first reading of Watchmen, it felt like a movie. Why does it have to **be** a movie?

Think of what will have to be lost. Is it worth it?

• **Terry Gilliam**

p.s. Happy 50th Birthday, Alan

KEN MEYER, JR.

Left: *Ken Meyer Jr. has been working in comics, games, and as a designer and illustrator (traditional and digital) for close to 20 years. See his work at www.kenmeyerjr.com.*
Illustration ©2003 Ken Meyer Jr.
Rorschach ©2003 DC Comics.

ACKNOWLEDGMENTS

The editors would like to thank for their kind assistance:
Elizabeth Rimmer at the ADI
Raimondo Mandis at AIMA

For our ingenious title:
Dave Whitwell

For assisting with vital contact information:
Greg McElhatton, Chris Staros, Joel Meadows, Dez Skinn at Comics International, Dave Whitwell, Bryan Talbot, Steve Lawton, Diana Schutz, Eric Reynolds, Jose Villarrubia, Jackie Estrada, Alan Barnes and Dominic Preston at 2000AD/Rebellion, Paul Gravett, Heidi MacDonald, Jean-Marc Lofficier, Guy Delcourt, Thierry Mornet, Ian Pyle, Peter Doherty, Simon Powell, Stephen Camper, Melinda Gebbie, Steve Leialoha, Tito Faraci, Davide Barzi, Alberto Ponticelli, Fabrizio Lo Bianco, Marco Rizzo and many more forgotten.

For being generally fine chaps:
Doug TenNapel and Jay Eales

For their kind permission to reprint their rare materials:
Dave Sim, Ken Meyer, Jr. Dame Darcy and Michael T. Gilbert.

For production assistance:
Brett Warnock, Gerhard and Jackie Estrada

For the original creators' website resource:
Roberto Ledda

For translation duties:
Paolo Livorati, Marco Abate, Tiziana Chiriaco, Michele Fioraso and Alessio Ligas.

For their vigorous promotion and donation of advertising space:
Filip Sablik and all at Diamond Distributors and Previews

For her kind assistance and inexhaustible patience:
Anouk Hurbutt at Quebecor Printing

For the promotional efforts of the online community:
www.ultrazine.org, www.comicon.com/pulse, www.borderlinemagazine.co.uk, www.popimage.com, www.rorschachonline.it, www.comicbookresources.com, www.ubcfumetti.com, www.digitalwebbing.com, www.newsarama.com, www.comicus.it, www.artbomb.net, www.fumetti.org and www.alanmoorefansite.com.

And of course:

All contributors to this book, who have kindly donated their work and time free of charge.

And finally, Alan Moore, for his kind permission and assistance, without whom this book would not have been possible.

smoky man dedicates this book to his mother. A very special thanks to Elide for her patience and love.

Gary would like to dedicate this book to his girlfriend Mandy who hasn't seen much of him these last three months.

— **smoky man, Gary Spencer Millidge & Omar Martini**

GARY SPENCER MILLIDGE
Pages 11-22 following:
Millidge is writer and illustrator of his self-published **Strangehaven** comic book series and wishes to apologise to all the journalists, artists, copyright holders and photographers whose work he has plundered for the following biography of the great man. Strip © 2003 Gary Spencer Millidge.

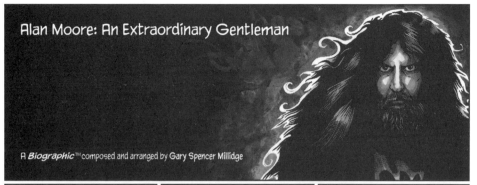

Alan Moore: An Extraordinary Gentleman
A Biographic™ composed and arranged by Gary Spencer Millidge
Northampton.
The centre of England geographically, culturally, economically and politically.
NORTHAMPTON
Birthplace of perhaps one of the most singularly creative minds of our generation and certainly the greatest comics writer of the modern age.
18 November 1953.
ART: RICK VEITCH
Alan Moore was born to Ernest and Sylvia at St. Edmunds Hospital, a converted workhouse.
He was born with no useful sight in his left eye and no hearing in his right ear.
At least I'm balanced.
Even so, he craftily managed to avoid wearing glasses until he was fifteen years old.
ART: KEVIN NOWLAN
The family home was a three bedroom, Victorian mid-terraced council house with no indoor toilet and a tin bath filled with hot water boiled from a "copper".
You'd think it was Henry VIII's time.
Even the street he grew up in was partly lit by gas.
ART: STEVE PARKHOUSE/KEVIN NOWLAN
ART: OSCAR ZARATE
Alan's eccentric, superstitious and highly religious grandmother watched over him and his younger brother, Mike, as his parents went out to earn the daily crust.
Ernest was a labourer for the local brewery and later dug holes for the electricity board until he retired. Sylvia worked at a local printers.
Young Alan was pretty much left to his own devices and began to map out his own universe.
He amused himself by reading children's versions of Greek and Norse legends, Robin Hood and Hiawatha, the more fantastical the better.
No. 440–JULY 8th,
THE TOPP
MICKEY THE MONKEY
He also read British humour comics like Topper and Beezer and liked to copy the pictures onto cheap paper.
But it was at the age of seven that he discovered some American comics on a market stall.
Detective COMICS
ACTION COMICS
It was 1961 and Moore found himself on the ground floor of the silver age of American comics.

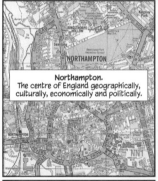

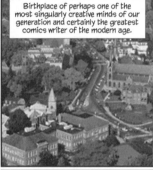

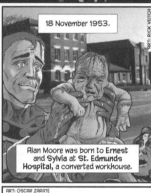

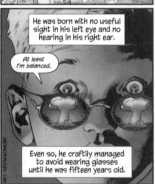

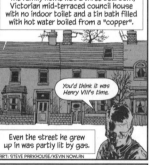

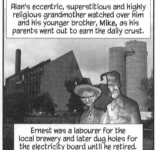

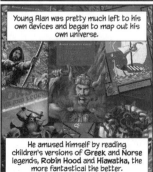

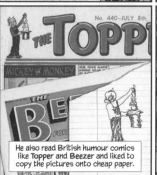

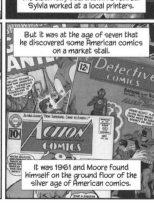

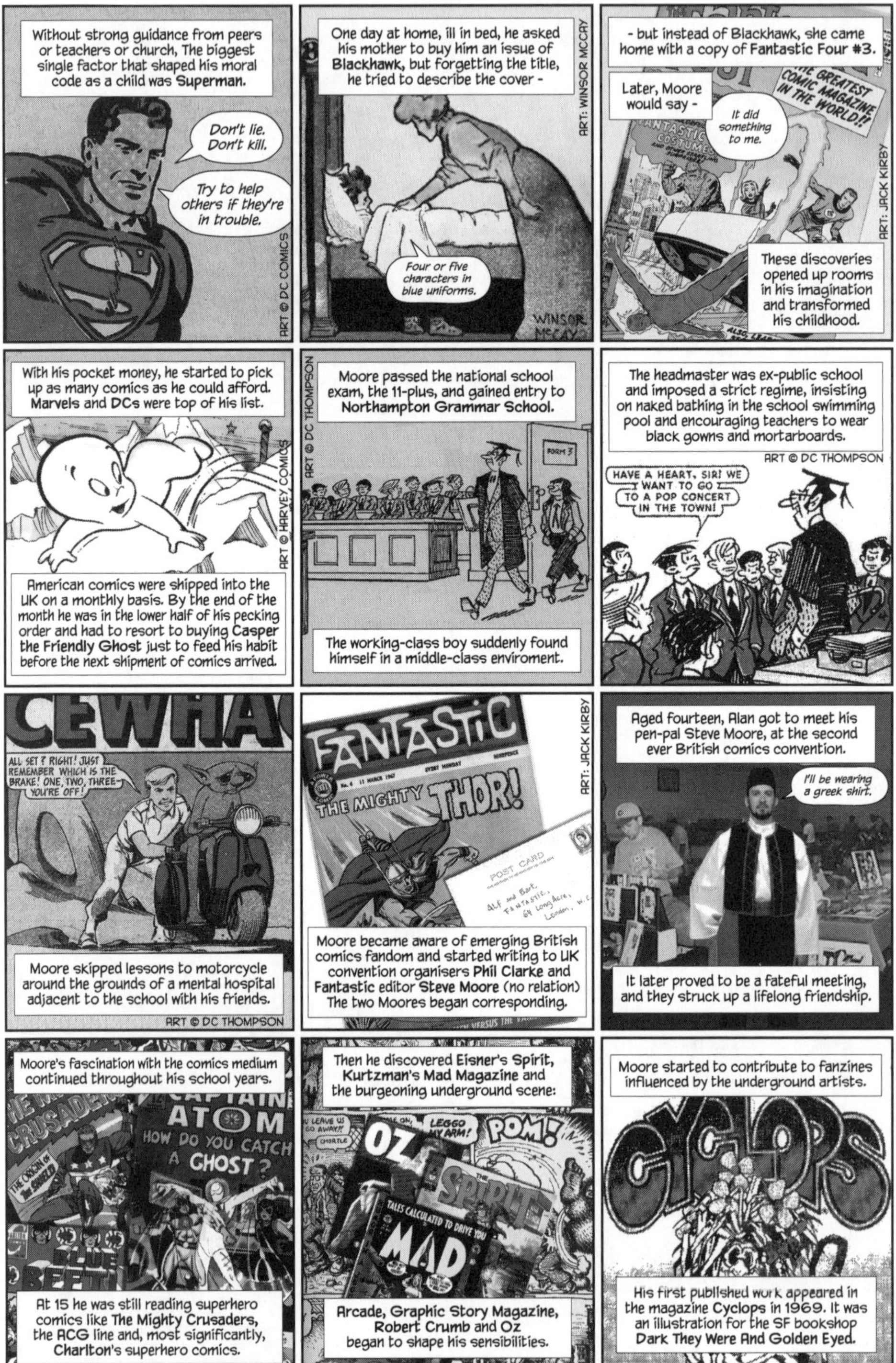
Without strong guidance from peers or teachers or church, The biggest single factor that shaped his moral code as a child was **Superman.**
Don't lie. Don't kill.
Try to help others if they're in trouble.
ART © DC COMICS
One day at home, ill in bed, he asked his mother to buy him an issue of **Blackhawk,** but forgetting the title, he tried to describe the cover -
Four or five characters in blue uniforms.
ART: WINSOR MCCAY
WINSOR MCCAY
- but instead of Blackhawk, she came home with a copy of **Fantastic Four #3.**
Later, Moore would say -
It did something to me.
THE GREATEST COMIC MAGAZINE IN THE WORLD!!
These discoveries opened up rooms in his imagination and transformed his childhood.
ART: JACK KIRBY
With his pocket money, he started to pick up as many comics as he could afford. **Marvels** and **DCs** were top of his list.
ART © HARVEY COMICS
American comics were shipped into the UK on a monthly basis. By the end of the month he was in the lower half of his pecking order and had to resort to buying **Casper the Friendly Ghost** just to feed his habit before the next shipment of comics arrived.
Moore passed the national school exam, the 11-plus, and gained entry to **Northampton Grammar School.**
ART © DC THOMPSON
FORM 3
The working-class boy suddenly found himself in a middle-class enviroment.
The headmaster was ex-public school and imposed a strict regime, insisting on naked bathing in the school swimming pool and encouraging teachers to wear black gowns and mortarboards.
ART © DC THOMPSON
HAVE A HEART, SIR! WE WANT TO GO TO A POP CONCERT IN THE TOWN!
ALL SET? RIGHT! JUST REMEMBER WHICH IS THE BRAKE! ONE, TWO, THREE-YOU'RE OFF!
Moore skipped lessons to motorcycle around the grounds of a mental hospital adjacent to the school with his friends.
ART © DC THOMPSON
FANTASTIC
THE MIGHTY THOR!
POST CARD
Alf and Bart, FANTASTIC, 69 Long Acre, London, W.C.
ART: JACK KIRBY
Moore became aware of emerging British comics fandom and started writing to UK convention organisers **Phil Clarke** and **Fantastic** editor **Steve Moore** (no relation) The two Moores began corresponding.
Aged fourteen, Alan got to meet his pen-pal Steve Moore, at the second ever British comics convention.
I'll be wearing a greek shirt.
It later proved to be a fateful meeting, and they struck up a lifelong friendship.
Moore's fascination with the comics medium continued throughout his school years.
CAPTAIN ATOM
HOW DO YOU CATCH A GHOST?
BLUE BEETLE
At 15 he was still reading superhero comics like **The Mighty Crusaders,** the **ACG** line and, most significantly, **Charlton**'s superhero comics.
Then he discovered **Eisner's Spirit, Kurtzman's Mad Magazine** and the burgeoning underground scene:
LEGGO MY ARM!
POM!
OZ
THE SPIRIT
TALES CALCULATED TO DRIVE YOU MAD
Arcade, Graphic Story Magazine, Robert Crumb and **Oz** began to shape his sensibilities.
Moore started to contribute to fanzines influenced by the underground artists.
CYCLOPS
His first published work appeared in the magazine **Cyclops** in 1969. It was an illustration for the SF bookshop **Dark They Were And Golden Eyed.**

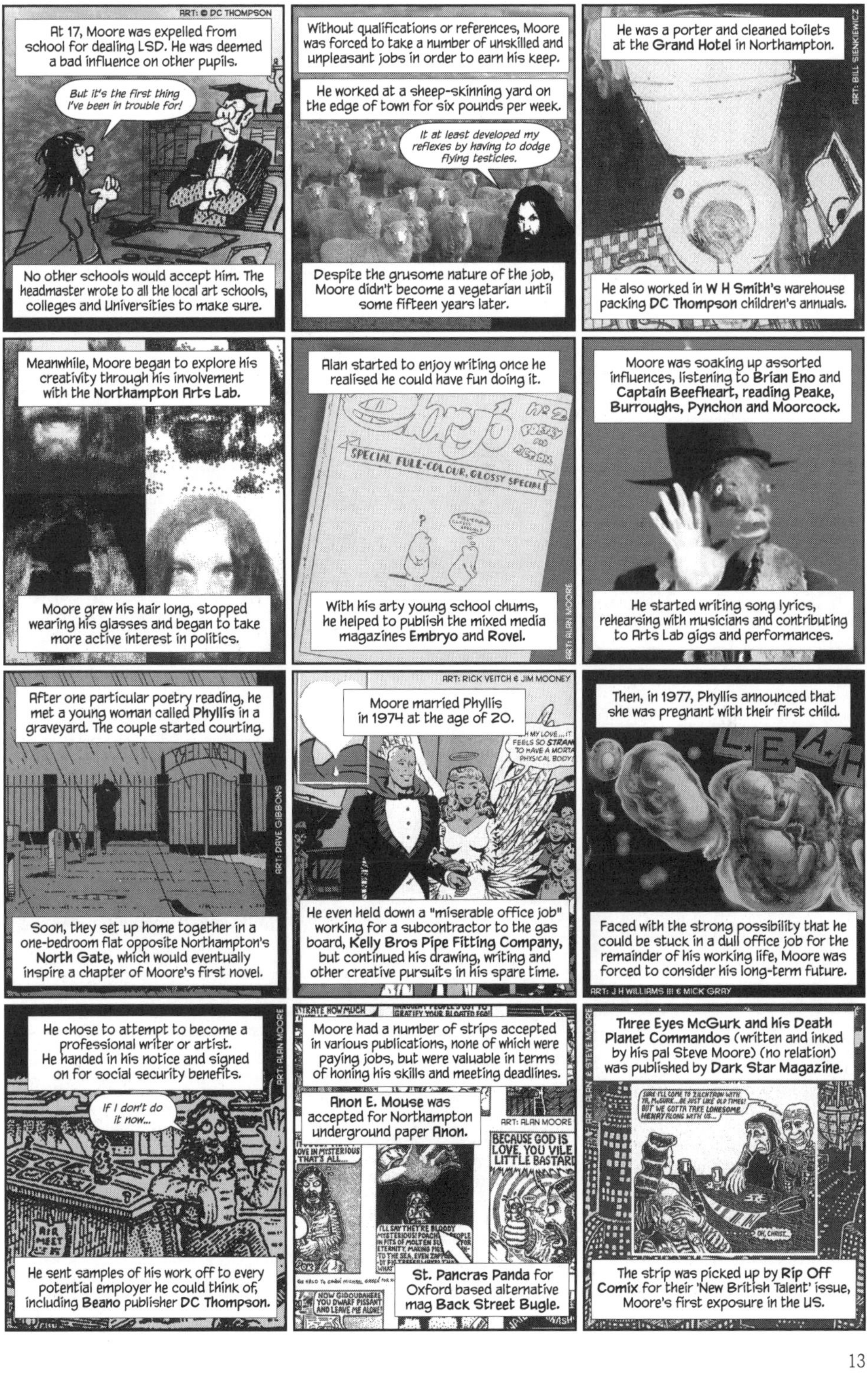

ART: © DC THOMPSON
At 17, Moore was expelled from school for dealing LSD. He was deemed a bad influence on other pupils.
But it's the first thing I've been in trouble for!
No other schools would accept him. The headmaster wrote to all the local art schools, colleges and Universities to make sure.
Without qualifications or references, Moore was forced to take a number of unskilled and unpleasant jobs in order to earn his keep.
He worked at a sheep-skinning yard on the edge of town for six pounds per week.
It at least developed my reflexes by having to dodge flying testicles.
Despite the grusome nature of the job, Moore didn't become a vegetarian until some fifteen years later.
He was a porter and cleaned toilets at the Grand Hotel in Northampton.
ART: BILL SIENKIEWICZ
He also worked in W H Smith's warehouse packing DC Thompson children's annuals.
Meanwhile, Moore began to explore his creativity through his involvement with the Northampton Arts Lab.
Moore grew his hair long, stopped wearing his glasses and began to take more active interest in politics.
Alan started to enjoy writing once he realised he could have fun doing it.
SPECIAL FULL-COLOUR, GLOSSY SPECIAL
ART: ALAN MOORE
With his arty young school chums, he helped to publish the mixed media magazines Embryo and Rovel.
Moore was soaking up assorted influences, listening to Brian Eno and Captain Beefheart, reading Peake, Burroughs, Pynchon and Moorcock.
He started writing song lyrics, rehearsing with musicians and contributing to Arts Lab gigs and performances.
After one particular poetry reading, he met a young woman called Phyllis in a graveyard. The couple started courting.
ART: DAVE GIBBONS
Soon, they set up home together in a one-bedroom flat opposite Northampton's North Gate, which would eventually inspire a chapter of Moore's first novel.
ART: RICK VEITCH & JIM MOONEY
Moore married Phyllis in 1974 at the age of 20.
He even held down a "miserable office job" working for a subcontractor to the gas board, Kelly Bros Pipe Fitting Company, but continued his drawing, writing and other creative pursuits in his spare time.
Then, in 1977, Phyllis announced that she was pregnant with their first child.
Faced with the strong possibility that he could be stuck in a dull office job for the remainder of his working life, Moore was forced to consider his long-term future.
ART: J H WILLIAMS III & MICK GRAY
He chose to attempt to become a professional writer or artist. He handed in his notice and signed on for social security benefits.
ART: ALAN MOORE
If I don't do it now...
He sent samples of his work off to every potential employer he could think of, including Beano publisher DC Thompson.
Moore had a number of strips accepted in various publications, none of which were paying jobs, but were valuable in terms of honing his skills and meeting deadlines.
Anon E. Mouse was accepted for Northampton underground paper Anon.
ART: ALAN MOORE
BECAUSE GOD IS LOVE, YOU VILE LITTLE BASTARD
NOW GIDOUDAHERE YOU DWARF PISSANT AND LEAVE ME ALONE!
St. Pancras Panda for Oxford based alternative mag Back Street Bugle.
ART: ALAN & STEVE MOORE
Three Eyes McGurk and his Death Planet Commandos (written and inked by his pal Steve Moore) (no relation) was published by Dark Star Magazine.
OH, CHRIST...
The strip was picked up by Rip Off Comix for their 'New British Talent' issue, Moore's first exposure in the US.

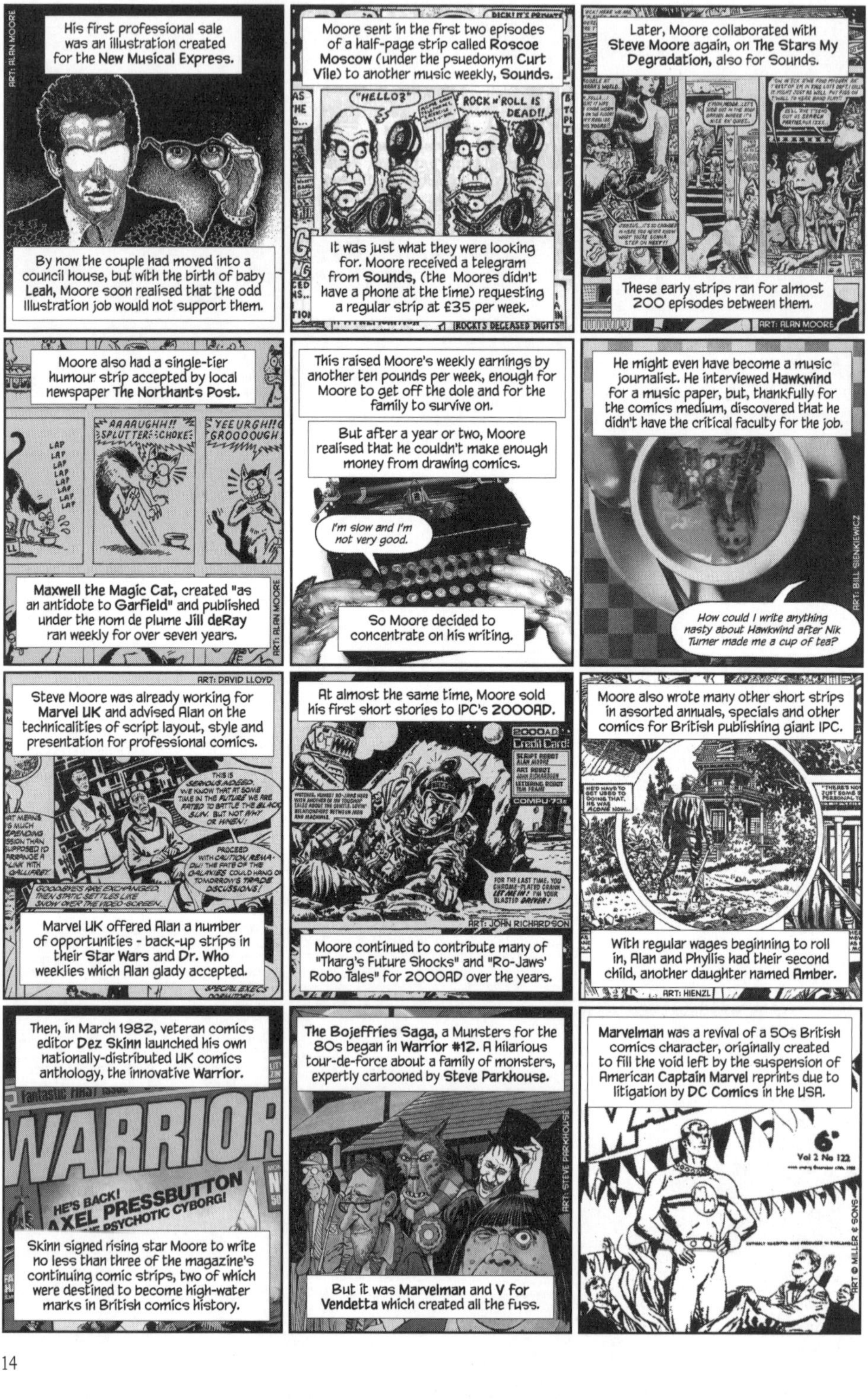
ART: ALAN MOORE
His first professional sale was an illustration created for the New Musical Express.
By now the couple had moved into a council house, but with the birth of baby Leah, Moore soon realised that the odd illustration job would not support them.
Moore sent in the first two episodes of a half-page strip called Roscoe Moscow (under the psuedonym Curt Vile) to another music weekly, Sounds.
"HELLO?"
ROCK N'ROLL IS DEAD!!
It was just what they were looking for. Moore received a telegram from Sounds, (the Moores didn't have a phone at the time) requesting a regular strip at £35 per week.
ROCKY'S DECEASED DIGITS!!
Later, Moore collaborated with Steve Moore again, on The Stars My Degradation, also for Sounds.
These early strips ran for almost 200 episodes between them.
ART: ALAN MOORE
Moore also had a single-tier humour strip accepted by local newspaper The Northants Post.
AAAAUGHH!! SPLUTTER CHOKE
YEEURGH!! GROOOOUGH
LAP LAP LAP LAP LAP LAP LAP
Maxwell the Magic Cat, created "as an antidote to Garfield" and published under the nom de plume Jill deRay ran weekly for over seven years.
ART: ALAN MOORE
This raised Moore's weekly earnings by another ten pounds per week, enough for Moore to get off the dole and for the family to survive on.
But after a year or two, Moore realised that he couldn't make enough money from drawing comics.
I'm slow and I'm not very good.
So Moore decided to concentrate on his writing.
He might even have become a music journalist. He interviewed Hawkwind for a music paper, but, thankfully for the comics medium, discovered that he didn't have the critical faculty for the job.
ART: BILL SIENKIEWICZ
How could I write anything nasty about Hawkwind after Nik Turner made me a cup of tea?
ART: DAVID LLOYD
Steve Moore was already working for Marvel UK and advised Alan on the technicalities of script layout, style and presentation for professional comics.
Marvel UK offered Alan a number of opportunities - back-up strips in their Star Wars and Dr. Who weeklies which Alan glady accepted.
At almost the same time, Moore sold his first short stories to IPC's 2000AD.
2000AD Credit Card
ART: JOHN RICHARDSON
Moore continued to contribute many of "Tharg's Future Shocks" and "Ro-Jaws' Robo Tales" for 2000AD over the years.
Moore also wrote many other short strips in assorted annuals, specials and other comics for British publishing giant IPC.
With regular wages beginning to roll in, Alan and Phyllis had their second child, another daughter named Amber.
ART: HIENZL
Then, in March 1982, veteran comics editor Dez Skinn launched his own nationally-distributed UK comics anthology, the innovative Warrior.
WARRIOR
HE'S BACK! AXEL PRESSBUTTON
PSYCHOTIC CYBORG!
Skinn signed rising star Moore to write no less than three of the magazine's continuing comic strips, two of which were destined to become high-water marks in British comics history.
The Bojeffries Saga, a Munsters for the 80s began in Warrior #12. A hilarious tour-de-force about a family of monsters, expertly cartooned by Steve Parkhouse.
ART: STEVE PARKHOUSE
But it was Marvelman and V for Vendetta which created all the fuss.
Marvelman was a revival of a 50s British comics character, originally created to fill the void left by the suspension of American Captain Marvel reprints due to litigation by DC Comics in the USA.
6d
Vol 2 No 122
ART © MILLER & SONS

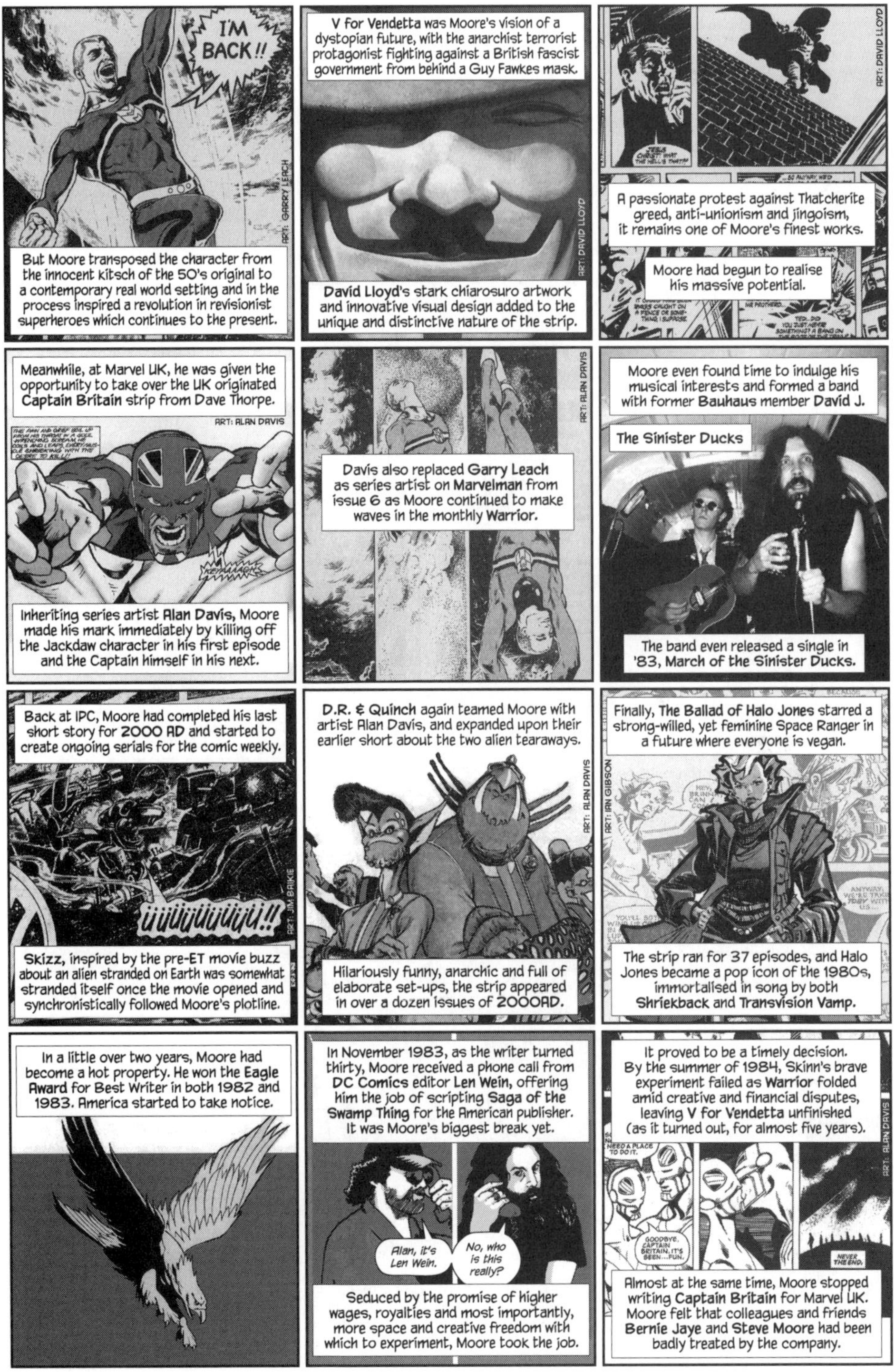
I'M BACK!!
ART: GARRY LEACH
But Moore transposed the character from the innocent kitsch of the 50's original to a contemporary real world setting and in the process inspired a revolution in revisionist superheroes which continues to the present.
V for Vendetta was Moore's vision of a dystopian future, with the anarchist terrorist protagonist fighting against a British fascist government from behind a Guy Fawkes mask.
ART: DAVID LLOYD
David Lloyd's stark chiarosuro artwork and innovative visual design added to the unique and distinctive nature of the strip.
ART: DAVID LLOYD
A passionate protest against Thatcherite greed, anti-unionism and jingoism, it remains one of Moore's finest works.
Moore had begun to realise his massive potential.
Meanwhile, at Marvel UK, he was given the opportunity to take over the UK originated Captain Britain strip from Dave Thorpe.
ART: ALAN DAVIS
Inheriting series artist Alan Davis, Moore made his mark immediately by killing off the Jackdaw character in his first episode and the Captain himself in his next.
ART: ALAN DAVIS
Davis also replaced Garry Leach as series artist on Marvelman from issue 6 as Moore continued to make waves in the monthly Warrior.
Moore even found time to indulge his musical interests and formed a band with former Bauhaus member David J.
The Sinister Ducks
The band even released a single in '83, March of the Sinister Ducks.
Back at IPC, Moore had completed his last short story for 2000 AD and started to create ongoing serials for the comic weekly.
ART: JIM BAIKIE
Skizz, inspired by the pre-ET movie buzz about an alien stranded on Earth was somewhat stranded itself once the movie opened and synchronistically followed Moore's plotline.
D.R. & Quinch again teamed Moore with artist Alan Davis, and expanded upon their earlier short about the two alien tearaways.
ART: ALAN DAVIS
Hilariously funny, anarchic and full of elaborate set-ups, the strip appeared in over a dozen issues of 2000AD.
Finally, The Ballad of Halo Jones starred a strong-willed, yet feminine Space Ranger in a future where everyone is vegan.
ART: IAN GIBSON
The strip ran for 37 episodes, and Halo Jones became a pop icon of the 1980s, immortalised in song by both Shriekback and Transvision Vamp.
In a little over two years, Moore had become a hot property. He won the Eagle Award for Best Writer in both 1982 and 1983. America started to take notice.
In November 1983, as the writer turned thirty, Moore received a phone call from DC Comics editor Len Wein, offering him the job of scripting Saga of the Swamp Thing for the American publisher. It was Moore's biggest break yet.
Alan, it's Len Wein.
No, who is this really?
Seduced by the promise of higher wages, royalties and most importantly, more space and creative freedom with which to experiment, Moore took the job.
It proved to be a timely decision. By the summer of 1984, Skinn's brave experiment failed as Warrior folded amid creative and financial disputes, leaving V for Vendetta unfinished (as it turned out, for almost five years).
ART: ALAN DAVIS
NEED A PLACE TO DO IT.
GOODBYE, CAPTAIN BRITAIN, IT'S BEEN...FUN.
NEVER THE END.
Almost at the same time, Moore stopped writing Captain Britain for Marvel UK. Moore felt that colleagues and friends Bernie Jaye and Steve Moore had been badly treated by the company.

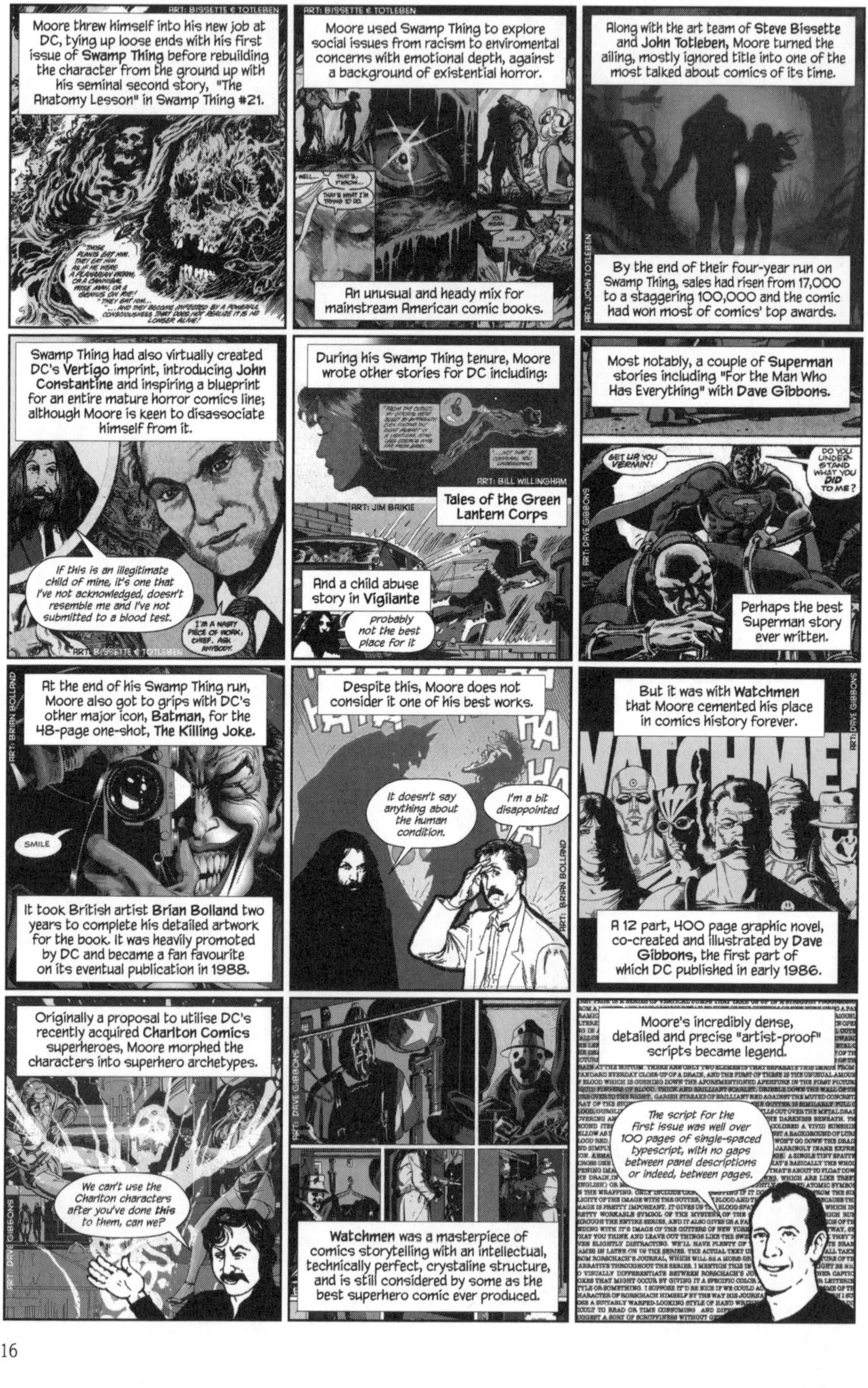
ART: BISSETTE & TOTLEBEN
Moore threw himself into his new job at DC, tying up loose ends with his first issue of Swamp Thing before rebuilding the character from the ground up with his seminal second story, "The Anatomy Lesson" in Swamp Thing #21.
ART: BISSETTE & TOTLEBEN
Moore used Swamp Thing to explore social issues from racism to enviromental concerns with emotional depth, against a background of existential horror.
An unusual and heady mix for mainstream American comic books.
Along with the art team of Steve Bissette and John Totleben, Moore turned the ailing, mostly ignored title into one of the most talked about comics of its time.
ART: JOHN TOTLEBEN
By the end of their four-year run on Swamp Thing, sales had risen from 17,000 to a staggering 100,000 and the comic had won most of comics' top awards.
Swamp Thing had also virtually created DC's Vertigo imprint, introducing John Constantine and inspiring a blueprint for an entire mature horror comics line; although Moore is keen to disassociate himself from it.
If this is an illegitimate child of mine, it's one that I've not acknowledged, doesn't resemble me and I've not submitted to a blood test.
I'M A NASTY PIECE OF WORK, CHIEF. ASK ANYBODY.
ART: BISSETTE & TOTLEBEN
During his Swamp Thing tenure, Moore wrote other stories for DC including:
ART: BILL WILLINGHAM
Tales of the Green Lantern Corps
ART: JIM BAIKIE
And a child abuse story in Vigilante
probably not the best place for it
Most notably, a couple of Superman stories including "For the Man Who Has Everything" with Dave Gibbons.
GET UP, YOU VERMIN!
DO YOU UNDERSTAND WHAT YOU DID TO ME?
ART: DAVE GIBBONS
Perhaps the best Superman story ever written.
ART: BRIAN BOLLAND
At the end of his Swamp Thing run, Moore also got to grips with DC's other major icon, Batman, for the 48-page one-shot, The Killing Joke.
SMILE
It took British artist Brian Bolland two years to complete his detailed artwork for the book. It was heavily promoted by DC and became a fan favourite on its eventual publication in 1988.
Despite this, Moore does not consider it one of his best works.
It doesn't say anything about the human condition.
I'm a bit disappointed
ART: BRIAN BOLLAND
But it was with Watchmen that Moore cemented his place in comics history forever.
ART: DAVE GIBBONS
A 12 part, 400 page graphic novel, co-created and illustrated by Dave Gibbons, the first part of which DC published in early 1986.
Originally a proposal to utilise DC's recently acquired Charlton Comics superheroes, Moore morphed the characters into superhero archetypes.
We can't use the Charlton characters after you've done this to them, can we?
ART: DAVE GIBBONS
ART: DAVE GIBBONS
Watchmen was a masterpiece of comics storytelling with an intellectual, technically perfect, crystaline structure, and is still considered by some as the best superhero comic ever produced.
Moore's incredibly dense, detailed and precise "artist-proof" scripts became legend.
The script for the first issue was well over 100 pages of single-spaced typescript, with no gaps between panel descriptions or indeed, between pages.

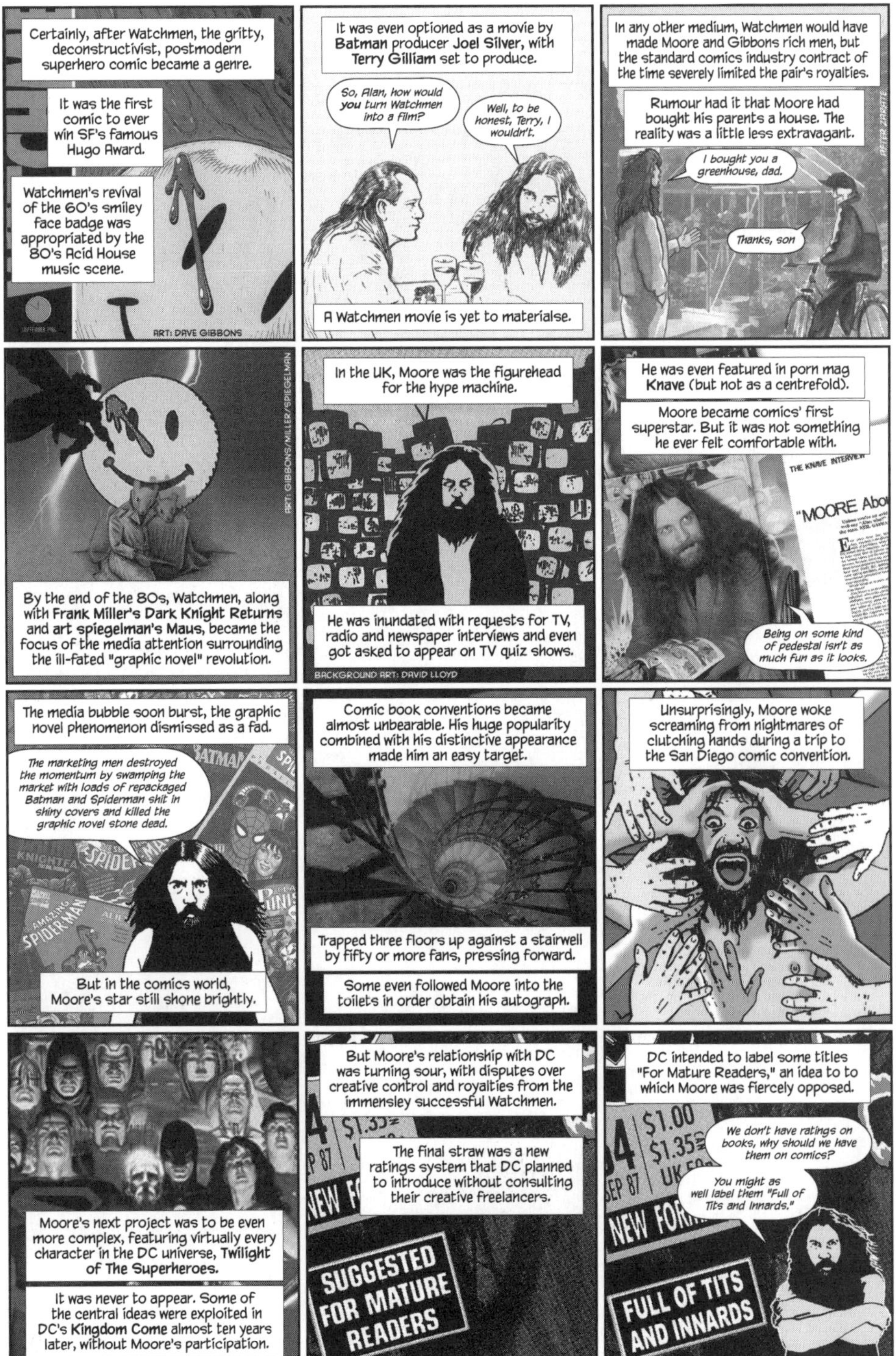

Certainly, after Watchmen, the gritty, deconstructivist, postmodern superhero comic became a genre.
It was the first comic to ever win SF's famous Hugo Award.
Watchmen's revival of the 60's smiley face badge was appropriated by the 80's Acid House music scene.
ART: DAVE GIBBONS
It was even optioned as a movie by Batman producer Joel Silver, with Terry Gilliam set to produce.
So, Alan, how would you turn Watchmen into a film?
Well, to be honest, Terry, I wouldn't.
A Watchmen movie is yet to materialse.
In any other medium, Watchmen would have made Moore and Gibbons rich men, but the standard comics industry contract of the time severely limited the pair's royalties.
Rumour had it that Moore had bought his parents a house. The reality was a little less extravagant.
I bought you a greenhouse, dad.
Thanks, son
ART: GIBBONS/MILLER/SPIEGELMAN
By the end of the 80s, Watchmen, along with Frank Miller's Dark Knight Returns and art spiegelman's Maus, became the focus of the media attention surrounding the ill-fated "graphic novel" revolution.
In the UK, Moore was the figurehead for the hype machine.
He was inundated with requests for TV, radio and newspaper interviews and even got asked to appear on TV quiz shows.
BACKGROUND ART: DAVID LLOYD
He was even featured in porn mag Knave (but not as a centrefold).
Moore became comics' first superstar. But it was not something he ever felt comfortable with.
THE KNAVE INTERVIEW
Being on some kind of pedestal isn't as much fun as it looks.
The media bubble soon burst, the graphic novel phenomenon dismissed as a fad.
The marketing men destroyed the momentum by swamping the market with loads of repackaged Batman and Spiderman shit in shiny covers and killed the graphic novel stone dead.
But in the comics world, Moore's star still shone brightly.
Comic book conventions became almost unbearable. His huge popularity combined with his distinctive appearance made him an easy target.
Trapped three floors up against a stairwell by fifty or more fans, pressing forward.
Some even followed Moore into the toilets in order obtain his autograph.
Unsurprisingly, Moore woke screaming from nightmares of clutching hands during a trip to the San Diego comic convention.
Moore's next project was to be even more complex, featuring virtually every character in the DC universe, Twilight of The Superheroes.
It was never to appear. Some of the central ideas were exploited in DC's Kingdom Come almost ten years later, without Moore's participation.
ART: ALEX ROSS
But Moore's relationship with DC was turning sour, with disputes over creative control and royalties from the immensley successful Watchmen.
The final straw was a new ratings system that DC planned to introduce without consulting their creative freelancers.
SUGGESTED FOR MATURE READERS
DC intended to label some titles "For Mature Readers," an idea to to which Moore was fiercely opposed.
We don't have ratings on books, why should we have them on comics?
You might as well label them "Full of Tits and Innards."
FULL OF TITS AND INNARDS

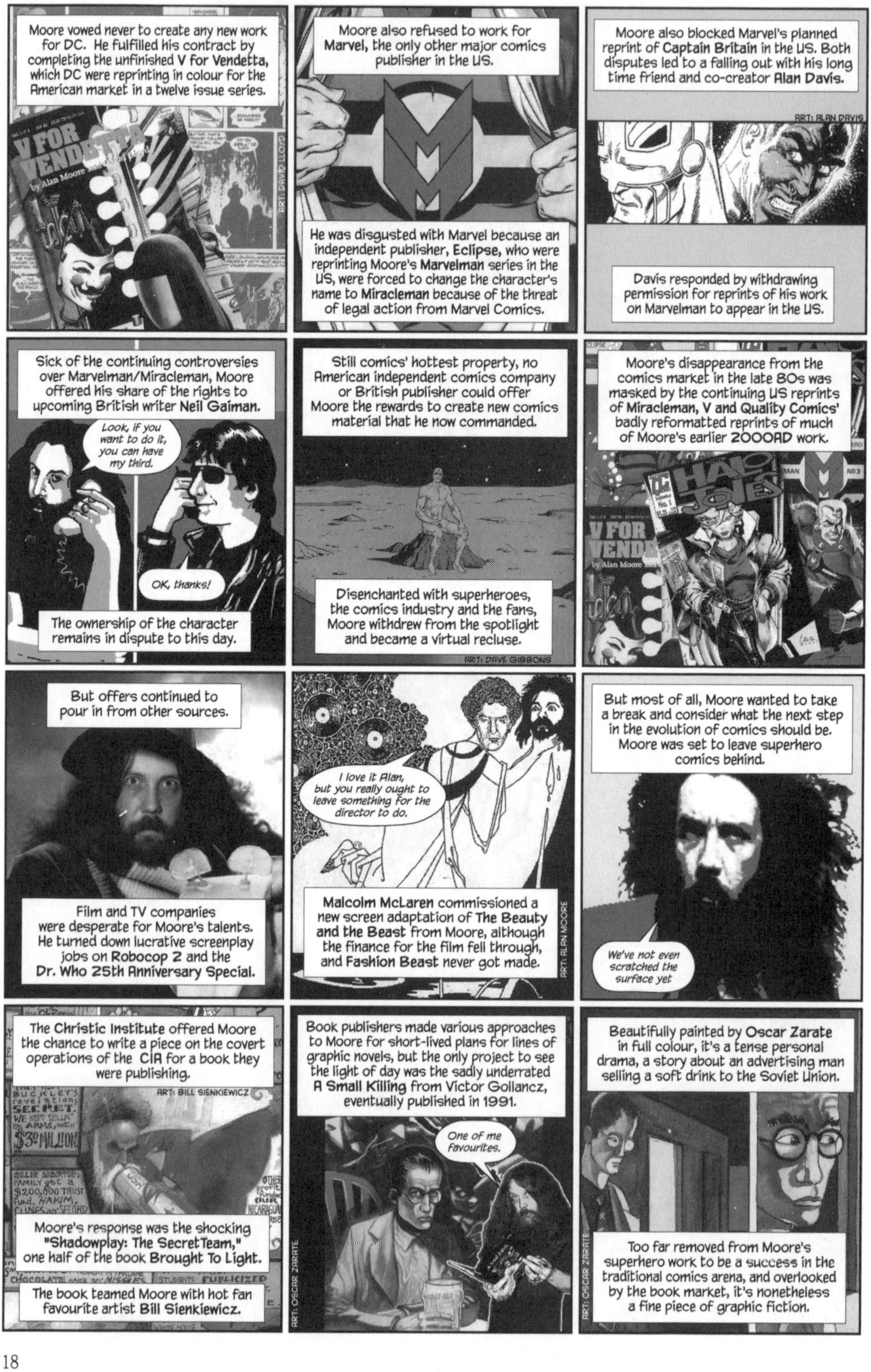
Moore vowed never to create any new work for DC. He fulfilled his contract by completing the unfinished V for Vendetta, which DC were reprinting in colour for the American market in a twelve issue series.
V FOR VENDETTA
ART: DAVID LLOYD
Moore also refused to work for Marvel, the only other major comics publisher in the US.
He was disgusted with Marvel because an independent publisher, Eclipse, who were reprinting Moore's Marvelman series in the US, were forced to change the character's name to Miracleman because of the threat of legal action from Marvel Comics.
Moore also blocked Marvel's planned reprint of Captain Britain in the US. Both disputes led to a falling out with his long time friend and co-creator Alan Davis.
ART: ALAN DAVIS
Davis responded by withdrawing permission for reprints of his work on Marvelman to appear in the US.
Sick of the continuing controversies over Marvelman/Miracleman, Moore offered his share of the rights to upcoming British writer Neil Gaiman.
Look, if you want to do it, you can have my third.
OK, thanks!
The ownership of the character remains in dispute to this day.
Still comics' hottest property, no American independent comics company or British publisher could offer Moore the rewards to create new comics material that he now commanded.
Disenchanted with superheroes, the comics industry and the fans, Moore withdrew from the spotlight and became a virtual recluse.
ART: DAVE GIBBONS
Moore's disappearance from the comics market in the late 80s was masked by the continuing US reprints of Miracleman, V and Quality Comics' badly reformatted reprints of much of Moore's earlier 2000AD work.
V FOR VENDE
But offers continued to pour in from other sources.
Film and TV companies were desperate for Moore's talents. He turned down lucrative screenplay jobs on Robocop 2 and the Dr. Who 25th Anniversary Special.
I love it Alan, but you really ought to leave something for the director to do.
Malcolm McLaren commissioned a new screen adaptation of The Beauty and the Beast from Moore, although the finance for the film fell through, and Fashion Beast never got made.
ART: ALAN MOORE
But most of all, Moore wanted to take a break and consider what the next step in the evolution of comics should be. Moore was set to leave superhero comics behind.
We've not even scratched the surface yet
The Christic Institute offered Moore the chance to write a piece on the covert operations of the CIA for a book they were publishing.
ART: BILL SIENKIEWICZ
Moore's response was the shocking "Shadowplay: The Secret Team," one half of the book Brought To Light.
The book teamed Moore with hot fan favourite artist Bill Sienkiewicz.
Book publishers made various approaches to Moore for short-lived plans for lines of graphic novels, but the only project to see the light of day was the sadly underrated A Small Killing from Victor Gollancz, eventually published in 1991.
One of me favourites.
ART: OSCAR ZARATE
Beautifully painted by Oscar Zarate in full colour, it's a tense personal drama, a story about an advertising man selling a soft drink to the Soviet Union.
Too far removed from Moore's superhero work to be a success in the traditional comics arena, and overlooked by the book market, it's nonetheless a fine piece of graphic fiction.
ART: OSCAR ZARATE

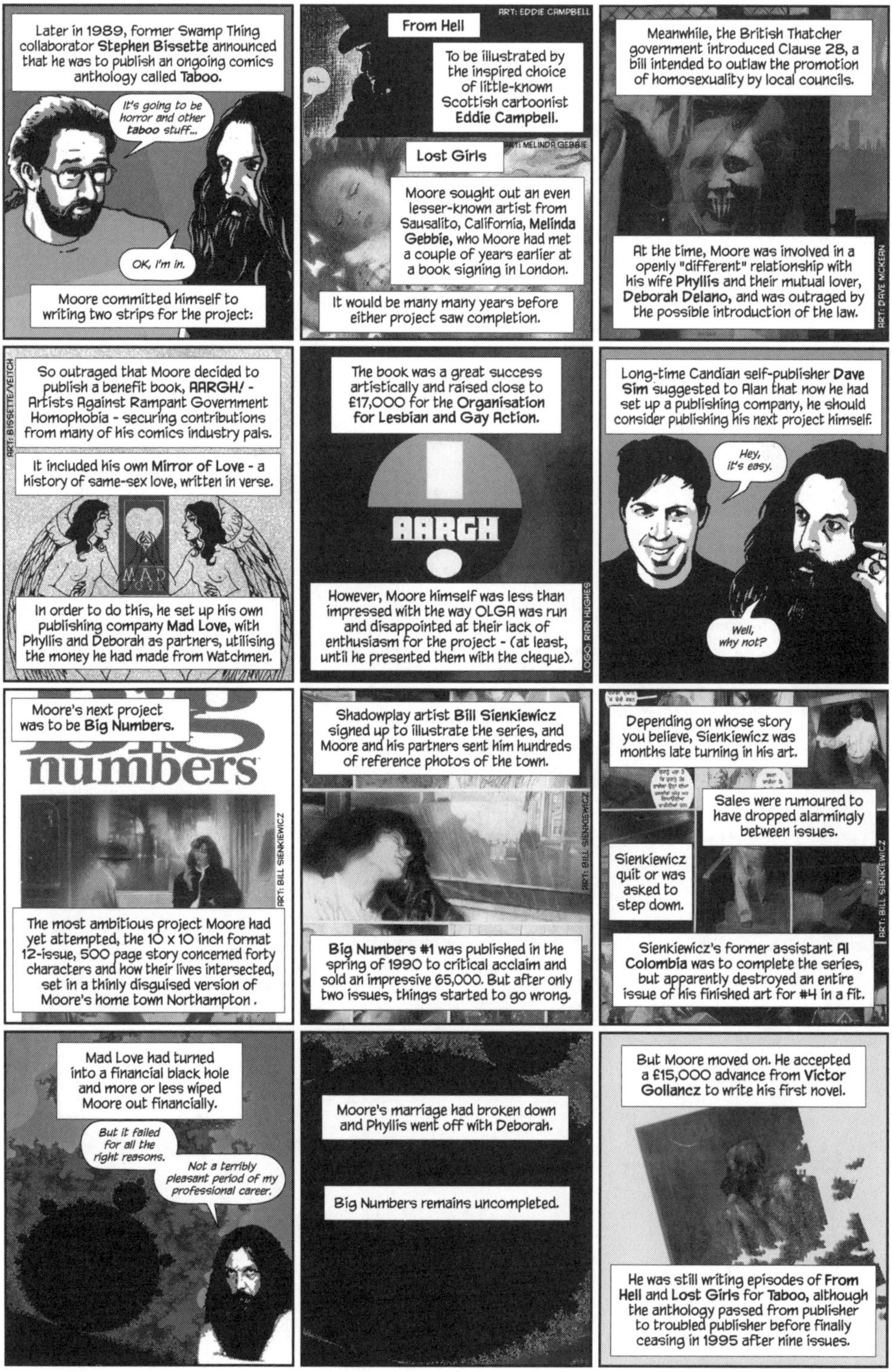
Later in 1989, former Swamp Thing collaborator Stephen Bissette announced that he was to publish an ongoing comics anthology called Taboo.
It's going to be horror and other taboo stuff...
OK, I'm in.
Moore committed himself to writing two strips for the project:
ART: EDDIE CAMPBELL
From Hell
To be illustrated by the inspired choice of little-known Scottish cartoonist Eddie Campbell.
ART: MELINDA GEBBIE
Lost Girls
Moore sought out an even lesser-known artist from Sausalito, California, Melinda Gebbie, who Moore had met a couple of years earlier at a book signing in London.
It would be many many years before either project saw completion.
Meanwhile, the British Thatcher government introduced Clause 28, a bill intended to outlaw the promotion of homosexuality by local councils.
At the time, Moore was involved in a openly "different" relationship with his wife Phyllis and their mutual lover, Deborah Delano, and was outraged by the possible introduction of the law.
ART: DAVE MCKEAN
ART: BISSETTE/VEITCH
So outraged that Moore decided to publish a benefit book, AARGH! - Artists Against Rampant Government Homophobia - securing contributions from many of his comics industry pals.
It included his own Mirror of Love - a history of same-sex love, written in verse.
In order to do this, he set up his own publishing company Mad Love, with Phyllis and Deborah as partners, utilising the money he had made from Watchmen.
The book was a great success artistically and raised close to £17,000 for the Organisation for Lesbian and Gay Action.
AARGH
However, Moore himself was less than impressed with the way OLGA was run and disappointed at their lack of enthusiasm for the project - (at least, until he presented them with the cheque).
LOGO: RIAN HUGHES
Long-time Candian self-publisher Dave Sim suggested to Alan that now he had set up a publishing company, he should consider publishing his next project himself.
Hey, it's easy.
Well, why not?
Moore's next project was to be Big Numbers.
numbers
ART: BILL SIENKIEWICZ
The most ambitious project Moore had yet attempted, the 10 x 10 inch format 12-issue, 500 page story concerned forty characters and how their lives intersected, set in a thinly disguised version of Moore's home town Northampton .
Shadowplay artist Bill Sienkiewicz signed up to illustrate the series, and Moore and his partners sent him hundreds of reference photos of the town.
ART: BILL SIENKIEWICZ
Big Numbers #1 was published in the spring of 1990 to critical acclaim and sold an impressive 65,000. But after only two issues, things started to go wrong.
Depending on whose story you believe, Sienkiewicz was months late turning in his art.
Sales were rumoured to have dropped alarmingly between issues.
Sienkiewicz quit or was asked to step down.
ART: BILL SIENKIEWICZ
Sienkiewicz's former assistant Al Colombia was to complete the series, but apparently destroyed an entire issue of his finished art for #4 in a fit.
Mad Love had turned into a financial black hole and more or less wiped Moore out financially.
But it failed for all the right reasons.
Not a terribly pleasant period of my professional career.
Moore's marriage had broken down and Phyllis went off with Deborah.
Big Numbers remains uncompleted.
But Moore moved on. He accepted a £15,000 advance from Victor Gollancz to write his first novel.
He was still writing episodes of From Hell and Lost Girls for Taboo, although the anthology passed from publisher to troubled publisher before finally ceasing in 1995 after nine issues.

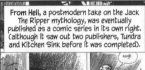

From Hell, a postmodern take on the Jack The Ripper mythology, was eventually published as a comic series in its own right. (although it saw out two publishers, Tundra and Kitchen Sink before it was completed).

ART: EDDIE CAMPBELL

It soon became clear that Moore was putting together an incredibly complex, exhaustively researched magnum opus.

It was to take ten years before From Hell was finally completed, but it was the first of Moore's works to appear on the big screen.

It's not as good as the book.

ART: EDDIE CAMPBELL

Whatever you think of the movie, Moore and Campbell's book remains a masterpiece of the comics medium.

Eddie Campbell later published the entire series in one massive 600 page volume.

Lost Girls, which Moore describes as post-feminist pornography, was also picked up by Kitchen Sink.

ART: MELINDA GEBBIE

There's probably not a sexual act that couldn't be made beautiful with enough layered crayon effects.

It lasted only two issues before the publisher went belly up.

The full 240 page story is finally to be published in a single full colour hardcover by Top Shelf in 2004, some 15 years after it began.

ALAN MOORE   MELINDA GEBBIE

ART: MELINDA GEBBIE

Meanwhile, Moore and Gebbie's union on the page spilled over into real life and romance blossomed between the two co-creators.

Moore also reformed his pop band **The Emperors of Ice Cream** with **Tim Perkins** and played various gigs over a period of two years.

He says, 'There's wrong and there's right, there's black and there's white and there is nothing, nothing in-between,' that's what Mr. A says.

"Mr. A" by The Emperors of Ice Cream

But by 1993, with his comics output trickling to a halt, Moore was fast becoming the forgotten man of comics.

Then he made a dramatic and unexpected return in the most unlikely of places.

Spawn #8, from the newly-formed **Image Comics** (a breakaway group of artists from Marvel who set up their own company), was Moore's first published superhero work since since 1987.

ART: TODD MACFARLANE

Moore's reasoning behind this unexpected move was a desire to save the ailing comics industry by returning them to their roots.

He was depressed that his **Watchmen** series was inadvertently responsible for creating the entire genre of ironic and cynical superhero comics which now dominated the marketplace.

I want to make escapist literature for thirteen year old boys, not dark and gritty junk for forty-something men

He was also motivated by the fact that **Image** were making serious inroads in a market long dominated by **Marvel** and **DC**.

ART: VEITCH & TOTLEBEN

He also scripted the mini-series **1963**, a pastiche-cum-homage to Jack Kirby and the innocent fun of the early years of Marvel Comics.

BY HELIOPOLIS, HOW CAN I PROTECT GREAT #4 FROM THESE NIGHT DEMONS WHEN I'M BURDENED WITH A MORTAL STOWAWAY?

ART: VEITCH & TOTLEBEN

1963 reunited him with artists like Gibbons, Bissette and Rick Veitch.

Moore's income from the high-selling Image titles was very welcome after the lean years following Mad Love's collapse.

On the day Moore turned forty, made another decision which surprised even his family and closest friends. He was to become a magician.

Magic and art are more or less analogous.

Both are the creation of something out of nothing.

ART © DC THOMPSON

He formed a "secret society of two" with his old friend **Steve Moore** to discuss their emerging ideas of magic, language, conciousness and art.

Less than two months later, on 7 January 1994 during an eight hour ritual, Moore claims to have raised a second century Roman snake diety called Glycon.

A god is the idea of a god.

ART: IPC MAGAZINES LTD.

The idea of a god is a god.

Alan and Steve expanded their society into a loose knit cabal of various artists, musicians and occultists, including Tim Perkins, David J, Melinda Gebbie and John Coulthart.

A truly magical organisation in that it doesn't actually exist.

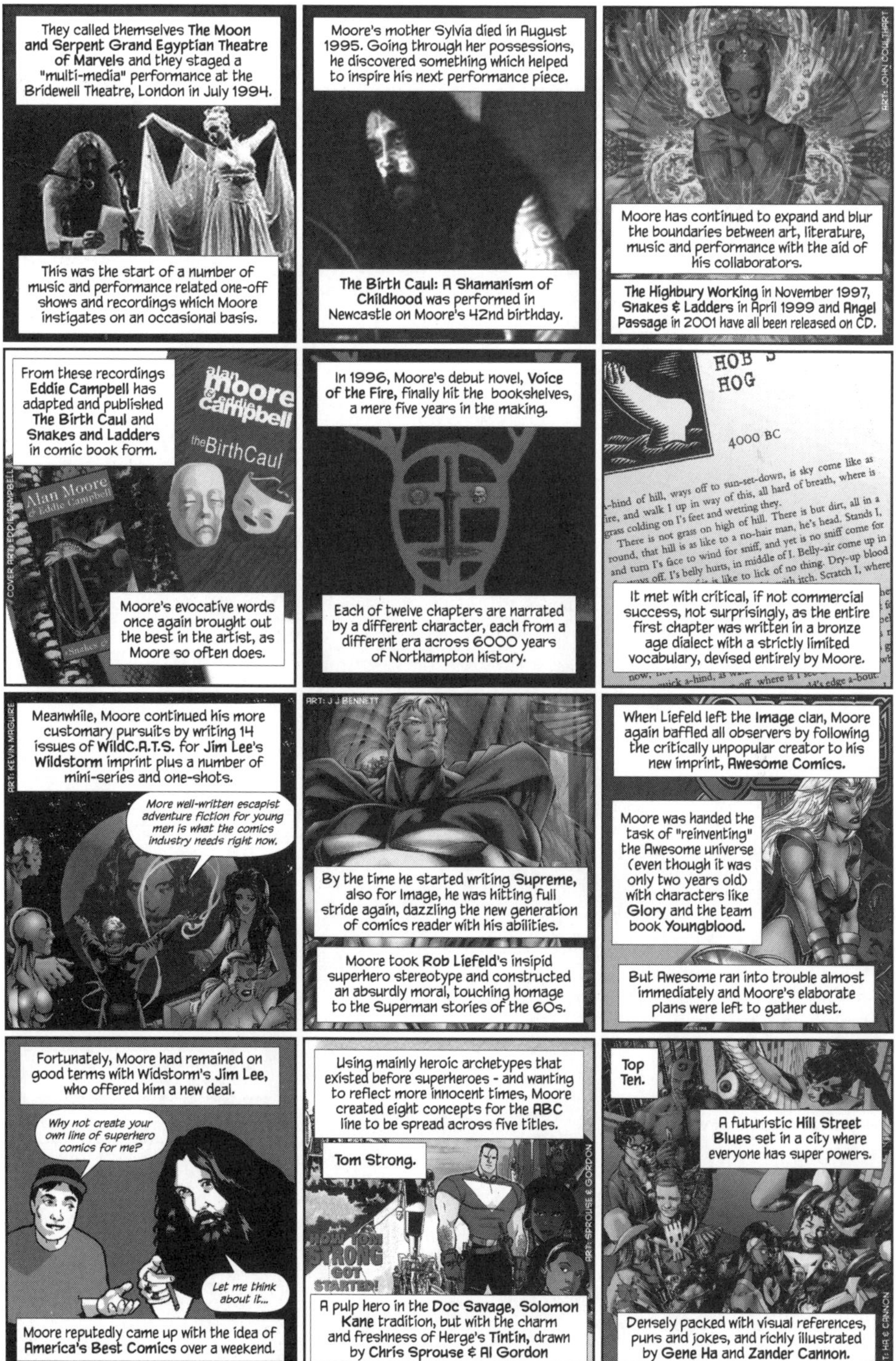

They called themselves **The Moon and Serpent Grand Egyptian Theatre of Marvels** and they staged a "multi-media" performance at the Bridewell Theatre, London in July 1994.
This was the start of a number of music and performance related one-off shows and recordings which Moore instigates on an occasional basis.
Moore's mother Sylvia died in August 1995. Going through her possessions, he discovered something which helped to inspire his next performance piece.
The Birth Caul: A Shamanism of Childhood was performed in Newcastle on Moore's 42nd birthday.
ART: JOHN COULTHART
Moore has continued to expand and blur the boundaries between art, literature, music and performance with the aid of his collaborators.
The Highbury Working in November 1997, **Snakes & Ladders** in April 1999 and **Angel Passage** in 2001 have all been released on CD.
From these recordings **Eddie Campbell** has adapted and published **The Birth Caul** and **Snakes and Ladders** in comic book form.
alan moore & eddie campbell
theBirthCaul
Alan Moore & Eddie Campbell
COVER ART: EDDIE CAMPBELL
Moore's evocative words once again brought out the best in the artist, as Moore so often does.
In 1996, Moore's debut novel, **Voice of the Fire,** finally hit the bookshelves, a mere five years in the making.
Each of twelve chapters are narrated by a different character, each from a different era across 6000 years of Northampton history.
4000 BC
It met with critical, if not commercial success, not surprisingly, as the entire first chapter was written in a bronze age dialect with a strictly limited vocabulary, devised entirely by Moore.
ART: KEVIN MAGUIRE
Meanwhile, Moore continued his more customary pursuits by writing 14 issues of **WildC.A.T.S.** for **Jim Lee's Wildstorm** imprint plus a number of mini-series and one-shots.
More well-written escapist adventure fiction for young men is what the comics industry needs right now.
ART: J J BENNETT
By the time he started writing **Supreme,** also for Image, he was hitting full stride again, dazzling the new generation of comics reader with his abilities.
Moore took **Rob Liefeld's** insipid superhero stereotype and constructed an absurdly moral, touching homage to the Superman stories of the 60s.
When Liefeld left the **Image** clan, Moore again baffled all observers by following the critically unpopular creator to his new imprint, **Awesome Comics.**
Moore was handed the task of "reinventing" the Awesome universe (even though it was only two years old) with characters like **Glory** and the team book **Youngblood.**
But Awesome ran into trouble almost immediately and Moore's elaborate plans were left to gather dust.
Fortunately, Moore had remained on good terms with Widstorm's **Jim Lee,** who offered him a new deal.
Why not create your own line of superhero comics for me?
Let me think about it...
Moore reputedly came up with the idea of **America's Best Comics** over a weekend.
Using mainly heroic archetypes that existed before superheroes - and wanting to reflect more innocent times, Moore created eight concepts for the **ABC** line to be spread across five titles.
Tom Strong.
HOW TOM STRONG GOT STARTED!
ART: SPROUSE & GORDON
A pulp hero in the **Doc Savage, Solomon Kane** tradition, but with the charm and freshness of Herge's **Tintin,** drawn by **Chris Sprouse & Al Gordon**
Top Ten.
A futuristic **Hill Street Blues** set in a city where everyone has super powers.
Densely packed with visual references, puns and jokes, and richly illustrated by **Gene Ha** and **Zander Cannon.**
ART: HA & CANNON

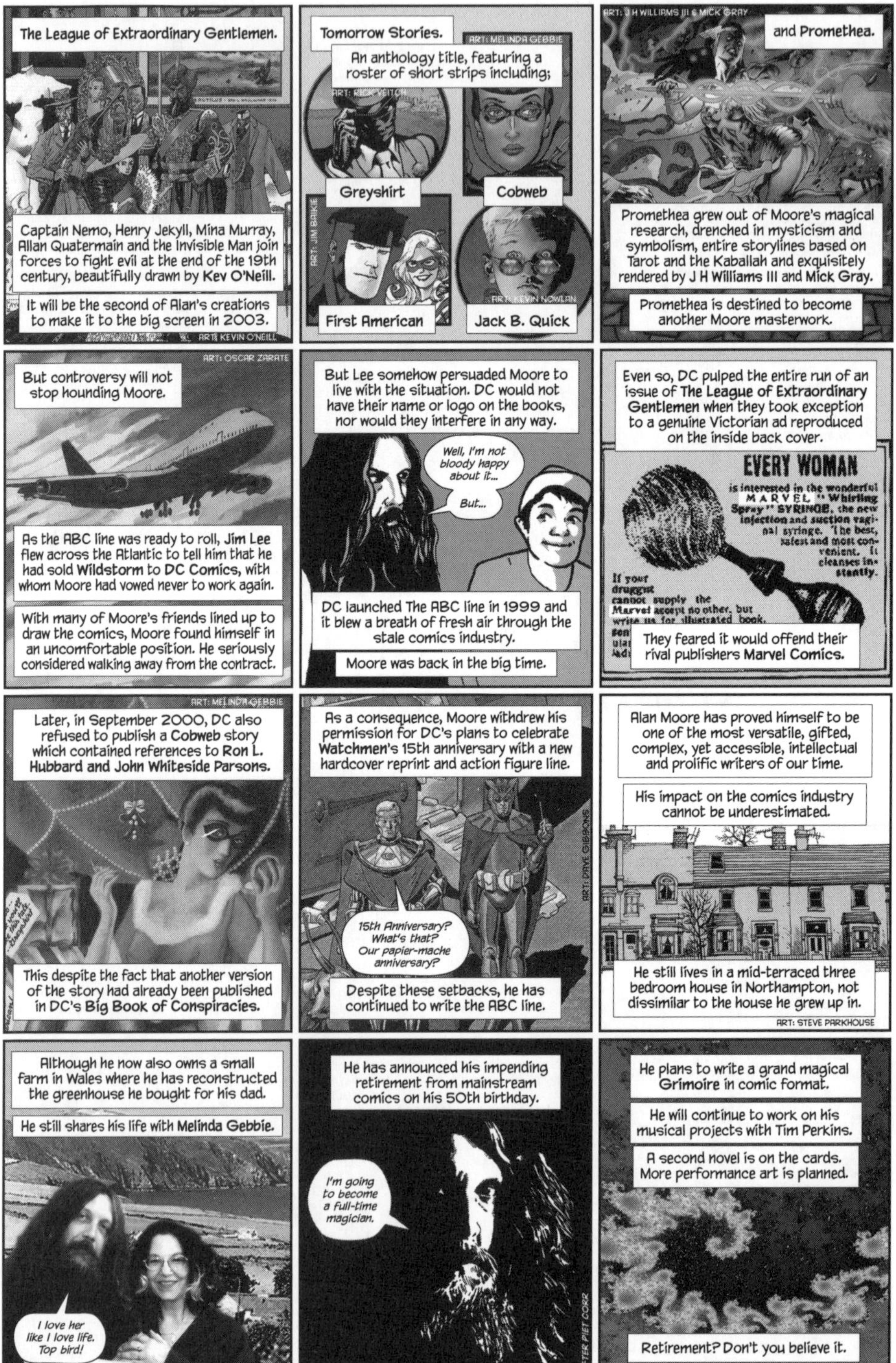

The League of Extraordinary Gentlemen.
Captain Nemo, Henry Jekyll, Mina Murray, Allan Quatermain and the Invisible Man join forces to fight evil at the end of the 19th century, beautifully drawn by Kev O'Neill.
It will be the second of Alan's creations to make it to the big screen in 2003.
ART: KEVIN O'NEILL
Tomorrow Stories.
An anthology title, featuring a roster of short strips including;
ART: RICK VEITCH
ART: MELINDA GEBBIE
Greyshirt
Cobweb
ART: JIM BAIKIE
ART: KEVIN NOWLAN
First American
Jack B. Quick
ART: J H WILLIAMS III & MICK GRAY
and Promethea.
Promethea grew out of Moore's magical research, drenched in mysticism and symbolism, entire storylines based on Tarot and the Kaballah and exquisitely rendered by J H Williams III and Mick Gray.
Promethea is destined to become another Moore masterwork.
ART: OSCAR ZARATE
But controversy will not stop hounding Moore.
As the ABC line was ready to roll, Jim Lee flew across the Atlantic to tell him that he had sold Wildstorm to DC Comics, with whom Moore had vowed never to work again.
With many of Moore's friends lined up to draw the comics, Moore found himself in an uncomfortable position. He seriously considered walking away from the contract.
But Lee somehow persuaded Moore to live with the situation. DC would not have their name or logo on the books, nor would they interfere in any way.
Well, I'm not bloody happy about it...
But...
DC launched The ABC line in 1999 and it blew a breath of fresh air through the stale comics industry.
Moore was back in the big time.
Even so, DC pulped the entire run of an issue of The League of Extraordinary Gentlemen when they took exception to a genuine Victorian ad reproduced on the inside back cover.
EVERY WOMAN
is interested in the wonderful MARVEL "Whirling Spray" SYRINGE, the new injection and suction vaginal syringe. The best, safest and most convenient. It cleanses instantly.
If your druggist cannot supply the Marvel accept no other, but write us for illustrated book.
They feared it would offend their rival publishers Marvel Comics.
ART: MELINDA GEBBIE
Later, in September 2000, DC also refused to publish a Cobweb story which contained references to Ron L. Hubbard and John Whiteside Parsons.
This despite the fact that another version of the story had already been published in DC's Big Book of Conspiracies.
As a consequence, Moore withdrew his permission for DC's plans to celebrate Watchmen's 15th anniversary with a new hardcover reprint and action figure line.
ART: DAVE GIBBONS
15th Anniversary? What's that? Our papier-mache anniversary?
Despite these setbacks, he has continued to write the ABC line.
Alan Moore has proved himself to be one of the most versatile, gifted, complex, yet accessible, intellectual and prolific writers of our time.
His impact on the comics industry cannot be underestimated.
He still lives in a mid-terraced three bedroom house in Northampton, not dissimilar to the house he grew up in.
ART: STEVE PARKHOUSE
Although he now also owns a small farm in Wales where he has reconstructed the greenhouse he bought for his dad.
He still shares his life with Melinda Gebbie.
I love her like I love life. Top bird!
He has announced his impending retirement from mainstream comics on his 50th birthday.
I'm going to become a full-time magician.
AFTER PIET CORR
He plans to write a grand magical Grimoire in comic format.
He will continue to work on his musical projects with Tim Perkins.
A second novel is on the cards. More performance art is planned.
Retirement? Don't you believe it.

MEA CULPA, ALAN MOORE

MICHAEL T. GILBERT

Michael T. Gilbert has written and drawn everything from Superman, Batman, Dr. Strange, Elric, Mickey Mouse and Donald Duck in his 30-year career in comics He created the monster-fighting hero, Mr. Monster and lives in Eugene, Oregon with his wife, Janet.

Text © 2003 Michael T. Gilbert.

I did a bad, bad thing. Sorry, Alan, old bean, old chap, old sock.

Sorry world.

It all started in 1985, when I first "met" Alan Moore. Actually it didn't start there really, but I thought it might be a clever way to flashback into some amusing Alan Moore anecdotes for Alan's 50th birthday. Turns out it's not all that clever, but "Oh well, Pip! Pip!" and all that rot. I'm sure you'll forgive me, gentle reader.

Anyway, back in '85 I was churning out Mr. Monster pages in my Berkeley, Cal. studio when my soon-to-be wife Janet rushed in. *"Michael! Michael! Alan Moore's on the phone!"* Did I mention she was quite excited?

I was pretty excited myself.

A few weeks earlier, I'd sent DC a postcard gushing over their newly revived *Swamp Thing* series, and Alan's startlingly original take on the character. Which is not to sneeze at the contributions of artists Steve Bissette and John Totleben. Together the three made the series one of my all-time favourites. But this is an Alan Moore tribute, so...
DC passed on my post to Alan and he gave me a ring from Jolly Olde England, (no small deal in the Gilbert household, I assure you!) I was tickled when Alan told me how much he'd loved The Wraith, a funny-animal Spirit knock-off I did back in the mid-70s. For my money, any British bloke who'd even heard of The Wraith was a friend for life! But I'd been impressed with Alan even before his DC stint, with his Marvelman's scripts for *Warrior* magazine. And I wasn't alone.

For better or worse, Alan was quickly becoming a comic book superstar, though you wouldn't know it to talk to him. On the phone he came off like a regular chap, as indeed he is. Although a highly *irregular* regular chap, if you know what I mean. Long-story-short, we had great fun chatting about old comics and the like, and I suggested that we collaborate on a Mr. Monster story together.

For those unfamiliar with the character, Mr. Monster's the world greatest monster-fighter. I'd started the character in 1984 as a tongue-in-cheek tribute to the pulp heroes of the 30s and 40s. A year later, he got his own series. Bill Loebs and Dave Stevens had already helped me draw Mr. Monster, but I was curious to see what a different writer might do. Needless to say, I was thrilled when Alan offered to write a 10 or 12-page story for our 3rd issue.

Months later I received one of Alan's "everything-and-the-kitchen-sink" scripts. Mouth agape, I chugged through his 32 single spaced typewritten pages. For a 16 page story no less! I believe he apologized for making the story a bit longer than he'd intended. Yeah — like I was really crying!
As I recall, Alan's script began with descriptions of him waking up, tossing the cat aside and putting a page in the typewriter. Real letter-to-a-pal, stream-of-consciousness stuff that was quite entertaining. Alan's story was even more so.

Describe a panel? Forget it! Kid stuff. Alan seduced his collaborators with his vivid word-pictures. Everything the artist needed to know was described, then he'd toss in a few more subtle background details for good measure. These details weren't necessarily art descriptions, but mind-paintings designed to inspire the artists. Whatever it was, it worked. Alan's Kurtzman-esque tale about the environmentalist garbage-monster, Sadie Mutz, was a joy to draw. Which makes me feel even worse about the bad, bad thing I did.

Ah, but we'll get to that...

In the 80s, Alan continued to surpass himself. His brilliant *Watchmen* series (drawn by artist Dave Gibbons) kept me on the edge of my seat, issue-by-issue. *Swamp Thing?* That comic just got better and better. Then he wrote a number of one-shot stories for DC, including a classic two-part Superman story that was both touching and inspirational.

In short order, Alan began scooping up Eisner, Kurtzman and Kirby Awards the way ordinary mortals scoop up cheese puffs.

Meanwhile, Alan and I worked out a deal with DC and Eclipse to produce a Mr. Monster/Swamp Thing crossover. This was possibly the first such agreement between a mainstream publisher and one of the small independents. Unfortunately, just as we finished plotting the story (a romp through the horror worlds of various old comic book companies), DC and Alan suffered a rancorous divorce and the project was scrapped.

He vowed never to work for them again, and DC lost one of their most fertile creators.

Luckily, Alan had plenty of other projects to keep him busy. There was *Miracleman* (formerly *Marvelman*) for Eclipse, *Lost Girls* and *From Hell* for Taboo and Tundra's ill-fated *Big Numbers* series. Ah yes, *Tundra*...

I like to think it was Tundra's fault. Yes, indeed. If not for them, I would never have been in England at all. And the bad, bad thing never would have happened. No indeed. So it's their fault, see?

Tundra. In the early 90s Teenage Mutant Ninja Turtles-magnate Kevin Eastman built his very own comic company. Foolish boy! He brought Alan and Steve Bissette on board — and Steve smuggled me and Mr. Monster aboard the S. S. Tundra. It was fun while it lasted.

In the year or two I was there, I produced three different Mr. Monster titles, and two book collections. Alan wrote a story for my Mr. Monster spin-off, *Kelly*, starring MM's sexy gal Friday. Two of his cartoonist pals drew his tale, and I suspect that's why he squeezed it into his schedule.

And say! How could I forget to mention the gory, exquisitely-detailed Mr. Monster pin-up Alan drew for the MM book collection? Yes, he also dabbles in art. Talented boy, that Alan!

Tundra was a good deal all around. We got to create some great comics, and Kevin was able to rid himself of great gobs of excess cash that were cluttering the offices. He got rid of at least a couple of carts of cash when he flew half the Tundra crew to England for *UKCAC91*. That's the 1991 *United Kingdom Comic Art Convention*, for those who haven't had the pleasure. I was one of about a dozen cartoonists and god-know-how-many staffers who *did*, courtesy of the ever-flowing "turtle-money."

Plane tickets, room and board were all on Tundra's tab. Yes indeed, that was but one of many brilliant financial decisions that quickly sank the company.

But I gotta tell you, that was one terrific convention — maybe my best ever! First class all the way, lads. I got to meet Simon Bisley, Neil Gaiman, Garry Leach and other equally impressive British cartoon luminaries.

ALAN MOORE

Right: *A rare illustration by Alan Moore himself for an issue of Michael T. Gilbert's* **Mr. Monster** *magazine. Illustration ©2003 Alan Moore. Mr. Monster © Michael T. Gilbert.*

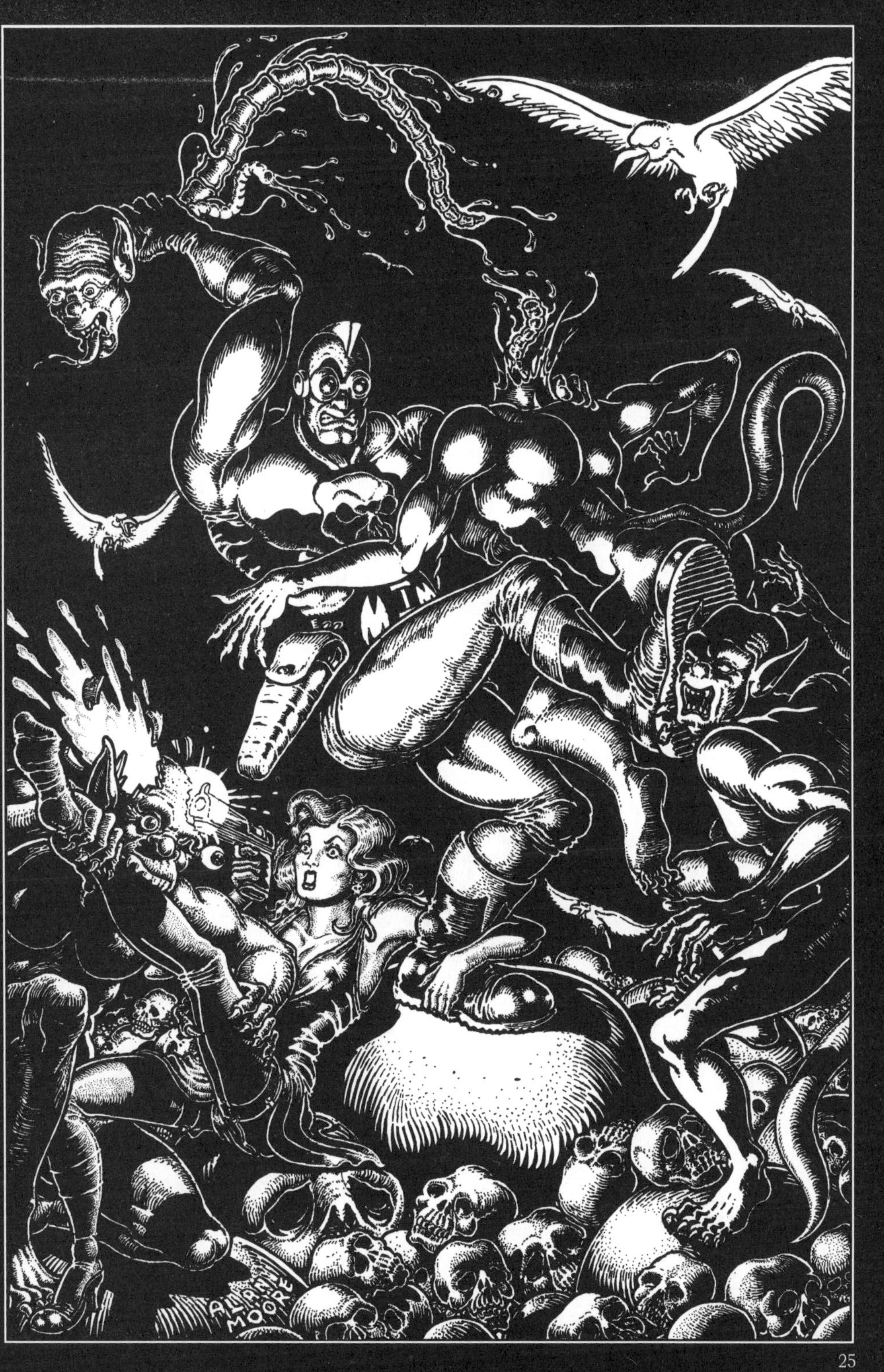
ALLAN
MOORE

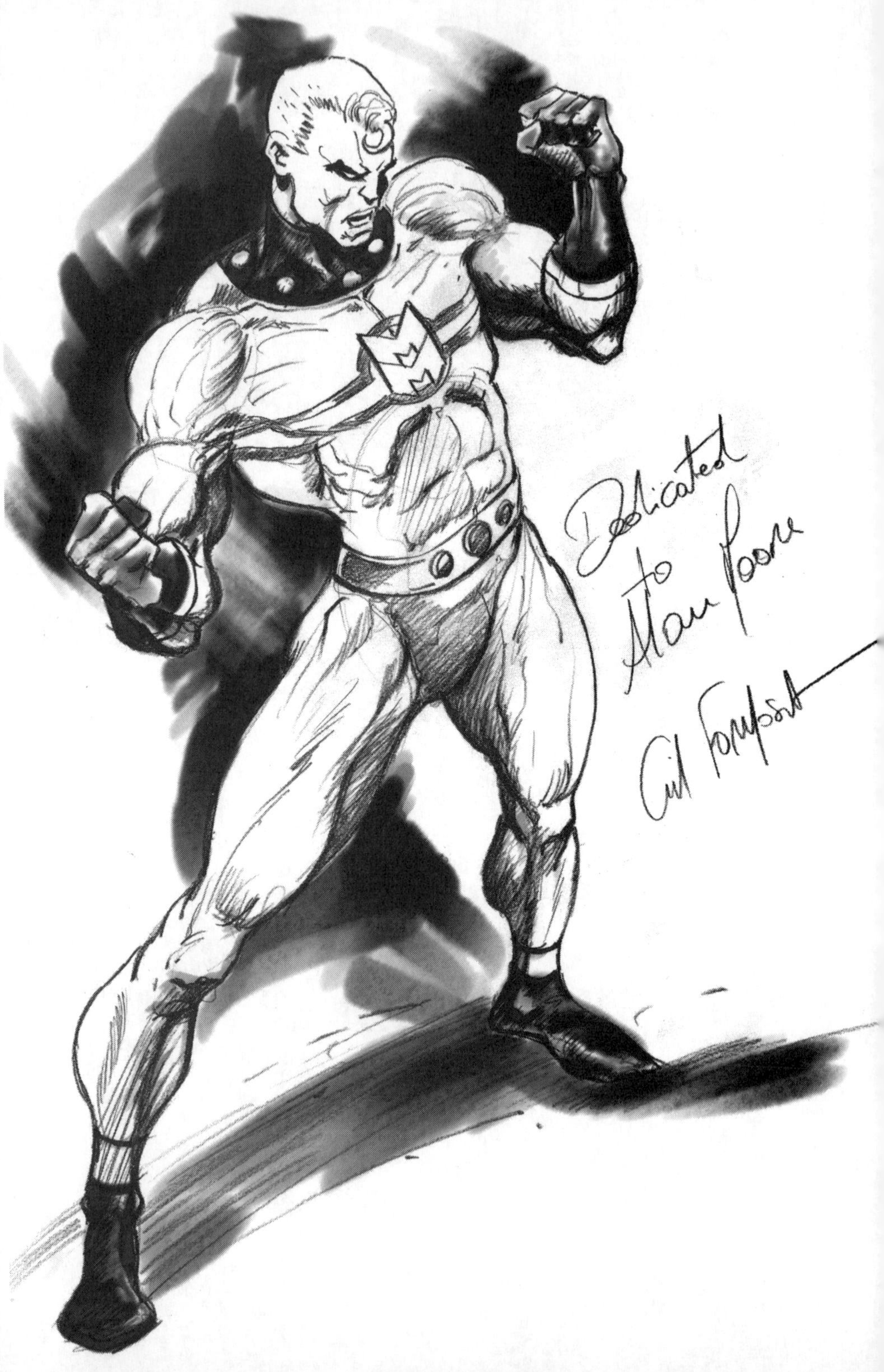
Dedicated to Alan Moore

Garry illustrated Alan's early Marvelman stories, and later co-edited A-1 magazine with fellow limey Dave Elliott. After the con, Garry gave me a personal tour of London's best comic shops. Or is that "shoppes?" Probably the latter, as some were situated in 400 year-old buildings! Nothing like that in the states, mate!
I still have some of the cheap black-and-white British reprints Garry turned me on to, featuring American comics from the 40s to the 60s. These often had stories from different, long-defunct companies in a single book. Wow!

Oh, yeah— I also visited Westminster Abbey and similar tourist must-sees. But you don't want to hear about that, now do you? This trip was my first overseas and remains a very, very fond memory.

Unfortunately, the universe has a way of balancing the good with the bad. Hence the bad, bad thing I did to Alan.

Which I will now tell you about.

It began right after the UK convention. I'd hoped to see Alan there, but he was a no-show at the show. I was told he'd recently sworn off cons after experiencing some good-natured stalking by adoring fans. They just loved the guy too much.

We should all have those problems.

We were phone pals, but I'd only met Alan in the flesh once, briefly, at the '86 San Diego Comicon. I say briefly because Alan was running from a crowd of bloodthirsty adoring fans (see above!). As I recall, they were brandishing Alan Moore effigies encased in Mylars® inscribed with the Moore family crest. I also seem to recall flaming torches being brandished, but I won't swear to it. Quite a scene, man!

But that was years earlier. Now that I was in Alan's backyard, I wanted to pay him a slightly longer visit. Little did I know...

I gave him a call after the con and, good-natured bloke that he is, Alan invited me to stay overnight. Good thing too, as the train ride from London seemed to go on for hours! Who knew England was that big? Hell, who knew *Europe* was that big?

The train eventually stopped at Northampton, a small working-class town in the middle of nowhere. By then I was feeling a bit under the weather. Runny nose, sneezing, that sort of thing. Lack of sleep and germ-infested airplane air was catching up with me. With the convention over, I was happy to start my real vacation. And what better way to begin than a visit with Alan Moore?

As much as I was looking forward to getting together, I was still a bit apprehensive. By 1991, Alan was already quite the media darling and I wasn't quite sure what to expect.

First there were all his awards. He'd won with such crushing regularity that the Eisner and Kurtzman committee guys began buying his trophy-labels in bulk, just to save printing costs. Ambitious graphic novels like *From Hell, Lost Girls,* and *Big Numbers* oozed like golden honey from his magic fingers. In his spare time Alan was busy writing novels, screenplays and God-knows-what-else. Then of course there were dark rumours about his arcane experiments with forbidden drugs, strange sex — and the occult. *Brrrr!*

Frankly it was all a bit intimidating.

Luckily, my pal Steve Bissette was also staying the night, so I wasn't all

GIL FORMOSA

Left: *Gil Formosa is one of the hottest commercial artists in France; he has illustrated ad campaigns for Coca-Cola, Heinz, Disney, Kellogg, Levi-Strauss and Honda. He's also illustrated several children's books featuring Tex Avery's characters, and designed numerous animated television series and video games. Illustration ©2003 Gil Formosa. Marvelman © 2003 copyright holder.*

that worried. Steve may even have been on the train with me, but it's hard to remember 12 years later. Regardless, I was glad he was joining us. When I arrived at the station, Alan was waiting.

Alan Moore stood roughly eight feet tall. His flowing black beard and intense eyes could have given Rasputin a run for his money. On that forlorn train station in the middle of nowhere, one thought kept running through my disease-ridden head again and again.

"Jeeze, Alan — *shave!!*"

Ha. Only kidding, Alan. *Kid-ding!*

After we arrived at Alan's flat he gave us the grand tour. What a mess! And I mean that in a good way, of course. Glorious chaos is what it was. Alan's studio floor was heaped six feet deep with comics and graphic novels. It's a wonder he could find anything amongst the rubble, but somehow he did. (Did I mention that Alan's also an ace detective?)
I made a mental note to dump my entire comic collection on my floor when I got home. Anything to improve my writing, I say! Later, Alan brewed us a spot of tea and the three of us chatted.

That afternoon I met Alan's charming young daughters. He'd been recently divorced, and the girls were visiting daddy. Later we took a short ride to see Alan's gal-pal, Melinda Gebbie. The two were working on their *Lost Girls* series, and Melinda's pages were quite striking.

Oddly enough, I'd met Melinda years earlier. In the 70s, we were both members of the "Ground-Under Cartoonists" — a loosely-knit group of San Francisco-based cartoonists. A dozen of us met every couple of weeks or so, and our ever-changing membership included Roger May, Larry Rippee and Trina Robbins. With one or two exceptions, we were all third-stringers in the underground comix pantheon, but we had fun griping, shooting the bull and drawing.

Melinda probably doesn't remember, but she and I even went on a date once. Back in '76 we grabbed a bite to eat and visited San Francisco's legendary *City Lights* bookstore, home of the original "beat" poets. I hadn't seen or heard from her for in at least a decade. Now she was in England, dating Alan. Weird!

If I'd imagined I was going to have tons of private time with Alan, reality soon set me straight. He was a comic book super-star, and the phone was constantly ringing. Shortly after I arrived, a couple of German TV guys showed up to interview Alan. Me, Steve, Melinda and Alan arranged to have lunch with them at some nearby Indian restaurant. We walked there in the hot, muggy air.

It seemed about a 100 miles away, but that may have just been the cold-bugs messing with my mind. I tried to pick up some cold pills along the way, but the stores were closed. Many U.S. drugstores are open 24/7, so it's easy to get spoiled. Not here!

The small restaurant had no air conditioning, which seems to be the norm in England. But the food was tasty, and if memory serves, the TV guys even picked up the tab. Cool.

Through it all, Alan in the centre of this storm, answering questions, making witty observations, cooking for the entire restaurant (did I mention Alan's a master chef?). It was exhausting just to watch. Perhaps this level of activity wasn't the norm, but I suspect otherwise.

ERIC SHANOWER

Right: *Eric Shanower writes and illustrates* **Age of Bronze,** *the award-winning comic book series from Image Comics retelling the Trojan War story. Illustration ©2003 Eric Shanower.* Promethea *©2003 America's Best Comics, LLC.*

28

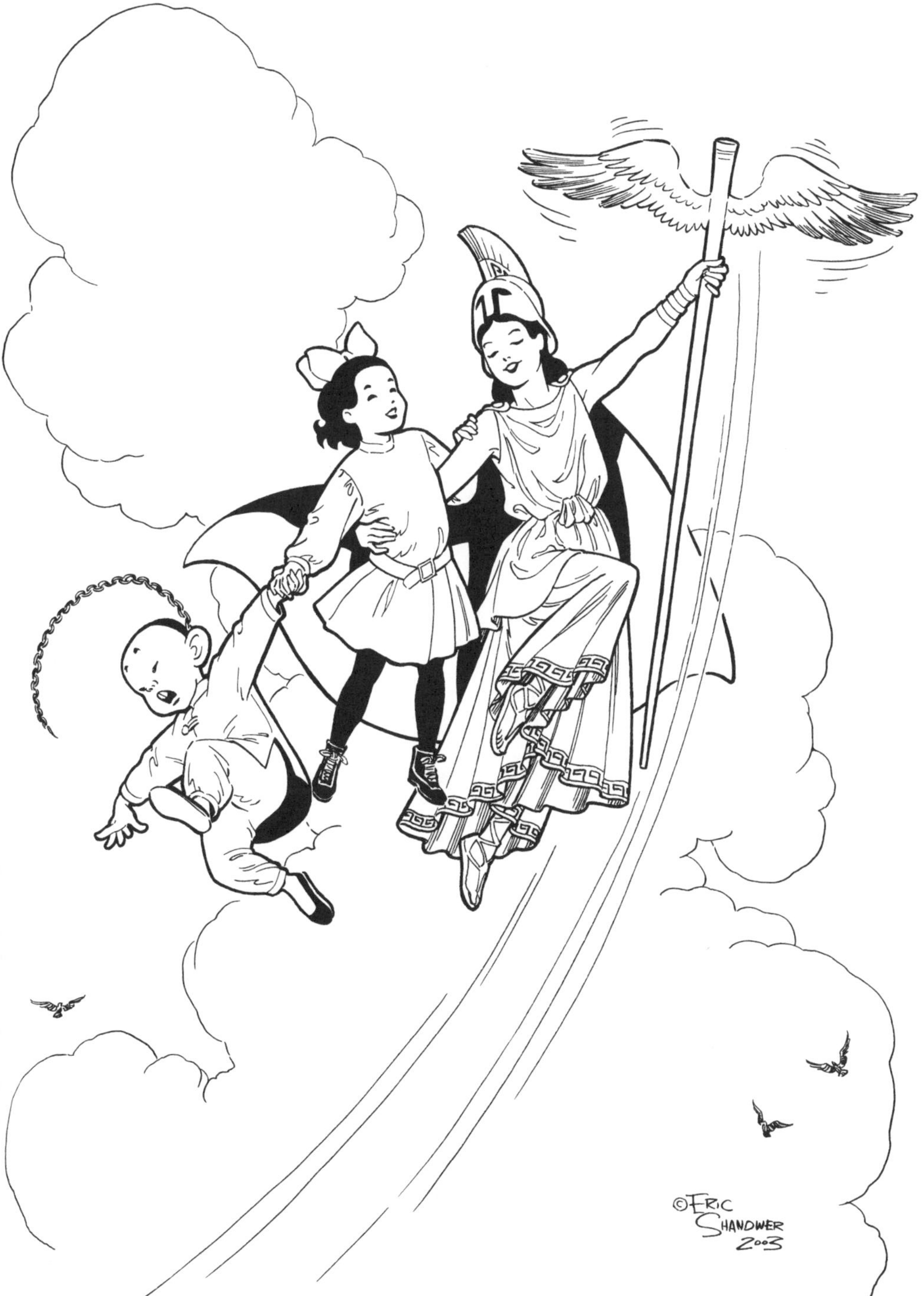
©ERIC SHANDWER 2003

Back home later that night, Alan passed around a fragrant, oddly overstuffed hand-rolled cigarette. Later, he played a tape featuring a song he and his mates had cut. Say, did I mention that Alan plays music too? Heck, he probably builds rockets in his spare time!

Anyway, we all had a fine time talking until bedtime. The sun wasn't *quite* up yet, as I recall. I bunked with Steve Bissette, and gabbed some more. They call it "sleep-talking" in England. Or so I'm told.

The next day, my cold was worse than ever. I was sneezing up a storm, and blowing through handkerchiefs at an alarming rate. Finally, Alan took pity on me. The stores were open now, so we stopped at a nearby "chemist." We call 'em drugstores in my part of the world, but I prefer the English version. There's something much more arcane and spooky about getting cold tablets at a "chemist."

I popped a couple of tablets and my sneezing stopped. Even my running nose finally took a rest. Thank you, Mr. Chemist!

From there I headed back to London — and then back to the states with enough England stories to bore my friends for months! And now, lest I bore you too, gentle reader, I'll bid you adieu.

Hope you enjoyed my little Alan Moore story and...

Eh? What's that, gentle reader? You say I *forgot* something?

Oh. That's right. I promised to discuss the bad, bad thing I did to Alan, didn't I? OK. Fair enough. Here goes...

Remember that cold? Well, Alan caught it. Must've been in bed for two whole days. During that dark, dark time he *didn't* finish three screenplays he'd been working on. Gone forever.

A 1700-page sequel to Dante's *Divine Comedy* (in the original *old Italian!*), five life-changing graphic novels, and three breakthrough comic book series were never completed. All lost.

He didn't compose his brilliant *Grunge Band Harmonica Concerto in D Minor.* Or the Shakespearean sonnet, two Madrigals, and 243 perfectly-pitched haikus. Nor did he paint that Botticelli homage.

World hunger persists because Alan, practically at death's door due to my cold bug, was too weak to recite the mystic spell he'd written to cure that particular problem.

And all because I sneezed.

Sorry Alan, old bean, old chap, old sock.

I should've visited Maggie Thatcher!

The End

• **Michael T. Gilbert**

BRAD MELTZER

Right: *Brad Meltzer is the acclaimed author of the best selling novels* **The Tenth Justice, Dead Even, The First Counsel** *and the recent* **The Millionaires.** *His books have been translated into over a dozen languages. He played himself as an extra in Woody Allen's* **Celebrity** *and recently wrote DC's* **Green Arrow** *comic book. www.bradmeltzer.com. Text ©2003 Brad Meltzer. Page design by Gary Spencer Millidge*

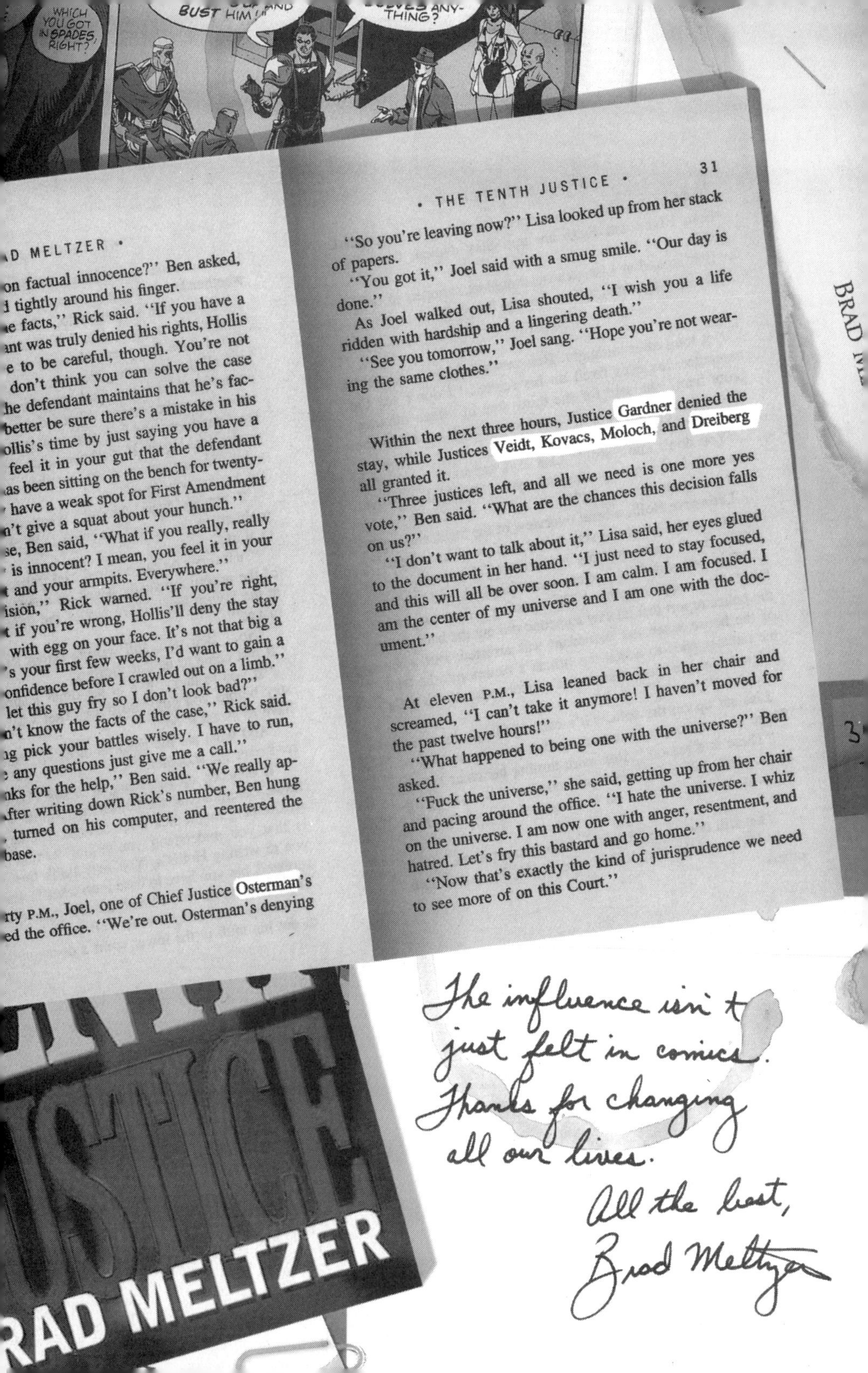
WHICH YOU GOT IN SPADES, RIGHT?
BUST HIM!
D MELTZER •
on factual innocence?'' Ben asked,
d tightly around his finger.
e facts,'' Rick said. ''If you have a
ant was truly denied his rights, Hollis
e to be careful, though. You're not
don't think you can solve the case
he defendant maintains that he's fac-
better be sure there's a mistake in his
ollis's time by just saying you have a
feel it in your gut that the defendant
as been sitting on the bench for twenty-
have a weak spot for First Amendment
n't give a squat about your hunch.''
se, Ben said, ''What if you really, really
is innocent? I mean, you feel it in your
and your armpits. Everywhere.''
ision,'' Rick warned. ''If you're right,
if you're wrong, Hollis'll deny the stay
with egg on your face. It's not that big a
's your first few weeks, I'd want to gain a
onfidence before I crawled out on a limb.''
let this guy fry so I don't look bad?''
n't know the facts of the case,'' Rick said.
g pick your battles wisely. I have to run,
any questions just give me a call.''
nks for the help,'' Ben said. ''We really ap-
fter writing down Rick's number, Ben hung
turned on his computer, and reentered the
base.
rty P.M., Joel, one of Chief Justice Osterman's
ed the office. ''We're out. Osterman's denying
• THE TENTH JUSTICE • 31
''So you're leaving now?'' Lisa looked up from her stack of papers.
''You got it,'' Joel said with a smug smile. ''Our day is done.''
As Joel walked out, Lisa shouted, ''I wish you a life ridden with hardship and a lingering death.''
''See you tomorrow,'' Joel sang. ''Hope you're not wearing the same clothes.''
Within the next three hours, Justice Gardner denied the stay, while Justices Veidt, Kovacs, Moloch, and Dreiberg all granted it.
''Three justices left, and all we need is one more yes vote,'' Ben said. ''What are the chances this decision falls on us?''
''I don't want to talk about it,'' Lisa said, her eyes glued to the document in her hand. ''I just need to stay focused, and this will all be over soon. I am calm. I am focused. I am the center of my universe and I am one with the document.''
At eleven P.M., Lisa leaned back in her chair and screamed, ''I can't take it anymore! I haven't moved for the past twelve hours!''
''What happened to being one with the universe?'' Ben asked.
''Fuck the universe,'' she said, getting up from her chair and pacing around the office. ''I hate the universe. I whiz on the universe. I am now one with anger, resentment, and hatred. Let's fry this bastard and go home.''
''Now that's exactly the kind of jurisprudence we need to see more of on this Court.''
BRAD MELTZER
The influence isn't just felt in comics. Thanks for changing all our lives.
All the best,
Brad Meltzer

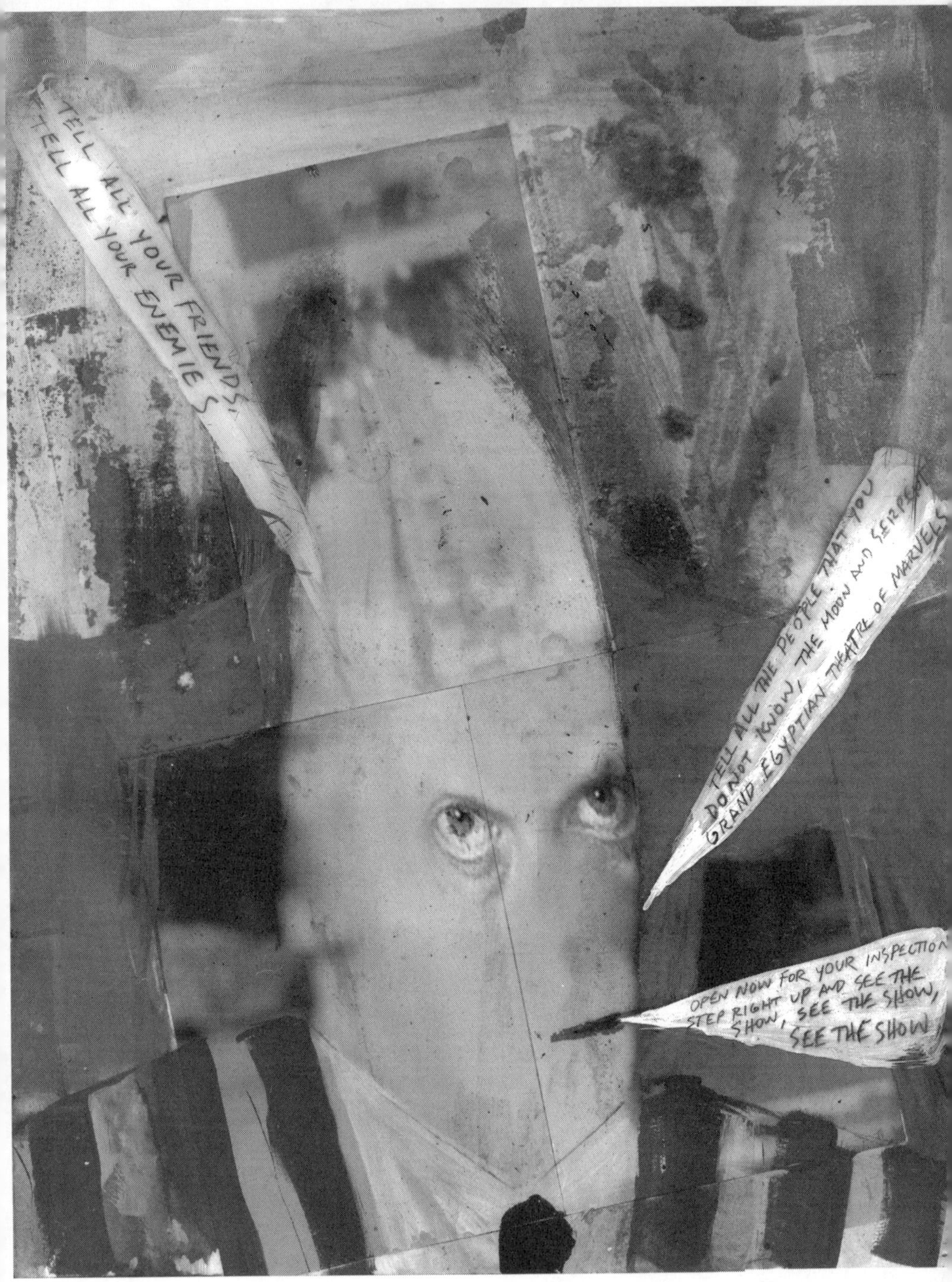
TELL ALL YOUR FRIENDS,
TELL ALL YOUR ENEMIES
TELL ALL THE PEOPLE THAT YOU DO NOT KNOW, THE MOON AND SERPENT GRAND EGYPTIAN THEATRE OF MARVELS
OPEN NOW FOR YOUR INSPECTION STEP RIGHT UP AND SEE THE SHOW, SEE THE SHOW, SEE THE SHOW

I've never met Alan Moore, but one of my favorite comic's jobs was painting Alan's "The Hair of the Snake That Bit Me" for "Negative Burn." It was a song, rather than a story. I began without a pag count and only vague circus images suggested by the lyrics. I was s into it that I painted all 8 pages in a week. Thanks Alan___Bill Koeb

ALAN MOORE AND THE MYSTERY OF TRANSUBSTANTIATION

GIUSEPPE PILI

Giuseppe Pili is an Italian writer who has worked in theatre, cinema, television and comics.
Text ©2003 Giuseppe Pili.

When we solve a riddle or crack an enigma, our spirit is pervaded by a subtle pleasure. Are we enticed by the complexity of the enigma, by the riddle-maker's skill, or by the confirmation of our abilities? There is no use in trying to tell these elements apart: their mutual permeation is the alchemy underlying the game.

There definitely is a difference between playing and being on the receiving end of a narrative – it depends on our degree of involvement. Listening or reading implies some passivity, while playing forces us into a direct confrontation.

We might define Moore's stories as "ludic interactions". Calling them "games" would be reductive: they are complex and refined challenges, which gradually screen the players. Going one step further, we could even talk of true initiations into Moore's world. We learned that the Master does not speak to just anybody, but only to those who have the talent – or the burden – of understanding stories first with the mind and only then with the heart. Admittedly, this pleases us. The symmetries, the references, the ellipses, the paraphrases, the quotations are all part of an architecture which entices and hypnotises us. Once we get trapped inside Moore's reality, we become its prey: we no longer understand where our everyday experience ends and his realism begins, we cannot tell a true dialogue from a simulation à la Moore.

We know the game well and we want to play it, if possible, with minimal variations. As we read the first page, the opening panel sweeps us away: the opening lines are complex and convoluted. We are bewildered, but not frightened: we know that, at the right moment, the Master will guide us. Then a structure begins to take shape. Recognisable, reassuring elements start to appear. For us, it is a relief; luckily, we are not completely at the mercy of Chaos. We have an irrational faith in the existence of an eventual Meaning and with Moore there is always a Meaning. Thus, as we keep reading, we become aware that what was originally obscure had its own justification after all. The second half of the story discloses the first and we feel the thrill. "Brilliant"... "how does he do it"... "how does he manage"... "such a balance of form"... "such daring geometry". Our passion lights up very gradually and is incomprehensible to those who do not live inside their mind.

PEDRO MOTA

Page 34 following:
Pedro Mota is the co-author of A Linguagem da BD (The language of Comics), and curated the largest retrospective exhibition of Alan Moore's work to date for the Amadora International Comics Festival in Portugal in 2002.
Text ©2003 Pedro Mota.

ANDRÉ CARRILHO

Page 35 following:
André Carrilho is an award-winning illustrator, cartoonist and caricaturist, born in Portugal in 1974. His most recent assignments have included caricatures for The New York Times and The Independent on Sunday.
Illustration ©2003 André Carrilho.

The ending succeeds in squaring the circle. We reassemble the pieces of the jigsaw in a moment of self-complacency. Here comes a retroactive aesthetic delight, exquisitely intellectual. We are pervaded by an unconscious and narcissistic pleasure in our abilities. We have understood Alan Moore. We have rightfully been initiated into his Church of Mysteries. Our lips have received the Host of his spirit.

Through the might and magic of this artistic transubstantiation, Alan Moore is no longer the creator of the magic. Now he has become both the magic itself and its officiants. He is part of us.

Reciprocity is the secret of his fascination: after the last page, irrespective of the man living in Northampton, Alan Moore is us.

• **Giuseppe Pili**

BILL KOEB

Left: Bill Koeb is a painter and illustrator who lives in North Carolina with his wife and son. He has illustrated stories for Vertigo and Marvel, and drawn a few of his own short pieces for Vanguard.
Illustration ©2003 Bill Koeb.

ALAN ON THE OTHER SIDE OF THE MIRROR

ALAN ON THE OTHER SIDE OF THE MIRROR

If there is a central theme in Alan Moore's work, it is the appeal to the affirmation of the individual and individual responsibility. Taking full responsibility for their actions, including both successes and failures, nothing can stop individuals in their process of discovery, of their own identity and universal dimension. Moore has also questioned the legitimacy of others (namely super-heroes) to define standards of normality and morality. This appeal to the responsibility of the individual is transmitted in many forms, but comics - this unique form of communication that appeals simultaneously to both halves of the brain - has been a privileged vehicle.

The mastery of different genres and formats in comics is one of the characteristics that define Alan Moore, the comic writer. But he prefers to demonstrate another one: the talent for collaboration, a deep knowledge of the people he works with and how to bring up the best in them. At first glance, Alan Moore's famously detailed scripts would seem to give very little room for the artist's creativity. But, in fact, those meticulous scripts reflect the vision of the artist into words, in a comprehensive and objective way of representation that, of the two people collaborating, only the writer is capable of doing. As a result, the final artwork reflects and translates the vision of the writer regarding such basic aspects as rhythm and composition, in a presentation that only that particular artist is able to produce. The work of Alan Moore in comics and in collaboration is, itself, a conscious experience of continuous discovery of knowledge. And this is perhaps the best parallel one can establish with his discovery of magic. For Alan Moore, writing and magic, two of the fields that Hermes looks after, are strongly connected. There's no significant difference between the two.

To be a writer means to have the ability to transmit anything to the reader, to transform him or her witness it. This involves the transmission of true emotion. This effort of sincerity and generosity that Moore puts into his work is, in turn, what his collaborating artists usually point out in Alan, the human being.

As a writer, his brilliance in characterization, ambiance and storytelling, and mastery of the English language has led Moore into experimenting in new directions in comics, taking this popular medium to a higher, and more demanding level. Using the metaphor of fractal mathematics, Fiction and Reality are redefined, by adjusting the point of view while accepting the complexity of what would be a more realistic and human form of relationship with the world. History becomes identified with Fiction, as associations and memories are constructed from the perception of our senses. It is the renewed believe in Myths, which defy the linear structure of both History and Fiction, with their permanent presence. "All myths are true, Moore writes. Given that they last longer, they are even truer than the so-called "Real World". This perspective is redefining the Fantasy and Historical Fiction genres. As Moore puts it: "Arriving to the conclusion that ideas are forms that exist in the idea-space, and that our mind can travel it, we can conceive, in this same space, forms of life, and interaction between different forms of life. And without the barrier of time: people from the past, people from the future, and even natives of this space, creatures consisting only of ideas, complex ideas that had become self-conscientious. There you can explain all the ghosts, demons, angels that exist in human imagination. These things exist in our mind and are real. But they aren't real in the same way that physical things are. They are two different kinds of reality: mental and physical".

On the other side of the mirror, we are privileged spectators of the conscious voyages that Alan Moore makes to the world of the mental reality, to the idea-space, the kingdoms of imagination, fiction, dream and fantasy. In each trip, he pushes further the possibilities of the mind and the possibilities of comics.

Pedro Mota, Amadora 2003

illustration by André Carrilho >>>>

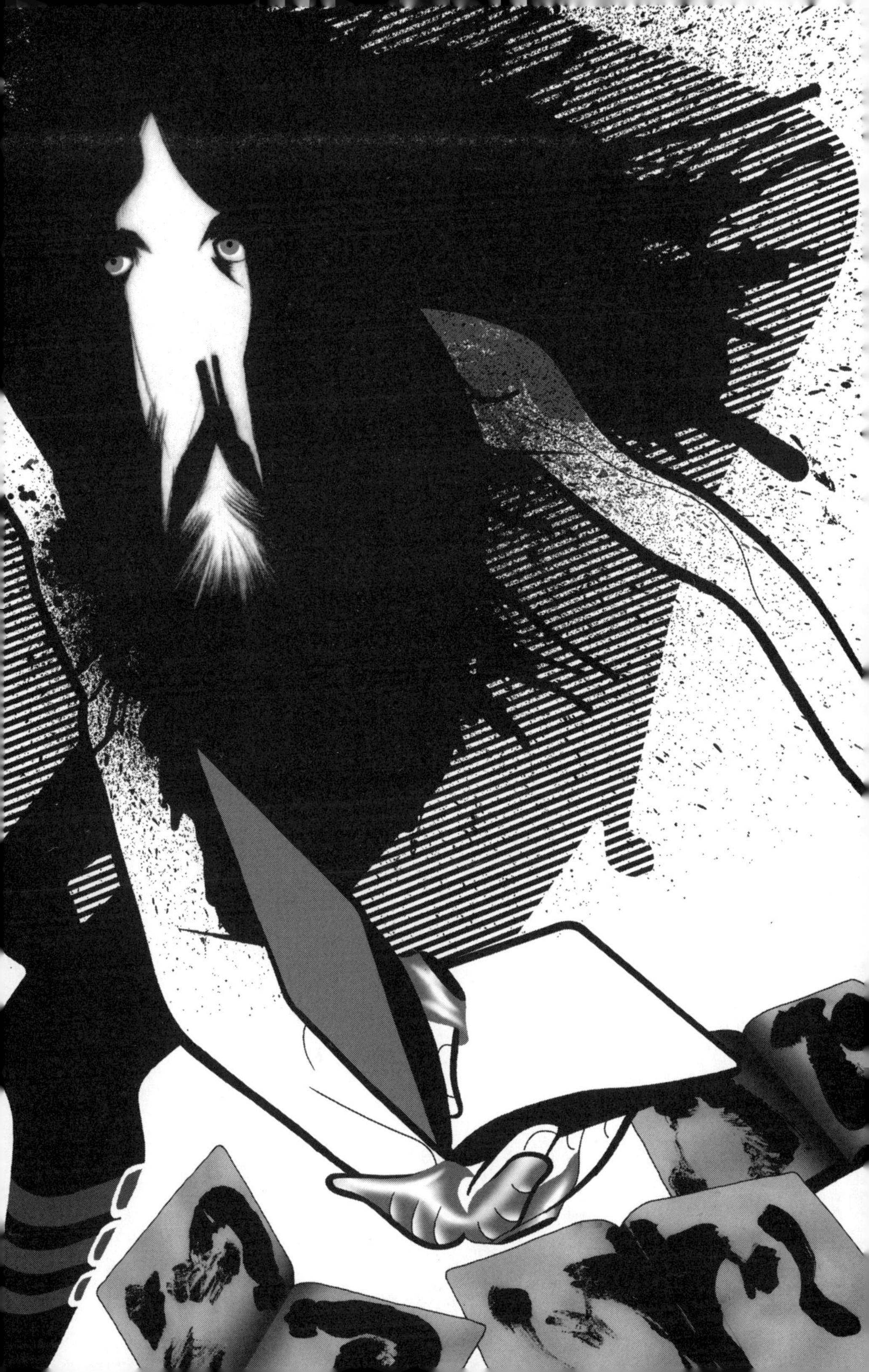

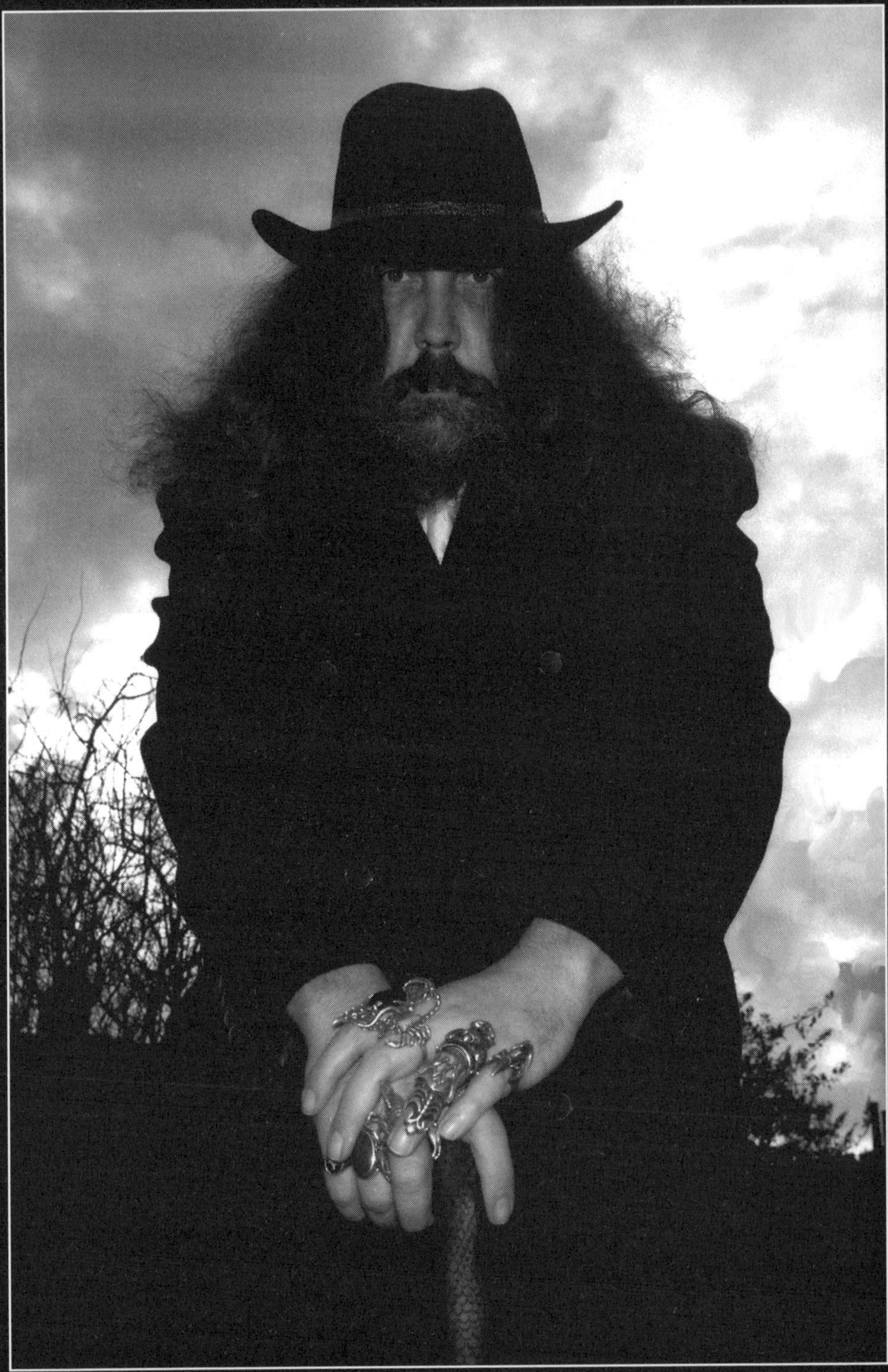

RANDOM THOUGHTS

LEN WEIN

Len Wein is the creator of **Swamp Thing** and has been a comics writer for over 30 years. He was also editor-in-chief at Marvel Comics and has written for film, TV and video games.

Text ©2003 Len Wein.

Some random thoughts about Alan Moore (which somehow seems appropriate):

1) The first time I called Alan, he refused to believe I was me.

I wish I could remember at this late date exactly what it was that prompted me to call Alan when I was looking for a new writer to take over *Swamp Thing*. I know I had been a fan of Alan's work on *2000 A.D.* and so he seemed an interesting choice as writer, assuming, of course, he was available and so inclined. I got his phone number somehow, made the international phone call, and Alan answered on the third ring. I introduced myself, told Alan I had an offer to make him, and he hung up on me.

When I called back, assuming the connection had been broken accidentally, I introduced myself again. Alan's reply: "No, who is this really?" And he started going through a list of his mates, trying to figure out who had put me up to this and why. It took me quite a while to convince Alan I was indeed me, and that I was interested in offering him work in the States, on my own precious baby. It took a lot of cajoling and convincing to talk Alan into taking on the assignment, but I'm glad he did. The changes he made on Swamp Thing helped to revolutionize the art form, his language was pure music. Under Alan, the graphic narrative suddenly grew up. And the comic book industry has never been the same since.

2) The first time I met Alan, I couldn't believe he was he.

DC Comics sent me to London to interface with what was then becoming a growing number of British creators who had started working on the DC books in Alan's wake. People like Dave Gibbons, Kev O'Neill, so many others. We met in a local Pub, and Alan was the last to arrive. He came strolling in, eyes wild, that long tangle of hair and beard whipping in the breeze, looking for all intents and purposes like the mad monk Rasputin returning from a two-week bender. He was wearing a suit that was 40 years out of style, the jacket and pants cuffs each several inches too short, a ruffled shirt, a narrow tie in a piano keyboard pattern, garish socks that matched nothing on earth, and (if I'm recalling correctly) a top hat.

Alan apologized for being late, but explained that he had been at the optometrist, having his eyes checked. He explained that the sight in one eye was perfect, but the other not so much. The Doctor had recommended glasses with appropriate lenses. Alan said he had considered getting a monocle instead for the one bad eye, but had decided against it. "Why?" I asked, foolishly.

Alan replied, "Well, frankly, I was afraid wearing a monocle might make me look a bit odd."

And, that, in a couple of quick anecdotes, is Alan Moore.

All the best, my friend. Long may you wave.

DAVIDE BARZI

Pages 38-39 following:
Davide Barzi is an Italian comics writer, journalist and critic.
Strip ©2003 Davide Barzi/Oskar.

OSKAR

Oskar works as penciler and inker on the Italian comics classic **Alan Ford** . He is also the co-creator, with writer Davide Barzi, of the small press comics series **No Name**.
Strip ©2003 Davide Barzi/Oskar.
The League of Extraordinary Gentlemen ©2003 Alan Moore and Kevin O'Neill.

PIET CORR

Left: Piet Corr a.k.a. **pietdesnapp** is a freelance photographer and lecturer, born in Northampton. His work has been exhibited in galleries and libraries all over England.
Photograph ©2003 Piet Corr.

• **Len Wein**
Los Angeles, CA
April, 2003

SandokAlan

Davide Barzi (story) & Oskar (art)

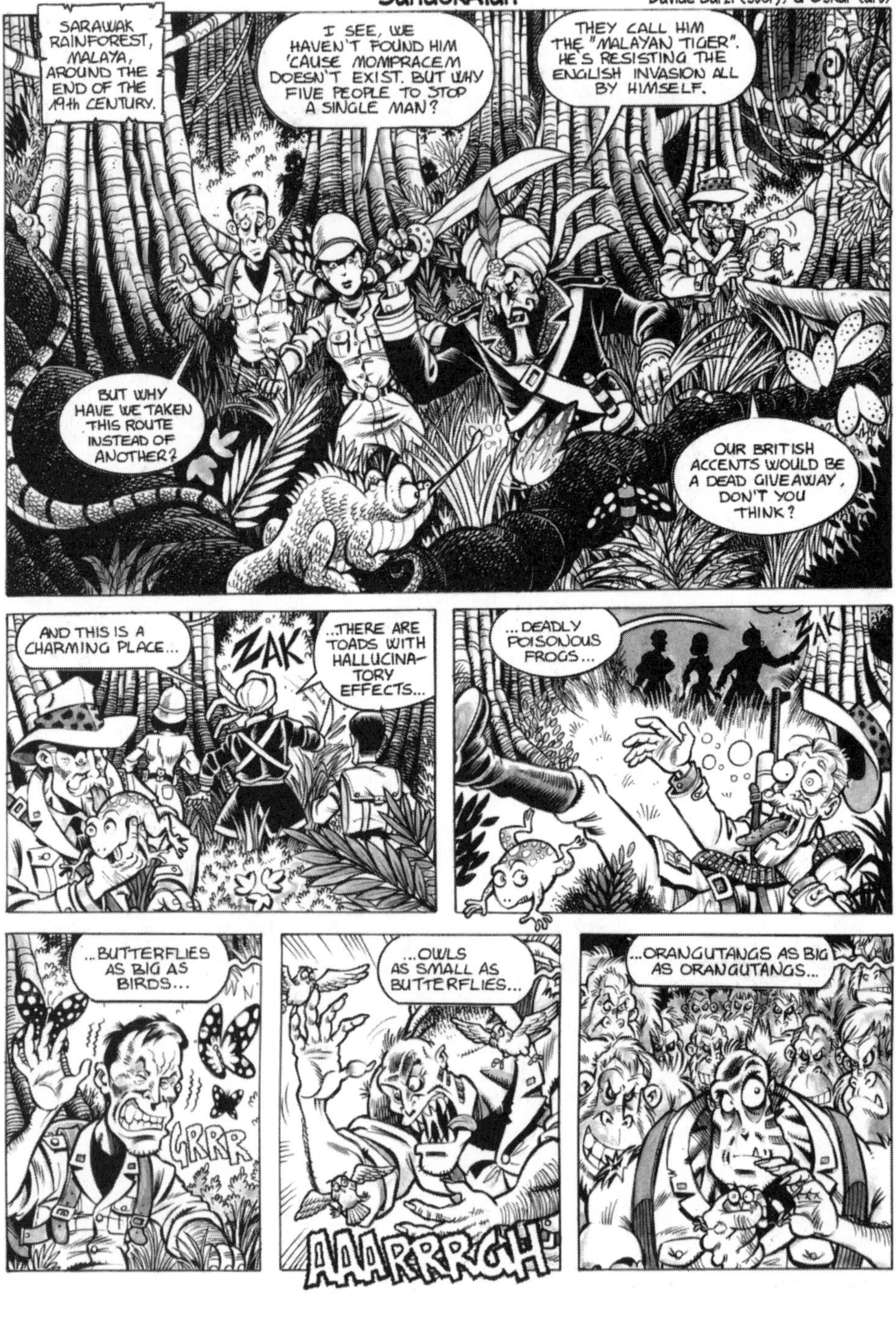
SARAWAK RAINFOREST, MALAYA, AROUND THE END OF THE 19th CENTURY.
I SEE, WE HAVEN'T FOUND HIM 'CAUSE MOMPRACEM DOESN'T EXIST. BUT WHY FIVE PEOPLE TO STOP A SINGLE MAN?
THEY CALL HIM THE "MALAYAN TIGER". HE'S RESISTING THE ENGLISH INVASION ALL BY HIMSELF.
BUT WHY HAVE WE TAKEN THIS ROUTE INSTEAD OF ANOTHER?
OUR BRITISH ACCENTS WOULD BE A DEAD GIVEAWAY, DON'T YOU THINK?
AND THIS IS A CHARMING PLACE...
ZAK
...THERE ARE TOADS WITH HALLUCINATORY EFFECTS...
...DEADLY POISONOUS FROGS...
ZAK
...BUTTERFLIES AS BIG AS BIRDS...
GRRR
...OWLS AS SMALL AS BUTTERFLIES...
AAARRRGH
...ORANGUTANGS AS BIG AS ORANGUTANGS...

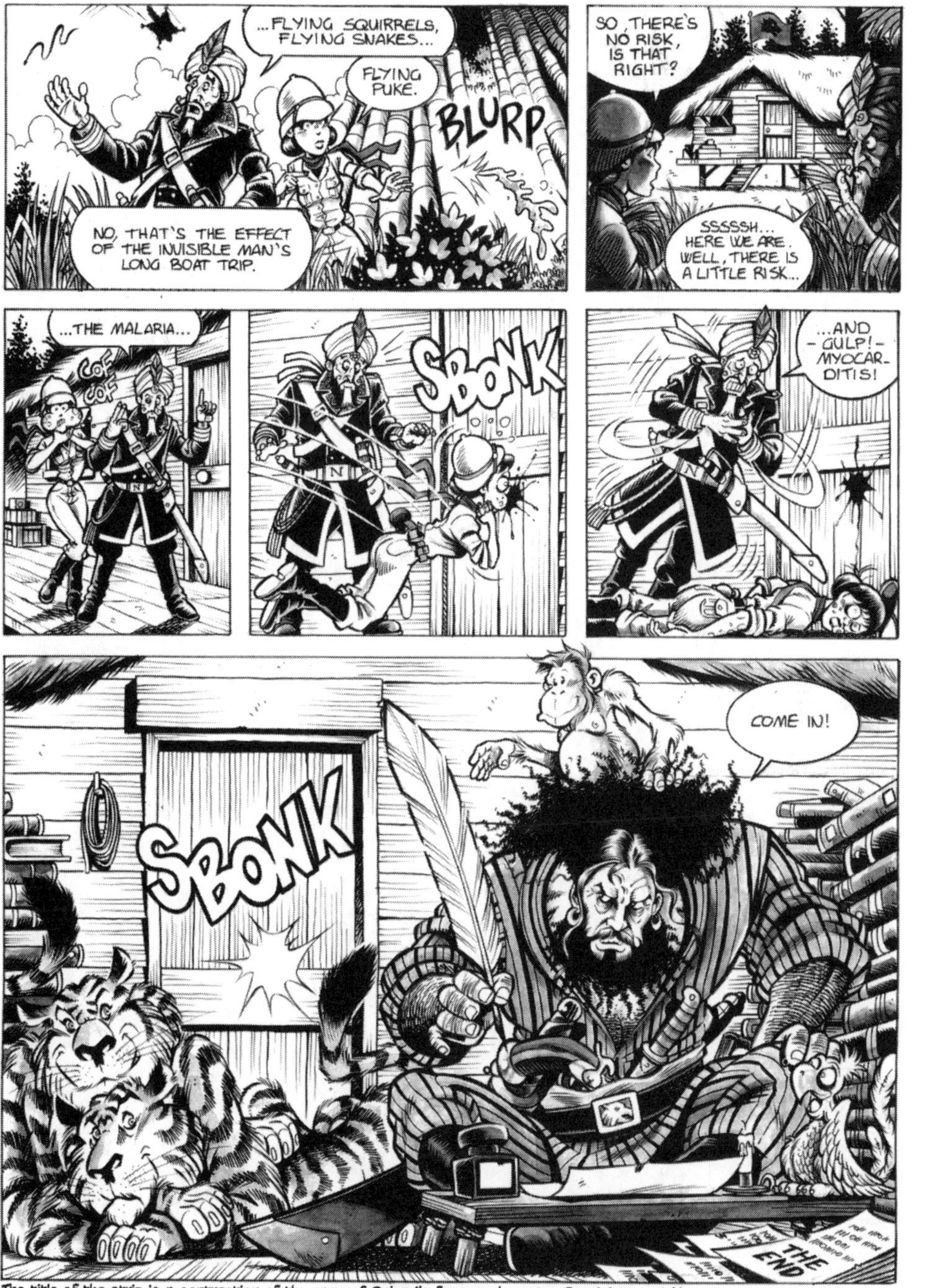
...FLYING SQUIRRELS, FLYING SNAKES...
FLYING PUKE.
BLURP
NO, THAT'S THE EFFECT OF THE INVISIBLE MAN'S LONG BOAT TRIP.
SO, THERE'S NO RISK, IS THAT RIGHT?
SSSSSH... HERE WE ARE. WELL, THERE IS A LITTLE RISK...
...THE MALARIA...
COF COF
SBONK
...AND - GULP! - MYOCAR-DITIS!
COME IN!
SBONK
THE END

The title of the strip is a contraction of the name of Salgari's famous character Sandokan and Alan...

UNWRAPPING THE BIRTH CAUL

MARC SINGER

Marc Singer teaches English at the University of Maryland and sits on the executive committee of ICAF, the International Comic Arts Festival. His articles have appeared in **JNT:** **Journal of Narrative Theory,** **African American Review,** and the **International Journal of Comic Art,** where he regularly reviews academic books about comics.

Text ©2003 Marc Singer.

The past few years have seen a tremendous creative output from Alan Moore, ranging from the completion of *From Hell* to the launching of America's Best Comics. But one of his richest, and most enigmatic, works of this period has been *The Birth Caul*, a "shamanism of childhood" (1) that examines the connections between our language, our identity, and our perceptions of the world.[1] First delivered as a performance at the Old County Court in Newcastle-upon-Tyne on November 18, 1995, and later adapted into comic book form by Moore's *From Hell* collaborator Eddie Campbell, *The Birth Caul* is a moving meditation on the loss of Moore's mother and on the myriad other losses that come with time and maturity.

Like *From Hell*, which Moore was writing at the time of his performance, *The Birth Caul* presents an essentially Romantic view of history as a tragic fall into a modern world that has lost some vital connection to its raw and violent past. Where *From Hell* brings us a gory Sir William Gull hectoring a crowd of unseeing, unhearing office-park drones, telling them, "Your days were born in blood and fires, whereof in you I may not see the meanest spark! Your past is pain and iron! Know yourselves! ... I am with you always!" (10: 21), *The Birth Caul* opens with a quick and depressing lecture on the history of Newcastle, which Moore presents as a long tumble from the pain and mystery of the Iron Age to a pestilent profusion of McDonalds and Pizza Huts. Moore, like Gull, looks to a bloody anatomical symbol to rediscover the primitive energy and meaning he and his peers have lost. He tells his audience, "We have wandered too far from some vital totem... something central to us that we have misplaced and must find our way back to... guided by some ancient bloodstained chart" (8). That totem, that bloodstained chart, is his mother's birth caul.

But *The Birth Caul* is far more than just a recapitulation of ideas that Moore has presented elsewhere. His Romantic and tragic concept of *cultural* history prepares his audience for an equally Romantic, tragic view of *personal* development—if all of English society has fallen from some primitive state of grace, then so too have all of us as individuals, over the course of our own lives. Moore therefore follows his historical overview with a series of flashbacks that depict the stages of development in a regression from early adulthood to adolescence, childhood, infancy, and finally back to prenatal existence. (In Campbell's adaptation these flashbacks illustrate the life of an audience member at Moore's Old County Court performance, creating a communal narrative that matches Moore's use of the collective "we" in his narration of these scenes.) *The Birth Caul* assumes an essentially gnostic view of child development, in which each earlier stage possesses an intuitive perception of the world that its successors have long forgotten.

Notes:

[1] Unless otherwise noted, all parenthetical references are to Moore and Campbell, The Birth Caul, Eddie Campbell Comics, 1999. For clarity's sake I have assigned page numbers to the unpaginated comic book, beginning the labeling with the first page of text and creators' credits.

To recover this primal state of consciousness, Moore must reverse not only our stages of development but also our faculties of language and self-awareness. Paradoxically, *The Birth Caul* uses language to erase language, but it nevertheless does so in a manner surprisingly consistent with some of the preeminent models of cognitive development. These models can potentially resolve Moore's linguistic contradictions; conversely, however, Moore's narrative also offers some important revisions of these theories. In articulating its own model of child development, *The Birth Caul* not only claims that we have lost some primal understanding of and connection to the world, it actively attempts to undo that loss by reversing time, self, and language.

GIANLUCA COSTANTINI

Left: Gianluca Costantini is one of the most productive artists in today's Italian underground comics scene. He is not only a comics author but also an illustrator, webmaster and organizer of comics events. www.gianlucacostantini.com. Illustration © 2003 Gianluca Costantini

On the first page of Campbell's adaptation, Moore says the birth caul "documents a personal Atlantis, a pre-verbal dreamtime, a naive shamanic state rich with abandoned totems" (1); he spends much of the rest of the work attempting to recover these totems by regressing his narrative consciousness to a state that predates language. This theme first comes to prominence in the second flashback episode, in which Moore and Campbell have reverted their audience-surrogate character back to preadolescence. The episode opens with the child staring at a butcher's window and at "the ritual centrepiece, a massive ox-tongue" that Moore employs, appropriately enough, as a totem of language: "the symbol of our power, of the divide between us and the other beasts, severed and dressed upon this public altar" (28). Because its sacrifice insures humanity's linguistic power, Moore uses the tongue to initiate *The Birth Caul*'s most detailed exploration of the mysteries of language.

The remainder of the childhood episode on pages 28 to 33 focuses primarily on the prices we pay for our mastery of language. Moore describes the child's acquisition of language—although possibly he refers to his own, since he writes this passage in the first-person singular rather than the more communal plural that marks most of the flashbacks' narration—in violent, mythic terms similar to those he has used to describe the ox-tongue: "They hanged me from a tree branch by my wrists and this is how I learned the words. They caved the underground den in on top of me and crawling like a lugworm through the smothering black dirt... I learned the words" (31). From the rituals of premature burial and Odin-like hanging, Moore gains the power of words.

The next two pages, however, abandon these mythological metaphors to describe a more realistic and conventional process of language acquisition, one that instructs children in socialization and obedience. In a passage that Campbell illustrates with images of childhood tribulations and schoolroom punishments, Moore writes,

> the language of a larger world is on us. We absorb its glossary of smack and panic... Sat knock-kneed at desks, we master an unmentioned alphabet of retribution and approval, become fluent in the lexicon of cross and tick and gold adhesive star. and this is how the tongue is severed, dressed, made fit for public consumption. (32)

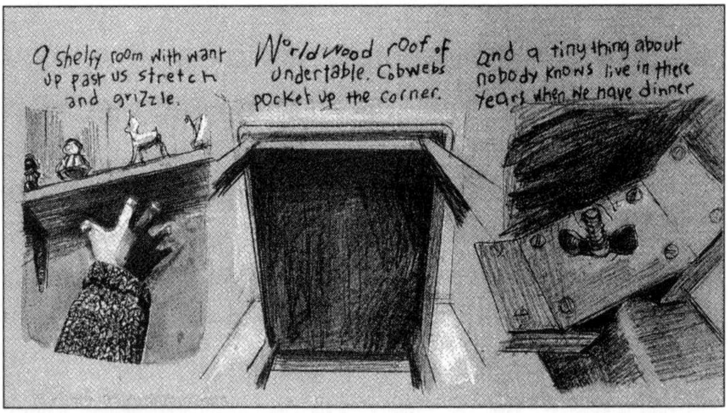
a shelfy room with want up past us stretch and grizzle.
Worldwood roof of undertable. Cobwebs pocket up the corner.
and a tiny thing about nobody knows live in there years when we have dinner
Fig. 1: from The Birth Caul, page 37.
© 2003 Alan Moore and Eddie Campbell

Here Moore adds some more common sacrifices to the metaphors of ox-tongue and gallows-tree; for children, learning language frequently means learning a punitive code of behavior. It also means losing the private language of home, as "Words we are allowed at home are confiscated. We become aware that the terrain behind our front door is unnervingly unique" (32). Language is instructing the child in difference and separation, a theme to which *The Birth Caul* will soon return.

But language carries an even more fundamental loss, one that Moore says we incur long before school and its torments. He writes, "Already something has been lost; a certain sight, a certain voice. Unable to recall more than the vaguest shape or flavour now as it recedes from us into that speechless fog before we knew the dazzle of the word, when form was all of our vocabulary" (33). In the next flashback episode, Moore attempts to illuminate that speechless fog by projecting his imagination, and the audience-surrogate figure, back into the preverbal state of infancy. With creatively mangled syntax, and with Campbell providing appropriately disjointed layouts and scribbled handwriting to complement him, Moore attempts to reproduce a preverbal consciousness (fig. 1). Many of the infant's insights are merely childlike misperceptions that invest mundane objects with animistic power: lawn ornaments that can talk (38), for example, or the underside of a simple table transformed into "Worldwood roof of undertable" (37), both a Tree of Life and a vault of heaven.

More boldly, though, Moore also claims that prelinguistic children perceive time quite differently than adults, implying that our sense of linear chronology is learned, if not outright imposed, by language or experience. The infant in *The Birth Caul* has not yet learned to recognize the divisions between past, present, and future. He senses "already that we are living long ago, like waistcoat whisker men the light got in and spoiled"—here Campbell introduces a fading nineteenth-century photograph (39)—and possesses a remarkable presentiment of mortality. The child thinks,

dead is birthday party... day one gran is be dead and just to think of it is almost now. day one is dad and mum be dead and it is now we cry and cry. and day one is a thing worse that we not can think about and cry and cry and cry and it is now and it is now. (40)

Either this child is perceiving all time as the present, or he has attained some more subtle awareness of time as a state of constant decay, a message in keeping with Moore's tragic conception of cultural and personal development.

Either way, it is probably safe to say that we don't commonly think of these insights as the work of a toddler. Yet Moore argues that we have simply lost our memory of these preverbal realizations, because of language but also because of an even more basic act of division whose precise moment in our development he attempts to capture: the forgetting happens "one sudden morning when us first think that we thinking and before it what we can't remember in the nothing came from" (41). The first moment of reflexive self-awareness also prompts our first amnesia, our loss of the gnosis that precedes not only our language but our most basic sense of self.

This argument is surprisingly consistent with some of the twentieth century's most prominent models of developmental psychology. Psychologist Jean Piaget claims, in *The Child and Reality* (1973), that children begin life in a stage of "sensorimotor intelligence" (10) in which they have no symbolic or linguistic faculties and draw no distinctions between subject and object, self and other; he also argues in *The Child's Conception of Time* (1946) that children do not easily grasp temporal concepts or distinguish them from spatial ones because they have a static concept of time (*Essential Piaget* 564). Piaget calls this a "temporal egocentrism" (*Essential Piaget* 565) that, like the sensorimotor egocentrism that fails to distinguish between self and other, projects their sense of self forwards and backwards across time. In the words of Hayden White, at the earliest stages of development "there is only the timeless, spaceless experience of the Same" (8). While Piaget's account of preverbal timelessness differs from Moore's—the psychologist describes a lack of awareness of time, not preternatural perceptions across it—both authors claim that this timeless experience is lost after children gain the powers of speech and symbolic operations.

Moore's linguistic and temporal regressions also bear some interesting resonances with Jacques Lacan's theories of psychoanalysis. Lacan claims that two orders, the "imaginary" and the "symbolic," alienate us from the "Real" order of direct, traumatic presence. The imaginary order is marked, Lacan argues, by the child's formation of ego and self-image during the "mirror stage" of first self-awareness; the symbolic order follows by introducing children to signification, teaching them the difference between signifiers and the objects they signify. Signification and selfhood both separate children from the Real, ushering them into a world of difference and alienation (Lacan 65; see also Evans 159-60). While Moore does not adhere to Lacan's theories as closely as he matches Piaget's model of cognitive development, he nevertheless provides an interesting case study in his attempt to revert back to a state of consciousness unhindered by the divisions of language, self, and symbol.

This attempt leads to the innermost moment in his narrative regression (though not its earliest moment), a recollection of consciousness before birth. Campbell's art and Moore's narration depict the first flicker of fetal consciousness from inside the womb, where Moore can pronounce that "the birth caul is the honest silence of ourselves" (42)—that is, a state that predates language and therefore a state where people "only are" (42), a state of being without any object or qualifier. The next page continues the depiction of a prelingual Eden; Moore describes the birth caul, amidst a torrent of metaphors, as "our sole identifying luggage label in the waiting room before they call our name and being named we are no more a part of everything" (43). Thus language not only destroys the infant's heightened awareness of past and future, it also sets the first boundaries around the self through the act of naming. The birth caul is a remnant of that last moment before language is imposed upon us, before we are delivered into the world where "self and time surrounds us" (44).

Yet even this moment before birth does not satisfy Moore as the origin of the self, and so he presses still farther back in time. *The Birth Caul* reverts through the stages of fetal development, past conception, beyond even copulation, back into some mysterious phylogenetic swamp from which Moore speculates we have arisen. This non-place (which Campbell can depict only metaphorically through quotations from Bosch and Hokusai; fig. 2) is the source of our creation, a river or sea whose waters Moore now pushes backwards over the "ocean wall of definition separating us from other. dashing it aside as if it were no more than words" (47). In fact, throughout the narrative that wall *has* been nothing more than words, as Moore has argued that language severs self from other, past from present. By reversing time and unspooling language, Moore hopes to undo the most basic boundaries of our selfhood as "verse by verse the song unwrites itself back to the word, the syllable... The cold white page" (47). In this total absence of language humanity can regain—or, at least, Moore can imagine—its first gnosis, the first unity that existed before the self. Moore's reversal of time and language therefore carries us back down the evolutionary ladder, back to our component elements, to the creation of those elements, to the creation of the universe and finally to the void that preceded it, in which we might finally understand "where we are come from" (48).

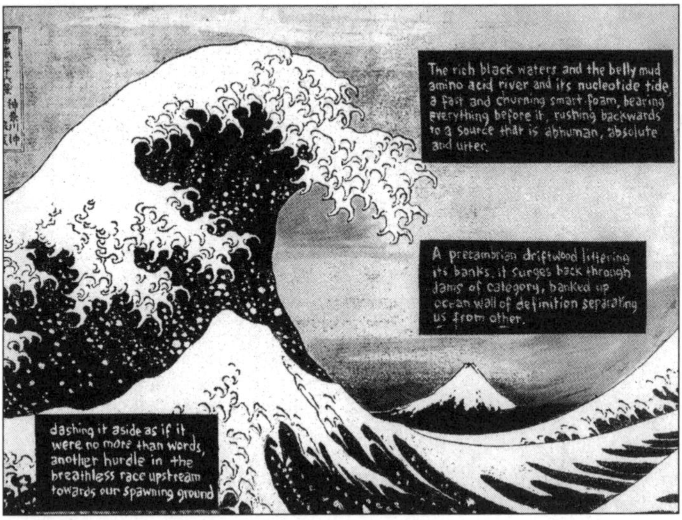
The rich black waters and the belly mud amino acid river and its nucleotide tide a fast and churning smart foam, bearing everything before it, rushing backwards to a source that is abhuman, absolute and utter.
A precambrian driftwood littering its banks. it surges back through dams of category, banked up ocean wall of definition separating us from other.
dashing it aside as if it were no more than words, another hurdle in the breathless race upstream towards our spawning ground

Fig. 2: from The Birth Caul, page 47.
© 2003 Alan Moore and Eddie Campbell

At this moment, however, when we might finally learn the ultimate source of our creation, when Moore twice promises to reveal the birth caul's final meaning, language fails Moore and his audience alike: "And our lips are... sealed" (48). What is remarkable about this failure is not its ill timing, however, but that it has not happened sooner. Moore has been describing a state of consciousness before birth for nearly a sixth of his narrative, states before language for nearly a third, but only at the end does his own language fail to represent that prelingual gnosis that should by definition be unrepresentable. The true mystery, then, is not only what lies behind the final, unspoken unveiling of the birth caul, but also how Moore's writing has so long sustained a narrative whose goal is to shed all language.

The richness of Moore's narration only exacerbates this internal contradiction; it is both ironic and unsurprising that the same work that tries to undo language should feature such a characteristically Moorish command of it. The same vocabulary that Moore struggles so fiercely to discard furnishes him with a cornucopia of insights, such as his pithy and unforgivingly accurate characterizations of teenage arguments: "Embittered slanging matches that occur nowhere save on some spite streaked astral plane" (21). Or pubic hair: "the insignia of a forbidden order, a werewolf freemasonry from which we are as yet excluded" (31). Or this ultimate statement on adolescence: "We confuse rebellion with a hairstyle" (23). For all that Moore tries to unwrite his language, *The Birth Caul* is utterly dependent on it—never moreso than when the narrative regresses back to the primal seas of creation, a state so unimaginable and unrepresentable it can only be rendered metaphorically through Moore's full linguistic power.

However, we may be able to explain or at least better understand this paradox by turning to the same theories of psychological development that support Moore's gnostic concept of childhood. Under Lacanian theory, for example, *The Birth Caul*'s recovery of an undivided, presymbolic subject can *only* be attempted through the symbolic realm of language, because we can only imagine prior states through the lens of the symbolic (Evans 97-98, 202-203). However, Lacan also argues that language can never hope to represent the terminus of Moore's journey, what Lacan might term the Real, since the Real belongs to another order entirely, "outside language and inassimilable to symbolisation" (Evans 159). To the extent that Moore declines to represent the prenatal experience, hinting at it only through the blank spaces of the "cold white page" (47) or the dark and silent void in which eyes, ears, and lips are sealed (48), he would appear to agree that language can never truly convey the Real.

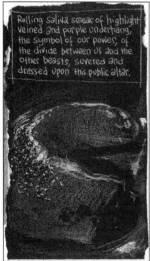

Rolling saliva smear of highlight
veined and purple underhang,
the symbol of our power, of
the divide between us and the
other beasts, severed and
dressed upon this public altar.
Fig. 3: from The Birth Caul, page 28.
© 2003 Alan Moore and Eddie Campbell

But Moore is hardly beholden to Lacanian psychoanalysis; in fact, he departs from Lacan in a number of other key areas. Perhaps most significantly, and refreshingly, Moore does not base his narrative of child development on any Oedipal struggles over the presence or lack of the phallus. Lacan regards the phallus as a "privileged signifier," the initiator of the symbolic order and the only absolute guarantor of meaning in a world whose symbols are otherwise relational and unfixed (Evans 143); Moore, on the other hand, creates a counter-sign that will undo its symbolic power. The birth caul functions as a kind of anti-phallus, delivered to Moore through a matrilineage; it comes from his late mother and leaves his "grandmother's birth-blood in unlikely carmine stains against the blue paper" (3). This maternal totem enables him to reverse the symbolic divisions of self and other, signifier and signified that Lacan assigns to the phallus. Interestingly, Moore also opposes the birth caul to another totem, the aforementioned ox-tongue, which receives the following overtly phallic description: "veined and purple underhang, the symbol of our power" (28; fig. 3). By overtaking the ox-tongue, by effacing the linguistic power that it symbolizes, the birth caul creates the possibility for a return to the states of consciousness that existed before language, signification, and self-awareness divided us from each other and from our world.

But this explanation still doesn't resolve the apparent contradiction of using language to revert to a prelingual gnosis. However, historian Hayden White points to a potential resolution in his analysis of Piaget's model of cognitive development.

In his introduction to *Tropics of Discourse* (1978), White considers the possibility of rhetorically reversing Piaget's model, of reverting to earlier modes of intelligence, in terms that prove startlingly prescient of *The Birth Caul*:

> To be sure, an unconscious or unintended lapse into a prelogical mode of comprehending reality would merely be an error or, more correctly, a regression... But such lapses, when undertaken in the interest of bringing logical thinking itself under criticism and questioning either its presuppositions, its structure, or its adequacy to an existentially satisfying

relationship to reality, would be poetry... Metaphorical consciousness may be a primitive form of knowing in the ontogenesis of human consciousness in its passage from infancy to maturity, but insofar as it is the fundamental mode of poetic apprehension in general, it is a mode of situating language with respect to the world every bit as authoritative as logic itself. (10)

This is precisely what Moore has done in *The Birth Caul*, regressing his own language back to presymbolic and metaphoric modes of consciousness in order to critique language for its separation of self from other. If this regression is still paradoxical, relying on language to unmake language, White at least demonstrates how such paradoxes are perfectly consistent within Piaget's model.

In other words, Moore does not need to abandon all language in order to critique it; he can instead excavate earlier states of consciousness. Piaget "stresses that in the process of development, a given mode of cognition is not so much obliterated as preserved, transcended, and assimilated to the mode that succeeds it" (White 10), sustaining the trace of the older forms and thereby making possible White's (and Moore's own) speculations on the potential of reverting to earlier, prelogical and prelinguistic modes of consciousness. Moreover, in White's model the first and most fundamental mode of consciousness—corresponding to Piaget's infantile, sensorimotor stage—is that of metaphor (White 5, 12), the same tactic to which Moore resorts in the final, prenatal pages of *The Birth Caul*. Because Moore cannot represent this primal state through any more literally descriptive, metonymic modes of language, he appropriately relies upon the earliest mode that White and Piaget describe. Under White's reading of Piaget, then, Moore's linguistic command in *The Birth Caul* is not a logical impossibility but rather the only feature that makes his narrative possible, as Moore's metaphoric gifts are the nearest means of approximating the earliest modes of human consciousness.

This final testimony to the power, rather than the paradox, of Moore's language seems an appropriate note on which to end this article, since that language is one of Moore's major contributions to comics. Set aside for a moment all the brilliant genre deconstructions and the headline-grabbing graphic novels—they've received ample praise elsewhere. But Moore also deserves our accolades simply for bringing the art of comics scripting, the very words through which comics stories are told, to new levels of grace and sophistication. In a medium where "narration" is too often confused for a terse "Elsewhere" or a breathless "Meanwhile," Moore continues to remind us that language can convey mood, emotion, and meaning in comics as well as it does in the best prose.

Like most American readers my age, I would imagine, I was first exposed to that gripping and unforgettable language when I picked up a copy of *Saga of the Swamp Thing* back in the mid-eighties. There on the first page was this poetic description of my home town, courtesy of Doctor Jason Woodrue by way of Alan Moore:

It's raining in Washington tonight. Plump, warm summer rain that covers the sidewalks with leopard spots. Downtown, elderly ladies carry their houseplants out to set them on the fire escapes, as if they were infirm relatives or boy kings. (Moore, Bissette, et al 1)

Never mind that a few years later I would learn that Moore had almost certainly never been to Washington when he wrote this; by then it was too late to matter. Those lines somehow remain fixed in my memory as a perfect portrait of summer in Washington, and as a perfect example of Moore's linguistic gifts. Alan Moore may indeed be unable to escape his language in *The Birth Caul*, and for that I am eternally grateful.

• **Marc Singer**
University of Maryland

Works Cited:

Evans, Dylan. *An Introductory Dictionary of Lacanian Psychoanalysis*. London: Routledge, 1996.

Lacan, Jacques. *Écrits. A Selection*. Trans. Alan Sheridan. London: Tavistock, 1977.

Moore, Alan, Steve Bissette, John Totleben, and Rick Veitch. "The Anatomy Lesson." *Saga of the Swamp Thing* 21. New York: DC Comics, 1983.

Moore, Alan, and Eddie Campbell. *The Birth Caul*. Paddington, Australia: Eddie Campbell Comics, 1999.

——. *From Hell*. Paddington, Australia: Eddie Campbell Comics, 1999.

Piaget, Jean. *The Child and Reality: Problems of Genetic Psychology*. Trans. Arnold Rosin. New York: Grossman, 1973.

——. "The Child's Conception of Time." Trans. A. J. Pomerans. 1946. *The Essential Piaget*. Howard E. Gruber and J. Jacques Vonéche, eds. New York: Basic Books, 1977. 547-75.

White, Hayden. "Introduction: Tropology, Discourse, and the Modes of Human Consciousness." *Tropics of Discourse*. Baltimore: Johns Hopkins University Press, 1978. 1-25.

ANGUS McKIE

Pages 47-50 following:
Still best known for his classic **So Beautiful, So Dangerous** *strip for Heavy Metal, McKie continues to work as an illustrator, colourist and designer. www.angusmckie.com. Strip ©2003 Angus McKie .*

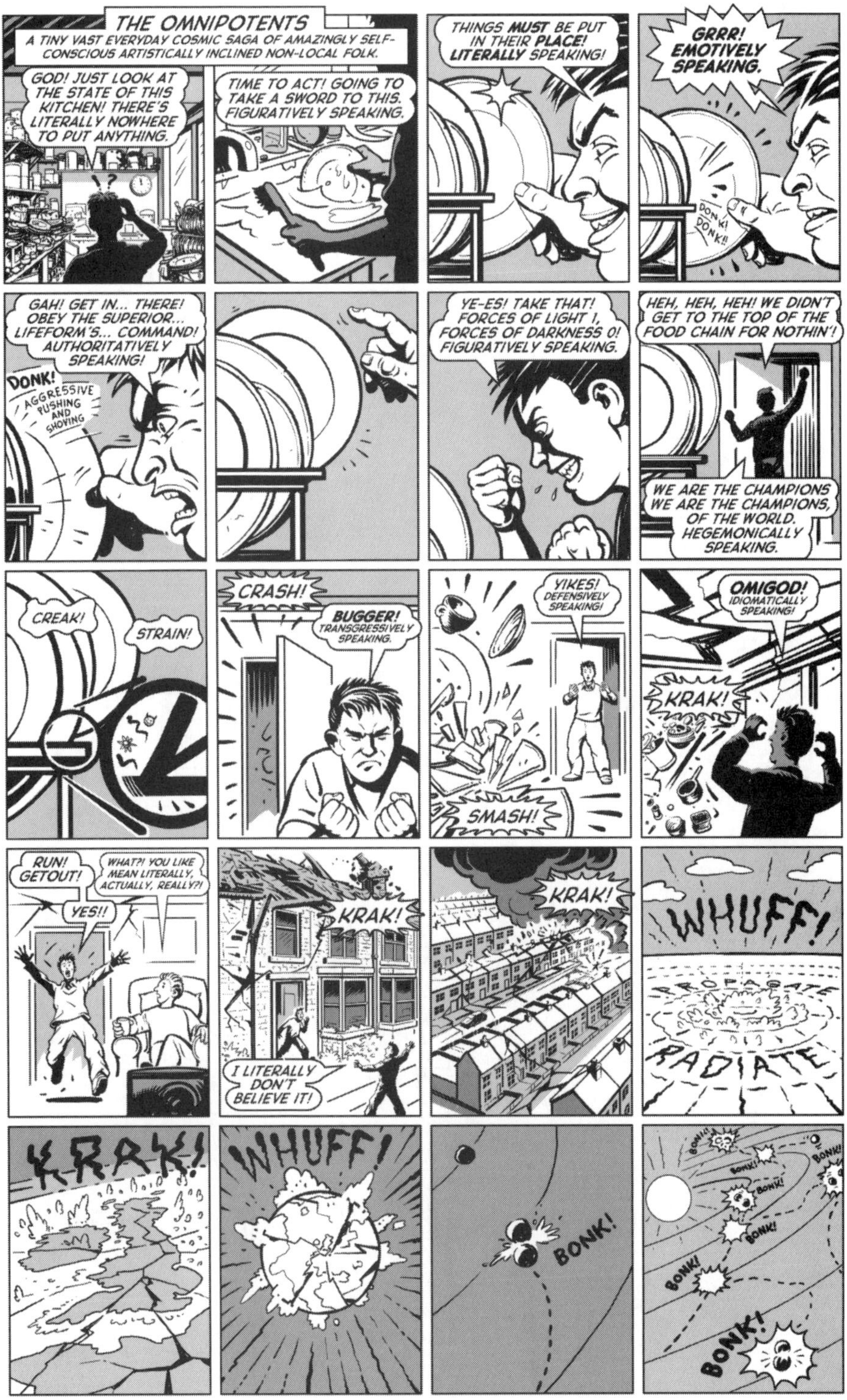
THE OMNIPOTENTS
A TINY VAST EVERYDAY COSMIC SAGA OF AMAZINGLY SELF-CONSCIOUS ARTISTICALLY INCLINED NON-LOCAL FOLK.
GOD! JUST LOOK AT THE STATE OF THIS KITCHEN! THERE'S LITERALLY NOWHERE TO PUT ANYTHING.
!?
TIME TO ACT! GOING TO TAKE A SWORD TO THIS. FIGURATIVELY SPEAKING.
THINGS MUST BE PUT IN THEIR PLACE! LITERALLY SPEAKING!
GRRR! EMOTIVELY SPEAKING.
DON-K! DONK!!
GAH! GET IN... THERE! OBEY THE SUPERIOR... LIFEFORM'S... COMMAND! AUTHORITATIVELY SPEAKING!
DONK!
AGGRESSIVE PUSHING AND SHOVING
YE-ES! TAKE THAT! FORCES OF LIGHT 1, FORCES OF DARKNESS 0! FIGURATIVELY SPEAKING.
HEH, HEH, HEH! WE DIDN'T GET TO THE TOP OF THE FOOD CHAIN FOR NOTHIN'!
WE ARE THE CHAMPIONS WE ARE THE CHAMPIONS, OF THE WORLD. HEGEMONICALLY SPEAKING.
CREAK!
STRAIN!
CRASH!
BUGGER! TRANSGRESSIVELY SPEAKING.
YIKES! DEFENSIVELY SPEAKING!
SMASH!
OMIGOD! IDIOMATICALLY SPEAKING!
KRAK!
RUN! GETOUT!
WHAT?! YOU LIKE MEAN LITERALLY, ACTUALLY, REALLY?!
YES!!
KRAK!
I LITERALLY DON'T BELIEVE IT!
KRAK!
WHUFF!
PROPAGATE
RADIATE
KRAK!
WHUFF!
BONK!
BONK!
BONK!
BONK!
BONK!
BONK!
BONK!

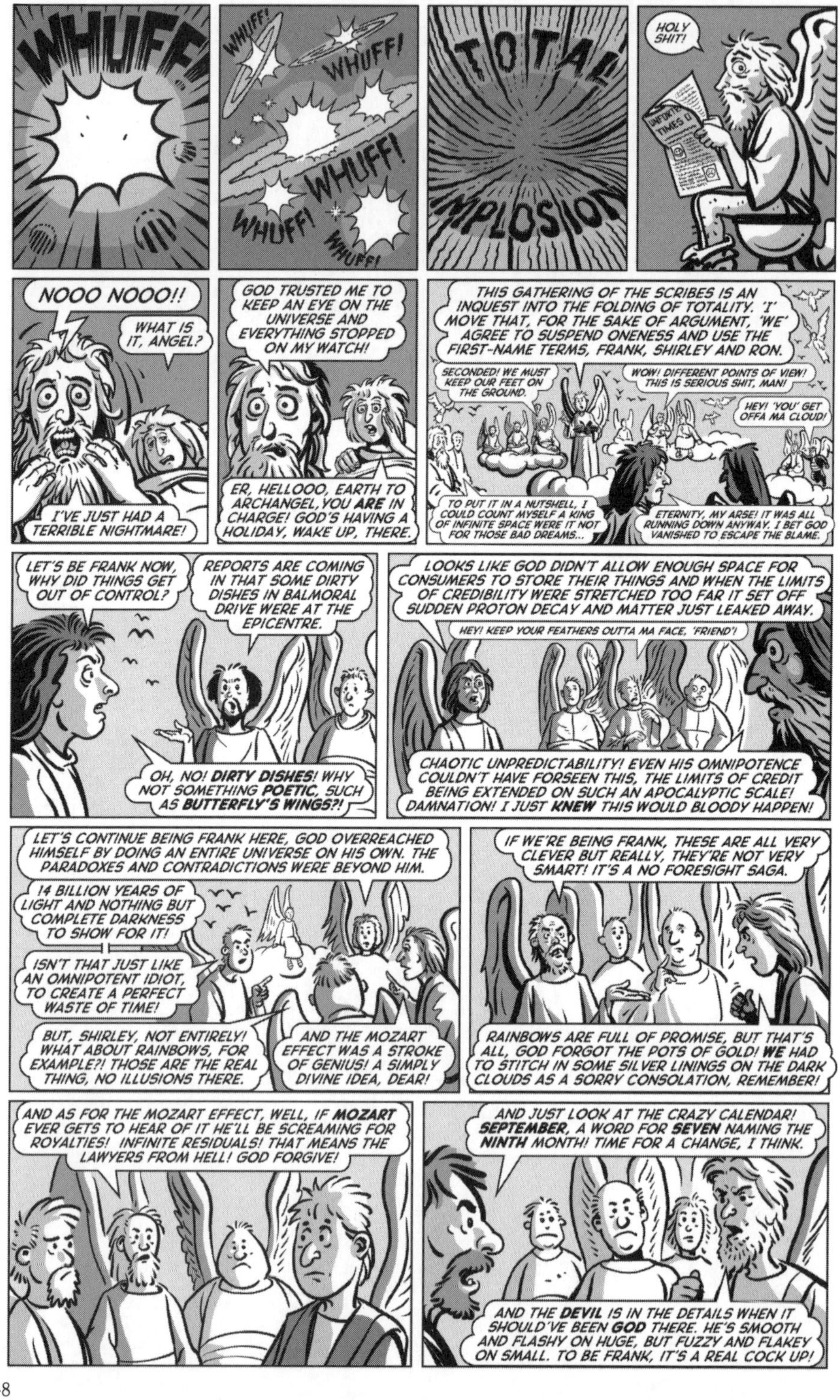
WHUFF!
WHUFF!
WHUFF!
WHUFF!
WHUFF!
WHUFF!
WHUFF!
TOTAL
IMPLOSION
HOLY SHIT!
NOOO NOOO!!
WHAT IS IT, ANGEL?
I'VE JUST HAD A TERRIBLE NIGHTMARE!
GOD TRUSTED ME TO KEEP AN EYE ON THE UNIVERSE AND EVERYTHING STOPPED ON MY WATCH!
ER, HELLOOO, EARTH TO ARCHANGEL, YOU ARE IN CHARGE! GOD'S HAVING A HOLIDAY, WAKE UP, THERE.
THIS GATHERING OF THE SCRIBES IS AN INQUEST INTO THE FOLDING OF TOTALITY. 'I' MOVE THAT, FOR THE SAKE OF ARGUMENT, 'WE' AGREE TO SUSPEND ONENESS AND USE THE FIRST-NAME TERMS, FRANK, SHIRLEY AND RON.
SECONDED! WE MUST KEEP OUR FEET ON THE GROUND.
WOW! DIFFERENT POINTS OF VIEW! THIS IS SERIOUS SHIT, MAN!
HEY! 'YOU' GET OFFA MA CLOUD!
TO PUT IT IN A NUTSHELL, I COULD COUNT MYSELF A KING OF INFINITE SPACE WERE IT NOT FOR THOSE BAD DREAMS...
ETERNITY, MY ARSE! IT WAS ALL RUNNING DOWN ANYWAY. I BET GOD VANISHED TO ESCAPE THE BLAME.
LET'S BE FRANK NOW, WHY DID THINGS GET OUT OF CONTROL?
REPORTS ARE COMING IN THAT SOME DIRTY DISHES IN BALMORAL DRIVE WERE AT THE EPICENTRE.
OH, NO! DIRTY DISHES! WHY NOT SOMETHING POETIC, SUCH AS BUTTERFLY'S WINGS?!
LOOKS LIKE GOD DIDN'T ALLOW ENOUGH SPACE FOR CONSUMERS TO STORE THEIR THINGS AND WHEN THE LIMITS OF CREDIBILITY WERE STRETCHED TOO FAR IT SET OFF SUDDEN PROTON DECAY AND MATTER JUST LEAKED AWAY.
HEY! KEEP YOUR FEATHERS OUTTA MA FACE, 'FRIEND'!
CHAOTIC UNPREDICTABILITY! EVEN HIS OMNIPOTENCE COULDN'T HAVE FORSEEN THIS, THE LIMITS OF CREDIT BEING EXTENDED ON SUCH AN APOCALYPTIC SCALE! DAMNATION! I JUST KNEW THIS WOULD BLOODY HAPPEN!
LET'S CONTINUE BEING FRANK HERE, GOD OVERREACHED HIMSELF BY DOING AN ENTIRE UNIVERSE ON HIS OWN. THE PARADOXES AND CONTRADICTIONS WERE BEYOND HIM.
14 BILLION YEARS OF LIGHT AND NOTHING BUT COMPLETE DARKNESS TO SHOW FOR IT!
ISN'T THAT JUST LIKE AN OMNIPOTENT IDIOT, TO CREATE A PERFECT WASTE OF TIME!
BUT, SHIRLEY, NOT ENTIRELY! WHAT ABOUT RAINBOWS, FOR EXAMPLE?! THOSE ARE THE REAL THING, NO ILLUSIONS THERE.
AND THE MOZART EFFECT WAS A STROKE OF GENIUS! A SIMPLY DIVINE IDEA, DEAR!
IF WE'RE BEING FRANK, THESE ARE ALL VERY CLEVER BUT REALLY, THEY'RE NOT VERY SMART! IT'S A NO FORESIGHT SAGA.
RAINBOWS ARE FULL OF PROMISE, BUT THAT'S ALL, GOD FORGOT THE POTS OF GOLD! WE HAD TO STITCH IN SOME SILVER LININGS ON THE DARK CLOUDS AS A SORRY CONSOLATION, REMEMBER!
AND AS FOR THE MOZART EFFECT, WELL, IF MOZART EVER GETS TO HEAR OF IT HE'LL BE SCREAMING FOR ROYALTIES! INFINITE RESIDUALS! THAT MEANS THE LAWYERS FROM HELL! GOD FORGIVE!
AND JUST LOOK AT THE CRAZY CALENDAR! SEPTEMBER, A WORD FOR SEVEN NAMING THE NINTH MONTH! TIME FOR A CHANGE, I THINK.
AND THE DEVIL IS IN THE DETAILS WHEN IT SHOULD'VE BEEN GOD THERE. HE'S SMOOTH AND FLASHY ON HUGE, BUT FUZZY AND FLAKEY ON SMALL. TO BE FRANK, IT'S A REAL COCK UP!

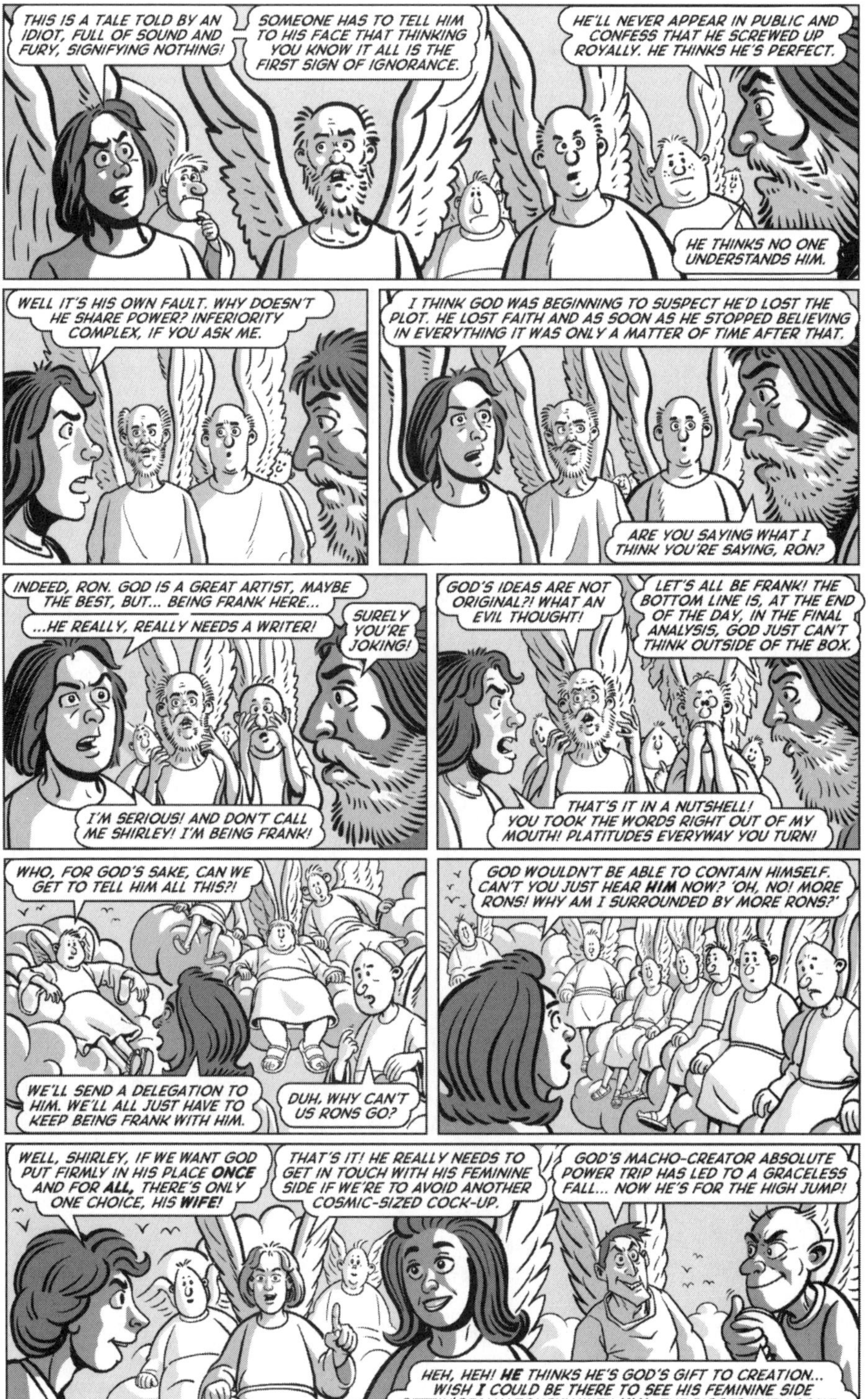
THIS IS A TALE TOLD BY AN IDIOT, FULL OF SOUND AND FURY, SIGNIFYING NOTHING!
SOMEONE HAS TO TELL HIM TO HIS FACE THAT THINKING YOU KNOW IT ALL IS THE FIRST SIGN OF IGNORANCE.
HE'LL NEVER APPEAR IN PUBLIC AND CONFESS THAT HE SCREWED UP ROYALLY. HE THINKS HE'S PERFECT.
HE THINKS NO ONE UNDERSTANDS HIM.
WELL IT'S HIS OWN FAULT. WHY DOESN'T HE SHARE POWER? INFERIORITY COMPLEX, IF YOU ASK ME.
I THINK GOD WAS BEGINNING TO SUSPECT HE'D LOST THE PLOT. HE LOST FAITH AND AS SOON AS HE STOPPED BELIEVING IN EVERYTHING IT WAS ONLY A MATTER OF TIME AFTER THAT.
ARE YOU SAYING WHAT I THINK YOU'RE SAYING, RON?
INDEED, RON. GOD IS A GREAT ARTIST, MAYBE THE BEST, BUT... BEING FRANK HERE...
...HE REALLY, REALLY NEEDS A WRITER!
SURELY YOU'RE JOKING!
I'M SERIOUS! AND DON'T CALL ME SHIRLEY! I'M BEING FRANK!
GOD'S IDEAS ARE NOT ORIGINAL?! WHAT AN EVIL THOUGHT!
LET'S ALL BE FRANK! THE BOTTOM LINE IS, AT THE END OF THE DAY, IN THE FINAL ANALYSIS, GOD JUST CAN'T THINK OUTSIDE OF THE BOX.
THAT'S IT IN A NUTSHELL! YOU TOOK THE WORDS RIGHT OUT OF MY MOUTH! PLATITUDES EVERYWAY YOU TURN!
WHO, FOR GOD'S SAKE, CAN WE GET TO TELL HIM ALL THIS?!
WE'LL SEND A DELEGATION TO HIM. WE'LL ALL JUST HAVE TO KEEP BEING FRANK WITH HIM.
DUH, WHY CAN'T US RONS GO?
GOD WOULDN'T BE ABLE TO CONTAIN HIMSELF. CAN'T YOU JUST HEAR HIM NOW? 'OH, NO! MORE RONS! WHY AM I SURROUNDED BY MORE RONS?'
WELL, SHIRLEY, IF WE WANT GOD PUT FIRMLY IN HIS PLACE ONCE AND FOR ALL, THERE'S ONLY ONE CHOICE, HIS WIFE!
THAT'S IT! HE REALLY NEEDS TO GET IN TOUCH WITH HIS FEMININE SIDE IF WE'RE TO AVOID ANOTHER COSMIC-SIZED COCK-UP.
GOD'S MACHO-CREATOR ABSOLUTE POWER TRIP HAS LED TO A GRACELESS FALL... NOW HE'S FOR THE HIGH JUMP!
HEH, HEH! HE THINKS HE'S GOD'S GIFT TO CREATION... WISH I COULD BE THERE TO SEE HIS FEMININE SIDE GETTIN' REALLY TOUCHY WITH HIM. THE BIGGER THEY COME...

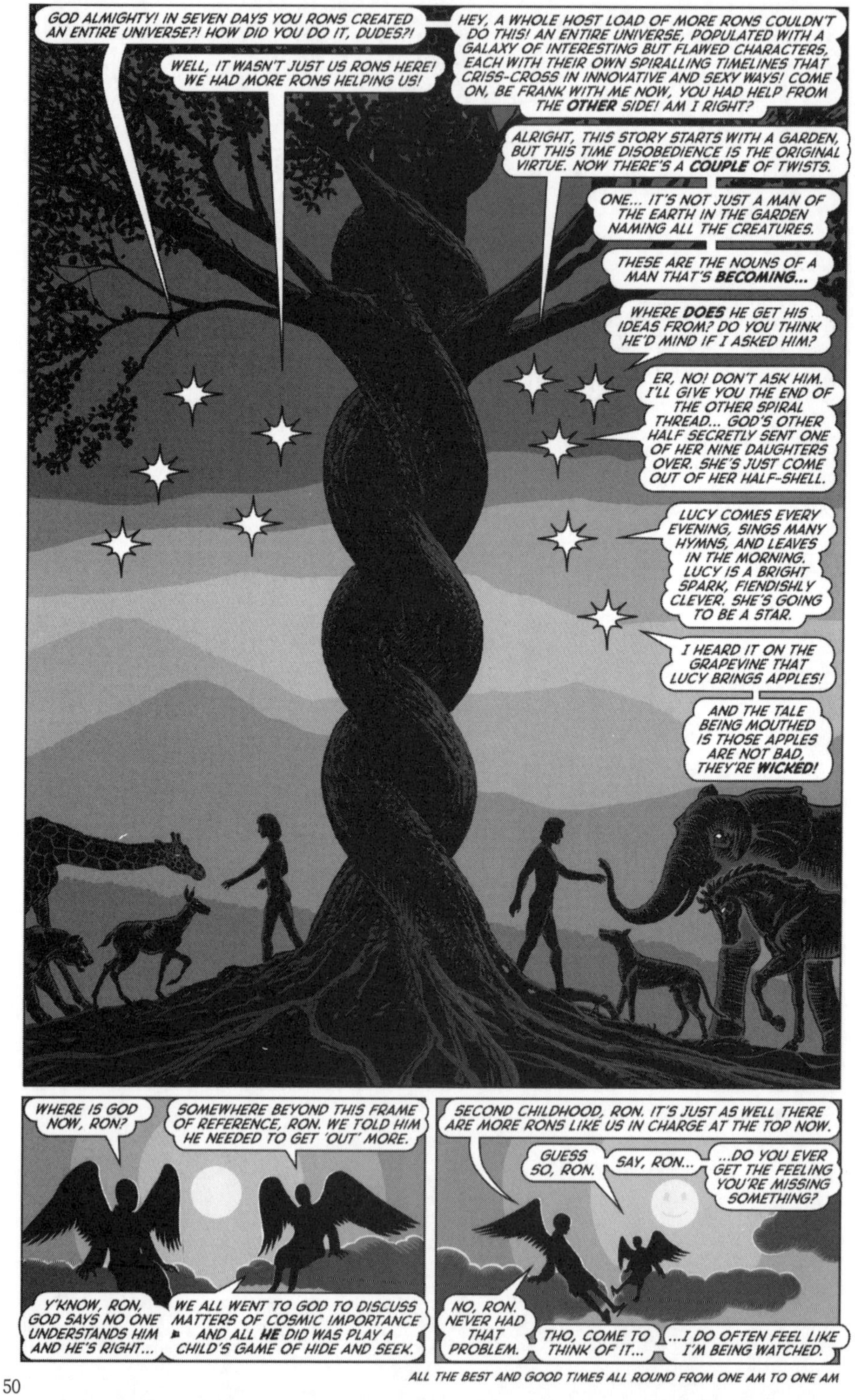

GOD ALMIGHTY! IN SEVEN DAYS YOU RONS CREATED AN ENTIRE UNIVERSE?! HOW DID YOU DO IT, DUDES?!
WELL, IT WASN'T JUST US RONS HERE! WE HAD MORE RONS HELPING US!
HEY, A WHOLE HOST LOAD OF MORE RONS COULDN'T DO THIS! AN ENTIRE UNIVERSE, POPULATED WITH A GALAXY OF INTERESTING BUT FLAWED CHARACTERS, EACH WITH THEIR OWN SPIRALLING TIMELINES THAT CRISS-CROSS IN INNOVATIVE AND SEXY WAYS! COME ON, BE FRANK WITH ME NOW, YOU HAD HELP FROM THE **OTHER** SIDE! AM I RIGHT?
ALRIGHT, THIS STORY STARTS WITH A GARDEN, BUT THIS TIME DISOBEDIENCE IS THE ORIGINAL VIRTUE. NOW THERE'S A **COUPLE** OF TWISTS.
ONE... IT'S NOT JUST A MAN OF THE EARTH IN THE GARDEN NAMING ALL THE CREATURES.
THESE ARE THE NOUNS OF A MAN THAT'S **BECOMING...**
WHERE **DOES** HE GET HIS IDEAS FROM? DO YOU THINK HE'D MIND IF I ASKED HIM?
ER, NO! DON'T ASK HIM. I'LL GIVE YOU THE END OF THE OTHER SPIRAL THREAD... GOD'S OTHER HALF SECRETLY SENT ONE OF HER NINE DAUGHTERS OVER. SHE'S JUST COME OUT OF HER HALF-SHELL.
LUCY COMES EVERY EVENING, SINGS MANY HYMNS, AND LEAVES IN THE MORNING. LUCY IS A BRIGHT SPARK, FIENDISHLY CLEVER. SHE'S GOING TO BE A STAR.
I HEARD IT ON THE GRAPEVINE THAT LUCY BRINGS APPLES!
AND THE TALE BEING MOUTHED IS THOSE APPLES ARE NOT BAD, THEY'RE **WICKED!**
WHERE IS GOD NOW, RON?
SOMEWHERE BEYOND THIS FRAME OF REFERENCE, RON. WE TOLD HIM HE NEEDED TO GET 'OUT' MORE.
Y'KNOW, RON, GOD SAYS NO ONE UNDERSTANDS HIM AND HE'S RIGHT...
WE ALL WENT TO GOD TO DISCUSS MATTERS OF COSMIC IMPORTANCE AND ALL **HE** DID WAS PLAY A CHILD'S GAME OF HIDE AND SEEK.
SECOND CHILDHOOD, RON. IT'S JUST AS WELL THERE ARE MORE RONS LIKE US IN CHARGE AT THE TOP NOW.
GUESS SO, RON.
SAY, RON...
...DO YOU EVER GET THE FEELING YOU'RE MISSING SOMETHING?
NO, RON. NEVER HAD THAT PROBLEM.
THO, COME TO THINK OF IT...
...I DO OFTEN FEEL LIKE I'M BEING WATCHED.

ALL THE BEST AND GOOD TIMES ALL ROUND FROM ONE AM TO ONE AM

HOMAGE TO CORNUCOPIA

MICHAEL MOORCOCK

Moorcock began his career at 16, working first for a number of British comics including **Tarzan Adventures, Cowboy, Thriller Picture Library, Sun, Comet, Eagle**. He later became a vanguard author, creator of **Jerry Cornelius** and **Elric**, pioneering editor, journalist, critic, and rock musician. He is currently writing an **Elric** graphic novel with Walter Simonson for DC.

Text ©2003 Michael Moorcock.

Although we have been in a movie together (Iain Sinclair's *The Cardinal and the Corpse; or, A Funny Night Out*) I have as far as I recall only met Alan Moore once, at a party given for a Jerry Cornelius book by my crooked but idiosyncratic publisher Allison and Busby. We got on well and I was impressed enough to start following his work. He hadn't at that time made a big name in the popular arena, but I couldn't fail to be impressed by someone who sported an even wilder crop of hair than my own and whose eye carried the same sort of mad, uncompromising glint. Here, it seemed to me, was a genuine visionary, a generous risk-taker, someone barmy and bolshy enough to follow his own dream no matter what.

As someone who started his career as a teenager editing *Tarzan Adventures* and writing dialogue and text for old Hal Foster 'Tarzan' strips (because I preferred to reprint Foster and Hogarth over the less interesting artists who followed them and because the pages came without English versions), and who earned the bulk of his early living writing *Cowboy Picture Library, Thriller Picture Library, Karl the Viking* and *Olac the Gladiator* strips for Fleetway, I have to admit that I never saw what Alan saw in comics. My generation, who included some excellent writers and brilliant artists, like Hampson, Bellamy, the Embeltons and Don Lawrence, simply saw comics as a way of earning a decent living. We did our best to make the strips as good as possible, within their terms, but we understood the medium to be about as permanent and respected as the daily newspapers we also worked for. We had no idea that there were people out there who were actually beginning to take note of the best of us. Our ambition was to get out of comics and into something more satisfying, whether it be novels or film-work. Our employers gave us limited scope for any ambition and the idea of using our work to say something substantial about the world was simply beyond our capacity to imagine!

My own idealism did, indeed, focus on popular art-forms, but I saw science fantasy as the way to go. In common with writers like Ballard, Disch, Sladek and a few others, I was trying to produce a form robust enough to carry the most sophisticated and furious ideas of my generation and carry them to a popular audience. Others chose film, music or broadcasting. We were all part of the same movement, whatever medium we chose.

As soon as I could I put comic work behind me and while 'Danny and his Time Machine' and 'Zip Nolan of the Highway Patrol' funded some early issues of *New Worlds*, I began to try to produce engaged and angry experimental fiction which reflected the modern world and appealed to an audience tired of the failures of contemporary modernism. For a while I saw 'intellectual' comic strips as an affectation of the French and while I enjoyed Moebius and Druillet (with whom I also worked), I wasn't at all sure that this wasn't a reverse of what I envisioned – that is, work using popular forms to get across traditionally 'serious' ideas to a popular audience. The French adoption of comics, at that time, I saw more as a sort of cultural raiding. These aren't opinions I've retained and I tell you all this to describe my own prejudices and biases of those days. In short, I simply couldn't see the possibilities of the graphic novel.

I think many of us would have remained as sceptical if it hadn't been for the work of one man, who began to come into his own with a series of DC comics questioning the nature of charismatic power and asking us who was watching 'The Watchmen'. While there had been attempts to humanise and, indeed, sentimentalise super-heroes (*Spiderman*, for instance), no American, as far as I know, had ever questioned the actual nature of the super-hero and his relationship to the fascism we had recently defeated as well as the neo-fascism which began to spring up almost as soon as Hitler lay, a messy suicide, in his bunker or Mussolini was hoisted upside down at the hands of Italian partisans. What was especially substantial about Moore's work was not the innovations, the new riffs on the superhero theme, but the fundamental questioning of the nature of power and those we invest with power. What British musicians did for American rock and roll, Moore began to do consistently for American comics. Without affectation or loss of impact, he used the graphic novel to confront the serious issues of his day. In this tradition he followed such popular cartoonists as Gilray and Hogarth, of course. Few genuine innovators are not moralists, from Bunyan and Blake to the present, but the trick is to entertain a broad audience while getting those moral points across.

It is maybe an irony that the angry moralist is generally an innovator – — they have to be, since the old forms have, for their purposes, become corrupted or stale. It is equally ironic that they are usually followed by enthusiastic admirers who take their innovations and produce sophisticated riffs without understanding the sense of social outrage which inspired them. I have seen many come after Moore, but only one or two (Bryan Talbot, for instance) have understood what drives him and what his innovations are actually able to do. As others take up his notions and milk them to death, Moore leaves them his carrion and, showing the stuff of a genuine trailblazer, moves on to fresh, new territories.

So it's fair to say that Moore changed the comics field forever. Almost everything produced these days is produced in the climate he created. Any work of ambition, which seeks to confront social issues, must refer to him. And it's also fair to repeat as often as possible that Moore, unlike some innovators, has remained uncomfortably original, temperamentally unable to rest on his laurels or to exploit his early dynamic. While the movie version of *From Hell* might have brought in the Johnny Depp fans, it's clear that it ripped the heart out of the Moore original, as such movies often do. Moore was not producing another crossword puzzle speculation on the identity of the Whitechapel monster, he was writing another parable about power and its uses and abuses.

And that, of course, is also the background to his wonderfully entertaining new series *The League of Extraordinary Gentlemen*, which inhabits the world of late Victorian and Edwardian imperialism only to examine it, confront it, subvert it and so cast a cold eye on contemporary imperialism, manifested in the deeds

NABIEL KANAN

Right: *Nabiel Kanan from Derby in England has been writing and drawing graphic novels since 1989, including the acclaimed* **Exit** *and more recently* **Lost Girl** *and* **The Birthday Riots** *for NBM. His new comics series* **Midnight** *will be released in 2003. Illustration ©2003 Nabiel Kanan. All characters ©2003 their respective copyright owners.*

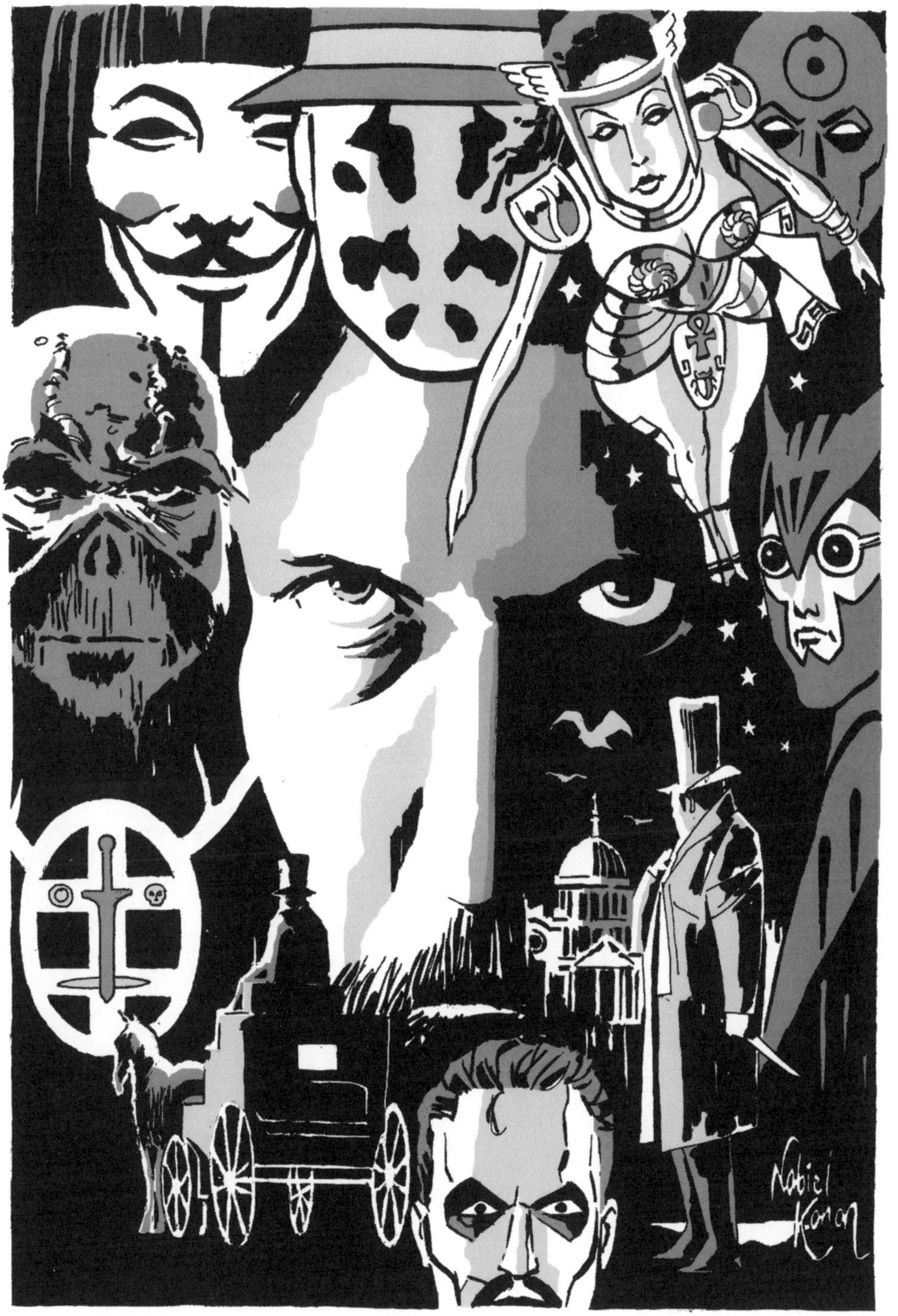
Nabiel Kanan

and actions of George W. Bush and his yapping dancing papillon Tony Blair.

Moore has produced a series which at its most popular level calls on our nostalgia for a world in which unselfconscious white men defended and expanded European and US empires, putting down rebellious 'natives', whether in the Middle East, India, Africa or the American homeland, giving their lives to preserve the expansionist values of the nation states they served. While he never labours his metaphors and allegories, they are always present, always speaking to the concerns and sensibilities of the modern reader.

Alan Moore has a generous soul, a cornucopian talent, an inventive mind, a fine social eye and a righteous politicial anger. He is also an outstanding entertainer. In his recent series, he has offered his readers all kinds of extra fun and adventure, as well as some delightful parodies, but at all times, frequently with sparing subtlety, he never ceases to confront the moral, political and social issues which continuously concern him. This is why he is still the best, why he has commanded so much respect for so many years and why, I am sure, he will continue to command respect for many years to come.

> **• Michael Moorcock,**
> The Old Circle Squared,
> Lost Pines,
> Texas
> January '03

JEFF SMITH

Right: *Artist and writer Jeff Smith has spent much of the last ten years working on his self-published comic book* **Bone** *which has appeared in sixteen languages around the world and has earned its author numerous top awards. He lives in Columbus, Ohio with his wife Vijaya live with their Great Dane, Euclid. Illustration ©2003 Jeff Smith. Fone Bone is ©2003 Jeff Smith. All other characters ©2003 their respective copyright owners.*

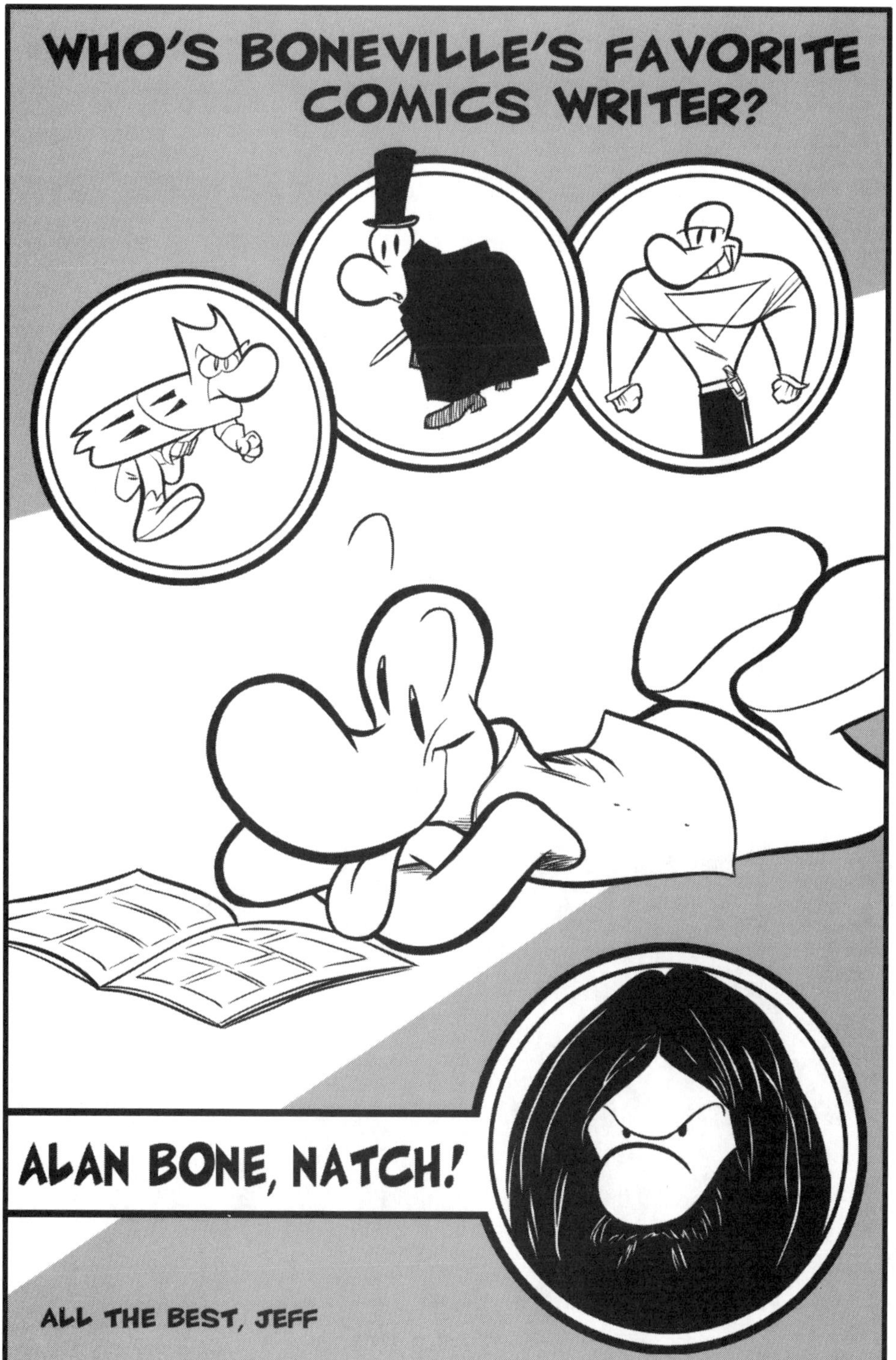
WHO'S BONEVILLE'S FAVORITE COMICS WRITER?
ALAN BONE, NATCH!
ALL THE BEST, JEFF

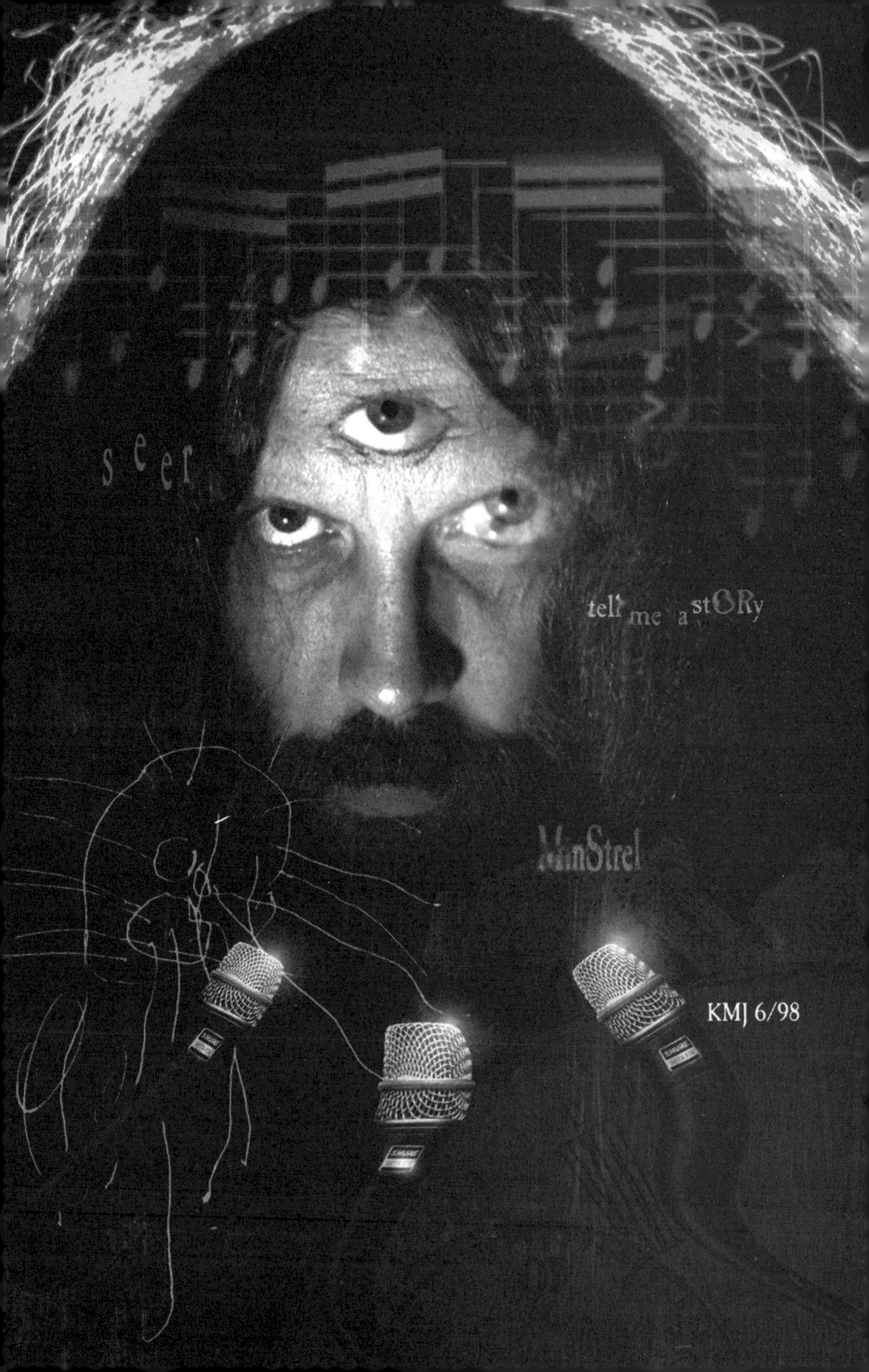
seer
tell me a stORy
MinStrel
KMJ 6/98

THE SCORPIO BOYS IN THE CITY OF LUX SING THEIR STRANGE SONGS

for Alan Moore

NEIL GAIMAN

Neil Gaiman became one of the top writers in modern comics with the fantasy series **Sandman** *for DC and has since become a best selling novelist with his books* **Coraline** *and* **American Gods***, and a screenwriter for film and TV.*
Poem ©2003 Neil Gaiman.

The Scorpio Boys in the city of Lux sing their strange songs
and smear the windows of your car with cheap rags,piss on your doorstep.
It's lucky to see them. If you see them you won't die today.

There's an old man. He's all that stands between us and the End of the World.
The End of the World knocks on his door once or twice a week,
they have cake and tea and a chat, and crumpets in the winter, and a battle of wits.
So far the old man is winning, the world only ends every now and again.
We don't remember it ending. We're from this go around.

Oh, they stare, the Scorpio Boys, it's an act of magic of course
if you believe in them at all. If you see them you'll be lucky. So damn lucky.

Beaten up and left for dead by the Piltdown Men
singing *we are we are the Piltdown men we are we are*
they stumble down the roads of the cities of twilight
breaking bottles and puking in gutters,
someone finds you and picks you up and carries you home.
Maybe it was us. You never know.

A cigarette traces a shape in the air,
Something made out of light and smoke, so you know it's magical
someone says it's lucky and who knows what will happen?
Stranger things happen in cities. Even small cities.

Take Lux, for example: a city that isn't even there,
Like all cities it is a magical description,
a way of making impossible things happen at a distance,

like a poem or a whisper or a saucer filled with ink —
you can stare into it, or dip your pen.
Either way it will take you to invisible places,
open a door in your hearts to us,
sharp-nosed and shabby genteel, with ink-spots and cinder-burns on our clothes.

When there are enough of us, we will become a city.

Doing it because we believe in it. Because the stories need to be described.
And come to us for their faces.

• **Neil Gaiman**

KEN MEYER, JR.

Left: *Ken Meyer Jr. has been working in comics, games, and as a designer and illustrator (traditional and digital) for close to 20 years. See his work at www.kenmeyerjr.com.*
Illustration ©2003 Ken Meyer Jr.

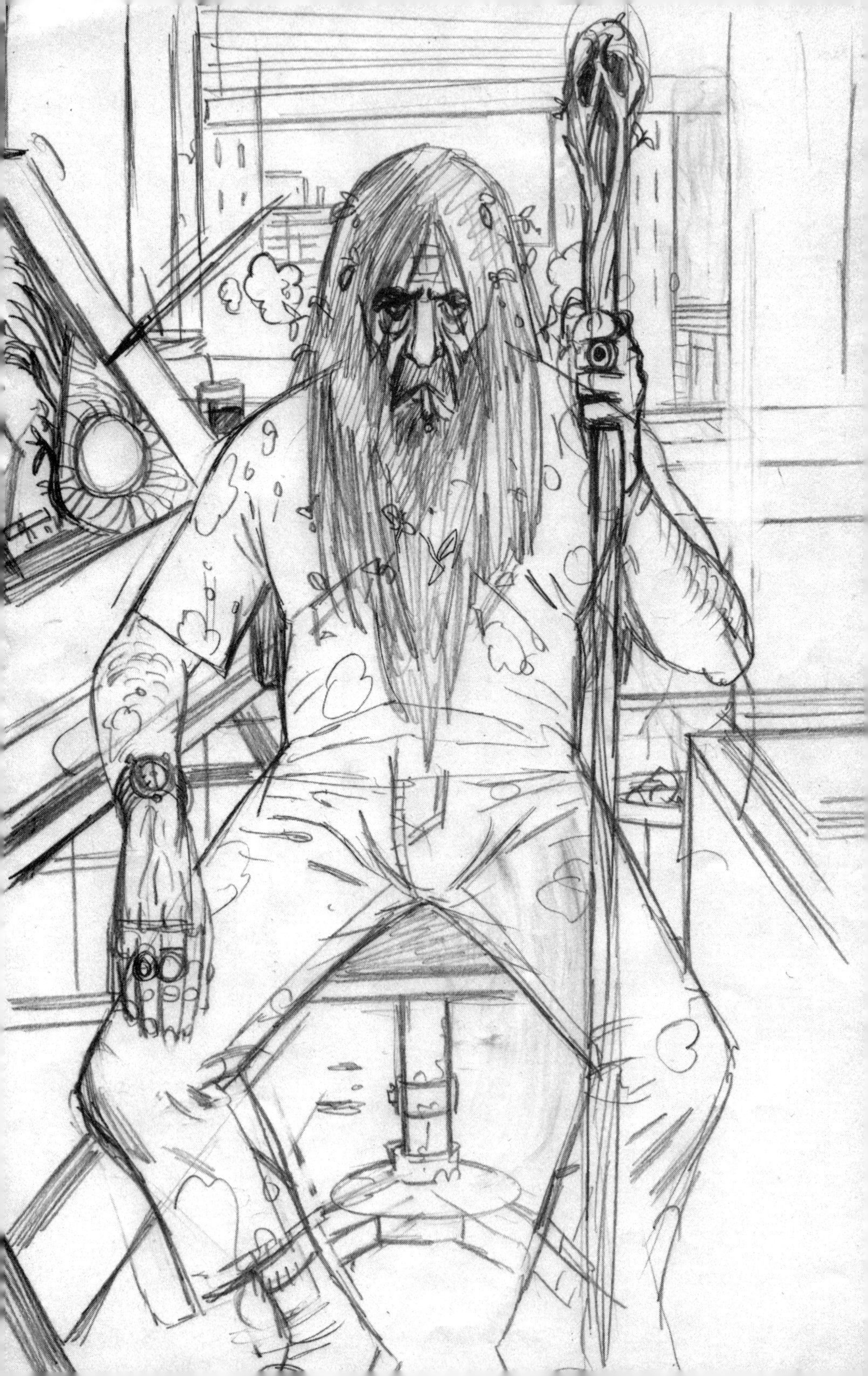

THE OTHER SWAMP THING

DYLAN HORROCKS

Born in New Zealand, Horrocks is the writer/artist of the graphic novel **Hicksville** *which was named a book of the year by The Comics Journal. More recently he's written* **The Names of Magic** *miniseries and the monthly title* **Hunter: the Age of Magic** *for DC/Vertigo, and is currently working on the creator-owned* **Atlas.** *www.hicksville.co.nz. Text ©2003 Dylan Horrocks.*

Not long ago I was developing a series for Vertigo, centered on the exploits of a comics company and its various employees. The twist was that all the comics they published were entirely true and their stars (Doctor Occult, Adam Strange, the Phantom Stranger, the Swamp Thing and other such DC-Vertigo characters) were all real people. There was a small team of cartoonists, each of whom was given the job of following around one of those heroes and recording their adventures and everyday lives accurately and truthfully in the form of a monthly comic book.

One of those cartoonists was going to be a thinly disguised version of Alan Moore (or at least the 1980s Alan Moore), who would shamble into the editorial office once a month, his legs caked with mud from the Louisiana swamp, his long hair and beard full of twigs and leaves and nesting insects, his breath sweet with whatever hallucinogenic fruit he'd recently chewed, to drop a pile of paper on the editor's desk. Then with a grunt, this mysterious cartoonist would turn and go, heading back to his beloved swamp, leaving behind a trail of mud and strange aromas and, of course, the latest issue of Swamp Thing. His comic, of course, would be beautiful – a magical, moving masterpiece, full of philosophical musings and profound insight into the human condition and our place in the natural world. It would also be trippy, sexy, pungent and disturbing.

When I described this project to the incredibly talented young cartoonist Chris McLoughlin (who'd drawn a guest-artist issue of **Hunter: the Age of Magic**), he was so taken with it that he went home and drew this sketch, which summed my idea up perfectly. Needless to say, the project was eventually turned down, although I still intend to do it one day (stripped of its DC properties, of course). But here, for posterity, is Chris's perfect sketch of the *other* Swamp Thing: the mystical magus of Louisiana...

• **Dylan Horrocks**

WILLY LINDHOUT
with STEVEN de RIE

Pages 60-63 following:
Belgian cartoonist Willy Linthout has just completed his 100ᵗʰ **Urbanus** *graphic novel in collaboration with the 'real' Urbanus, the movie actor and stage artist. Linthout has also embarked on a new series,* **Roboboy,** *published by Dupuis.* **Steven de Rie** *is assistant to Lindhout and also creator of his own series, the best known being* **The Silent Witness.** *Strip ©2003 Willy Lindhout. Urbanus is ©2003 Willy Lindhout. All other characters ©2003 their respective copyright owners.*

CHRIS McLOUGHLIN

Left: *Chris McLoughlin was born in Liverpool in 1971. He is currently working with writer David Moyes on* **Holmes: The Detective Monkey** *for Editions Carabas in France. Illustration ©2003 Chris McLoughlin Concept ©2003 Dylan Horrocks*

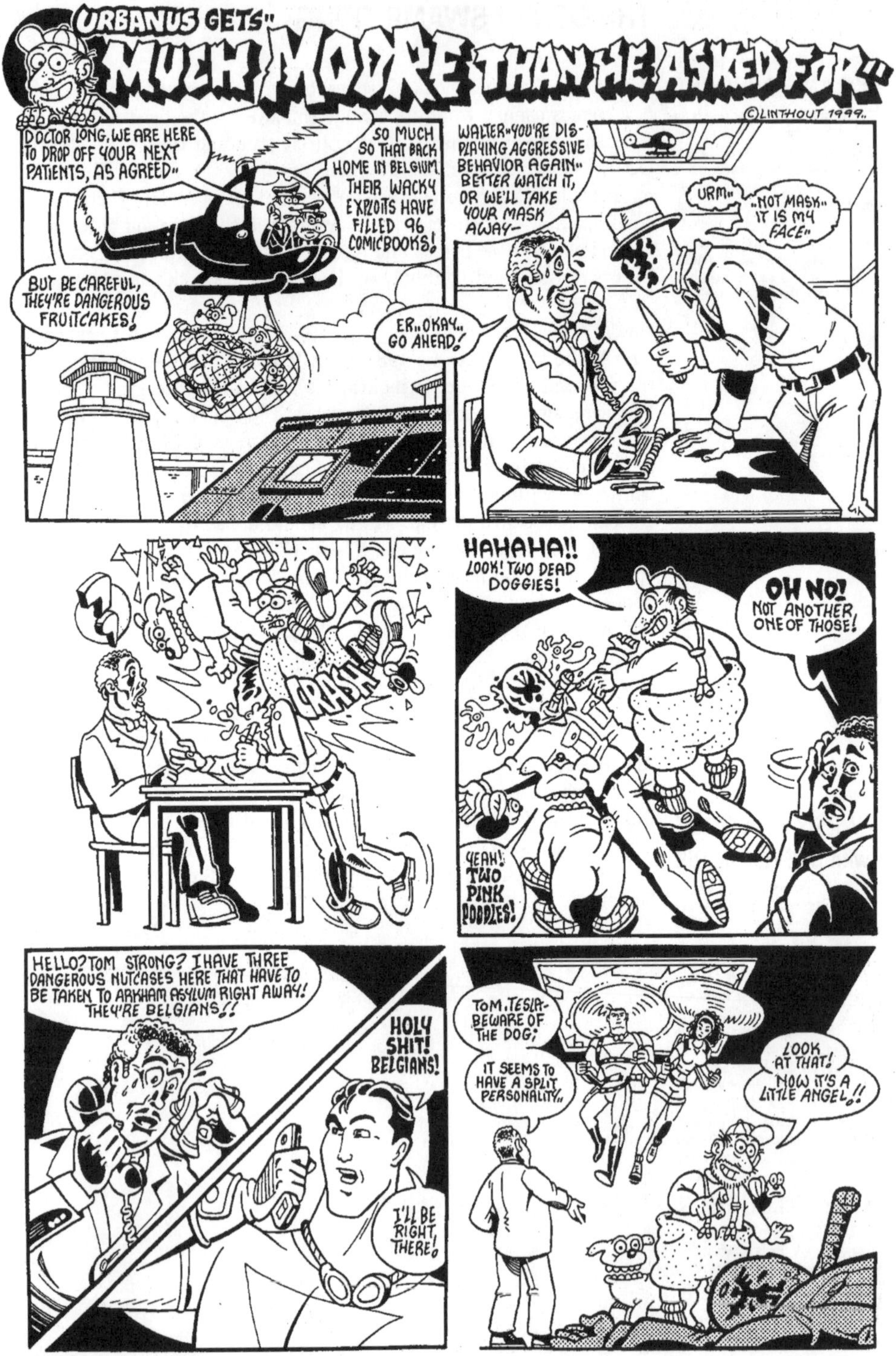
URBANUS GETS "MUCH MOORE THAN HE ASKED FOR"
©LINTHOUT 1999.
DOCTOR LONG, WE ARE HERE TO DROP OFF YOUR NEXT PATIENTS, AS AGREED"
SO MUCH SO THAT BACK HOME IN BELGIUM THEIR WACKY EXPLOITS HAVE FILLED 96 COMICBOOKS!
BUT BE CAREFUL, THEY'RE DANGEROUS FRUITCAKES!
ER.. OKAY.. GO AHEAD!
WALTER.. YOU'RE DISPLAYING AGGRESSIVE BEHAVIOR AGAIN.. BETTER WATCH IT, OR WE'LL TAKE YOUR MASK AWAY-
URM..
"NOT MASK.. IT IS MY FACE"
CRASH
HAHAHA!! LOOK! TWO DEAD DOGGIES!
OH NO! NOT ANOTHER ONE OF THOSE!
YEAH! TWO PINK POODLES!
HELLO? TOM STRONG? I HAVE THREE DANGEROUS NUTCASES HERE THAT HAVE TO BE TAKEN TO ARKHAM ASYLUM RIGHT AWAY! THEY'RE BELGIANS!!
HOLY SHIT! BELGIANS!
I'LL BE RIGHT THERE!
TOM, TESLA- BEWARE OF THE DOG;
IT SEEMS TO HAVE A SPLIT PERSONALITY..
LOOK AT THAT! NOW IT'S A LITTLE ANGEL!!

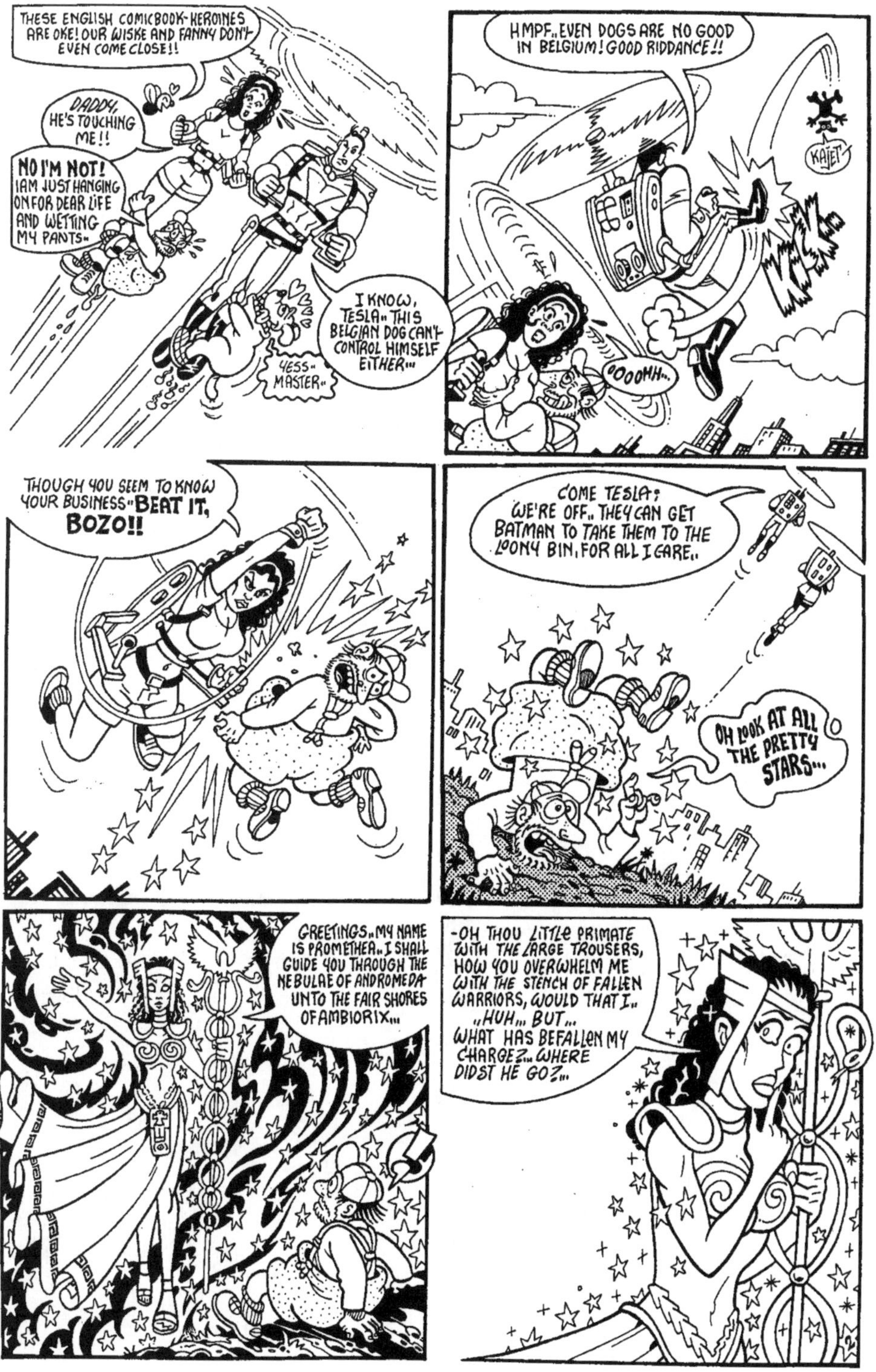
THESE ENGLISH COMICBOOK-HEROINES ARE OKE! OUR WISKE AND FANNY DON'T EVEN COME CLOSE!!
DADDY, HE'S TOUCHING ME!!
NO I'M NOT! I AM JUST HANGING ON FOR DEAR LIFE AND WETTING MY PANTS..
I KNOW, TESLA.. THIS BELGIAN DOG CAN'T CONTROL HIMSELF EITHER...
YESS.. MASTER..
HMPF.. EVEN DOGS ARE NO GOOD IN BELGIUM! GOOD RIDDANCE!!
KAJET
KICK
OOOMH..
THOUGH YOU SEEM TO KNOW YOUR BUSINESS.. BEAT IT, BOZO!!
COME TESLA: WE'RE OFF.. THEY CAN GET BATMAN TO TAKE THEM TO THE LOONY BIN, FOR ALL I CARE..
OH LOOK AT ALL THE PRETTY STARS...
GREETINGS.. MY NAME IS PROMETHEA.. I SHALL GUIDE YOU THROUGH THE NEBULAE OF ANDROMEDA UNTO THE FAIR SHORES OF AMBIORIX...
-OH THOU LITTLE PRIMATE WITH THE LARGE TROUSERS, HOW YOU OVERWHELM ME WITH THE STENCH OF FALLEN WARRIORS, WOULD THAT I.. ..HUH.. BUT... WHAT HAS BEFALLEN MY CHARGE?.. WHERE DIDST HE GO?..

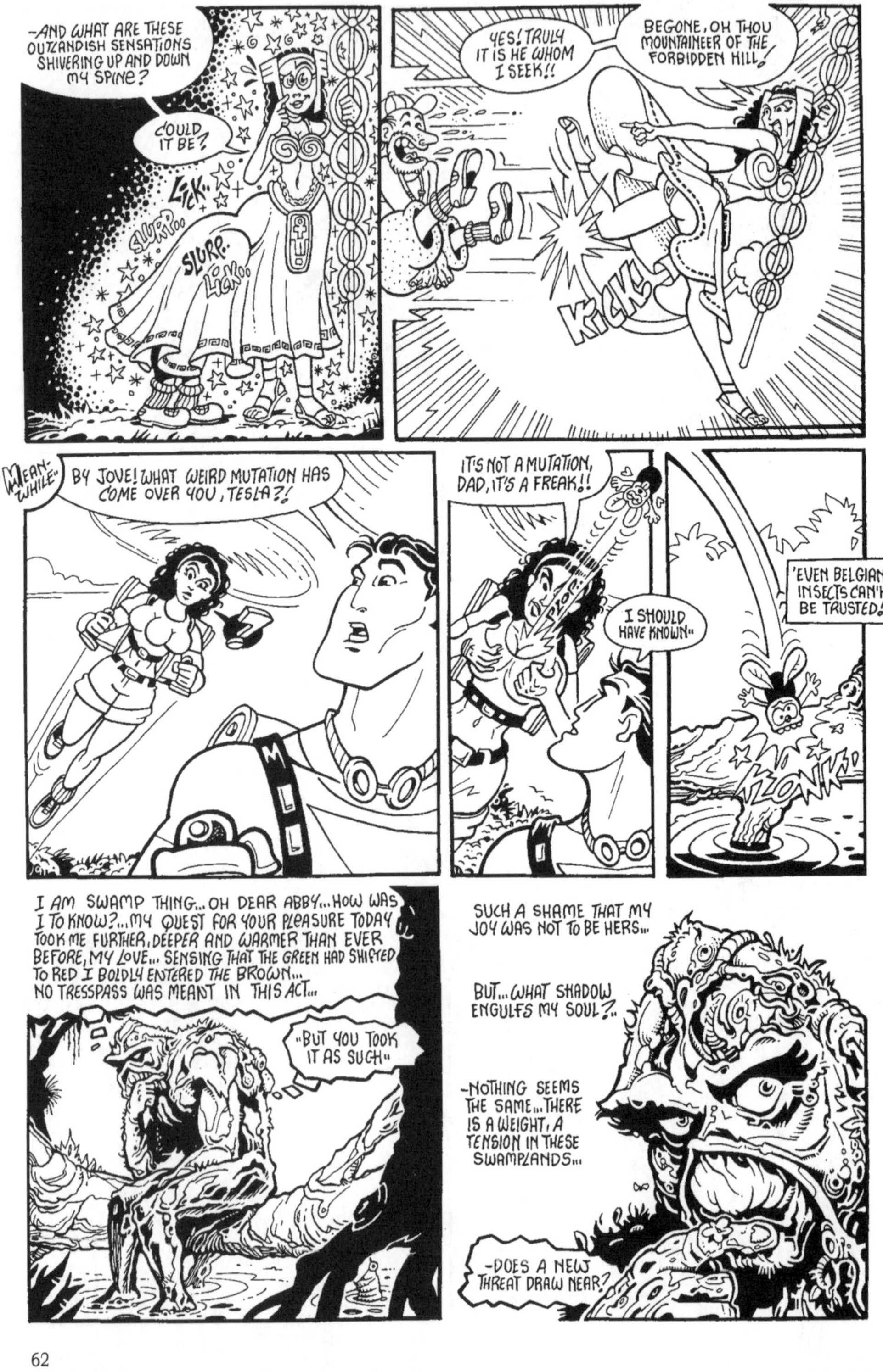
-AND WHAT ARE THESE OUTZANDISH SENSATIONS SHIVERING UP AND DOWN MY SPINE?
COULD IT BE?
LICK
SLURP
SLURP
LICK
YES! TRULY IT IS HE WHOM I SEEK!!
BEGONE, OH THOU MOUNTAINEER OF THE FORBIDDEN HILL!
KICK
MEANWHILE
BY JOVE! WHAT WEIRD MUTATION HAS COME OVER YOU, TESLA?!
IT'S NOT A MUTATION, DAD, IT'S A FREAK!!
PLOP
I SHOULD HAVE KNOWN
'EVEN BELGIAN INSECTS CAN'T BE TRUSTED!'
KLONK
I AM SWAMP THING... OH DEAR ABBY... HOW WAS I TO KNOW?... MY QUEST FOR YOUR PLEASURE TODAY TOOK ME FURTHER, DEEPER AND WARMER THAN EVER BEFORE, MY LOVE... SENSING THAT THE GREEN HAD SHIFTED TO RED I BOLDLY ENTERED THE BROWN... NO TRESSPASS WAS MEANT IN THIS ACT...
"BUT YOU TOOK IT AS SUCH"
SUCH A SHAME THAT MY JOY WAS NOT TO BE HERS...
BUT... WHAT SHADOW ENGULFS MY SOUL?..
-NOTHING SEEMS THE SAME... THERE IS A WEIGHT, A TENSION IN THESE SWAMPLANDS...
-DOES A NEW THREAT DRAW NEAR?

"...THE ATMOSPHERE...THE SMELLS OF THE SWAMP ARE...DIFFERENT... BUT,...DO OTHERS SENSE THIS AS WELL? DOES THIS GREY VEIL ONLY SHROUD MY HEART OR ENCOMPASS THE ENTIRE GREEN?"

"SNIF·SNIF"

"LE BAJOU EST DIFFERENT"

"ABBY?...DO YOU FEEL IT TOO? SOMETHING...DIFFERENT...AN INTERNAL TENSION THAT IS A SENSATION AS WELL?"

"!☆#@!"

"IT IS CLEAR NOW...I MUST PURSUE THIS ALONE...AS USUAL..."

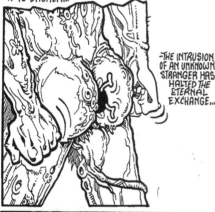

-AND THEN IT REVEALS ITSELF TO ME...THE ANCIENT CYCLE BETWEEN MYSELF AND THE SWAMP...AND HOW IT IS BROKEN...

-THE INTRUSION OF AN UNKNOWN STRANGER HAS HALTED THE ETERNAL EXCHANGE...

-NO COURSE IS LEFT TO ME BUT TO FOCUS ALL MY STRENGTH IN ONE THRUST,,,ONE ENORMOUS ERUPTION...

"A GENTLE RICHNESS TRAVELS THROUGH MY BOWELS..."

"...OH SWEET RELEASE..."

"...AND THE BOND... BETWEEN ME AND THE GREEN IS FORGED ONCE MORE..."

"SNIF... SNIF..."

"LE BAJOU EST MAGNIFIQUE..."

"LAISSEZ LES BONTEMPS ROULER!"

C'MON GUYS,,, ALL THESE WEIRDO'S HAVE DIRTY MINDS... WE ARE WAY TOO CLASSY FOR THAT"

"PHEW!AMEDEE- WHERE HAVE YOU BEEN?YOU STINK!"

"LET'S GO HOME!"

"BELGIUM"

STORY&ART WILLY LINTHOUT & STEVEN.

WEARING ALAN MOORE

It is always the same old story. Think about when either famous pop stars or attractive TV presenters are interviewed about the last book they read. It is always, invariably, something by Hermann Hesse, Stephen King, or *The Manifesto of The Communist Party* (strangely enough, nobody ever reads *Das Capital*...).

Probably they think (and the same holds for the public, or so it seems) that there is no chance that you can be considered stupid, if you have read Hesse. Or, better, if you <u>say</u> that you have read Hesse.

The use of the literary "name", in the head of the VIP, becomes analogous to a fashion brand: something comfortable, often to be shown off in public. Like a Ralph Lauren jumper or a Versace suit...

It seems like a ridiculous behaviour, something to joke about (maybe taking the piss out of Beckham), but if we reflect carefully, something similar has been happening in comics for about 15 years.

Whether preview editions, interviews or collections introductions, the result does not change. In comics, the name that needs to be brought up is the one of Mr. Alan Moore from Northampton.

Moore, amongst the comics cognoscenti, has obtained this status, almost embarrassingly so: if his name is not mentioned during an interview, it's a mistake that's almost a crime.

The fact that Moore is (almost) a compulsory reference, though, demonstrates the greats skills and immense talent of the Man with the Beard.

In fact, while the previously mentioned TV personalities try to ease the pressure using lazy references, who mentions Moore's name does it as a precise choice and, most of all, after he's read his book. It is not a minor distinction. Moore is acclaimed *first among equals* by both his colleagues and the readers. This has been going on for over a decade. In the very fickle world of entertainment, where trends and taste change very quickly (too quickly, if you ask me), I think it's not too bad, really.

The late great Italian actor Carmelo Bene liked to define himself "a living legend". Today, this definition can be attributed (at least, this is the case in comics) only to Alan Moore.

The production of the great English writer has covered, sometimes in an almost schizoid fashion, every sub genre of comics available on the US market. It is probably a well known fact in Europe (but maybe not in America) that Moore wrote everything between the groundbreaking *From Hell* and *Whatever Happened to the Man of Tomorrow?*.

The "living legend" Moore holds a very remarkable record: not only does he unite critics and fans in the unconditional praise for his work, but the man from Northampton also makes fans among any kind of audience. As it is always the case for a true Prince of Darkness, Moore's aficionados range from the flaccid sixty-something to the spotty teenager.

Moore's public is really unclassifiable, from loyal mainstream superhero readers (the ones who enjoy only the trendiest Wildstorm comics) to radical "indie" supporters. In any other mass media, this is simply inconceivable.

Today fame and respect seem to be obtainable only by selling out, trying to please the vilest instincts of the masses. Check the TV, if you don't believe me. What is supposed to be "popular" becomes "vulgar".

But there is someone who reminds us it does not have to be this way.

Long live, Mr. Alan Moore, and thanks for everything.

• **Antonio Solinas**

ANTONIO SOLINAS

*Antonio Solinas is the co-founder and staff writer of **Rorschach**, the popular Italian weekly newsletter devoted to comics art.*
Text ©2003 Antonio Solinas.

METAPHROG

Pages 65-69 following:
*Metaphrog are the duo from Scotland responsible for **Strange Weather Lately**, **The Maze** and the multiple award nominee **Louis - Red Letter Day**. Two more acclaimed scary-cute stories featuring Louis are already published. www.metaphrog.com.*
Strip and Louis ©2003 Metaphrog.

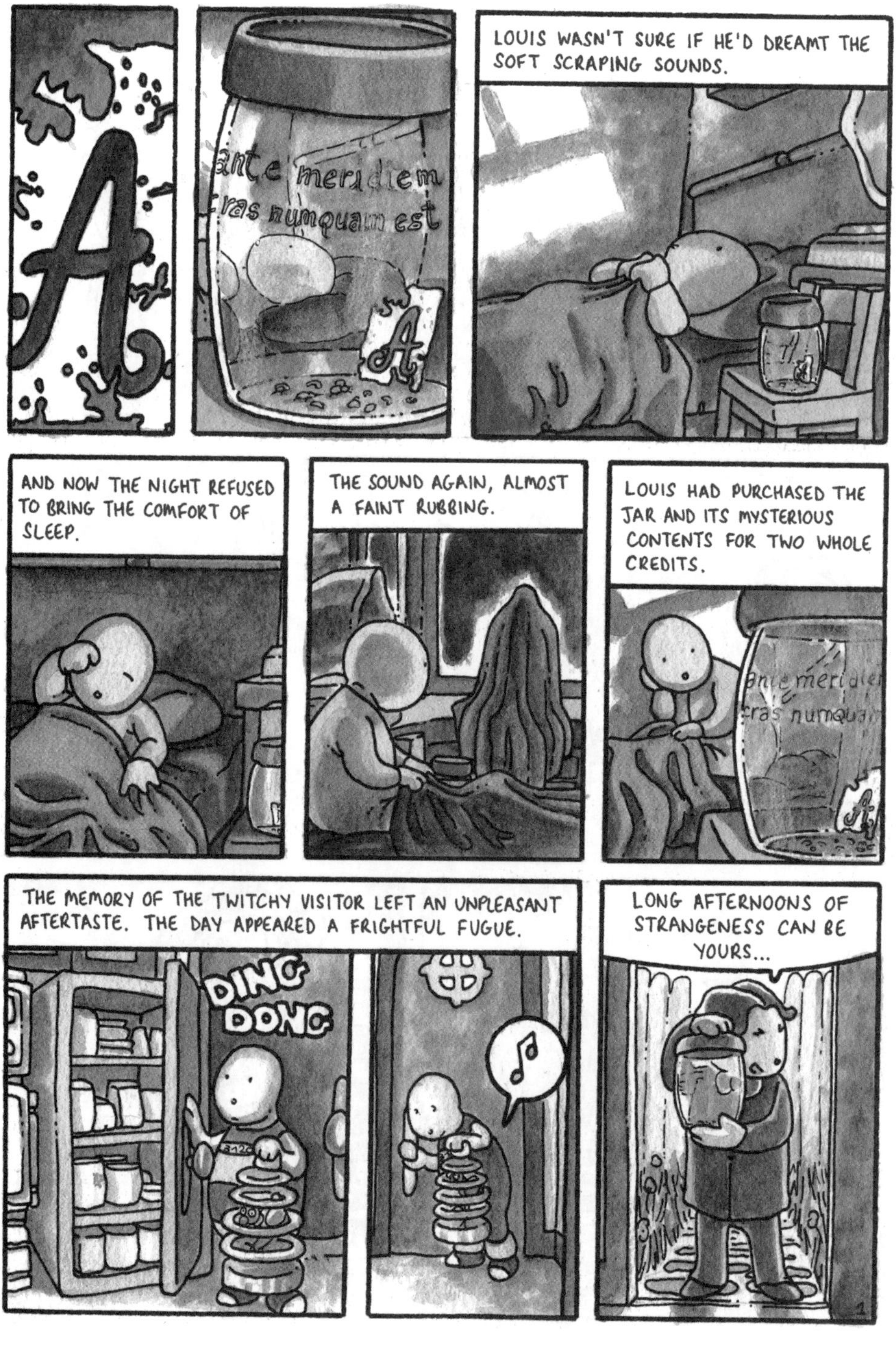
ante meridiem
cras numquam est
LOUIS WASN'T SURE IF HE'D DREAMT THE SOFT SCRAPING SOUNDS.
AND NOW THE NIGHT REFUSED TO BRING THE COMFORT OF SLEEP.
THE SOUND AGAIN, ALMOST A FAINT RUBBING.
LOUIS HAD PURCHASED THE JAR AND ITS MYSTERIOUS CONTENTS FOR TWO WHOLE CREDITS.
THE MEMORY OF THE TWITCHY VISITOR LEFT AN UNPLEASANT AFTERTASTE. THE DAY APPEARED A FRIGHTFUL FUGUE.
DING DONG
LONG AFTERNOONS OF STRANGENESS CAN BE YOURS...

NOURISHED EXCLUSIVELY ON BOOKS WHOSE PAGES HOLD...

... THE VERY KEY OF DREAMS, PAPER OF A PRECIOUS PLANT FROM SEVEN DISTANT MISTY HILLS...

...HALLUCINATORY BRUSHWOOD, *Aloe roman* (THAT'S LATIN YOU SEE.)

A DEAD YET MORDANT TONGUE. APT FOR SUCH A NOBLE WORM.

NOW I CAN'T SLEEP.

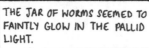

THE JAR OF WORMS SEEMED TO FAINTLY GLOW IN THE PALLID LIGHT.

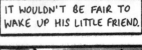

IT WOULDN'T BE FAIR TO WAKE UP HIS LITTLE FRIEND.

LOUIS WONDERED IF FC DREAMED IN MECHANICAL SLEEP.

FLIPPI -NECK !!!

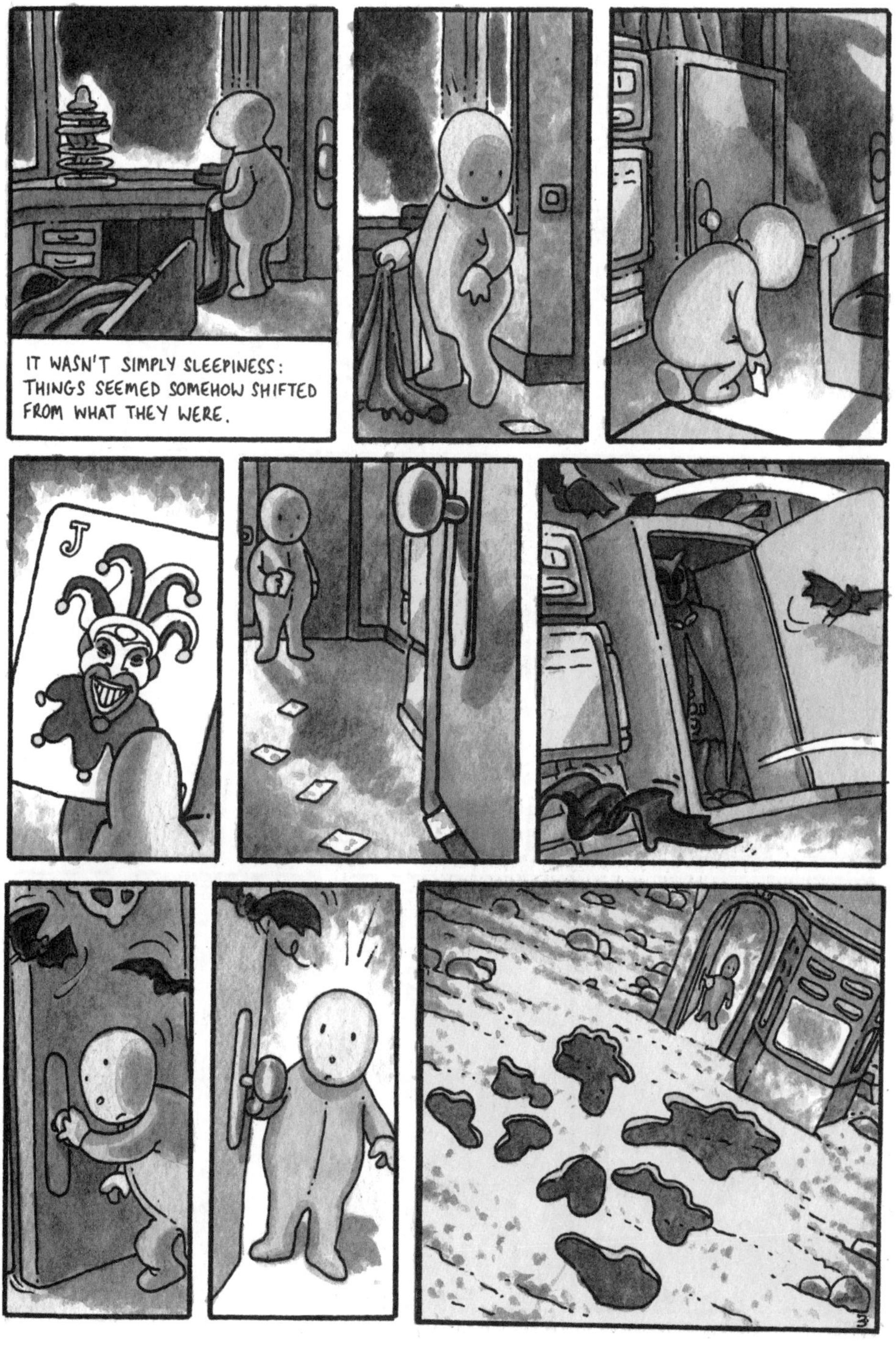
IT WASN'T SIMPLY SLEEPINESS: THINGS SEEMED SOMEHOW SHIFTED FROM WHAT THEY WERE.
J

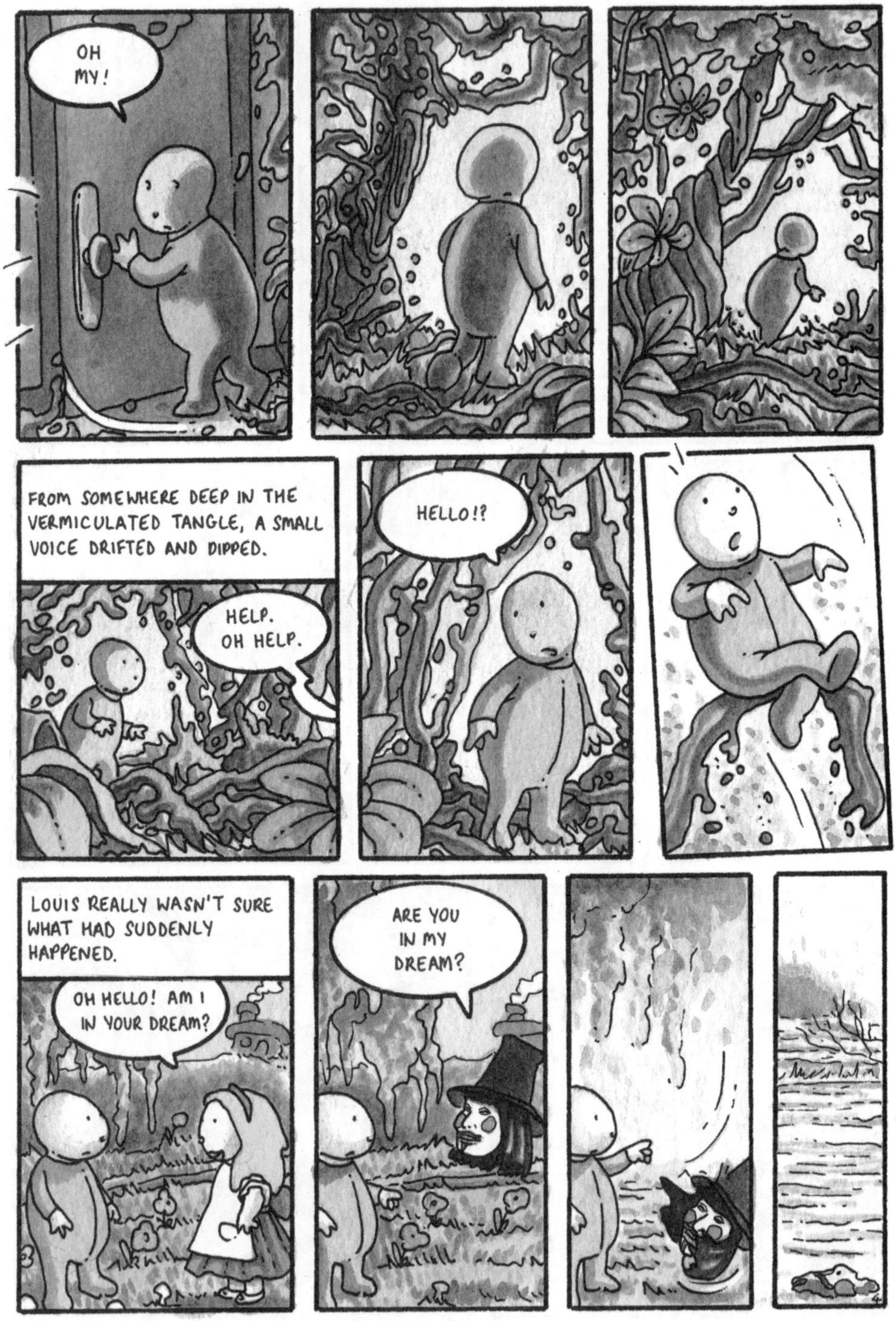
OH MY!
FROM SOMEWHERE DEEP IN THE VERMICULATED TANGLE, A SMALL VOICE DRIFTED AND DIPPED.
HELP. OH HELP.
HELLO!?
LOUIS REALLY WASN'T SURE WHAT HAD SUDDENLY HAPPENED.
OH HELLO! AM I IN YOUR DREAM?
ARE YOU IN MY DREAM?

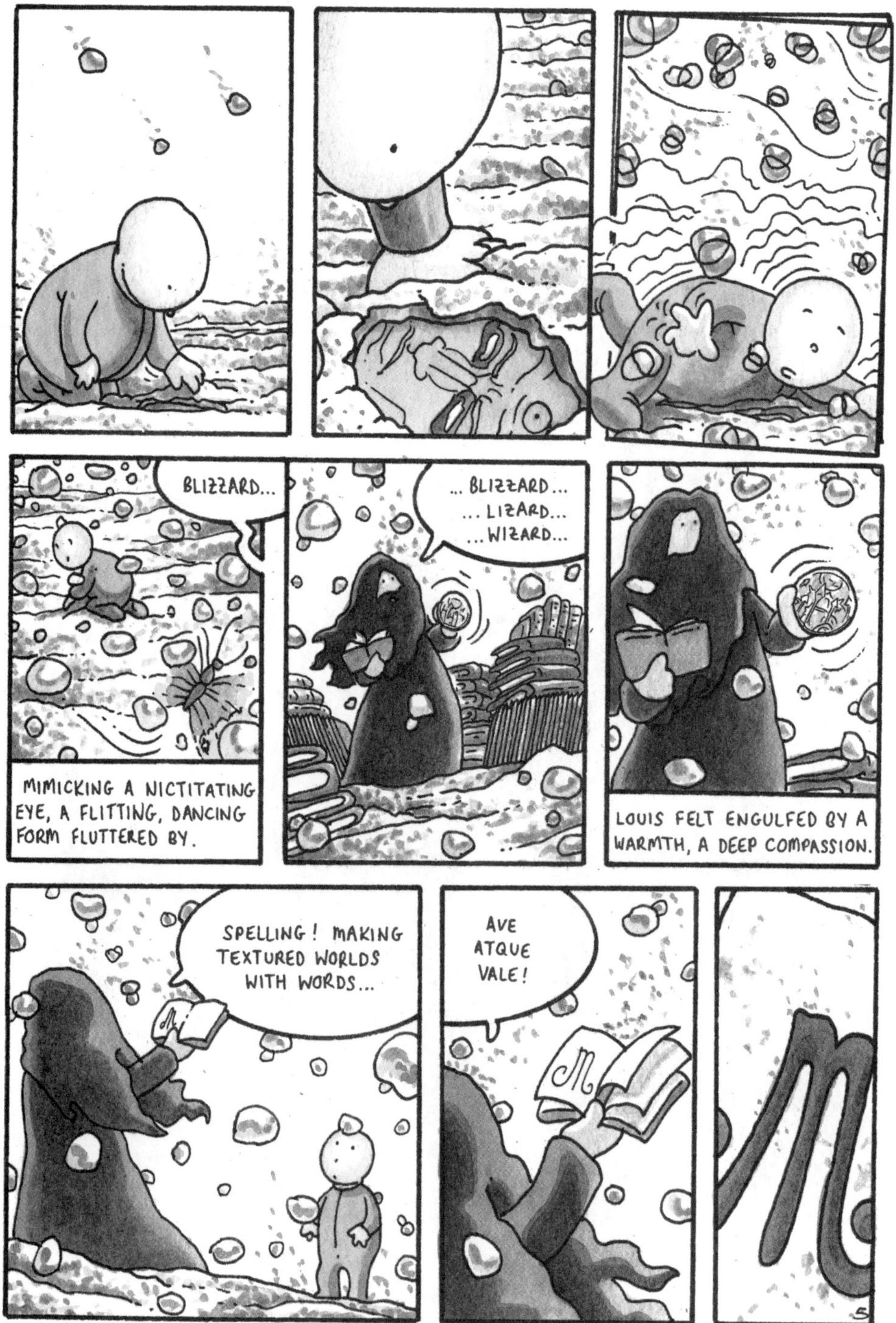
BLIZZARD...
MIMICKING A NICTITATING EYE, A FLITTING, DANCING FORM FLUTTERED BY.
... BLIZZARD... ... LIZARD... ... WIZARD...
LOUIS FELT ENGULFED BY A WARMTH, A DEEP COMPASSION.
SPELLING! MAKING TEXTURED WORLDS WITH WORDS...
AVE ATQUE VALE!
5
metaphrog 2003

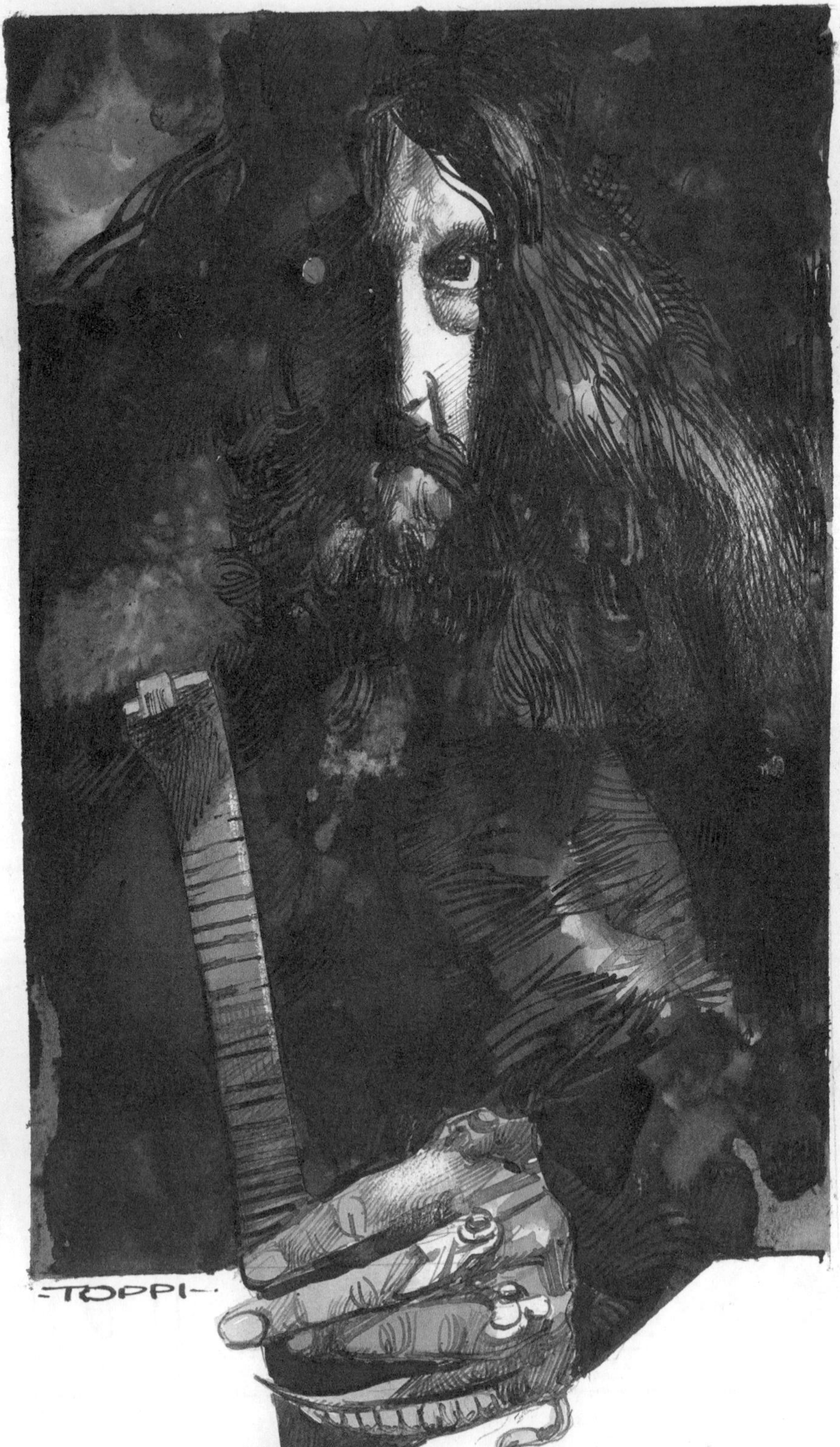
-TOPPI-

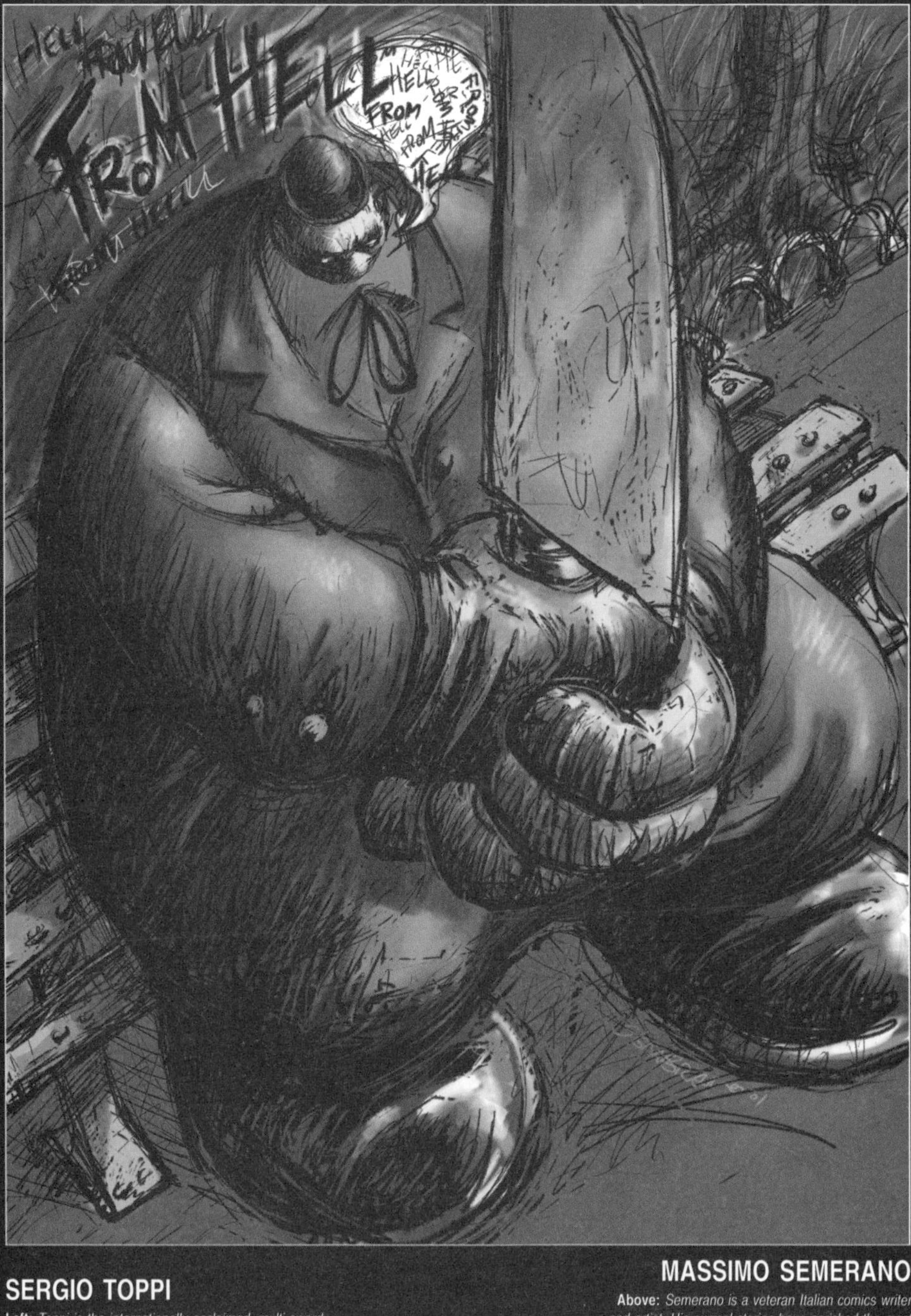
FROM HELL

SERGIO TOPPI

Left: *Toppi is the internationally acclaimed, multi-award winning Italian master of comics and illustration. Following his exhibition in Paris during 2002-03,* **Le Figaro** *defined him as an "immense" artist and compared his art to the works of Döre, Klimt and Schiele.*
Illustration ©2003 Sergio Toppi.

MASSIMO SEMERANO

Above: *Semerano is a veteran Italian comics writer and artist. His surreal stories have enriched the most important Italian comics magazines, such as* **Dolce Vita, Frigidaire, Fuego** *and* **Cyborg.** *He wrote* **Pop 666,** *published in USA by Fantagraphics Books.*
Illustration ©2003 Massimo Semerano.
From Hell © 2002 Alan Moore/Eddie Campbell.

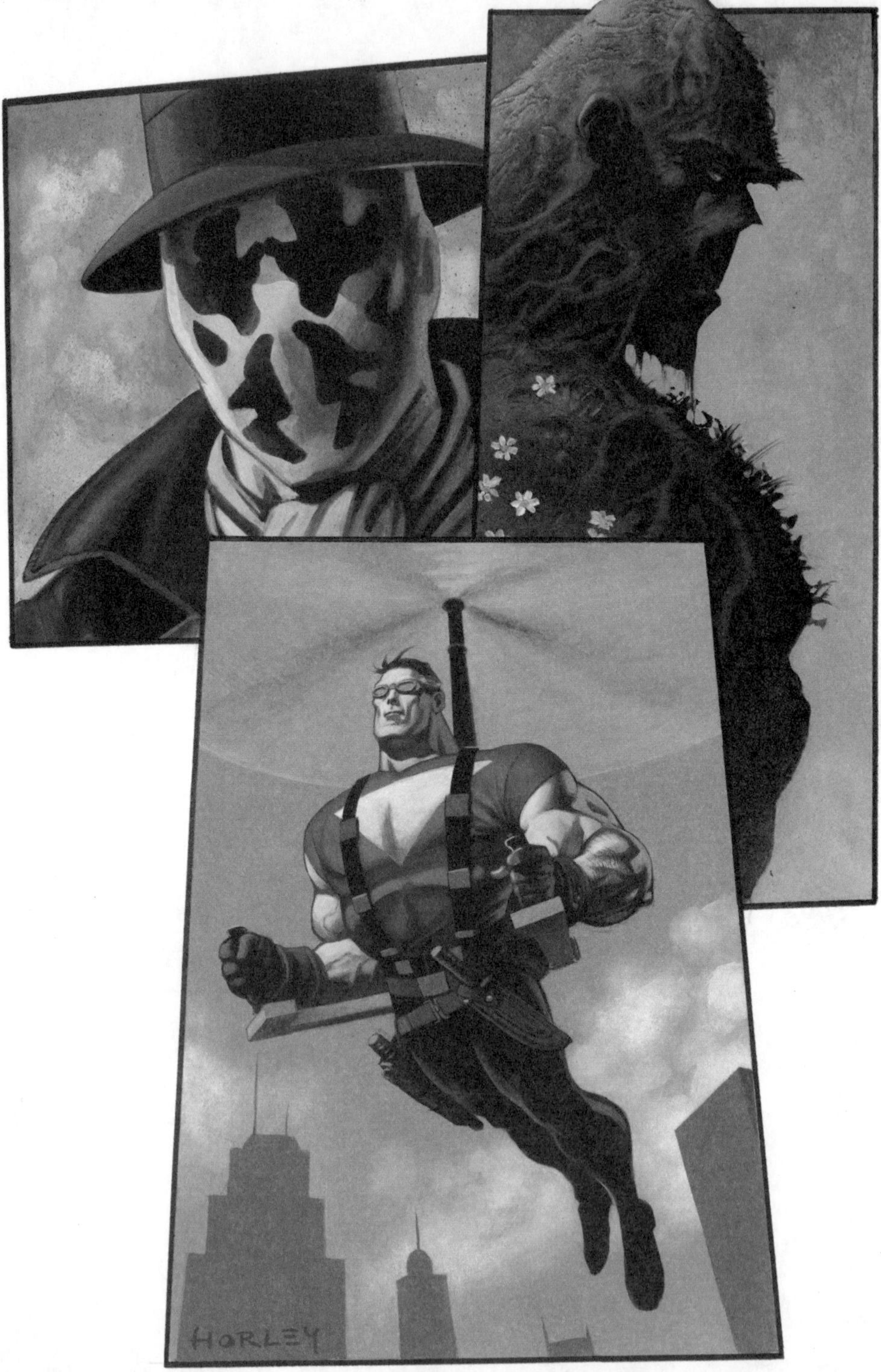
HORLEY

WHY I HATE ALAN MOORE

STEVE NILES

Steve Niles is the writer of **30 Days of Night** (soon to be a movie produced by Sam Raimi), **Criminal Macabre** and **Hellspawn**. Originally from Washington DC, Steve now resides in Los Angeles with his wife Nikki and their three black cats.
Text ©2003 Steve Niles.

There are signposts in life, crossroads, and for me Alan Moore is one of those markers.

I'd never heard of Alan Moore when I first read comics. I was strictly a Marvel kid with the occasional defection to Creepy, Swamp Thing and Batman. By the time I was 14, I'd given up on them. I sold my collection and used the money to buy stereo equipment and some other teen supplies, and I thought comic books were behind me for good. I stopped thinking about them. No more Spiderman, no more Fantastic Four. After a short lifetime of reading and collecting, I was done.

A few years went by. I was in Washington D.C. visiting my dad on one of those terminally awkward, post-divorce weekend visits. There was a comic store in Georgetown. Completely unaware I'd abandoned funny books my Dad slapped me with some cash and sent me into the store.

I was stunned. Comics had changed since I fled the scene. There seemed to be some excitement brewing in the musty little shop. Something sinister and fun. There was a guy behind the counter. His name was Don and he demanded I buy a title. He said if I liked horror (and I did) I had to buy The Swamp Thing by Alan Moore. He shoved a copy in my face and added the bait.

"It's the first comic from one of the big boys WITHOUT the comic's code."

Really? Sounds like trouble. I was sold. Wrap it up!

I read Alan Moore's Swamp Thing and was hit by the narrative like a locomotive. I was shocked, and happily appalled. Here was a comic that hit me on a gut level, spoke to me like I was a...a...well, a reader. There wasn't any of the guarded storytelling I'd grown used to and out of.

That's really the thrust of this little ditty... Alan Moore dragged me back into comic. I was out and I had no intention of looking back because comics had become a thing of my childhood, colorful little stories which had no place in my blooming adult life... until Moore came along with his scary and sophisticated, cutting and gripping tale of a swamp creature lost in an impossible nightmare.

I never left comics again and I blame Alan Moore. Every time I pick up a title I hope it will have the impact of that first issue of Swamp Thing, the first appearance of Constantine, or the first time Abby and Alec kissed.

And now, All these years later, I'm still in and into comics, I still read everything Moore writes. That guy Don from the comic store? He grew up to be Don Murphy, the producer of Moore inspired films From Hell and League of Extraordinary Gentlemen.

Small, weird, weird world.

So why do I hate Alan Moore? There are two reasons really. The first for dragging me back into comics. What would my life had been like if I hadn't read that issue of Swamp Thing? I'll never know. I'm knee-deep in the shit now, anxiously awaiting the next issue of LoEG.

ALEX HORLEY

Left: Born in Italy, Horley has worked as illustrator for all the major comics companies including **Heavy Metal**, Marvel, Image and DC Comics. His latest project is the painted miniseries **Lobo Unbound**. www.alexhorley.com
Illustration ©2003 Alex Horley.
Rorschach & Swamp Thing are both ©2003 DC Comics.
Tom Strong ©2003 America's Best Comics, LLC.

The second reason I hate Alan Moore, and this is the big one, is because the man is as close to the perfect comic writer as we may ever see. He manipulates the medium to its fullest potential, juggling words and pictures effortlessly, and always managing to amaze.

I guess both reasons are sort of the saying the same thing; I hate Alan Moore because he makes comics worth while. The bastard.

• **Steve Niles**
Los Angles
March 30 2003

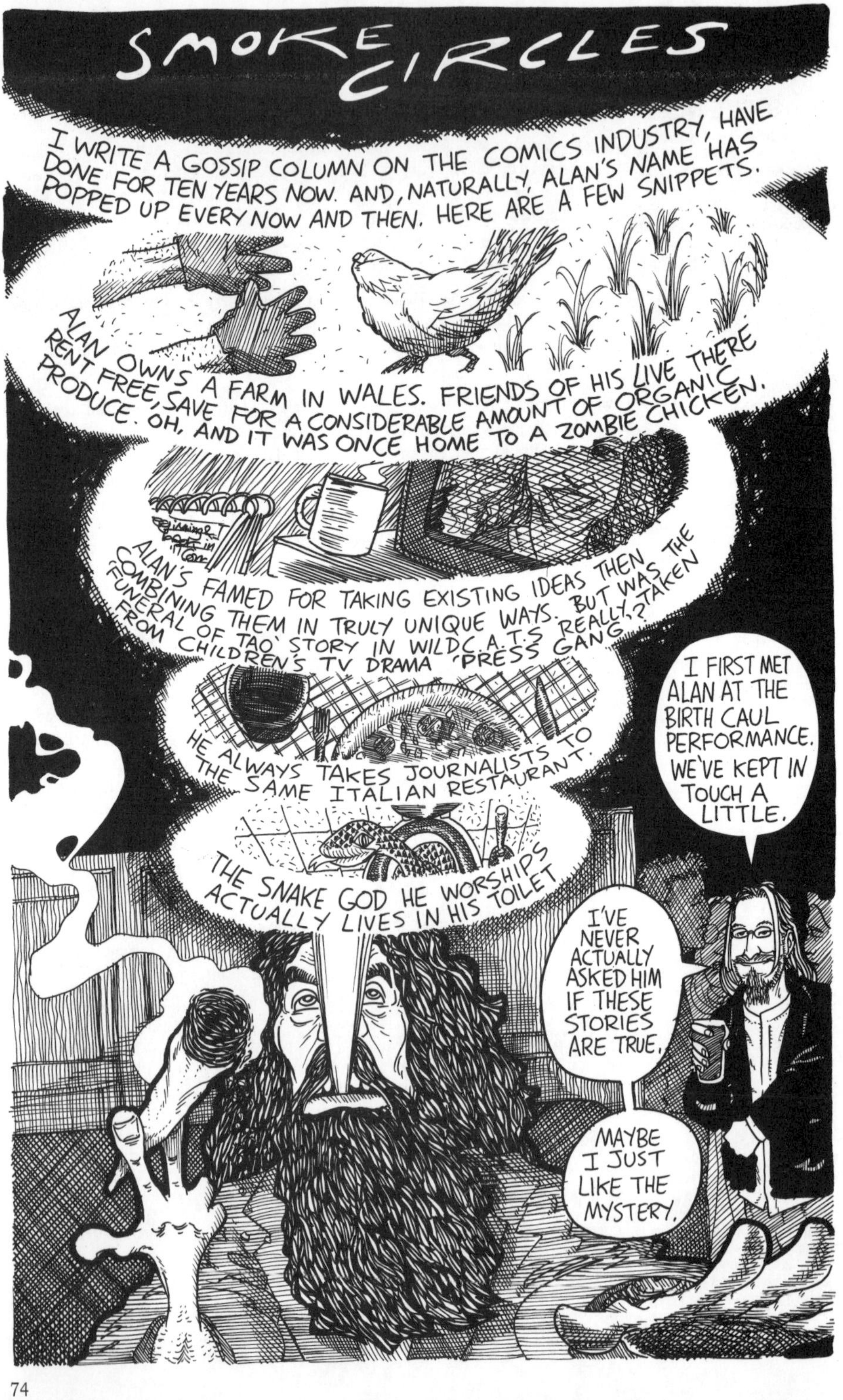
SMOKE CIRCLES
I WRITE A GOSSIP COLUMN ON THE COMICS INDUSTRY, HAVE DONE FOR TEN YEARS NOW. AND, NATURALLY, ALAN'S NAME HAS POPPED UP EVERY NOW AND THEN. HERE ARE A FEW SNIPPETS.
ALAN OWNS A FARM IN WALES. FRIENDS OF HIS LIVE THERE RENT FREE, SAVE FOR A CONSIDERABLE AMOUNT OF ORGANIC PRODUCE. OH, AND IT WAS ONCE HOME TO A ZOMBIE CHICKEN.
ALAN'S FAMED FOR TAKING EXISTING IDEAS THEN COMBINING THEM IN TRULY UNIQUE WAYS. BUT WAS THE 'FUNERAL OF TAO' STORY IN WILDC.A.T.S REALLY TAKEN FROM CHILDREN'S TV DRAMA 'PRESS GANG'?
HE ALWAYS TAKES JOURNALISTS TO THE SAME ITALIAN RESTAURANT.
THE SNAKE GOD HE WORSHIPS ACTUALLY LIVES IN HIS TOILET
I FIRST MET ALAN AT THE BIRTH CAUL PERFORMANCE. WE'VE KEPT IN TOUCH A LITTLE.
I'VE NEVER ACTUALLY ASKED HIM IF THESE STORIES ARE TRUE.
MAYBE I JUST LIKE THE MYSTERY.

MOORE MORALITY

DYLAN HORROCKS

Born in New Zealand, Horrocks is the writer/artist of the graphic novel **Hicksville** *which was named a book of the year by The Comics Journal. More recently he's written* **The Names of Magic** *miniseries and the monthly title* **Hunter: the Age of Magic** *for DC/Vertigo, and is currently working on the creator-owned* **Atlas.** *www.hicksville.co.nz. Text ©2003 Dylan Horrocks.*

I still remember the first time I noticed Alan Moore's name. I was 15 or 16 and an avid reader of the British weekly comic 2000AD, which I would pick up every Thursday on the way home and happily lose myself in for half an hour with an after-school snack. This must have been around 1982, because ET was going great guns at the boxoffice and I guess the editors of 2000AD wanted to cash in on that with a cheap imitation of their own. To their credit they gave the job to Alan Moore. The resulting serial was called SKIZZ and by the end of the first episode I knew this was much more than a cheap Spielberg ripoff. I looked up the name of the writer (or 'script droid' as 2000AD wryly put it) who'd taken such a lame brief and turned it into a tense, funny, moving and politically provocative story (complete with witty references to Alan Bleasdale's searing indictment of the unemployment-economy, "Boys from the Blackstuff"). It was an easy name to remember: "Alan Moore". Before long, it was a name no-one could ignore.

American fans usually view "Swamp Thing" and "Watchmen" as Moore's breakthrough stories - the books with which he changed comics forever. Personally, I'm struck by how the key elements of what makes Moore so special are there from the very beginning: the ability to take a trashy formula or forgettable character and shape them into something fresh, profound and beautiful - while at the same time managing to impart a genuinely respectful sense of what was precious about the original. The humour, the literacy, the intelligent political analysis, the technical virtuosity, the sincerity and warmth. And above all (for me), a deep and genuine moral core to his work.

I don't think it's possible to overstate how influential Alan Moore's work has been in the English-speaking comics world. I still hear echoes of "Marvelman" in almost every superhero comic I pick up these days - usually pale, shallow echoes, but they're there nonetheless (and don't get me started on "Watchmen"). "Swamp Thing" effectively gave birth to the entire body of work known as Vertigo Comics (though it's still better than any of them). And now ABC Comics is hauling the mainstream comic in a whole new direction again - actually in two or three new directions (and how many retro-styled tribute covers have we seen since "Promethea" and "Tom Strong" started the trend?).

The extent of this influence is our blessing and Moore's curse. A curse because most of the work that has come in his wake has stolen some superficial elements of Moore's narrative style or tone, while failing to notice what makes his comics REALLY good. Because by trying to make mainstream comics grow up, all he managed (in many cases) was to push them into a rowdy, obnoxious, pretentious adolescence. I love the fact that now, with "Tom Strong", Moore is gently leading us back to childhood again.

But as influential as Moore has and continues to be, that's not what really makes me love his work. It's the work itself. From odd forgotten 80s gems like "Captain Britain" to the phenomenal "From Hell", from ephemeral humour strips like "The Bojeffries Saga" to the deeply serious political manifesto "V for Vendetta", from accessible 'mainstream' adventure stories like "Tom Strong" to the labyrinthine, intensely personal "Birth Caul", Moore's work is always a masterpiece. Sure - he's one of the greatest craftspeople we've ever had. But even that's not the real issue for me.

RICHARD JOHNSTON

Left: Johnston started out as a self-publishing cartoonist on his **Dirtbag** *and* **X-Flies** *series but is better known in his capacity as a comics journalist and rumour monger with columns like* **Lying In The Gutters** *at www.comicbookresources.com. Cartoon ©2003 Richard Johnston.*

Let me tell you about the moment I realised just how lucky we are to have him in our strange little literary ghetto. You remember the issue of "Top Ten" when there's been an accident at a teleportation pad? Much of that issue consists of one of our heroes sitting with two of the accident's victims as they slowly die. They talk, they cry, they struggle with fear, they wait for the inevitable. This came as something of a surprise to me, since the previous issues of "Top Ten" had basically been an entertaining and playful spin on TV cop shows. Suddenly, out of the blue - this! At first, I even thought Moore had inserted the incident as black comedy - which seemed uncharacteristically callous of him. But as the issue unfolded, I realised - with that shiver up the spine I associate with so much of Moore's work - that he was putting me through something much worse - and much more valuable. I don't know if this issue was written out of the same impulse that led to "The Birth Caul," but it had the same effect on me. By the last page, I was in tears. It was genuinely moving in the way that only the most sincere and meaningful work can be. Moore was facing the reality of death, not unafraid but free of illusions and sentiment. The closest thing to that issue I can think of is the long passage in "War & Peace" where Andrei is dying.

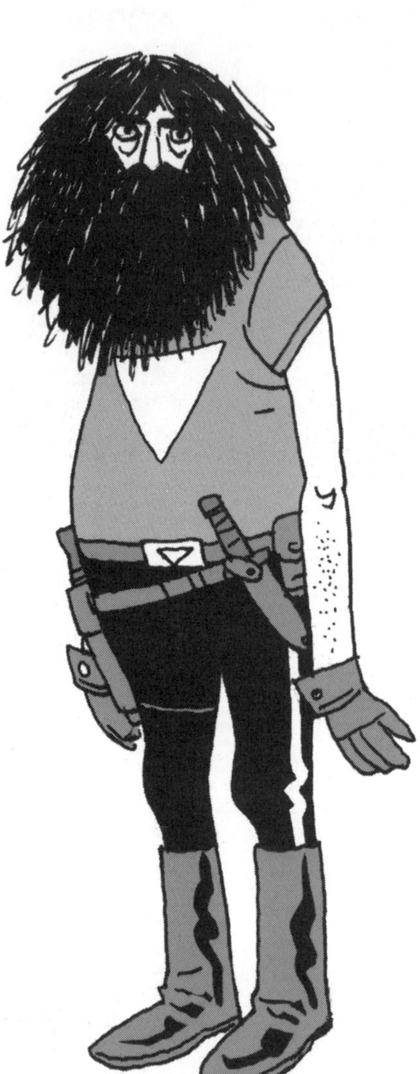

It was impressive, sure - but ultimately I don't give a shit about impressive. I wasn't crying because Moore had written the thing so damn well. I was crying because he'd taken all his own grief and the lessons he'd learnt from it and had distilled them into this crazy little comic about superheroes and interdimensional travel. He'd given us a gift, carefully copied from the scars on his own heart.

That's what I mean when I say that what really makes Alan Moore's work special is its morality. His work is pure and sincere. And utterly, deeply humane. It was clear in SKIZZ and it's clear in everything he's written since. It was radiantly clear in "This is Information" - his contribution to one of the 9-11 benefit books. Moore's story was intelligent, moving and profoundly mature. He even managed to express perfectly my own complex ambivalence towards the American comics industry's response to the events of September 11. Once again, I was grateful to the man who could pull this off - not because it was a good comic; but because he said what someone needed to say.

I don't care if he worships an ancient snake god and summons demons in his spare time. I would trust Alan Moore with my soul. And every time I pick up one of his comics, that's exactly what I do.

• Dylan Horrocks

Above: *Illustration ©2003 Dylan Horrocks. Tom Strong ©2003 America's Best Comics, LLC.*

GIL FORMOSA

Below: *Gil Formosa is one of France's hottest commercial artists and is currently producing covers for French comics publisher Semic. Cartoon ©2003 Gil Formosa. The League of Extraordinary Gentlemen ©2003 Alan Moore and Kevin O'Neill.*

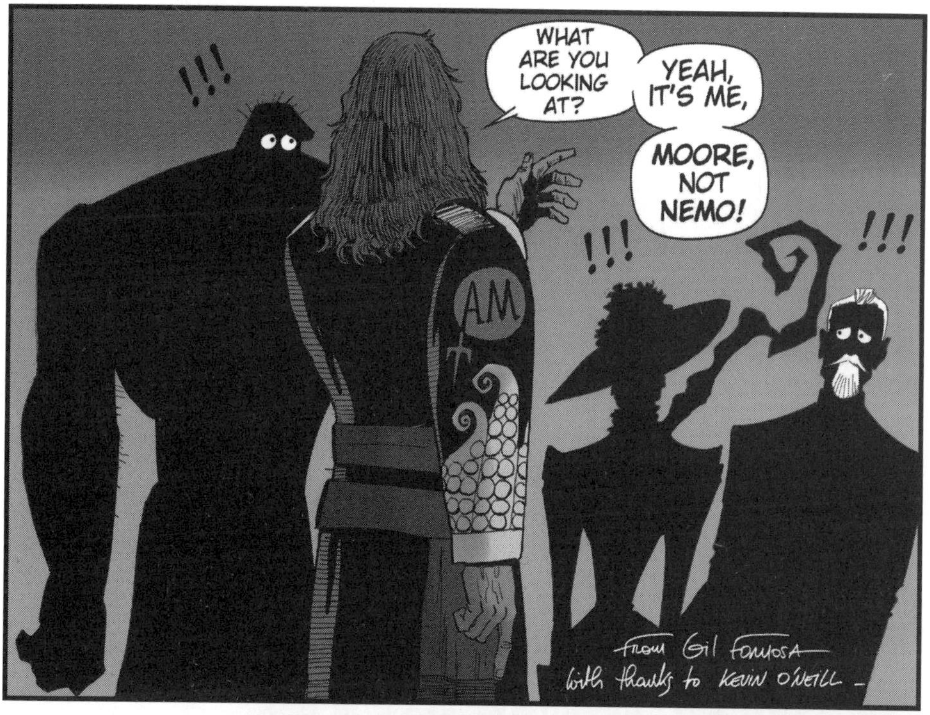
!!!
WHAT ARE YOU LOOKING AT?
YEAH, IT'S ME,
MOORE, NOT NEMO!
!!!
!!!
AM
FROM GIL FORMOSA
with thanks to KEVIN O'NEILL

HOWARD CHAYKIN

Chaykin started out in his comic career as assistant to Gil Kane and went on to freelance for every company in the business. He later pioneered the graphic novel format with books like **Empire** *and created* **American Flagg!** *for First Comics in the 1980s. Although he moved on to write for TV and film, he is currently co-writing* **American Century** *for DC. Text ©2003 Howard Chaykin.*

Simply put, Alan Moore is the best writer American comic books have had since Harvey Kurtzman—and since, in my opinion, Harvey was the best writer comics have ever seen, that's high praise.

• Howard Chaykin

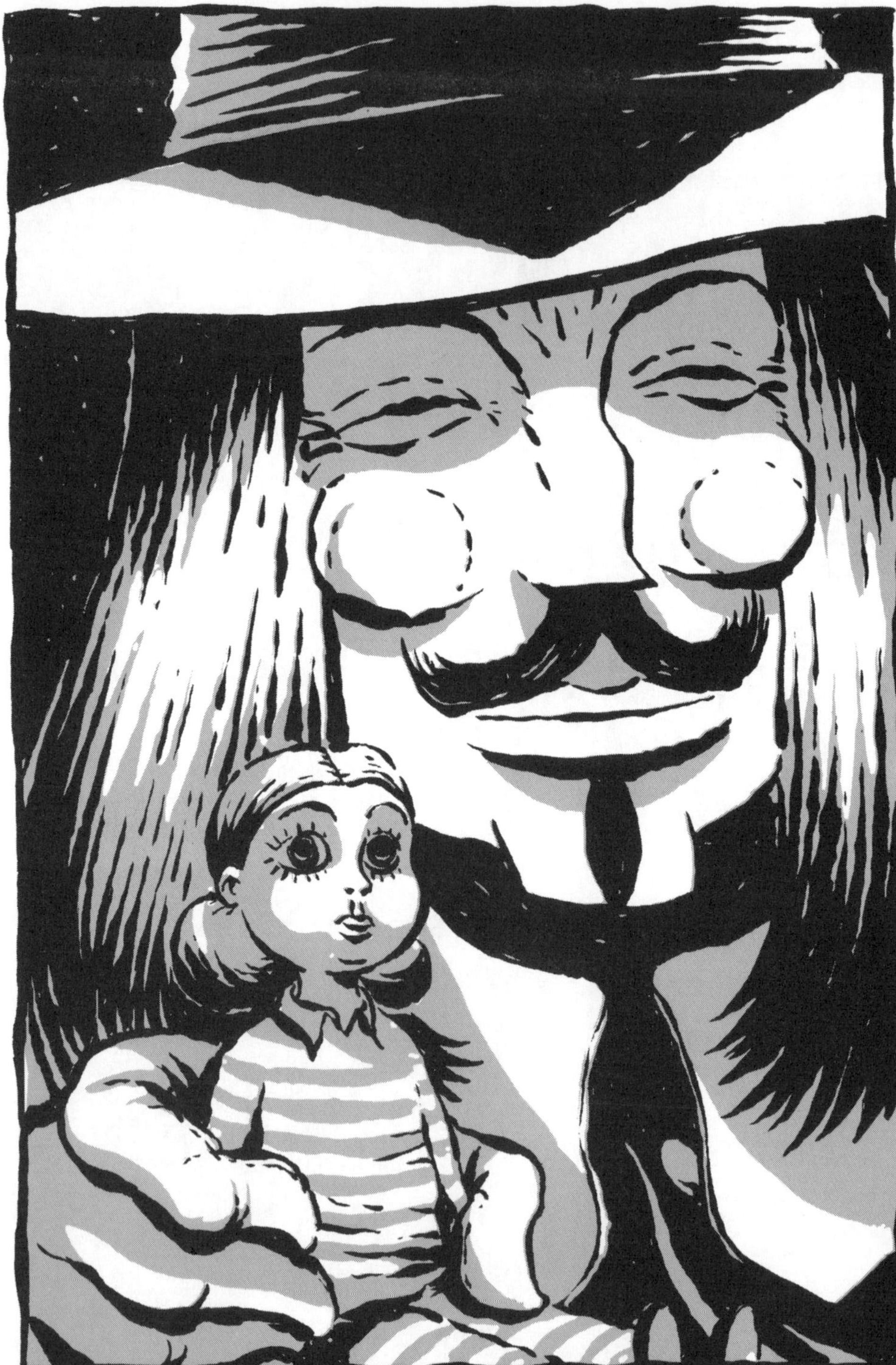

POISONED CHALICE

PAT MILLS

Pat Mills began his comics career at DC Thomson as editor on their romance comics, but moved on to IPC where he wrote **Charley's War** for Battle and created **Sláine, A.B.C. Warriors** and **Nemesis the Warlock** for **2000AD**. In the US, he is better known for his work on **Marshal Law, Metalzoic** and **Batman**.
Text ©2003 Pat Mills.

I recall with immense admiration a scene in Alan's V for Vendetta where the Archbishop of Canterbury, or similar prelate, having committed some loathsome and perverted crime, is fed a poisonous host by V. This act of unholy communion was superbly choreographed by Alan's script and beautifully and darkly illustrated by David Lloyd. The exact details of the scene are vague now; yet the emotions it provoked are still powerful in my mind, so I hope my recollection is correct. Of all Alan's writings this scene always comes back to me again and again.

Firstly, because - whilst I have a high regard for all his work - this is the one scene I truly envy and wish I'd written. I can recall thinking when I first read it, many years ago, "Damn! Why didn't I think of that?"

Secondly, because - especially in this day and age - it is usually practitioners of my own ex-religion of Catholicism that are rightly subjected to critical scrutiny by writers of fiction and non fiction. So it is was original and different of Alan to focus on the English High Anglican tradition that is far more skilful than Catholicism at hiding its dark side.

Having researched High Anglicanism myself for some time, I've become aware of just how curious it really is; and how truly sinister and offensive its dark side can be. Therefore I've always wanted to ask Alan his inspiration for this scene.

Because I know that any scene worth writing and reading must come from the heart and resonate with truth. Otherwise it's just the usual comic book crap which Alan's work never is. Whatever his inspiration on this occasion, I was delighted to revel in this very special scene where such an unpleasant authority figure as the Archbishop is subjected to such appropriate and legitimately cruel punishment. In fact, I think V let him off lightly. I'd personally like him to have suffered a little longer.

It's surely a mark of a writer's talent if he can trigger this kind of powerful emotional response in the reader. And even now, recalling that scene this evening, co-incidentally in the week of Guy Fawkes, the role model for V, I still find myself praying to my own Gods that there are poison hosts waiting for everyone of the perverts in the Anglican and Catholic religions.

I suppose I should now conclude with something humorous or flip, but I'm afraid - for me - that would be inappropriate. Because there was never anything humorous or flip about V. It resonated with an important and serious truth; and there is nothing humorous about the real life evil it highlighted in the guise of fiction.

One day I hope to write a similar scene where an avenger pays one of these so-called "Men of God" a visit. Probably with a hammer, nails and two crossed beams of wood. Thank you for your inspiration, Alan.

• **Pat Mills**, November 2002

CARLA SPEED McNEILL

Pages 80-82 following:
McNeill came out of nowhere with her self-published **Finder** comic book series which has now been collected into three trade paperback collections and counting.
www.lightspeedpress.com.
Strip ©2003 Carla Speed McNeill.

MICHELE PETRUCCI

Left: Michele Petrucci is a rising Italian comics talent. He is the creator of two graphic novels, **Keires** and **Sali d'argento**, for Innocent Victim, also published in France by Vertige Graphic.
Illustration ©2003 Michele Petrucci.
V For Vendetta © DC Comics.

CALL & RESPONSE

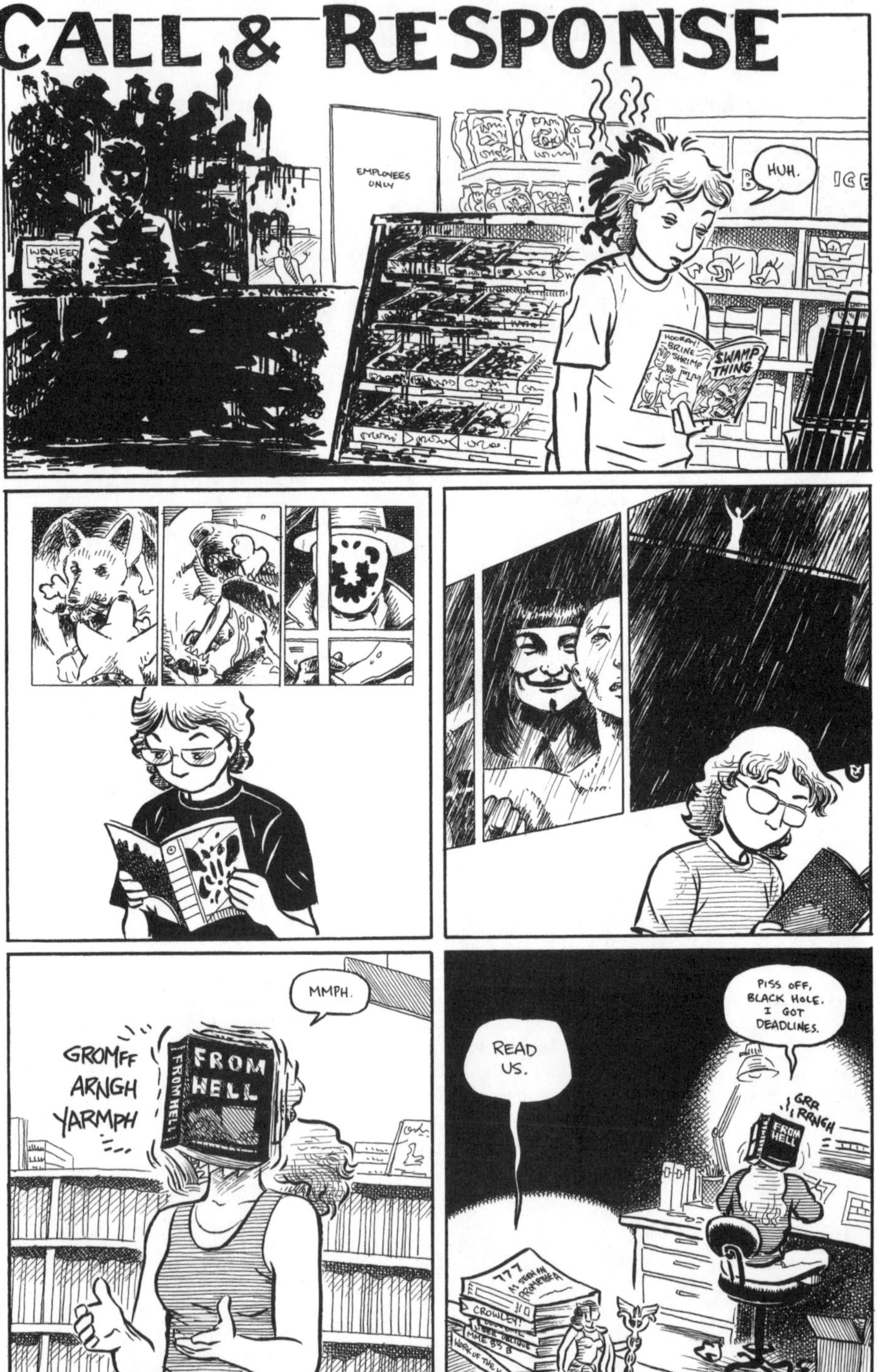
EMPLOYEES ONLY
HUH.
HOORAY! BRINE SHRIMP
SWAMP THING
MMPH.
GROMFF ARNGH YARMPH
FROM HELL
READ US.
PISS OFF, BLACK HOLE. I GOT DEADLINES.
GRR RRNGH
FROM HELL
777 AS SEEN IN PROMETHEA
CROWLEY!

I HAVE NO PROPER PERSPECTIVE ON ALAN MOORE. HIS BLAST RADIUS IS FAR TOO LARGE.

I VALUE HIM AS A VERY CLEAR WRITER ABOUT SOME DEEPLY STRANGE SHIT. A MAN ABLE TO SPEAK RATIONALLY ABOUT INESCAPABLY IRRATIONAL THINGS.

A TRUE AMPHIBIAN, TO USE HIS OWN TERM.

HE'S A NUMEROLOGIST WITHOUT NUMBERS. CHANCE CONNECTIONS AND RESONATING REPETITIONS ARE THE SPINE OF ALL HIS WORK. HE RARELY GOES FAR INTO A BOOK HE CARES ABOUT WITHOUT FIRING OFF A SUPER-DENSE STREAM-OF-CONSCIOUSNESS DREAM SEQUENCE.

IN HIS SPOKEN-WORD PIECES, HE SEEKS TO PUT HIS AUDIENCE INTO ANOTHER PLACE BY MEANS OF WORDS AND IMAGES -- AND WHATEVER ELSE HE CAN PUT TO HIS PURPOSE.

I'VE NO DOUBT THEY'RE EXTREMELY POWERFUL.

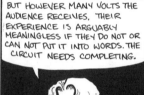

BUT HOWEVER MANY VOLTS THE AUDIENCE RECEIVES, THEIR EXPERIENCE IS ARGUABLY MEANINGLESS IF THEY DO NOT OR CAN NOT PUT IT INTO WORDS. THE CIRCUIT NEEDS COMPLETING.

ALL THAT CURRENT'S GOT TO GROUND ITSELF **SOMEWHERE**, OR IT BURNS OUT SOMETHING VITAL. SO WHAT'S **MY** RESPONSE?

WHAT OF HIS **CAN** I RECEIVE AND RETURN?

WHAT MACHINERY IN ME DOES HIS ELECTRICITY VIVIFY?

JUST A SEC.

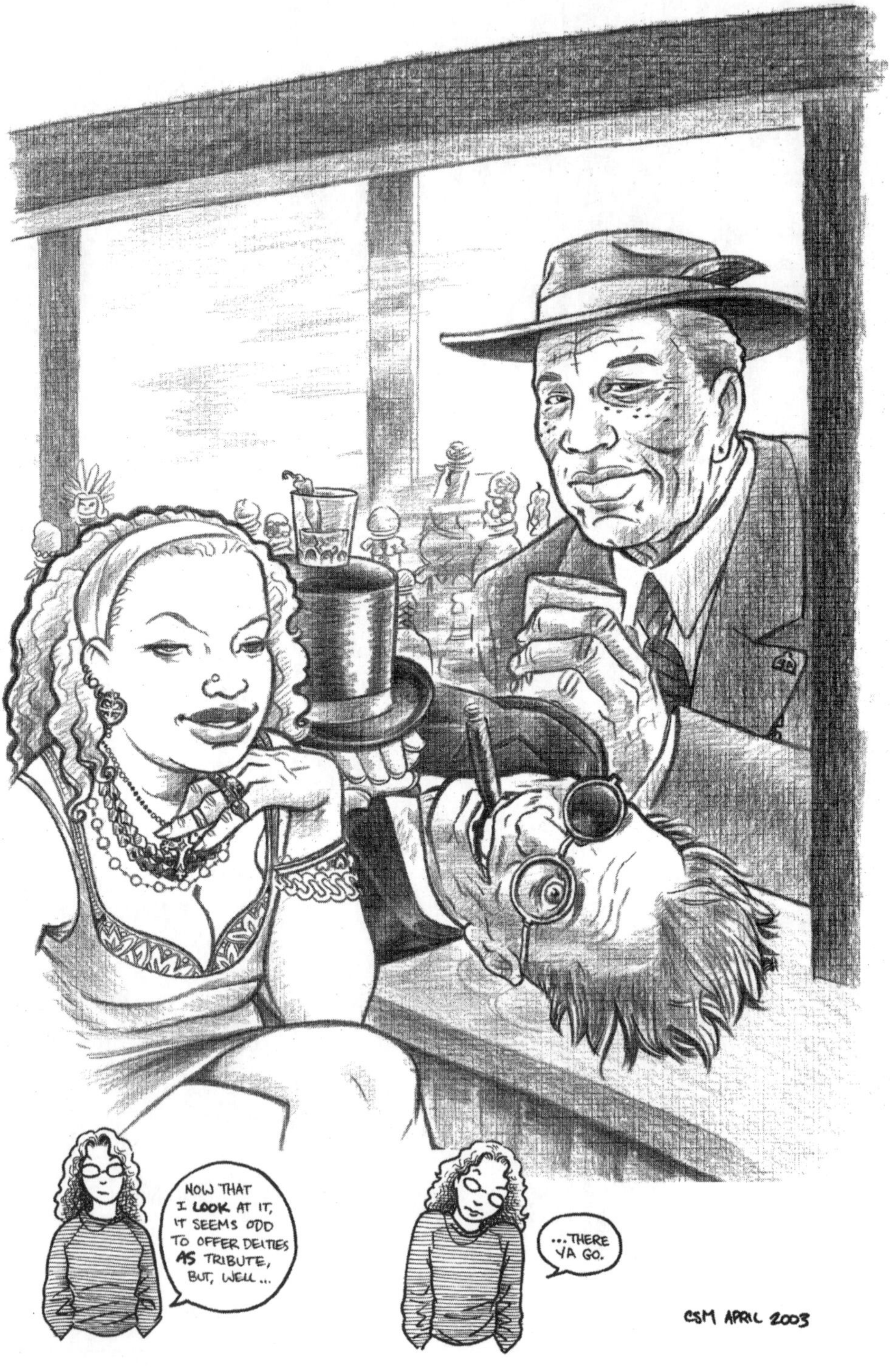
NOW THAT I LOOK AT IT, IT SEEMS ODD TO OFFER DEITIES AS TRIBUTE, BUT, WELL...
...THERE YA GO.
CSM APRIL 2003

SEX, VAMPIRES AND CHRISTMAS SHOPPING

STEVE PARKHOUSE

Steve Parkhouse has worked on countless strips for British comics including **The Spiral Path** *and* **The Bojeffries Saga** *for Warrior.*

Text ©2003 Steve Parkhouse.

I first met Alan Moore in 1971. He was about sixteen or seventeen at the time, and I was five years older. I'd just started working at IPC Magazines as a comics sub-editor on titles such as Whizzer and Chips and Buster and mysteriously named prototypes like JNP 49.

Though professing to be producing new comics all the time, IPC Juveniles were simply regurgitating ideas that were fifty years old. Recycling was the name of the game. Editorial staff were paid next to nothing, installed in draughty old buildings with creaking office furniture and expected to co-exist with the rats, the debris and the general malaise of Farringdon Street and its depressing environs.

It was a cottage industry; inhabited by middle-aged men in cardigans who smoked pipes. You could see them in the works canteen, spooning down vast quantities of jam roly-poly and custard while discussing the latest developments in model aircraft design. The very suggestion of producing something new in the comics field would be met with glazed and vacant incredulity.

In this world, Dan Dare was the apotheosis of comics creation. The Eagle comic was the altar upon which everything else was sacrificed. There was another company somewhere in Scotland, in the heathen land beyond the Wall where another clutch of juveniles was being produced by middle-aged men in cardigans and pipes. They had different titles, but were basically the same.

Sitting across from him at the table of a small café, just around the corner from the Bookends bookshop in West London, I was struck by Alan's demeanour. He was very, very young – but very, very funny. He was undeniably a performer. Very quick, irreverent and totally refreshing.

For the next three years I was engaged in the regurgitation of fifty-year old material, until finally I could stand it no longer and quit. I had occasional glimpses of Alan's work – or the odd message conveyed through Steve Moore – another IPC sub-editor – who'd been a long standing friend of Alan's. But we never actually met again until ten years later.

In the interim, I had learned something of the craft of storytelling. I could draw a cartoon or two in about half a dozen styles – and was ploughing a strange and somewhat lonely furrow as a freelance illustrator. I had kept various contacts since IPC days – the most notable being Dez Skinn and Paul Neary, both of whom had been involved in setting up a British office for Marvel Comics. Everybody talked a lot about doing something new. Every time comics people get together, beer flows with the conversation and great, majestic vistas unfold of unlimited creativity. There's invariably a wistful edge to these conversations – largely because people recognise the fact that comics have never been a true part of British culture. Comics are, and always have been, regarded as children's entertainment and are consequently marginalised in the national psyche.

So, in the early Eighties, when Dez Skinn commissioned me to start work on a new title called Warrior – I assumed it was another pipe-dream.

I managed to cook up a few things to keep my interest going, but I was totally unprepared for what was to come. And what was to come was Marvelman.

Drawing for a living is a strange occupation. People outside the business assume that it's an "interesting" job, maybe full of bizarre characters and exciting situations. That's only partially true. For the most part, drawing comics, like everything else, consists of hard graft and uninteresting chores. Inking, to name but one. The joy of

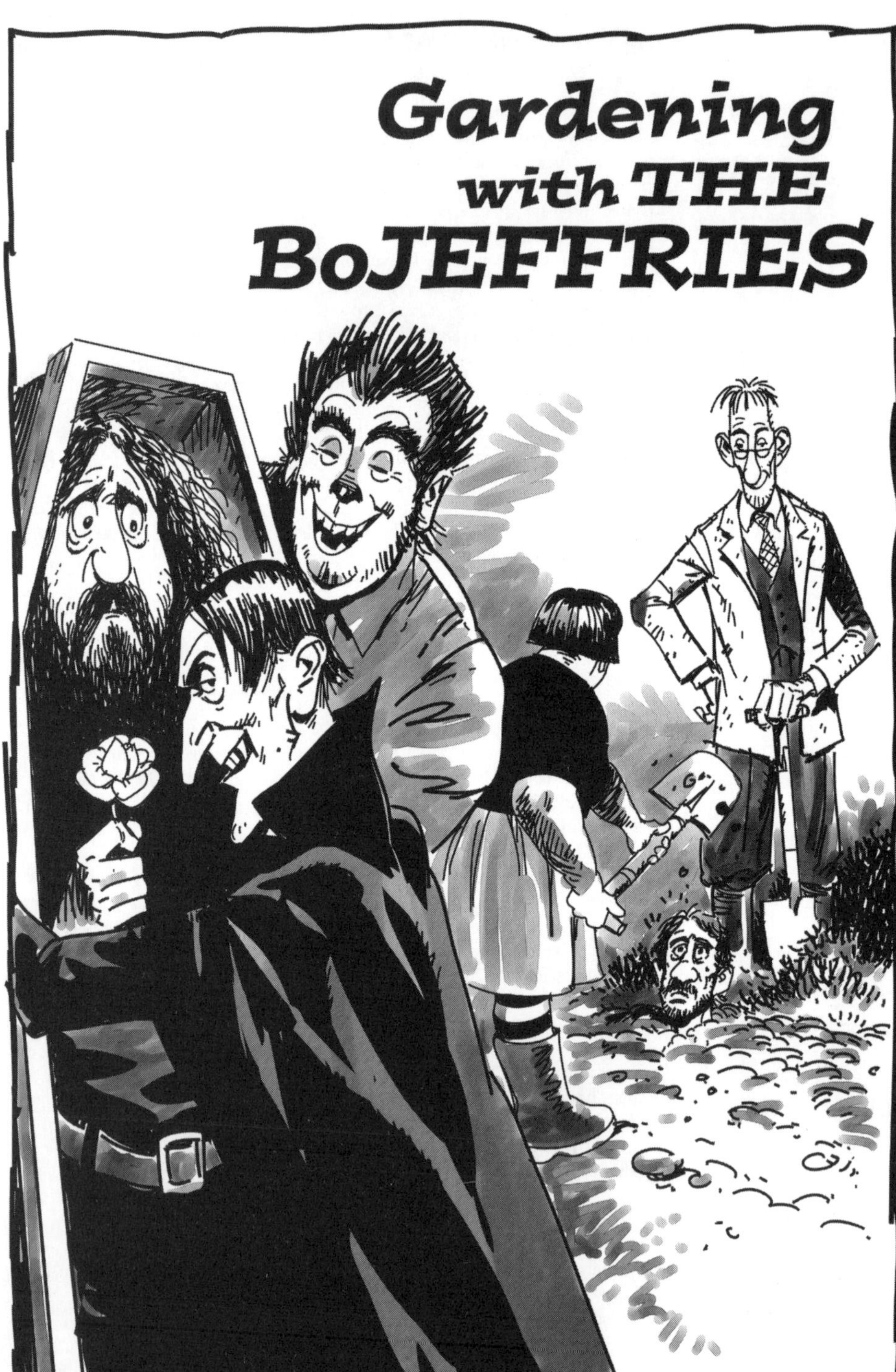
Gardening
with THE
BoJEFFRIES

the work is in the original creation, telling the story with rough pencilling work. Getting the artwork "camera ready" is the tedious part, often involving disappointment and lots of reworking.

During the long, isolated and sometimes stressful hours, one's mind turns to the whole question of "why we do it."

For the most part, we are working on flimsy fantasies, peopled by two-dimensional characters speaking ridiculous dialogue dreamed up by ten-a-penny hacks. At their best, comics are mildly entertaining kitsch. At worst...well, at worst they're simply tomorrow's wood pulp.

When the first few issues of Warrior were in preparation, I was visiting Dez Skinn's editorial bullpit on a regular basis. On one occasion I walked into Dez's office to find a very large man with a very large beard looking at some of my artwork. He introduced himself as Alan Moore – and we briefly reminisced about our first meeting. We also went into the time-honoured routine of: We Must Work Together Some Time. Yeh, right.

As I went on my way, I had no idea that Alan was the kind of person who actualises things. Whether his motivation springs from some inner hunger (especially at that time) or a genuine wellspring of creativity, we have never discussed. I guess it's a large portion of both – and an excelent balance it is. But nevertheless, within a very short time Alan presented me with a choice of three different scenarios that he'd been working on.

Now here's the <u>really</u> strange part. Here there is a risk of wandering into thickly-wooded hinterlands of esoteric musings. We had agreed to do something funny. We had agreed that Mad magazine had more or less monopolised comics humour for far too long. I had been working on an extraordinarily dark and difficult piece called Spiral Path, my attempt to put together a totally un-scripted comic. I was exhausted. I was suffering from hallucinations and nightmares. My house was haunted, one of my oldest friends had been abducted by aliens, and my cat had been run over by a tractor.

I was longing to draw cartoons again. I had a vague notion of domestic humour with a strongly surreal twist. When the Bojeffries Saga appeared in the post, it was the beginning of a healing process for me that has spanned many years.

This was a script written by a person who had experienced many trials and tribulations. Though still young, he was a parent of girls (like me) He was a performer, a poet, a songwriter...a voracious reader (like me)...a person of seemingly vast eclectic knowledge (I wish). He was undeniably a dreamer (like me)...in fact we shared the same dreams, literally. And yet he had a grasp of the human drama that revealed a huge undertow of compassion and understanding. There was no cynicism, only affection.

In subsequent scripts, he displayed the peculiar talent that almost every other collaborating artist finds agreement with: *the ability to write exactly what the artist wants to draw.*

Even though he confessed that sometimes every phrase of the Bojeffries had to be chiselled from granite, he never compromised on quality or commitment. And that involvement made The Bojeffries an unparalleled joy for me to work on.

Like all the best magicians, Alan brings forth ideas from the cornucopia of his mind with a flourish and a panache that disguises the hard work beneath. His power to amaze us conceals an equally amazing feat: these are no flimsy fantasies. They may be fantastical, but at no time does he stray from his true task of illuminating the human condition. His stories are invariably written from the experience of a life truly lived, with a human scale and dimension woven through them like a thread of gold.

STEVE PARKHOUSE

Left: *Illustration ©2003 Steve Parkhouse.*
The Bojeffries ©2003 Alan Moore & Steve Parkhouse.

And in the case of the Bojeffries, they are very, very funny.

I confess, I read the first three issues of Warrior with a sinking heart. The power and potency and absolute "adultness" of Marvelman was blowing everything else away. Alan had stepped from the wings with a prodigious talent, and like a grown-up amongst so many children had simply shown us the way.

He seemed to bring a novelist's sensibility to the craft of writing comics, but in a way that no novelist has ever managed to achieve. He had arrived at exactly the right time, when comics were floundering in a swamp of their own making. We all wanted something new, but nobody had the road map. It had occurred to very few people that maybe comics should be about life as we know it, based on our own experiences. I suspect this is because the milieu of comics seems permanently adolescent in nature.

I know that Alan's writing encouraged me to draw from a different perspective. To observe from life – the life I saw around me, rather than aping the techniques of established artists.

As more issues of Warrior appeared, my heart stopped sinking and I relaxed into simply acknowledging the emergence of a gifted and inspirational writer.

Through the combined efforts of Dez Skinn and the writers and artists of Warrior, the doors of the cottage industry had been well and truly breached. Battered down, in fact.

There are still those pipe-dreamers who wait patiently for the resurrection of the Eagle.

But I don't think it's gonna happen.

The old paradigm has gone.

Alan Moore has seen to it.

• **Steve Parkhouse**
Carlisle, Cumbria
October 2002

MARK
BUCKINGHAM

Right: Buckingham started as inker
on DC's Vertigo titles such as
Hellblazer, Sandman, Shade and
Death but is probably best known for
his artwork on the Neil Gaiman issues
of **Miracleman.**
Illustration ©2003 Mark Buckingham.

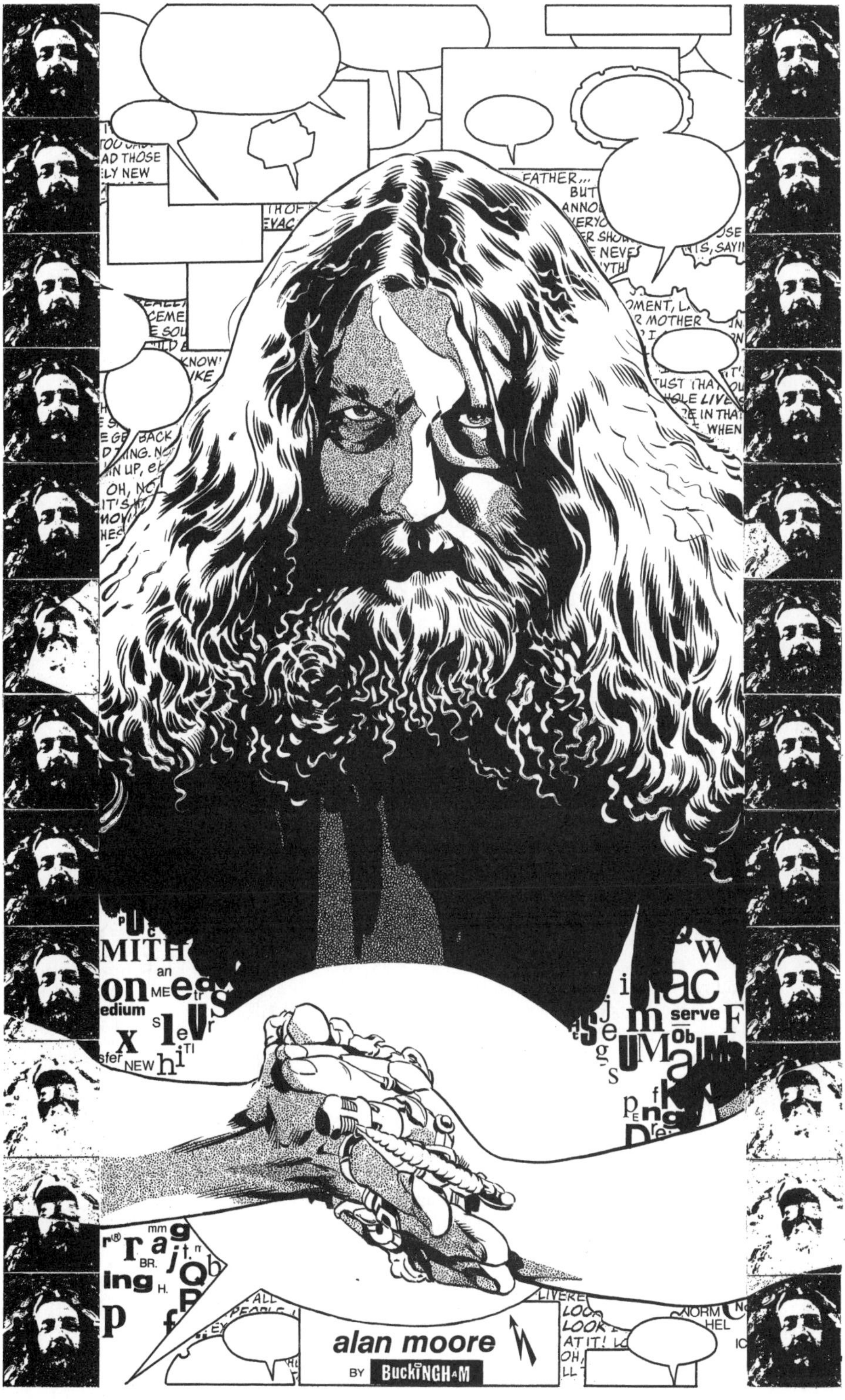
alan moore
BY BUCKINGHAM

QUANTUM STRINGS

The latest theory of the universe is that it's made of a bunch of quantum strings that vibrate together to create matter. What can I say about Alan Moore, except that our respective strings seem to intersect and create even odder patterns?

JEAN-MARC LOFFICIER
text ©2003 Jean-Marc Lofficier

Once upon a time, we both worked for Dez Skinn, or was it for Marvel U.K, or both? It's like stalactites and stalagmites, I could never tell them apart anyway. Alan did some of his earliest writings for the *Doctor Who* comic based on the renowned BBC series, and at the same time, I was penning articles for *House of Hammer* and *Starburst*. Then, against all odds, I, a Frenchman living in California, went on to write the *Doctor Who Programme Guide*. This is why the title of this tribute echoes that of the very first *Doctor Who* story — "An Unearthly Child," for those of you unfamiliar with that worthy British institution.

Another intersection? I remember first meeting Alan at the San Diego Comicon, poolside, at the hotel. *Watchmen* was being published, so it must have been in '86. We talked about Dez Skinn and old comics. I mean, things like *The Spider*, *Steel Claw*, that I'd read in French translations many years before. I think Alan killed them all in an early chapter of *Captain Britain*. That mischievous desire to play with other people's toys and sneak them into our stories is another connection. Alan (reportedly) got in trouble at DC when he snuck Pogo into *Swamp Thing*, and I Tintin in *Teen Titans*. Naughty, naughty.

At about the same time, Randy and I were supposed to write a book for Dark Horse with Mark Nelson that would have pitted intelligent dinosaurs against a cast of thinly-disguised French fictional heroes and historical characters, such as Henri Poincaré and Mata-Hari. That fell by the wayside, as many projects do, but the idea refused to die. Four years ago, it resurfaced when French artist Gil Formosa suggested the three of us do a steampunk series for publisher Albin Michel. That became *Robur*, our homage to Jules Verne and H. G. Wells and the other French heroes of yesteryear.

Meanwhile, Randy and I had collaborated with the utterly brilliant Kevin O'Neill on a short comic story intended to launch an animated feature — it was finally published as *Nightspeeder* in France in 2001 — and, during a short visit to Los Angeles, Kevin told us his next project was gong to be a book with Alan entitled *League Of Extraordinary Gentlemen!*

Later, I was fortunate to help, first with the French translation of Dupin's dialogue in Volume 1, then with tidbits of information which I had gathered for a French Science Fiction encyclopedia (published in 2000 by McFarland in the U.S.). In one of the many, delightful in-jokes spread throughout the book, Kevin identified me as the author of a secret report on a very real 1906 French pulp Martian explorer, *Docteur Omega*. (In Vol. 2, No. 3, Page 14, Panel 7. Go look it up.)

So, when the time came to prepare this homage, all those strands that connect us jumbled and tangled and crossed in my mind. Which is why this vignette mixes up Doctor Who and Doctor Omega, Robur and a mildly manic portrayal of its authors, and even authentic period illustrations by E. Bouard, tying these various quantum strings into one, neat thank you ribbon!

• **Jean-Marc Lofficier**

RANDY & JEAN-MARC LOFFICIER
Pages 89-92 following:
Jean-Marc & Randy have written many comic-book stories for Marvel and DC including **Dr. Strange**, **Superman** and **Batman** and are currently writing four regular series for Semic. They are also the authors of **The Dr. Who Programme Guide** and numerous other non-fiction books and have written animation scripts for TV.

GIL FORMOSA
Formosa's first comics work was **The Legend Of Chevalier Cargal** in 1981, since then he has illustrated ad campaigns for Coca-Cola, Heinz, Disney, Kellogg, Levi-Strauss and Honda. He is currently working with Jean-Marc & Randy on **Robur**. Strip and Robur are ©2003 Jean-Marc & Randy Lofficier/Gil Formosa.

AN UNEARTHLY GENTLEMAN

• A Tribute to ALAN MOORE •

Randy & Jean-Marc Lofficier (Writers) • **Gil Formosa** (Artist)

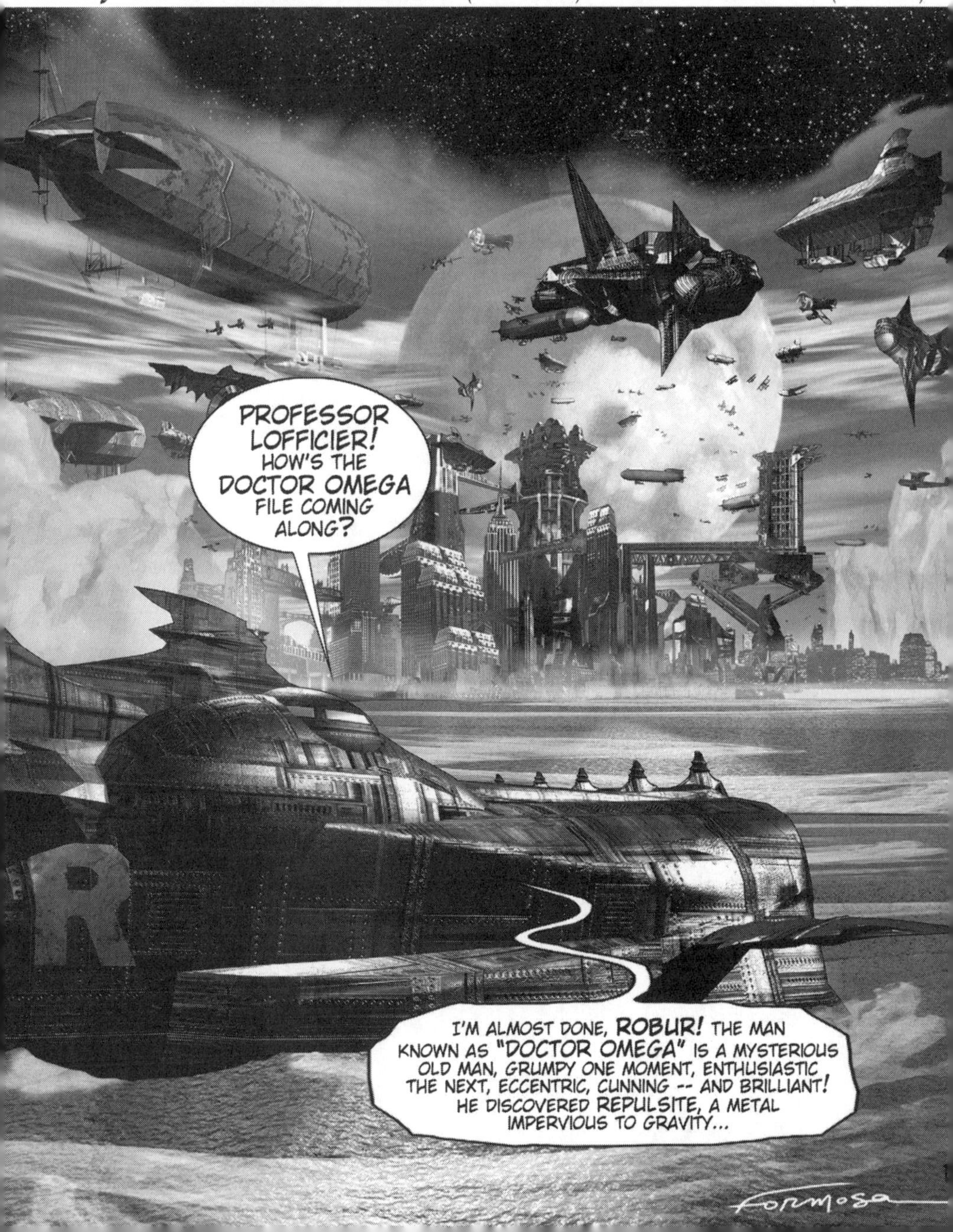
PROFESSOR LOFFICIER! HOW'S THE DOCTOR OMEGA FILE COMING ALONG?
I'M ALMOST DONE, ROBUR! THE MAN KNOWN AS "DOCTOR OMEGA" IS A MYSTERIOUS OLD MAN, GRUMPY ONE MOMENT, ENTHUSIASTIC THE NEXT, ECCENTRIC, CUNNING -- AND BRILLIANT! HE DISCOVERED REPULSITE, A METAL IMPERVIOUS TO GRAVITY...
R
Formosa

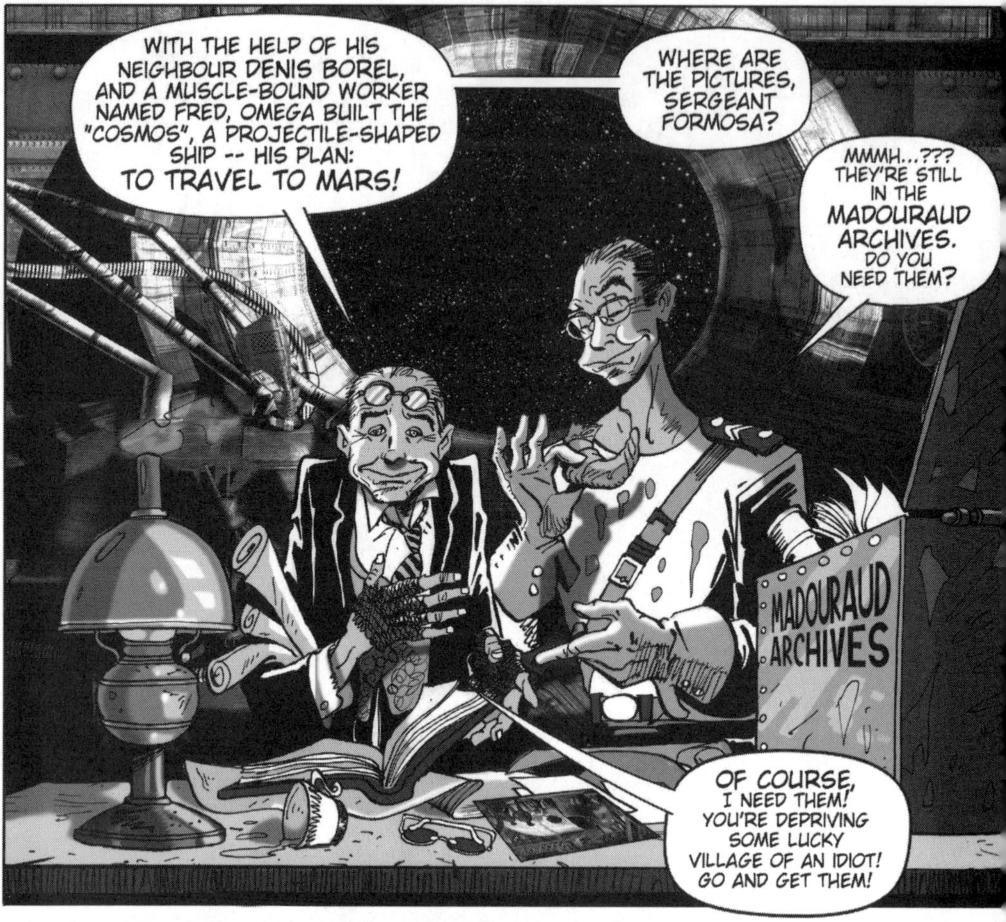
WITH THE HELP OF HIS NEIGHBOUR DENIS BOREL, AND A MUSCLE-BOUND WORKER NAMED FRED, OMEGA BUILT THE "COSMOS", A PROJECTILE-SHAPED SHIP -- HIS PLAN: TO TRAVEL TO MARS!
WHERE ARE THE PICTURES, SERGEANT FORMOSA?
MMMH...??? THEY'RE STILL IN THE MADOURAUD ARCHIVES. DO YOU NEED THEM?
MADOURAUD ARCHIVES
OF COURSE, I NEED THEM! YOU'RE DEPRIVING SOME LUCKY VILLAGE OF AN IDIOT! GO AND GET THEM!

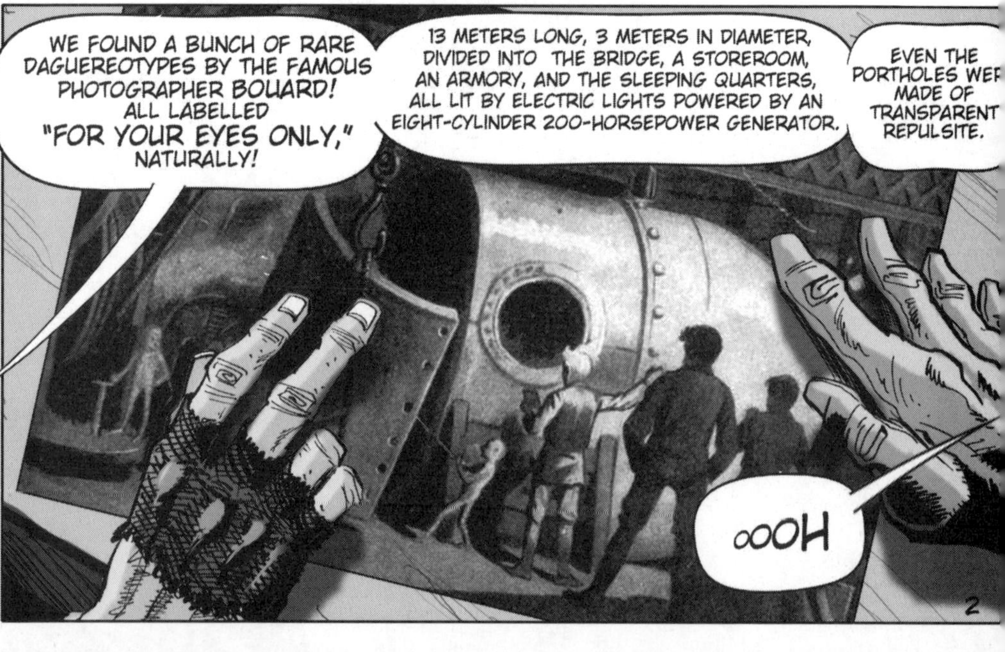
WE FOUND A BUNCH OF RARE DAGUEREOTYPES BY THE FAMOUS PHOTOGRAPHER BOUARD! ALL LABELLED "FOR YOUR EYES ONLY," NATURALLY!
13 METERS LONG, 3 METERS IN DIAMETER, DIVIDED INTO THE BRIDGE, A STOREROOM, AN ARMORY, AND THE SLEEPING QUARTERS, ALL LIT BY ELECTRIC LIGHTS POWERED BY AN EIGHT-CYLINDER 200-HORSEPOWER GENERATOR.
EVEN THE PORTHOLES WER MADE OF TRANSPARENT REPULSITE.
OOOH

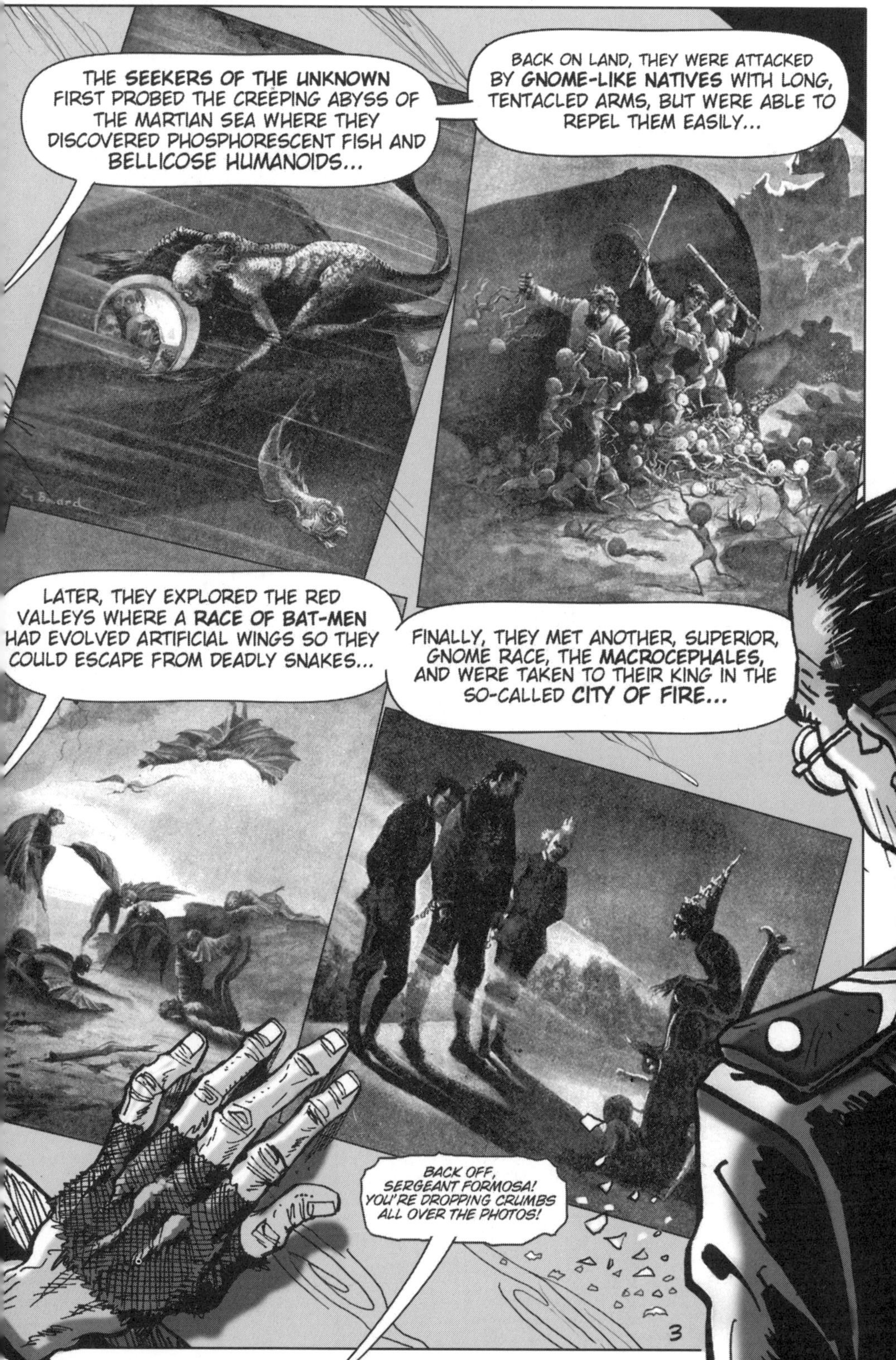
THE SEEKERS OF THE UNKNOWN FIRST PROBED THE CREEPING ABYSS OF THE MARTIAN SEA WHERE THEY DISCOVERED PHOSPHORESCENT FISH AND BELLICOSE HUMANOIDS...
BACK ON LAND, THEY WERE ATTACKED BY GNOME-LIKE NATIVES WITH LONG, TENTACLED ARMS, BUT WERE ABLE TO REPEL THEM EASILY...
LATER, THEY EXPLORED THE RED VALLEYS WHERE A RACE OF BAT-MEN HAD EVOLVED ARTIFICIAL WINGS SO THEY COULD ESCAPE FROM DEADLY SNAKES...
FINALLY, THEY MET ANOTHER, SUPERIOR, GNOME RACE, THE MACROCEPHALES, AND WERE TAKEN TO THEIR KING IN THE SO-CALLED CITY OF FIRE...
BACK OFF, SERGEANT FORMOSA! YOU'RE DROPPING CRUMBS ALL OVER THE PHOTOS!

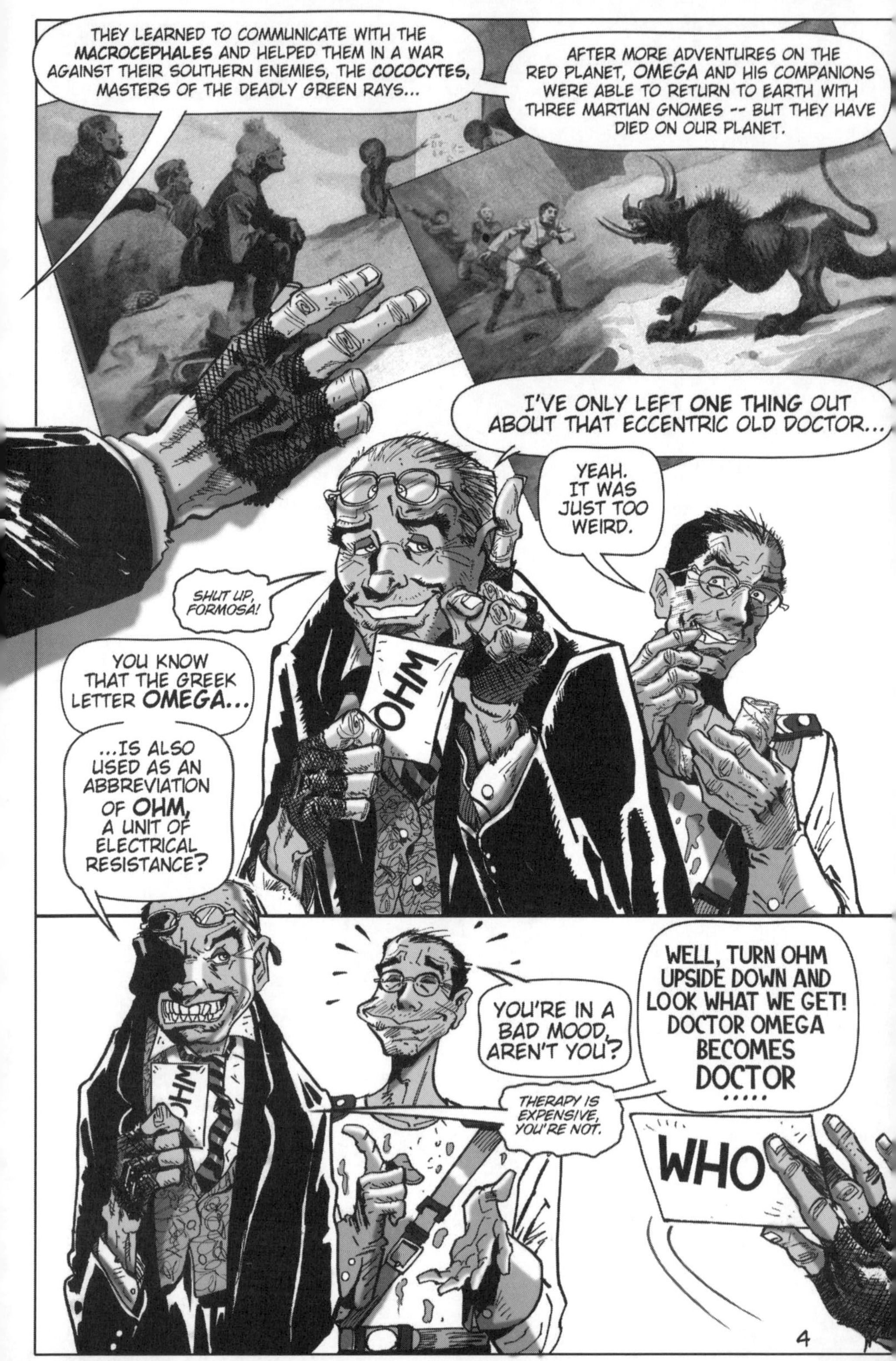

THEY LEARNED TO COMMUNICATE WITH THE MACROCEPHALES AND HELPED THEM IN A WAR AGAINST THEIR SOUTHERN ENEMIES, THE COCOCYTES, MASTERS OF THE DEADLY GREEN RAYS...
AFTER MORE ADVENTURES ON THE RED PLANET, OMEGA AND HIS COMPANIONS WERE ABLE TO RETURN TO EARTH WITH THREE MARTIAN GNOMES -- BUT THEY HAVE DIED ON OUR PLANET.
I'VE ONLY LEFT ONE THING OUT ABOUT THAT ECCENTRIC OLD DOCTOR...
YEAH. IT WAS JUST TOO WEIRD.
SHUT UP, FORMOSA!
OHM
YOU KNOW THAT THE GREEK LETTER OMEGA...
...IS ALSO USED AS AN ABBREVIATION OF OHM, A UNIT OF ELECTRICAL RESISTANCE?
OHM
YOU'RE IN A BAD MOOD, AREN'T YOU?
WELL, TURN OHM UPSIDE DOWN AND LOOK WHAT WE GET! DOCTOR OMEGA BECOMES DOCTOR .....
THERAPY IS EXPENSIVE, YOU'RE NOT.
WHO

WALT SIMONSON

Simonson began drawing comics professionally in 1972, working on such titles as **Dr. Fate, The Metal Men, The Incredible Hulk** *and* **Batman.** *He went on to write and draw the award-winning* **Mighty Thor** *in 1983 and has since worked on many other titles such as* **X-Factor, the Fantastic Four** *and* **Gen-13.**

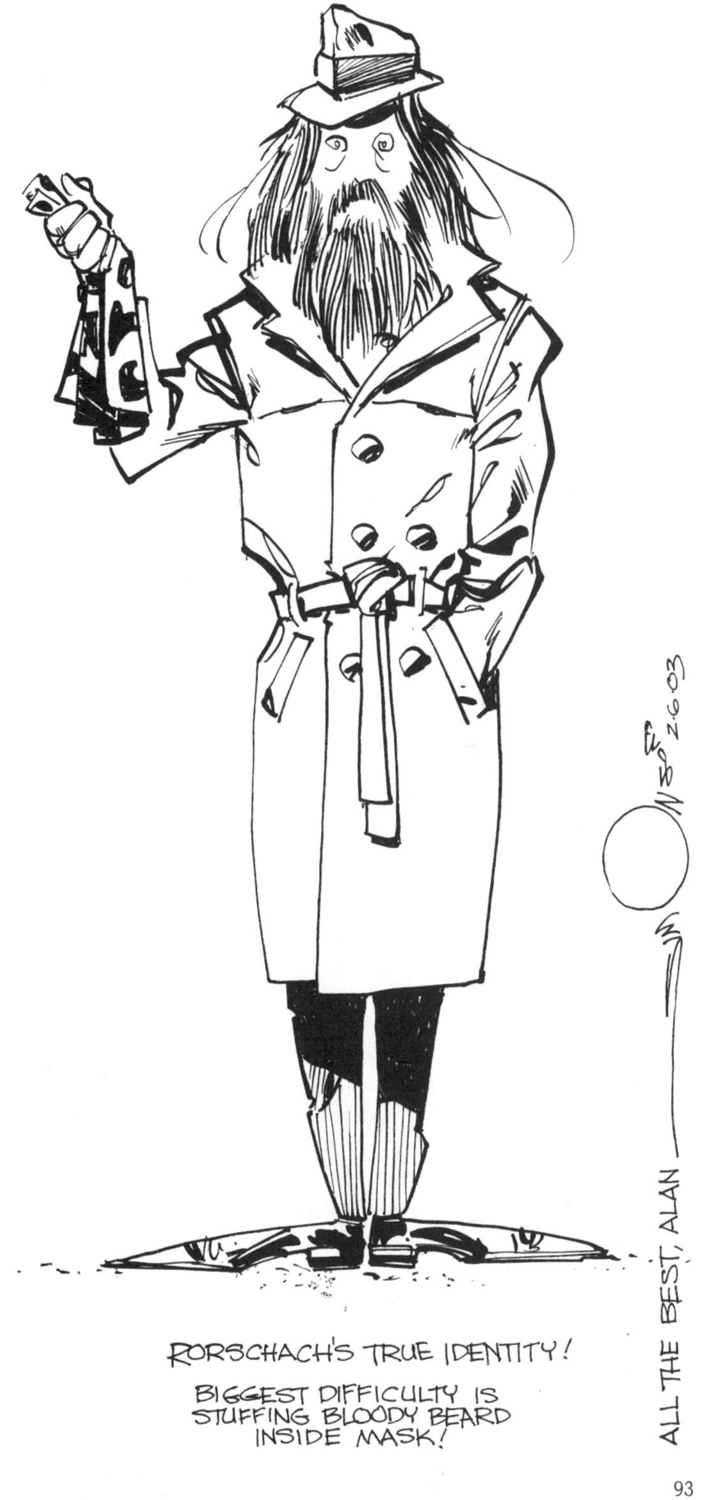
RORSCHACH'S TRUE IDENTITY!
BIGGEST DIFFICULTY IS STUFFING BLOODY BEARD INSIDE MASK!
ALL THE BEST, ALAN
2.6.03

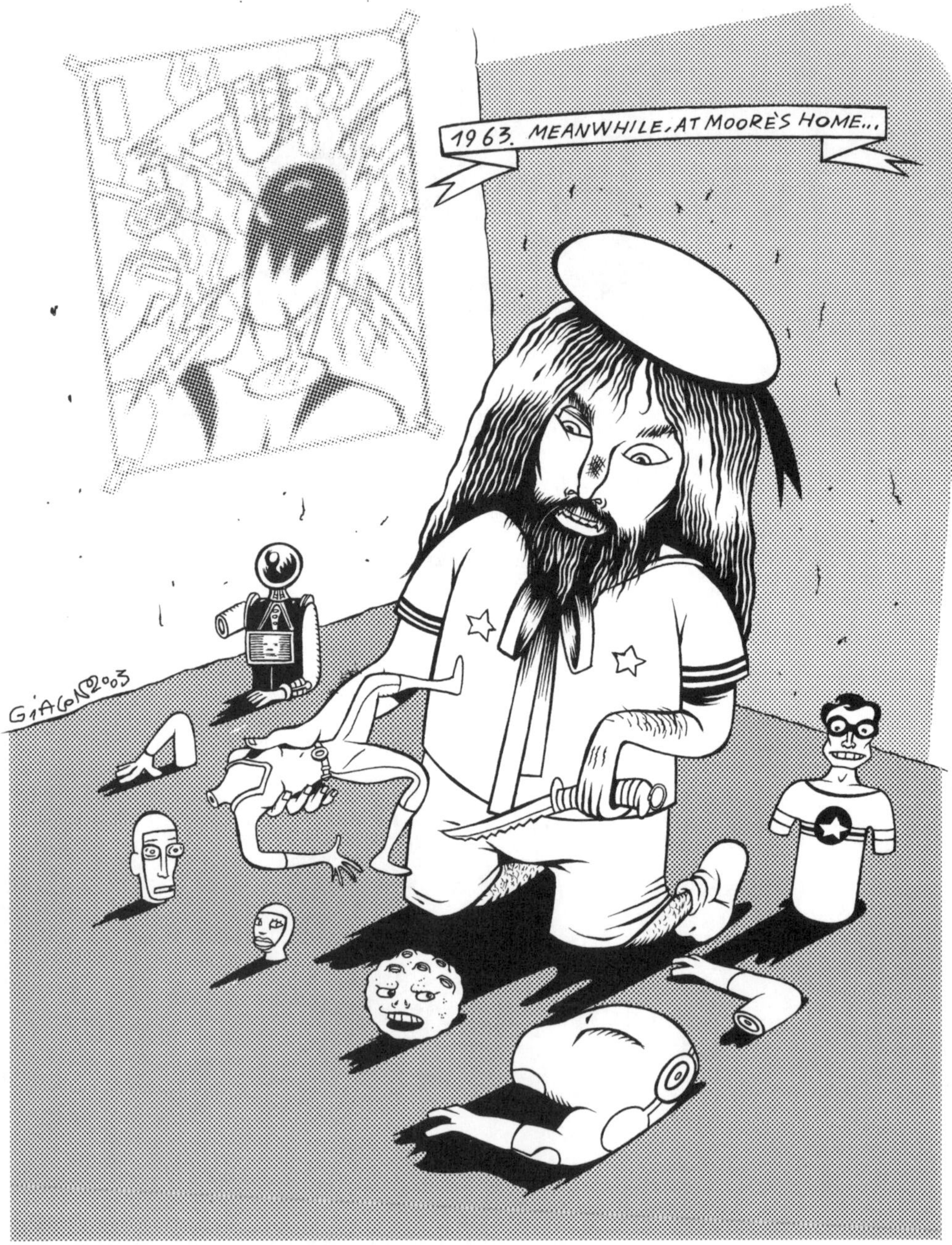
1963. MEANWHILE, AT MOORE'S HOME...
GIACON 2003

YOUNG ALAN MOORE in
"SAGA OF THE VILE THING"

DARREN SHAN

Darren Shan is the best selling Irish author of Children's horror classics including **The Vampire Prince, Tunnels of Blood** *and* **Cirque Du Freak,** *the movie rights of which have already been snapped up by Warner Bros. His latest book in the Adventures of Darren Shan series is* **Killers of the Dawn.** *Story ©2003 Darren Shan.*

November 18th, 1963. In America, president John F Kennedy is four days away from a decisively deadly date with destiny. In Britain, a young band of mop-tops from Liverpool are about to release their second album (it will hit stores in Britain on the same day that a "rubber bullet" hits president Kennedy) and will soon go on to conquer pop charts across the globe. The world stands on the brink of great social, cultural and technological changes. By the end of the decade everything will have altered, faster than previously imagined possible. It is a time of upheaval and revision. We could throw our gauntlet down in any corner of this brave new world and find individuals of wondrous imagination and courage, heralds of the age of evolution. We could alight in Moscow, New York, Berlin, London. But the metropolises of the world have been exhaustively documented. Let us instead set our sights on a grey, cold town in middle England, and one of its younger, more anarchic inhabitants. The town is Northampton, scene of two apparently unconnected, but preternaturally linked, petty crimes. And our focal spirit is ten year old Alan Moore, perpetrator of the humbly heinous acts. Let us observe ...

•

"Who the hell would steal Santa's beard?" constable Constantine asked rhetorically.

"I dunno," the unfortunately named Curt Vile muttered. "The bleeder hit me over the back of me head while I wasn't looking. Mugging a poor old guy like me in a Santa suit — he must be the spawn of Satan!"

Curt was lying across the pavement, redolent in a baggy red costume. He had black boots, the crimson suit, a white fur rimmed hat. All he lacked was the beard to complete the perfect yuletide picture.

"What you doing in that get-up anyway?" constable Constantine asked. "Christmas is miles off."

"Thought I'd get in early on the act this year," Curt said. "Another couple of weeks and you won't be able to move for street Santas. Figured I'd beat them to the punch and make a bit of cash before the rush starts."

"Begging, eh?" constable Constantine exclaimed, ever quick to pounce on the subtlest of clues. "You're nicked, mate!"

Curt rubbed his bare chin and grimaced. "So much for the spirit of Christmas!"

•

Meanwhile, several streets away, Roscoe Moscow (as he was known to the local kids) was carrying out an emergency stock inventory. Roscoe sold and repaired bicycles from a small side-street shop. The shop had been burgled many times since opening day. He'd learnt a long time ago not to leave any money in the till, and to only keep tired old bikes in the shop (the good ones he kept in the spare rooms of his home). Thieves still pestered him, making off with equipment and the battered old bikes, or smashing up the contents of the shop for pure, bitter fun. But this was the strangest break-in yet.

"I don't get it," Roscoe sighed, inventory completed. "Who'd go to all the trouble of breaking in just to take a single can of black spray paint?"

•

MASSIMO GIACON

Left: *Massimo Giacon has had his bizarre comics published in most major Italian comics magazines. He is also a musician, a performer and a designer for Philips, Swatch and Alessi. Illustration ©2003 Massimo Giacon. 1963 characters ©2003 Alan Moore, Rich Veitch & Steve Bissette.*

"Yo-ho-Huxley," Alan Moore grunted, studying his reflection in a broken shard of mirror. He was wearing the long, shaggy Santa Claus beard, sprayed a delicious shade of midnight black. The paint can rested on the waste ground behind him. His fingers were smudged from the paint, but he'd been careful not to get it on his clothes — his mother would have his guts for garters if she found out about this!

"Not bad," Alan said, admiring his reflection. Even at that tender age there was something supernaturally piercing in his gaze. His grandmother said he had the eyes of an old man who'd seen much of the world, and worlds beyond. ("Aye," his Dad had deadpanned. "And I bet the old fart was glad to get rid of 'em.")

"That's decided then," Alan said, removing the beard and laying it down next to the paint can. "I'll grow me own as soon as I can." The beard suited him. He should have been born with one. Thinking about it, he wondered if he had — maybe his grandmother had shaved it off. He smiled at the image of a baby with a beard. He imagined his mother's reaction: "Ernest! Help! Me fanny's coming away on the baby's head!" Maybe he'd write a story about it ... But no. He doubted his parents would see the funny side of that. Genitalia were unacceptable in his work at this moment in time. A few months ago he'd written a story about a lizard with both a penis and vagina (he'd called it "A hypersexual lizard") — when his father stumbled across it, it had been like a replay of the wrath God visited upon Sodom and Gomorrah.

Alan turned his back on the painted beard ("One day ...") and went exploring the warren of the Northampton back streets. Today was his tenth birthday, a special time in a boy's life, the start of his ascent towards adulthood. Alan knew he had a lot of growing yet to do, but he had moved beyond the boundaries of basic childhood, and from today there could be no going back. He'd reached double figures — he was into big numbers now.

He should have been in school, but how could he waste a magical day like this on lessons? If he was to have children, and they were to ask him how he'd celebrated his tenth birthday, how was he to respond? "Oh, I went to school like normal and got caned for knowing more than the teachers." No. Better to be able to say he'd marked the occasion with a statement of his individuality and freedom of spirit. Some would have called his avoidance of school truancy — but Alan regarded it as valid, liberating, soul-enhancing rebellion.

Trudging around Northampton, careful not to be seen by anybody who might know him, keeping to the shadows, elusive, hidden. Many children would have felt lonely, bored, scared in his position. But not Alan. With his imagination for company, he was never alone. He sought amusement in it while he walked, the hours passing swiftly, far swifter than they ever did in school.

He was a super-hero, Batman, fighting the Joker. No, better than that, he was his own super-hero, a character of his own invention. He was Jimmy Muscles ... No, something even sturdier ... Tommy Strong! Born in the tropics, possessor of incredible strength (not too sure how he came by his powers, but that wasn't important), married to a beautiful, resourceful woman, guardian of mankind.

In his head he fought a dozen battles, in the present, the future and the past. All zones were accessible to Tommy Strong. He could follow his enemies to the ends of the earth and through the torrid, twisted, tunnels of time itself.

But even super heroes have to stop for lunch. Alan made a seat of a wooden crate next to a deserted factory and made quick work of his sandwich and apple. He was thirsty. A bottle of coke would have been perfect, but he lacked the funds, so he settled for some cool clear water from a rain barrel. A bunch of teddy boys passed as he was drinking from his cupped hands. They laughed at him and threatened to dunk him in the barrel. Alan said nothing while they passed – he'd been dunked before, so he didn't doubt the seriousness of the threat – but once they were out of earshot he cursed them vilely, ending with a thumping snort of "Fashion beasts!"

As he was leaving, in the opposite direction to the teddy boys, he noticed a watchman inside the factory, standing by one of the windows, bored out of his brain, idly watching the skyline. Alan studied the watchman for a while. The glass of the window was badly stained, and if Alan shifted slightly from foot to foot, the stains appeared to spread across the watchman's face, altering his appearance. Alan wondered if anyone else was watching the watchman — glancing around at the grey neighbouring buildings, he didn't think so.

Eventually the watchman retreated, perhaps to view the town from a different window. Alan moved on, becoming Tommy Strong again. He fought space monsters, Nazis, and giant spiders. He had the idea for a creature half human and half spider — "Cobweb," he called it. Cobweb was a man to begin with, but then Alan imagined it as a woman, alluring and sensual, destroying and devouring those she loved.

In his mind, Cobweb proved too much of a threat for Tommy Strong — he was rendered helpless by his love for her. But not to fear — Alan simply invented a team of friends for Tommy, super heroes of all sorts, with a variety of powers. Jack Quickly, the Number One American, Greycoat — courageous, capable, loyal allies, one and all. But he needed a name for the team, something catchy. How about the Association of Extraordinary Gentlemen? Hmm ... He liked it, but he sensed he could do better. He'd have to sleep on this one ...

After a series of taxing, life-threatening adventures, Alan wound up by the gates of his school, ten minutes before classes finished for the day. This way he could take the ordinary route home and not raise any suspicions if he was spotted by his neighbours.

On the stroke of three o'clock, the pupils came streaming out, chattering, yelling, laughing, excited by their freedom. Alan kept to the shadows of the houses opposite the school gates, waiting for the crowd to pass, so he could follow just behind them. As he waited he spotted Hilary Jones, a girl from his class. She wasn't the prettiest girl in school, but Alan had a warm spot for her. She had a lovely smile which gave him butterflies in his stomach every time he saw it. In his mind's eye Hilary was no mere human girl — she was an angel, with a hidden glowing halo, sent to brighten up the lives of mere mortal men. He was not worthy of her, and would never be her boyfriend or husband, but perhaps he could write a poem in honour of her one day — or a ballad.

When most of the children had passed – and all the teachers – Alan slipped out of hiding, fell in behind the stragglers, and made his way home, adopting the most innocent expression his mischievous little gargoylian face could manage.

•

Alan spent much of the afternoon ensconced in his bedroom, reading. On his bed lay a thick edition of Frankenstein: Or the Modern Prometheus (Alan had underlined the word "Prometheus" on the inside cover — he quite liked the sound of it), which Alan was enjoying immensely. There were also several Jack the Ripper tomes stacked in one corner of the room, which he dipped into at frequent intervals. Alan was intrigued by the Ripper, and thought he knew who the killer might have been, but he wasn't prepared to make a claim just yet, not until he'd done a bit more research.

Most of the time, though, he read comics. Comics were his first and abiding love. He boasted a collection of ageing, tattered, dog-eared, but golden treasures. Batman, Superman, Captain Britain, Marvelman — fantastic stuff! He liked to draw his own comics – he'd have a go at a Tommy Strong story soon – but he feared his lack of artistic ability might work against him in the long run. Perhaps he'd just write stories when he grew up, and get other people to draw them. Not as much fun as drawing them himself, but better than not working in the medium at all.

When he wasn't reading, Alan was scribbling in either his ABC or Top Ten notebooks. Alan loved to make lists and play with words. In the Top Ten pad he'd compose lists of his favourite comics, songs, TV shows, movies, as well as his top ten diseases, scourges, implements of torture, and so on. In the ABC book, Alan would jot down all the letters of the alphabet, meditate a while to blank his mind, then gaze at the letters and write down whatever words occurred to him, starting at A and rapidly working his way through to Z. He had hundreds of ABC lists, compiled in several bulging paper folders which his mother – a printer – had been able to procure for him.

Alan was nearing the end of his latest list – "R for rorschach, S for supreme, T for time travel, U for UFO, V for vendetta" – when his mother called him down for supper. He quickly complete the list – "W for watchmen, X for x-ray (again!), Y for young blood, Z for zzzzzzz" – then raced for the kitchen.

•

His mother had offered to throw a party for him, but Alan didn't believe in making a big deal out of birthdays, even one as important as his tenth. So apart from a small cake and a slightly nicer dinner than normal, it was a typical meal. Alan had opened his presents that morning – books and comics for the most part, as well as some clothes – but his mother had held a few surprises back for him, which provided some excitement after dinner. The presents were nothing extra special – another book, a game of Snakes and Ladders, a small magician's set of tricks (he'd received the same set the year before, and had mastered the tricks within a couple of days, but Alan was a diplomatic boy and said nothing of this minor faux pas).

He played a few games of Snakes and Ladders with his parents, then spent some time playing with the cat on the kitchen floor. The cat's name was Maxwell. An elderly, straggly mongrel, missing half an ear, nicked and scratched in many places — a real cat. Alan liked Maxwell — he felt they were kindred spirits. He told the cat of his day and how he'd celebrated his birthday, safe in the knowledge that the cat wouldn't betray his confidence. He started to tell Maxwell a story about a modern day kidnapper-cum-ripper who abducted young ladies – "Lost Girls" became the title, once Alan had worked out where the story was heading – but then a neighbour arrived and Maxwell bolted — the cat wasn't fond of company.

Alan strolled through to the living room to see which of the neighbours had come a-calling. He discovered one of the Bojeffries clan, sitting chatting with his mother. The Bojeffries woman – there were so many of them, Alan never bothered to remember their names – had a baby with her, and was showing what looked like some kind of parchment to Alan's mother.

"A birth caul," she said. "Covered her head like a wee cap. We thought Glory – that's what we's called her – we thought she was deformed to begin with, but it was only the caul."

Alan was interested in the birth caul – he hadn't seen one before – but his mother shooed him away before he could examine it properly. She didn't like him poking his nose into "women's stuff". Her son was a bit too curious for her liking. There were certain things which men – and boys, certainly! – had no business knowing about.

Muttering blackly to himself, Alan went to sit beside the fire. (He had no interest in television, though a new programme, due to start five days later, sounded like it might be worth his while — according to the grapevine, it was all about a time-travelling doctor.) He stared into the flames for a while, then cocked his head sideways. His grandmother had told him you could hear people talking if you listened closely to the flames. She hadn't said whether the speakers were spirits, or if the flames served as some sort of telephonic system for the living. Alan listened intently for a long time, but there was no voice in this fire, and eventually he abandoned his post and returned to his room, to read and scribble some more.

•

Later that night, tiring of his notebooks and well-thumbed comics, Alan turned his hand towards writing some stories of his own. He wasn't sure how writers wrote comic stories – did they draw a rough version of each page and write in the dialogue, or did they just describe the contents of the page? – so he'd experimented with several methods. Tonight he wrote a Tommy Strong story as straightforward prose, figuring he could adapt it at a later stage if he liked the feel of it.

Alan had a good feeling about Tommy Strong. He was on to a winner with this one. It might take him a while to truly capture the character, develop his world and bring him to light, but he was sure, when he did, that the Tommy Strong comic would sell like hot cakes — he'd make a small killing!

After the Tommy Strong adventure, he tried to think of some new characters, to use in other stories. He jotted down a series of names, but none really grabbed him. He took a break about nine o'clock and returned to the kitchen. His throat was exceedingly dry and he needed something to quench the thirst. As he stood in the kitchen, gulping down water, he played around with the word "quench". A nice word, possibly one he could adapt for a character ...

Back in his room, he wrote the word down, replaced the "e" with an "i" (for no good reason other than it pleased him), then tried to find another name to go with it — "Quinch" sounded to him like one half of a partnership. Perhaps a doctor. Dr so-and-so and Quinch. Not bad, except he couldn't find the right name for the doctor, no matter how hard he tried. In the end he left it as "Dr and Quinch" and resolved to work on it again in the morning.

Some more doodling, a bit more reading, then Alan was ready for bed. He undressed, checked his underpants for skizz marks (his grandmother's phrase), visited the bathroom, said goodnight to his parents, then tucked himself in.

"So," he thought in the darkness, staring at the cloudy night sky through a crack in the curtains. "Ten years old. Not a bad day. A bit on the quiet side, but what can you expect in Northampton! I'm sure, when I'm bigger, I'll live somewhere big and fabulous. That'll be much more exciting. Who knows — for my fiftieth, maybe I'll be celebrating my birthday on the moon!"

As Alan lay in bed, slowly drifting into the realm of slumber, he ran a few more story lines through his head. He often thought of good ideas late at night, on the verge of sleep, and sometimes he wouldn't nod off until one or two in the morning. But not tonight. Ideas weren't coming to him easily, and he didn't want to work too hard on his birthday. He could chase ideas the next day. "Tomorrow," he muttered, making a comfortable space for his head in the exact middle of the pillow. "Lots of time for stories tomorrow ... write all the stories I want ... tomorrow ... stories ..."

And with that, young Alan Moore twitched, scratched his chin, then surrendered to the forces of Lord Morpheus, to dream of beards ... and wonders.

The End.

TITO FARACI

Pages 100-101 following:
Tito Faraci is one of the most well-loved and versatile Italian comics writers. He writes **Dylan Dog** *for* **Bonelli, Mickey Mouse** *for Disney Italia and* **Diabolik** *for Astorina.*

PASQUALE FRISENDA

Italian artist Pasquale Frisenda is staff penciler and regular cover artist of Bonelli Comics' monthly western series **Magico Vento***.*
Strip ©2003 Tito Faraci/Pasquale Frisenda. All characters are ©2003 their respective copyright holders.

• **Darren Shan**

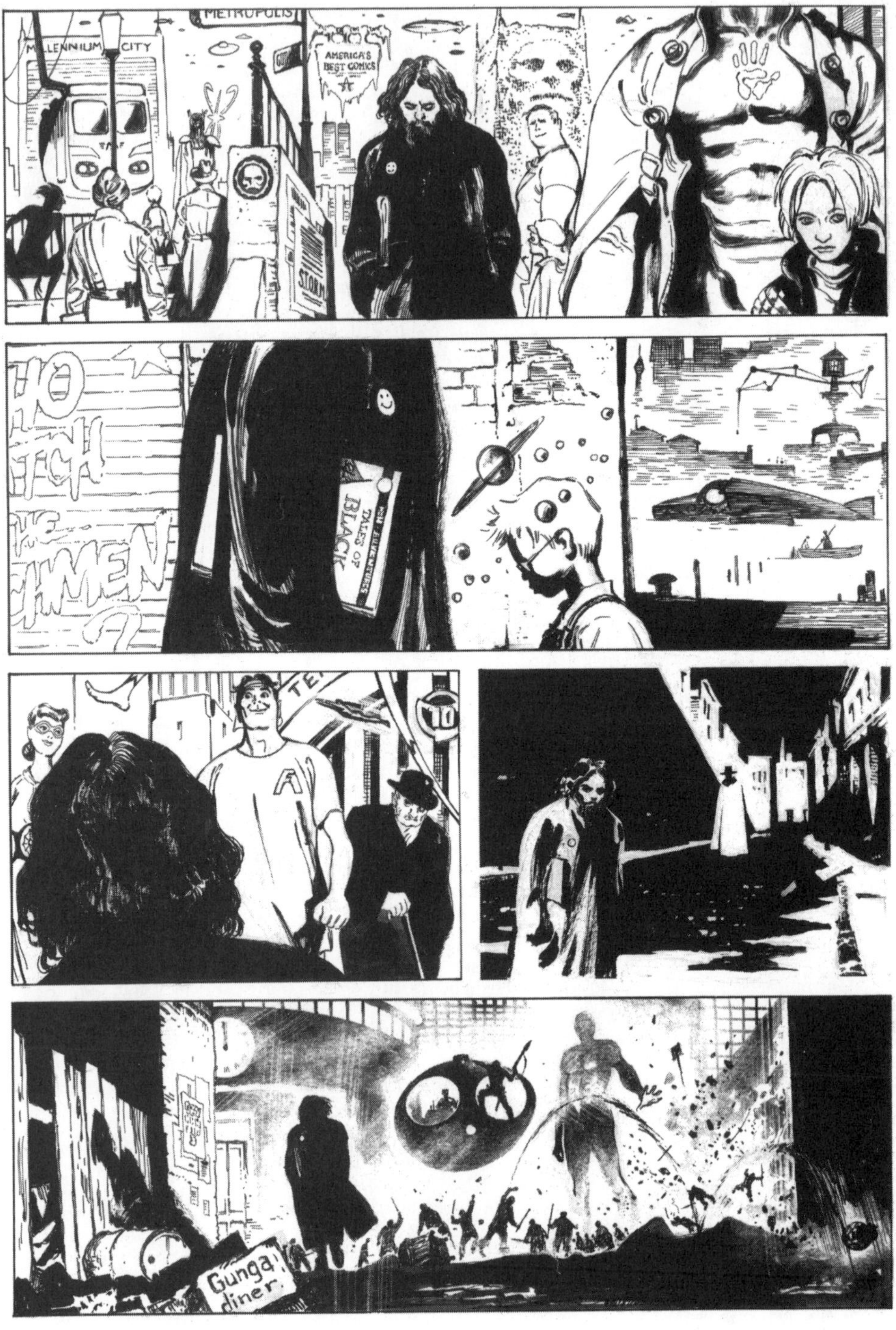

METROPOLIS
MILLENNIUM CITY
AMERICA'S BEST COMICS
S.T.O.R.M.
TALES OF BLACK
Gunga diner

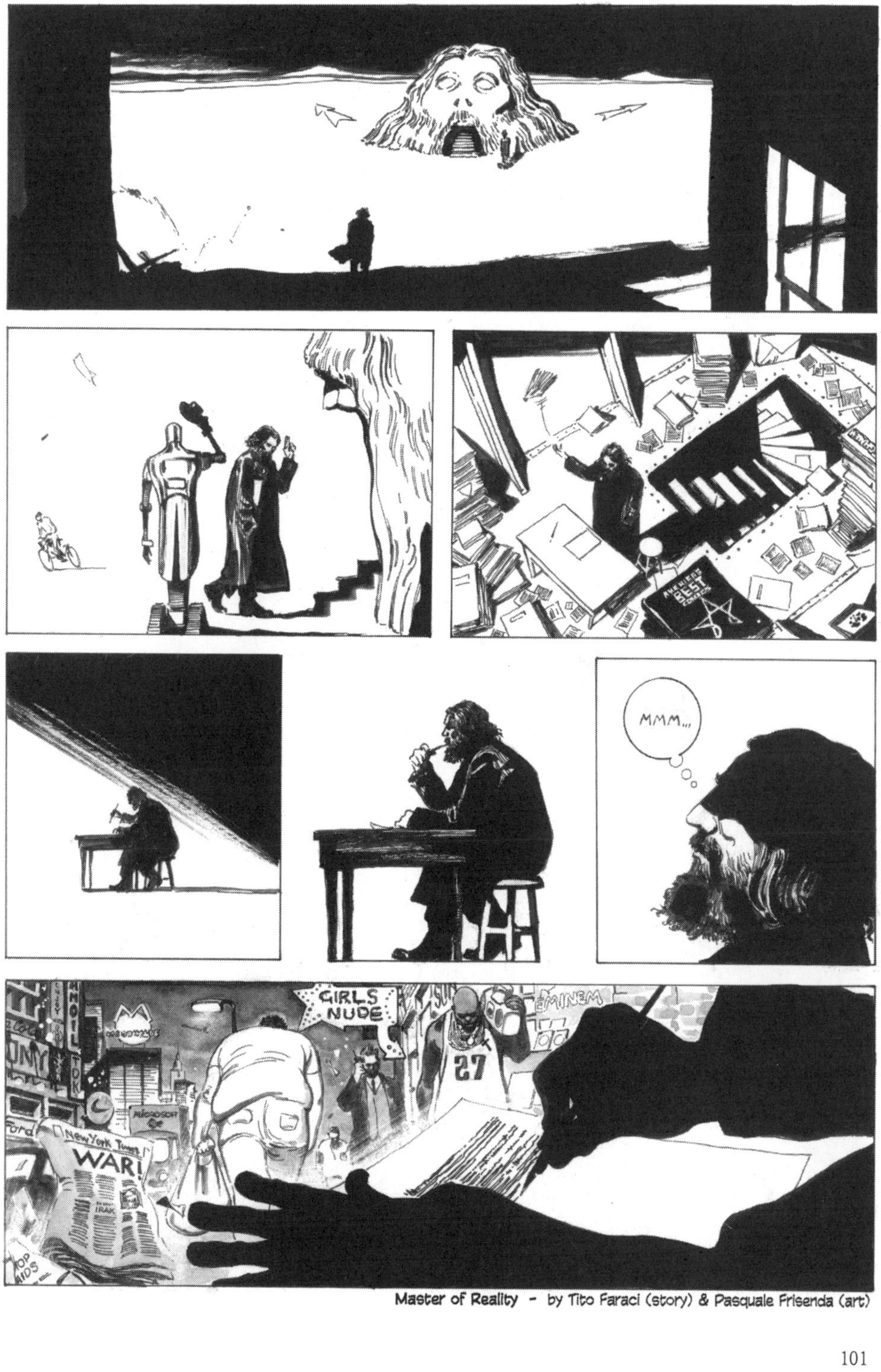
MMM...
GIRLS NUDE
EMINEM
27
New York Times
WAR!
IRAK

Master of Reality - by Tito Faraci (story) & Pasquale Frisenda (art)

ALAN MOORE: I KNEW HIM WHEN...

In the early 80s I met Alan Moore. He was as grand and imposing as anyone I've ever encountered. The beard, the hair, the manner: a showman in essence, an entertainer with more than the vaguest hint of menace. He was waxing eloquent about his first proper series for 2000AD - Skizz - and how several elements he'd included mirrored actions in ET (the movie it was to 'echo' in the grand 2000 tradition) even though he hadn't seen it while writing. He was witty and self-deprecating and I was going to have to tell him that I was working with him. I feared for my life.

At the time, I was scuttering at the edges of comics, trying to snatch scraps of work. Links with the Society of Strip Illustration led to odd jobs, the latest of which was to work on a semi-animated movie called 'Ragnarok'. Designed by my pal Bryan Talbot, it was to be written by Alan.

At this point, I had encountered Alan's name in 2000AD Future Shocks, in the astonishingly re-invigorated Captain Britain and of course, in Warrior. The chance of working with him was daunting - he had become a legend overnight so it seemed. I met him at a London Comics Con (at some hotel, somewhere—all I remember is the hair-raising and life threatening journey on the back of a motorbike to get there) where he surprised me by knowing who I was and what I'd done in fanzines. Mine'n'Mark Farmer's strip 'Moonstone' was reaching a conclusion, and I'd written myself into a corner. Alan asked how it'd be resolved; I said I dunno... any ideas? To my amazement he offered to write the final episode, wrapping up my over-complicated alternate reality/time travel paradox epic, which he did beautifully in four pages.

Pleased with the result (and from the work Mark and I did on Ragnarok, I hope) he recommended us to Bernie Jaye at Marvel UK. He'd sent in a parody strip of Frank Miller's Daredevil run, and attached our names to the script. After a bit of reluctance, she took us on board. From then on, we were comics professionals.

Thanks to Alan's good graces, we'd gotten through the comics Catch-22: 'No one will hire you until someone hires you.' I imagine this book is full of artist and writers who speak well of Alan and how he helped along their careers. It's not too extreme to say that without Alan, UK and US comics would look different today. He championed people he thought needed the break and - as one of them - I'm eternally grateful to him.

Happy 50th!

• **Mike Collins**

MIKE COLLINS

Mike Collins has been a writer and artist for British and American comic books for more than fifteen years and has worked on **Superman, Batman, Wonder Woman, X-Men, Spider-man,** and **Daredevil.** He's also worked on licensed titles like **Star Trek, Dr.Who, Transformers** and **Thundercats.**
Text ©2003 Mike Collins.

Right: Peter Cannon: Thunderbolt, the revived Charlton hero Collins wrote and drew for DC in the early 90s—and his Watchmen universe counterpart, **Ozymandias.**

J. H. WILLIAMS III

Pages 104-105 following:
Born In Roswell, New Mexico (home of the UFO), Williams worked on many projects for comics companies including Marvel and DC before teaming up with Alan Moore for Promethea from the first issue. He resides with his lovely wife, Wendy, in California.
Illustration & text ©2003 J H Williams III.

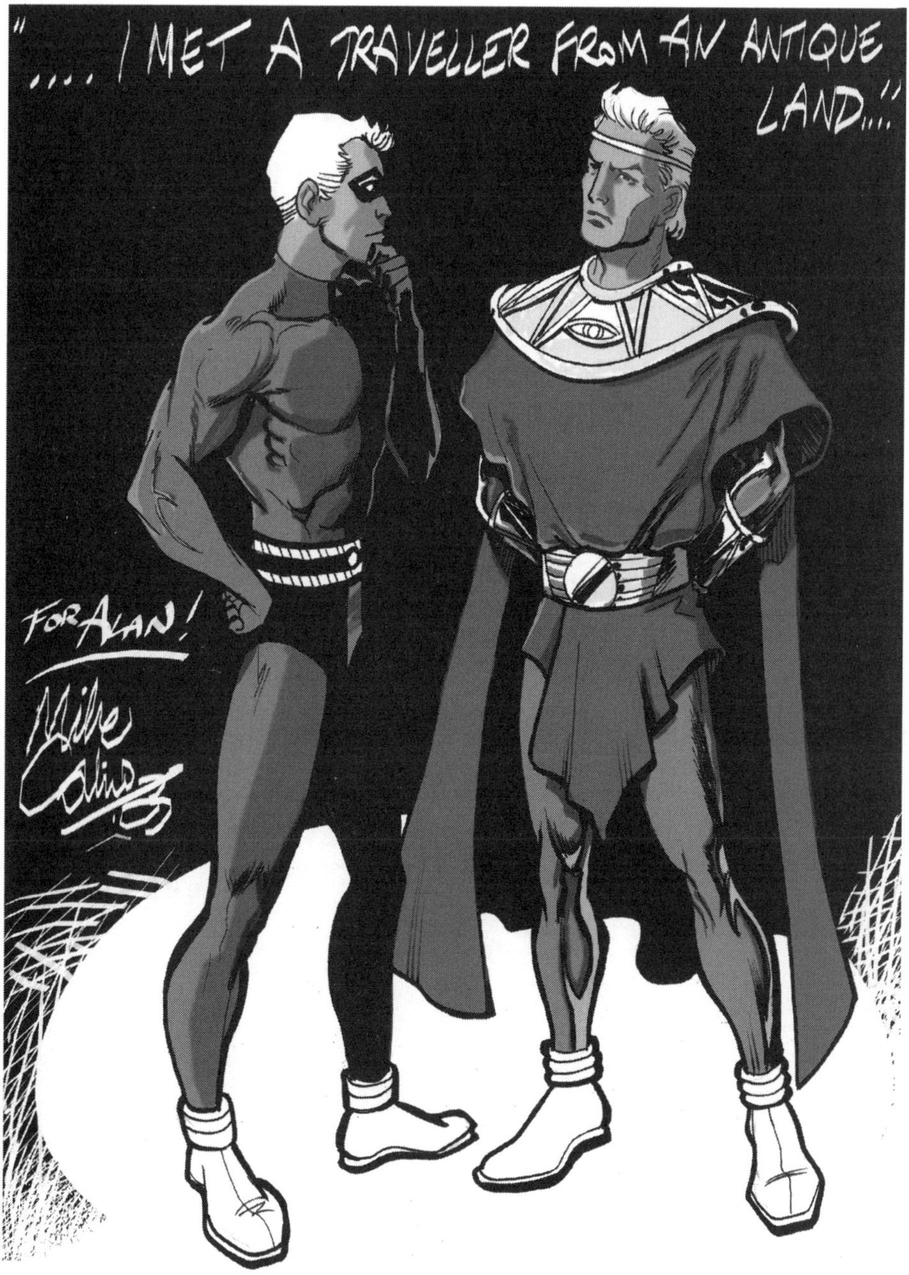
"....I MET A TRAVELLER FROM AN ANTIQUE LAND...!"
FOR ALAN!
Mike Collins

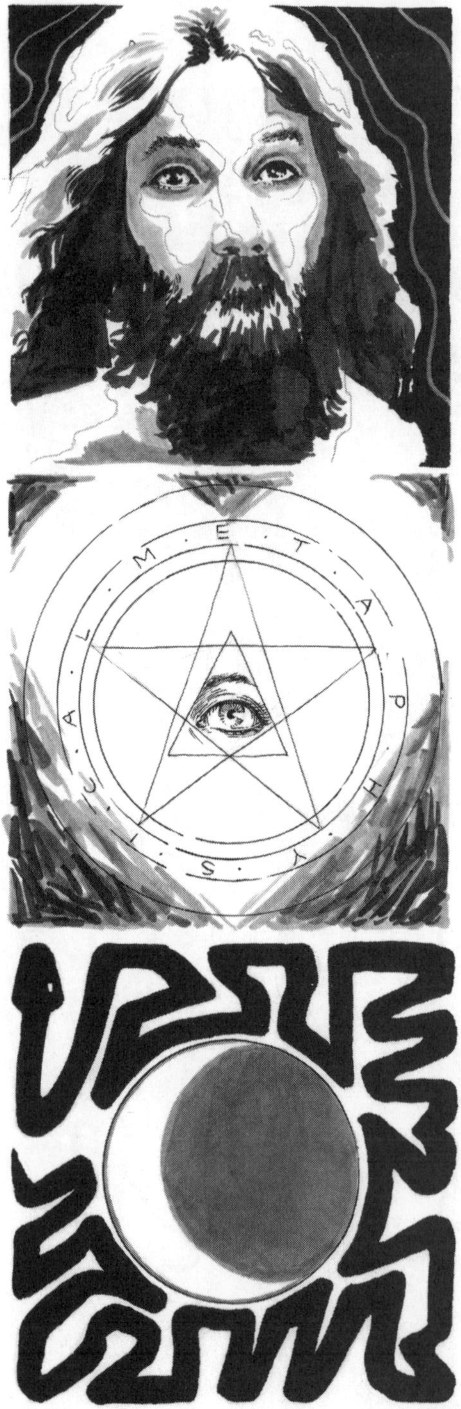
METAPHYSICAL
PORTRAIT

ART

TRANSLATED IMAGINATION
FROM THE INNER REACHES OF MIND
WAY BEYOND THE RINGS OF SATURN

AND BACK AGAIN

KEPT WITHIN A HEARTFELT PULSE
BUT TOUCHING OUTWARD
SO OTHERS MAY FEEL IT
A KEEN EYE FOR WORDS

ALAN

SPEAKS TO US

WITH THAT HEARTFELT PULSE

WE FEEL

WE LOVE

WE APPRECIATE

SO THAT WE MAY SHARE
THE BEAUTY OF FANTASTIC DREAMS
OPENING OUR MINDS TO POSSIBILITY
FROM AWE TO INSPIRATION
RISE AND REVERBERATE

MOON AND SERPENT
METAPHYSICAL PORTRAIT

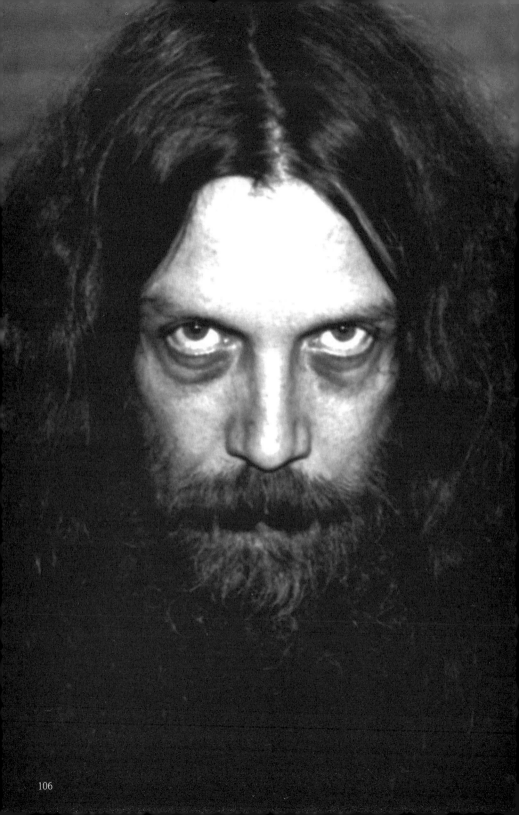

THE DARK SIDE OF THE MOORE:
An Interview conducted by Omar Martini

OMAR MARTINI

Omar Martini, who has worked as an editor and translator, is the co-founder of the Italian independent comics publishing house Black Velvet Editrice. Interview ©2003 Omar Martini.

I'd like to ask you some questions about your performances and your thoughts in general on history, not simply on comic books. Since here in Italy few people have written about this particular area of your work, I'd like to ask why you chose to start with those particular readings, those performances – The Moon and Serpent Grand Egyptian Theatre of Marvels, The Birth Caul - that is, what kind of subjects do you choose and how do you work on them?

Okay. In my teenage years, I was a member of the Northampton Arts Lab, which was an experimental art organization that was popular in England during the '60s. While working with the Arts Lab I did performances, I did poetry readings, I performed sketches, I wrote some songs and performed them, so basically there's always been an element of performance in what I like to do. However, it was in 1993-94 that I decided to become a magician.

Yes. I read about it.

What that meant was that I intended to find out what Magic was and practice it. One of the first impulses that came to me when I decided to practice magic was the familiar impulse (for me) of trying to turn it in something creative. So along with my musical partners David J (of Bauhaus and Love & Rockets) and Tim Perkins (a brilliant local musician), we put together a kind of collage of different things. There were some songs that had already been written but that seemed appropriate, there were some new pieces that we composed on the spot. We kind of put all these things together and this coincided with the performance that Blast Furnace Records and Iain Sinclair the writer were putting on at the Bridewell Theatre. We did a performance there, really enjoyed it. The whole idea for the format, the idea for the work... had all arisen out of thin air. One part of it was that we were actually talking about the building where the performance was taking place, we were talking about the surrounding environment, the surrounding area of London. This seemed to give the work a power and immediacy, in that the audience found themselves listening to a work that was talking about the place they were sitting in and was talking about the night they were sitting there. It became quite intense and personal. So we decided to carry this on, the next performance we did was... I stress that these are one-off performances, we never repeat them. I didn't really like the standard rock'n'roll idea of...

Of repeating...

You write your album, you then go out and do gigs on the road, playing the same songs every night. You hope that somewhere along the line you're going to have enough time to write songs for your next album. It didn't seem like that was much fun to me. So what we decided to do was, we do these things, put an immense amount of work into them, and only perform them once, with the idea that we could produce a CD that would bring them out in a more permanent form. The next thing we did was for a Newcastle Arts Organization. They wanted us to go there and perform for them. That was the piece that turned into *The Birth Caul*. Again, it was probably more polished than the first piece, we got a little bit more of an idea of what we were doing, but it was still a very powerful and resonant piece, it was a good performance. I was very pleased with that.

PIET CORR

Left: *Piet Corr a.k.a.* **pietdesnapp** *is a freelance photographer and lecturer, born in Northampton. His work has been exhibited in galleries and libraries all over England. Photograph ©2003 Piet Corr.*

I saw some photos and I also read and translated Eddie Campbell's adaptation of The Birth Caul. I found it really interesting and the particular thing was that at every reading I found some pieces... I understood something more than on each previous reading.

Well, all the pieces that we do we try to make them very dense, they generally deal with large subjects and we've got generally about an hour to do them all, without them

107

seeming rushed, and then they've got a kind of structure to them so that they would build nicely in the audience's mind and consequently we've got to get immense amount of detail into these things. I think that actually at the performances they can be a little overwhelming. The audience can't possibly... by the time they've paused to fully appreciate one line, they've missed the next two. But that's fine. I quite like the idea of overwhelming the audience's normal critical faculties.

You have this densely written language in one stream, then you've got very complex music in one other stream, you've got theatrics, maybe a fire breather... you've got synchronised psychedelic film collage... this sort of multimedia approach again, goes very much back to my Arts Lab days. I'm starting to appreciate it more because it almost... when the mind of the audience is taking in more information every second than it can handle, the effect of all these things become something like... perhaps psychedelic drugs, a kind of fugue state, where there are too many vectors of information occurring at once. So the mind tends just to give up and be carried along by the flow. Even if they're not taking in the meaning of every word, every sentence, I think that they are certainly soaking up all of the emotion and the general feeling of the thing. So I'm not too worried if they can't get it all at the first hearing.

We did The Birth Caul, and then we were offered a performance at the Highbury Garage, which again I decided that we would do as a "site specific" performance, it would be about Highbury. I have kind of adopted the belief that anywhere you could find enough interesting stories to make a performance if you dig deep enough. However, when we first looked at Highbury, it seemed that there wasn't anything there at all that was of any interest. So we started to dig a bit harder... and eventually the theory was vindicated.

Do you choose the subject according to the place or do you have something specific in mind before you decide to start writing for a new performance?

Well, in this case it was simply that Chris Brook who I'd met during my association with the K Foundation - the KLF, as they used to be called - Chris had got a series of nights in Highbury, so it was the fact that we were offered this performance in Highbury that told us what the event was about. Then we let the information that we unearthed shape the final performance. The unique character of any area is something that you can only reveal by this kind of excavation.

It's like... as an example, the piece that we did after Highbury, a year or something later, maybe two years later, was the Red Lion Square performance *Snakes & Ladders*, which Eddie Campbell has done an adaptation of and the album will be put by RE: Records, same as the other two albums... but with that we were talking about Holborn, which is an area of North London, which isn't very far away from Highbury, another area of North London. But the kind of historical events and characters that are associated with the two areas are completely different, and that tends to give a different flavour to each of the environments. Highbury turned out to have a lot of stories that revolved around drugs, around phantasmagoria, freak shows, it had a more hallucinatory atmosphere, there was something freakish, something sexual... a lot of "sex, drugs and rock'n'roll" over the centuries at Highbury. Whereas with Holborn and the Red Lion Square performance we found something that was perhaps less flashy, but more profound. We found a lot of resurrections, we found some genuine visions, some redeeming visions, things like that. It's purely the area itself that we tried to allow to tell its own story and to reveal its own unique character.

So, with say, *The Birth Caul*, how we arrived at the idea for that one ... because, there was a part of *The Birth Caul* which was talking about the area of Newcastle in which we performed it, but what *The Birth Caul* was mostly about came from me, David J and Tim Perkins: we did a magic ritual. The purpose of the ritual was to try and find out exactly what we should do next in terms of performance. What came out of the ritual was 3 to 4 hours of inspired enthusiastic talk about our childhood. Now, we figured out from that, whatever our next performance was about, it was going to have a large part of it that was talking about our childhood, infancy, teenage years.

When the Arts Foundation that was putting on *The Birth Caul* asked us what kind of venue we would like to do the performance at, we told them that our preference was to perhaps do it at a disused school or somewhere that seemed to have some relevance to the childhood theme. Now, they couldn't find a school, they found us a Victorian Court Room, which was a magnificent building, a lovely place to do a performance. We were a bit disappointed because it didn't seem to have any relationship to this childhood theme, but we decided to do it there anyway because it felt right. Now, the performance was in November; by the August of that year we still hadn't got any more than that initial idea, of something to do with childhood. It was during that August that my mother died and while looking through her effects, we found this piece of blue bandage wrapping, with this membrane stuck to it that had originally belonged to my grandmother and which had been passed down and which we recognized as a birth caul. There was something so powerful and talismanic about this object, it seemed to me to be almost... almost talking about birth, the pre-uterine state, it seemed to be talking about the womb, childhood, it seemed to be a kind of inspirational thing, around which we could compose this story of life and death, of childhood and birth, and... all of these other areas that we could talk about. So that's how *The Birth Caul* came to be the piece of work that it was. It was only after we had done the performance that we found out that birth cauls are mentioned on the first pages of *David Copperfield* by Charles Dickens, when they try to sell David Copperfield's birth caul and the person who buys it is not a fisherman - they traditionally prize birth cauls very highly - but the person who buys David Copperfield's birth caul is a barrister, or a lawyer. It turns out that barristers and lawyers also prize birth cauls as, apparently, they had worn birth cauls upon their heads to denote wisdom. Which is presumably the origin of the barrister's wig. So it turned out that by performing it at the Court we'd done in the perfect place...

It makes sense...

It all made perfect sense. This is the way most of these things come together. If they're meant to happen then they generally... if you can just kind of work without purpose, you have to kind of float in a way, to just drift generally towards your goal without having much idea of direction or control. If you can gather the nerve to do that, then you generally find that everything turns out perfectly, you know? I think that's answered your question.

Yes, I think so. I would like to talk more about your performances. I read also in some works and also in the text that you wrote for the Locus+ website that you usually work for a couple of weeks to a month to write the performances before you perform them. But during this period, do you usually write some other works or do you usually work only on this performance? Do you have some sort of schedule or does this kind of writing absorb you completely?

Well, what I have to do is, if I have deadlines with my regular work, then I have to get them out of the way first. What's generally happened with the CDs so far is that it's taken about two weeks to compose and record and produce the music. It also takes about two weeks to write all the words. That said, it might be that if I've got, say, to get another four to six pages of Promethea to J. H. Williams III during that week, then I will perhaps write four pages of Promethea in one morning, type them up, spend the rest of that afternoon/evening working on the performance piece; the next day perhaps doing another couple of pages of Promethea in the morning... I mean, I like it to be as continuous as possible, and with the Blake piece that we did, that was very absorbing. I was very conscious that I wanted to do something that would be worthy of William Blake, not to do something that was as good as William Blake but to do something that would not be an insult to William Blake. So I was feeling kind of pressured. I felt that I'd got this Eighteenth/Nineteenth Century ghost standing behind my shoulder, and if I wrote a phrase that was too dull, I would kind almost hear him tutting or sighing; if I wrote a phrase that was too elaborate, I'd hear the same thing. They were very demanding, I tried to make them my very best writing. It's like... they have to be intense because they're going into just a single hour where you've got one chance to get it right and so I put a great deal of work into all the pieces, with that in mind.

How do you collaborate with David J and Tim Perkins, your musicians? Do you first write down everything and then talk with them or...

What happens tends to vary... with the first album, the Bridewell performance, there were a couple of songs that had already been written, one of them I had written the lyrics first, then David J put the music to those lyrics, another one where me and Tim Perkins... I think there were two songs, where me and Tim Perkins just sat down and he had been playing me the song as he worked it out, and I was working on the lyrics more or less at the same time. Now, what generally tends to happen - at least these days - remember that David J is out of the picture, Dave has been over in America for some years so he's not really been in the loop - but these days, when Tim and me work together, what I generally prefer to do is to give Tim an idea of the overall structure of the piece. Like with the Blake thing, I said Okay, there's going to be four sections: the first one will do with his early life, and that would be Innocence; then we'll deal with the turmoil of his middle life - that would be Hell; we'll then do something about his later years, when he was an old man, that would be Experience; then, we would do the final section, which would be jubilant, psychedelic and we'll be talking about William Blake as kind of spirit coursing through history, that would be Heaven. Tim suggested that we also had an overture, so he could give more musical structure to the piece - I've got no problem with that - so then Tim started to work upon the four main musical pieces, with me sometimes putting in suggestions, some of which he would take notice of, some of which he wouldn't. Then, when he got the music finished, I wrote the words around the music, which I do by sitting down with a tape recorder and a stopwatch. I go through, say, the first ten minute track, making scribbled notes, that the first ten seconds have got a ghostly twinkling atmosphere, and then after ten seconds French horns come in and there's fifteen seconds before jangly guitars come in, and then twenty seconds before there's some other change in the music, and then I'll go through... get the general impression of what the music sounds like. Let that influence how I write the words and I also write them in verses of ten/fifteen/twenty seconds. Or however long that it takes me to say them. So that I would be able to read them along with the music and it would be all completely synchronised, which is a bit hair-raising when you're doing it live: you have to count in your head, you know, you reach a certain point in the music and you think "right, now I've got to count to twenty before I start to talk again".

But it is very effective, very powerful because it sounds... I think it's a bit like circus horses. People tend to think that the horses are dancing to the music, but in fact they're not. The orchestra is playing along to the movements of the horses, which it makes look like the horses are dancing. That's something like what I do... Tim creates that in whatever style he fancies and then I have to put the words in and around the music. So that it sounds as if the words were written first and the music was written afterwards, whereas in fact it's the other way round. We just get a really perfect synchronization sometimes. I don't think it would be possible were we writing the words first because if I were writing the words first they would tend to have quite predictable, rhythms and rhyme schemes, it would limit Tim too much in terms of what he could do with the music. If he does the music first he has no limitations and then I've got the challenge of fitting in the right words around the musical structure that he's given me.

It sounds really interesting, but also a little complicated.

It's quite scientific! [laughs]

It's very mathematic.

Yes, we have to be very precise. All right, sometimes it doesn't end up being quite as precise as we hoped, but it's generally pretty tight. The way the film and the dance and the fire breathing and everything kind of synchronises in within it. That also works very nicely.

But are the CDs a recording of the performances or are you doing them in a studio?

One of them [is a live recording]. But all of the performances have taped music to which I do a reading. Now, it's a bit like... now I don't know if you've seen the David Lynch film *Mulholland Drive*...

Yes.

They say: "Hay no banda"... there is no band. The only CD that is actually performed live is *The Birth Caul*. *The Birth Caul* because Charrm Records had got the recording equipment: they had it all set up so that we could record that live. So when you listen to *The Birth Caul*, that is absolutely as it was performed on the night... there's no special effects added or anything like that, you hear it exactly as it was on that night. All the other ones, because we did not have the facilities to record it or the recording turned out to be unusable... what we did was, we took the music that we used in our backing tape and I simply put a new vocal over the top; did a second reading and put that down. So the only truly live one is *The Birth Caul*.

So in some ways the other ones are live and in some ways they aren't.

Yes, that's it. They're a recreation of the live performance: we use the same music, the same tapes and I do the same reading over the top, so it's a recreation of the live performance.

Are you planning more performances or are you too busy with your other commitments?

Taking a break at the moment... but as far as *The Moon & Serpent Grand Egyptian Theatre of Marvels* goes, we kind of got the feeling that... there's been a kind of progression over the four or five albums that we've done so far: the first one - because we did not know what we were doing – is perhaps the most incoherent. I was talking about Magic when I hadn't got the faintest idea what I was talking about. It's the roughest of the lot because we were inventing form as we went along. In the subsequent performances we became more and more confident and they became more and more polished. This culminated in *The Angel Passage*, the William Blake performance. Now, that is the most polished complex thing, either musically or lyrically that we have ever done. It also doesn't really have a fraction of the same eerie power that the first recording had, when we made less sense, when we were less polished and less aware of what we were doing, we produced more powerful material, more genuinely magical material. So what we want to do is... me and Tim will chill out for a while, kick back, finish a couple of projects and have a rethink; go back to our initial roots, where we haven't got any idea of what we were doing, we haven't got any idea there's going to be a CD, when we haven't got any idea that it would be performed anywhere: we were just doing it because it felt that it was the thing to do. We want to try to get back to that naive state, then take it from there. So, there's probably going to be quite a pause while we strip away a lot of the sophistications that we've built up over this past, what, nearly ten years.

I would like to talk with you about two other subjects. The first one is history. One can certainly notice that you're interested in history and it comes out in many of your works. For example, as you said The Birth Caul is your history, but also kind of Great Britain's history and the Universe's history; Voice of the Fire is Northampton's history, with also some piece of contemporaries history in the sequence with the TV news, and "The First American" sometimes is some kind of history of the media; Supreme, of course, is some sort of recap of Superman's history. So it seems that you have a strong interest in history: it's like as if by your retelling you may change it a little bit and maybe to have something better. Is it correct? Why is history so present and so strong in your work?

Well, I try to see things in four dimensions. I feel that if we regard Time as a fourth dimension, then in order to have any sense of what we as individuals mean, what our lives mean, we really have to know where those lives came from, how we got to this current position, whether as personally or in terms of cultures, nations, you know, entire histories running back to the Palaeolithic. All these things seem fascinating to me, also the information that is buried in history… it's like seams of gold, that are still valuable, are still useful and are there for anybody who has the patience to do a little bit of digging.

For example, there is a big historical part in most of the CDs, so… now, the way I regard that is… I believe that to a certain extent we are creatures of our environment, I think that our environment reflects us and I think that we come to reflect our environment. Now, if you are living in a squalid tower block, if you are living in a shit heap, eventually you'll probably come to the conclusion - at least subconsciously - that you are shit. If you are living in a rattrap, you'll think you're probably a rat, and you'll probably modify your behaviour accordingly. Now, me, I live in a terraced house in Northampton which has got stars all over the ceiling, strange idols, stained glass: it looks pretty mad but it also… it looks a little bit like a temple. Now if you're living in a temple you'll perhaps get the idea after a while that you're some sort of [laughter] of divinity, or high priest or something, which might be delusional, but it feels a lot better than thinking you're a rat. I think that if I had to walk down the grey fairly miserable streets of Northampton everyday of my life, or London, if I have to be visiting London, as I shall be this Friday… a walk down one of those streets can be an entirely negative experience. You can notice nothing but the litter, the ugly graffiti, the urban decay. However, if you happen to know something about the history of that street - it can be personal history, something you did there when you were a twenty year old, when you were teenager, when you were a child - or family history, this is were your auntie lived back in the '30s, or the little gems of genuine local history…

I mean, where I'm sitting in this perfectly ordinary street, as I pointed out, I think, in *Voice of the Fire*, that just down the road there's the church where Francis Crick, who discovered DNA, went to Sunday School, next door to that is the cricket ground, where Samuel Beckett, the author of Waiting for Godot, he played cricket against Northampton. I can imagine this very Samuel Beckett cricket match, you know, where you have two old fielders, at the edges, saying, "Well, shall we… shall we go back to the Pavilion?" and the other one says "Yes." And then neither of one would move. He was up in Northampton quite a bit because he was come to visit Lucia Joyce, James Joyce' daughter, who was in the mental asylum, next door to where I used go to school. Same mental asylum John Clare died in, the Northampton poet, one of the best nature poets in the English language. Also a Jack the Ripper suspect, J. K. Steven, died there. Michael Jackson, Dusty Springfield, various celebrities were stopped in there to recuperate at various points.

Knowing all these things means that even the most dull and ordinary little streets suddenly can take on a wealth of meaning. A journey down Market Street can have your head buzzing with lively information. It's a completely different experience to walking down the same street when you don't know anything about it. I think that if we are to value the present and to really get as much as we can out of each present moment, it would help if we understood how this moment has arisen, if we understood the past, if we understood how incredibly rich and savage and beautiful our history can be. There is information like old things in the past and if we can unearth them I think we can use them to enrich our present existence.

So the presence of history in your work is some kind of looking back to see why we have reached this state and also to impart information.

Yeah. The whole of *From Hell*, in some senses, was… it seemed to me that looking at most of the technological or political or artistic or literary advances of the Twentieth Century, most of them could be traced back to the 1880s. Most of them, like France invading Indochina in the 1880s which lead to the Vietnam war… the Michelson-Morley experiments would lead, of course, to Einstein and the atom bomb, you know?

What struck me was that if the 1880s were the Twentieth Century in miniature, then maybe the Jack the Ripper murders were the absolute fulcrum of the 1880s. So, this is were I came up with the concept for *From Hell,* where we actually have the final murder - William Gull is more or less acting as a midwife in the gory birth of the Twentieth Century. It was trying get people to see the connectiveness of things, to see the shapes that exist in history, the things that link events, sometimes coincidences, sometimes sort of threads of meaning. But I think that people could kind of see things from that perspective, they just have a much richer experience of life.

Very interesting! The other subject I'd like to talk about - in part you have already answered- is why you chose Northampton as the stage for most of your works, for example Big Numbers, Voice of the Fire *and, in some way,* The Birth Caul *as well. Has Northampton a specific meaning for you or is it simply because it's your city, the place where you live and that you know the best?*

Perhaps all of those are true. I was born in Northampton, I believe that my family for the last several generations have originated in Northampton, may indeed, have always lived in Northampton. Despite the fact that Northampton is by no means a pretty or a beautiful town, it's a town that I feel a deep emotional connection to. It is the centre of MY universe... however, because I am a reasonably clever writer, I can probably make a case by saying that actually Northampton is the centre of THE universe. Practically, anything of any importance that could ever happen [laughs] generally kind of comes out of Northampton in some peculiar way, like... America, for example: George Washington's grandparents, Benjamin Franklin's great-grandparents emigrated from Ecton and Seagrave in Northamptonshire after the English Civil War and went to America. The village crest of Barton Seagrave in Northamptonshire is bars and motes, which is the heraldic name for stars and stripes. So, the American flag... yeah, that's probably based upon an obscure Northampton heritage crest. So, we've got DNA being sorted out at the Sunday school just down the road... Saint Patrick passed through Northampton on his way to throw the snakes out of Ireland... this was the capital of Britain throughout the Saxon period, this is where Thomas Beckett was tried, where Mary Queen of Scots was beheaded... you just try to find out all of these things... Buffalo Bill and Annie Oakley and Sitting Bull...

Did they come to Northampton?

...they performed on the little park, which is about a hundred yards, two hundred yards from where I'm now. I noticed a chimney pot on one of the houses near the racecourse that's got this bearded face carved onto it. Which at first I thought was perhaps Jesus or Moses... then I realised that it's got a cowboy hat and that in fact it was Buffalo Bill. They carved him on to commemorate the race course thing... it's like parliamentary democracy, the idea of having parliaments or presidents, things like that, rather than kings or queens, that was all started at Naseby, when Oliver Cromwell won the British civil war and introduced the idea of parliamentary democracy, the first in the world.

I also think that I can make for a pretty good case for Northampton being the absolute centre of the universe, but I think that probably anybody could about anywhere that happened to be dear to them if they were prepared to do the work... you know, wherever you are standing is the centre of the Universe [laughter]. If you are prepared to do the work you can probably come up with a very convincing case for that. Yes, I accept that Northampton is just another ordinary British town, no different from any other. At the same time, to me is a magical place that is very much historically, and in almost every other respect, the exact centre of England, if not the centre of the Universe.

Really very fascinating. I saw something like that some weeks ago because here in Bologna there was a visual performance made by Greenaway. He did this short film, at about I think 15-18 minutes showing some of the most important moments of history in Bologna and it was very striking because it seemed that so many things have happened here that no one could have ever imagined.

I believe it's true everywhere, but it's always marvellous and surprising when you found out about these things. This town where you live all your life, where you suddenly found out that all these marvellous things happened there that you had no idea about. When you start to do the research, the whole town comes to life; you see it in a completely new light.

There is a public library near my house and there are some old photos from the past and there are some more recent photos of the same place 30-40 years later. It's really striking to see the differences: maybe within your life span, you don't notice these changes much, but in a larger span there are some incredible changes.

Sure. I've been a big sucker for collections of local photographs. When they publish books of history of Northampton in photographs... I love these books because I find they give enormous pleasure and they break my heart. I'm looking at these places that I remember from my childhood and it's a delight to see them again and it's kind of painful to realize that they're not there and that they haven't been there for thirty years now. I think that... I don't like nostalgia because I think it's unhealthy. Nostalgia is a clinging to the past as a kind of denial of the future... that's not healthy at all. On the other hand, taking energy from the past in order to create some sort of future... that seems to me to be valuable and a noble thing.

Is information the most important thing and not to long for something past?

Not to long for something that is lost, you know... oh, how lovely it was when I was twelve... it was lovely when all of us were twelve. It's never going to happen again [laughter]. You know, like with *The Birth Caul*: I was able to look back at what it was like when I was twelve and to get some meaning from it, some information, some value, you know, that is useful to me and was hopefully useful to the people who heard the record. That's the way to approach the past, as something that is living, is healthy, vital, ongoing, you know, not to treat the past as some pretty mausoleum of dead memories that you go and make a fetish of. That's wrong, you know? The past is still alive, nothing ever dies. It's this kind of momentum, this energy that carries us through time and through our lives. It's a living thing... the people that are gone, the buildings that are gone ... they're not really gone, you know? They still exist in some sort of platonic space.

Understood. Since we have talked about your novel Voice of the Fire, *are there any plans for your next novel?*

The next novel it got... abandoned for a period. It was something I was going to do when Faith Booker, my editor, had asked me to do another book for Gollancz. I really liked Faith, so I really wanted to do another book for her. But then Gollancz fired her so I wasn't very happy with them. She was the only reason I was working for them because I liked her as a friend. So I kind of put aside any ideas of doing a novel... maybe some point in the future... you know, give it a couple of years when I've tied up all the comics work.

*Chris Staros was very kind and showed me the work you are doing with José Villarrubia, *Mirror of Love *and the new edition of* Voice of the Fire...

Yes, I'm very excited about both those projects.

It's certainly interesting to see that you still have some sort of fascination with the written word, since they're such different works from your comic titles. Why did you decide to do a new edition of these two works?

Well, I mean, I suppose the short answer is because José suggested it. It seemed like such a wonderful idea because *The Mirror of Love* is something that I've always been proud of. I think that at the time it was written it was probably the only comprehensive guide to gay culture anywhere... which is horrifying! I mean, this was 1988, '89 or something, and there weren't any comprehensive histories of gay culture. I believe that are still only very, very few, so the fact that The *Mirror of Love* has appeared just once in a benefit magazine and has never been reprinted... when José suggested that he could turn it into something quite different, into a beautifully produced, memorable book with photographs, you know? And the images that I've seen so far that he's produced have got that incredible passion that José brings to his work... they're wonderful images.

For *Voice of the Fire* the idea of an American edition sounded good and when José suggested that he could do portraits of each of the characters, that sounded very good to me, especially because that meant he had to do a portrait of me for the final chapter, and he has done. And I have to say that thanks to José's digital magic he's managed to make me look like an absolute Love God. I fell in love with myself all over again looking at Jose's pictures [laughs], you know, they're fantastic-looking things. José has a real visionary sense to his work and I just really wanted to see what he did with the stuff from *Voice of the Fire*.

So, yes, both of those projects are very dear to me... what you were saying about the fact that I do still have a strong affection to the word and not just for the pictures... I'd say that my first allegiance is to the word. I think that writing, just writing words is more pure than writing comic strips. I mean, I think that the comics strip is a wonderful art form of its own, it's a technology of its own, but the language, the essential word itself... these are the essential technologies. I think language is a technology that we've not begun to tap the full potential of. It's a technology upon which all other technologies are based. That's why I have the "logy" bit, the end of "techno"... I mean, writing is about technique, writing's about body of knowledge... that's what technology means, you know. Language is an inexhaustible technology, the things that we could do with it... like I say, I don't think that we've really scratched the surface. You're always going to find me involved in whatever forms the word takes... there's going to be words behind it somewhere.

In fact, one of the things that fascinate me about your work is the use you make of technology in such different ways. Sometimes you are able to do something poetic with technology. I'm thinking, obviously to some passages from Watchmen, *but also there are some striking images in the text of* The Birth Caul, *where you are able to focus some specific meanings with some scientific images.*

Well, in *Snakes & Ladders* we take that probably even further, where we've got a discourse upon the creation of the universe and its formation...
I don't just read occult books, but I also read New Scientist magazine every week and try to keep up with all the latest ideas, and I think that there is as much poetry in some of the ideas about quantum physics, about DNA, about science... I think that you should be able to find as much poetry in the most ultra-modern things as you can in the most rustic, beautiful, natural scenery. You should be able to find as much poetry in a dirty urban street as you can in a bucolic natural setting. Poetry is a kind of tool with which we try to understand the world and so it's important that poetry be able to talk about technology, to talk about science, to talk about the things that we know now, because otherwise poetry gets left behind and becomes more and more useless, and those particular areas continue to develop without any poetry in them. I think that both of those outcomes are to be avoided, if possible. I try to find what is magical or marvellous in anything, whether that actually be something from the field of Magic or whether it be from the field of physics or whether it be from ordinary urban life. There's generally something pretty marvellous about almost everything. It's just a matter of... if something is boring to you it's probably because you're not looking hard enough, you know. If you were to look a bit harder, a bit closer you'd suddenly see that it was in fact the most marvellous thing in the universe.

Some of your past work was very experimental... for example, the incomplete Big Numbers, or Lost Girls, which was a different approach to the erotic/pornographic genre, From Hell, of which we have already talked about ... what does it mean to experiment with comics medium? Do you think that there are still some unexplored zones in this medium?

I can see very little BUT unexplored zones. The areas that we have explored are tiny. You know, even in some stories I did for America's Best Comics, just the odd little story here or there... we did one issue of *Promethea*, which is entirely based upon using the 22 Tarot cards to tell the complete history of the Universe, with accompanying anagrams of "Promethea"... that's probably the most experimental story I have ever done. I really didn't know if it would be possible to do that.

Reading Promethea *is really challenging because of the text, of the ideas and the information it contains on Magic, the Kabala, things like that...*

The storytelling in *Promethea* has some strange things in it. Then, there was an issue of *Tomorrow Stories*, where we had, a *Greyshirt* story, that was all about a building, with 4 panels in each page, one for each floor of the building, they were all in different times...

Yes, I remember it...

It's something you couldn't do in any other medium other than comics... which I haven't seen done in comics before... it took a little bit of working out, but... yeah, in every field that I work I don't like the idea of doing something which has been done before... I don't even like the idea of doing something that I'VE done before. I've got a very low boredom threshold. If you know that something you're going to do is going to work, there's probably no point in doing it. If you know it's going to work it's because you've done it before and it's starting to get tame and safe... this is one of the reasons why we've decided to break down everything we've done so far on the new CD, halt progress on the musical front and try to get back to a more genuinely experimental state where we don't know what we're doing because... it's how I've always been.
To return to the beginning of this conversation, constant experimentation was one of the main tenants of the Arts Lab movement. Everything could be experimental art... it was the '60s, you know, you couldn't go to the toilet without it being experimental. I suppose I'm very much a child of the '60s, there's a voracious hunger for something new, you know, all the time, something new. I guess I probably do have that in my work.

Never play safe and try to do something different every time.

Yeah, of course it gets progressively more difficult to find something more extreme to do. This is probably why I had to become a magician when I was 40. I couldn't think of [laughs] anything I hadn't done... I had to do something pretty extreme. But of course, when I'm 50 in about a years' time, I shall have to try to become... I dunno, an axe murderer or something.

You have anticipated my next question. What are you planning to do for your 50th birthday? When you were 40 you decided to become a magician. Have you already planned something?

Yes. I'm going to pretty much wrap up the entire ABC line of comics, I'm going to pull out of mainstream comics, I'm going to disappear for a couple of years, at least... who knows? Maybe forever. I'm going to concentrate on things... probably more in the kind of things we discussed tonight, concentrate on things that don't have to make money, where it doesn't matter to me if nobody buys them [laughs]... where I could just to do what exactly I want to do. That's my plan when I become 50. It's not much of a plan because part of it involves... I don't want to know what I'm going to be doing when I'm 50. That's part of the fun. Yeah, I suppose when I get to 50, I want to have a complete lack of certainty, security [laughs] or any of those things that most people really want by the time they're 50. I want insecurity, uncertainty... you know, I mean... in short, my audience can rest assured I will be happy with whatever it is I'm doing.

Since you wrote Brought to Light *and your recent short story with Melinda Gebbie, "This is Information," do you think that there is any future for political comics or comics that try to spread a social message?*

Well, YEAH... I mean, I think there's certainly a future for political comics if there is a future for anything. We'll have to see whether George Bush and Tony Blair launch their war against Iraq on November 5th, whether Saddam Hussein throws more scuds into Tel Aviv like he did last time, whether Ariel Sharon nukes Baghdad as he has more or less threatened to, whether the rest of the Arab states come into it, I mean... if there's a future for anything, there's a future for political comics. I want to hedge my bets on that question until, say, early next year if we're all still here then... if there's a future for anything, if there's a future for any of us, there's a future for political comics and I should love to be doing them. I really enjoyed doing "This is Information" with Melinda... I wish I could have perhaps been a bit more outspoken, but they were very worried that... the Americans are very sensitive.

Well I don't know if, for example, in England you have heard about the scandal that happened this day at the Film Festival in Venice for the movie on September 11 made by eleven directors...

Yeah, I heard about it, yeah...

There has been some scandal because they said it was "un-American"...

Well, one of the things I really want to do when I'm 50 is that I don't want to work for big American companies anymore. A lot of my very best friends, my girlfriend... are American. I love some American people but I've got to say that as a nation... they want to grow up. Yes, it was terrible what happened to the Twin Towers, but in the rest of the world we've all been having the shit bombed out of us since Guernica. Digging people out of rubble is kind of business as usual everywhere in the world apart from America.

Last year I read a couple of books by Noam Chomsky and Gore Vidal that said the same thing: "Ok, it was terrible, it was a really huge disaster, but for the rest of the world it was business as usual..."

Yeah, especially, you know... please, don't stand there and say, "Why does everybody hate us? We didn't do anything!" because that shows a complete ignorance of history, of the world situation, of reality... yes, you did do something, that's why they did something. If you start investigating that a bit, then maybe, you know, you'll come to some sort of understanding or realisation about these things. But... yeah, you know... I mean, like, Marvel have asked me to take part in another book they're doing, which is a pro-peace book, but... I don't know. They're planning on it coming out in April, when we'll probably almost certainly still be embroiled in a war against Saddam Hussein, if that goes ahead. I'm not sure that I feel comfortable in doing something with an American company talking about how the world should be at peace, when America is dragging the world to the brink of Armageddon, mainly to keep the oil companies happy. So, I'm still thinking about it... and if I come up with something really good to do that would work for me then maybe I'll do it. Otherwise, I won't.

• Interview with Alan Moore conducted by **Omar Martini** on 09/09/2002

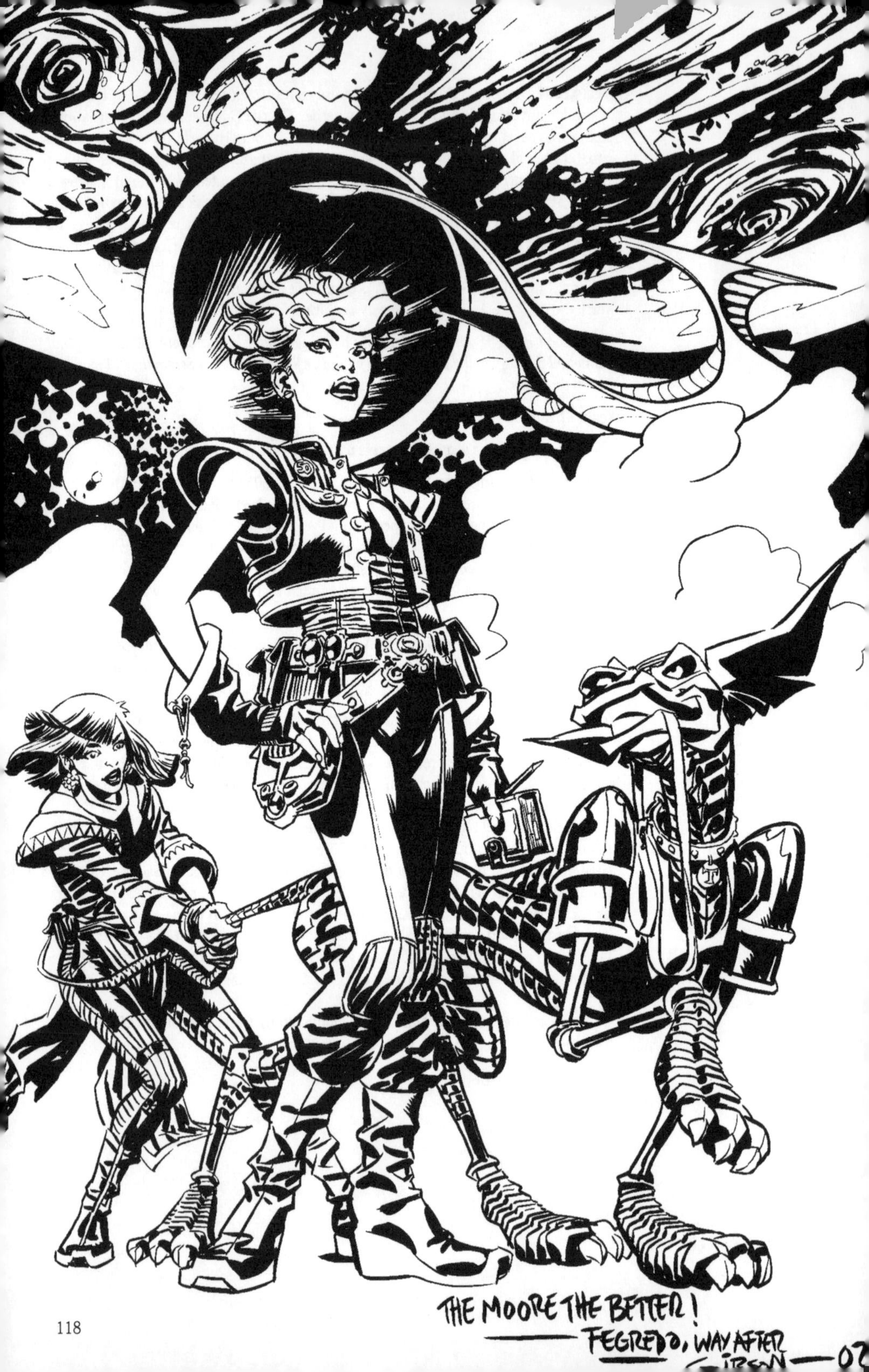
THE MOORE THE BETTER!
— FEGREDO, WAY AFTER

PICK UP THE PHONE

ANTONY JOHNSTON

Antony Johnston is the author of **Frightening Curves, Three Days In Europe** and **Rosemary's Backpack.** He has adapted several Alan Moore prose works into comic form for Avatar Press, including **The Courtyard** and **Another Suburban Romance.** Antony lives in southern England with his girlfriend.

Text ©2003 Antony Johnson.

I can't do it. I can't pick up the phone.

Rewind: I'm eleven years old. I read comics. When I grow up, I'm going to draw them. I know this, in the unconscious reaches of my juvenile heart. I *know* it. And the comic I will work for is called 2000AD.

Understand, this was a time when 2000AD wasn't the only boy's comic on the newsstands. ACTION, BATTLE, SCREAM, EAGLE... Seemed like every six months there'd be a new comic launched, a new way to spend that pocket money. And spend it I did. Who needs sweets when you can have *comics?*

But there was never any question that 2000AD was the superior comic. Some of us read other comics too. Some of us - well, me - read pretty much *every* other comic too. But in the playground, on the way home from school, wherever you went in my world, *everyone* read 2000AD.

EAGLE had DOOMLORD, and DEATH WISH. SCREAM had THIRTEENTH FLOOR. BATTLE had CHARLEY'S WAR. ACTION had ACTION FORCE.

But 2000AD had D.R. & QUINCH, and SKIZZ, and HALO JONES, and ABELARD SNAZZ, and these amazing TIME TWISTERS that bent your mind out of shape.

2000AD had Alan Moore. But I didn't realise it.

Forward a year or two: somewhere in the darkness, a switch is thrown. A light bulb comes on above my head. And I realise, for the first time, that a comic doesn't just come into being. An artist doesn't just sit down and draw stuff until a comic bursts from his head fully formed like Athena.

Someone actually sits down and writes a story. And someone else sits down and draws it. And someone *else* sits down and puts the letters on.

And some people write more than one story.

Great Scott!

That was it. That was when I began reading credits. This would culminate in my current state, a state where I must read the indicia of a novel, where I must watch the credits of a movie, where I perplex my friends by nodding and saying, "Oh yeah, them" in a knowledgable grunt when I see casting companies credited on screen.

It all started here. With 2000AD. And Alan Moore.

Naturally, I was going to write *and* draw my stories, because I was *special*. And my prepubescent plagiarism logically went, well if *he* writes really good stories, I should read them and re-read them, because they'll teach *me* how to write really good stories.

Bear in mind, at the time I was also blatantly copying Steve Dillon's artwork.

DUNCAN FEGREDO

Left: Duncan Fegredo has been drawing comics for a lot longer than he likes to admit and should know better. When he questions the futility he reaches for his battered volumes of Halo Jones, just to clarify why he wanted to draw comics in the first place. He is currently drawing **Ultimate Adventures** for Marvel. Illustration ©2003 Duncan Fegredo. Halo Jones is ©2003 Rebellion.

Forward another year or two. My stories are, of course, still crap. Even I can tell that. Doesn't stop me exactly, but despondency is starting to set in. I'm fourteen years old, and hardly anyone I know still reads comics. We've all started playing roleplaying games instead. My parents don't have the faintest idea what this comics lark is about. Frankly, they're amazed I'm still reading them.

These are the dark days. I have no-one to turn to. No-one knows my pain. (Insert other teenage angst here as appropriate.)

Then. Then, my local TV station repeats a late-night series made the year before, called ENGLAND, THEIR ENGLAND. It showcases unusual British talents and success stories. I can't remember what the rest were - doubtless people who run proper businesses, with big buildings and machines and everything - but this one, I remember.

It is called MONSTERS, MANIACS AND MOORE. Oh, yes.

I duly set the VCR.

Like the tape I would have some years later of Bill Hicks' RELENTLESS performance, MM&M would get to know the inside of my parent's VCR very well indeed in a short space of time. I had, in my clumsy teenage fashion, found a guru.

The programme taught me three major things about Alan Moore.

1) He is fucking bonkers. (See 2)
2) He is probably the most sane person on earth. (See 1)
3) He is from Northampton.

Wait a minute! *Northampton?* That's just down the road from me! My great-grandfather still lives there!

From that day on, my confidence never wavered. It was possible to come from a working-class family (check), to have a distinctly average formal education (check), to be *from the Midlands* (check), and yet still write comics. Great comics, at that.

I could do it. I was *going* to do it. I had it all planned out.

And then along came beer, sex, more beer, and... Well, I carried on reading comics. For a bit. But, you know - *sex*. And *beer*. Comics didn't stand a fucking chance.

Forward: what about this bloody phone? Yeah, yeah, I'm getting to that.

So it's early 2000. A few months previously, I'd started reading comics again. Because I'd decided I wanted to write them.

(The intervening time is a long and largely boring story. All you need to know is that my art skills never progressed beyond the age of sixteen, and that's not saying much. A writer, then.)

So this friend of mine, this guy I've gotten to know since entering the now-largely-online comics community, asks me if I want Alan Moore's phone number. Do what, I say. He repeats the offer. Just don't tell anyone where you got it, he says, or Alan will fucking kill me. Go on then, I reply. Why not?

Half a millisecond after I write it down, I realise why not: *I can never call this number.*

I mean, since I last read an Alan Moore comic he's stopped going to conventions. He's become a magician. He doesn't even have an internet connection, for heaven's sake! This man clearly does not want to be randomly contacted by some star-struck old fanboy. And this star-struck old fanboy does not want to approach publishers and have them think, "Fuck, this is that guy Alan Moore told me was stalking him. Reject! Reject!"

Paranoia does horrible things to your brainmaggots, I can tell you.

So I didn't use it. I was terrified to my core.

Forward again: it's 2002, and I've just been approached by Avatar to adapt a short Alan Moore story into comic form. After picking myself up off the floor, I do just that. It goes well. Alan seems to like my stuff, and what I've done with his story.

Piiiiick meeeee uuuuup, whispers the phone. *Phooooone hiiiiiim.*

No. Abject terror, it turns out, is a powerful deterrent. Who knew?

Forward again: it's later in 2002. I get an email from the producer of the FROM HELL movie. He's interested in one of my comics, wants to talk about maybe optioning

ROBIN SMITH

Right: *Born on Merseyside, Robin Smith worked for 2000AD for six years and drew the original Alan Moore script-droid. He now makes a living as a freelance artist. Survived by Lucy, Emma and Sophie. Illustration ©2003 Robin Smith.*

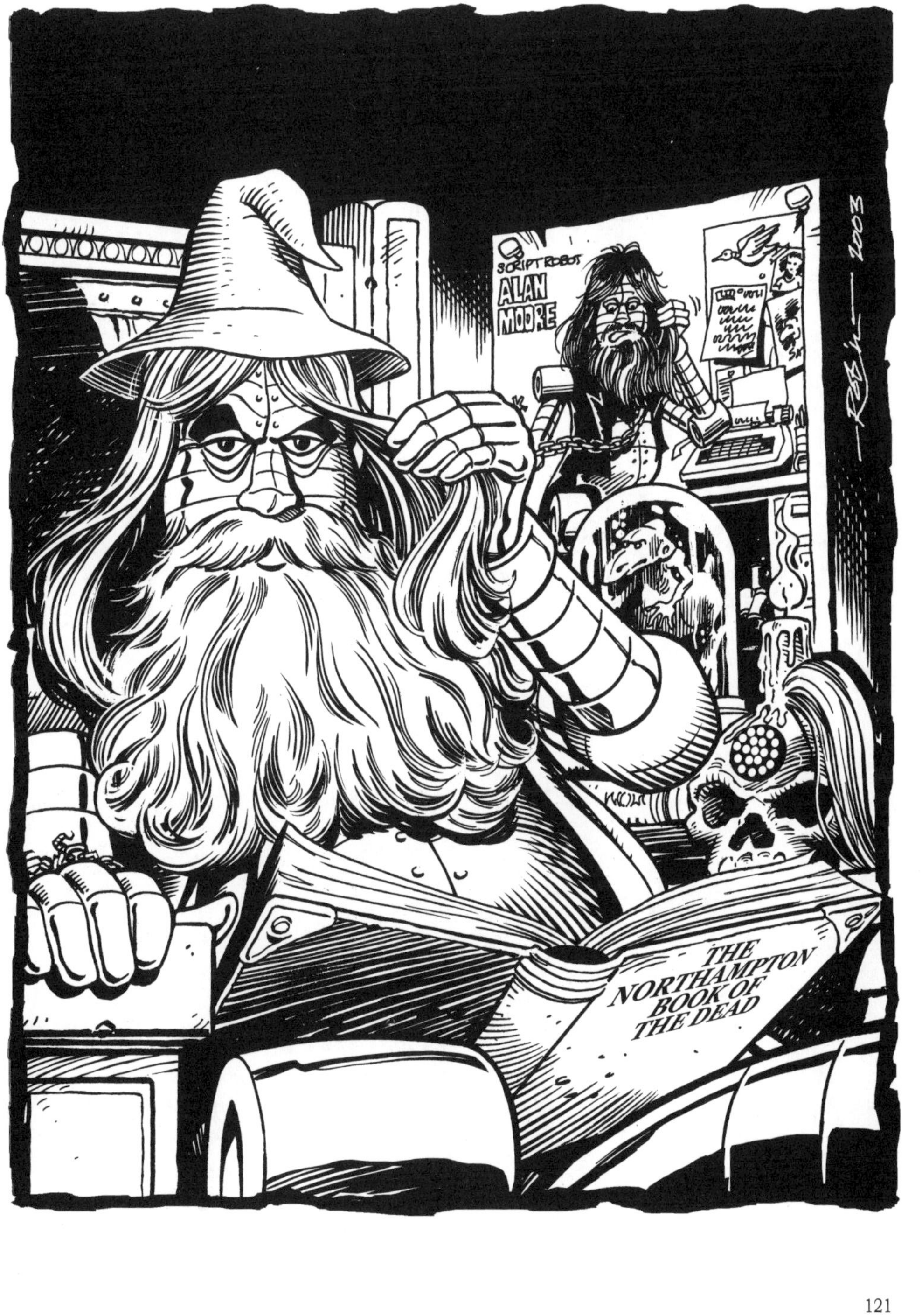
SCRIPT ROBOT
ALAN MOORE
THE NORTHAMPTON BOOK OF THE DEAD

it. Now, by this time I've already had some first-hand experience of producers, and realised that they're just like everyone else; some are good people, some are fuckwits, and it's sometimes hard to tell which camp someone falls into until you've already wasted hours on the phone.

So I look up the guy's credentials. Turns out he's produced some damn good films. Friends tell me "Yeah, he's for real. He's a good guy." But these are people who live and breathe the movie industry. I want an objective opinion, from someone who isn't afraid to speak their mind.

I can tell you're ahead of me, here.

I am literally shaking as I pick up the phone. Every possible response runs through my head. *"Who the fuck are you and how did you get this number?"* surfaces with alarming regularity.

I can't do it. I can't pick up the phone. He's not going to know who the hell I am. Why should he?

Deep breath. I remind myself that this is nothing to do with comics. Nothing to do with the adaptations I've done of this man's work. Nothing to do with me being a fanboy. This is business. Everyone's told me he's a nice guy, so long as you're not wasting his time or trying to rip him off.

Yeah, like that helps me any. I'm still shaking, and now my throat feels like a camel's gonads to boot.

I pick up the phone.

"Hello, is that Alan?"

"Yes." *(Christ, his voice is deep! Jesus fuck, does he chew gravel or something?!)*

"Alan, it's Antony Johnston—"

"Oh, hello Antony. How are you...?"

• **Antony Johnston**
17/03/03
England

HOWARD CRUSE

Right: *Howard Cruse's most recent book of collected comic strips is* **Wendel All Together.** *He is also the author and illustrator of the internationally award winning graphic novel* **Stuck Rubber Baby.** *Cartoon ©2003 Howard Cruse. Batman © DC Comics.*

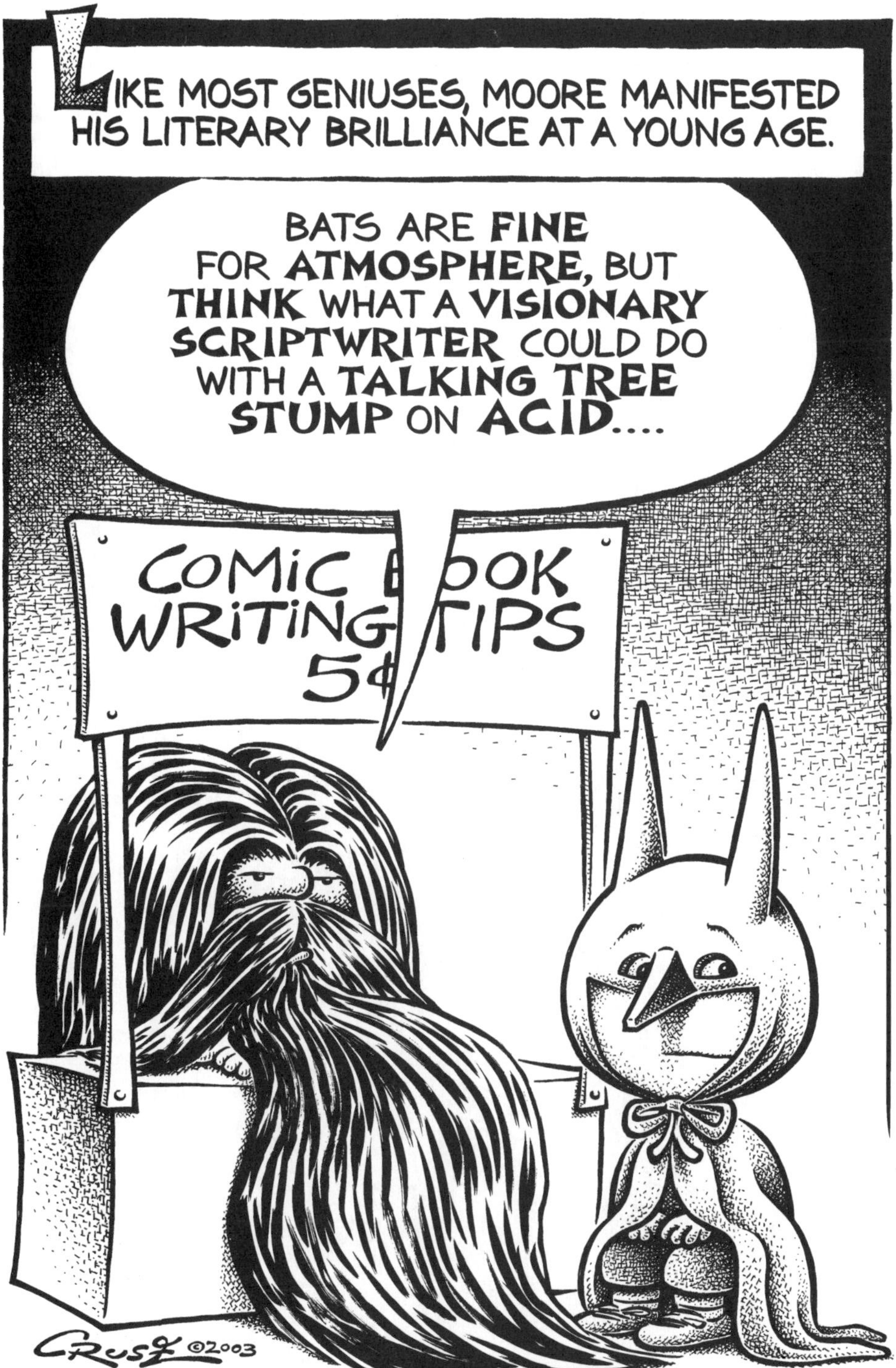
LIKE MOST GENIUSES, MOORE MANIFESTED HIS LITERARY BRILLIANCE AT A YOUNG AGE.
BATS ARE FINE FOR ATMOSPHERE, BUT THINK WHAT A VISIONARY SCRIPTWRITER COULD DO WITH A TALKING TREE STUMP ON ACID....
COMIC BOOK WRITING TIPS 5¢
CRUSE ©2003

Bryan Talbot
2003

THE MAGICIAN

MARCELLO ALBANO

Marcello Albano has been working in the Italian comics market as writer and penciler since the '80s. He is the co-writer of the revisionist Italian superhero **Radar**. Text ©2003 Marcello Albano.

RICH KOSLOWSKI

Pages 126-128 following:
Rich Koslowski has been writing and drawing comics for ten years, starting with his self-published title, **The 3 Geeks** and later, **Geeksville**. His ambitious graphic novel, **Three Fingers** was published by Top Shelf last year. He is a lifelong fan of comics and just happens to think that Alan Moore is a genius. Strip and Gil Lenderthol are ©2003 Rich Koslowski.

BRYAN TALBOT

Left: Bryan Talbot has written and drawn a huge variety of comics from the underground **Brainstorm!** to superhero stories featuring **Batman** and **Judge Dredd**. He has also illustrated stories for Vertigo's **Sandman** and **Fables**, but is best known for his graphic novels **The Adventures Of Luther Arkwright, Heart Of Empire** and **The Tale Of One Bad Rat.**
Illustration ©2003 Bryan Talbot.

It's very difficult for someone who works in the comics field to talk about Alan Moore. For two reasons: the first one is that the Northampton-based magician is the BEST writer who has ever graced the medium. The second reason is that Alan is, maybe, the ONLY comics writer in the world.

Writing comics is not a real job. People who do it often have a degree in the Humanities and aspire to write for television, cinema, web sites and magazines, if they do not nourish the dream to write the Big Novel. Comics are just a small part of their literary interests. They are often so busy trying to avoid the "expressive restraints" of the comics page, that they don't care at all to verify if these restraints are real or just the result of a prejudice.

Alan has spent his whole career doing exactly the opposite. He didn't get any formal higher education. After having let himself be expelled from high school for dealing Acid and having lived the years of the sexual revolution in the ARRGH community, he was (for a short time) a musical journalist; since 2000 AD, the legendary British magazine, he never again left the comics medium.

Even his novel, *Voice of The Fire*, is a comic without pictures as his From Hell is a novel in comics form.
What I mean is that in those works there are storytelling techniques which are possible ONLY in comics: in the first case, I am referring to the first chapter, where the cavemen talk in a Neolithic English (Alan loves creating new languages; in comics the understanding of his neologisms is supported by the pictures; in the second case, on the contrary, it gives the impression of a conversation fading out, an effect made by the progressive shrinking of the lettering...

Alan explores the possibilities of comics, discovering an immense cave whose limits are clearly known only to himself. The bearded hippie is not interested in exploring other media. His discovery, apparently a simple one, is that FREEDOM OF EXPRESSION in comics is limited only by talent and by the skill of who is using it.

After having spent the first half of his career killing characters (his first issue on *Captain Britain* was a bang: in a four-page sequence he kills the whole cast of the series, main character included) and moving all the social criticism and odd surrealism of the "Undergrounds" into the comics mainstream. Alan took a long sabbatical and resigned from his role as minor post-modern genius. Then he came back, with general surprise, in the guise of Great Wizard and as a devotee of Crowley, Dee and Spare.

In this new phase what amazes the most is the incredible quantity of his new creations. It almost seems that he is repenting for having put the last nail in the coffin of the superhero genre, by trying to magically reanimate the corpse.
After their iconoclastic fury has vanished, Alan's stories lose their dark and apocalyptic tone and get crowded with characters that we would never expect to meet again. Here they are, they all come back: the super-dog, the super-ape, the planet where the good guys are the bad ones and vice versa ... no hero is really dead; there is no character in the imaginary realm who can do it.

Moore owns the key for the Limbo where all the untold stories have their place. It is a secret garden where aliens with two bodies run after women dressed in protective girdles and the Trojan War is still raging.

There, growing like a vine around their own story, the Knights of the Holy Grail, Supergirl, Alexander The Great and Jack The Ripper with his Mary Kelly are all living together. You have just to evoke them and they will reply.

Obviously, to do this you need to be a magician ...

• **Marcello Albano**

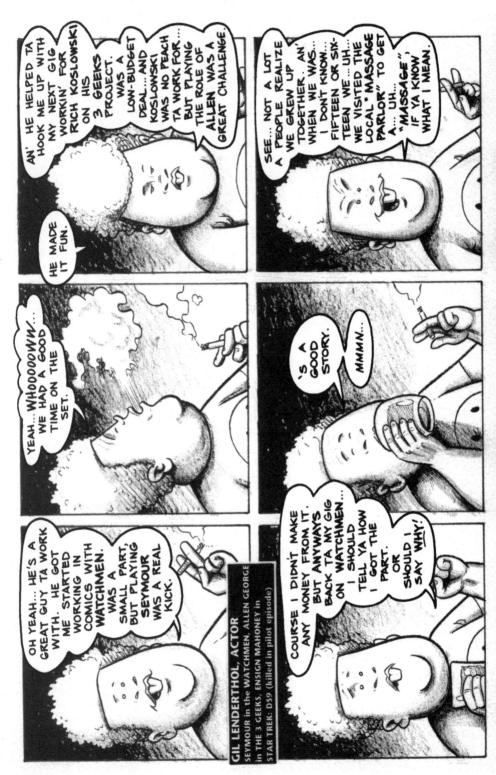

AN' HE HELPED TA HOOK ME UP WITH MY NEXT GIG WORKIN' FOR RICH KOSLOWSKI ON HIS 3 GEEKS PROJECT. WAS A LOW-BUDGET DEAL... AND KOSLOWSKI WAS NO PEACH TA WORK FOR... BUT PLAYING THE ROLE OF ALLEN WAS A GREAT CHALLENGE.

HE MADE IT FUN.

SEE... NOT A LOT A PEOPLE REALIZE WE GREW UP TOGETHER... AN' WHEN WE WAS... I DON'T KNOW... FIFTEEN OR SIXTEEN WE... UH... WE VISITED THE LOCAL "MASSAGE PARLOR" TO GET A... UH... "MASSAGE", IF YA KNOW WHAT I MEAN.

YEAH... WHOOOOOWW... WE HAD A GOOD TIME ON THE SET.

'S A GOOD STORY.

MMMN...

OH YEAH... HE'S A GREAT GUY TA WORK WITH. HE GOT ME STARTED WORKING IN COMICS WITH WATCHMEN. WAS A SMALL PART, BUT PLAYING SEYMOUR WAS A REAL KICK.

GIL LENDERTHOL, ACTOR
SEYMOUR in the WATCHMEN, ALLEN GEORGE in THE 3 GEEKS, ENSIGN MAHONEY in STAR TREK: DS9 (killed in pilot episode)

COURSE I DIDN'T MAKE ANY MONEY FROM IT. BUT ANYWAYS BACK TA MY GIG ON WATCHMEN... I SHOULD TELL YA HOW I GOT THE PART. OR SHOULD I SAY WHY!

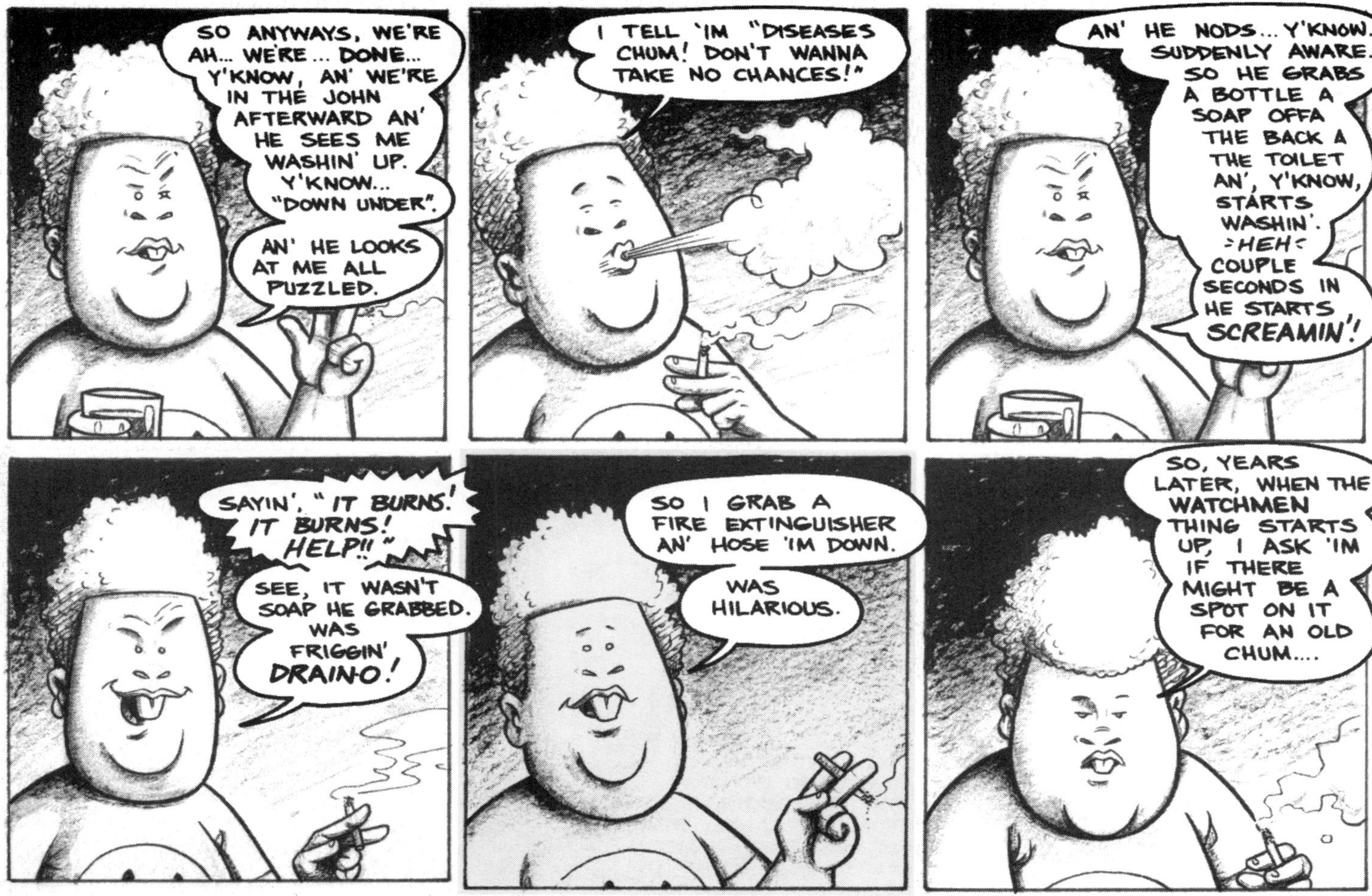
SO ANYWAYS, WE'RE AH... WE'RE... DONE... Y'KNOW, AN' WE'RE IN THE JOHN AFTERWARD AN' HE SEES ME WASHIN' UP. Y'KNOW... "DOWN UNDER".
AN' HE LOOKS AT ME ALL PUZZLED.
I TELL 'IM "DISEASES CHUM! DON'T WANNA TAKE NO CHANCES!"
AN' HE NODS... Y'KNOW... SUDDENLY AWARE. SO HE GRABS A BOTTLE A SOAP OFFA THE BACK A THE TOILET AN', Y'KNOW, STARTS WASHIN'. =HEH= COUPLE SECONDS IN HE STARTS SCREAMIN'!
SAYIN', "IT BURNS! IT BURNS! HELP!!"
SEE, IT WASN'T SOAP HE GRABBED. WAS FRIGGIN' DRAIN-O!
SO I GRAB A FIRE EXTINGUISHER AN' HOSE 'IM DOWN.
WAS HILARIOUS.
SO, YEARS LATER, WHEN THE WATCHMEN THING STARTS UP, I ASK 'IM IF THERE MIGHT BE A SPOT ON IT FOR AN OLD CHUM....

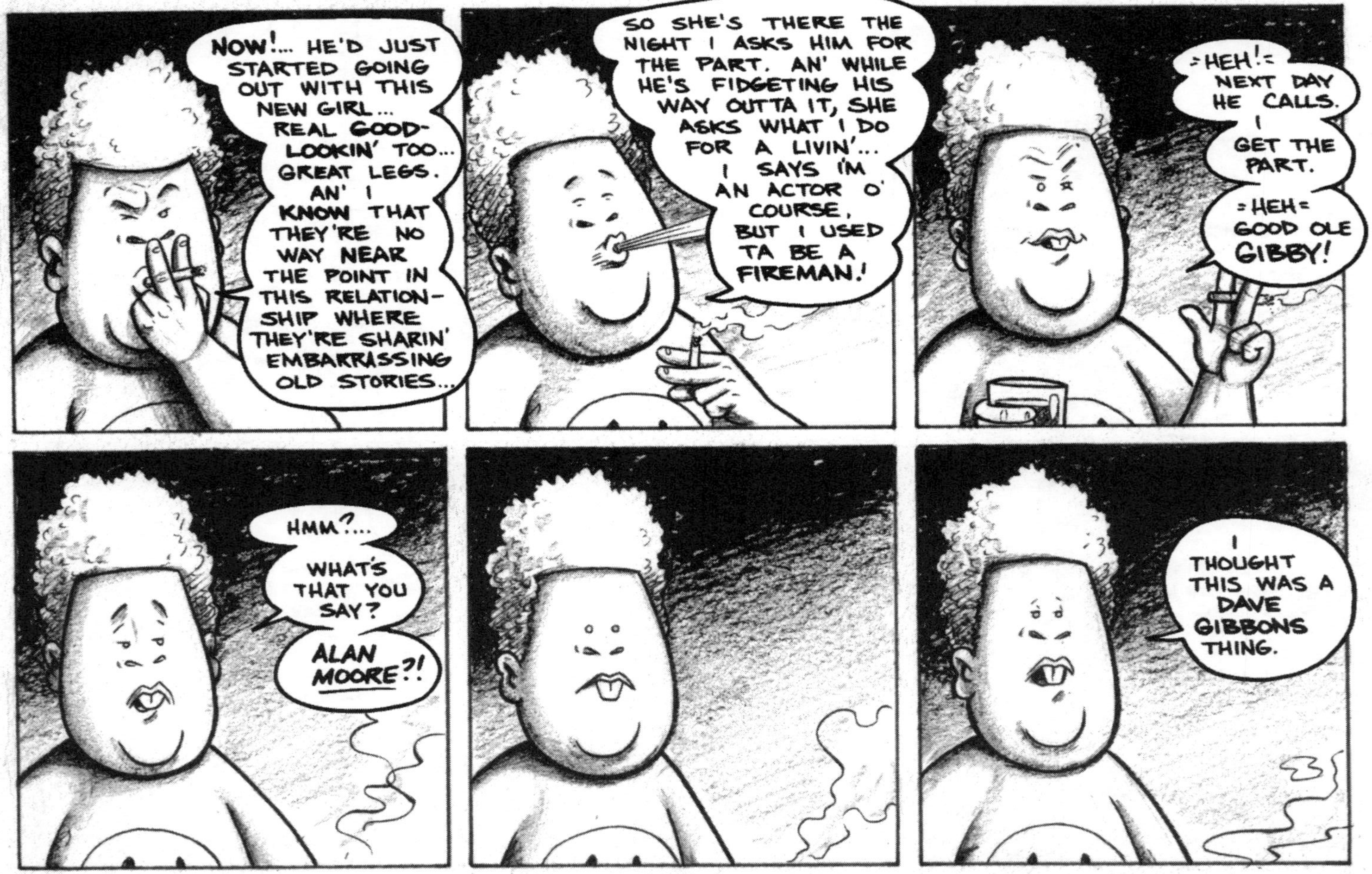
NOW!... HE'D JUST STARTED GOING OUT WITH THIS NEW GIRL... REAL GOOD-LOOKIN' TOO... GREAT LEGS. AN' I KNOW THAT THEY'RE NO WAY NEAR THE POINT IN THIS RELATION-SHIP WHERE THEY'RE SHARIN' EMBARRASSING OLD STORIES...
SO SHE'S THERE THE NIGHT I ASKS HIM FOR THE PART. AN' WHILE HE'S FIDGETING HIS WAY OUTTA IT, SHE ASKS WHAT I DO FOR A LIVIN'... I SAYS I'M AN ACTOR O' COURSE, BUT I USED TA BE A FIREMAN!
=HEH!= NEXT DAY HE CALLS.
I GET THE PART.
=HEH= GOOD OLE GIBBY!
HMM?...
WHAT'S THAT YOU SAY?
ALAN MOORE?!
I THOUGHT THIS WAS A DAVE GIBBONS THING.

RUTTING IN FREE-FALL:
Moore & Bissette/Zulli's Act of Faith

JOSÉ ALANIZ

José Alaniz, Ph.D. in Comparative Literature from the University of California - Berkeley, writes on Russian comics, disabilty in superhero comics and Alan Moore. His work has appeared in the International Journal of Comic Art. In fall, 2003, he will begin teaching in the Department of Slavic Languages & Literatures at the University of Washington-Seattle. Text ©2003 José Alaniz.

It is false to imagine that breaking the sexual taboos means a return to nature as exemplified in the animals, and yet the behavior forbidden by the taboos is like that of animals. ... Indeed, the sexual functions of animals have aspects which bring us close to the inner experience as we consider them attentively. – Georges Bataille

[I]f we accept the most basic psychoanalytic premise that original objects are lost, whether owing to the entrance into the symbolic, as Lacan puts it, or simply because the mother or breast must eventually be given up by the child, then we must likewise agree that the whole of infantile and adult sexuality – including the genital sexuality usually considered the "normal" route for sexual instincts – is perverted, or swerved away, from its original object. – Linda Williams

Alan Moore, Stephen Bissette & Michael Zulli's short story "Act of Faith," a tiny (non-continuity) episode in the environmentalist-minded 1980s comics series *the Puma Blues,*[1] makes an explicit linkage between human and animal sexuality. More boldly, it contends, through a fetishistic unnamed narrator, that only such cross-species imaginary leaps can attain the vertiginous heights of true erotic fulfillment, recalling Bataille's formulation that "the sex taboo [is] fully seen in transgression ... it is only really present in more complex forms in which the quality of transgression is stressed progressively more and more." *(Erotism,* 107-08)

But in what ways can we truly call this story "transgressive"? Do Moore, et al's complex confessional narrative, visual puns and wordplay constitute an "escape" to a liberatory *ars erotica naturae,*[2] or merely the imposition of established human (read: male) sexual norms onto a passive wilderness? In other words – its authors prompt us to ask – is "Act of Faith" more an act of *bad* faith? The four-page story, told through a reminiscing 26-year-old male narrator, describes the mating ritual of two "rays" – mutated mantas that have evolved out of water to swoop the skies. With only their "giant livers" to process the innumerable toxins of a poisoned future USA, the rays stand on the brink of extinction – only 30 or so remain; like the actual American bald eagles which they clearly reference, these fanciful creatures figure as living national symbols of a natural world gone awry through man's errant stewardship. High above a toxic reservoir, the rays copulate in free-fall, helpless against gravity and thus courting death (again, mimicking the mating strategies of eagles). The voyeuristic narrator, meanwhile, anxiously masturbates, climaxing "just before they hit the water, peeled apart, a splash that never came, but oh God I did. I did." (46) The use of animals as symbols and/or barometers of a natural world in peril has, of course, a very long literary pedigree. To pick just one recent example out of the burgeoning nature writing canon, William Ashworth uses the image of a dying seal as a "stand-in" for a deteriorating environment:

It lay half on its side, its flanks heaving with the effort of breath ... Black eyes, with plenty of self-awareness still in them, locked onto mine. There was a soundless gape of defiance, but the animal was clearly too weak to do anything more. (2)

Ashworth invokes the dying seal as an opening for questions of, among other things, personal mortality, as does Virginia Woolf in her more famous, proto-nature writing essay, "The Death of the Moth":

One could only watch the extraordinary efforts made by those tiny legs against an oncoming doom which could, had it chosen, have submerged an entire city, not merely a city, but masses of human beings; nothing, I knew, had any chance against death. ... O yes, he seemed to say, death is stronger than I am. (374-75)

Notes:

The author wishes to extend a word of appreciation to the participants of his Comparative Literature 1B course, "'Back' to 'Nature,'" conducted in Spring, 2003, at the University of California-Berkeley, without whose insights this paper would not be what it is.

The epigraphs come from Bataille's Erotism, pg. 94 and Williams' Hard Core, pg. 272.

1. Long defunct, the Puma Blues tackled issues of environmental degradation, government cabals and alien intervention in a near-Schopenhaurian mode of despair and wit. One of its main characters was a puma on the prowl. The manta rays also appeared frequently throughout the series' run in the late 1980s. Of its creators, artist Michael Zulli would achieve the most mainstream success; he went on to work on various projects for DC's Vertigo imprint.

2. In The History of Sexuality, Michel Foucault identifies two "great procedures for producing the truth of sex": the Orientalist ars erotica of gnostic mysticism and pleasure "first and foremost in relation to itself"; and our own more recent scientia sexualis, which emphasizes the transmission of knowledge-power, through, among other things, scientific measurement and study of sexual phenomena and the confession. See pgs. 53-73. An ars erotica naturae would involve non-human insights for producing an art of sex.

129

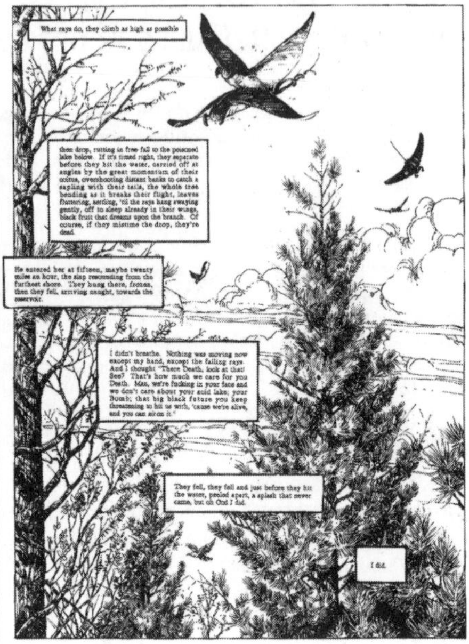
What rays do, they climb as high as possible
then drop, rutting in free-fall to the poisoned lake below. If it's timed right, they separate before they hit the water, carried off at angles by the great momentum of their coitus, overshooting distant banks to catch a sapling with their tails, the whole tree bending as it breaks their flight, leaves fluttering, settling, 'til the rays hang swaying gently, off to sleep already in their wings, black fruit that dreams upon the branch. Of course, if they mistime the drop, they're dead.
He entered her at fifteen, maybe twenty miles an hour, the slap resounding from the furthest shore. They hung there, frozen, then they fell, arriving naught, towards the reservoir.
I didn't breathe. Nothing was moving now except my hand, except the falling rays. And I thought "There Death, look at that! See? That's how much we care for you Death. Man, we're fucking in your face and we don't care about your acid lake; your Bomb; that big black future you keep threatening to hit us with, 'cause we're alive, and you can sit on it."
They fell, they fall and just before they hit the water, peeled apart, a splash that never came, but oh God I did.
I did.

Left: art from "An Act of Faith," Puma Blues #20 © 2003 Moore, Bissette & Zulli

Both these passages, I wish to emphasize, exploit a natural process (death), represented by a denizen of the natural world (an animal), as a metonym to evoke not a natural but an inner, psychological landscape.[3] Our knowledge of Woolf's long depression and subsequent suicide, in fact, cannot but influence our reading of lines like "oncoming doom" and "death is stronger than I am." The moth, so to speak, gets lost in the shuffle.

Such readings underscore the move in much recent environmentalist thought away from the metaphysical views of Deep Ecology, which deems nature a wholly separate and "sacred" space ideally left unsullied by man, to an appreciation of nature as always and already imbricated with human culture - a nature overlaid with historically-determined human presumptions, traditions and values, and indeed *constructed* largely by the human psyche and its desires.

Certainly the anonymous male narrator in "Act of Faith" derives a deep satisfaction from "peeping" on the rays, imposing his own desires on the natural world.[4] Structured by his gaze, the wilderness overflows with phallic imagery ("erect" trees; branches intertwined by a ray's sensuous tail; violent acrobatic sex: "He entered her at fifteen, maybe twenty miles an hour, the slap resounding from the furthest shore" [46]). The female ray's circular snout and lamprey-like mouth clearly recall the *vagina dentata* of male dread and Freudian phantasmagoria; throughout the piece, the sex/death link prevails: "Skimming low across the caustic reservoir she slaps her tail down twice, three times, flirting with pain and teasing death to make her sex more sharp, more sweet." (45) Moreover, the panels appear almost uniformly in the shape of elongated rectangles - with the "orgasm" panel (a full splash page) the largest rectangle of all (46).[5]

These sorts of representations constitute a problem for feminist critics like Elizabeth Grosz, who see them as anything but innocent descriptions of natural phenomena; rather, they seem little more than reifications of male sexuality writ large:

> ... for some men, animal sex and even insect sex hold immense fascination because they represent motifs, themes and fantasies that are close to what might be understood as a masculine imaginary, to a masculine mode of representation of self and other. (295)[6]

Worse, these "colonizations" of the natural world by the imperial male gaze, Grosz argues, seek to reinscribe human femininity along rigidified norms. The male renders everything "not-male" either in his own image or as threatening - witness our common cultural associations regarding the "predatory" sexual practices of the Praying Mantis or the Black Widow (both gendered female, and both transformed in our imaginations into man-eating "femme fatales")[7]:

3. Unlike Ashworth and Woolf (who either lock gazes or have physical contact with the animals), Moore/Bissette/Zulli's narrator does not directly interact with the natural objects of his vision; he seems to operate solely as an observer, outside nature looking in. In this essay I try to demonstrate how he is in fact interacting with it on a perhaps more fundamental level.

4. We should take the term "natural world" advisedly: the rays themselves, thanks to a profoundly polluted 21st century environment, are man-made, products of human-induced mutation. In what sense, then, can we call them "natural"? (It goes without saying, of course, that as made-up creatures in a sci-fi story, the rays are in yet another fashion "man-made." They were not even "invented" by Moore, but by Puma Blues *creators Stephen Murphy & Michael Zulli. On all these levels, the rays are already "sullied" and "unnatural.")*

5. We can compare this boundary-smashing splash panel to several other instances of orgasm in Moore's work, especially Dottie's climax in Lost Girls *no. 2 ("The Twister"). The instance from* Swamp Thing *I cite below also qualifies as a sort of surreal extended splash across several pages. These designs visually foreground the liberatory powers of orgasm, its capacity to carry the subject beyond earthly constraints; as in "Act of Faith," many of these illustrations portray an upward lift or temporary escape from gravity.*

6. One of the most notorious literary instances of a male-oriented thanatopic depiction of nature (figured as woman-bashing) occurs in William Golding's The Lord of the Flies. *He portrays the slaughter of a wild sow as a gang rape, with boys turned into soulless "hunters" who "fulfill" upon her "inch by inch" with their spears, reenacting their trauma of abandonment by punishing the Mother. Most disturbingly, Golding intimately describes the terror and torment of the sow and the hunter's delight in inflicting it; they sadistically joke, "Right up her ass!" (135)*

> [A]ny attempt to understand female pleasures and desires on the models provided by male sexuality and pleasure risks producing a model of female sexuality that is both fundamentally reliant on heterosexual norms of sexual complementarity or opposition, and that reduces female sexuality and pleasure to models, goals and orientations appropriate for men and not women – models, in short, which reduce female sexuality to versions of male sexuality. (279)[8]

Grosz specifically objects to depictions, like that in "Act of Faith," which link the feminine erotic to the thanatopic (as in the "femme fatale" instance cited above), noting that "by linking sexual pleasure to the concept of death (the 'little death')[9], woman is thereby cast into the category of the non-human, the non-living, or a living threat of death." (284)[10]

While not refuting Grosz's objections to such sins of linkage by male authors, I will argue that "Act of Faith" does not commit them – at least not in a conventional sense. Certainly the male narrator does seem to encroach upon nature from without, imposing his phallic gaze on the rays' "natural" courtship, deriving his deepest voyeuristic pleasure from their coupling, essentially turning them into porn actors in animal drag for his consumption. As outlined above, he (along with the authors) also associates the female ray with the monstrous, the deathly and the victimized in familiarly misogynist ways. In this sense, we can say that the story privileges a specifically (human, Western, late 20th-century) male version of sexuality at the expense of other forms.

All the same, Grosz's feminist critique cannot account for all the narrator's fetishistic motivations in "Act of Faith." Rather, he seems – to put it bluntly – very turned on by the rays themselves. In their tryst he finds the (fictitious, fanciful) romantic purity of "natural" erotic fulfillment which he has failed to locate within his own species. In the words of Midas Dekkers, he has "let [him]self go," and found "true satisfaction" by giving in to interspecies difference (3):

> Sex is something that by definition you have with another being [sic],[11] whether of the same or a different sex, someone of the same race or a more exotic choice. Every sexual encounter is a breaking of bounds, an intrusion into an alien realm, every sexual encounter retains a whiff of bestiality. (2)

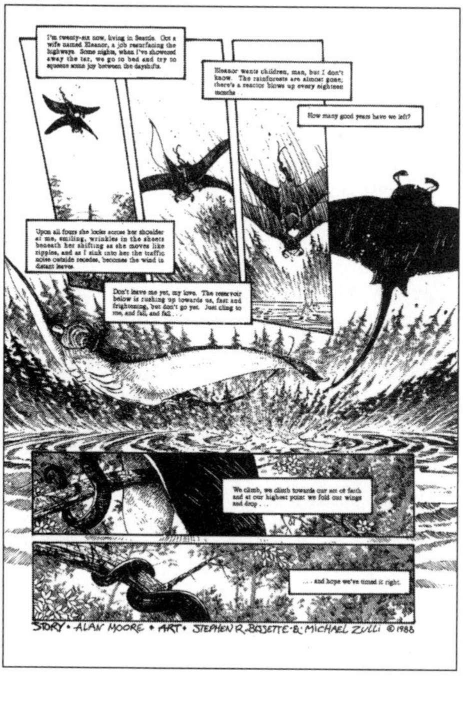

I'm twenty-six now, living in Seattle. Got a wife named Eleanor, a job resurfacing the highways. Some nights, when I've showered away the tar, we go to bed and try to squeeze some joy between the dayshifts.
Eleanor wants children, man, but I don't know. The rainforests are almost gone; there's a reactor blows up every eighteen months . . .
How many good years have we left?
Upon all fours she looks across her shoulder at me, smiling, wrinkles in the sheets beneath her shifting as she moves like ripples, and as I sink into her the traffic noise outside recedes, becomes the wind in distant leaves.
Don't leave me yet, my love. The reservoir below is rushing up towards us, fast and frightening, but don't go yet. Just cling to me, and fall, and fall . . .
We climb, we climb towards our act of faith and at our highest point we fold our wings and drop . . .
. . . and hope we've timed it right.
STORY • ALAN MOORE • ART • STEPHEN R. BISSETTE • & • MICHAEL ZULLI ©1988

Or more than a whiff, in the narrator's case. Moore's text in "Act of Faith" provides numerous clues to its protagonist's outré sexual preference.

Page 44:

To begin with, he is not "from without" nature at all; as a teenage "reservoir guide" he actively works *in* nature (at least whatever polluted form of it remains in the dystopic future America of *the Puma Blues),* and in nature he finds sexual satisfaction (he begins working there at 15, in the Spring, the mating season for many species).

7. I cite this example from Wild Sex, *one of a burgeoning number of titles devoted to the scandalous love lives of animals: "[The Praying Mantis] turns and falls on her lover and begins munching him for an after-sex snack. Sometimes the male has not even finished copulating before she begins nibbling away at him. Fortunately his sex drive is so strong he is able to continue even while being slowly eaten away." (262) This comes from a chapter called "Fatal Love."*

8. Grosz's essay, in fact, seeks to "clear the air of certain key projections," to "dispel accounts which bind women too closely to representations of men's or animals' sexuality." (280)

9. Grosz refers here to la petite mort, *colloquial French for orgasm.*

10. She is to some extent writing after Roger Callois, the French sociologist who has extensively addressed the wonders of mimicry in the natural world and the cultural resonances produced by the "sexually ravenous" Praying Mantis.

11. Puzzlingly, Dekkers excludes autoeroticism as a legitimate form of sex. Yet, as Woody Allen notes in Annie Hall: *"Hey, don't knock masturbation. It's sex with someone I love."*

Right: art from "An Act of Faith," Puma Blues #20
© 2003 Moore, Bissette & Zulli

Conversely, he declares "Massachusetts" (the artificial human construct that demarcates and segments the natural landscape) a "sex-free zone." He comes to that opinion when, thinking others will find his insights into ray mating behavior as fascinating as he does, he tries to share them with an "unescorted chick."[12] These lame (not to mention bizarre) attempts at sexually connecting with girls are rebuffed: "I guess not everybody's turned on by mutated skates humping. It never worked ... except on me." Unlike the others, he prefers to sit, "sniffing the blossoms," while his ray-induced erection passes.

The narrator finds human females inadequate in other ways. He cannot trust them. They either coldly refuse his advances, or haphazardly shift identities in his "indecisive" fantasies. He only experiences arousal if they wear a diaphanous nightgown or leather (i.e., an animal's skin), as does Donna Fein.[13] These efforts fail to raise the cowed narrator's spirits (or anything else), until he "notice[s] the rays."

Page 45:

The female ray "leads," as do the human females, but in identifying with the powerful, confident male ray, our narrator feels inspired, not snubbed: "My cock leapt with her lashing tail, as if attached to a fishing line." He feels literally connected to the rays through an imaginary cord; hooked, man is "caught" – seduced – by the animal, rather than the other way around. Here, as throughout the story, the human ("Bring a child into a world like this ... man, that's a death-defying act of faith.") is confused with the animal ("They breed so recklessly ... but don't we all?"). Moore relentlessly reduces the distance between the two: "I felt the sharp, warm pebbles upon the bank beneath me through my jeans .../ ... just feet between them ... inches ... millimeters ..."

Page 47:

The story concludes not only with a link established between human and animal sexuality, but – in a reversal of Grosz's formulation – the "colonization" of the former by the latter; the narrator, now grown up, has "gone over to the other side," represented by his moving from Massachusetts to Seattle (from one coast to another, geographically about as far apart as one can get and still remain in the contiguous US). While he has ostensibly left nature by working to resurface highways (which nonetheless probably takes him into remote areas of the northwest), he nightly "shower[s] away the tar" of modern industrial life. Though married, he feels reluctant to have children, citing the state of the environment and a sense of apocalyptic doom – putting concern for nature above his personal life.

"Act of Faith's" last four captions secure the narrator's perception of life and sex purely in terms of his beloved (imaginary) rays. His wife Eleanor[13] looks "across her shoulders" at him, "[u]pon all fours," as they make love. This sexual position, of course, most closely resembles that of many animals in the wild, as Sigmund Freud noted in the Wolf-Man case.[14]

The wrinkles in the sheets beneath her meld into ripples on the reservoir made by post-coitus rays (visually underscored by the fourth, borderless panel), while the city life he nominally leads (represented by traffic noise) "recedes, becomes the wind in distant leaves." The deceptive word "distant" is belied by the fact that the narrator has immersed himself so intimately and thoroughly in the spectacle of the "mutated skates humping" that he can only describe sex with his wife in terms of "the reservoir below, rushing up towards us," "and fall, and fall," "at our highest point we fold our wings and drop," etc. We may of course read this language as the overcooked metaphor of romanticism, as amorous purple prose ("Do not leave yet, my love."). But the narrator's long-standing obsession with the rays, his clear disenchantment with females of his own species and his alienation from urban life all suggest a more devastatingly literal reading.

Our protagonist experiences a familiar cognitive dissonance – familiar because we all, of course, idealize our lovers. The narrator, however, has idealized his lover beyond the human (Bissette/Zulli's art emphasizes this; "Act of Faith" has textual

12. The narrator uses a slang term for woman derived, not coincidentally, from an animal, i.e., a baby chicken, further conveying his biocentric frame of mind.

13. Two women's names appear in the story, and they both profoundly problematize the narrator's relation to the opposite sex. We can read Donna Fein ("Fine Lady") as fine in the sense of attractive ("She's fiiine."). However, Donna, from the Latin Domina, *"mistress or ruler of the home," implies a domineering figure (the Latin partly shares this meaning with the Gaelic* Domhnall, *"ruler of the world," from which the English "Donald" and "Donna" derive). "Fein," from the German, can be read as "refined" or perhaps "overly fastidious." "Donna Fein" therefore represents a threatening, tyrannical figure who refuses to cooperate even in the narrator's fantasies. His wife Eleanor, meanwhile, bears the name of a medieval queen, Eleanor of Aquitaine, who fought in the Second Crusade, married (and messily fell out with) two kings and in 1179 led an insurrection of her sons against their father, her second husband Henry II of England. In the overall scheme of "Act of Faith," therefore, the name Eleanor alludes to feminine power, duplicity, intimidation and the peril of uncontrolled reproduction. Eleanor possibly derives from Helen, the woman whose abduction by (or maybe elopement with) Paris launches the Trojan War. (Male) authors from Homer to Shakespeare have portrayed Helen as fickle, callous and a slut, a woman insensitive to the fact that her fabulous beauty leads to the suffering of others.*
Moore, incidentally, had by this time written at least one other story dealing with male paranoia over female deceit. In "Mortal Clay," (Batman Annual *no. 11, DC Comics, 1987) the supervillain Clayface obsesses over a clothing store mannequin, delusionally projecting his lurid desires and fears upon it.*

14. This more ferarum, *and its manifestation in the witnessed primal scene, has all sorts of repercussions for Freud's subject, the Wolf-Man (the son of a Russian landowner with a phobia of wolves), one of the most famous cases in the psychoanalytic literature.*

references to *homo sapiens*, but the pictures are completely people-free). The rallying cry of the Deep Ecologists, Thoreau's "In Wildness is the preservation of the world," takes on an added twist: In Wildness is the sexual salvation for the narrator.[15] But I would like to point out another way in which "Act of Faith" fulfills a transgressive function. This has to do with its depiction of orgasm.

For Linda Williams, the subtextual mission (impossible) of much cinematic pornography has been "the obsessive attempt of a phallic visual economy to represent and 'fix' the exact moment of the sexual act's involuntary convulsion of pleasure" (113) as part of an overall will to visual knowledge. Out of this mission emerged the genre convention of the "Money Shot" (ejaculation) to depict male orgasm. Female orgasm, however, proved immune to visual representation, and so could only be hinted at, suggested, metaphorized – in short, "faked" – through various devices that pornography used to penetrate that "invisible place."[16] To varying degrees all these devices proved unsatisfactory; female orgasm lies outside representation, despite the male porn viewer's repeated attempts to "fix" it.

But, of course, male orgasm too escapes visual (or any) representation, no less than the female variety; it also resides in an "invisible place." The Money Shot may signify an "involuntary convulsion of pleasure," but as a device, a shorthand, it merely serves as the marker of a phenomenon that exists only partly in the realm of the visibly physical.[17] Orgasm, no less than nature, may be overlaid with cultural assumptions, but also like nature, it is to a considerable extent irrepresentably other. I do not argue that men's and women's orgasms are the same, only that they, as Williams puts it, belong to the same economy of desire. (273)

Orgasm's resistance to representation has consequences. It often opens a space for utopian expressions of ultimate community, of a breakdown between self and other. Grosz, writing after the philosopher Alphonso Lingis, describes orgasm this way:

The subject ceases to be a subject, giving way to pulsations, gyrations, fluxes, secretions, swellings, processes over which it can exert no control and to which it only wants to succumb. Its borders blur, seep, liquefy, so that, for a while at least, it is no longer clear where one organ, body or subject stops and another begins. (290)

Grosz's (genderless) description of orgasm, i n t r i g u i n g l y , approximates those of Moore, with the critical difference that Moore adds *species* to the list of blurred borders. (This was no recent innovation for Moore, a writer working in sci-fi, horror and fantasy, marginalized genres that not uncommonly deal with alternative sexualities.) Even before "Act of Faith" he had written on interspecies sex. In the early *Swamp Thing* story "Rite of Spring," for example, Abigail Cable and "Alec" the earth elemental enjoy a form of b o u n d a r y - m e l t i n g

15. *This hints at why Moore maintains the anonymity of the narrator; the confession of illicit, "abnormal" desire performed pseudonymously or anonymously is a staple of pornographic literature, e.g.* The Story of O.

16. *In the 1972 film* Deep Throat, *for example, the heroine's orgasmic ecstasy is represented through rapid-fire cutting to shots of* Love American Style-*type fireworks and a space rocket launch.*

17. *Williams acknowledges this, calling erection and ejaculation a "limited and reductive way" to depict male pleasure. (49) I would add that orgasm in any case does not necessarily equal ejaculation (e.g., nocturnal emissions, occasional instances of ejaculation at death, Tantric orgasm without ejaculation), rendering the Money Shot still more inadequate as an index of male pleasure. Authors can resort only to metaphorical representations, like Moore/Gibbons's wry depiction of the Owlship "ejaculating" fire in* Watchmen *(interestingly, the Owlship itself is also a combination of the natural and the cultural/mechanical), or the narrator's frenzied reinscription of desire onto a phallicized natural world in "Act of Faith." For my money, these perverse "Money Shots" convey the tragicomic idiosyncrasy of male orgasm far better than most porn films.*

Right: from Watchmen #7 *by Alan Moore & Dave Gibbons.*
© 1986/87 DC Comics.

conjugal communion equal parts psychedelic, mystical and sexy. Note how its "bio-erotic" language echoes Lingis/Grosz's:

Above: from Swamp Thing #34 by Alan Moore, Steve Bissette & John Totleben.
© 1984 DC Comics.

The bark encrusts my flanks. The moss climbs my spine to embrace my shoulders ... We ... are ... one creature ... and all ... that there *is* ... is in *us* ... ... there is no contradiction ... only the pulse. The pulse within the world. Within us. Within me. It throbs. It breathes. In the world, in its fibers ... The pulse quickens, strands tighten, draw taut, a clenched glove in my stomach ...Underground, buried claws wound the soil ... Savage furrows fill with moisture ... A fish twists ... the bubbles rise ... the world pulses ... and shudders ... with life ... and death ... with tide ... and magma ... With me. With him. ... (200-203)

In both these passages, orgasm and the sex act itself are about unity, erasing divisions between individuals. So too in "Act of Faith" the false male-female-animal trichotomy dissolves as outlined above, through an intricate blending of the visual, textual, bestial, cultural, and sexual, and finally orgasmic, through a narrator who "sees" through the eyes of a ray.

In a world still overly wedded to gender norms, and where elaborate mechanisms maintain strict divisions between the human and the animal, nature and culture, in such a world to advance the idea that we are all of a flesh, that we can love polymorphously, and that such commingling bears its own stark beauty as well as vertiginous danger – danger as if falling from a great height – that does indeed amount to a transgressive, death-defying act of faith.

• **Jose Alaniz**

Works cited and consulted:

Ashworth, William. The Left Hand of Eden, Oregon State University Press, 1999.
Bataille, Georges. The Tears of Eros [1961], trans. Peter Connor, San Francisco: City Lights Books, 1989.
——————————. Erotism: Death & Sensuality [1957], trans. Mary Dalwood, San Francisco: City Lights Books, 1986.
Burt, Jonathan. Animals in Film, London: Reaktion Books, 2002.
Cronon, William. "The Trouble with Wilderness, or, Getting Back to the Wrong Nature" in Uncommon Ground, ed. Cronon, New York: Norton & Company, 1995, pgs. 471-499.
Dekkers, Midas. Dearest Pet: On Bestiality, trans. Paul Vincent, New York: W.W. Norton, 1994.
Foucault, Michel. The History of Sexuality: An Introduction, Volume I, New York: Vintage, 1978.
Freud, Sigmund. "The Case of the Wolfman: From the History of an Infantile Neurosis" [1915] in The Wolf-Man By the Wolf-Man, ed. Muriel Gardiner, New York: The Noonday Press, 1991, pgs. 153-262.
Golding, William. The Lord of the Flies, New York: Perigee, 1954.
Grosz, Elizabeth. "Animal Sex: Libido as Desire and Death" in Sexy Bodies: The Strange Carnalities of Feminism, ed. Grosz and E. Probyn, New York: Routledge, 1995, pp. 278-300, accessible at <http://www.hsph.harvard.edu/rt21/concepts/GROSZ.htm>.
Moore, Alan & Bissette, Stephen & Zulli, Michael. "Act of Faith" in the Puma Blues, vol. 1, no. 20, 1988, pgs. 44-47.
Moore, Alan & Bissette & Totleben, "Rite of Spring" in Swamp Thing: Love & Death, , New York: DC Comics, 1985, pgs. 185-206 [reprint of Swamp Thing, vol. 2, no. 34, 1984].
Murphy, Stephen & Zulli, Michael. the Puma Blues, Book One: Watch that Man, Haydenville, MA: Mirage Studios, 1988.
Williams, Linda. Hardcore: Power, Pleasure and the Frenzy of the Visible, Berkeley: University of California Press, 1989.
Windybank, Susan. Wild Sex: Way Beyond the Birds and the Bees, New York: St. Martin's Press, 1991.
Woolf, Virginia. "The Death of the Moth" [1942] in The Norton Book of Nature Writing, ed. Robert Finch & John Elder, New York: Norton, 1990, pgs. 374-77.
< http://www.behindthename.com/>
<http://www.womeninworldhistory.com/heroine2.html>

RICK VEITCH

Right: Rick Veitch has written and drawn many comics over the past 20 years, including **Teenage Mutant Hero Turtles and Swamp Thing**, as well as creating his own comic book series like **Rare Bit Fiends**, which was featured in Life magazine. He's currently drawing **Greyshirt** for Alan Moore's Tomorrow Stories. Strip ©2003 Rick Veitch.

RARE BIT FIENDS

Rick Veitch

· DREAM 1997 · COMICS 2003 ·

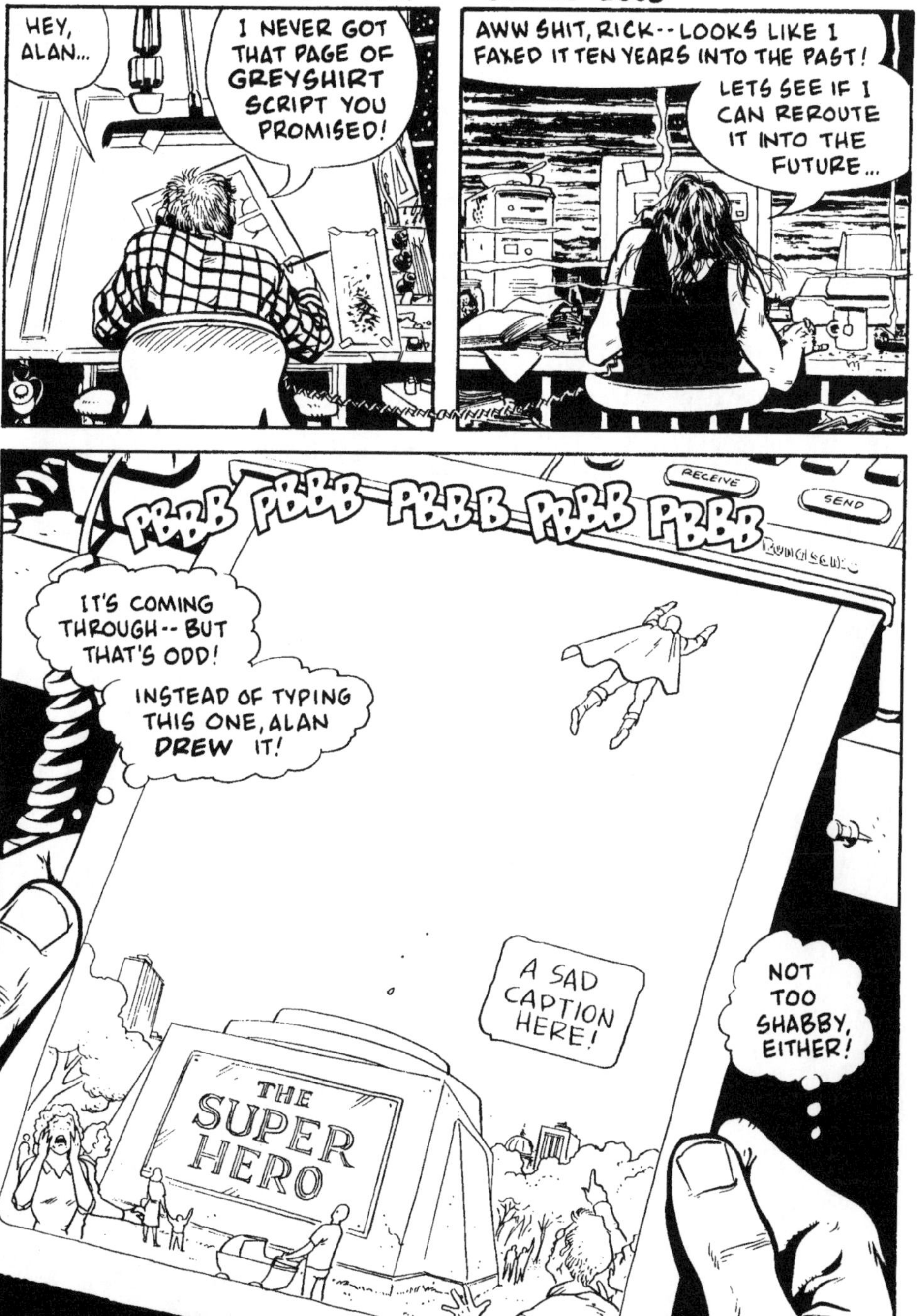

HEY, ALAN...
I NEVER GOT THAT PAGE OF GREYSHIRT SCRIPT YOU PROMISED!
AWW SHIT, RICK-- LOOKS LIKE I FAXED IT TEN YEARS INTO THE PAST!
LETS SEE IF I CAN REROUTE IT INTO THE FUTURE...
RECEIVE
SEND
PBBB PBBB PBBB PBBB PBBB
IT'S COMING THROUGH-- BUT THAT'S ODD!
INSTEAD OF TYPING THIS ONE, ALAN DREW IT!
A SAD CAPTION HERE!
THE SUPER HERO
NOT TOO SHABBY, EITHER!

ALAN HAS RED HAIR

Alan has red hair, red skin, red eyes.
He has tiny constellations on his face and
gods in his arms.
He has heroes on his fingertips and
flocks of dragons in his chest.
Alan has dark avengers on his lips and
jungles on his skin.
He has murderers under his fingernails.
He has an Aleph in his skull.
Alan has a garden where he rests.
Green leaves fall from the trees,
covering him, like ideas, like sunspots.
Alan has a little room in Northampton,
like a Babylonian library.
Alan sows storms.
Alan conceives worlds,
conceives universes in one day, in an instant.
Alan has red hair, red skin, red eyes.

ALABARCEZ MENDONÇA

*Alabarcez Mendonça was born In Godoy, Argentina in 1974. He has worked as art assistant to Leo Fernandez, Marcelo Frusin and currently Eduardo Risso. Sucking their brains out, more likely.
Poem ©2003 Alabarcez Mendonça.*

EDUARDO RISSO

Right: *Risso made his name as a comics illustrator in Italian magazines like* **Eroticon, Satiricon** *and* **Puertitas.** *In 1997 he drew* **Alien: Ressurection** *for American publisher Dark Horse but is probably best known for his art on DC/Vertigo's award-winning series* **100 Bullets.**
Illustration ©2003 Eduardo Risso.

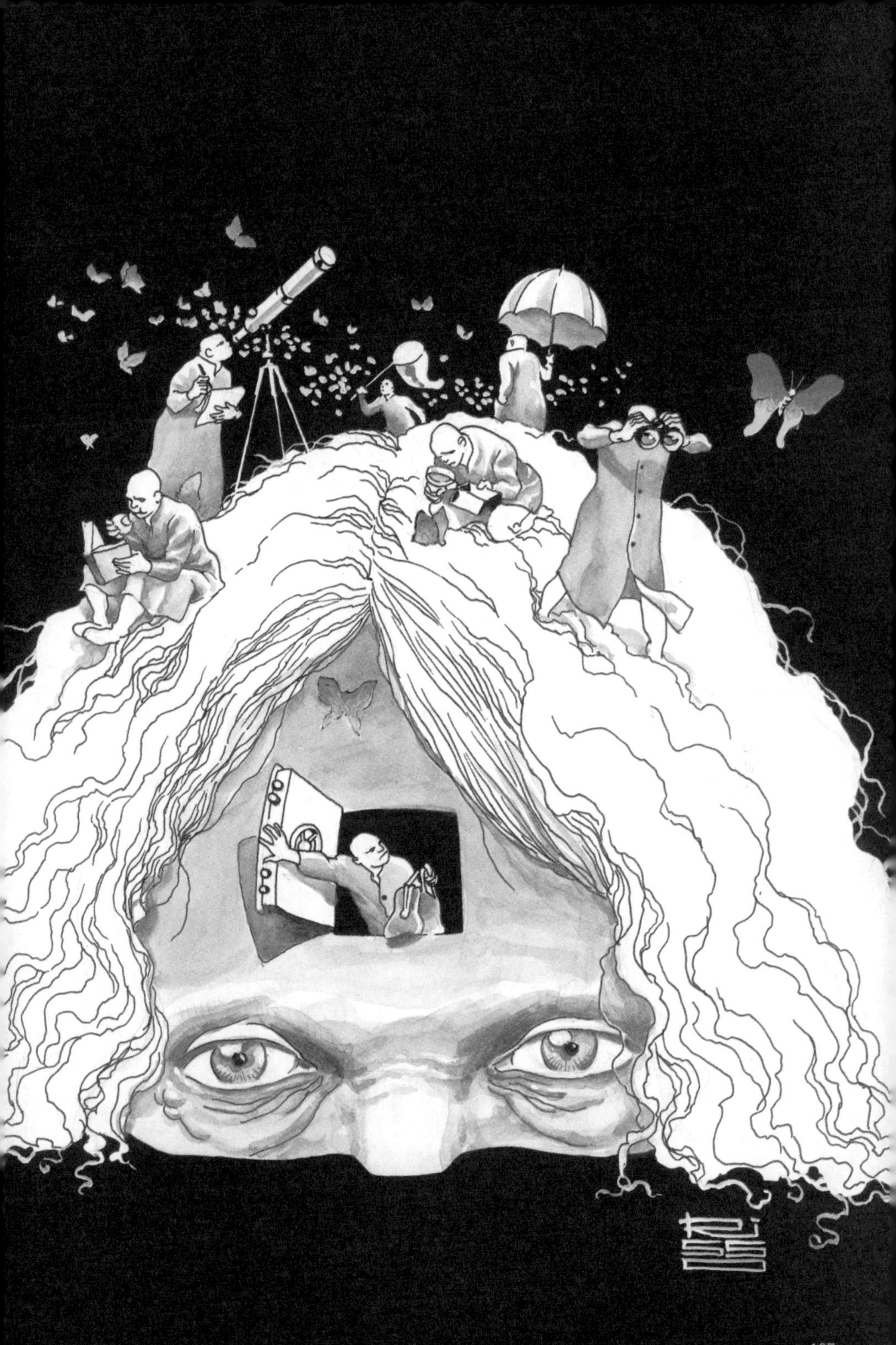

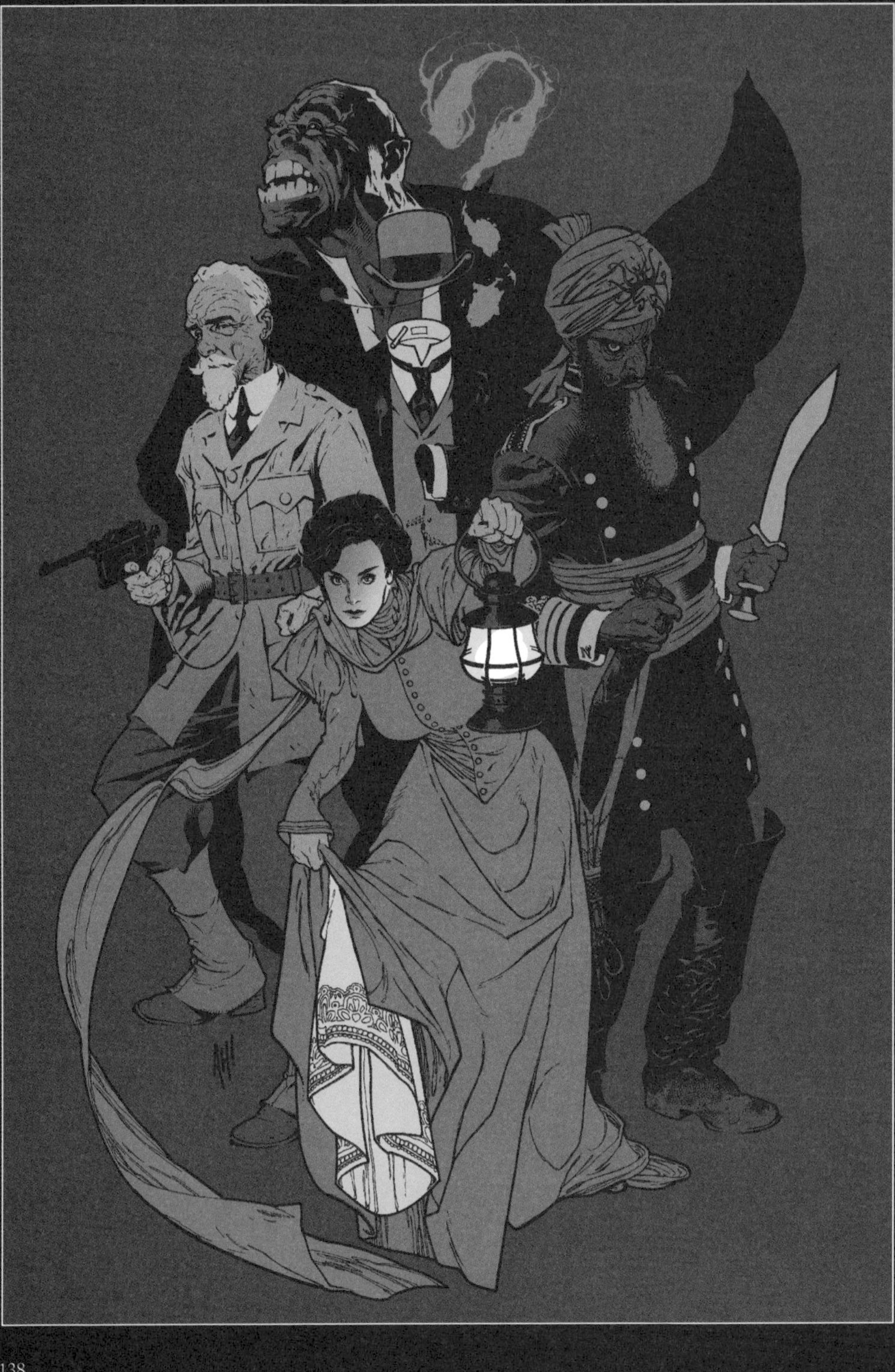

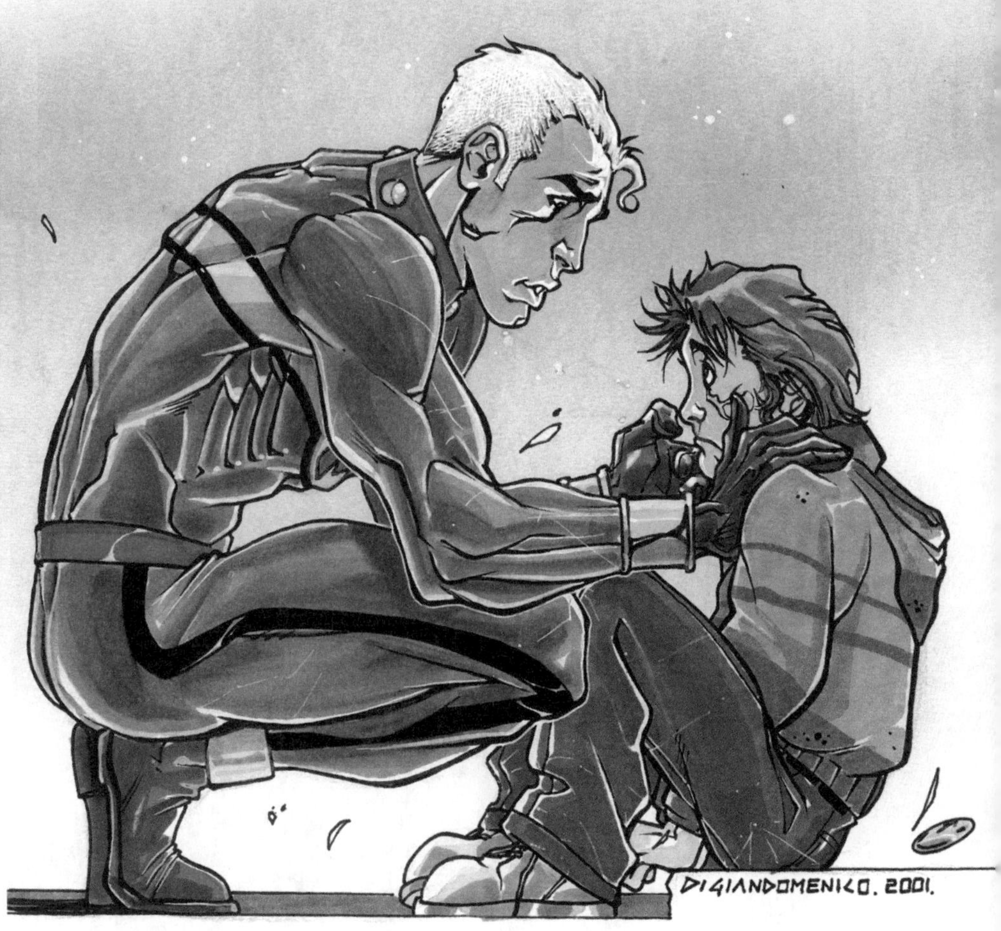
DI GIANDOMENICO. 2001.

ADAM HUGHES

Left: *Adam Hughes started his meteoric rise in the comics industry on titles such as* **Justice League, Legionnaires, Star Trek, Ghost** *and* **Gen 13** *and is now in great demand for his classy cover art, currently on DC's* **Wonder Woman.**

ASHLEY WOOD

Pages 140-141 following: *Award winning Australian illustrator and comic book artist Ashley Wood has worked for Dreamworks, Warner Bros., Random House, Todd MacFarlane Productions and Marvel Comics. His most recent comics works are IDW Publishing's* **Popbot** *and Wildstorm/DC's* **Automatic Kafka.** *www.ashleywood.com*

CARMINE DI GIANDOMENICO

Above: *Carmine di Giandomenico is the artist of the Italian steam-punk miniseries* **Le avventure di Giulio Maraviglia** *and the dystopian graphic-novel* **La Dottrina.** *He also drew storyboards for Tsui Hark's* **Double Team** *and Martin Scorsese's* **Gangs of New York.**

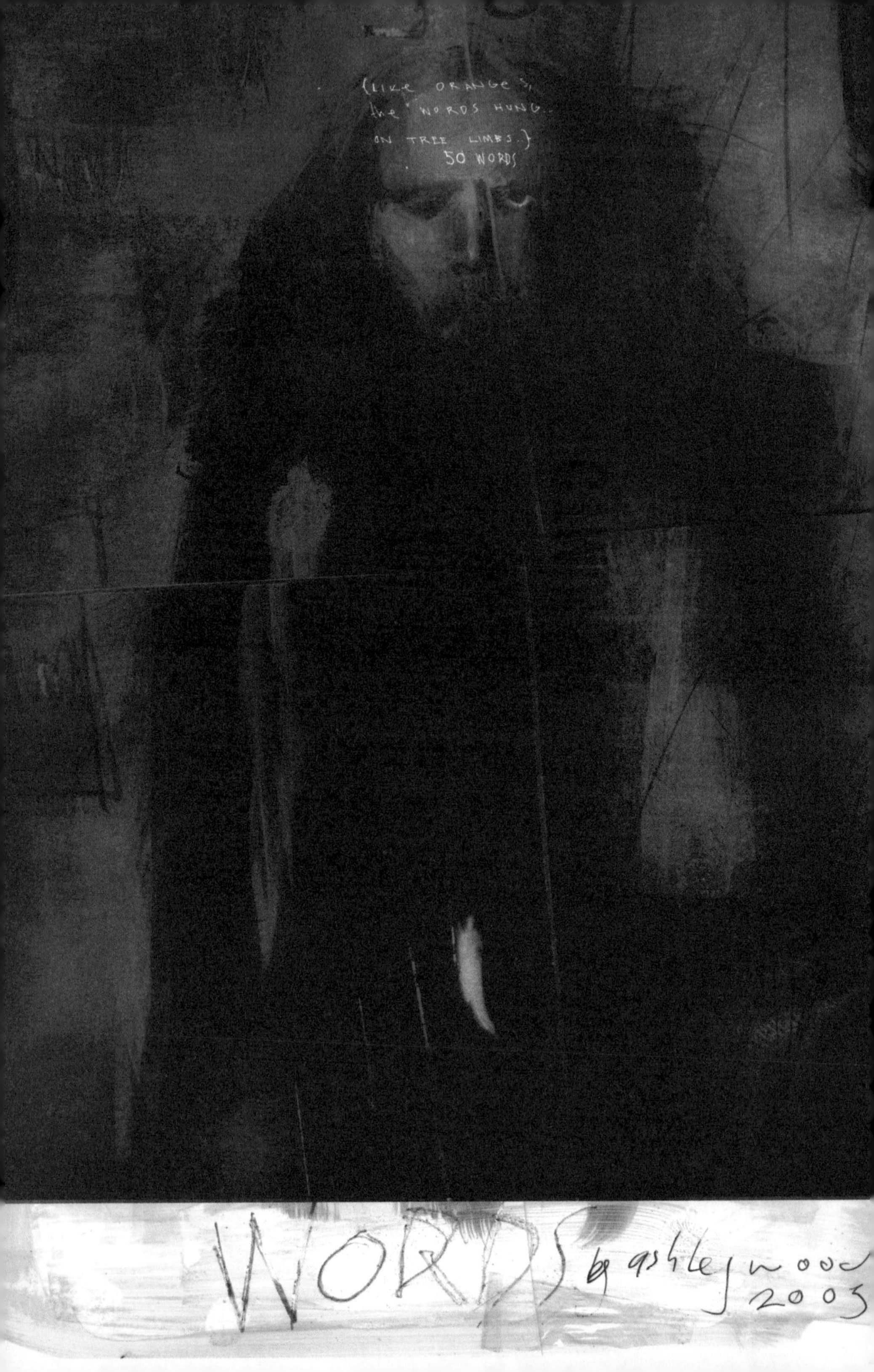
{LIKE ORANGES, the WORDS HUNG.. ON TREE LIMBS..}
50 WORDS
WORDS by ashley wood 2005

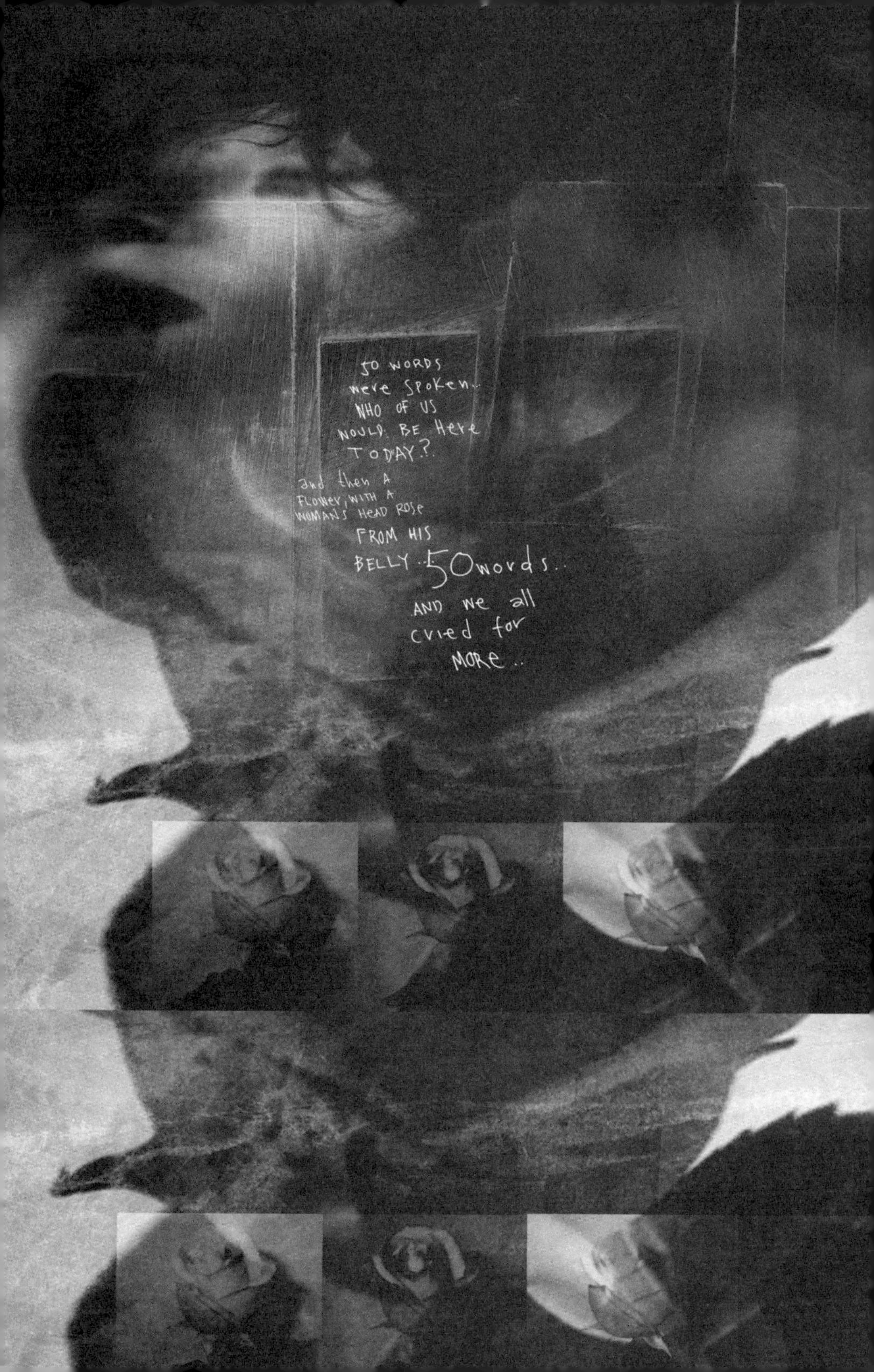
50 WORDS
were spoken..
WHO OF US
WOULD BE Here
TODAY?
and then A
FLOWER, WITH A
WOMAN'S HEAD ROSE
FROM HIS
BELLY .. 50words..
AND we all
cried for
MORE..

ANDY SMITH

Above: *Andy Smith has been a comic artist for over a decade and has worked for all the major publishers. He is currently pencilling* **The First** *for Cross Gen and has a new book out titled* **Drawing Dynamic Comics.**
Illustration ©2003 Andy Smith
Tom Strong ©2003 America's Best Comics. LLC.

AL DAVIDSON

Right: *Al Davison, currently lives in Peckham, London, with his wife Maggie. He is currently working on a second volume of his autobiography* **Spiral Cage.** *Volume 1 is about to be re-published by Active Images*
Illustration ©2003 Al Davidson

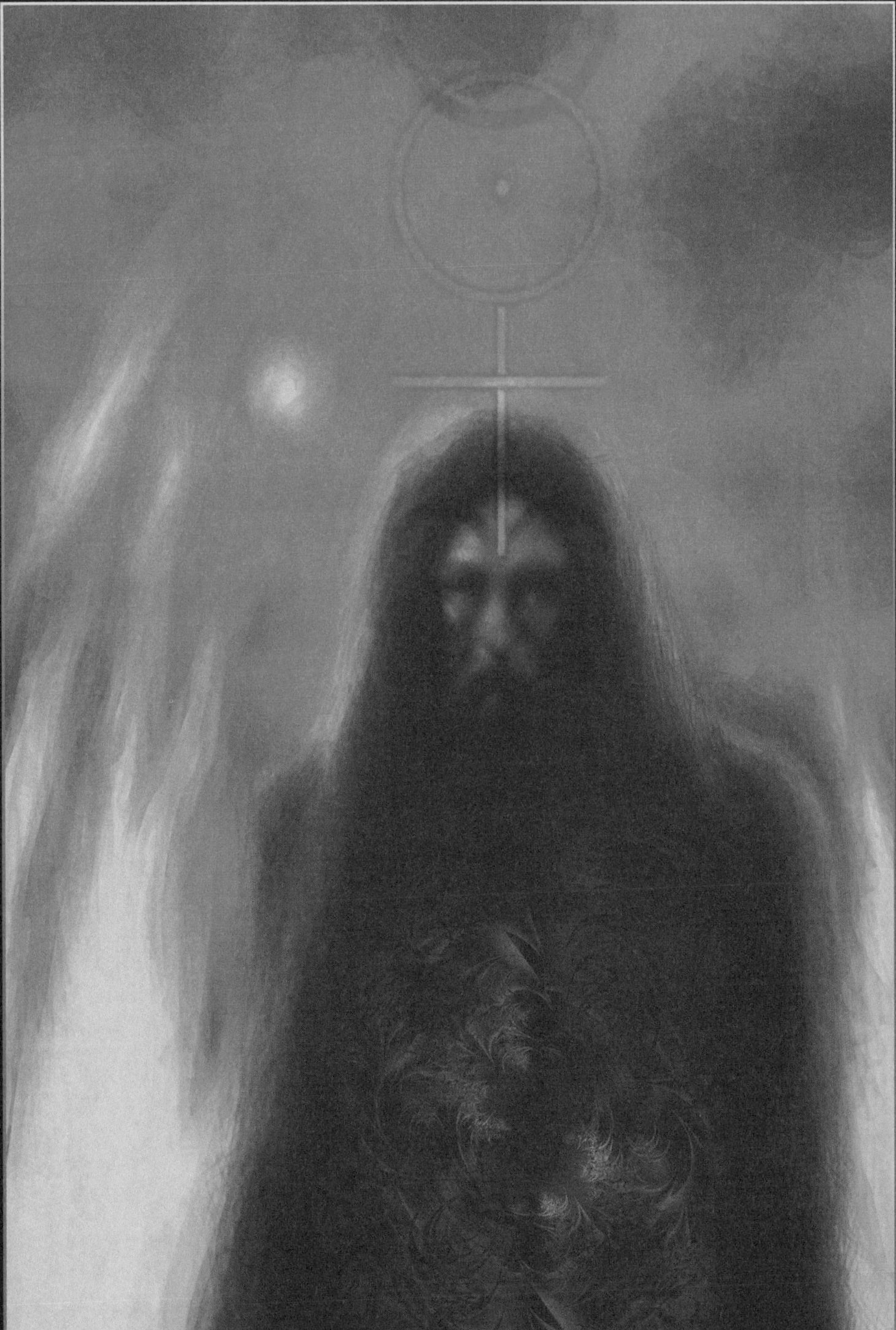
'Voice of the Fire'
Al Davison

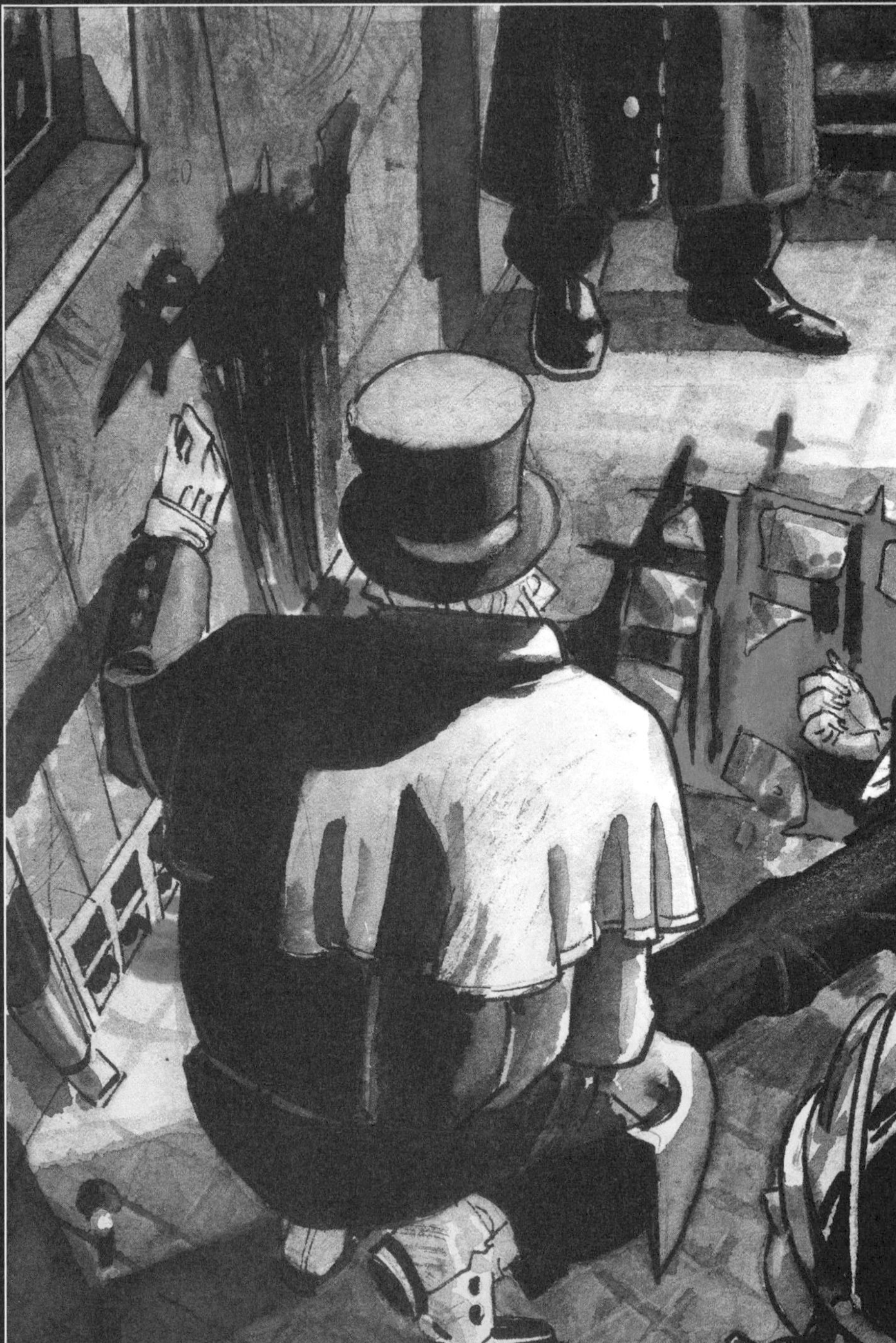

INTO HER DEAD BODY:
Moore & Campbell's From Hell

JOSÉ ALANIZ

José Alaniz, Ph.D. in Comparative Literature from the University of California - Berkeley, writes on Russian comics, disabilty in superhero comics and Alan Moore. His work has appeared in the International Journal of Comic Art. In fall, 2003, he will begin teaching in the Department of Slavic Languages & Literatures at the University of Washington-Seattle. Text ©2003 José Alaniz.

The value attached to the narrative in the representations of real events arises out of a desire to have real events display the coherence, integrity, fullness, and closure of an image of life that is and can only be imaginary.
– Hayden White, "The Value of Narrativity in the Representation of Reality"

In all our efforts to describe the past, to list the simple facts of history, we are involved in fiction.
– Alan Moore, Introduction to *From Hell: The Compleat Scripts, Vol. 1*

The historical record states that in the fall of 1888, in the Whitechapel slums of East London, within the space of a few weeks, at least five prostitutes fell victim to a sadistic murderer or murderers – never apprehended – that we have come to know as Jack the Ripper.

With no motive for the atrocities ever definitively proven, the panic-stricken city found no shortage of speculation as to the killer's identity: a mad butcher, a syphilitic surgeon, an evil Jew, the Masons, the Queen's own agents. The sensationalistic press (including of course the lurid, proto-comic penny dreadful) proffered its own conjectures; as the cultural historian Judith R. Walkowitz and others have noted, the JTR case proved the precursor to the modern-day media circus. Meanwhile, the "facts" spoke for themselves. The London *Times* reported on the fifth and final (?) victim, Marie Kelly (killed and mutilated in her home at 13 Miller's Court on November 9) through a veritable catalog of atrocity:

The poor woman lay on her back on the bed, entirely naked. Her throat was cut from ear to ear, right down to the spinal column. The ears and nose had been cut clean off. The breasts had also been cleanly cut off and placed on a table which was by the side of the bed. The stomach and abdomen had been ripped open, while the face was slashed about, so that the features of the poor creature were beyond all recognition. The kidneys and heart had also been removed from the body, and placed on the table by the side of the breasts. The liver had likewise been removed, and laid on the right thigh. The lower portion of the body and the uterus had been cut out, and these appeared to be missing. The thighs had been cut. A more horrible or sickening sight could not be imagined.[1]

These details, albeit "factual" (journalistic), cannot help us to truly understand the ordeal of Marie Kelly, an indigent whore, probably about 25 years old, born to a poverty and misery themselves unimaginable. At least through the penny dreadful, which fed such lurid details to a sensation-starved public, we get some sense of understanding; narrative, fictional convention, black hats and evil hearts, make an unspeakable tragedy like Marie Kelly's at least consumable – and for many, titillating. Alan Moore & Eddie Campbell's *From Hell,* a self-described "melodrama in 16 parts," also and self-consciously provides such narrative coherence, such titillation. Through meticulous attention to/manipulation of historical detail and the look of the period – derived from photographs and Victorian-era engravings – *From Hell* bestows JTR with a motive (Masonic intrigue at the service of a royal cover-up), an identity (the misogynist, cult-obsessed Queen's Surgeon Sir William Withey Gull) and, most crucially, narrative closure.

Chapter 10, "The Best of All Tailors," speculates extensively on the climactic Kelley murder and dismemberment; as the most stomach-turning and, for many, unreadable portion of the novel, it seems to challenge most effectively the idea of historiography's mission to make palatable and coherent the most chaotic, unknowable, private events. Ultimately I will argue that it does indeed successfully challenge that notion, but not through a gross, gory splatterfest calculated to revolt the faint of heart. On the contrary, Moore & Campbell seek to lure the reader literally into "the still-warm corpse of history itself," as Moore puts it, enacting in parodic, literalistic microcosm

Notes:

1. Quoted in, among numerous other sources, <http://www.historybuff.com/library/refLT111088.html>.

EMILIANO MAMMUCARI

Left: *Mammucari is the young artist of Italian small press successes* ll Dono Nero *and* Povero Pinocchi *(Montego). He is on the staff of the upcoming series* John Doe*(Eura Editorial). Illustration ©2003 Emiliano Mammucari.*
From Hell *© 2002 Alan Moore/Eddie Campbell.*

the greater critical project of the novel. In so doing, they "dissect" and interrogate the ways all of us (as subjects "in" history) imagine the past.

Left: from From Hell, Chapter 10. ©2003 Alan Moore & Eddie Campbell

The chapter's opening is classically penny dreadful, set in near-pitch blackness, with our killer in a black top hat, brandishing a blade before the frightened damsel. Pure icon: faces obscured, indistinct, dialogue restricted to the merest convention ("oh no Murder! Help!"), the seven-panel progression almost reminiscent of silent film imagery. "Jack" emerges from darkness to wreak his evil.

But that recognizable image of JTR (what we might call the literary-historical figure) disappears by the third page; murder committed, "Jack" disrobes and the lights come on, revealing the aged, portly Dr. Gull.

The repetitive, static, mostly nine-panel layouts over the next several pages evoke *both* the matter-of-fact progression of Kelly's bodily demolition as well as a sense of historical suspension, emphasizing the (mad) universality and timelessness of Gull's sacrificial psycho-drama. The panels' flat replication of compositional elements underscores the plot, in which Gull imagines himself in contact with the mythological creation story of the Enuma Elish. In that ancient story, the storm god Marduk slays the primeval dragon Tiamat, a symbol of primordial chaos, in order to remold her various parts into the world, much as Gull is dismantling Kelly's corpse in a ritual that will "save [her] from time" and make the two of them "inextricable within eternity."

Even when Gull's mystical reveries transport him to a late 20th-century office full of computers, ball-point pens and women who "all but show their sexes," the small-panel layouts, minimal variation of shot angles and repeated compositions retain the sense of timelessness and ahistoricity in Gull's sacrificial rite. The comics medium's unique *modus operandi* of storytelling through pictorial juxtaposition makes this sense of "timelessness" possible; we read comics panel by panel, but our eye also takes in the entirety of each page's layout all at once. Every panel thus "happens" simultaneously[2]; we have a concurrent sense of the particular and the general in comics which Moore/Campbell enhance in their compositions to foreground the "mythic" aspects of their story.

Yet Gull's mythopoeic rite has its hiccups. On page 11, panel four, as in other moments throughout the chapter[3], Gull is jolted out of his reverie, and turns to face the

Chapter
Ten
The Best
of
All Tailors
Hello?

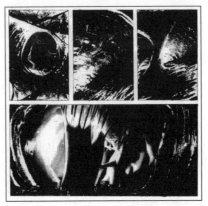

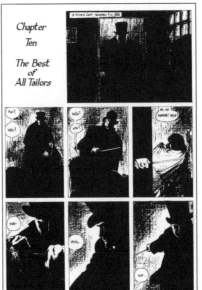

2. Scott McCloud elucidates this "simultaneity" most incisively in Understanding Comics, *pg. 104.*

3. Page 13, panel 7; page 15, panel 4; page 23, panel 4. I especially want to emphasize the "staginess" of these panels; it seems as if at these points of rupture Gull grows cognizant of an audience watching him. The room takes on the features of a dramatic set. In terms set forth by the art historian Michael Fried, Gull in these moments of "staring back," Gull swings from a mode of "absorption" to one of "theatricality."

Left: from From Hell, Chapter 10. ©2003 Alan Moore & Eddie Campbell

Right: from From Hell, Chapter 10. ©2003 Alan Moore & Eddie Campbell

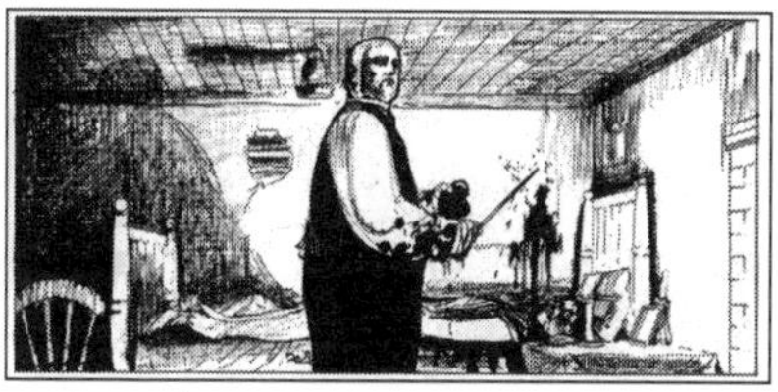

reader. The "altar" upon which he enacts his timeless, mythical psychodrama degenerates into a merely squalid room where a man has killed and dismembered a woman. There's an almost palpable sense of embarrassment, exposure, bathos. But Gull doesn't get the worst of it. The reader, the voyeuristic spectator consuming this atrocity, also stands exposed, revealed as co-conspirator, indeed as manufacturer of JTR's alleged "immortality." For who creates it and perpetuates it with ever-eager relish if not we ourselves, through reading? Might our undying, eye-driven fascination with JTR indeed betray a fetishization of an immortality we more anonymous selves will never achieve?[4]

Elsewhere, Moore has formulated this idea of immortality in terms of his pseudo-Platonic "Idea Space" concept:

> We cannot establish a real material, physical identity for the being we call JTR ... JTR, in a very real sense, never actually had a physical existence. He was a collage creature, made from crank letters, hoaxes and sensational headlines. He exists wholly in Idea Space, looking forward from our books of theory and our fictions, from our slasher films and our contemporary mythology of serial murder, from the pages and appendices of *From Hell.* He is unencumbered by a physical body or human identity. He has transcended human reality to become, like it or not, one of our *immortals.*
>
> In a sense, it might also be said that in choosing his victims, he elected them to the same extra-human estate that he himself was destined for. Five anonymous Whitechapel women now live in the realm of legend forever, are translated from weak and ailing flesh into symbols, martyrs, saints of a kind. ... If the realm of concept and consciousness is, as I believe it to be, truly the realm of the sacred, then in the crucible of the Whitechapel murders, both killer and victims were in a sense "made holy."[5] (emphasis added)

The amoral notion of a vicious killer or killers called JTR amounting to nothing more than some Baudrillardian simulacrum, bereft of any physical existence beyond that provided by an economy of signs ("Idea Space"), invites a critique of Moore's tidy formulation, if for no other reason than that JTR was real enough to the five women he/they eviscerated, strangled and killed.

Elizabeth Bronfen grapples with a similar conundrum of representation ("real" vs. simulacrum) in her seminal study *Over Her Dead Body: Death, Femininity & the Aesthetic.* If figures such as JTR and his victims have been inducted into a timeless "immortality," enabling us as readers and viewers access to their ghostly "lives," then critics such as Bronfen wrench us back to considerations of the price at which such "immortality" and "access" is purchased.

In her discussion of Swiss artist Ferdinand Hodler's 1914/15 sketches of his dying mistress Valentine God¾-Darel, Bronfen advances something more than their oft-commented poignancy and stoic frankness. She asks:

> What do we see when we see these images? Does God¾-Darel become visible? Is her experience of dying transmitted? The paradox is the following. In order to be "sharable," her experience of the death process has to be translated beyond the boundaries of her real body – the private into the public world of signs – but this act of figuration or representation forecloses the real. The "unsharability" of pain results from its resistance to language. Transforming the real body experience of death into an objectified form mitigates the violence posed by the real.(46)[6]

Bronfen argues that these drawings occlude the very real dying of its subject, citing reviews that praise Hodler's work as an allegory of the artist's courageous confrontation with death. God¾-Darel herself suffers an erasure – not unlike that of the "real" Marie Kelly – precisely by being turned into a symbol meant for someone

4. In the From Hell *epilogue, "Dance of the Gull Catchers," and in one of his most fascinating short pieces of the 1990s, "I Keep Coming Back," Moore (and his collaborator on the latter Oscar Zarate) comments on the "necrotourism" industry that has emerged in the areas of Whitechapel associated with the murders. Intriguingly, the story is told in a "first-person" view that emphasizes the visual consumability of tragic events, even remote ones.*

5. See the Sim/Moore correspondence elsewhere in this volume

6. Elsewhere she asks: "Does articulating death always mean turning it into a meaningful event, into a narrative moment? How is the meaning of the represented death process as a sequence of events contingent on the discursive position of its spectators?" (40) Hodler produced more than 70 of these sketches, capturing his subject's physical deterioration over time. The continuity and unity of the subject matter in these pieces, Bronfen remarks, invites us to read them as a narrative sequence.

else's purposes. Bronfen calls this process a "violence of representation" that severs the (feminine) body from its actual materiality and historical context (44).

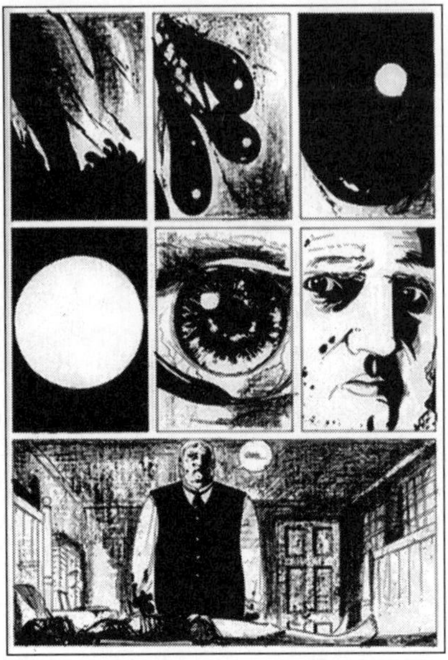

Left: from From Hell, Chapter 10. ©2003 Alan Moore & Eddie Campbell

Similarly, and for much higher political stakes, Diana Taylor agonizes over the physical fate of *los desaparecidos,* those who vanished during Argentina's Dirty War military crackdown of the 1970s/80s. In *Disappearing Acts* she writes:

... the *desaparecidos* are, by definition, always already the object of representation. The flesh and blood victims, forcefully absented from the sociopolitical crisis that created them, left no bodies. Those disappeared. The victims reemerged as icons, either as "subversives" (for the military government) or as the "disappeared" (for the Madres and other human rights activists) – powerful, conflicting images that reintroduced the missing into the public sphere as pure representation. Somewhere behind the images, and simultaneously occluded and eliminated by them, one imagines the "real bodies" ... the reality of their ordeal becomes unreal to us through the very process of trying to illuminate them. (140)[7]

I bring up the plight of Valentine God¾-Darel and *los desaparecidos,* of course, to directly relate it to the victims of JTR. Bronfen and Taylor's readings remind us that Gull/"Jack's" removal of Marie Kelly's face by violence serves not only to erase her own identity, but also to impose another, that of paradigmatic victim; the cutting knife acts also as a brush with which to paint on a new face *(FH,* Chapter 10, pgs. 4-5).

We also cannot ignore the fact that the violence of representation in *From Hell* (and the JTR case) is enacted specifically on feminine subjects, figures already made essentially powerless through circumstances of class, historical happenstance and sexual/gender repression. Moore & Campbell visually illustrate the dilemma of the feminine in 1888 London through the still-living Marie Kelly's half-dressed supine pose *(FH,* chapter 9, page 17, panel 1). The posture and composition directly quote the well-known Scotland Yard photograph of the ghastly, mutilated human remains found at 13 Miller's Court. The panel thus figures Kelly's doomed victimhood in a patriarchal system that can cast her only as object of desire (trope of "feminine mystery" subject to the male gaze) or as corporeal remains (trope of another mystery - death). In either case, she has no agency to shape her role as mere cipher of repulsion/fascination.

The chapter ends with Gull completing his masonic rite, dressing (visually taking on once more the black mantle of "Jack") and, after some reflection, disappearing into the London night. Icons of helpless whore victim and black-hatted killer set into their proper historical space, roles assigned, heirarchy established: history – that urgent imposition of narrative coherence we impose on the past – is secured. And yet.

"The Best of All Tailors," literally at its heart, undermines such an easy reading. Tellingly in light of Bronfen and Taylor's critiques of representation, it does so at the level of the material feminine body.

7. Taylor goes on:

The photos paraded by the Madres, for example, are powerful evocations of their loved ones that, arguably, inadvertently hide the very violence they aim to reveal. The smiling, forever youthful faces communicate an image of personal wholeness and integrity that elides the decomposed "real" bodies. The photos, like magic fetishes, keep the dead and brutalized forever "alive." They tempt us to see them as "natural," and transparent manifestations of the "real." Thus it seems treasonous to resist that view by insisting on the iconic quality of these photographs. (142)

This opposition of the marginalized "real" body vs. the privileged iconic body recalls a like treatment of corporeality in Moore & Gibbon's 1986 work, Watchmen *(the subject of another paper), as exemplified in Rorschach's death scene. Briefly, Jon Osterman/Dr. Manhattan (the timeless "icon") slays Rorschach (the time-trapped body), thereby enacting the superhero genre's "preference" for the clean, sleek, fascistic superhuman body over the fleshly, stinking, ugly, oozing, imperfect, human body of someone like Rorschach, the failed hero. To underscore the point, Rorschach leaves a bloody, organic puddle after his murder by the iconic, upright Osterman.*

All this underscores a similar process in From Hell, *whereby Gull introduces the "anonymous," wretched Marie Kelly into the realm of the "immortal" Idea Space.*

8. Gilman notes the Victorian-era physician's role in examining the post-suicide prostitute's corpse "was to examine and dissect the body condemned to death by its fall from grace. And that body becomes the object of study, the corpse to be opened." (265). Intriguingly, he cites an 1890 painting by the Spanish artist Enrique Simonet Lombardo, "And She had a Heart, too" (Y tenía corazón), which encapsulates the notion of the doctor as privileged "viewer" of the dead female body's interior. Standing over a dissected whore's cadaver, the aged physician holds the dead woman's heart in his hand, contemplating it – an eerie echo of Gull's handling of Kelly's heart, in a work painted a mere two years after the actual Kelly's demise. The reader may view the painting at <http://averroes.cec.junta-andalucia.es/~gabearte_malaga/ ba/imagenes/teniac.jpg>.

Michel Foucault and other historians tell us that since the rise of modern anatomical studies in the early Renaissance, to gaze into the human body is to conquer its truth, to own all the eye surveys, immediated. As Foucault writes in *The Birth of the Clinic*:

The gaze plunges into the space that it has given itself the task of traversing ... In anatomo-clinical experience, the medical eye must see the illness spread before it, horizontally and vertically in graded depth; as it penetrates into the body, as it advances into its bulk, as it circumvents or lifts its masses, as it descends into its depths.(136)

The medical gaze subsumes all it surveys into its store of knowledge. This is certainly what Gull, through his positivist colonizing eye, expects during his dissection of Kelly's corpse. To see into woman, to open her up and decipher her, is to conquer – to put the finalizing stamp on her for eternity, as Moore describes and Bronfen/Taylor lament.

But once more, a hiccup.

As Gull cuts, we accompany him, through a series of mysterious panels, into her dead body, into the "warm corpse of history itself," and find ... an inscrutable bioscape: eye repulsed, benumbed, at sea. Medical gaze cast adrift (pages 12-13). The ray of vision bounces back; narrative coherence (historiography's mission) falls apart; the indecipherability of these biomorphic images form a wall – the body itself. The unfinalizable corpus, ultimate agent of the "real" – that unassimilable something which stands outside the symbolic order and which reasserts itself with the inevitability of death – is finally immune to our conquering gaze. At the heart of "history's corpse," we find darkness, illegible shapes.[8]

For all its meticulously researched period detail, its baroque conspiracies and intricate allegorical dissection of an era, *From Hell* is finally a novel about our incapacity to know, the limits of any epistemology. Gazing into her dead body, into the twin mysteries of death and the past, we, like Gull, helplessly see only our own reflection.

• **José Alaniz**

Works cited and consulted:

Bronfen, Elizabeth. Over Her Dead Body: Death, Femininity & the Aesthetic, New York: Routledge, 1992.

Foucault, Michel. The Birth of the Clinic, New York: Vintage, 1994.

Fried, Michael. Absorption and Theatricality: Painting and the Beholder in the Age of Diderot, University of Chicago Press, 1988.

Gilman, Sander. "'Who Kills Whores?' 'I Do,' Says Jack: Race and Gender in Victorian London" in Death & Representation, ed. by Elizabeth Bronfen & Sarah Goodwin, Baltimore: Johns Hopkins Press, 1993, pgs. 263-284.

Laqueur, Thomas. Making Sex: Body and Gender from the Greeks to Freud, Harvard University Press, 1990.

McCloud, Scott. Understanding Comics, Northhampton: Kitchen Sink Press, 1993.

Moore, Alan & Campbell, Eddie. From Hell (Collected Edition), Paddington: Eddie Campbell Comics, 1999.

Moore, Alan & Zarate, Oscar. "I Keep Coming Back" in It's Dark in London, ed. Zarate, London: Serpent's Tail, 1996.

Moore, Alan. From Hell: The Compleat Scripts, Vol. 1, London: Borderlands Press, 1995.

Moore, Alan & Gibbons, Dave. Watchmen, New York: DC Comics, 1986.

Sinclair, Iain. "Jack the rip-off" in The Observer (UK), January 27, 2002, at <http://www.observer.co.uk/review/story/0,6903,639883,00.html>.

Taylor, Diana. Disappearing Acts: Spectacles of Gender and Nationalism in Argentina's "DirtyWar," Durham: Duke University Press, 1997.

Walkowitz, Judith R. City of Dreadful Delight: Narratives of Sexual Danger in Late-Victorian London, University of Chicago Press, 1992.

White, Hayden. "The Value of Narrativity in the Representation of Reality" in Critical Enquiry, vol. 7, no. 1, Autumn, 1980.

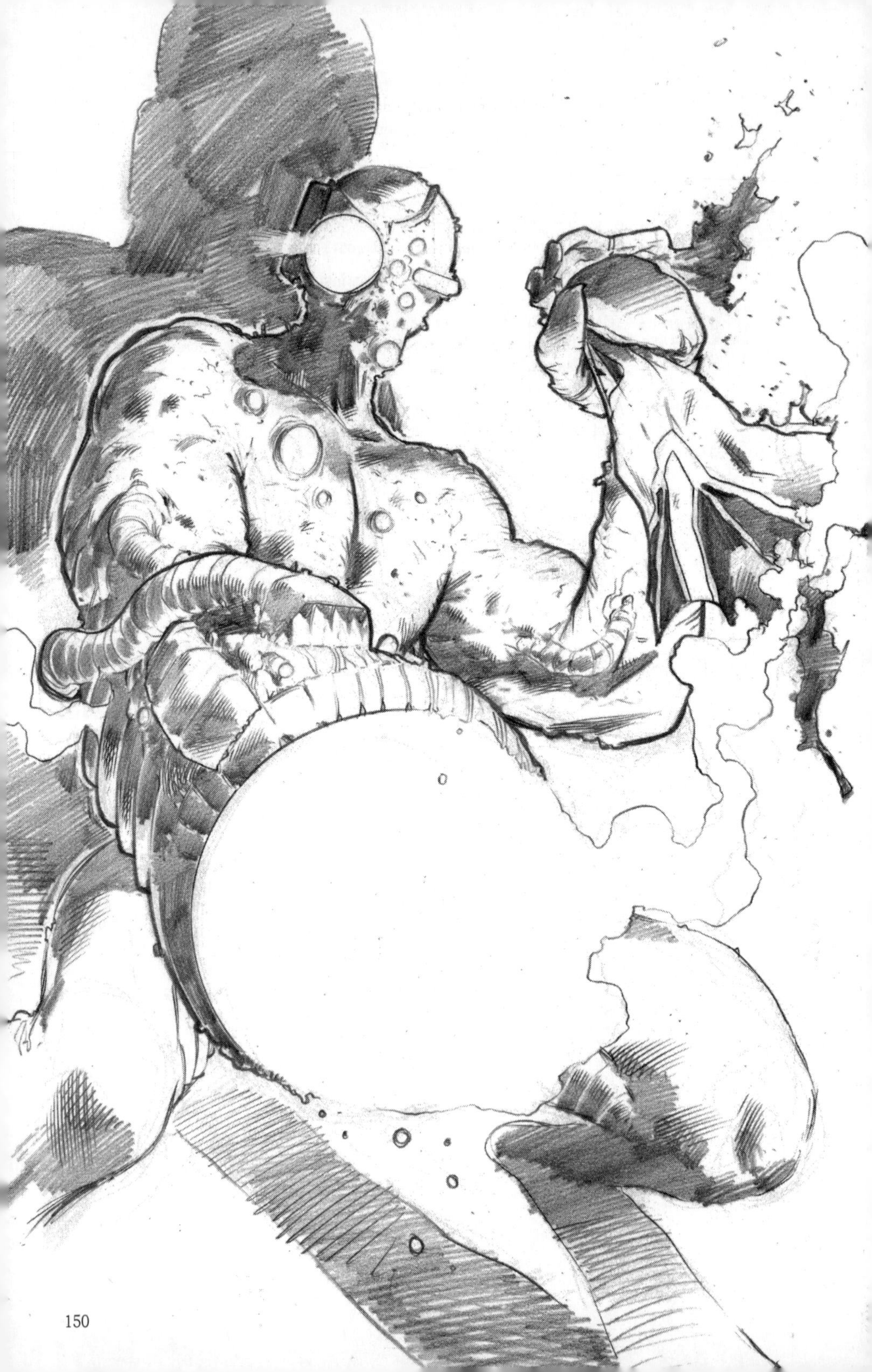

"Allow me to introduce you to The Fury...
It kills super-heroes."

ROB WILLIAMS

Rob Williams is the writer of the Com.X title Cla$$war.
Text ©2003 Rob Williams.

1983. I was 12-years-old. I liked comics. I liked bright, fun comics about super heroes who hit each other a lot. Justice League, Avengers, that type of thing. I liked Roy Of The Rovers, Whizzer And Chips and the Victor Book For Boys. I LIKED comics. Understand?

And then I got hold of a copy of Daredevils #1, and suddenly I loved comics.

Daredevils was a British black and white comic which, as well as reprinting classic Spider Man stories, also contained Frank Miller's Daredevil and Alan Moore and Alan Davis' Captain Britain.

Now, I wasn't sophisticated enough at the time to work out why these stories were better than anything else I had read up to that point – I just knew that they were. In the same way that I vaguely knew at the time that I had funny feelings about Erin Grey and her tight jump suits in Buck Rogers in the 25th Century.

I knew that I liked Alan Davis' artwork a lot. I also knew then that the Fury scared the life out of me. It still does.

Back to the future - 2003, where I'm 31, and women do not, sadly, all wear Erin Gray jump suits. Now I write comics, where I just used to just read them.

As a writer you're always looking for a character's high concept – to clarify for the readers what their motivations are. 20 years on, you can't get much more high concept than The Fury.

It kills super-heroes.

BATTON LASH

Pages 152-153 following:
*Batton Lash is the creator of **Wolff & Byrd, Counsellors of the Macabre,** published in the ongoing* **Supernatural Law** *comic book series. He is co-publisher, with his wife Jackie Estrada, of Exhibit A Press. www.exhibitapress.com Strip ©2003 Batton Lash.*

It is immensely strong, utterly ruthless, with the "logic of a computer. Intuition of a dog." It never stops. It keeps coming. "It runs like a retarded child" (Moore made us imagine how horribly it moves – how many comic writers do that?). It has a purity to it. It cares about nothing. Is distracted by nothing. It murders. It is the stuff of nightmares.

Reading the trade paperback of Captain Britain now The Fury still makes me feel like wetting myself with fear as poor Linda McQuillan did back then. It kills super-heroes? Yes. But it also made super-heroes better than they've ever been.

• Rob Williams

TREVOR HAIRSINE

Left: *Trevor Hairsine was one of the early contributors to Judge Dredd Megazine,. co-creating* **Harmony Krieg** *and illustrating many* **Judge Dredd** *stories and covers. He's also worked on such titles as* **Holocaust 12, Space Girls and Captain America.**
Illustration ©2003 Trevor Hairsine. The Fury and Captain Britain ©2003 Marvel Comics.

WHERE DOES HE GET HIS IDEAS?

by Bottom Cash '03

A BUNCH OF US *CARTOONISTS* LIKE TO GET TOGETHER ONCE A MONTH TO *TALK SHOP, GOSSIP,* AND GENERALLY *SHMOOZE* ABOUT *COMIC BOOKS* . . .

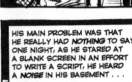

ONE NIGHT, *ALAN MOORE'S* NAME CAME UP, AND WE TALKED ABOUT HOW CLEVER AND INNOVATIVE HIS *IDEAS* ARE . . . AND WONDERED *WHERE* HE GETS THEM . . .

I *HAD* TO TELL THE GUYS A STORY I HEARD ABOUT ALAN MOORE . . . THAT HE'S INTO THE *OCCULT* AND GOES INTO THE *WOODS* TO *CONJURE UP* IDEAS . . .

OF COURSE, THE GUYS WERE *DOUBTFUL* . . . SO I TOLD THEM ABOUT A COMICS WRITER WHOM A FRIEND OF A FRIEND OF MINE KNOWS . . .

WELL, HE WAS A *WANNABE* COMICS WRITER. HE HAD A SALE HERE AND THERE, BUT MOSTLY HE *TALKED* A GOOD GAME . . . HE WAS LARGELY *UNMOTIVATED* . . .

HIS MAIN PROBLEM WAS THAT HE REALLY HAD *NOTHING* TO SAY. ONE NIGHT, AS HE STARED AT A BLANK SCREEN IN AN EFFORT TO WRITE A SCRIPT, HE HEARD A *NOISE* IN HIS BASEMENT . . .

HE WAS GOING TO *IGNORE* THE SOUND, BUT HIS *CURIOSITY* GOT THE BEST OF HIM. IN THE BASEMENT, HE NOTICED SOMETHING *COWERING* BEHIND SOME BOXES . . . IT SEEMED *WOUNDED* . . . MAYBE *LOST* . . .

AT FIRST, HE THOUGHT IT WAS A STRAY *CAT* . . . BUT AS HE TOOK A CLOSER LOOK, HE SAW THAT IT WAS *UNLIKE* ANYTHING HE'D EVER *IMAGINED* . . .

AND HE REALIZED THAT HE HAD COME UPON ONE OF ALAN MOORE'S *IDEAS* THAT HAD *LOST* ITS WAY!

CLICK

CAREFULLY, HE **GRABBED** THE WAYWARD IDEA AND TOOK IT AS HIS **OWN** . . .

HE PUT IT IN A **PET CARRIER** TO MAKE SURE IT WOULDN'T GET AWAY. HE COULDN'T BELIEVE WHAT HE HAD--ONE OF **ALAN MOORE'S** CONJURED IDEAS!

HE NOW HAD A **GOOD** IDEA-- EVEN THOUGH IT WAS ONE OF **ALAN MOORE'S**-- AND HE **KNEW** IT! THE TROUBLE WAS, HE LOOKED AT THE IDEA AS HIS **PET PROJECT**, AND HE WASN'T QUITE SURE WHAT TO **DO** WITH IT . . .

DURING THIS PERIOD, HE MANAGED TO WANGLE HIS WAY ONTO A "WRITER'S PANEL" AT A LOCAL COMIC BOOK CONVENTION. HE **BRAGGED** ABOUT HAVING A GREAT IDEA, BUT HE WAS PRETTY **VAGUE** ON WHAT **EXACTLY** THE IDEA WAS, AND HE GAVE NO **DETAILS** . . .

HE DIDN'T WANT TO TIP HIS HAND **TOO** MUCH ABOUT THE IDEA--HE WAS AFRAID HIS **PEERS** WOULD **STEAL** IT! CONFIDENT THAT HE HAD **LOCKED IN** A GREAT TALE, HE LET IT **SIT** WHILE HE CONCENTRATED ON **OTHER** MATTERS . . .

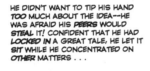

APTER WEEKS OF TAKING THE IDEA FOR **GRANTED**, HE WENT TO CHECK UP ON IT, AND MUCH TO HIS **HORROR**-- IT WAS GONE!

IT SEEMS THAT ALAN MOORE HAD BEEN ABLE TO GET HIS IDEA **BACK**. WHEN THE IDEA EVENTUALLY MANIFESTED ITSELF IN **PRINT**, THE PROCRASTINATING WRITER TOLD ANYONE WHO WOULD LISTEN THAT **HE'D** HAD THE IDEA **FIRST** . . . **BEFORE** ALAN MOORE . . .

BUT WHAT **COULD** HE HAVE DONE WITH THAT IDEA ANYWAY?

A LOT OF WRITERS STUMBLE ONTO **GREAT** IDEAS-- IT'S UP TO THE WRITER TO **MAKE** IT WORK!

OF COURSE--

WHAT MAKES MOORE'S IDEAS GREAT IS HOW HE **NURTURES** THEM WITH HIS **TALENT** . . . **FEEDS** THEM HIS **VIEWS** . . . GIVES THEM EVERYTHING HE'S **LEARNED** FROM HIS OWN **LIFE EXPERIENCE**

YEAH, BUT **STILL**--WHERE DOES HE GET THOSE IDEAS **FROM?**

I **TOLD** YOU-- IT'S HIS OWN SPECIAL **MAGIC** . . .

ITALIAN WITH ALAN

When I first met Alan Moore at Northampton train station back in 1998, I really wasn't sure what to expect. I had been editor of TRIPWIRE for six years and done a multitude of interviews but meeting the writer for the first time made me nervous. There was such a mystique and a legend attached to the man that the train journey up from London was a nerve-wracking experience.

Once we met at the station, we made our way up the hill to an Italian restaurant where Moore was greeted as if he was a regular there. So I'd be eating pizza with Alan Moore, which was a strange idea. As it happens, Moore didn't have pizza but pasta and then proceeded to order ice cream. We were in the restaurant for around three hours, filling two tapes very comfortably with the interview and I watched the restaurant go from lunchtime busy to afternoon lull. Once the interview finished, we made our way back from the restaurant to the train station, making a stop for me to take photos. We stopped at a churchyard near the station (the church's name escapes me) and on a windswept early autumn day in Northampton, I snapped a few shots of Moore, whose natural environment seems to be standing in a gothic Victorian setting. We parted company at the station and I went back to London.

Between 1998 and 2002, I interviewed Moore around five times (once for the shortlived Sci Fi World magazine and four for TRIPWIRE). We went back to the Italian place four of the five occasions, the last time I interviewed him, we did it at his house in Northampton, an address that even the local taxi driver was familiar with. On one of the occasions, we even went browsing together in Waterstones in Northampton, since I needed to track down a book for research for something I'm writing, and another time, we chatted about the TV programmes he enjoyed while wandering through the city centre, admitting a shared admiration for The Sopranos. I've even been into his local comic shop with him, which was one of the most surreal moments so far in my life. Each time I met him, I began to build up a picture of the man and although I can't admit to knowing him well, on the few times that I've met him, I've come to realise that Moore is one of comics' genuine characters: in person he comes across as sincere, likeable and very down to earth, which is ironic considering his public love of all things magical.

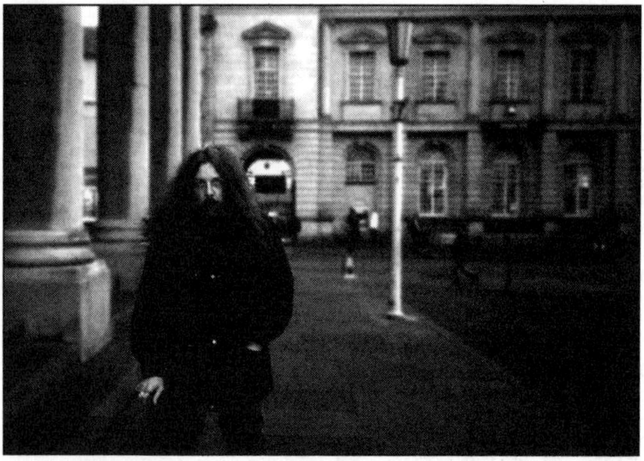

Above: *Photograph by Joel Meadows*

Moore has been one of the few ambassadors to the outside world, able to attract attention to this industry of ours in a positive and interesting way and we feel lucky that our good association with the man continues to this day.

• Joel Meadows

JOEL MEADOWS

Since 1992, Joel Meadows has been the editor of **Tripwire,** *The UK comic features magazine, interviewing top creators like Alan Moore, Frank Miller, Mike Mignola, Brian Bendis, Grant Morrison and more. His writing has also been published in* **The Guardian, The Independent on Sunday, SFX, Broadcast** *and* **Time Out.**
Text ©2003 Joel Meadows.

SEAN PHILLIPS

Right: *Sean Phillips has been drawing comics for over twenty years for everybody from DC Comics, Marvel and Dark Horse to Island Records and Twentieth Century Fox.*
Illustration ©2003 Sean Phillips.
John Constantine ©2003 DC Comics.

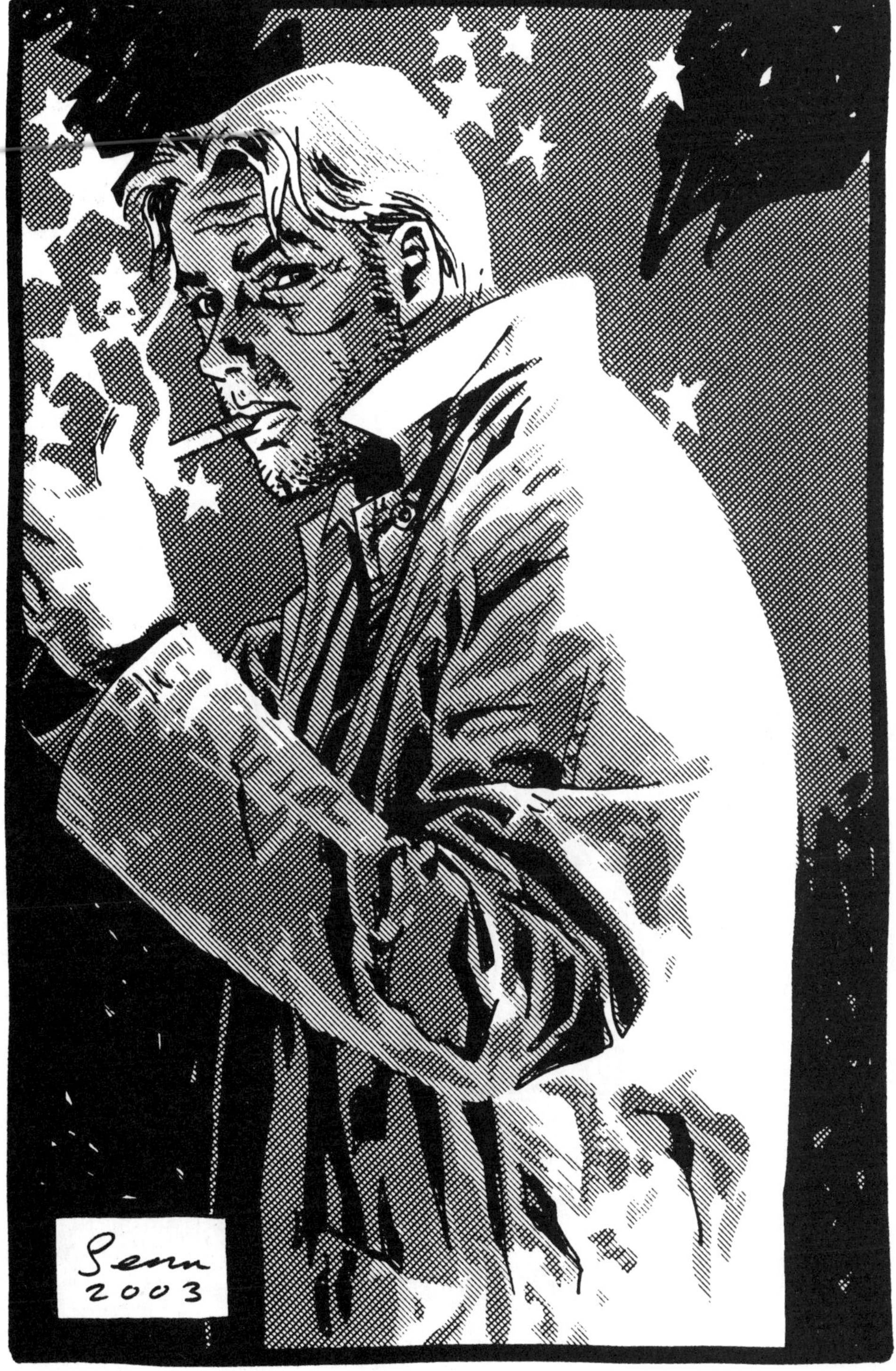
Sean
2003

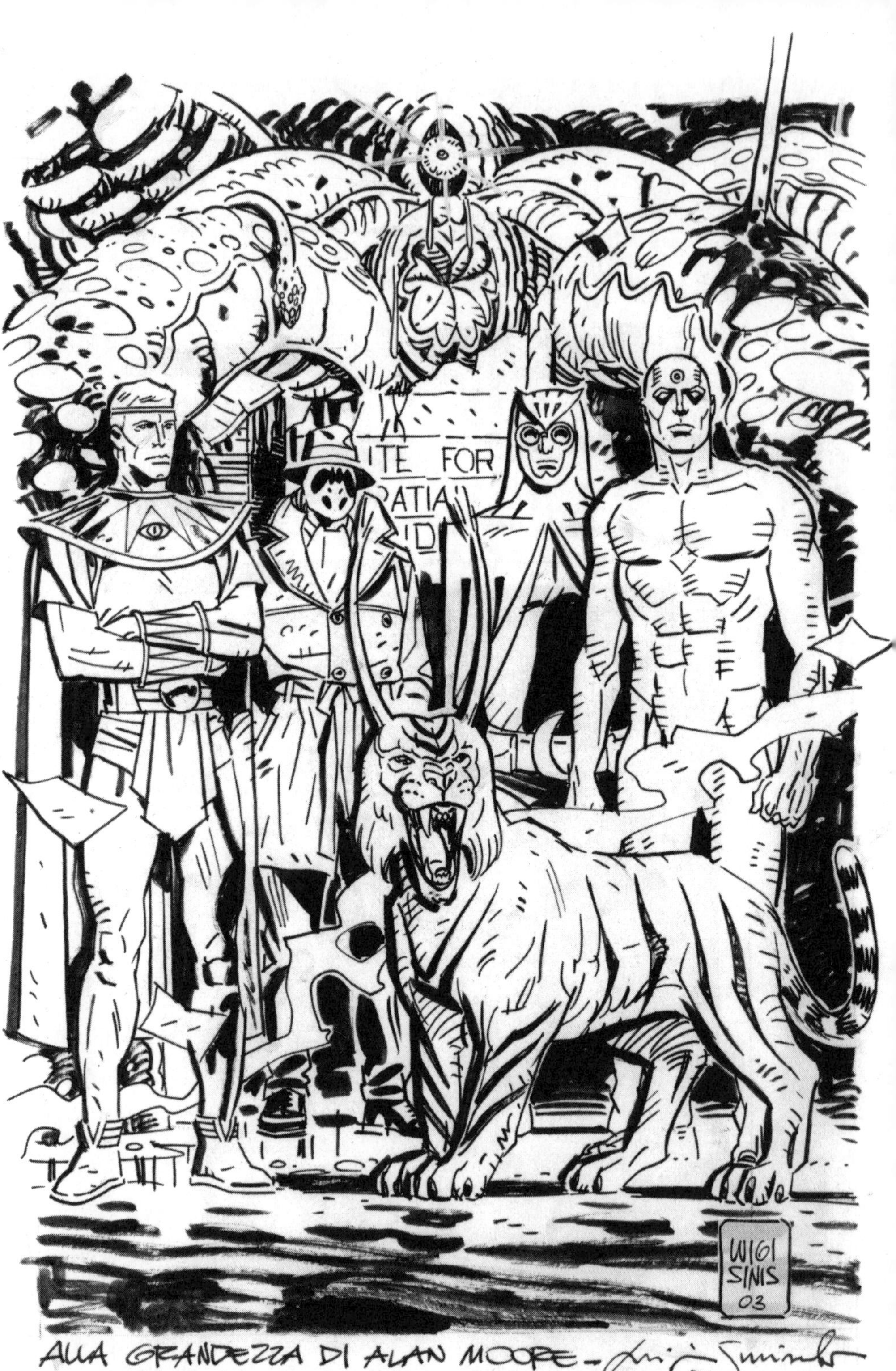
ITE FOR
LUIGI
SINIS
03

ALLA GRANDEZZA DI ALAN MOORE –

1986: THE MOTHER OF ALL YEARS

GARY PHILLIPS

Gary Phillips writes crime and mystery stories, and enjoys a good cigar now and then. Most recently he's produced the novels **The Perpetrators** from Ugly Town, **The Jook** and the **Midnight Mover** mini-series for Oni Press. Text ©2003 Gary Phillips.

Click, bang, do you remember? Nineteen eighty fuckin' six, man. There's only twenty-six letters to mix and match to describe the psychic impact that ocrica, that shake-up of the comics genre that tore down some tired, sorry ass approaches to the art form had on us fans and practitioners. What started out as a revamping of old school Charlton heroes turned into something that has rippled across the years and decades to where we are now.

Damn. And what helped spur this creation, what allowed his genie out of the keyboard, was because of some jive copyright entanglements. All because the suits upstairs didn't want no, you know, street-edge shit, no characters with flaws and depth and contradictory emotions being imposed and messing up their gaudy do-gooders.

So they let him retool and refit.

Who Watches the Watchmen was the gag, baby, the grand guffaw writ large across our collective minds when we couldn't wait, after being teased by those come-on ads, to read each successive issue of that mother of all story arcs.

But unlike say Orson Wells – and even he had more than one hand of Three Card Monty to dazzle the suckers – this dude this book is honoring has stepped up time and again and delivered. It's like Kobe hitting those threes 12 times in one game or the first time you got a peek of some hottie's panties when she crossed her legs and she winked at you. JAYZUS.

It stays with you, know what I'm sayin'?

It's as if the Comedian, that gloating, Hoyo de Monterrey smoking, Lee Harvey Oswald lone gunman nutbag on steroids and crank was still firing those nitro velocity rounds of his from that high window; causing dissension and distraction not in the social order, but in the over-ripe corpus delicti of the comics industry. Only those bullets don't sing death. They zing tracers of energy coursing through that body to resuscitate and educate us that indeed, this fumetti, this thing of ours has merit, has something to offer in the way of its unique storytelling methods.

DAME DARCY

Pages 158-169 following: Dame Darcy self-published the first issue of her comic book **Meat Cake** while at the San Francisco Art Institute in 1989. She also pursued a career as an actress with parts in local independent films and has developed a series of hand-crafted dolls that have earned her vast attention in the curious world of doll collecting. In 1999, acclaimed writer Alan Moore offered to collaborate with Darcy on a story for the ninth issue of **Meat Cake**. All he asked for in return was two Darcy dolls for his daughters. Strip ©2003 Alan Moore/Dame Darcy.

Watchmen brought me and so many others back to these four-color fables when many of us figured we'd outgrown them what with mortgages, car payments, and crowns on our teeth.

The stories of wonder and woe he's presented in fare like Swamp-Thing, V, Green Lantern, Supreme, Top Ten and League of Extraordinary Gentlemen keeps me addicted — keeps me wanting more badder than an alkie lining up in the morning outside the corner liquor store to bum change for his short dog of Old Smuggler.

But his stuff doesn't leave me with a hang over. His stuff makes me jealous and envious as a writer...and as an afficionado, all you can do is admire his skill that he's always honing, not content to do the same trick over and over but challenging himself to tell the best yarn he can again and again.

I wish Mr. Moore well on reaching his half-century mark. And here's hoping the next fifty — and that doesn't seem so preposterous given one is to understand he's been dipping into some sort of study of magiks - has him crafting tales that pleasure and bother the reader.

LUIGI SINISCALCHI

Left: Luigi Siniscalchi is staff penciller at Bonelli Comics. He has illustrated, and continues to work on, popular Italian comics series such as **Dylan Dog, Martyn Mystére, Nick Raider** and **Julia**. www.luigisiniscalchi.it. Illustration ©2003 Luigi Siniscalchi Watchmen ©2003 DC Comics

See? The Owl was wrong, it isn't all crap. It's all good, baby.

• **Gary Phillips**
Los Angeles, California, U.S.A.

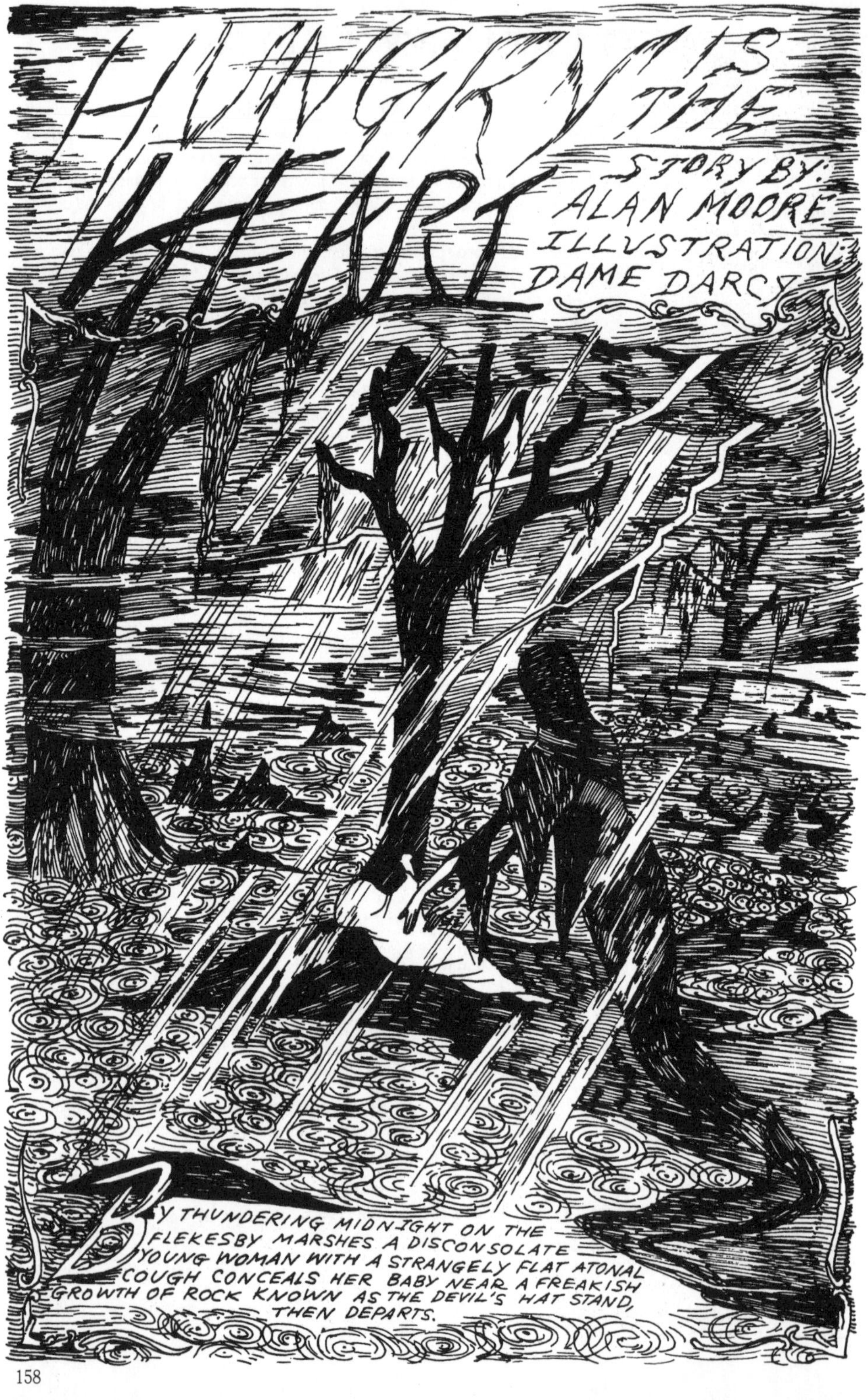
HUNGRY IS THE HEART
STORY BY: ALAN MOORE
ILLUSTRATION: DAME DARCY
BY THUNDERING MIDNIGHT ON THE FLEKESBY MARSHES A DISCONSOLATE YOUNG WOMAN WITH A STRANGELY FLAT ATONAL COUGH CONCEALS HER BABY NEAR A FREAKISH GROWTH OF ROCK KNOWN AS THE DEVIL'S HAT STAND, THEN DEPARTS.

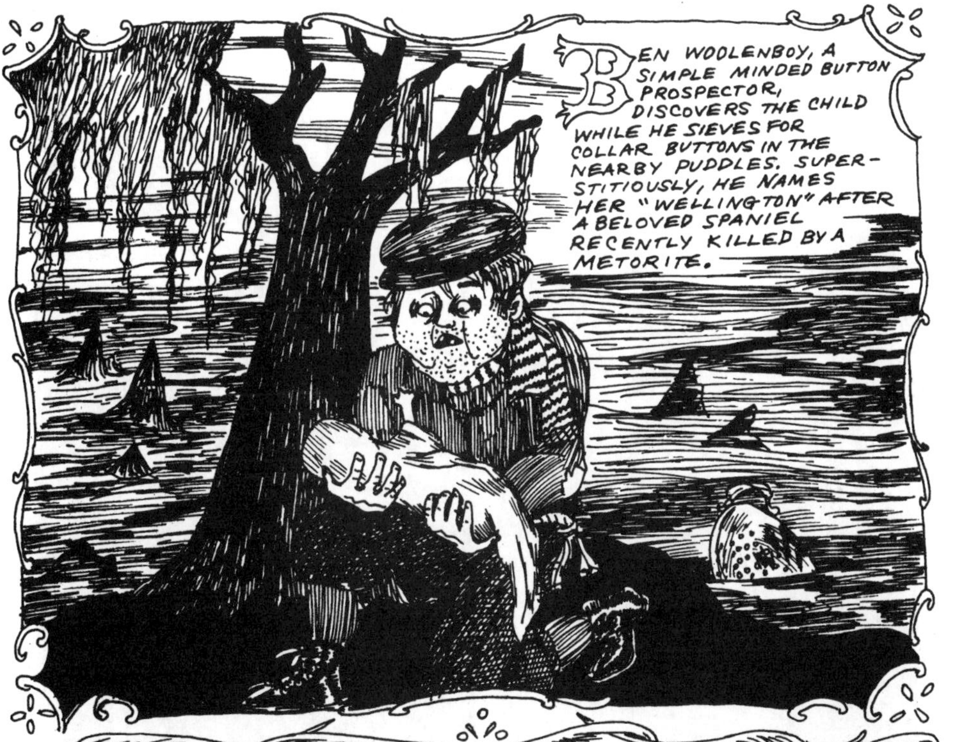
BEN WOOLENBOY, A SIMPLE MINDED BUTTON PROSPECTOR, DISCOVERS THE CHILD WHILE HE SIEVES FOR COLLAR BUTTONS IN THE NEARBY PUDDLES. SUPER-STITIOUSLY, HE NAMES HER "WELLINGTON" AFTER A BELOVED SPANIEL RECENTLY KILLED BY A METORITE.

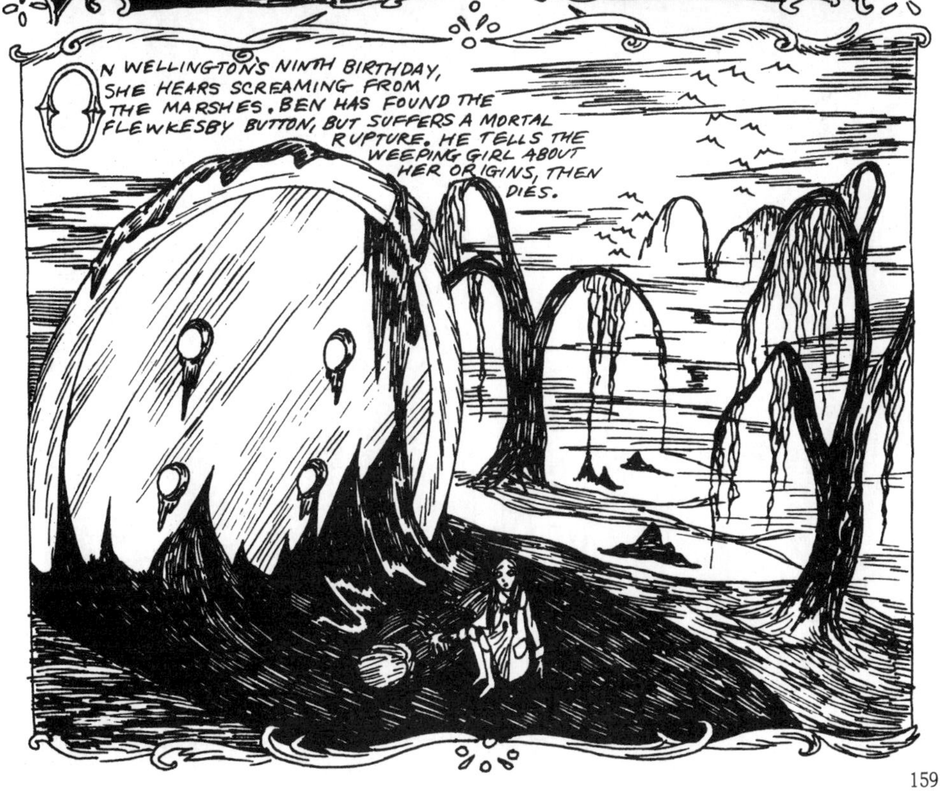
ON WELLINGTON'S NINTH BIRTHDAY, SHE HEARS SCREAMING FROM THE MARSHES. BEN HAS FOUND THE FLEWKESBY BUTTON, BUT SUFFERS A MORTAL RUPTURE. HE TELLS THE WEEPING GIRL ABOUT HER ORIGINS, THEN DIES.

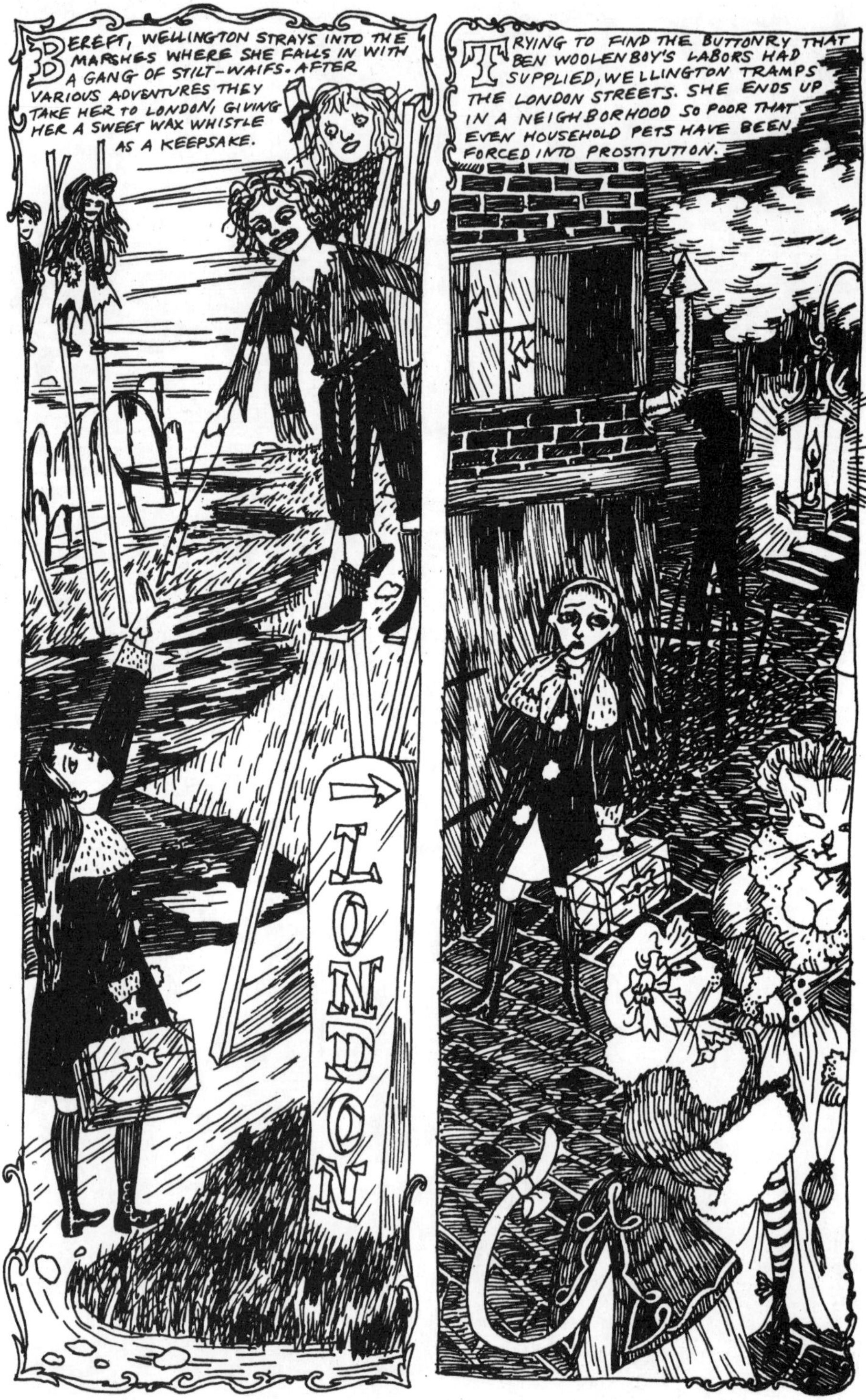
BEREFT, WELLINGTON STRAYS INTO THE MARSHES WHERE SHE FALLS IN WITH A GANG OF STILT-WAIFS. AFTER VARIOUS ADVENTURES THEY TAKE HER TO LONDON, GIVING HER A SWEET WAX WHISTLE AS A KEEPSAKE.
LONDON
TRYING TO FIND THE BUTTONRY THAT BEN WOOLENBOY'S LABORS HAD SUPPLIED, WELLINGTON TRAMPS THE LONDON STREETS. SHE ENDS UP IN A NEIGHBORHOOD SO POOR THAT EVEN HOUSEHOLD PETS HAVE BEEN FORCED INTO PROSTITUTION.

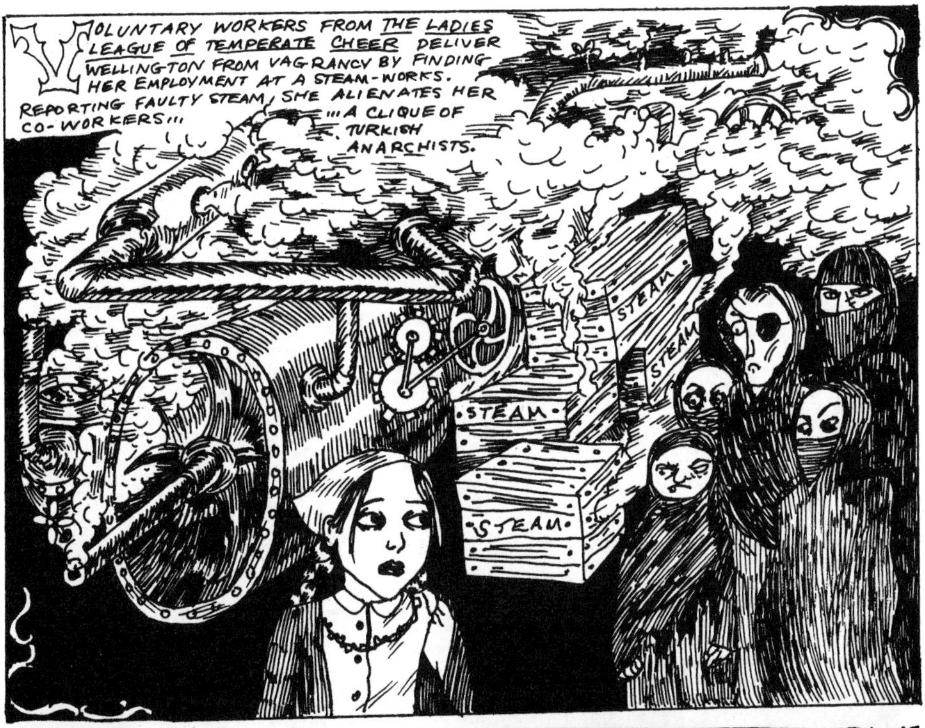
VOLUNTARY WORKERS FROM THE LADIES LEAGUE OF TEMPERATE CHEER DELIVER WELLINGTON FROM VAGRANCY BY FINDING HER EMPLOYMENT AT A STEAM-WORKS. REPORTING FAULTY STEAM, SHE ALIENATES HER CO-WORKERS...
...A CLIQUE OF TURKISH ANARCHISTS.
STEAM
STEAM
STEAM
STEAM

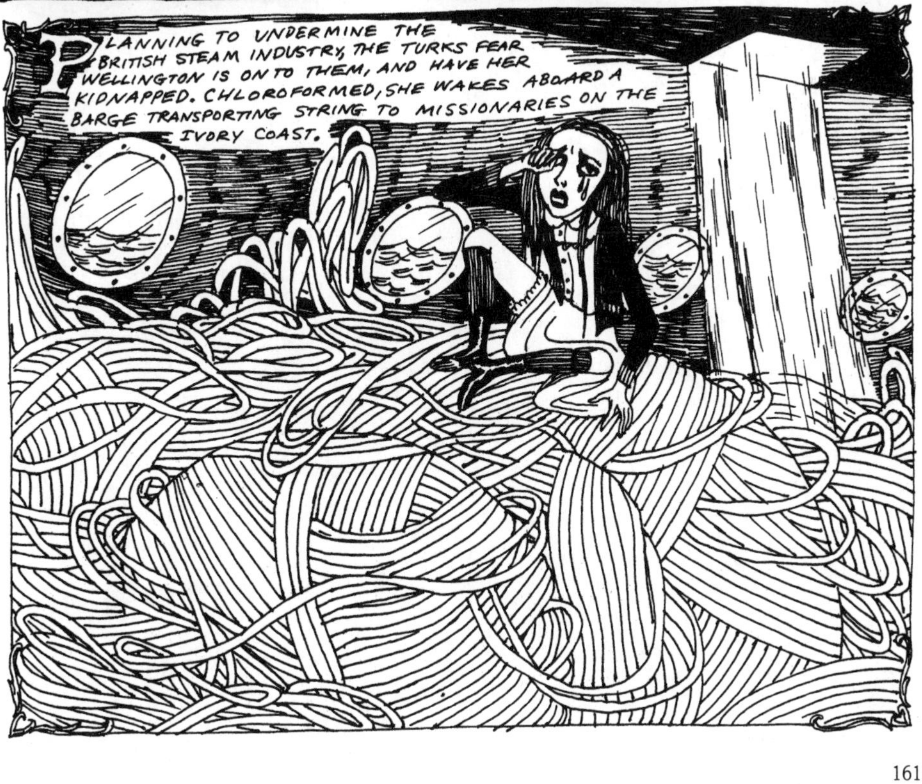
PLANNING TO UNDERMINE THE BRITISH STEAM INDUSTRY, THE TURKS FEAR WELLINGTON IS ON TO THEM, AND HAVE HER KIDNAPPED. CHLOROFORMED, SHE WAKES ABOARD A BARGE TRANSPORTING STRING TO MISSIONARIES ON THE IVORY COAST.

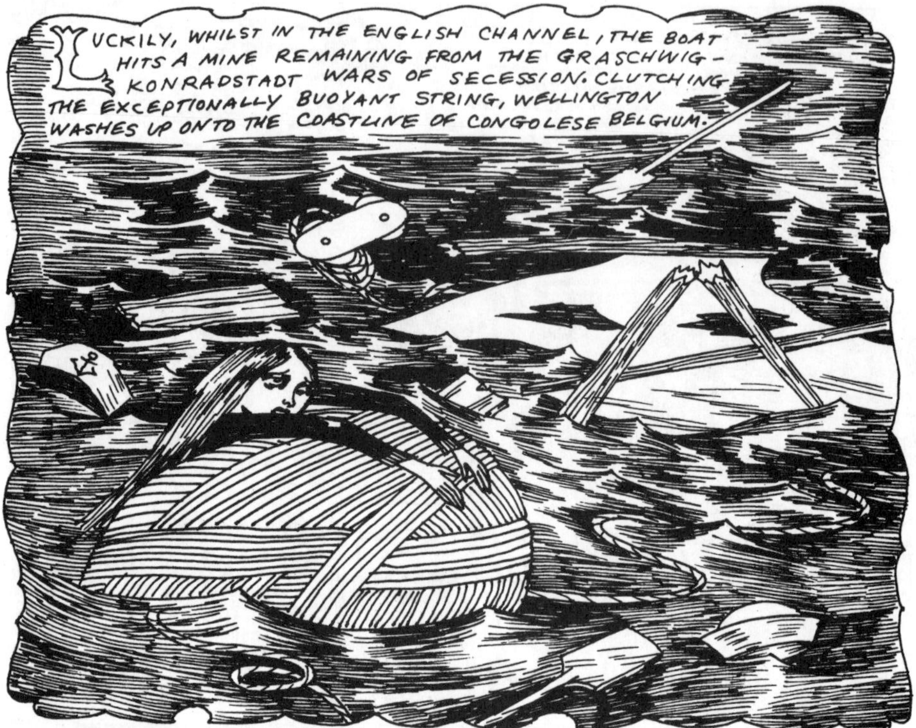
LUCKILY, WHILST IN THE ENGLISH CHANNEL, THE BOAT HITS A MINE REMAINING FROM THE GRASCHWIG-KONRADSTADT WARS OF SECESSION. CLUTCHING THE EXCEPTIONALLY BUOYANT STRING, WELLINGTON WASHES UP ONTO THE COASTLINE OF CONGOLESE BELGIUM.

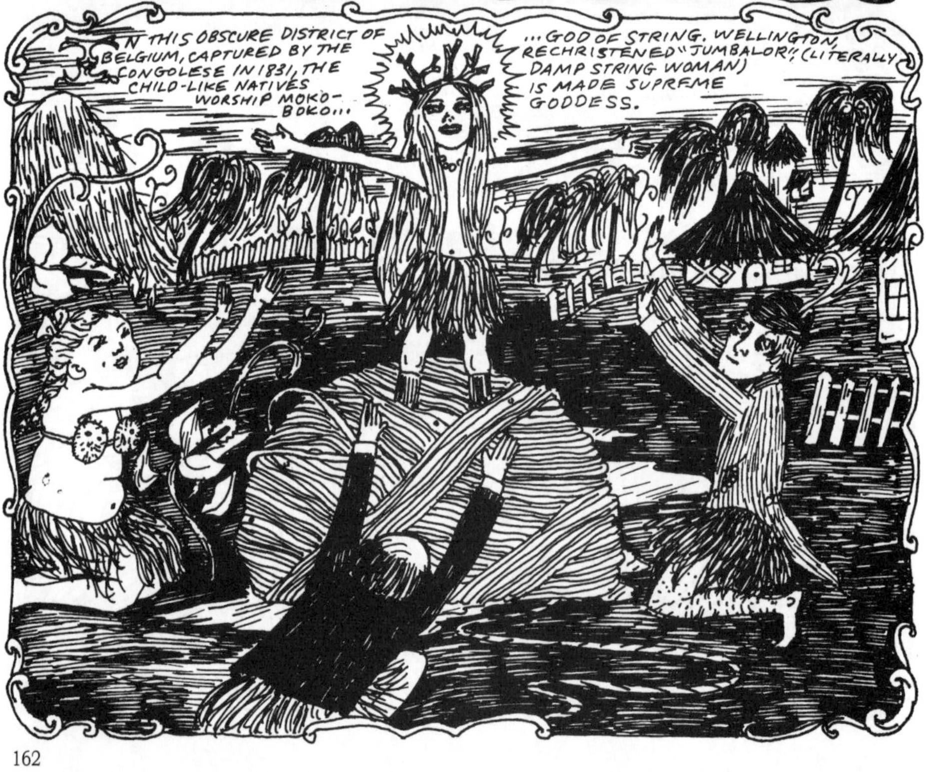
IN THIS OBSCURE DISTRICT OF BELGIUM, CAPTURED BY THE CONGOLESE IN 1831, THE CHILD-LIKE NATIVES WORSHIP MOKO-BOKO...
...GOD OF STRING. WELLINGTON, RECHRISTENED "JUMBALOR!" (LITERALLY DAMP STRING WOMAN) IS MADE SUPREME GODDESS.

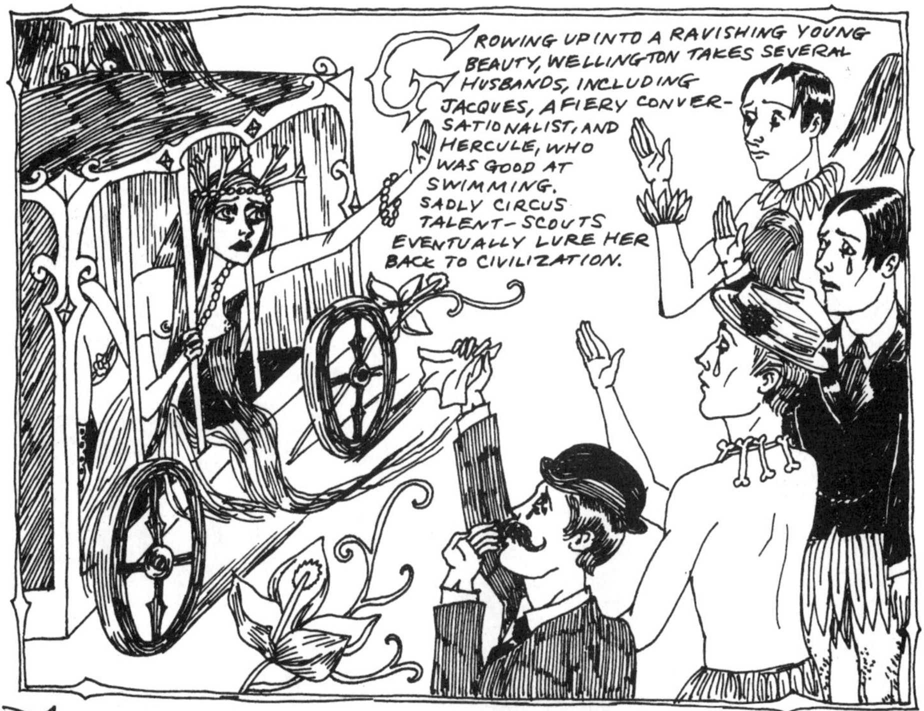
GROWING UP INTO A RAVISHING YOUNG
BEAUTY, WELLINGTON TAKES SEVERAL
HUSBANDS, INCLUDING
JACQUES, A FIERY CONVER-
SATIONALIST, AND
HERCULE, WHO
WAS GOOD AT
SWIMMING.
SADLY CIRCUS
TALENT-SCOUTS
EVENTUALLY LURE HER
BACK TO CIVILIZATION.

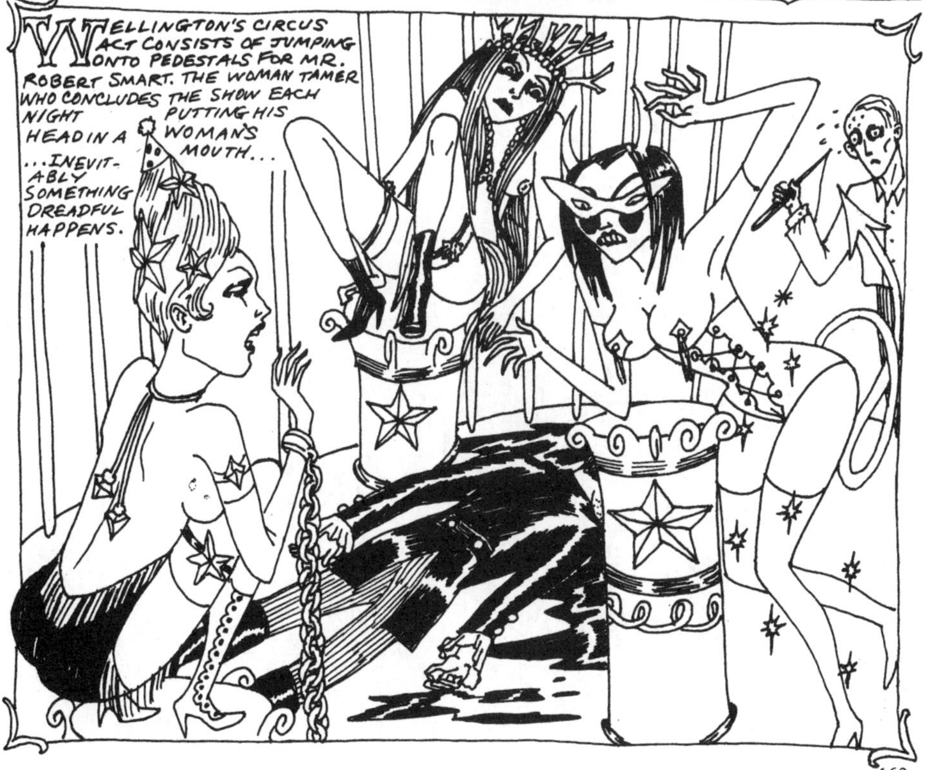
WELLINGTON'S CIRCUS
ACT CONSISTS OF JUMPING
ONTO PEDESTALS FOR MR.
ROBERT SMART. THE WOMAN TAMER
WHO CONCLUDES THE SHOW EACH
NIGHT PUTTING HIS
HEAD IN A WOMAN'S
MOUTH...
...INEVIT-
ABLY
SOMETHING
DREADFUL
HAPPENS.

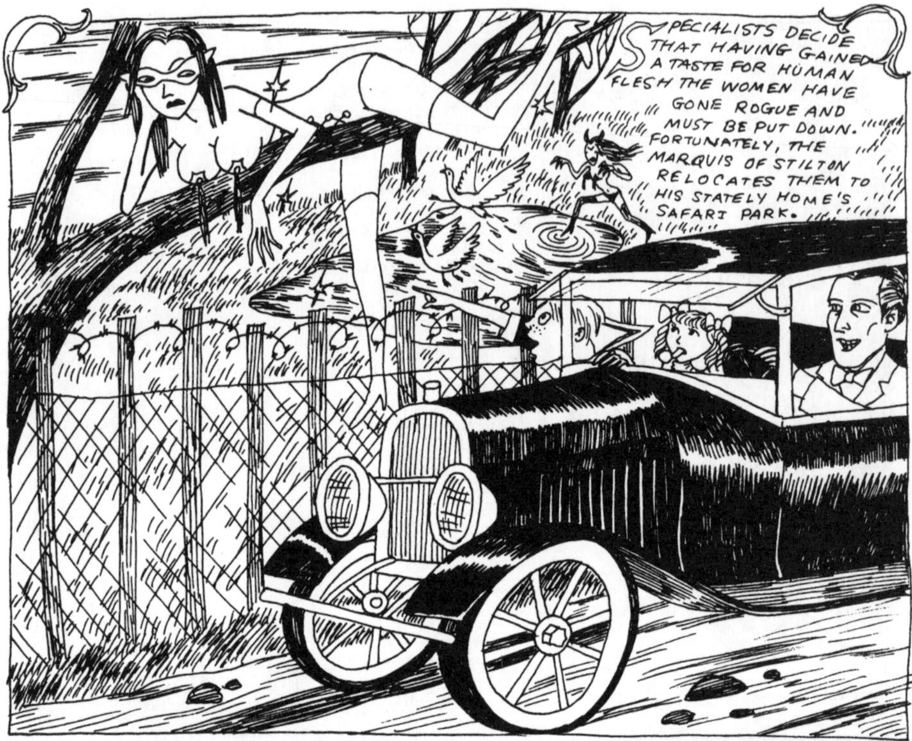
SPECIALISTS DECIDE THAT HAVING GAINED A TASTE FOR HUMAN FLESH THE WOMEN HAVE GONE ROGUE AND MUST BE PUT DOWN. FORTUNATELY, THE MARQUIS OF STILTON RELOCATES THEM TO HIS STATELY HOME'S SAFARI PARK.

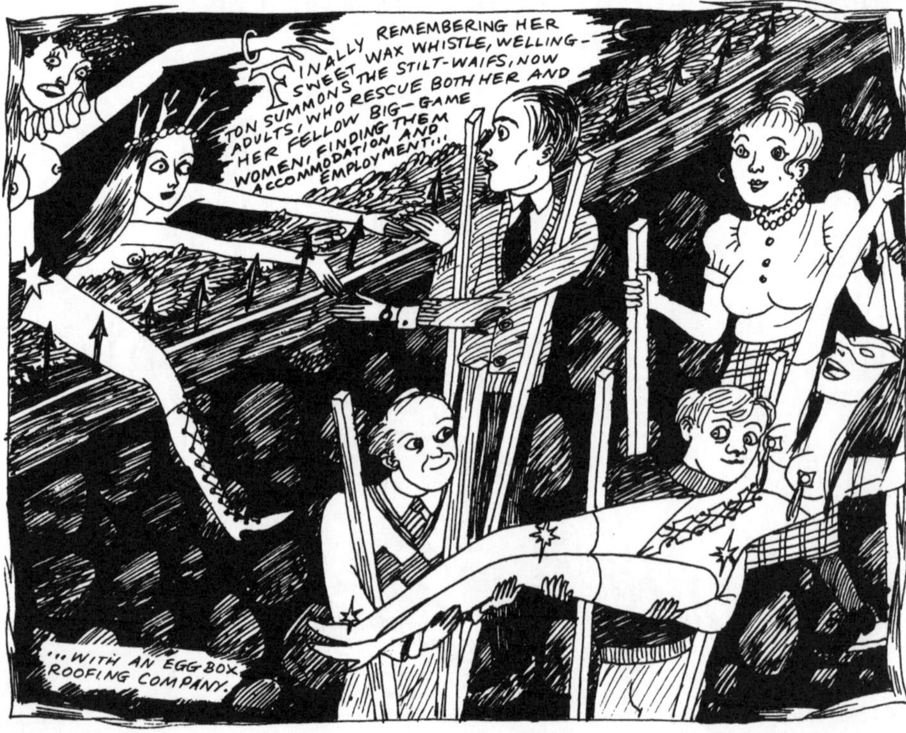
FINALLY REMEMBERING HER SWEET WAX WHISTLE, WELLINGTON SUMMONS THE STILT-WAIFS, NOW ADULTS, WHO RESCUE BOTH HER AND HER FELLOW BIG-GAME WOMEN, FINDING THEM ACCOMMODATION AND EMPLOYMENT...
...WITH AN EGG BOX ROOFING COMPANY.

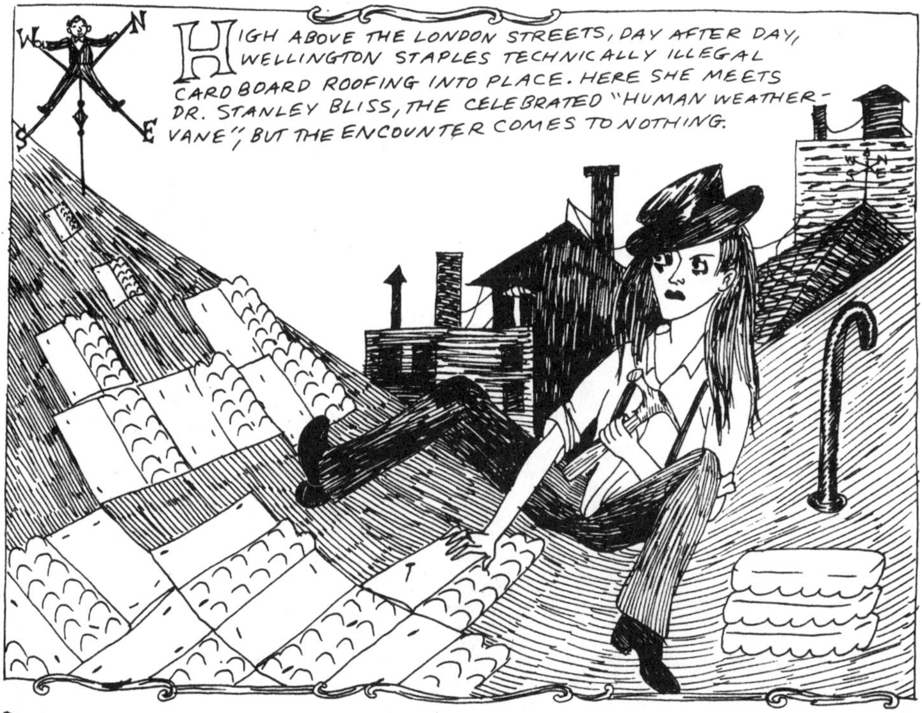
HIGH ABOVE THE LONDON STREETS, DAY AFTER DAY, WELLINGTON STAPLES TECHNICALLY ILLEGAL CARDBOARD ROOFING INTO PLACE. HERE SHE MEETS DR. STANLEY BLISS, THE CELEBRATED "HUMAN WEATHER-VANE", BUT THE ENCOUNTER COMES TO NOTHING.

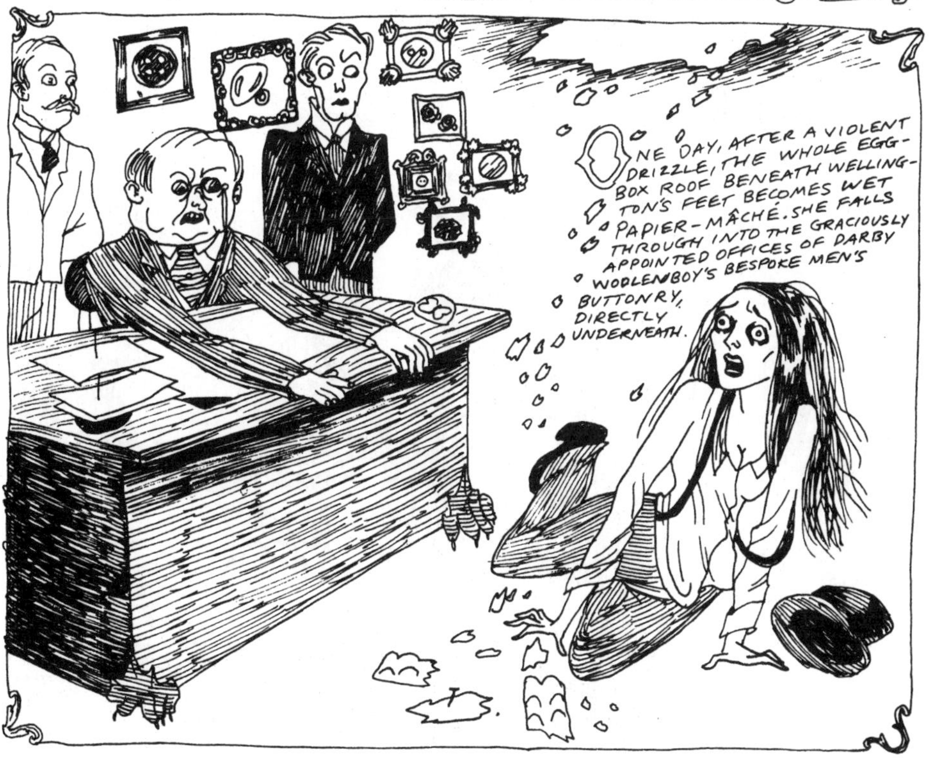
ONE DAY, AFTER A VIOLENT DRIZZLE, THE WHOLE EGG-BOX ROOF BENEATH WELLINGTON'S FEET BECOMES WET PAPIER-MÂCHÉ. SHE FALLS THROUGH INTO THE GRACIOUSLY APPOINTED OFFICES OF DARBY WOOLENBOY'S BESPOKE MEN'S BUTTONRY, DIRECTLY UNDERNEATH.

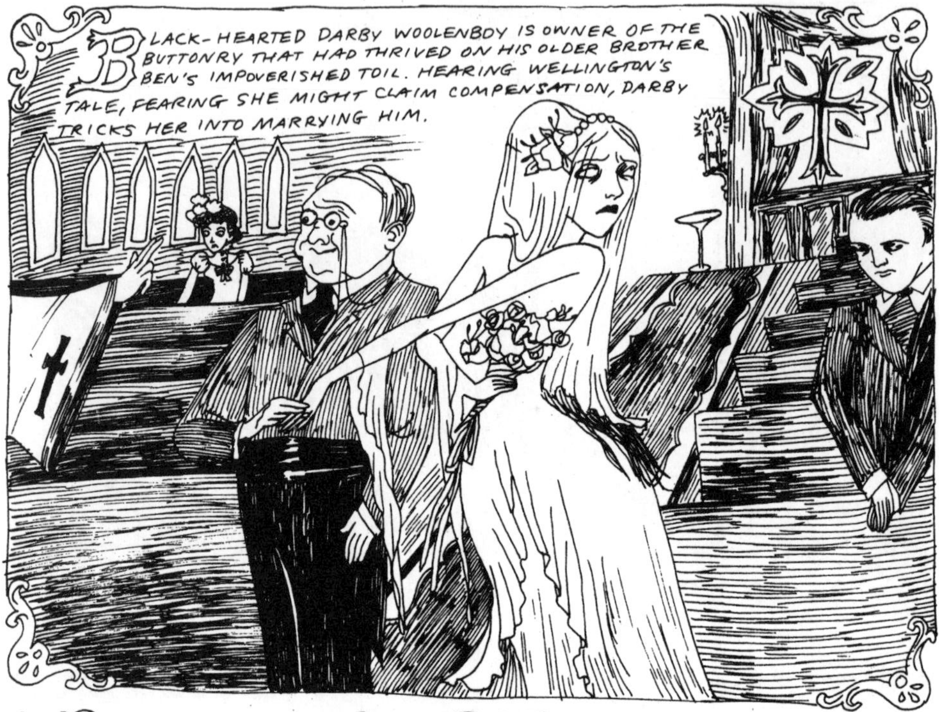
BLACK-HEARTED DARBY WOOLENBOY IS OWNER OF THE BUTTONRY THAT HAD THRIVED ON HIS OLDER BROTHER BEN'S IMPOVERISHED TOIL. HEARING WELLINGTON'S TALE, FEARING SHE MIGHT CLAIM COMPENSATION, DARBY TRICKS HER INTO MARRYING HIM.

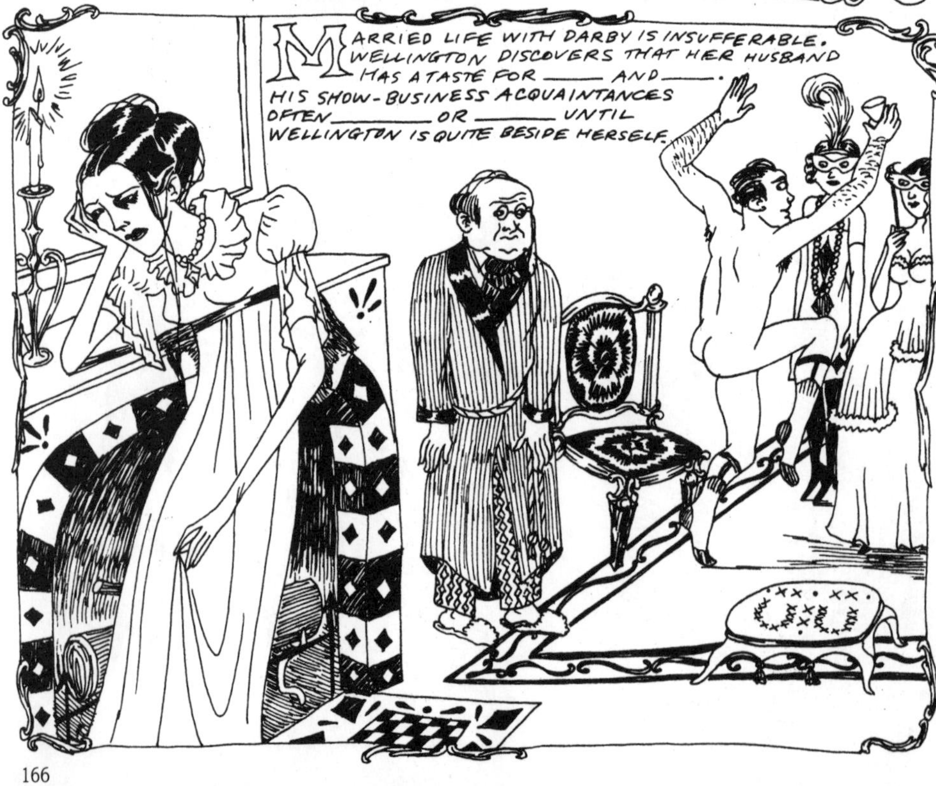
MARRIED LIFE WITH DARBY IS INSUFFERABLE. WELLINGTON DISCOVERS THAT HER HUSBAND HAS A TASTE FOR ____ AND ____. HIS SHOW-BUSINESS ACQUAINTANCES OFTEN ______ OR _____ UNTIL WELLINGTON IS QUITE BESIDE HERSELF.
!!
!!

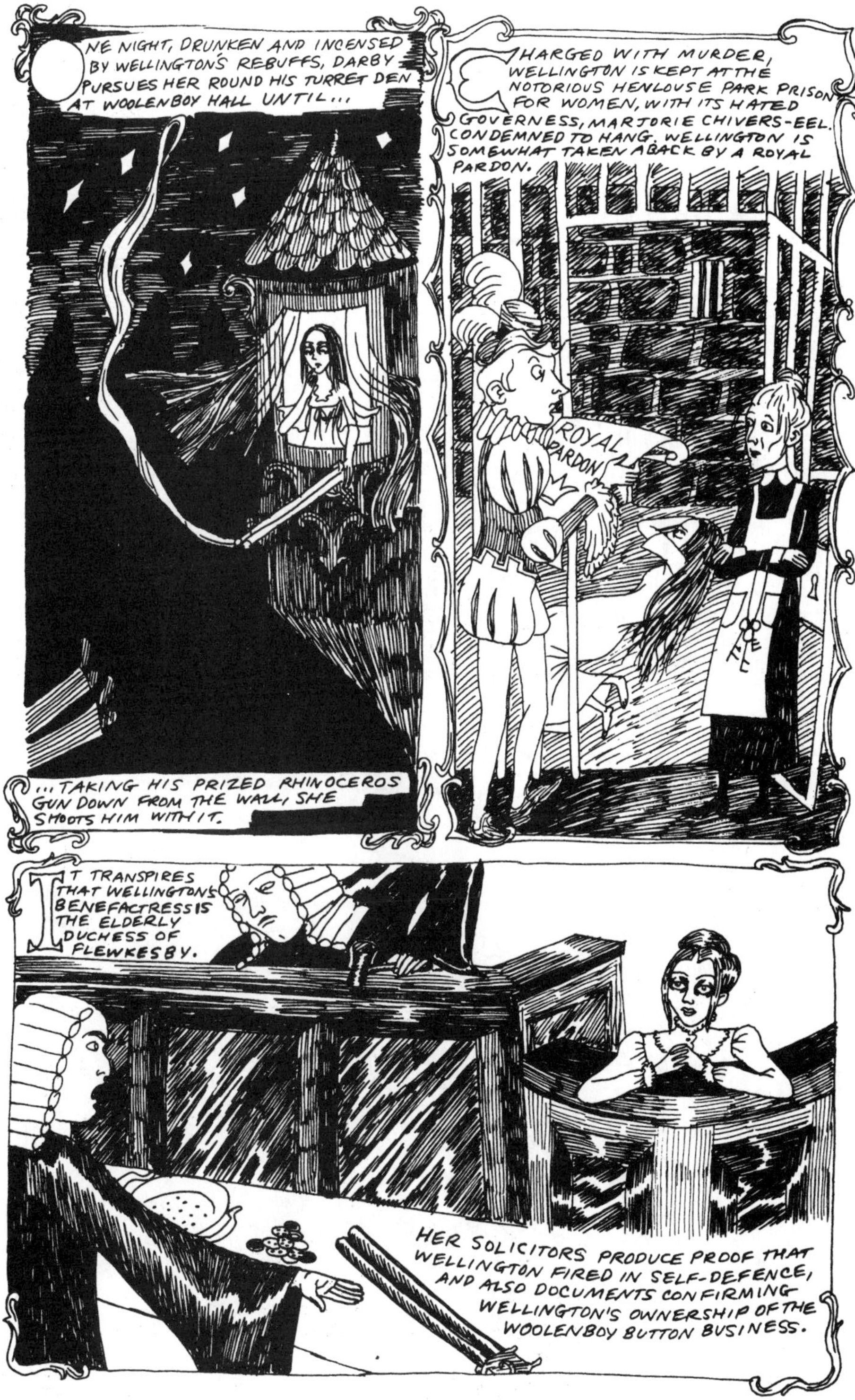
ONE NIGHT, DRUNKEN AND INCENSED BY WELLINGTON'S REBUFFS, DARBY PURSUES HER ROUND HIS TURRET DEN AT WOOLENBOY HALL UNTIL...
...TAKING HIS PRIZED RHINOCEROS GUN DOWN FROM THE WALL, SHE SHOOTS HIM WITH IT.
CHARGED WITH MURDER, WELLINGTON IS KEPT AT THE NOTORIOUS HENLOUSE PARK PRISON FOR WOMEN, WITH ITS HATED GOVERNESS, MARJORIE CHIVERS-EEL. CONDEMNED TO HANG. WELLINGTON IS SOMEWHAT TAKEN ABACK BY A ROYAL PARDON.
ROYAL PARDON
IT TRANSPIRES THAT WELLINGTON'S BENEFACTRESS IS THE ELDERLY DUCHESS OF FLEWKESBY.
HER SOLICITORS PRODUCE PROOF THAT WELLINGTON FIRED IN SELF-DEFENCE, AND ALSO DOCUMENTS CONFIRMING WELLINGTON'S OWNERSHIP OF THE WOOLENBOY BUTTON BUSINESS.

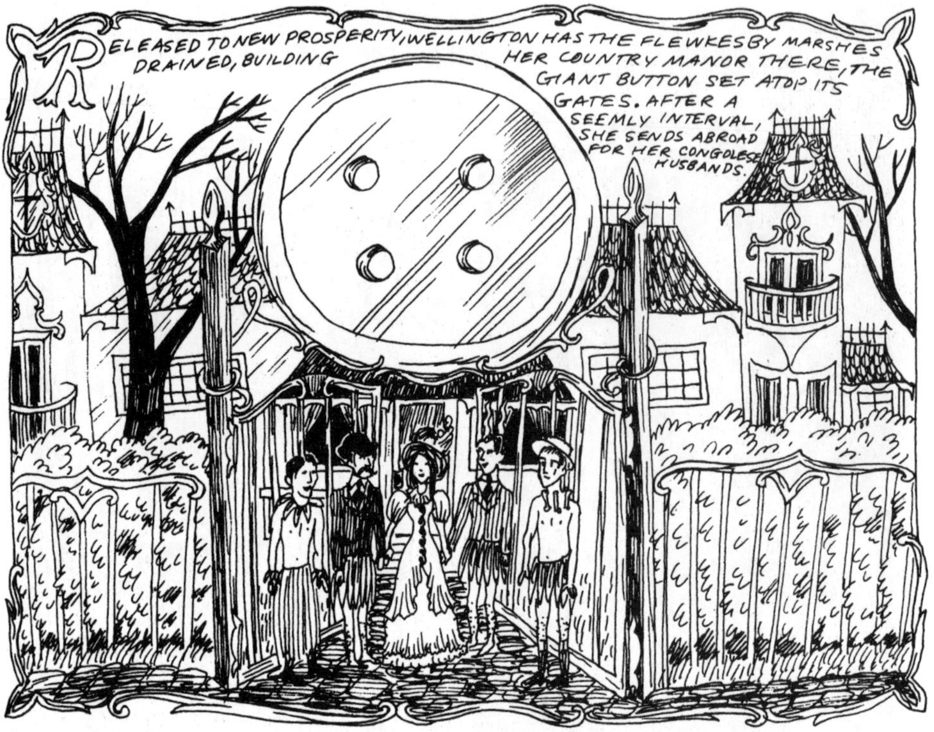
RELEASED TO NEW PROSPERITY, WELLINGTON HAS THE FLEWKESBY MARSHES DRAINED, BUILDING HER COUNTRY MANOR THERE, THE GIANT BUTTON SET ATOP ITS GATES. AFTER A SEEMLY INTERVAL, SHE SENDS ABROAD FOR HER CONGOLESE HUSBANDS.

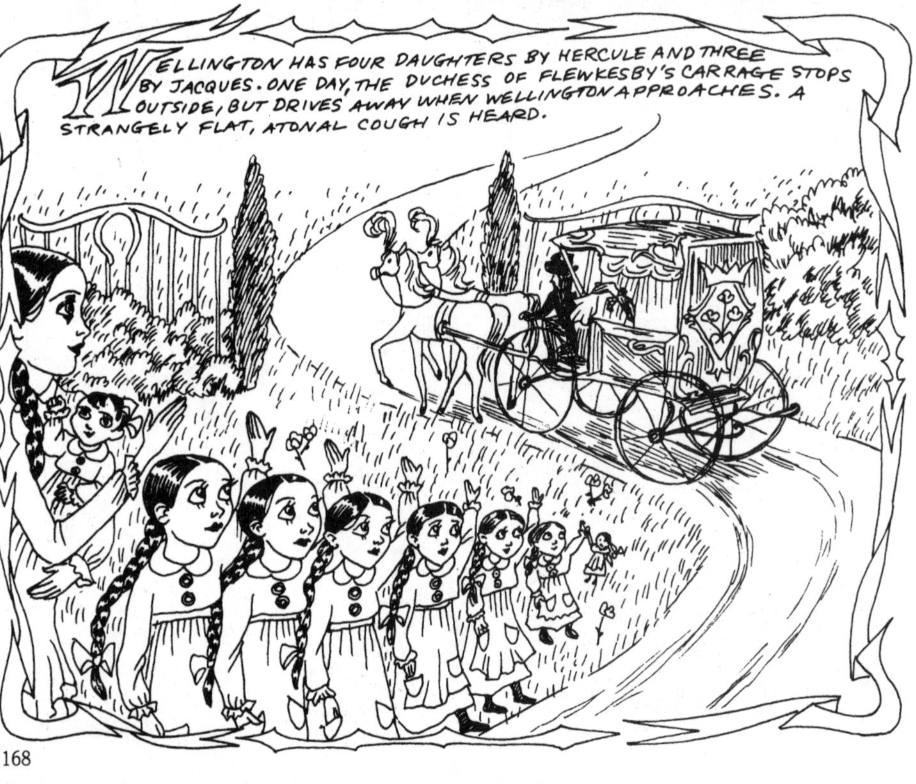
WELLINGTON HAS FOUR DAUGHTERS BY HERCULE AND THREE BY JACQUES. ONE DAY, THE DUCHESS OF FLEWKESBY'S CARRAGE STOPS OUTSIDE, BUT DRIVES AWAY WHEN WELLINGTON APPROACHES. A STRANGELY FLAT, ATONAL COUGH IS HEARD.

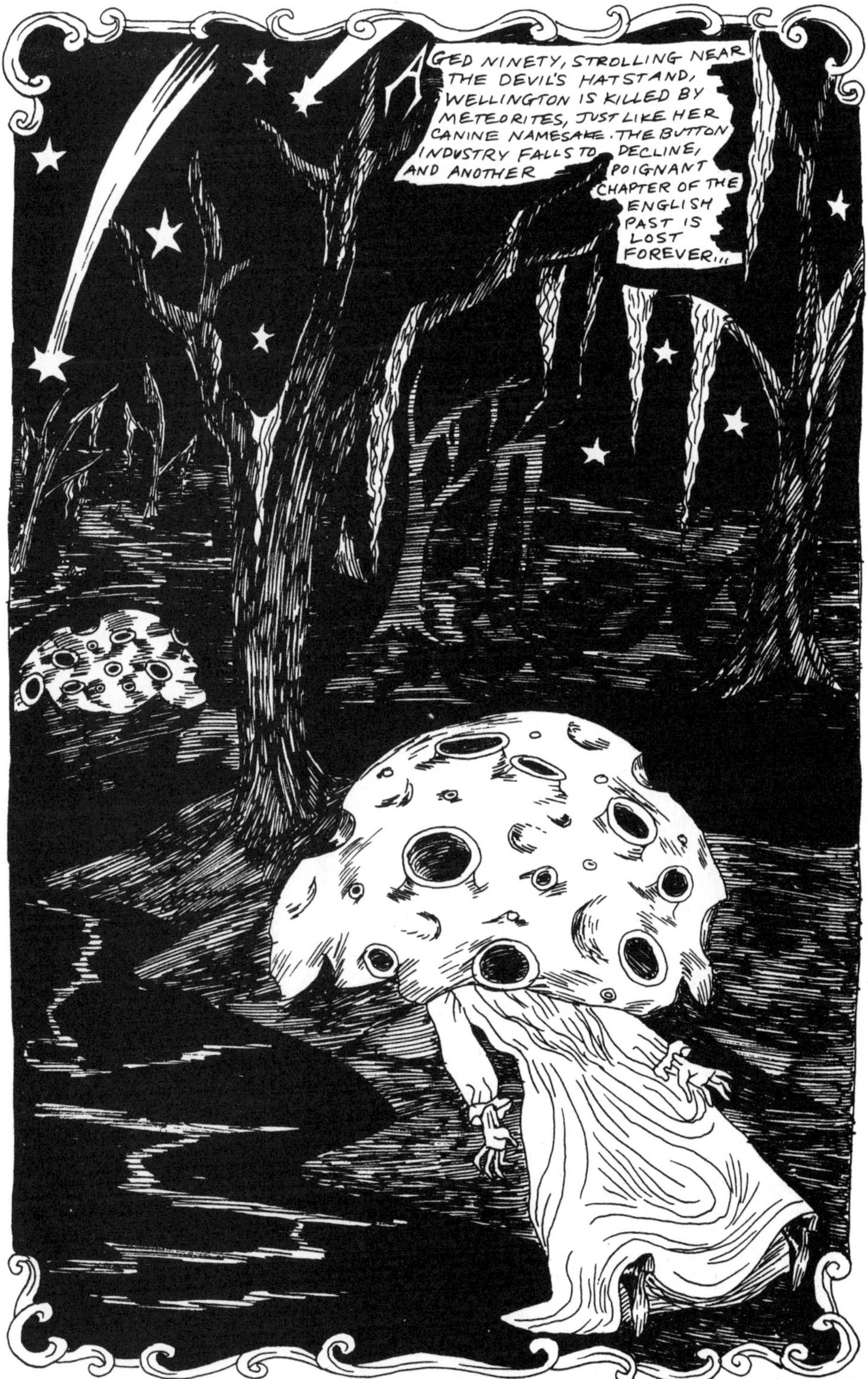
AGED NINETY, STROLLING NEAR THE DEVIL'S HATSTAND, WELLINGTON IS KILLED BY METEORITES, JUST LIKE HER CANINE NAMESAKE. THE BUTTON INDUSTRY FALLS TO DECLINE, AND ANOTHER POIGNANT CHAPTER OF THE ENGLISH PAST IS LOST FOREVER...

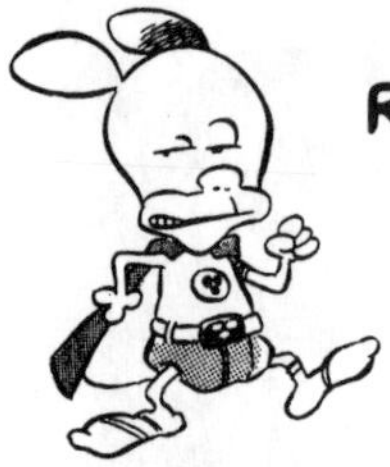

RAT-MAN FEATURING V FOR VENDETTA

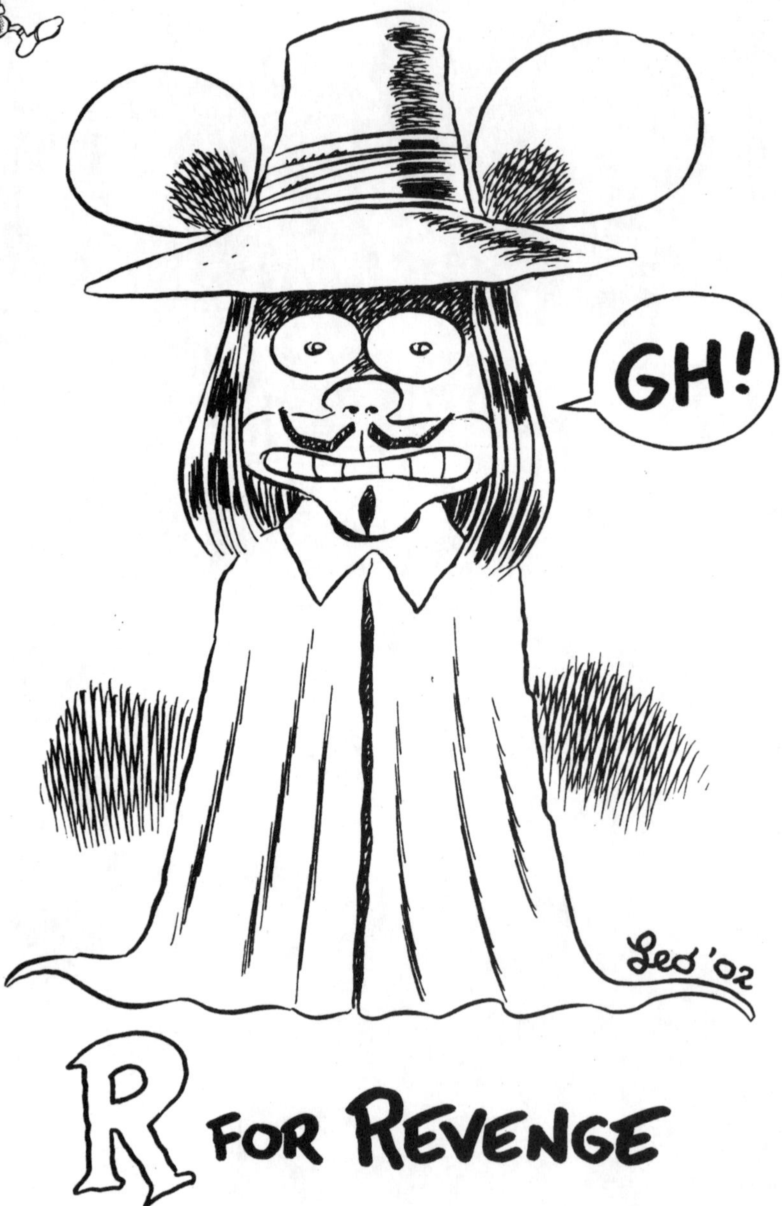
GH!
Leo '02

R FOR REVENGE

A READER'S VIEW

ADE CAPONE

Ade Capone is a veteran Italian comics writer with a 20-year career in the field. He has worked for Bonelli Comics, created the long-running **Lazarus Ledd** for Star Comics and translated the Italian edition of Alan Moore's run on **WildC.A.T.S.** Text ©2003 Ade Capone.

Everybody has written about Alan Moore, everything and its opposite. Therefore, I don't think I can add anything new, though I have read the English writer's work since the '80s, both as reader and as writer, trying to pinch a trick or two from the author of *V for Vendetta*.

One cannot deny that there is much to learn from reading Moore's works. What fascinates me the most is his ability to translate science into poetry. Think about Dr. Manhattan in *Watchmen* and the quote of the watchmaker Einstein.

Or *WildC.A.T.S.'* android, Spartan, who flies into the night, listening to every single sound, including the electrons in their quantum orbits. This was from a splash-page that I had the honour to translate for the Italian edition of the comic book, realizing how impossible it was to find a proper equivalent for sentences that sound in English, thanks to his precise terminology, just like music. Besides, every story by Moore is, in some sense, rock music; and Moore himself, in photographs, looks very much like a '70s rock-star, with his lucid and bohemian creative madness, which expresses itself perfectly in his two main narrative themes; one based on superheroes, the other on Old England. *The League of Extraordinary Gentlemen* is, in a sense, the union of the two.

But let's talk about the straight superheroes. Alan Moore has been a master in the superheroic arena, because with *Watchmen* (and, indeed, *The Killing Joke*) he wrote the definitive superhero story, mercilessly exposing their (super) human miseries. The fact is, in my opinion as a reader (as a writer I would not dare to express such a judgement), the story was, above all, definitive of the writer. And the proof is (again, in my opinion as a reader) that he was only able to reach such artistic heights again with *From Hell*, which was not about superheroes. His *WildC.A.T.S.* run was wonderful, that's true. And many things in *ABC Comics* are valuable. But they are not *Watchmen*, and they could not be, for the aforementioned reason. It's not surprising that, despite the excessive praise of critics too often looking at the author's name rather than the work itself, none of these more recent works have matched the sales and the success of *Watchmen*. And as far as I am concerned, the public is always right, especially when it's a public without any preconceptions against the new product of a great author. To put it simply, they liked these new things less because you can create a character like Dr. Manhattan (and company) once in your life, assuming you have enough genius. *From Hell*, on the other hand, being free from comparison to previous works, allowed Moore to free his genius once more, helped by the art of an Eddie Campbell who was at his peak and perfectly tuned to the script.

LEO ORTOLANI

Left: Leo Ortolani is the creator of the superhero parody **Rat-Man**, one of Italy's best selling comics, also published in Spain. www.rat-man.it. Illustration ©2003 Leo Ortolani. Rat-Man is ©2003 Leo Ortolani. V for Vendetta is ©2003 DC Comics.

Speaking as a writer, there's this to say, too; a writer, in his entire career, meets two, three at most, artists able to precisely render his soul. The others, good as they may be, will never be able to attain that full symbiosis which is necessary to create a masterwork. Alan Moore, the *"extraordinary writer"* halfway between steam

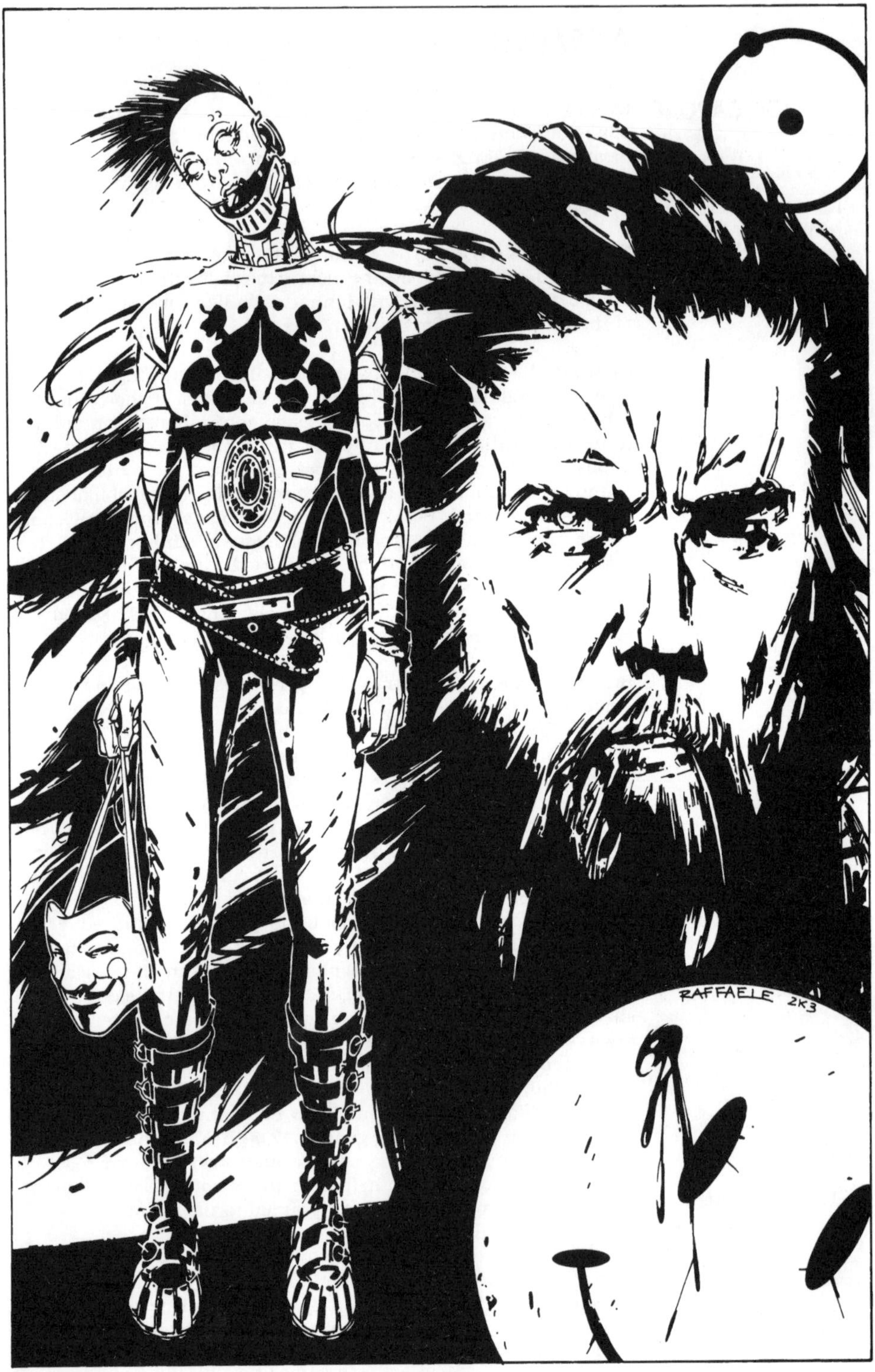
RAFFAELE 2K3

engines and quantum physics, found the other half of his creative coin in Dave Gibbons and Eddie Campbell. And those aren't people able or willing to bind themselves to periodical publication, with fixed deadlines, like the *ABC* line. Someone who possibly could have been Moore's third "ideal artist" was Travis Charest, the initial artist on his *WildC.A.T.S.* run. Sponsored by Star Comics at the Expocartoon convention in Rome, Travis told me how he was perfectly comfortable with Moore's very precise scripts. I thought that was odd, Travis being an artist who tends towards less detailed artwork (unlike, say, a Gibbons). We were at a dinner, the wine of the Roman Castles loosened our tongues. Laughing, Travis told me I was right. And that Moore did know that perfectly, too. But he set him totally free, putting the smallest details in the script anyway, so that Charest could "skip" them to obtain a more terse effect. Look (read!) those issues of *WildC.A.T.S.*, and you'll see how Travis managed it. Regrettably, his timetables didn't match the deadlines, and he had to leave the book. He did nothing else with Moore, and not much else in general.

Art and serialisation: a problem as old as the world, and probably with no solution. I think Alan Moore knows this all too well. Happy birthday, Alan... and thank you!

• **Ade Capone**, October 2002

WOODROW
PHOENIX

Pages 174-177 following:
Woodrow Phoenix has worked as cartoonist and illustrator for over 20 years. He is currently making a cartoon version of his Slave Labour series **Pants Ant.** *He lettered Alan Moore and Oscar Zarate's A Small Killing. That's him on page 24. Story and illustrations ©2003 Woodrow Phoenix.*

STEFANO
RAFFAELE

Left: *Stefano Raffaele has had comics published by Valiant, Marvel and Marvel Italy. He is the artist of the upcoming Dark Horse miniseries* **The Blackburne Covenant** *and Les Humanoids'* **Fragile.**
Illustration ©2003 Stefano Raffaele. All characters ©2003 their respective copyright holders.

I

The Wonderful Wardrobe of Alan Moore

by Woodrow Phoenix

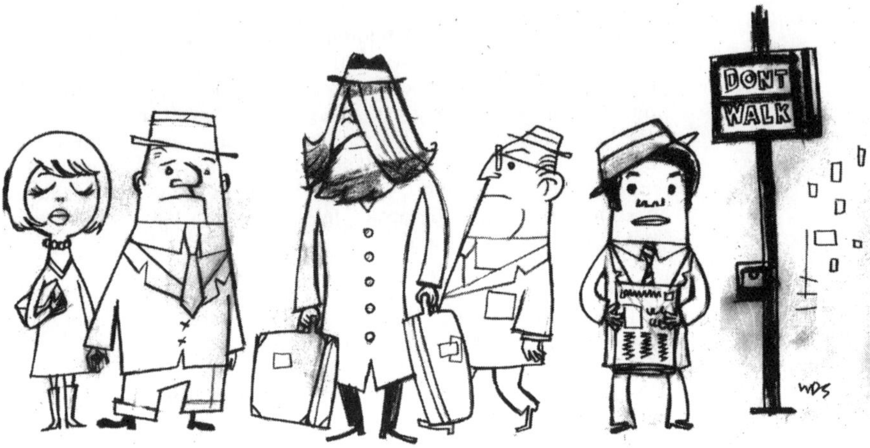
DONT
WALK

When Alan arrived in Mainstream City, he seemed to be the same as everyone else. He blended right in with all the residents with their hats and overcoats, though you might have noticed the fancier stitching and the rather higher than average quality material of his overcoat if you paid attention to such things.

He soon found himself a place to live and a job, made friends and went to church just like everybody else, but there was something about him that made him stand out. Eventually people figured out what it was. It was the way he dressed. Even though he wore the same things as everyone else, he wore them differently. It was all in the details. Hand finishing. Linings in unusual fabrics. Bias cutting. Seams that were stitched rather than fused or glued.

According to Alan there was nothing especially noteworthy about any of this. He came from a tradition of hard work and attention to detail, he said, and that was all there was to it.

II

However, while he had begun by branching out, by subtly altering the details of traditional tailoring, he began feel the restrictions of this approach. He decided to go further. He went off in entirely new directions with radical styles and some rather challenging choices of colour and fabric. People noticed. People talked. He became the focus of quite a lot of attention and speculation about what he might make next.

It was remarked upon that he never seemed to wear the same piece of clothing twice. He said it was true: there were so many styles in the world, why confine yourself to the same items over and over? Not long after that, Alan saw that his discarded clothes earmarked for recycling were vanishing from his rubbish bins only to turn up on the backs of other young men around town. They were obviously not quite as well fitting as when Alan wore them but they looked good enough to gain some attention of their own. Those who knew something about fashion recognised the source. They went to Alan to tell him about it and ask him to make clothes for them and finally he agreed.

He began to build quite a following for his unique tailoring style that took standard detailing and made it into something unexpected and new. There was quite a demand. He won prizes and appeared in magazine articles. Models competed to wear his styles in fashion spreads.

But then of course the knockoffs were thriving too. Alan could never hope to satisfy the hunger for his clothes by himself and it was unthinkable to hire assistants just to keep up with the orders. So the waiting list grew and sometimes people just couldn't wait any longer. Gradually, a whole industry grew up with no other purpose, it seemed, than to watch what Alan made and then replicate it more cheaply. He didn't take any of them seriously – they didn't have the patience or the imagination to copy more than the surface details. But it was tiring, all the same. The feeling of being on a treadmill was stronger every day until he knew he had to do something before his desire to create vanished for good.

Then he announced to all his clients that from now on he would be putting all his resources into something new.
He called it... the potatosack.

It didn't catch on right away. It was rough and scratchy, provided no pockets for credit cards or cellphones, came in only one colour and one size and was no good in the rain. It certainly didn't keep the cold out, either. But nobody wanted to be the one who didn't 'get it', so eventually everyone who was anyone was wearing the potatosack.

The fashion magazines wrote about it endlessly. It spread inexorably to the cheaper stores who also sold cutdown versions for children. And just when it looked like there could hardly be anyone left in the entire city who didn't own a potatosack, Alan was interviewed on TV. He was wearing one of his old suits. Why wasn't he in a potatosack?

—Because it's a joke, he said.
—You're all wearing sacks made for potatoes, he said.
—Look at you. They're impractical, ugly and itchy. They're not clothes. They're rough pieces of burlap. They're only fit for carrying potatoes. Why would anyone with any sense voluntarily wear one of those ridiculous things when they could be warm and dry and comfortable in actual garments?

Imagine it. Every line to the station's switchboards was instantly jammed and there were crazy scenes in the the studio as the entire audience rose up as one and rushed the stage, knocking lights, cameras, cameramen aside in their frenzy. At some point order was restored and that was when they realised that Alan had vanished. A vengeful crowd searched for him while potato sacks burned in the streets, but his apartment was empty, his bank accounts closed and his office bare.

Six months later, halfway around the world in Technical Town, several people began to notice an unusual kind of software in use at a few terminals around downtown cafés... but that's another story.

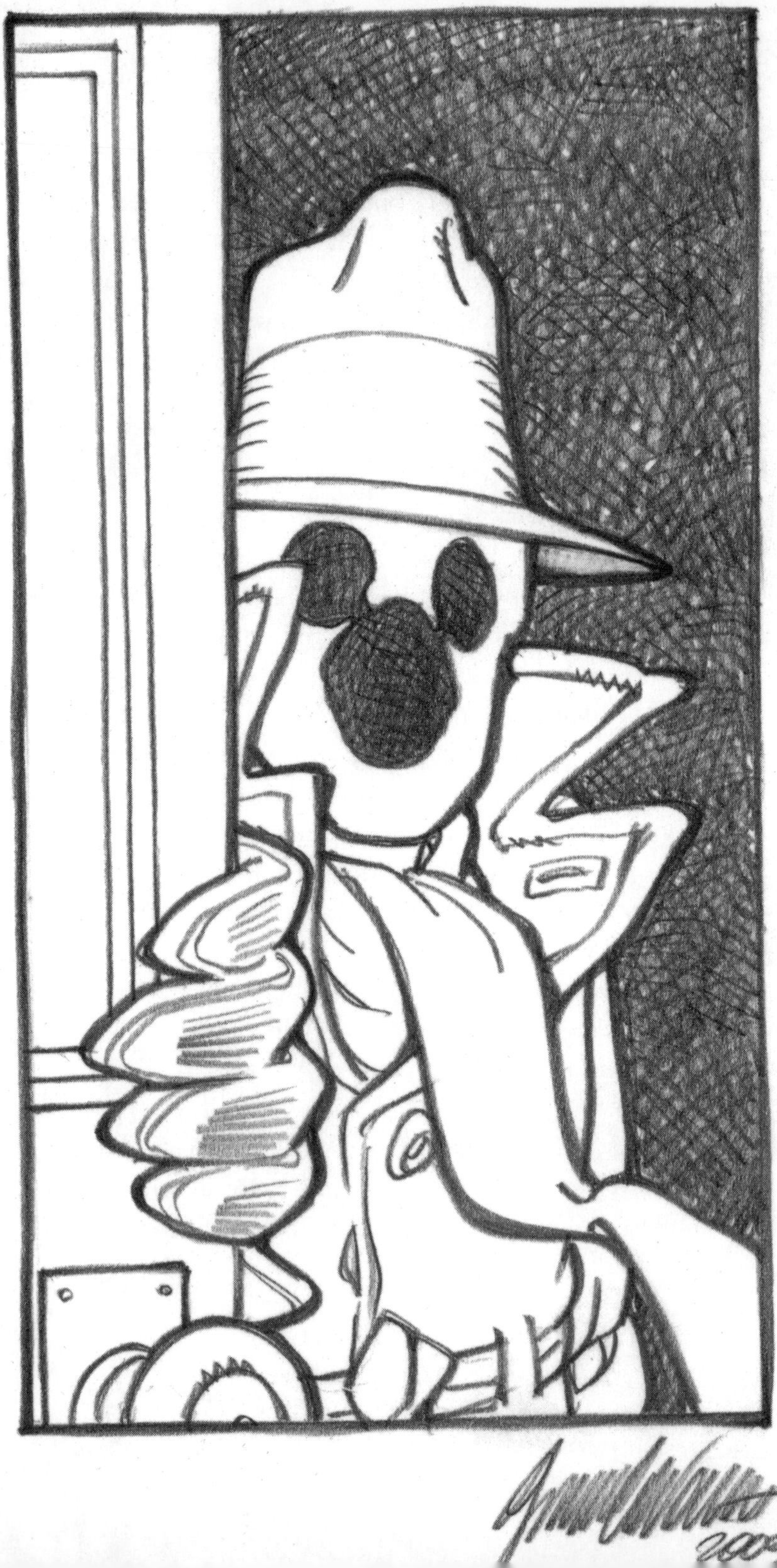

TIME

IGORT

Igort is a well-known Italian comics artist and publisher, who regularly works for Japanese publisher Kodansha. His latest graphic-novel **5 è il numero perfetto** *has been simultaneously published in Italy, France, USA, Canada, Germany, Holland, Spain, Greece and Portugal.* www.igort.com. *Text ©2003 Igort.*

Paris, late March, 2003

Earlier today I met a fellow artist, Oscar Zarate. As usually happens between authors, we talked about work over a cup of tea. You know, the things we are currently doing, those we are planning to do, our personal opinions of a certain publisher, the comics world in general. Very soon the conversation turned to an old piece of work done by Oscar and Alan Moore. Inevitably, I asked how it had felt to provide the art for *A Small Killing*, since I know Alan's scripts are extremely dense and packed with information. In this respect, Moore is not just famous, but legendary. To an artist, manoeuvring through thousands of details is never easy. "Usually with Alan, a panel takes up a whole page of the script with explanations", Oscar told Sampayo, who was sipping a Russian Earl Grey with us. These descriptions are quite precise and very visually oriented. Oscar said he had had no problems: the two of them had co-written the story and thus, for once, Moore did not need to resort to his minutiae, panel after panel, page after page.

Flashback

I recall my first impressions after reading *Watchmen*. It was the late Eighties. I had just founded a magazine called *Dolce Vita* and wanted to publish quality European comics; not just the same old stuff, but comics which would add something new to the medium. A few years earlier, along with Lorenzo Mattotti, Giorgio Carpinteri and others, I had co-founded what came to be known as the "Italian comics new-wave movement." It was a group of authors producing their own magazine, *Valvoline Motorcomics*. We were convinced that making the most of the medium's enormous potential and working on the language was the natural thing to do. We acted like a Surrealist group, with a mix of irreverence and irony which used to incense a part of Italian comicdom, especially the more conservative among our colleagues. After the *Valvoline* experience, then, I was finding myself again in the dual role of author and publisher. *Watchmen* struck me deeply because it was an extremely complex and multi-layered work, which had no use for the narrative shortcuts of American mainstream comics. The characters wore spandex, true, but could anyone call them "heroes?" Moore was ruthless with them. He completely rewrote the American myth from a European point of view. Moreover, *Watchmen* was a true epic: it took hours to read and on reaching the last page, one felt it was necessary to read it again and again to appreciate all its subtleties.

Another thing I admired in Moore was his mimetic ability to use mainstream tools to produce something different. In this case, the tool was the comic book format, which Moore was using as a *feuilleton*, as if he were a 19th Century French writer. To him, each issue was a chapter of a story that was much greater than the sum of its parts. The covers themselves were unusual in that they worked by subtraction: action was no longer in the foreground, replaced by a metaphysical look on objects which acted as traces, as memories of actions which had already taken place. Moore would also work with time, taking a step back and letting it do its job on people and things. To me, time was the true main character in the story. Fifteen years later, my opinion is still the same and I think it applies to all of Alan's works. What I admire in them is the absence of boundaries. Comics are not the only thing Moore reads and this shows in the way he conceives the story. This stems from an extremely broad notion of storytelling. *Watchmen* is full of stories which contain other stories, just like Russian dolls.

It is a many-voiced narrative, but at the same time also a meta-narrative, a

GIORGIO CAVAZZANO

Left: *Giorgio Cavazzano is the internationally acclaimed Italian Disney artist. His art can be seen in many European, USA and Brazilian magazines. Cartoon ©2003 Giorgio Cavazzano. Rorschach is ©2003 DC Comics.*

sum of different techniques (documents, letters, newspaper clippings, etc.). From this point of view, it is the closest thing to avant-garde art in the field of comics.

Paris, April 1st, 2003

I would like to stress that to me the importance of Moore's work lies not only in his use of different storytelling techniques, but also in the fact that this is done subtly and unobtrusively. He is first and foremost a great narrator. The reason why I wanted to write this homage to him is because I consider works such as *Watchmen* or *V for Vendetta* (to name just two) still perfectly relevant. They marked a watershed in the history of storytelling in the last twenty years. Unlike other books that came out more or less at the same time and today look mostly to have aged badly, Alan's works are still un-aged and ageless.

Flashback – Bologna, 1987

Alan's stories – and this happens very rarely otherwise – can be the subject of a narrative themselves. I recall a conversation with Giorgio Lavagna (a fellow writer and the singer in a band in the glory days of Italian New Wave) in which, lost in reverie, he waxed lyrical about the *Miracleman* book. He told me how Moore had retrieved a forgotten minor-league hero and rewritten his history. Pages from the original series, which had been cancelled many years before, were even used as part of the new stories and given a new life. The difference in style was justified by the plot which, if I remember rightly, involved moving between dimensions. Ever the great talker, Giorgio told me and Leila [Marzocchi] about the mechanics of the story, down to the personal details, while mimicking the characters' stances, facial expressions and hesitations.

This had an incredible effect on me and I remember I started looking everywhere for those hard-to-find back issues.

Well, I find Moore's ability to astonish even other writers, to have this effect which transcends the boundaries of both one's nation and one's ego, one of his most amazing traits. In my view, being able to pass on this great passion for narrative – for the act of telling itself – really means a lot.

In retrospect, even the blurbs on the back cover of the original paperback collection of *Watchmen* seem to have aged faster than the book itself. *Time Zone Magazine* described it as "the first true postmodernist superhero comic-book," *Time Out* as "a true novel." Today, these definitions sound inadequate. Dealing with an author who defies classification by creating categories of his own, they look like some garment one retrieves from a chest after fifteen years, wondering: "How on Earth was I able to squeeze into this?"

• **Igort,** Paris.

OSCAR ZARATE

Right: *Oscar Zarate studied architecture and worked in advertising in his native Argentina before moving to Europe. Zarate illustrated some children's books and made the comic adaptations* **Lenin for Beginners' Freud for Beginners,** *and* **Faustus.** *He's best known for his graphic novel collaboration with Alan Moore,* **A Small Killing,** *published by Gollancz. Strip ©2003 Oscar Zarate.*

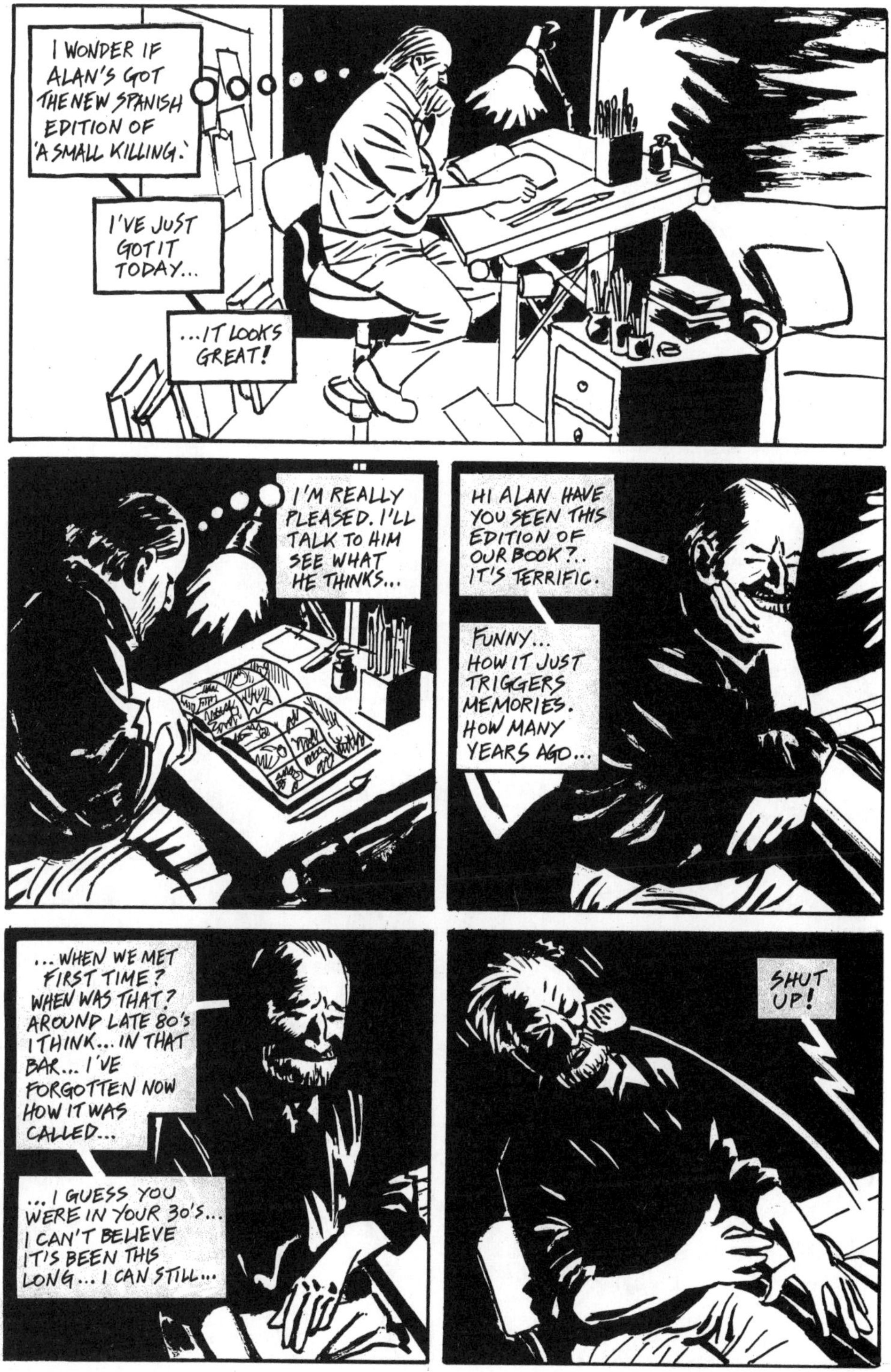
I WONDER IF ALAN'S GOT THE NEW SPANISH EDITION OF 'A SMALL KILLING.'
I'VE JUST GOT IT TODAY...
...IT LOOKS GREAT!
I'M REALLY PLEASED. I'LL TALK TO HIM SEE WHAT HE THINKS...
HI ALAN HAVE YOU SEEN THIS EDITION OF OUR BOOK?.. IT'S TERRIFIC.
FUNNY... HOW IT JUST TRIGGERS MEMORIES. HOW MANY YEARS AGO...
...WHEN WE MET FIRST TIME? WHEN WAS THAT? AROUND LATE 80'S I THINK... IN THAT BAR... I'VE FORGOTTEN NOW HOW IT WAS CALLED...
...I GUESS YOU WERE IN YOUR 30'S... I CAN'T BELIEVE IT'S BEEN THIS LONG... I CAN STILL...
SHUT UP!

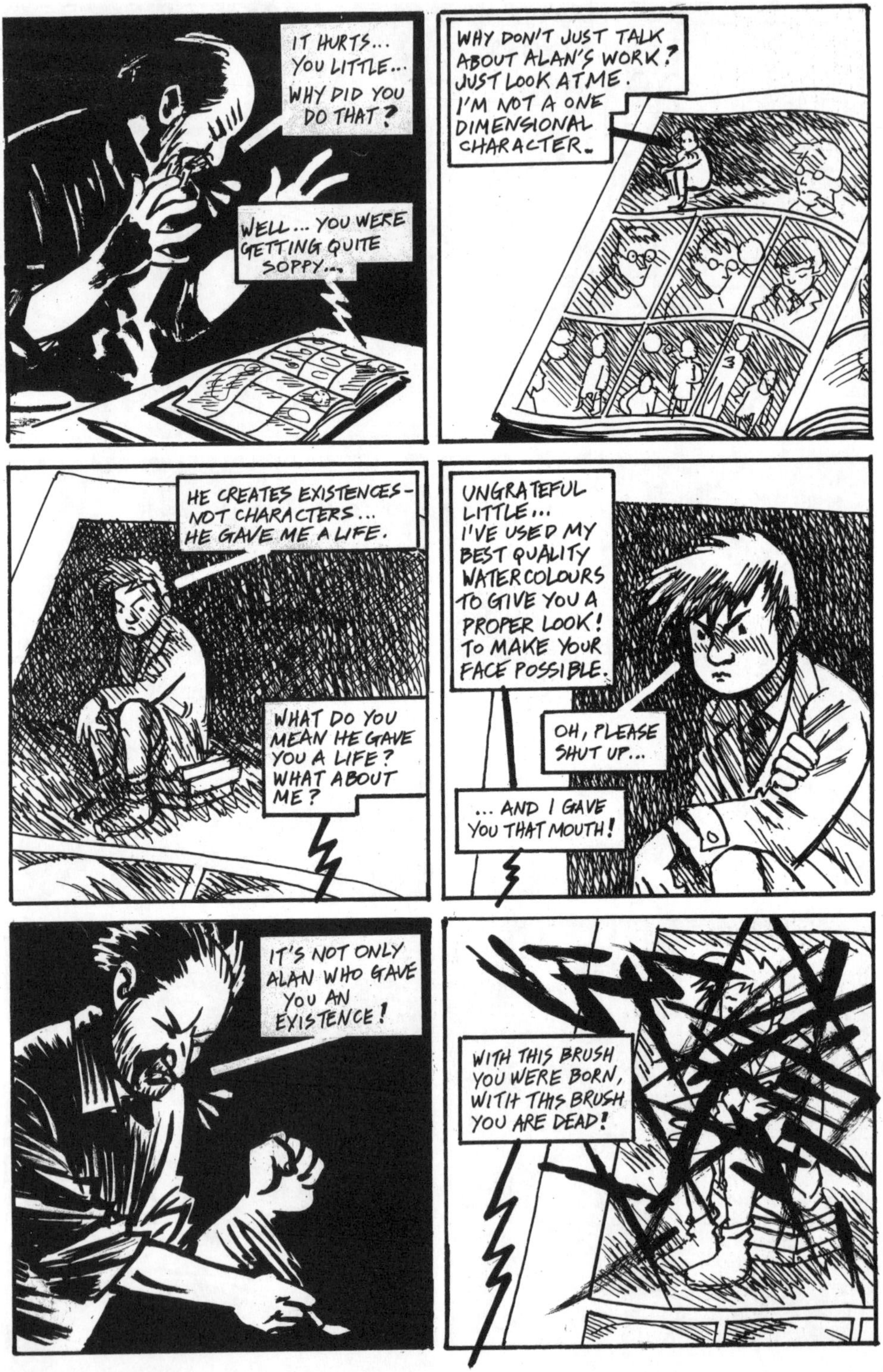
IT HURTS... YOU LITTLE...
WHY DID YOU DO THAT?
WELL... YOU WERE GETTING QUITE SOPPY...
WHY DON'T JUST TALK ABOUT ALAN'S WORK? JUST LOOK AT ME. I'M NOT A ONE DIMENSIONAL CHARACTER.
HE CREATES EXISTENCES - NOT CHARACTERS... HE GAVE ME A LIFE.
WHAT DO YOU MEAN HE GAVE YOU A LIFE? WHAT ABOUT ME?
UNGRATEFUL LITTLE... I'VE USED MY BEST QUALITY WATER COLOURS TO GIVE YOU A PROPER LOOK! TO MAKE YOUR FACE POSSIBLE.
OH, PLEASE SHUT UP...
... AND I GAVE YOU THAT MOUTH!
IT'S NOT ONLY ALAN WHO GAVE YOU AN EXISTENCE!
WITH THIS BRUSH YOU WERE BORN, WITH THIS BRUSH YOU ARE DEAD!

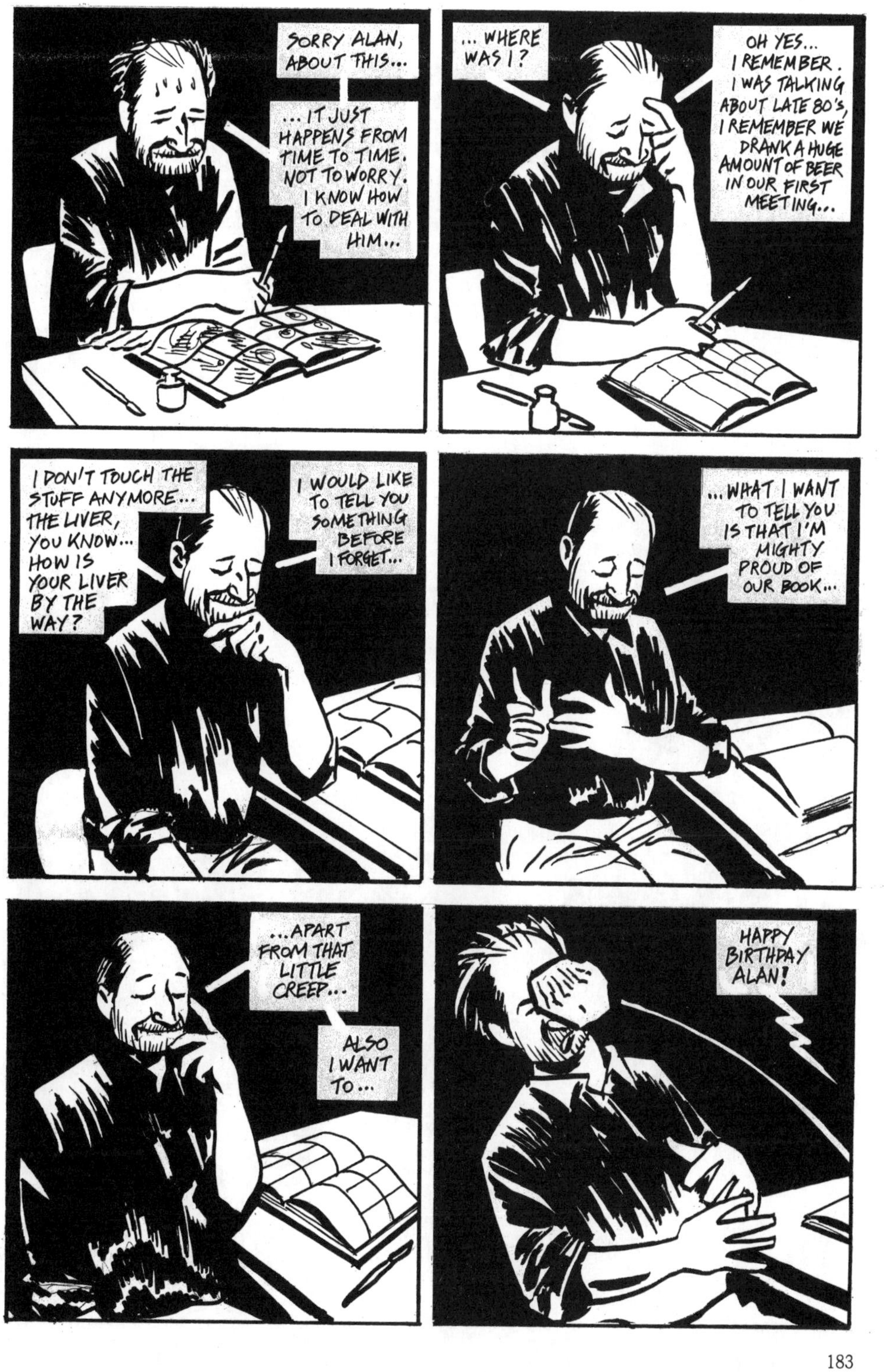
SORRY ALAN, ABOUT THIS...
... IT JUST HAPPENS FROM TIME TO TIME. NOT TO WORRY. I KNOW HOW TO DEAL WITH HIM...
... WHERE WAS I?
OH YES... I REMEMBER. I WAS TALKING ABOUT LATE 80'S, I REMEMBER WE DRANK A HUGE AMOUNT OF BEER IN OUR FIRST MEETING...
I DON'T TOUCH THE STUFF ANYMORE... THE LIVER, YOU KNOW... HOW IS YOUR LIVER BY THE WAY?
I WOULD LIKE TO TELL YOU SOMETHING BEFORE I FORGET...
... WHAT I WANT TO TELL YOU IS THAT I'M MIGHTY PROUD OF OUR BOOK...
... APART FROM THAT LITTLE CREEP...
ALSO I WANT TO ...
HAPPY BIRTHDAY ALAN!

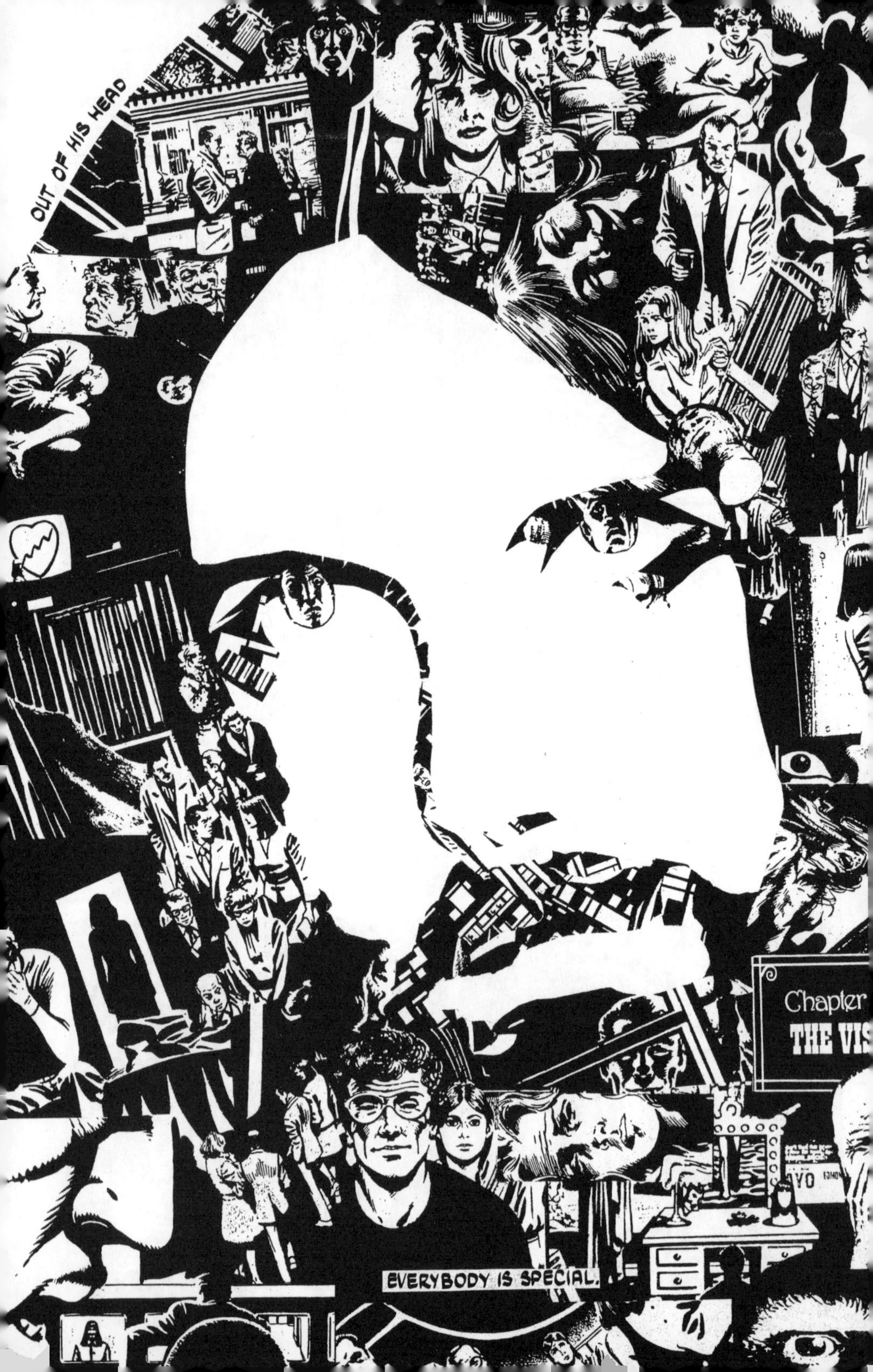
OUT OF HIS HEAD
Chapter
THE VIS
EVERYBODY IS SPECIAL.

A SMALL SENSE OF NOT BELONGING

ALESSANDRO BILOTTA

*Alessandro Bilotta is the Italian comics writer of steam-punk series **Le aventure di Giulio Maraviglia** (Montego) and dystopian graphic novel **La Dottrina** (Magic Press). Text ©2003 Alessandro Bilotta.*

Dear Sir Alan Moore,

I hope you will forgive me because I do not exist.

I arrived in Northampton in July of 1985 on a local train which took a strange route, stopping in a lot of small towns in the south. On the last exhausting part of the journey I fell asleep, breaking all the solid principles of diffidence and prudence which, to a great extent, are responsible for what I am today. Or, if you prefer, for what I am not. Just a second to realise that my Prince of Wales jacket was still folded in four on the seat in front of me, and I started running down the narrow corridor looking for a ticket inspector who could tell me if I had missed my stop. The train stopped at yet another town. "Bedford" the sign said. A man with good manners, but with clay on his shoes, explained in an apparently kind way that we would arrive in Northampton in half an hour's time. But I didn't trust him and so I asked the inspector who confirmed what he had said. Once back in my compartment I checked that the suitcase was still in the space above the seat in front of mine and then stayed standing so I would not fall asleep again.

The house was welcoming, shabby and clean. You got a smell of newness yet of already used. I don't know if you, Sir Alan, have ever bought a brand new car. Up to a little while ago I was not able to afford one. What you feel is something very like opening the box of a toy when you are a child. You are sure that that thing is yours because nobody has ever touched it before you. It is an inexact conclusion because someone will have taken that toy from the production line to put it inside the box. But the difference between that one and another bought in a flea market is, in my opinion, the smell. I can say that the sour smell of a material which has been kept in a box or in an environment which preserves its original characteristics can give the impression of being virgin. And give the apparent omnipotence to do with it what you will. Prints, shoes, motorcars and apartments are all part of this same olfactory category. To walk into a rented apartment or buy a used car is an experience which leaves no smell because someone has already consumed it.

The first time I saw you, Sir Alan, was in the Grosvenor Shopping Centre. I would tell a lie if I were to say it was intentional. It was one of my first days in Northampton and I was still trying to settle in, I was almost not thinking about you. Later this would make me reflect on the strange way human destinies pursue one another.

DAVID LLOYD

*Left: For over 20 years, David Lloyd has applied his electrifying talent to a host of comic book stories, bringing them to vibrant life with a stunning blend of cinematic technique and design skills. Widely known for **V for Vendetta**, and hardly known for anything else, he is currently exploring ways and means of expanding the markets for his work, as part of an enthusiastic, almost fanatical, and, quite possibly, futile, crusade to educate the broadest public available into the full realisation of the values of his craft. Illustration ©2003 David Lloyd. V for Vendetta ©2003 DC Comics.*

That hair, that beard and that dragging walk, what seediness, I thought. You were wearing a green spring jacket, with a military late-Seventies cut, the kind of jacket which was very popular with anti-militarists. Certainly not a designer jacket. And so I got the idea of following you as you made your way along the main aisle of the centre, your head down with that touch of agoraphobia which suits artists, like someone who is afraid that another person can pinpoint his own diversity. Like me who, in the midst of dozens of people, was afraid of losing you, and followed your unmistakable silhouette. You went into the bookshop of the shopping centre and asked an assistant at the cash desk if the book you had ordered had arrived. The assistant apologised for the further delay and added that it was not easy to find but that they had guaranteed it would be there on the Friday of the following week. I pulled out my notebook and made a careful note of the title and author of the book. You went towards the exit, stopping for a second to peep at the first of a series of calendars on sale next to the door, then you left disappearing from my sight. This time I did not follow you. I went over to the shelves of novels which were piled up according to the author's surname and searched for one which was not there, but could be easily found. I went over to the cash desk and asked if they had Camus' "The Stranger". The cashier got up and went over to the same point where I had looked for the book that was not there. That point which the inflexible alphabetical order had assigned to it. Returning to the cash desk he told me they did not have it, but that if I ordered a copy it would arrive in a short period of time. A question of two or three days. I left my surname and telephone number and headed towards the door. I took a step back to take a peep at the calendar which had caught your attention. It was illustrated by a certain Hokusai. Three days later an assistant took a copy of "The Stranger" from a shelf on which the books ordered by clients were piled up neatly behind the cash desk. The shelf was clearly visible and within everyone's reach. I peeped to see if your book had arrived, but it was too early. The bookshop was punctual in its delay.

On the Thursday evening of the following week the book was on the shelf. I could get close to it without any problem. You would pick it up only the next morning.

Returning home that evening I thought how much one of your fans would have envied me. Does the logic of the fanatic exist in the world of comic strips? I had met you, followed you, and got close to you. My glance had fallen on you recognising you as being different in the midst of hundreds of people. But I was not the slightest bit interested in your work, nor had I ever read anything you had written, because I don't read comics. Indeed I thought you were an illustrator, I didn't think there was a difference between the two roles, the person who writes the comic and the person who draws it. All this stimulated me and as soon as I got home from my suitcase I pulled out the last Superman Annual I had bought shortly before leaving. I read it and let it drop on the couch. I went over to the window and pulled the curtain aside a little to see your house on the other side of the road. The lights were on.

Did you know there is also a Northampton in America, in Massachusetts, and that there is even one in Australia? During my entire stay I always asked myself what they could have in common with yours. If, by some contorted destiny, they had illegitimately taken possession of some other detail which was not the originality of the name.

I found the neighbourhood horrible. A long row of houses which stretched as far as the eye could see like a long spinal chord of the fossil of a brachiosaurus disappearing around the curve of the horizon. These kind of panoramic monstrosities do not exist where I come from. They cannot even be compared with Hell, because there you imagine things to be in perpetual motion and constantly changing like inside the crater of a volcano. Northampton, on the other hand, looked like a motionless advertisement for a Fifties white goods company. Yet I liked it.

For my job I have travelled and still travel often. But I never get used to that feeling of being a stranger. Funny isn't it? How can someone who does not exist feel part of something? Every place I visit remains at a distance from me, everything is lovely and sometimes even welcoming, but it remains at a distance as if waiting for me to go back to where I came from and take back my own place. And so, when you travel, everything is like an invitation to a party, you are enjoying it, but you can't take off your shoes and fall asleep on the couch, because the very reason you feel well is because you do not belong to that place. It rolls off your back. And so, Sir Alan, I don't know if

CHARLIE ADLARD

Right: *In his real world Charlie lives in Shrewsbury with his wife, Lynette, son Dylan, and Ren and Stimpy, his cats...* In his other world, he is the artist of among other things,**The X-Files, The Establishment, Mars Attacks, Batman: Scarface** and **White Death.** *Illustration ©2003 Charlie Adlard. The League of Extraordinary Gentlemen ©2003 Alan Moore and Kevin O'Neill.*

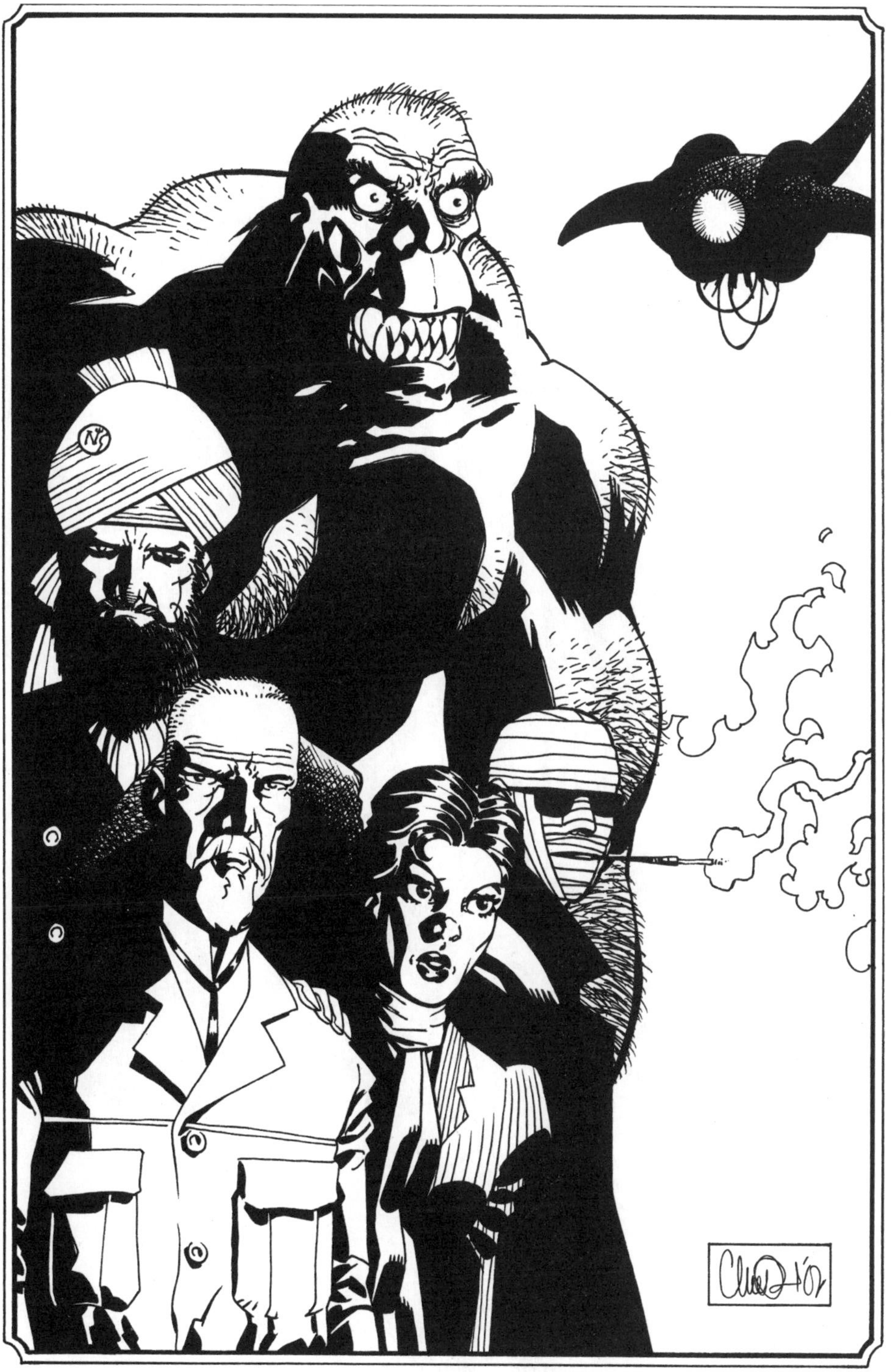

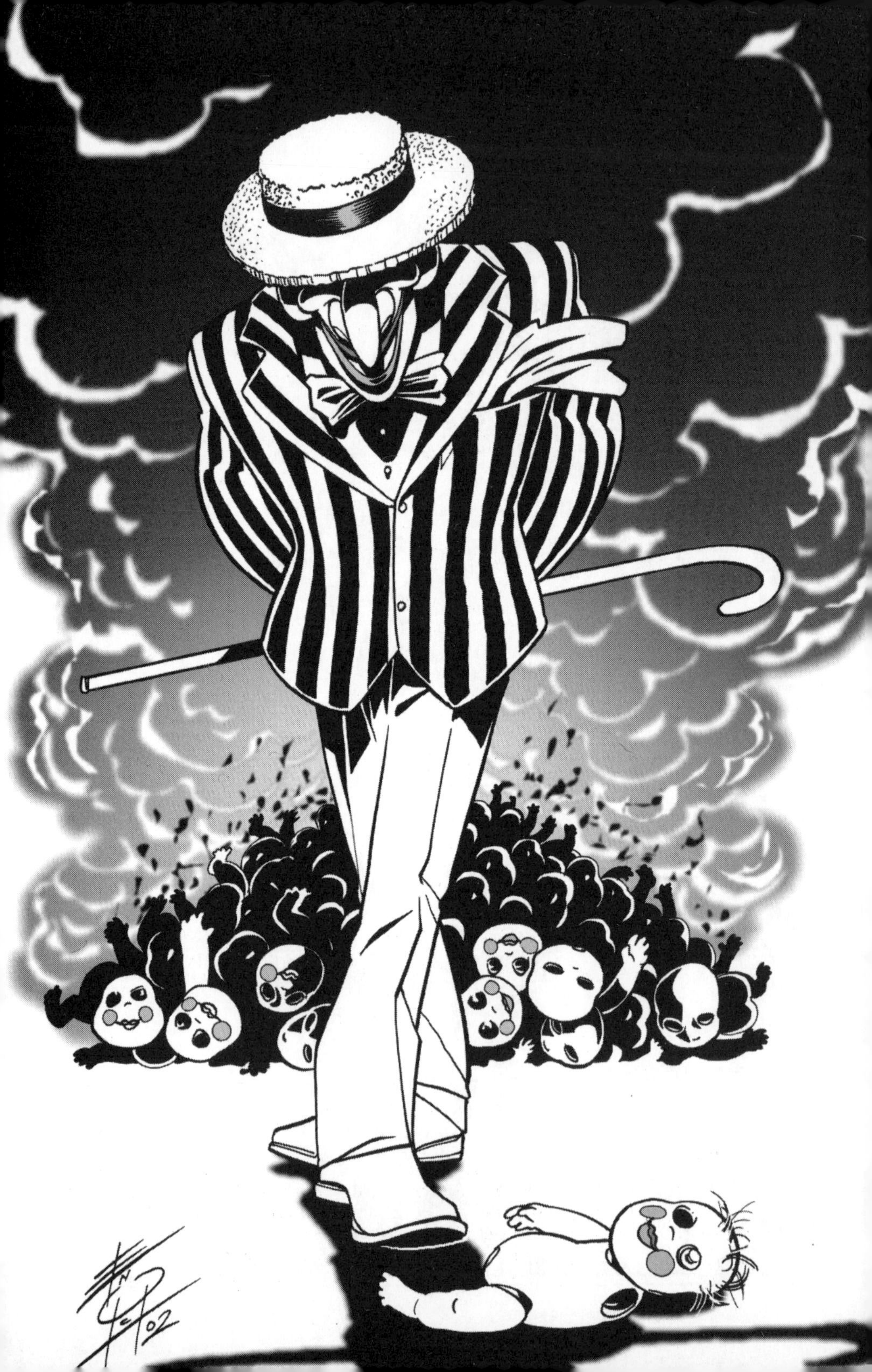

you agree, but finding oneself in another city, be it on business or holidays, makes it even more enjoyable, perhaps only because it is easier to accept. We don't belong to it and it does not belong to us. The next morning, after waking up, there is no traffic to make us late and no work to go to. Because we come from somewhere else. We are not there. In my case we do not even exist.

And so Northampton could even have poured cement over those few flowerbeds left along the road, the little houses could have squeezed even closer together like packets of cigarettes, that grey sky could even have made me keep the light on at ten in the morning. I was a spectator.

Next to the window Hokusai's calendar stared at me, open at the first page, January 1986, although it was July 1985. I stared at it in a dream while the lights of the house on the other side of the street filtered dimly through the design on the curtain and were imprinted on my retina. Two men crossed a bridge which seemed to be suspended in space. It must have been a rope bridge because under their weight it was bent almost into a V. Except for a detail which struck me about the two men, it would have been possible to lose oneself in the scene depicted. The impression was that of finding oneself higher up than the mountain tops, so much so as to be surprised that the birds managed to be so high up, violating an apparently virgin place. The bridge seemed to be beyond the clouds. But the two men caught my attention more than the rest. They both seemed to be intent and decided on the same destiny. Perhaps they barely knew one another, but they were both certain they had to go where they were going. Together and for the same reasons. But then why was only one of them carrying an enormous weight on his shoulders while the other following him was carrying practically nothing? Maybe the direction was the same, but the determination was not.

From the headphone I listened carefully to your conversations, you, Phyllis, Amber, Leah and Deborah. Presumably the book was at a transit point of the house, perhaps at the entrance. I waited until you had gathered all your conversations and left. I saw you get into the car, that embarrassing heap of tin which looked like a coffin. I waited a few minutes. Then I crossed the road and entered.

I have to admit it was a rash thing to do. It was not my business yet I felt it was my duty. As soon as I was out of your house I didn't head straight for my house, but turned left and once again recalled all the details of that strange experience. I started with those which were closest. Your living room, the bedroom and the smell of the clothes in the wardrobe. The bathroom, the children's room and the view from the window. The glass was a perfect frame for the house on the other side of the road, it was the same as all the others, yet at the same time more anonymous. The lights were off and maybe the person who lived there was asleep, but no, it was too early. There was nobody at home. Perhaps the lodger was at a party with friends, in a restaurant with a woman, or perhaps quite simply by himself at the cinema, comfortably seated watching the lives of others on a white sheet. Or better still, nobody lived in that house. Yes, that was probably the assumption closest to the truth. Often there is no need to travel with fantasy to seek the reality of facts. Sometimes the facts just don't exist.

LUCA ENOCH

Left: Luca Enoch is the Italian creator of Bonelli Comics' bi-annual series Gea. He is also the co-creator and writer of **Morgana**, a series published in France and the US by Humanoids. Illustration © 2003 Luca Enoch. V for Vendetta ©2003 DC Comics.

Then I was distracted by the thought of that huge horrible painting which hung on your wall. But I had learned that your genius often goes arm in arm with bad taste, although it is something I find unpardonable. In the meantime I had come close to a fence which enclosed a park. I sat down on it and fixed my gaze on a small lake inside the park. Then I picked up the thread of my thoughts again. What infinite coincidences had brought me there? Among the people I had just got to know in Northampton some of them had even been willing to become friendly with the newcomer. But I had not arrived, I was merely passing through. I even remember, Sir Alan, the time a policeman came round and wanted to use my house as a look out for your house. Really crazy, don't you think? Forgive the irony but don't worry, I refused. Sitting on that fence I was overcome by a profound sense of sadness and I remembered that Superman Annual you had written and which I had read a short time earlier. When Kal stops the fluctuations in the crater and descends to think, his gaze lost in space, followed by the anxious eyes of his son Van. The son asks for explanations and looks for a concrete word or gesture which only his father can give. But Kal, on the other hand, feels that everything is unreal, he himself is making contact with what is around him, he can no longer perceive a relationship with the outside world. Just as when one is desperate. And so he feels the world is moving away, although at the same time he is moving away from the world. Does this ever happen to you, Sir Alan? Do you ever get the impression, at times of great difficulty, that you are cut off from everything else? Do you get the impression that the more you try to recapture a rapport, the more it draws away like a floating feather when you try to grab it too violently? Do you never get the impression that you cannot even pronounce a word which comes close to describing all this?

I got down from the fence and returned to the two houses. One facing the other and so different. Yet so dependent one on the other, more so than you perhaps can even imagine. I opened the door of my house and crossed the hall without turning on the light, holding out one hand so as not to run into the door of my room. I opened it banging it against the almost full suitcase which was lying on the ground. I turned on the light. I gave one last look at the notes I had written carefully in pencil on a very long sheet of paper, of the kind they use in printers, and then threw it into the suitcase. I got undressed and sat for a while on the side of the bed stroking my thighs the wrong way up, letting the many little needles wake up and straighten up on my skin. I turned off the light and slept.

I don't know why I am telling this story of my brief stay only now, Sir Alan. Maybe because it concerns you very closely, maybe because I think you can understand. I hope you will forgive me because, after all, I have neither a face nor a soul. I hope you will forgive me for having allowed myself some boring dissertations, but then the people I used to know always said I was verbose. Ironic isn't it. After all, it is the people around us who are historians and biographers and, as historians and biographers, give their version of us. Which is the version that lasts in time. Now only a few people surround me, and the things I have told you are perhaps something of a liberation for me. I hope that one day, Mr Moore, you will want to tell the small story of a man who does not exist.

• **Alessandro Bilotta**

SHANNON WHEELER

Right: Shannon Wheeler is an old, bitter, man who lives and works alone in the rural backwoods of southern Arkansas. He has three cats and a goat. He's trying to teach them to dance. He's also the creator and publisher of **Too Much Coffee Man.** Strip ©2003 Shannon Wheeler.

ALAN MOORE

SHANNON WHEELER

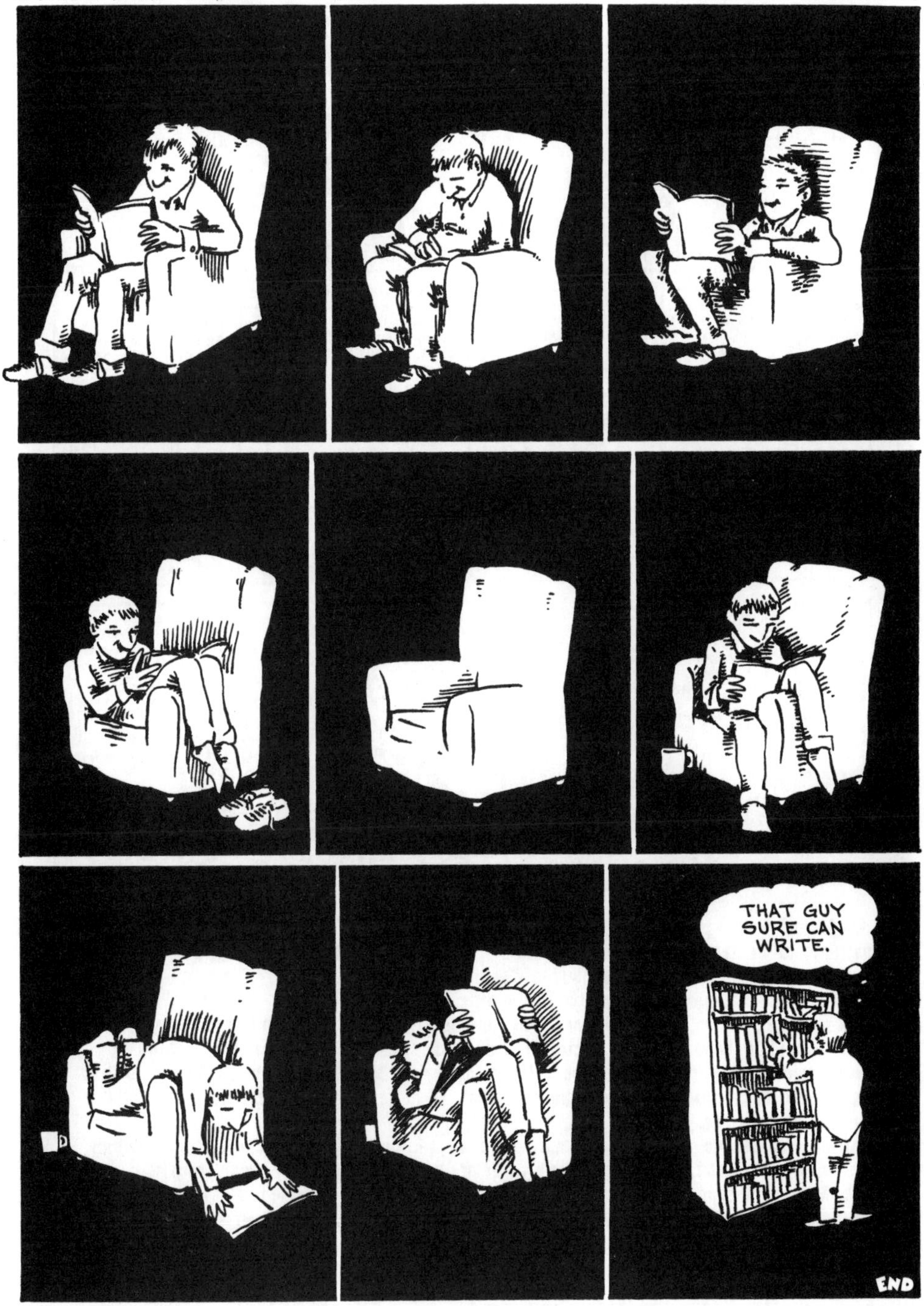

THAT GUY SURE CAN WRITE.
END

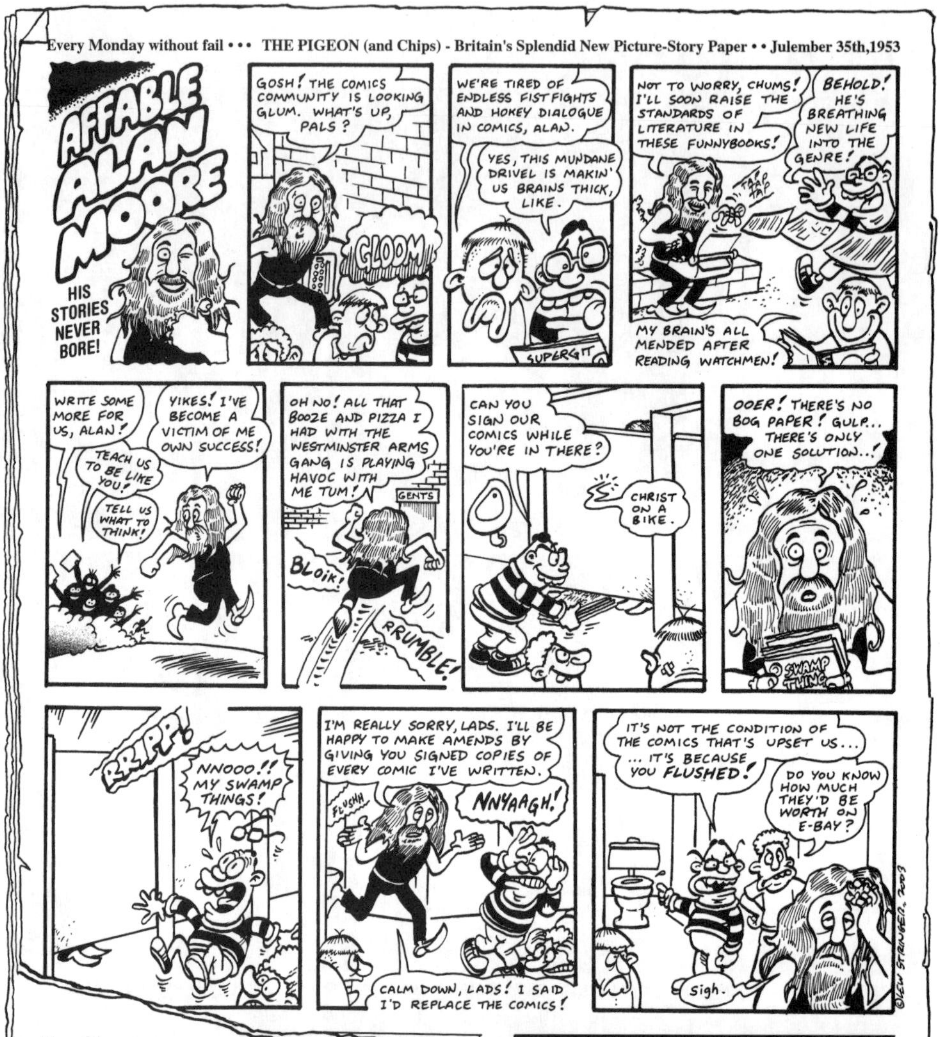
Every Monday without fail • • • THE PIGEON (and Chips) - Britain's Splendid New Picture-Story Paper • • Julember 35th,1953
AFFABLE ALAN MOORE
HIS STORIES NEVER BORE!
GOSH! THE COMICS COMMUNITY IS LOOKING GLUM. WHAT'S UP, PALS?
GLOOM
WE'RE TIRED OF ENDLESS FIST FIGHTS AND HOKEY DIALOGUE IN COMICS, ALAN.
YES, THIS MUNDANE DRIVEL IS MAKIN' US BRAINS THICK, LIKE.
SUPERGIT
NOT TO WORRY, CHUMS! I'LL SOON RAISE THE STANDARDS OF LITERATURE IN THESE FUNNYBOOKS!
BEHOLD! HE'S BREATHING NEW LIFE INTO THE GENRE!
TAP TAP
MY BRAIN'S ALL MENDED AFTER READING WATCHMEN!
WRITE SOME MORE FOR US, ALAN!
YIKES! I'VE BECOME A VICTIM OF ME OWN SUCCESS!
TEACH US TO BE LIKE YOU!
TELL US WHAT TO THINK!
OH NO! ALL THAT BOOZE AND PIZZA I HAD WITH THE WESTMINSTER ARMS GANG IS PLAYING HAVOC WITH ME TUM!
GENTS
BLOIK!
RRUMBLE!
CAN YOU SIGN OUR COMICS WHILE YOU'RE IN THERE?
CHRIST ON A BIKE.
OOER! THERE'S NO BOG PAPER! GULP... THERE'S ONLY ONE SOLUTION..!
SWAMP THING
RRIPP!
NNOOO!! MY SWAMP THINGS!
I'M REALLY SORRY, LADS. I'LL BE HAPPY TO MAKE AMENDS BY GIVING YOU SIGNED COPIES OF EVERY COMIC I'VE WRITTEN.
FLUSHH
NNYAAGH!
CALM DOWN, LADS! I SAID I'D REPLACE THE COMICS!
IT'S NOT THE CONDITION OF THE COMICS THAT'S UPSET US... ...IT'S BECAUSE YOU FLUSHED!
DO YOU KNOW HOW MUCH THEY'D BE WORTH ON E-BAY?
Sigh.

1001 STAMPS
that you can't use

Alan Moore was
instrumental in starting my career in comics.
Twenty years ago I regularly attended the Westminster Comic Marts in London and was producing fanzines at the time. Giants in the industry such as Dave Gibbons, Kev O'Neill, and Alan, had become good friends and were always supportive of my work. However, a stream of rejection slips from publishers was making me despondent. Then Alan introduced me to Marvel UK editor Bernie Jaye, encouraging me to send her samples of my work. Success! This first break led to lots of regular freelance work and I've been busy ever since.
Alan was selflessly encouraging for many newcomers in the business. The last time I saw him was in 1990. He was trying to avoid the crowds at Angouleme. (Not easy considering he was wearing a bright orange suit!) Although it's been many years since those fondly remembered Westminster marts, I've always appreciated the motivation he gave me. Thanks, Alan!
-Lew Stringer http://www.geocities.com/lewstringer

THE TIPPING POINT
Or: NOTES FROM THE PERIPHERY OF THE MAGUS

JAMES A. OWEN

James Owen started self-publishing his acclaimed **Starchild** *comic book in 1992. One of current projects from his Coppervale Press is a re-launch of the art magazine* **International Studio**.

Text ©2003 James A. Owen.

As far as professional affiliations go, I think my tenure as an Alan Moore collaborator was of shorter duration than that of anyone else in this book (with the possible exception of Brad Meltzer, whom, as far as I know, has not actually collaborated with Alan, but which, I hasten to point out for fear of jeopardizing my future collaborations-The *Incunabula Promethea* and The *Legion of Super Heroes* Graphic Novel, respectively-is no reflection on the talent of either of these gentlemen). Still, given the influence Alan had on the beginnings of my career (and has on it still), I was very pleased for the opportunity to express my admiration for the creator of a body of work without which my own career and work on *Starchild* would have been greatly diminished, if indeed, they would have happened at all. I say this, because outside of a general influence, outside of a brief acquaintenceship and collaboration, outside of his influence on the many mutual friends working in the medium, I can specifically thank Alan for the Tipping Point which was the catalyst for *Starchild* and all of my career which has followed.

•••••

Let me start at the beginning. In decades past, DC Comics had a remarkable program of publishing material in digest form, material both reprinted and new. It was sort of a pilot run for what is now known as the trade paperback industry, except the books were released at a quarter of the size and a tenth of the price. At some point in the early 1990's, they decided to discontinue this program (thereby relinquishing the small-format racks of grocery stores everywhere to *Archie*) but during the 1980's, one tradition which was trailblazing (for the time) was a yearly Blue-Ribbon Digest called *The Year's Best*. Granted, it meant the year's best *DC* comics, but considering (at the time) there was little else to choose from except for the ubiquious Marvel line, and the trailblazers *Cerebus* and *Elfquest*, it was a pretty high-quality package.

The 1985 edition is the issue that changed a few things, for me. It had the usual suspects (Wolfman, Levitz, Perez, Garcia Lopez) and a short *Green Lantern* story which, along with an earlier *Detective Comics* two-pager, convinced me that Len Wein is one of the great short-story writers of the last few generations. It also reprinted Alan Moore's first *Swamp Thing* story, "The Anatomy Lesson", from the 21st issue of the series. It was my first exposure to Alan Moore, as well as his talented collaborators Stephen Bissette (who has since become a friend and fellow traveller) and John Totleben (more about whom later).

Not quite the tipping point, but the beginning of a significant shifting nonetheless.

•••••

Then came *Watchmen*. Not much to say here. When I bought issue one on the first day of a family vacation, it had the same effect as if my mother had casually revealed that the family Ford Pinto could drive up the sides of buildings. Sort of a 'What the hell is going on here?' kind of response. When I bought issue twelve, on my way to the San Diego Comicon (where I met Alan's collaborator Dave Gibbons), the ending shook me enough I made my friend's dad stop the car in the middle of the desert so I could run around whooping and hollering at the top of my lungs.

LEW STRINGER

Left: *Lew Stringer has worked as a cartoonist for over 20 years, starting off by drawing strips like* **Snail-Man,** **Captain Wally** *and* **Robo Capers** *for the British Marvel weeklies. He created* **Combat Colin** *for Action Force and* **Tom Thug** *for Buster and currently contributes to* **Viz,** *the* **Beano** *and the Swedish comic,* **Herman Hedning.**

Strip and text ©2003 Lew Stringer.

Still not the tipping point, but I was beginning to pick up momentum.

•••••

There are books which have inspired me in my work, and I've written of them often:

193

The original run of *Elfquest*; *Nexus*; Frank Miller's *Ronin*; Paul Chadwick's *Concrete.* All have been an influence, and all inspired my earlier attempts at creating comics material. But the one singular influence-my personal Tipping Point-the book which forced me to push my own boundaries past emulation and into the desire to create something on as pure a level, was Book Three of *Miracleman*, "Olympus", by Alan Moore and John Totleben.

Anyone familiar with my inking style will see Totleben's obvious influence (amidst the Windsor-Smith grass and leaves), but until *Miracleman*, I'd never gone at it in earnest to see if I had boundaries. I found them more quickly than I expected to. Ever since, I have been trying to break them, and a number of new influences have taken hold. But, if nothing else inspires, a glance at any of the "Olympus" issues clears the road ahead and lets me get back to work.

A few years later, having established my chops as a professional in the comics' field, I decided that I never wanted to meet Alan Moore or John Totleben. I'd become prominent enough that many of the people I'd admired were now my personal friends, and the batting average was about a third of what I'd hoped for. For all of the Rick Veitchs and Wendy Pinis and Bernie Wrightsons (who are all decent human beings) there were a score more who either hated their work or hated others' hero worship of said work or both, but were loathe to give up either, and in the process had skipped over mere feet of clay-ness straight into an existence that was hell to witness and even worse to interact with.

On the opposite end were people with whom I'd grown closest, and who broght with them all of the challenges of a personal relationship. The difference was, when I had a let's-change-the-world discussion with an old pal from high school, a transcript of said discussion wasn't likely to appear in the next issue of *Cerebus*, wrapped in a cover spoofing one of my own characters from *Starchild* (among issues, I should point out, which also contained long transcriptions of a discussion with Alan Moore, whom I intended to never meet or speak with).

I'd decided it might be better not to know who your heroes were.

•••••

It's the latter end of 1994 and I'm talking on the phone with Alan Moore.

Joe Pruett, the editor of the anthology *Negative Burn*, had asked if I'd be interested in participating in a project called *The Alan Moore Songbook.* Since it gave me a legitimate reason to call Alan (Rick Veitch had given me his number-and Totleben's-a couple of years earlier) I trashed my earlier convictions and accepted. I scrolled through the twenty or so songs, skipping the ones obviously better suited to another artist (Art Adams for "Trampling Tokyo") and ended up with one that I thought had some nice, romantic overtures to it. There were a few cloudy parts (bad fax), but I glossed over them, giddy with the idea that I was going to be working with Alan Moore. Made some notes. Called him up. Did the usual chitchat, then went white when his first reaction to my choosing "Rose Madder' was to say that he was glad that one would be done by an artist able to do detail work, what with all of the sexual imagery and whatnot.

(The irony is only apparent when you know that I was raised in a community where, despite the evidence to the contrary at the high school, asexual reproduction was preached as the reality and nudity only existed in Italian painting and MTV).

I've never been so grateful for the concept of Metaphor in my life. We talked a few times, Alan liked my ideas, I illustrated the song, and, as I heard sometime later, Alan and Melinda liked it very much.

•••••

JAMES A. OWEN

Right: *Owen's recent illustration of* **Promethea** *as a gift for Moore. Illustration ©2003 James A. Owen. Promethea ©2003 America's Best Comics, LLC.*

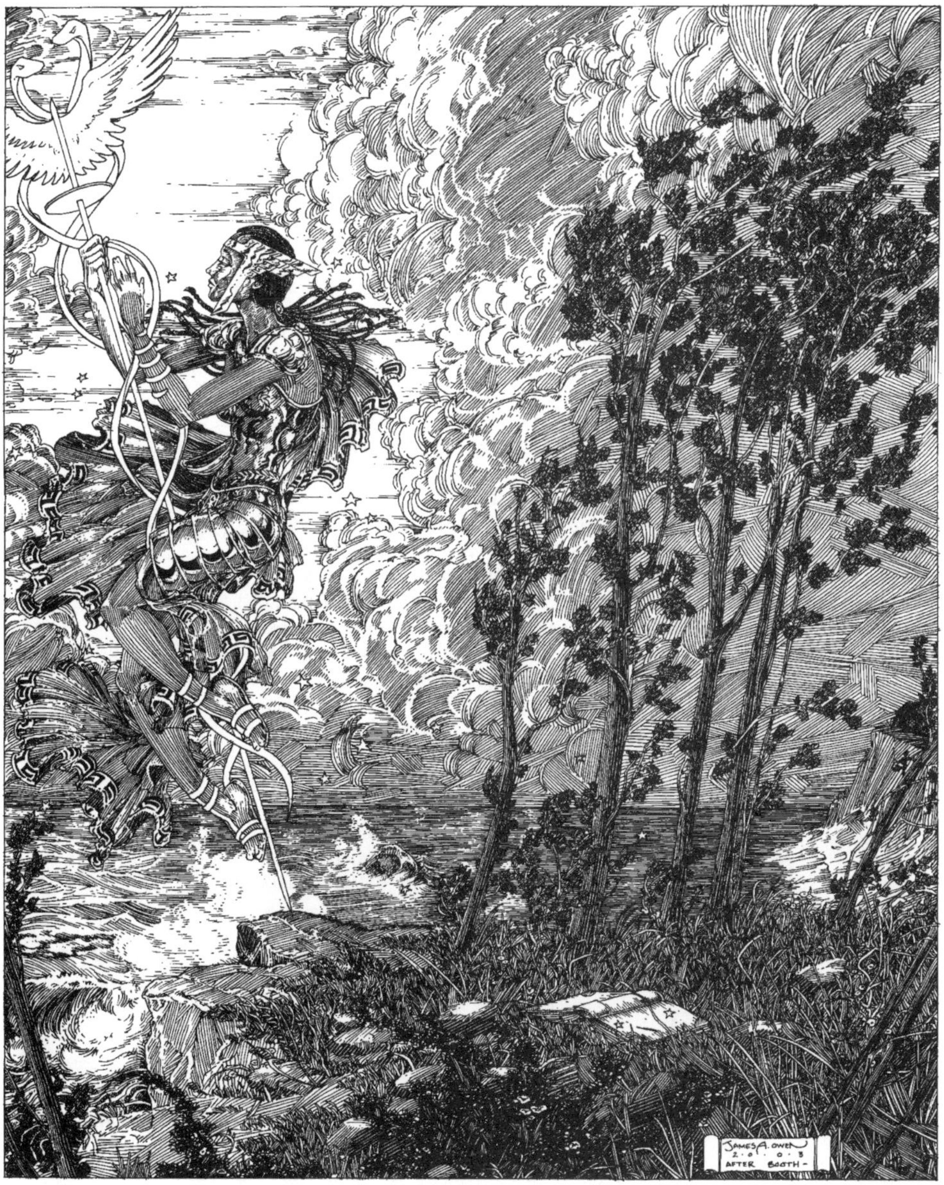
JAMES A. OWEN
2.0.0.3
AFTER BOOTH -

P R O M E T H E A

In Oakland at Wondercon several years ago, just after Alan's decision to enter seriously into the study of Magic (or Magick, as it were), Rick Veitch and I happened to have adjacent hotel rooms. We tended to be dinner companions when in the same city, and so we ended up turning in at about the same time each night. The first night, I awoke in the middle of a very lucid dream-thinking this would be good fodder for Rick's dream comic, *Rare Bit Fiends*-to see a veiled Alan sitting in the corner chair, talking. It became apparent after a moment or two that he wasn't talking to me, but to Rick. I spoke, and pointed this out to him. He replied that it didn't matter which room he was in-Rick would be able to hear him anyway-and continued his discourse. I went back to sleep.

The next morning, I asked Rick if he'd had any interesting dreams. He replied that he'd had all the usual menagerie-but also that he dreamed of the disembodied voice of Alan Moore, dropping some words of counsel or whatnot from afar.

"Not so far," I said. "He was in my room."

Rick then told me about Alan's new interest in Ideaspace, and Magick, and we talked about dreams and dreams of dreams, and I've never asked Alan exactly what he may have been doing that night, because I'm not sure I wanted to know. It was brief, and was directed at Rick, and I was more than happy to be on the periphery.

•••••

We're now at nearly the twenty year mark since I first heard of Alan Moore. I continue to hover at the periphery. Alan has been a part of my own stories, based on experiences both real and imagined; his collaborations seem to occur with artists who are my friends (my long friendship with Mick Gray being the inspiration for my *Promethea* illustration printed herein, the original of which will have been delivered by now, as a birthday gift for Alan); and his work continues to be an influence. At some point, I now expect we will become better acquainted personally-but considering he was comfortable dropping in on my hotel room and I was comfortable with him being there, I don't think it's going to be a problem.

I still haven't called John Totleben yet, though.

• **James A. Owen**
Taylor, Arizona
March, 2003

ART BROOKS

Pages 197-204 following:
Brooks is the writer of **Karol's Book, Azoth, Lvamp** *and the graphic novel* **The Outpost,** *all published in his native Spain. For Avatar in the US, he has adapted Alan Moore's songs into comic strips for the anthology* **Magical Mystery Moore.**

DANIEL ACUÑA

Acuña is a comic strip artist and magazine cover illustrator from Spain. His work includes art on **Claus & Simon, Snow Black & The Seven Samurais** *and the Roy Thomas scripted* **Anthem.**
Strip ©2003 Art Brooks & Daniel Acuña. All characters are ©2003 their respective copyright holders.

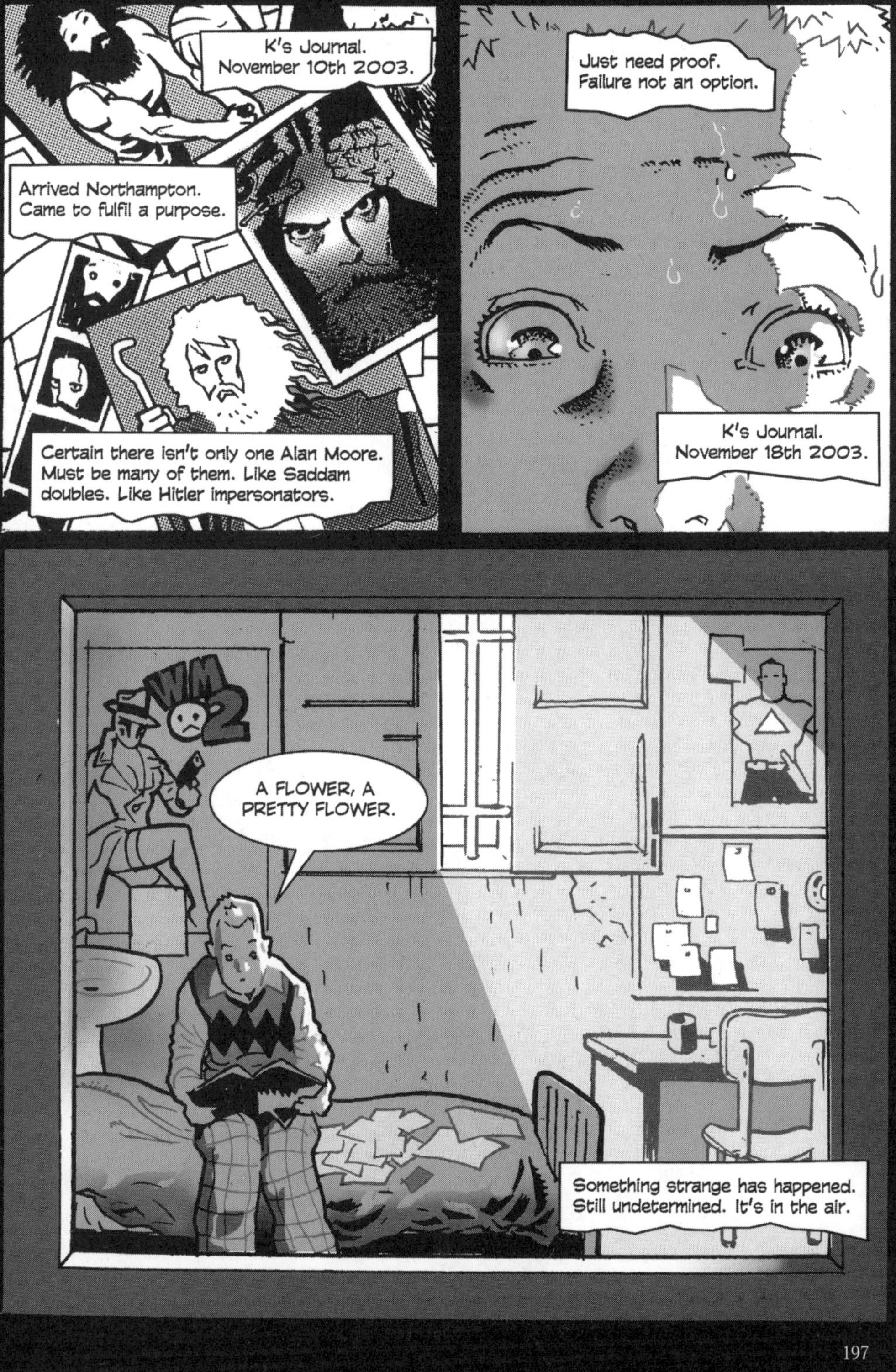
K's Journal.
November 10th 2003.
Arrived Northampton.
Came to fulfil a purpose.
Certain there isn't only one Alan Moore.
Must be many of them. Like Saddam
doubles. Like Hitler impersonators.
Just need proof.
Failure not an option.
K's Journal.
November 18th 2003.
WM 2
A FLOWER, A
PRETTY FLOWER.
Something strange has happened.
Still undetermined. It's in the air.

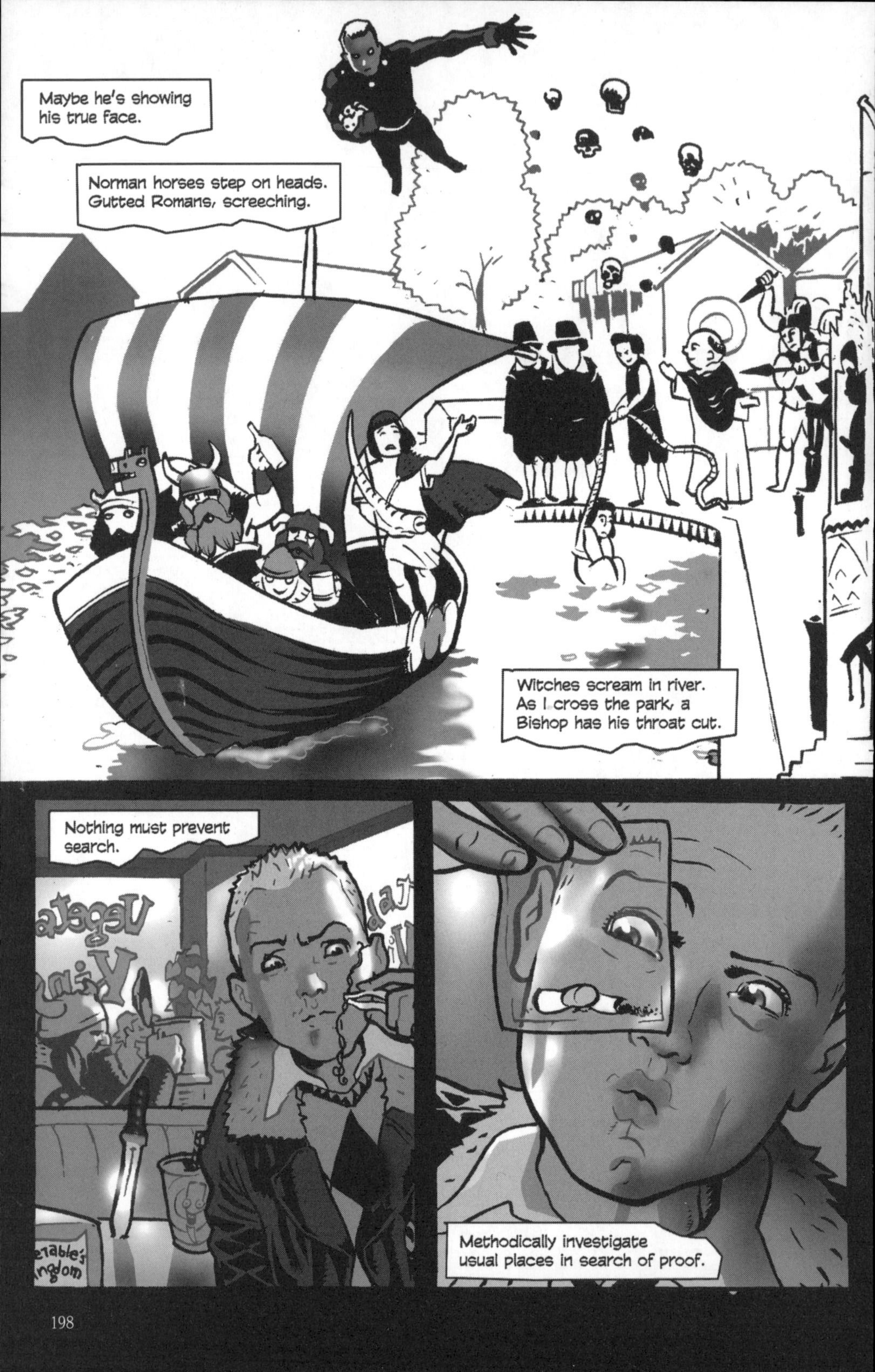
Maybe he's showing his true face.
Norman horses step on heads. Gutted Romans, screeching.
Witches scream in river. As I cross the park, a Bishop has his throat cut.
Nothing must prevent search.
Methodically investigate usual places in search of proof.

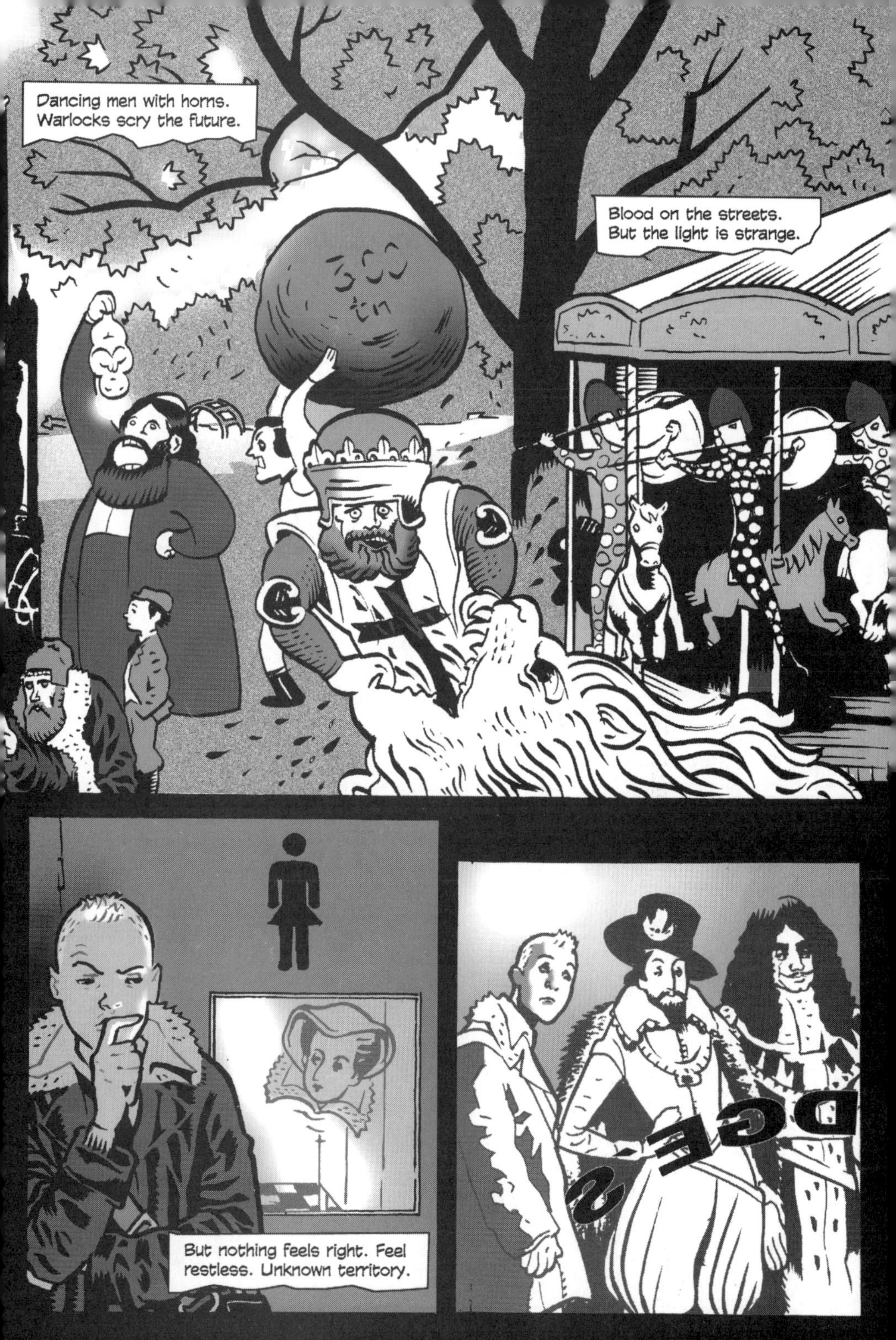

Dancing men with horns. Warlocks scry the future.
Blood on the streets. But the light is strange.
But nothing feels right. Feel restless. Unknown territory.

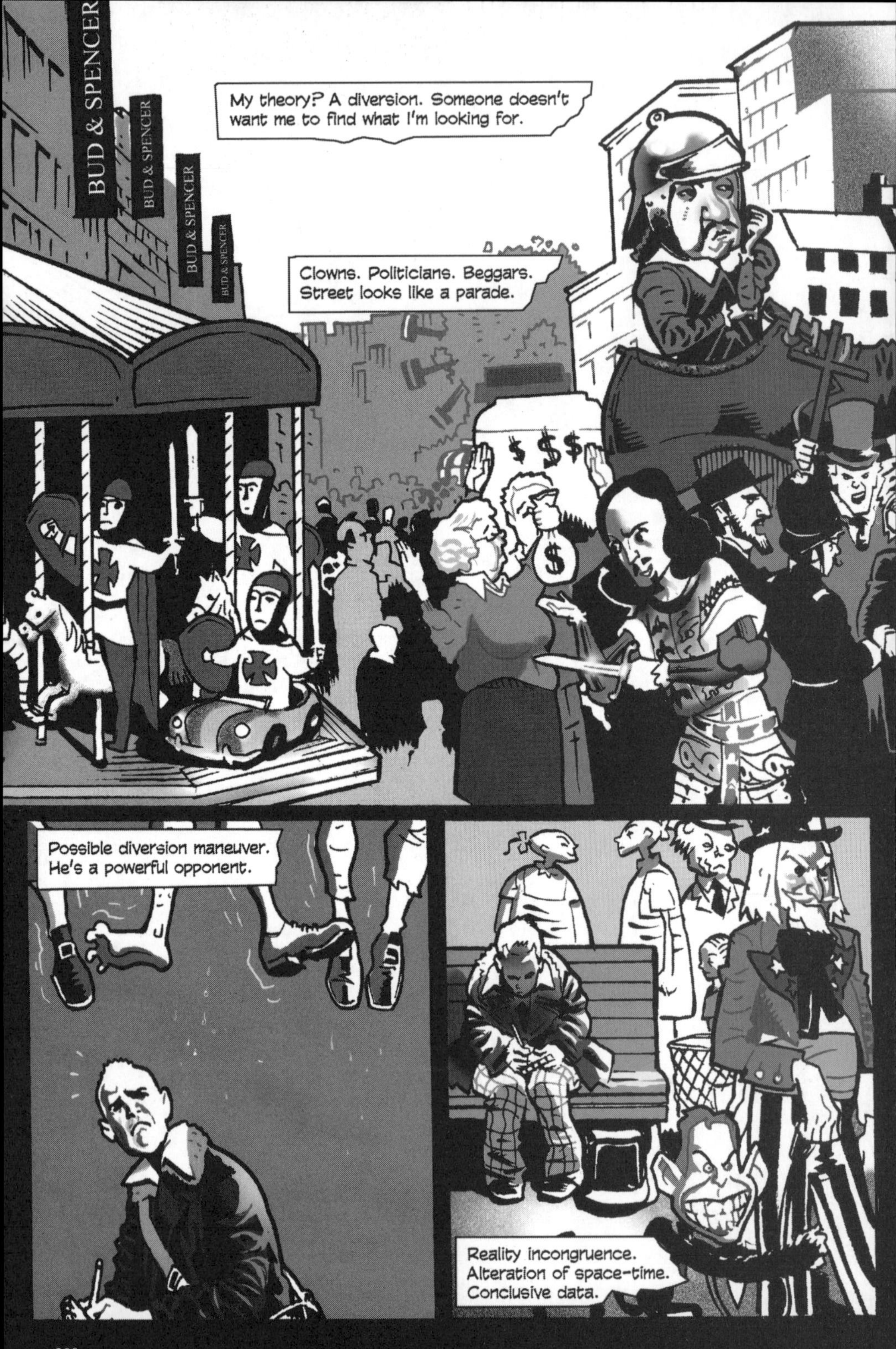
BUD & SPENCER
BUD & SPENCER
BUD & SPENCER
BUD & SPENCER
My theory? A diversion. Someone doesn't want me to find what I'm looking for.
Clowns. Politicians. Beggars. Street looks like a parade.
$ $ $
$
Possible diversion maneuver. He's a powerful opponent.
Reality incongruence. Alteration of space-time. Conclusive data.

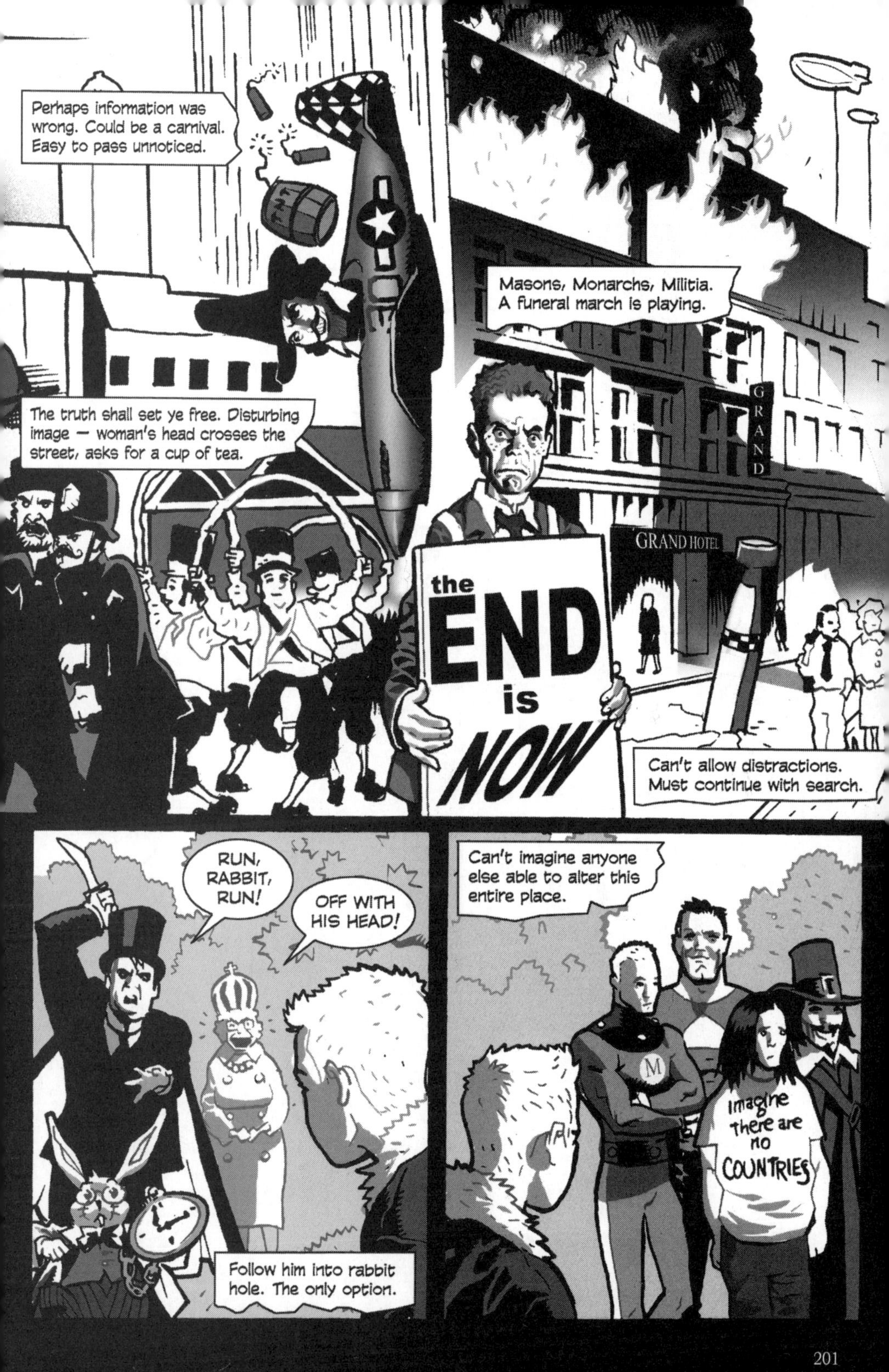
Perhaps information was wrong. Could be a carnival. Easy to pass unnoticed.
Masons, Monarchs, Militia. A funeral march is playing.
GRAND
GRAND HOTEL
The truth shall set ye free. Disturbing image — woman's head crosses the street, asks for a cup of tea.
the END is NOW
Can't allow distractions. Must continue with search.
RUN, RABBIT, RUN!
OFF WITH HIS HEAD!
Follow him into rabbit hole. The only option.
Can't imagine anyone else able to alter this entire place.
M
Imagine There are no COUNTRIES

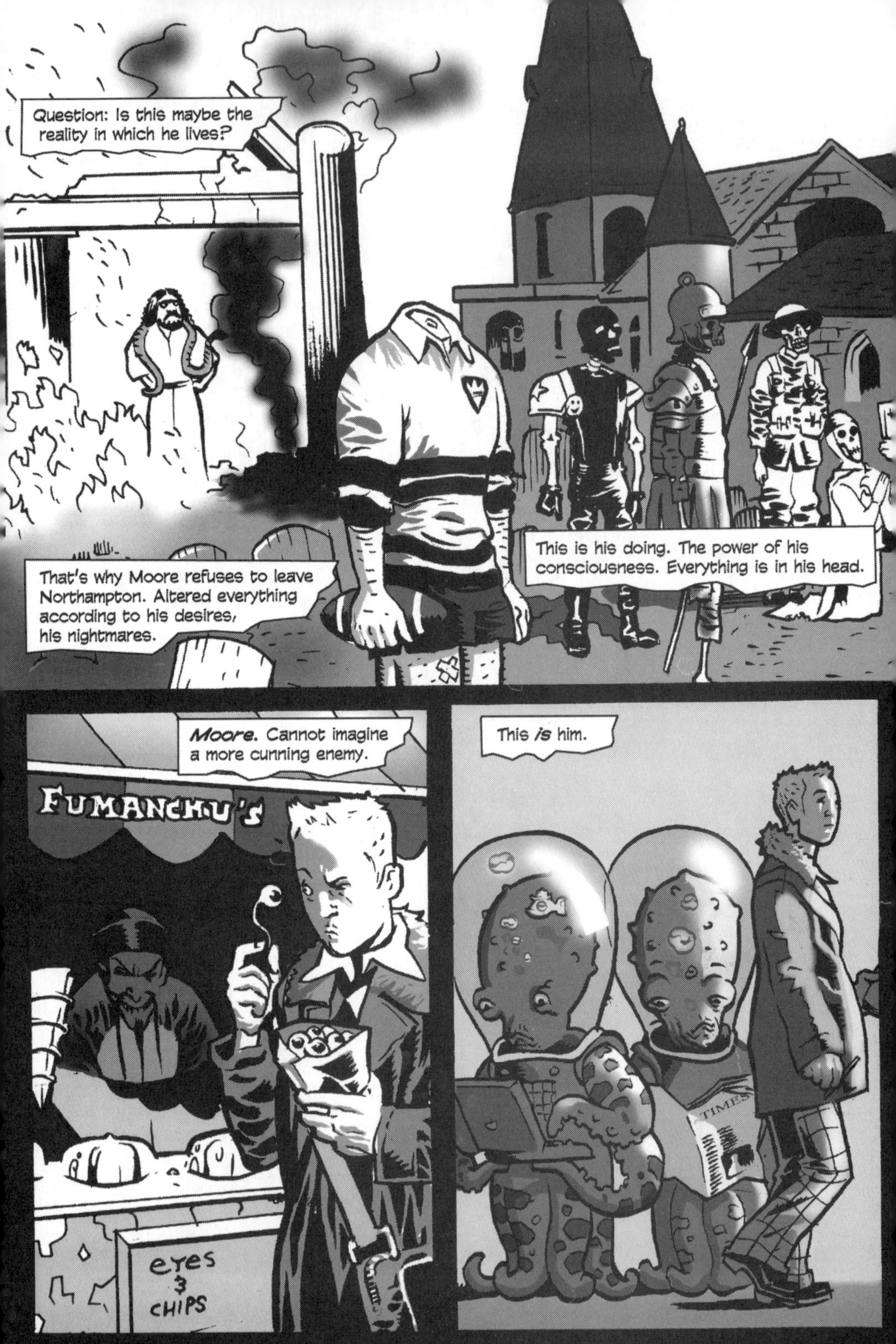
Question: Is this maybe the reality in which he lives?
That's why Moore refuses to leave Northampton. Altered everything according to his desires, his nightmares.
This is his doing. The power of his consciousness. Everything is in his head.
Moore. Cannot imagine a more cunning enemy.
FUMANCHU'S
eyes 3 CHIPS
This *is* him.
TIMES

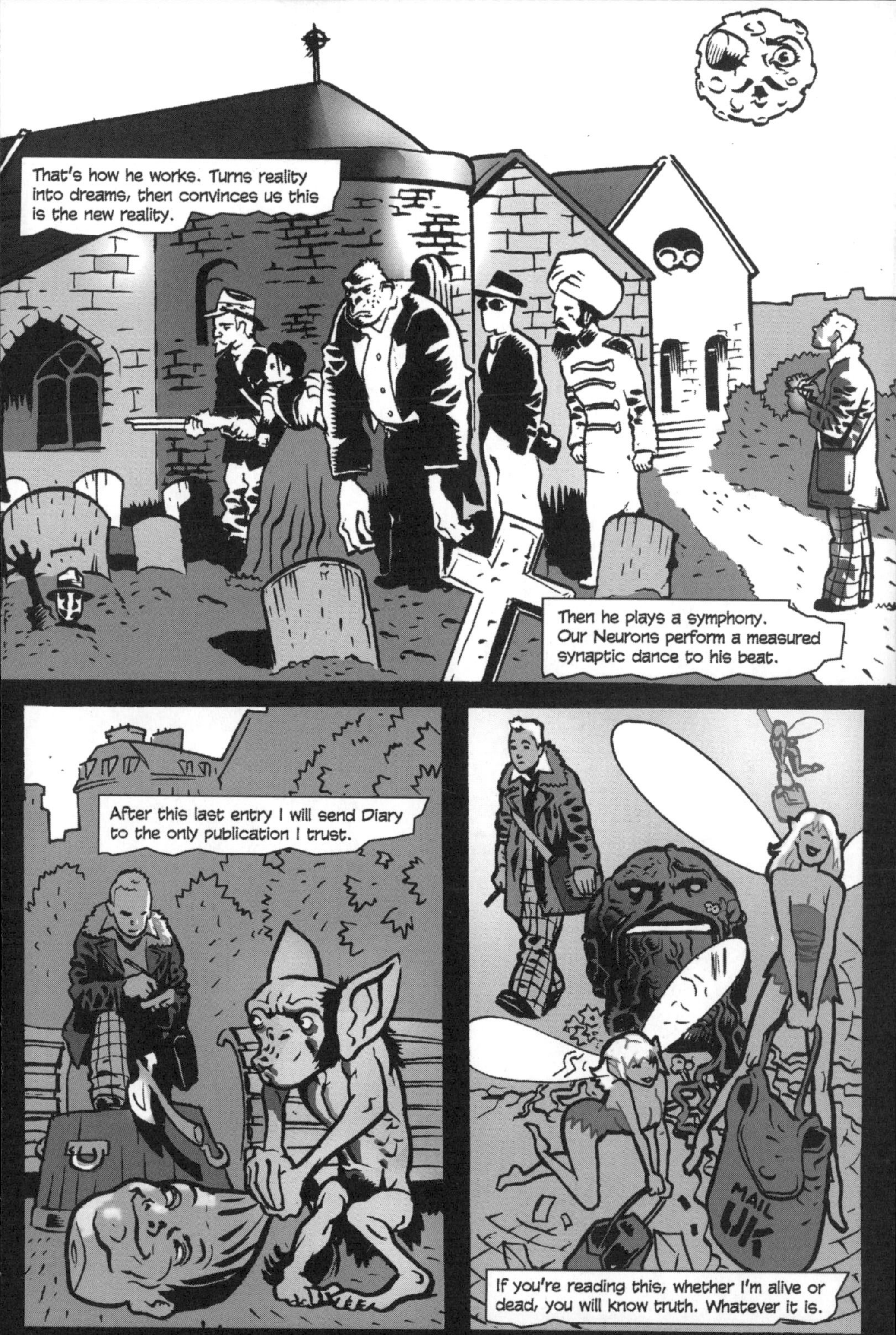

That's how he works. Turns reality into dreams, then convinces us this is the new reality.
Then he plays a symphony. Our Neurons perform a measured synaptic dance to his beat.
After this last entry I will send Diary to the only publication I trust.
MAIL
UK
If you're reading this, whether I'm alive or dead, you will know truth. Whatever it is.

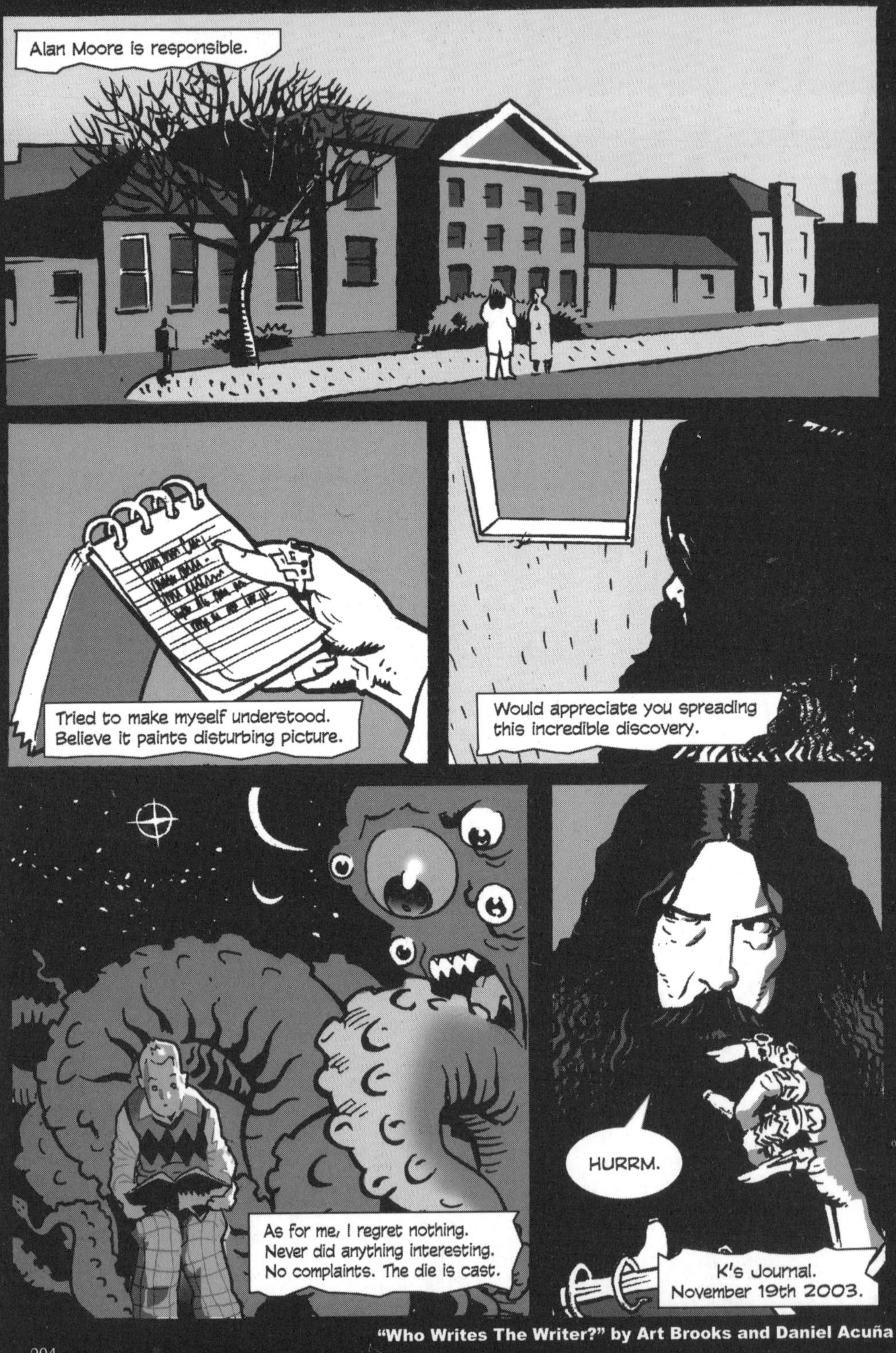
Alan Moore is responsible.
Tried to make myself understood. Believe it paints disturbing picture.
Would appreciate you spreading this incredible discovery.
As for me, I regret nothing. Never did anything interesting. No complaints. The die is cast.
HURRM.
K's Journal. November 19th 2003.

"Who Writes The Writer?" by Art Brooks and Daniel Acuña

HOW I LEARNED TO LOVE THE ALAN

MARK MILLAR

Mark Millar has written an eclectic little mix of books in the past including **The Authority, Superman Adventures, Swamp Thing** and **JLA**. At the moment, the Scotsman is writing **The Ultimates** and **Ultimate X-Men**, the two highest selling comics in the USA, as well as **Superman: Red Son** for DC Comics and the launch title for Marvel Comics revolutionary new Epic imprint.

Text ©2003 Mark Millar

Okay, I've got two Alan Moore stories and neither of them is particularly good, but they're mine and I love them and I'll share them with you right now if you have a minute to spare.

The first is probably the most embarrassing and features me, aged thirteen, showing- up at my first, very modest comic convention in the futuristic city of Glasgow back in 1983. I'd never heard of Alan Moore at that point, but my Dad had read in a newspaper that some Marvel Comics writers and artists were going to be appearing locally and eager young fans were invited to approach for autographs and sketches. Now bear in mind that I was thirteen years old (and a slightly stupid thirteen at that), but I showed up with a sketch pad and asked this preposterously tall man with a beard, Jesus hair and a fine 40s-style hat where I could find Stan Lee. He looked politely awkward and said that Stan wasn't here, but the Marvel UK boys were. He introduced me to such fledging superstars as Alan Davis, Gary Leach, Brian Bolland, Dave Gibbons and a fairly large number of people I'd never actually heard of before. It was one of those slightly surreal scenes where a weighty group of comic book pros were actually lining up to sketch and sign for a single, semi-detached young fan who was a little disappointed this line-up wasn't quite what he expected. Deep down, they knew that I wanted to save those blank A4 pages for slightly more important pros, preferably with American accents.

Flash-forward one year and Alan Moore is back in Glasgow again at one of those ill-attended Scottish Cons. He's instantly recognisable, of course, and knowing absolutely no-one else at the show I approach him as he thumbs through a bargain bin and ask him for his autograph. I've still never read any of his work at this point, but a friend had asked me to get some Warriors signed for him and it wasn't really much of an inconvenience. Mistaking me for someone who'd actually been reading this stuff, he asked me what I thought and, as bone-crushingly cringing as it is to admit now, I just pretended I was quite a fan and let Moore detail at length his upcoming plans for perhaps the two finest comic-strips of that very illustrious decade. But a strange thing happened as I tuned into his hypnotic, Northampton accent. I don't know if it was the Rasputin beard, the Svengali eyes or the fact that he was just invading my personal space to the point where I agreed with almost everything he suggested, but I became a convert. This slightly frightening-looking black and white stuff was a million miles from the four-colour shite I'd been eating up every month from Marvel and DC, but he made a fascinating case for it and, on the train home, I read every single word and hungered for more.

Next day, I begged my parents for cash and took off into town again on a mission to catch up on this guy's stuff. His fifth or six Swamp Thing was out so I had a few of them to catch up on, Warrior was at number twenty-one or so which meant I had a couple of blissful years of Marvelman, V For Vendetta, Bojeffries and various shorts to masticate over. As the weeks passed, I even started tracking down the smallest two and three page 2000AD stories this rising star had churned out on his way to the top and, best of all, I picked up every single issue of Bernie Jay's Daredevils; a monthly, black and white reprint magazine that not only featured all these Krigstein-like strips from some guy called Frank Miller, but page after page of a young Alan Moore who was writing everything he could get his hands on. Captain Britain, comic-book articles, cartoon strips and interviews; Daredevils gave Moore a forum to not only dazzle us with the stories, but also convert us to his rapidly growing cult by indoctrinating us with his opinions. Here was a grown-up talking about comics like they actually meant something and, when you're fourteen years old and living in the arse-end of nowhere, that's really quite alluring, you know.

My most poignant memory of Moore's articles (and I'm too lazy to dig it out to give you specific reference) was a piece where he wrote about his appreciation of 60s Marvel and his (really quite manly) love of Mister Stan Lee. His ode to Stan ended with an appreciation of his efforts that not only gave him years of pleasure as a child, but also built a foundation that meant that he and his peers could actually earn a comfortable living on the basis of Stan's hard graft. I remember being impressed with that at the time and feel the same way now as my rolling, easily-distracted eyes drift across my bookshelves and see a body of work from Moore which, more than anyone else of his period, promoted his craft and the medium he obviously has such a scary-looking erection for. My own snotty generation of British writers owe Moore for not only proving that it was possible to work for an American company while living on this miserable, rain-soaked rock, but we owe him a debt for inspiring us to write something better than that formulaic super-shite we'd probably be writing without him. Together with guys like Miller and Chaykin, he redefined the medium forever and, based on that bedrock, the biggest industry spike we've ever seen took place in the early nineteen nineties. But I think Moore deserves the credit for that foundation more than anyone else and I'll say that to their faces, dear reader. Moore was really our Stan Lee and he's pretty much the reason most of us are in a job.

By the way, before I go, I should probably point out that I never actually *got* that Alan Moore autograph for the pal in my old hometown. I was genuinely so mesmerized by Moore's loose chatter about an upcoming Superman annual and his eerily accurate vision of a totalitarian Britain that I completely forgot and only remembered once I'd opened my front door again. Like the bastard I am, instead of just admitting my mistake, I took the easy way out and clumsily forged his signature across a copy of Warrior issue one. To this day, that autographed cover hangs on his wall and I must admit that even I can feel some tiny twinge of guilt whenever I look at it. If you're reading this, mate, I'm so incredibly sorry, but I suppose it isn't *every* day that a writer gets to sign a book that good.

Cheers, Alan. Have a good one and may whatever dark forces you're channelling these days let you live forever at the expense of others.

• **Mark Millar,**
Glasgow
25th March 2003

TRINA ROBBINS

Right: *Trina Robbins has been writing and drawing comics and books – and paperdolls — for over thirty years. She lives in San Francisco with her partner, who draws comics, and two cats, who cover the house with their fur. She has one beautiful daughter. She loves shoes, vintage clothing, and Promethea.*
Paper doll ©2003 Trina Robbins. Marvelman ©2003 the copyright holder. V For Vendetta ©2003 DC Comics. Promethea ©2003 America's Best Comics, LLC.

ALAN MOORE'S CLOSET

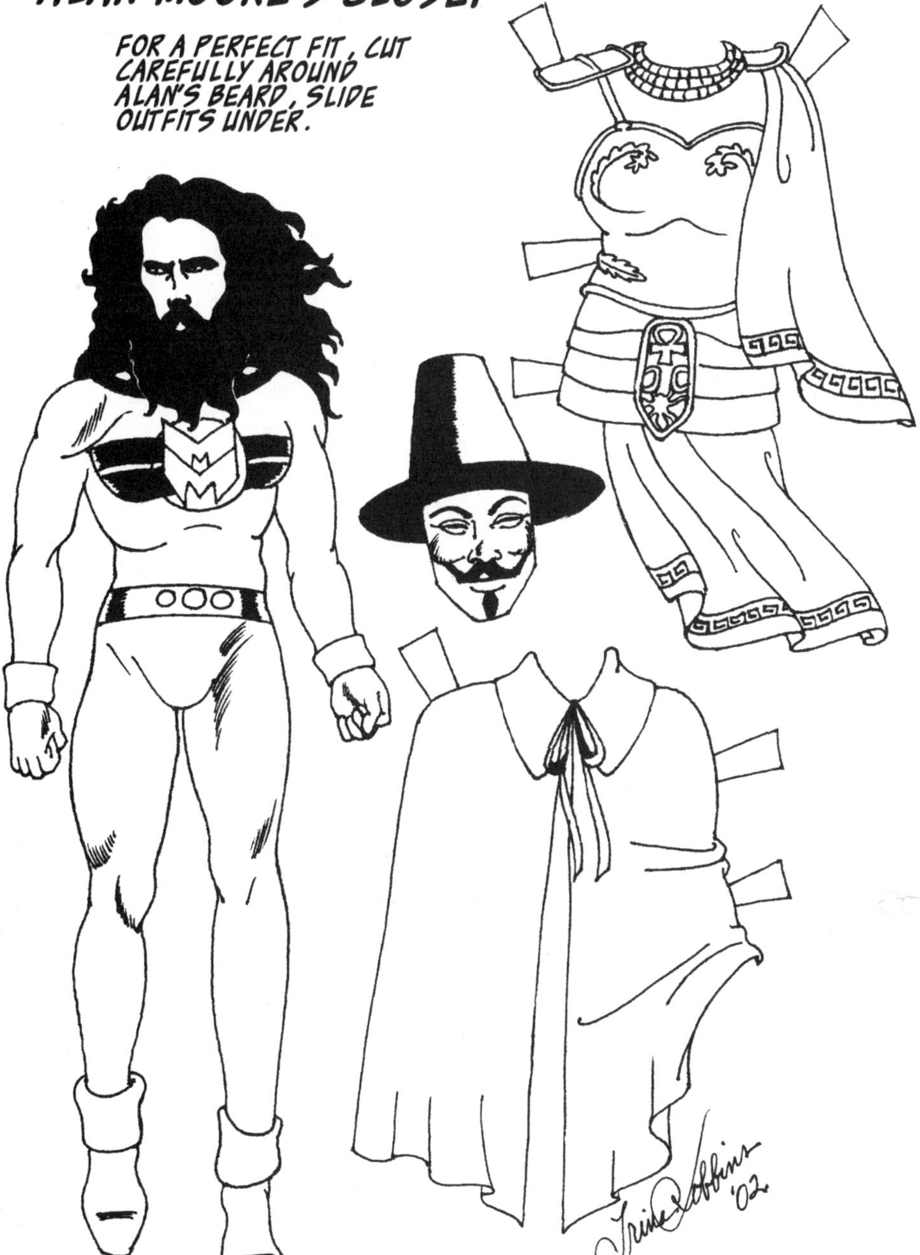
FOR A PERFECT FIT, CUT CAREFULLY AROUND ALAN'S BEARD, SLIDE OUTFITS UNDER.

THE ALANMOORY LESSON

Why do I like Alan Moore? "I like his way of writing" sounds trite. Perhaps it's better to say that I like his way of thinking.

I was struck by what he once said "My purpose is to create with joy." We should print it in block capitals on the walls behind our desks. "Creating with joy" is something that you seldom bear in mind: rather, you tend to worry about deadlines and about how better a script would have been if you had spent some more time on it. You also think about the things that you could do and that nobody is willing to finance, such as a good colour book, satisfactorily printed.
Finally, you live your job in a remorseful way, trying to think that, "it's just a job," that, "in substance what really matters is that you draw your pay." In this position creating is difficult enough and creating "with joy" becomes impossible. Honestly, I don't know if Alan Moore always creates "with joy." Maybe he himself doesn't know. Anyway, if fiction's aim is to convey emotions... well, when I read Moore's works I feel lots of emotions.

As an exacting and voracious reader, I must add that not all Moore's stuff is to my liking. His novel "Voice of the Fire" made me doze off after three chapters, "The Killing Joke" is full of incongruities and I think that The ABC line is a faultless but sterile virtuous exercise.
Anyway, at his best ("Watchmen", "From Hell", "Swamp Thing" and also the undervalued "A Small Killing"), Moore is really great.
I think his greatness consists - rather than in his well-known excellent technique - in the basic idea of his works and in his ability to re-invent himself over again, supplanting or revising the comics' rules, or even working rigorously inside them.

It is a typical English and American idea of art, the idea which named the dramatic works with a word - "play" – setting itself in opposition to the traditional Catholic-Communist dismal seriousness which still corrupts the Italian culture (comics included, authors and readers).

The rest – the legend around the Bard of Northampton's work, his never-ending panel descriptions to his illustrators, his narrative and graphic symmetries – doesn't impress me particularly.

That's technique, and technique – although excellent – can be learned.
You can't learn the ideas. That's another thing and that's what makes the difference.

• Michele Medda

MICHELE MEDDA

Michele Medda is the acclaimed Italian co-creator and staff writer of Bonelli Comics' successful sci-fi monthly series Nathan Never.
Text ©2003 Michele Medda

JOHN COULTHART

Pages 209-213 following:
John Coulthart divides his time as an illustrator, comic artist and CD and book designer. Since 1989 he has worked on the controversial **Lord Horror** *comic series and his adaptations of H.P. Lovecraft stories were collected in* **The Haunter of the Dark and other Grotesque Visions** *in 1999.*
Strip ©2003 John Coulthart.

32 SHORT LUCUBRATIONS CONCERNING ALAN MOORE

ON THE OCCASION OF HIS 50TH BIRTHDAY

A SEMIOTIC DIVERSION BY JOHN COULTHART

1 NOVEMBER 18TH
PART ONE: WRITING

The North Prospect of the Conuentuall Church of Westmynster.

Royal Chapels Choir & Transepts ADMIT ONE ADULT

86298

ON THIS DAY IN 1477, THE FIRST DATED BOOK WAS PRINTED IN ENGLAND.

'DICTES AND SAYENGES OF THE PHYLOSOPHERS' BY EARL RIVERS WAS ISSUED FROM THE CAXTON PRESS IN WESTMINSTER ABBEY.

2 ALAN MOORE WAS BORN IN NORTHAMPTON 476 YEARS LATER.

RUMOURS THAT HIS BIRTHPLACE WAS IN ROAMO LANE ARE WITHOUT FOUNDATION.

3

ALAN MOORE DRINKS GREAT QUANTITIES OF TEA.

4 INGREDIENTS: PLAIN CHOCOLATE (20%), SUGAR, WHEAT GLUCOSE SYRUP, WHOLE EGG, GELLING AGENT), DEXTROSE MONOHYDRATE, CONCENTRATED JUICE (8.4% ORANGE JUICE EQUIVALENT), CITRIC ACID, ...CTANT (GLYCERINE), EMULSIFIERS (E471, E475), VEGETABLE OIL, RAISING AGENTS (AMMONIUM BICARBONATE, DISODIUM DIPHOSPHATE, SODIUM BICARBONATE), NATURAL FLAVOURINGS, ACIDITY REGULATOR (SODIUM CITRATE), NATURAL COLOUR (CURCUMIN).

NUTRITION INFORMATION		
Average Values	Per Cake	Per 100g
Energy	203kJ	1620kJ
	48kcal	384kcal
Protein	0.5g	4.4g
Carbohydrate	9.2g	73.2g
of which Sugars	6.5g	52.0g
Fat	1.0g	8.1g
of which Saturates	0.5g	4.2g
Fibre	0.2g	1.3g
Sodium	Trace	0.1g
		1.0g FAT

HE ONCE ASKED ME WHERE I STOOD ON THE QUESTION OF BISCUITS.

BEING PUT ON THE SPOT IN THIS MANNER, I WAS FORCED TO CONFESS A PREDILECTION FOR McVITIE'S JAFFA CAKES.

5 MAY 29, 1982 35p

8.

BREAKING UP IS HARD TO DO

WERE YOU TALKING TO ME MISTER?

ALTHOUGH WE'VE WORKED TOGETHER ON A NUMBER OF DIFFERENT PROJECTS, OUR FIRST ENCOUNTER WAS INADVERTENT AND COINCIDENTAL.

THE PAGES OF 'SOUNDS' FOR MAY 29, 1982 CARRIED AN EPISODE OF THE COMIC SERIES 'THE STARS, MY DEGRADATION', WRITTEN AND DRAWN BY ONE "CURT VILE", ALAN'S NOM DE PLUME AT THE TIME.

THIS ISSUE ALSO FEATURED AN ADVERT SHOWING MY FIRST ILLUSTRATION WORK FOR HAWKWIND.

(DON'T ASK ME WHY THAT GUY IS WAVING A SAUSAGE.)

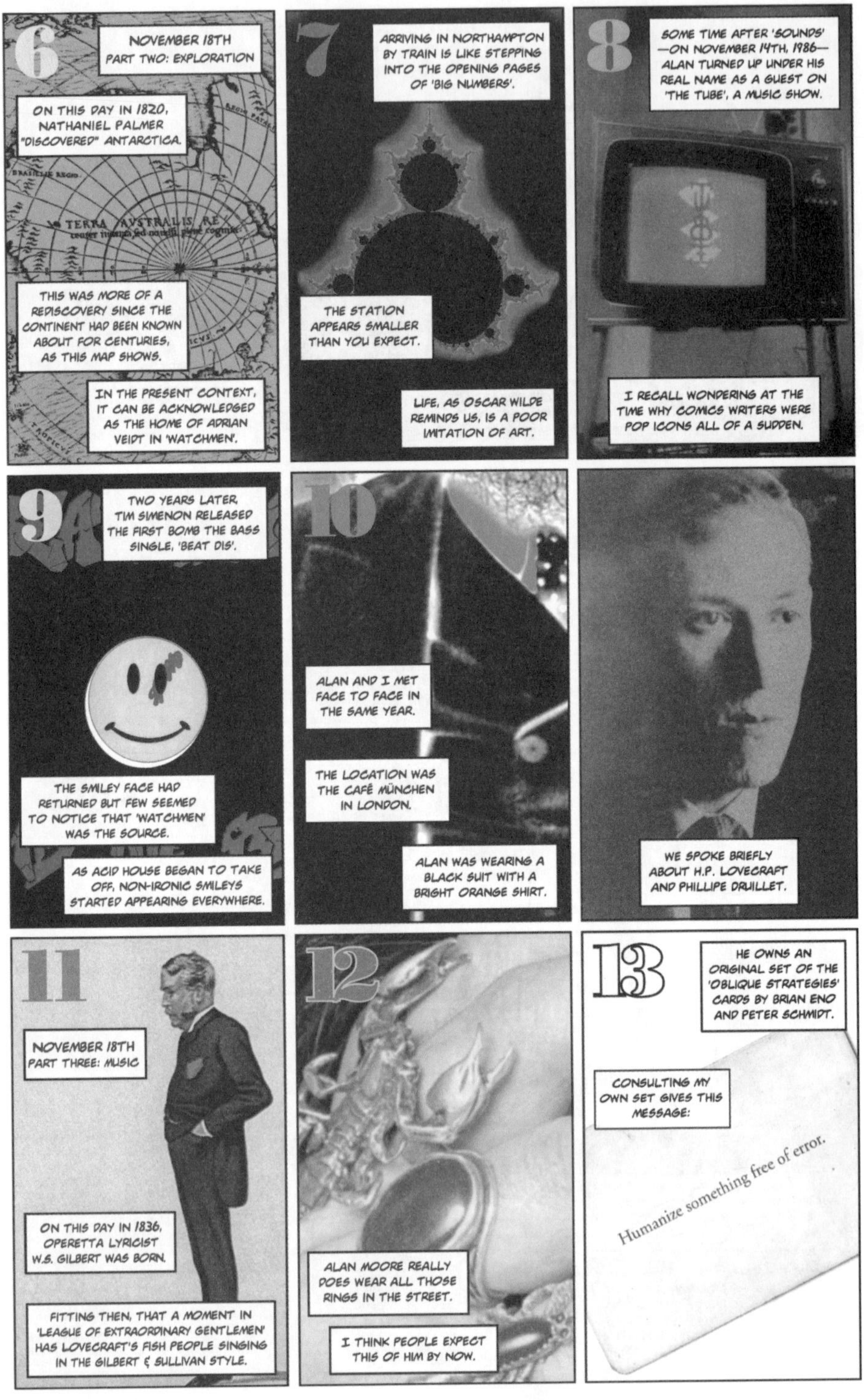
6
NOVEMBER 18TH PART TWO: EXPLORATION
ON THIS DAY IN 1820, NATHANIEL PALMER "DISCOVERED" ANTARCTICA.
TERRA AUSTRALIS
THIS WAS MORE OF A REDISCOVERY SINCE THE CONTINENT HAD BEEN KNOWN ABOUT FOR CENTURIES, AS THIS MAP SHOWS.
IN THE PRESENT CONTEXT, IT CAN BE ACKNOWLEDGED AS THE HOME OF ADRIAN VEIDT IN 'WATCHMEN'.
7
ARRIVING IN NORTHAMPTON BY TRAIN IS LIKE STEPPING INTO THE OPENING PAGES OF 'BIG NUMBERS'.
THE STATION APPEARS SMALLER THAN YOU EXPECT.
LIFE, AS OSCAR WILDE REMINDS US, IS A POOR IMITATION OF ART.
8
SOME TIME AFTER 'SOUNDS' —ON NOVEMBER 14TH, 1986— ALAN TURNED UP UNDER HIS REAL NAME AS A GUEST ON 'THE TUBE', A MUSIC SHOW.
I RECALL WONDERING AT THE TIME WHY COMICS WRITERS WERE POP ICONS ALL OF A SUDDEN.
9
TWO YEARS LATER, TIM SIMENON RELEASED THE FIRST BOMB THE BASS SINGLE, 'BEAT DIS'.
THE SMILEY FACE HAD RETURNED BUT FEW SEEMED TO NOTICE THAT 'WATCHMEN' WAS THE SOURCE.
AS ACID HOUSE BEGAN TO TAKE OFF, NON-IRONIC SMILEYS STARTED APPEARING EVERYWHERE.
10
ALAN AND I MET FACE TO FACE IN THE SAME YEAR.
THE LOCATION WAS THE CAFÉ MÜNCHEN IN LONDON.
ALAN WAS WEARING A BLACK SUIT WITH A BRIGHT ORANGE SHIRT.
WE SPOKE BRIEFLY ABOUT H.P. LOVECRAFT AND PHILLIPE DRUILLET.
11
NOVEMBER 18TH PART THREE: MUSIC
ON THIS DAY IN 1836, OPERETTA LYRICIST W.S. GILBERT WAS BORN.
FITTING THEN, THAT A MOMENT IN 'LEAGUE OF EXTRAORDINARY GENTLEMEN' HAS LOVECRAFT'S FISH PEOPLE SINGING IN THE GILBERT & SULLIVAN STYLE.
12
ALAN MOORE REALLY DOES WEAR ALL THOSE RINGS IN THE STREET.
I THINK PEOPLE EXPECT THIS OF HIM BY NOW.
13
HE OWNS AN ORIGINAL SET OF THE 'OBLIQUE STRATEGIES' CARDS BY BRIAN ENO AND PETER SCHMIDT.
CONSULTING MY OWN SET GIVES THIS MESSAGE:
Humanize something free of error.

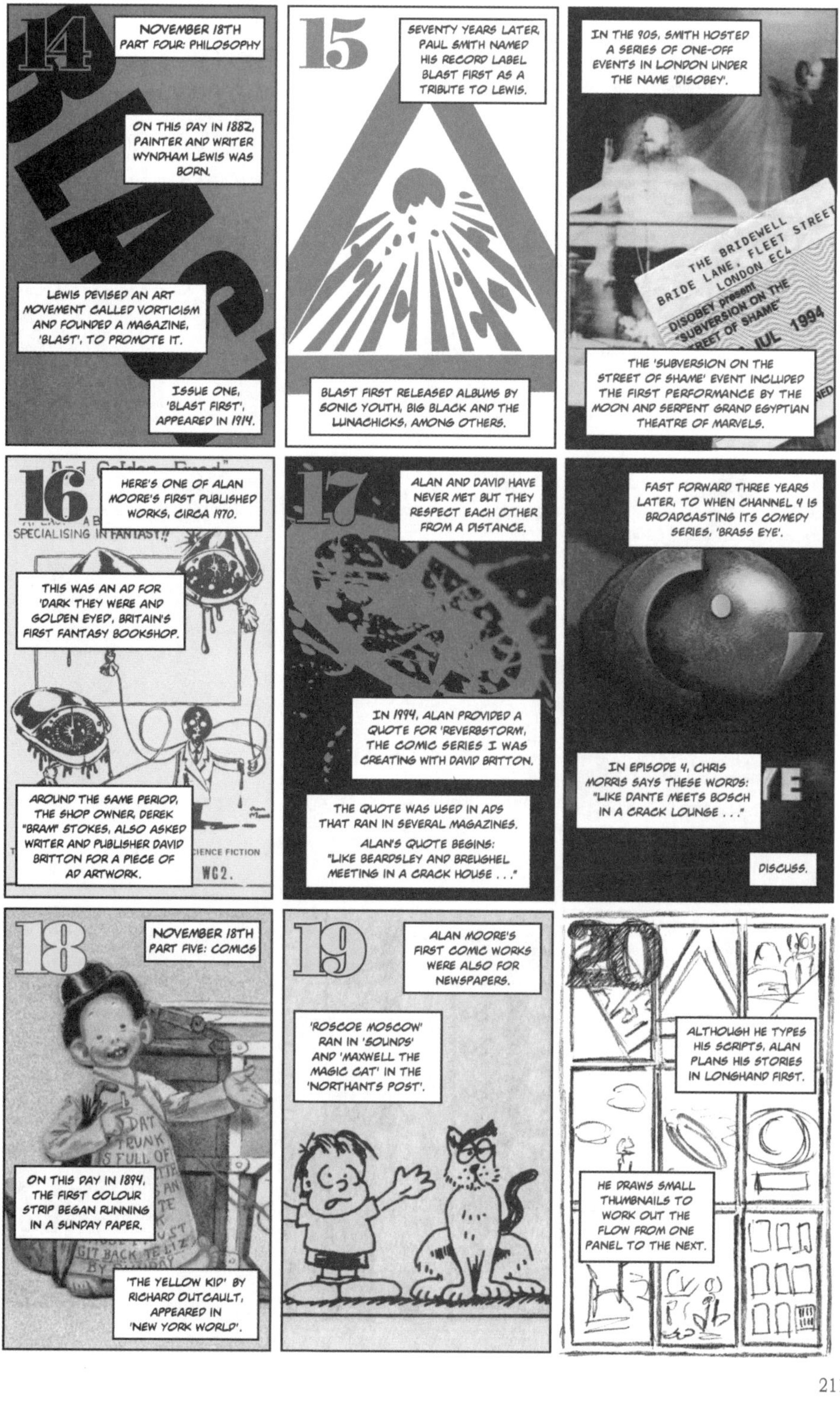

14
NOVEMBER 18TH
PART FOUR: PHILOSOPHY
ON THIS DAY IN 1882, PAINTER AND WRITER WYNDHAM LEWIS WAS BORN.
LEWIS DEVISED AN ART MOVEMENT CALLED VORTICISM AND FOUNDED A MAGAZINE, 'BLAST', TO PROMOTE IT.
ISSUE ONE, 'BLAST FIRST', APPEARED IN 1914.
15
SEVENTY YEARS LATER PAUL SMITH NAMED HIS RECORD LABEL BLAST FIRST AS A TRIBUTE TO LEWIS.
BLAST FIRST RELEASED ALBUMS BY SONIC YOUTH, BIG BLACK AND THE LUNACHICKS, AMONG OTHERS.
IN THE 90S, SMITH HOSTED A SERIES OF ONE-OFF EVENTS IN LONDON UNDER THE NAME 'DISOBEY'.
THE BRIDEWELL
BRIDE LANE, FLEET STREET
LONDON EC4
DISOBEY present
"SUBVERSION ON THE
STREET OF SHAME"
JUL 1994
THE 'SUBVERSION ON THE STREET OF SHAME' EVENT INCLUDED THE FIRST PERFORMANCE BY THE MOON AND SERPENT GRAND EGYPTIAN THEATRE OF MARVELS.
16
HERE'S ONE OF ALAN MOORE'S FIRST PUBLISHED WORKS, CIRCA 1970.
SPECIALISING IN FANTASY!!
THIS WAS AN AD FOR 'DARK THEY WERE AND GOLDEN EYED', BRITAIN'S FIRST FANTASY BOOKSHOP.
AROUND THE SAME PERIOD, THE SHOP OWNER, DEREK "BRAM" STOKES, ALSO ASKED WRITER AND PUBLISHER DAVID BRITTON FOR A PIECE OF AD ARTWORK.
WC2.
17
ALAN AND DAVID HAVE NEVER MET BUT THEY RESPECT EACH OTHER FROM A DISTANCE.
IN 1994, ALAN PROVIDED A QUOTE FOR 'REVERBSTORM', THE COMIC SERIES I WAS CREATING WITH DAVID BRITTON.
THE QUOTE WAS USED IN ADS THAT RAN IN SEVERAL MAGAZINES.
ALAN'S QUOTE BEGINS: "LIKE BEARDSLEY AND BREUGHEL MEETING IN A CRACK HOUSE . . ."
FAST FORWARD THREE YEARS LATER, TO WHEN CHANNEL 4 IS BROADCASTING ITS COMEDY SERIES, 'BRASS EYE'.
IN EPISODE 4, CHRIS MORRIS SAYS THESE WORDS: "LIKE DANTE MEETS BOSCH IN A CRACK LOUNGE . . ."
DISCUSS.
18
NOVEMBER 18TH
PART FIVE: COMICS
ON THIS DAY IN 1894, THE FIRST COLOUR STRIP BEGAN RUNNING IN A SUNDAY PAPER.
'THE YELLOW KID' BY RICHARD OUTCAULT, APPEARED IN 'NEW YORK WORLD'.
19
ALAN MOORE'S FIRST COMIC WORKS WERE ALSO FOR NEWSPAPERS.
'ROSCOE MOSCOW' RAN IN 'SOUNDS' AND 'MAXWELL THE MAGIC CAT' IN THE 'NORTHANTS POST'.
20
ALTHOUGH HE TYPES HIS SCRIPTS, ALAN PLANS HIS STORIES IN LONGHAND FIRST.
HE DRAWS SMALL THUMBNAILS TO WORK OUT THE FLOW FROM ONE PANEL TO THE NEXT.

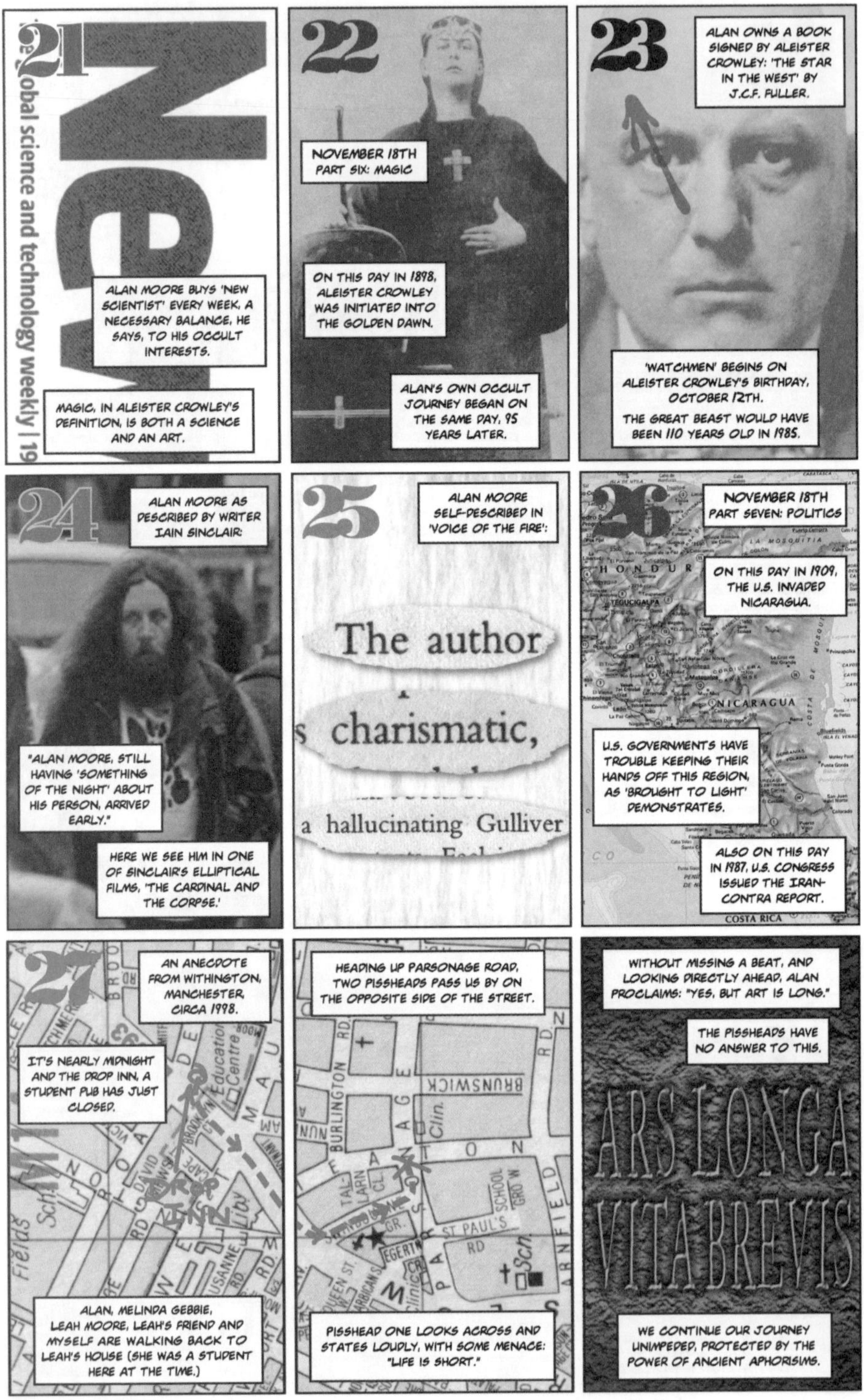
21
science and technology weekly | 19
ALAN MOORE BUYS 'NEW SCIENTIST' EVERY WEEK, A NECESSARY BALANCE, HE SAYS, TO HIS OCCULT INTERESTS.
MAGIC, IN ALEISTER CROWLEY'S DEFINITION, IS BOTH A SCIENCE AND AN ART.
22
NOVEMBER 18TH PART SIX: MAGIC
ON THIS DAY IN 1898, ALEISTER CROWLEY WAS INITIATED INTO THE GOLDEN DAWN.
ALAN'S OWN OCCULT JOURNEY BEGAN ON THE SAME DAY, 95 YEARS LATER.
23
ALAN OWNS A BOOK SIGNED BY ALEISTER CROWLEY: 'THE STAR IN THE WEST' BY J.C.F. FULLER.
'WATCHMEN' BEGINS ON ALEISTER CROWLEY'S BIRTHDAY, OCTOBER 12TH.
THE GREAT BEAST WOULD HAVE BEEN 110 YEARS OLD IN 1985.
24
ALAN MOORE AS DESCRIBED BY WRITER IAIN SINCLAIR:
"ALAN MOORE, STILL HAVING 'SOMETHING OF THE NIGHT' ABOUT HIS PERSON, ARRIVED EARLY."
HERE WE SEE HIM IN ONE OF SINCLAIR'S ELLIPTICAL FILMS, 'THE CARDINAL AND THE CORPSE.'
25
ALAN MOORE SELF-DESCRIBED IN 'VOICE OF THE FIRE':
The author
charismatic,
a hallucinating Gulliver
26
NOVEMBER 18TH PART SEVEN: POLITICS
ON THIS DAY IN 1909, THE U.S. INVADED NICARAGUA.
U.S. GOVERNMENTS HAVE TROUBLE KEEPING THEIR HANDS OFF THIS REGION, AS 'BROUGHT TO LIGHT' DEMONSTRATES.
ALSO ON THIS DAY IN 1987, U.S. CONGRESS ISSUED THE IRAN-CONTRA REPORT.
TEGUCIGALPA
NICARAGUA
COSTA RICA
27
AN ANECDOTE FROM WITHINGTON, MANCHESTER, CIRCA 1998.
IT'S NEARLY MIDNIGHT AND THE DROP INN, A STUDENT PUB HAS JUST CLOSED.
ALAN, MELINDA GEBBIE, LEAH MOORE, LEAH'S FRIEND AND MYSELF ARE WALKING BACK TO LEAH'S HOUSE (SHE WAS A STUDENT HERE AT THE TIME.)
HEADING UP PARSONAGE ROAD, TWO PISSHEADS PASS US BY ON THE OPPOSITE SIDE OF THE STREET.
BURLINGTON
BRUNSWICK
ST. PAUL'S
PISSHEAD ONE LOOKS ACROSS AND STATES LOUDLY, WITH SOME MENACE: "LIFE IS SHORT."
WITHOUT MISSING A BEAT, AND LOOKING DIRECTLY AHEAD, ALAN PROCLAIMS: "YES, BUT ART IS LONG."
THE PISSHEADS HAVE NO ANSWER TO THIS.
ARS LONGA VITA BREVIS
WE CONTINUE OUR JOURNEY UNIMPEDED, PROTECTED BY THE POWER OF ANCIENT APHORISMS.

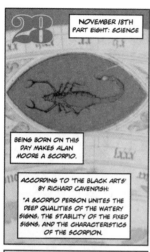

NOVEMBER 18TH
PART EIGHT: SCIENCE

BEING BORN ON THIS DAY MAKES ALAN MOORE A SCORPIO.

ACCORDING TO 'THE BLACK ARTS' BY RICHARD CAVENDISH:

"A SCORPIO PERSON UNITES THE DEEP QUALITIES OF THE WATERY SIGNS, THE STABILITY OF THE FIXED SIGNS, AND THE CHARACTERISTICS OF THE SCORPION.

"SCORPIOS ARE DARKLY SECRETIVE, INTENSE, PASSIONATE.

"THEY HAVE INVINCIBLE WILL-POWER, SHARP AND RESILIENT MINDS AND CHARACTERS.

"THEY HAVE A KNACK FOR ACQUIRING GREAT WEALTH. THEY ARE TERRIBLE AND RELENTLESS ENEMIES.

"THEY SHOULD KEEP THEIR FEET FIRMLY ON THE GROUND AND BE CAREFUL ABOUT THEIR DIET."

'FIRE WALK WITH ME' IS ONE OF ALAN'S FAVOURITE FILMS.

HEATHER GRAHAM APPEARS BRIEFLY AS ANNIE BLACKBURN.

TEN YEARS LATER SHE PLAYED PROSTITUTE MARY KELLY IN THE FILM OF 'FROM HELL'.

NOVEMBER 18TH
PART NINE: ART

ON THIS DAY IN 1962, THE DANISH PHYSICIST NIELS BOHR DIED.

BOHR IS MENTIONED IN 'VOICE OF THE FIRE' FOR HIS CONNECTION WITH NORTHAMPTON VIA THE CARLSBERG BREWERY.

HE IS MOST RENOWNED FOR HIS 'COPENHAGEN INTERPRETATION' OF QUANTUM MECHANICS.

THIS REGARDS THE EQUATIONS OF QUANTUM PHYSICS AS MATHEMATICAL MODELS WHICH HELP US CALIBRATE THE QUANTUM UNIVERSE.

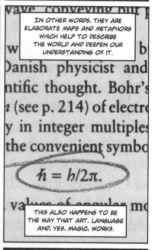

IN OTHER WORDS, THEY ARE ELABORATE MAPS AND METAPHORS WHICH HELP TO DESCRIBE THE WORLD AND DEEPEN OUR UNDERSTANDING OF IT.

Danish physicist and ntific thought. Bohr's (see p. 214) of electro y in integer multiples the convenient symbo

$$\hbar = h/2\pi.$$

THIS ALSO HAPPENS TO BE THE WAY THAT ART, LANGUAGE AND, YES, MAGIC, WORKS.

IT GOES WITHOUT SAYING—BUT I'LL SAY IT ANYWAY—THAT ALAN MOORE MANAGES TO DEEPEN OUR UNDERSTANDING OF THE WORLD AND BE DAMNED ENTERTAINING AT THE SAME TIME.

DID I SAY HE'S THE BEST?

WELL, OF COURSE, YOU KNOW THIS ALREADY, DON'T YOU?

NOVEMBER 18TH
PART TEN: FELICITATIONS

HAPPY BIRTHDAY, ALAN!

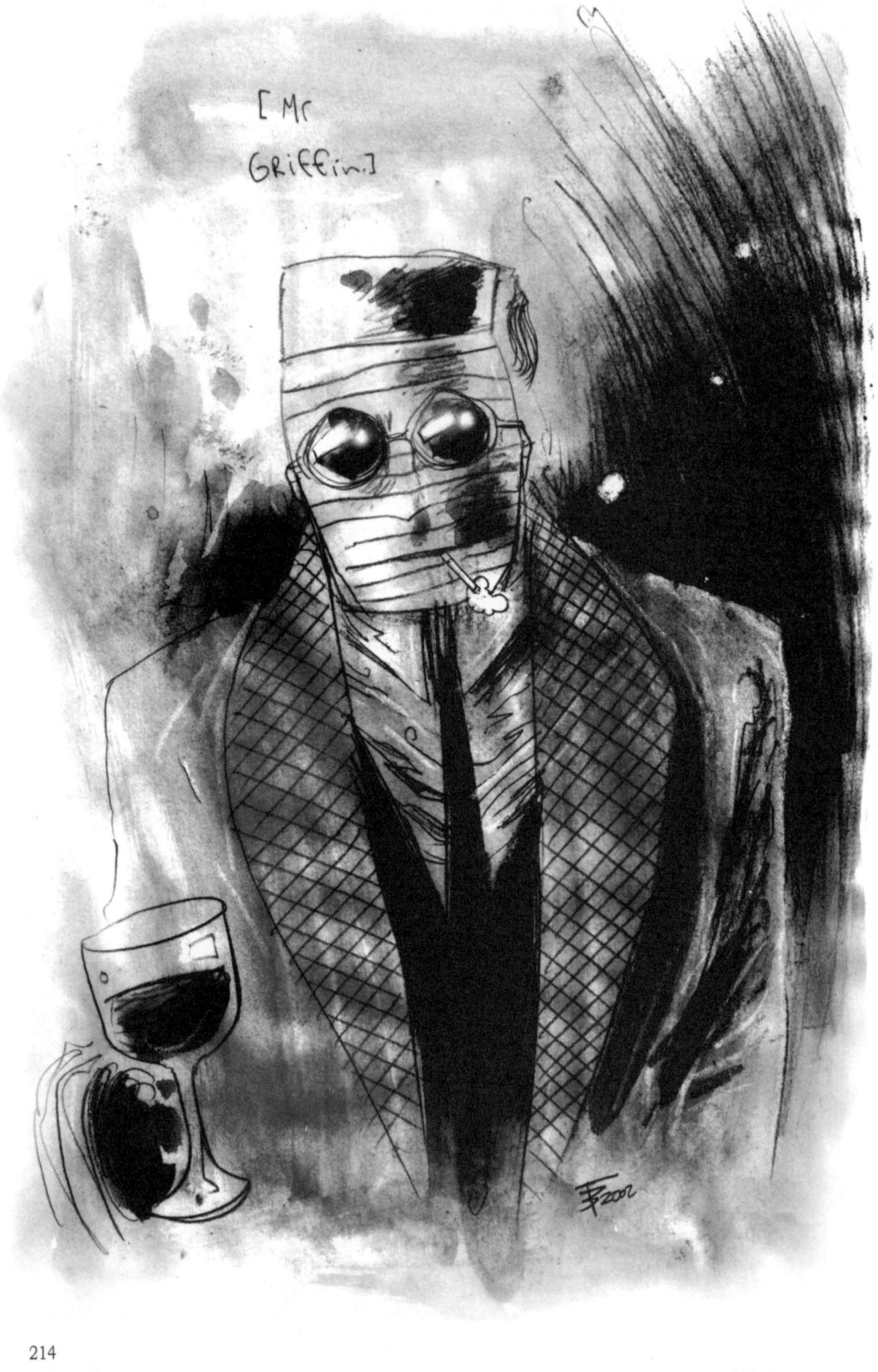
[Mr
Griffin]

BEN TEMPLESMITH

Left: *Templesmith is an Australian freelance illustrator
and comic book artist, his works include* **Hellspawn**
and IDW's **30 Days of Night**. *www.templesmith.com
Illustration ©2003 Ben Templesmith.
The League of Extraordinary Gentleman ©2003 Alan
Moore and Kevin O'Neill.*

SAM KIETH

Above: *Sam Kieth drew the first five issues of*
Sandman *before writing and illustrating* **The
Maxx** *for Image Comics in 1993, which
became a cartoon on MTV. Most recently he's
created* **Zero Girl** *and* **Four Women** *for DC.
Illustration ©2003 Sam Kieth.*

215

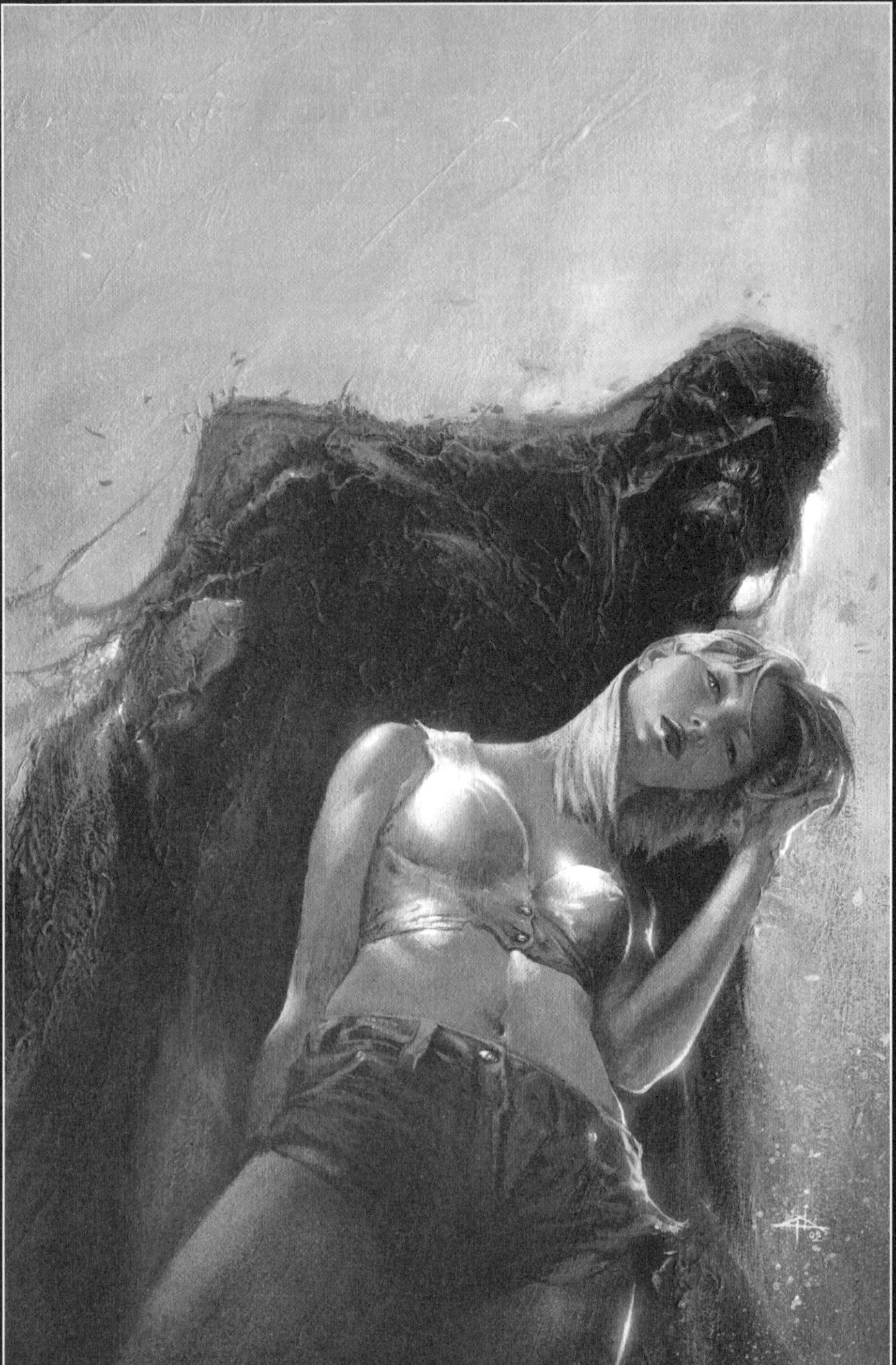

MR. MOORE AND ME

STEPHEN R. BISSETTE

*Stephen R. Bissette worked for 24 years in the comics industry, but is best known for his work on **Swamp Thing,** his anthology **Taboo, 1963** and **Tyrant.** He has also worked as book jacket illustrator, short fiction writer, lecturer, video columnist and has co-authored many non-fiction books on comics and horror movies. www.comicon.com/bissette Text ©2003 Stephen Bissette.*

I first met Alan Moore as most of you did: as a reader.

And upon first reading, I knew: this was magic.

When the first issue of WARRIOR was published in the UK a little over two decades ago, the vagaries of distribution permitted a few stray copies to wander into the US. Back in '82, I lucked into a copy at the Heroes World comic shop in New Jersey, and snapped it up.

Lo and behold, from the debut issue's first strip "Marvelman," I realized this was something fresh, a revelation, a new eruption in the international comics scene that was as bracing as the fateful first issue of METAL HURLANT had been back in '74 (which I was lucky enough to see upon its arrival in the US via Bud Plant's mail order service and my friend Jack). Here was the hoariest of comics traditions — transformation from mortal flesh to superhuman divinity with a mere spoken word — given weight and substance and conviction and — dare I say it? — vision.

I had precious little interest in, or use for, superhero comics, but this was different. This was promising. The writer of note, one Alan Moore, a name I'd never heard or read of, had his own superpower (not to forget his ink-slinging collaborator, Garry Leach, who boasted his own uncanny skills — but it's Alan I'm talking about here). Alan's voice, his mastery of words, and the engaging way in which he conceived and wrote a story — this story — was intoxicating.

At first reading, Alan taught me about the power of words, above and beyond the power latent in "Kimota!" or "Shazam!" As a working artist and struggling writer who constantly felt unable to elevate my own writing skills to the visions that danced in my heart and head, Alan became a teacher by example. Surely, THIS was the way to write a comic, the way it should have always been done.

By the time I'd read the first installment of Alan Moore and David Lloyd's "V for Vendetta," I knew this was perhaps more significant; this was art, touching me as few comics had since the American underground era.

This was better than different:

This was magic.

Little did I know, as I held WARRIOR #1 in my hands, that I would soon taste that magic even more intimately, and that it would change my life forever.

•

John Totleben and I met at the Joe Kubert School in 1977, where I was going into my second (and final) year as a member of the school's debut class, and John was blowing into Dover, New Jersey amid the second wave of students.

Tall, lanky, shaggy, and street-smart, 19-year-old John cut a mean Keith Richards figure new to the school. Sharing a deep and profoundly twisted affinity for all things grotesque, John and I hit it off immediately, though it was evident from the get-go that John could draw circles around every one of us at the school. Steeped in a surprisingly classical training via a specialized high school art curriculum, John's dazzling illustrative line echoed vital elements of his favorite artists — Franklin Booth, Virgil Finlay, Berni Wrightson — enhancing a style and vision that was distinctively John's and John's alone.

GABRIELE DELL'OTTO

Left: *Gabriele Dell'Otto is an Italian acclaimed artist and illustrator. He has worked for Panini Comics, Marvel USA and Marvel Germany. At present, he is cover artist for the US Marvel comic **The Call.** Illustration ©2003 Gabriele Dell'Otto. Swamp Thing ©2003 DC Comics.*

In John's universe, fast 'n' bulbous squids bred with stunning ravaged women to spawn Lovecraftian broods, and love poems sang of surf-washed gulls with their eye sockets pecked clean. And in his heart of hearts, John really wanted to have a shot at his all-time favorite comicbook character, Swamp Thing. He had already evolved his own take on the muck monster, delineated in stirring brush-and-ink renditions of the sorrow-eyed Swampy looking up from the mire, detailed in drunken conversations at the great parties classmates Tim and Beth Truman threw in their

Lake Hopatcong apartment wherein John described the notion of Swamp Thing growing edible potatoes from his body, and Rick Veitch (if memory serves) suggested the bon mot of their being hallucinogenic (ah, those parties).

Of course, DC Comics would never let such madness see print — but still, John could dream, and flesh out some of his concepts when the muse struck.

A few years later — after we had graduated from the Kubert School, shared a house in suburban Dover with our friends and fellow travelers Rick Veitch and Tom Yeates, and I had moved back to my home state of Vermont — John and I ended up having our shot at Swamp Thing, taking over the pencil (by me) and ink (by John) chores when our amigo Tom Yeates left SAGA OF THE SWAMP THING. To make a long story short, our stint began with the 16th issue, with the book already way behind schedule and sinking steadily in sales. Though the title was sliding like the House of Usher into the tarn, we had a shot, and we gave it our best.

One night in early 1983, during a phone conversation in which John and I agonized over the misdirection our stint as artists on DC Comics' SAGA OF THE SWAMP THING seemed to be going, we briefly fantasized how cool it would be if we could work with that new British comics writer, Alan Moore. Both John and I had scoured out each and every issue of WARRIOR as it slunk across the Atlantic at an increasingly erratic pace, and I'd begun to search for scarce-as-hen's-teeth issues of 2000 A.D. (well, they were scarce stateside) in hopes of finding more Moore. We imagined a kindred soul there, and then laughed off the conceit.

Above: One of John Totleben's early **Swamp Thing** revamps, reflecting his conception of the Wein/Wrightson character before his own tenure on the series with Alan Moore and Stephen Bissette; note the date beneath the signature (14 May 1982). At the time, Len Wein considered this approach "too extreme," but all that changed less than a year later when Alan Moore took over scripting the series.
Artwork ©1982 John Totleben.
Swamp Thing ©2003 DC Comics.

A couple of months later, we each received a phone call from our harried editor, Len Wein, he-who-had-co-created-Swamp-Thing when John and I were mere lads in high school scribbling monsters in ballpoint on the edge of our Algebra textbooks.

Though John lived in Erie, Pennsylvania, far from my southern Vermont mountainside abode, we shared the seismic shock of joy: Alan was to be the new SWAMP THING scribe, and we should prepare for a change of the guard.

Our amazement was only amplified when the first tentative contacts proved that Alan was, indeed, a kindred soul, and in more ways than we'd ever dared dream.

•

"Never having had the doubtless traumatic experience of collaborating with a colonial before, I thought I'd better take this opportunity to drop you a line, generally introduce myself, and let you know that I don't bear any grudges about your fathers coming over here in the war and having sexual intercourse with our mothers for Hershey Bars. I'd have probably done the same then myself in the circumstances." So began the first "long, tedious, and rambling" (Alan's words) letter — my first contact — from Alan back in May, 1983. That four-page single-spaced letter was far from being tedious or rambling: it was hilarious, invigorating, inspiring, incredible. After years of drawing from scripts crafted sans collaborative juice, fearing that John and I would never taste in mainstream comics the giddy pleasures we found when jamming on drawings with each other or Rick Veitch (indeed, my most intense and rewarding collaborations to that point had been those I'd savored with Rick), here was a writer hoping for something more than the assembly-line approach SWAMP THING had provided thus far:

"I suppose my basic attitude to the work is that what ends up on the printed page is the only important thing," Alan continued. "To that end, the script and art really have to be seen as one process, rather than as pictures over here and words over there.... it'd be a pretty dismal waste of potential if we didn't all have equal input into the work as a whole.... sometimes when I read through a comic, either indigenous or American, I get the impression that there's some horrible form of aesthetic territorial warfare going on. It looks like the writers are scribbling reams of luscious, dripping prose in an attempt to cover up the artwork while the artists get their own back by shoving huge looming women with grotesquely large tits in the foreground of every frame, even if the action takes place on the South face of the Matterhorn. For my part, being British and thus anxious to avoid causing a fuss, I like everybody to be friends.... So, if either you or John have any visual things you'd like to try out then let me know and I'll see if it's possible to work them into the plot.... Similarly any vague plot ideas you happen to have in the back of your minds... if they fit into the story as it's shaping up, then I'll use them." From the get-go, it was apparent that Alan's ego was not a driving determinative force; it was the genuine desire to seek, create, nurture that elusive plane of shared existence wherein physical parameters dissolve in the mingling of ideas and dreams, to be given form through lucid, skilled and forever shared work.

To that end, Alan went on to describe his work method, and his intended approach to the project at hand. "When I'm writing something, just to get the visual and narrative flow of the story, I tend to see it all unraveling visually inside my head. So, what I do is to breakdown all the sequences and pictures until they've got the right rhythm and timing and then provide pretty detailed panel descriptions."

That remains Alan's essential methodology, and it's brilliant; his scripts read and flowed like no other I'd ever laid eyes on (much less worked from) before that spring of '83. He thus established an approach to scripting comics that an entire generation has used as a foundation for their own efforts: yet another debt Neil Gaiman, Grant Morrison, Warren Ellis, et al owe to he-who-came-before.

There are comics that were written before Alan Moore, and comics that were written after his arrival; the division in my mind will forever remain marked by my reading of Alan's script to SAGA OF THE SWAMP THING #21, "The Anatomy Lesson," and I daresay history will bear out that out as a reality for the medium and the industry.

That first letter went on to detail Alan's personal preferences and prejudices ("... things I'd like to restrict are the use of sound effects and the use of stressed words in the narrative...") in his orientation to the craft and art of the medium. He efficiently identified what he saw as the problems of the series as it had existed up to that point, and his solutions were eloquent and perfectly in tune with John's and my own views — views Alan had no idea we shared. His views, in fact, were eerily in tune with those of the man from Erie, specifically the drawings John had done on his lonesome back in 1977, the very approach editor Len Wein had judged "too extreme" when John showed them to Len while assisting Tom Yeates (beginning with the second issue of SAGA).

Alan wanted "to emphasise the fact that [Swamp Thing] isn't in the least bit human... he's some sort of vegetable/animal hybrid, and his thought processes are not the same as ours. As an example of ways in which we could emphasize this visually, maybe it would be possible to include a couple of incredibly tight, nose-three-inches-away-from-him close ups, so that the reader can actually get a physical idea of just what this thing is made of... the little patches of pinmould and lichen spreading across the shoulder-blades, the places where stray seeds have rooted themselves in Swamp Thing's mass and rooted... maybe even the insect life which must obviously inhabit his body..." [Note: all ellipses in this paragraph are from Alan's original letter].

Furthermore, Alan shared John's and my own desire to steep the reader in the environment of the swamp itself; the prior 19 issues of the series had done everything possible to remove Swamp Thing from his element, much to the detriment of the character and comic. "For a few issues at least I'd like to have the strip actually set within the swamp... I'd like to make the swamp almost as important a character as Swamp Thing himself, giving the reader a real feeling of the teeming, mindless life that's slugging it out to the death in every square centimetre of Swampland, every second."

We were also leaning toward the same desire to elevate SAGA to the level of the horror literature and films we loved, rather than playing it safe working with the expected horror comics cliches; Alan expressed a love for the same writers, musicians, and filmmakers I loved, including Stephen King, Ramsey Campbell, Captain Beefheart, Nicolas Roeg, and "whoever it was who made the two Dr. Phibes films" (that would be Robert Fuest, of course).

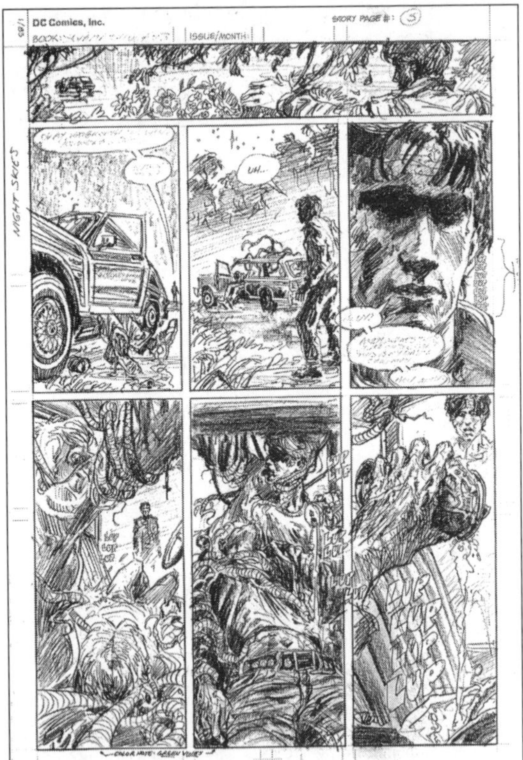
DC Comics, Inc.
STORY PAGE #: 3
ISSUE/MONTH
NIGHT SKIES
UH...

Overjoyed, John and I threw ourselves into the issue at hand — for John, inking (and essentially redrawing much of the) pencils for Alan's first issue, SAGA OF THE SWAMP THING #20, as I plunged into #21, "The Anatomy Lesson," which to my mind remains our finest collaborative effort. With self-effacing modesty we came to find typical, Alan referred to that script in his letter of July, 1983, as something "which I hope isn't too much of a disappointment."

It was, of course, fucking brilliant.

I mailed Alan our twelve pages of single-spaced typed story ideas, concepts we had shared with the prior writer of the series only to read later in an interview how offended he was by our presumption and input (see "Writer: Marty Pasko," COMICS INTERVIEW #34, 1986, page 13). Alan, on the other hand, immediately adopted two of the stories and continued to invite our most lunatic musings and ideas, from Nukeface to the Demon's resurrection, from put-upon female werewolves whose lycanthropy meshed with their 'time of the month' (a concept I'd previously pitched to HEAVY METAL in the context of an imaginary sf author's faux-biography) to the ghosts who haunted the Winchester estate (an issue that owed a debt to my friend Jim Wheelock). These he lovingly juxtaposed with his own seed concepts and fully-fleshed stories, from the opening volley co-starring Jason Woodrue, the Floronic Man, to the expansive American Gothic saga (finally, the comic truly became a saga).

*Above and page opposite: Script by Alan Moore, pencils by Stephen Bissette; a two page sequence from **Saga of the Swamp Thing #23:** the wake of Jason Woodrue, the Floronic Man, and a fine example of the Moore/Bissette/Totleben brand of suspense.*
Swamp Thing ©2003 DC Comics.

Even the most fleeting of notions fueled the volatile chemistry we all felt: "EDIBLE TUBERS??," began Alan's first letter to John (even John's name excited Alan: "does it really mean 'Deathlife'? What an incredible name. I don't suppose you'd care to sell it?"). "My god," Alan continued, "That's the most repulsive thing I've heard all morning! You can't possibly be suggesting that... Jesus Christ. What sort of loathsome and demented TransAtlantic sensibilities am I dealing with here? If you imagine for one moment that any Son of Albion would reduce himself to..." [Note: ellipses from original letter text].

Ah, but he would, and did, and we were all loathsome and demented in precisely the right way. It was the right time, the right team, the right character and comic, the right editor (as was Karen Berger, who picked up the reins from Len with issue #25), the right stuff, and we all felt the charge of it, though we were physically divided by oceans and half-a-continent. It was a rich cross-pollination of imaginations that was more than any one of us could have ever done alone, pushing us to explore and experience all we could for as long as possible.

It was the beginning of something unprecedented for us, and, as it turned out, for comics as a community, as a medium, and as an industry.

•

For a time, we all enjoyed the ride, and rolled with whatever punches came our way. Briefly disoriented by the curve-ball of the "Nukeface" story being bumped from Alan's planned SAGA OF THE SWAMP THING #29 to a later spot (#36-37, at editor Karen Berger's insistence), Alan apologized for the resulting replacement issue: "Having to rewrite 29 was a real fucking bastard... I could see Karen's point about the story being a bit slow and downbeat for a time when we were hoping to pull in new readers, but I was still heartbroken.... I'm sorry about the replacement story... I had to rush through it in three days in order to keep within any sort of schedule at all, and I'm still not sure about the end result."

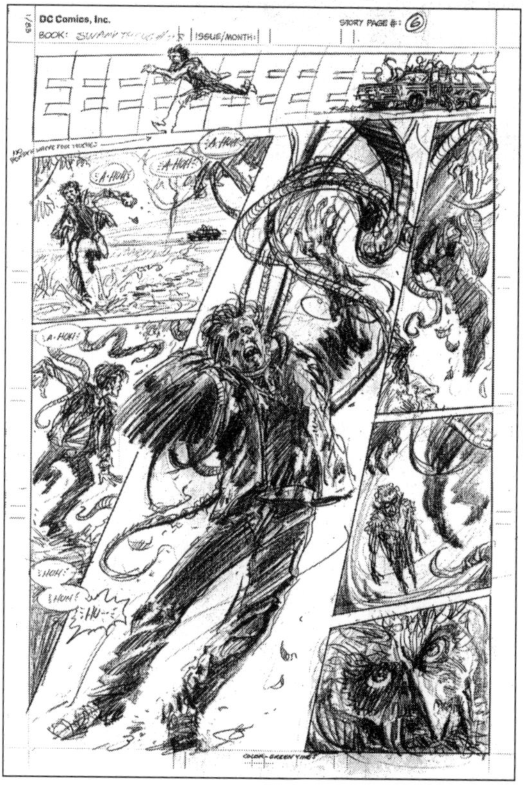

DC Comics, Inc.
BOOK:
ISSUE/MONTH:
STORY PAGE #: 6
A-HOH!
A-HOH!
A-HOH!
A-HOH!

That, of course, was the issue that lost us the Comics Code seal of approval, forever kicking down the doors that had kept mainstream four-color horror comics in a cage since October of 1954, and sent shivers up the spines of enough readers to create an outbreak of parasitic Tinglers. For that, Alan owed no one an apology — and John and I had the most fun we had ever had drawing a comic, a high I for one rarely tasted again.

•

If space permitted, I would continue this chronology — I have kept every letter, every script, and almost every sketch and scrap of paper that passed between us — but this is neither the time or venue. Another time, another place.

I could also detail those marvelous scripts, their clockwork precision tooled within conversational banter and sometimes over-abundant details of time, place, character, atmosphere, and intended effect. Perhaps you've been lucky enough to read a few yourself, perhaps not. Their heft, weight, and density is justifiably legendary, and most who comment on them note the quality of Alan's writing. Indeed, they were all lovely, never more so than when they reach their conclusion: "Final page now," Alan wrote for the culmination of SAGA OF THE SWAMP THING #34, "The Rites of Spring," the issue that began with a postcard from yours truly suggesting we do a single issue giving Abby and Alec a break from the horrors and let them just make love in the bayou; "and it's a full-page, full-figure shot of Swamp Thing and Abby standing there locked in their embrace. Surreally, the vines grow out of Swamp Thing and all over Abby, so that they look almost like two statues tied together by vines, miniature leaves sprouting elegantly here and there along the supple green stems. The idea of a woman and a plant-elemental kissing, with vines covering the woman and drawing her in to him, strikes me as a the sort of image that would have entertained the Pre-Raphaelites or the Symbolists... I see it as having that rich, mythical, lyric classicism to it, if you know what I mean. Behind

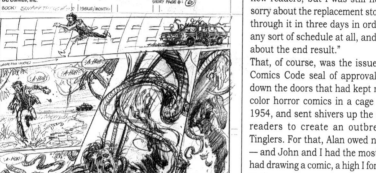

them as they kiss the sun settles, bloated and raw upon the treeline of the horizon, flooding the sky with powerful and bloody light."

How could John and I NOT give it our all? The results were rapturous enough to be stolen from the DC offices (though most of the issue was later returned to John and me, that page — and the issue's painted cover — is/are still among the stolen pages, so if you're looking at it now upon your own wall as you read this, aren't you a right shameless, nasty bastard? Give it back, please).

Not everyone was seduced by Alan's prose.

While visiting Al Williamson's Pennsylvania studio on an invite from Al, his wife Cory, and my friend Rick Veitch (who was working with Al at the time), I brought the current SWAMP THING pencils I was laboring over to Al's studio. Incredulous, Al hefted the script, asking if this was typical of Alan's work. I enthusiastically replied it was, and began to rhapsodize over how much fun they were to work from. Al screwed his face impatiently, flipping through the pages as I ranted on, and tossed it back into my lap saying, "How can you work from this? I just want to know where I am, who's hitting who, and where I'm off to next panel. This is WAR AND PEACE!"

I often wondered what a vet like Curt Swan made of that first script he'd received for "Whatever Happened to the Man of Tomorrow?" (SUPERMAN #423 and ACTION #583, 1986): however much editor Julie Schwartz had prepped Swan for his first glimpse of a Moore script, it must have been an initially daunting proposition once he held it in his (perhaps shaking) hands. Ever the gentleman, Alan's first lines were calculated to put his collaborators at ease: "Before we get this epic underway," that particular script began, "could I first say what a pleasure it is to be working with both of you, Curt, and you, George [Perez]. (Since I'm getting jaded and blase about working with Julie, I won't even give him a mention.) I hope that you both have as much fun as I'm going to working on this two-parter, and that you won't feel in any way confused or intimidated by the length of the script that follows...."

And so, the game began, and Alan's valentine to every Superman story Julie had ever edited and Curt had ever drawn was delivered, as sure as Cupid's arrow.

Alan's scripts were always like that: love letters to the artist, his partner of the moment, full of surprising laughs and insights and pokes and prods, ever at the service of the beautifully-built house each issue represented. Alan walked you through the hallways and rooms, made sure you knew where all the doors and windows and traps were so that ALL those involved could not only do their part, but make it their own, too.

Most of them began as if you had just joined Alan in a new excursion, "Wee Fellow Travellers," and indeed, that was most often the case. "Well, off we go," the script to SAGA OF THE SWAMP THING #50 enthuses, "I've got a spanking new typewriter ribbon, a couple of fresh reams of specially-made Croxley Script 'Funny-Sized English Typing Paper' (the actual brand name, believe it or not) and a new pad of carbon paper. What more could I ask for, except for perhaps a new brain and a peaceful, caring society?"

"I suppose that before I shove our tiny coracle out onto the wilder seas of incomprehension," Alan's script to SOTST #36 began, "I ought to explain a little bit about the story-structure of the piece in hand, just so you don't think that I've suffered a complete psychological breakdown as you read through the story. What I want to do is to break down the story into a number of self-contained stories, each narrated by a different character..." Though this surgically-crafted approach echoed that of many novelists — Bram Stoker's "Dracula" comes immediately to mind — it was a fresh template for a mainstream comic in the mid-1980s, and Alan went on to explain its direction.

Other details were for our eyes, and our eyes alone, never to be savored by the readers. Some were painfully personal and utterly tactile: consider this excerpt from the opening paragraph of SOTST #39's script: "What I'm trying to do here is to set up a sort of parallel between the values of a normal God-fearin', child-rearin' community against the values of the weird submarine vampire community. I'm sure you'll figure out what I mean as we go along. I should point out at this juncture that I've got a miserable cold at the moment. I feel so bloody terrible and badly-disposed towards the world that this episode is going to be unrelentingly horrible beyond the dreams of Caligula. Horror? Don't talk to me about horror... my nasal passages are currently like something out of H.P. Lovecraft's most grossly inhuman visions, and if I'm going to suffer then I'm going to make damn sure that everybody else does as well." Except for John and I; as always, we had a ball.

Let me distract you this procession of peripheral details excerpted from the panel descriptions for the opening page of "Strange Fruit," SOTST #42, set inside a cross-section of a coffin beneath the ground, in which the corpse within begins to stir. After an exquisitely detailed anatomical treatise on the minutia of the corpse itself, Alan goes a step further into Ladislas Starevitch territory by way of Sergio Aragones:

"(PANEL) 1: ...We can also see a number of small beetles running round inside the box, skittering over wood and bone with complete impartiality, doing whatever it is that beetles do under the ground... go to church, lend each other power tools, deliver newspapers, stuff like that. Apart from the beetles, nothing in the picture is moving. (PANEL) 2: Exactly the same shot, except that the beetles have changed position, scampering up the orbit of one eye socket perhaps before embarking upon a trip across the ochre planetoid of the skull. They look like they're having fun, but since they don't get any dialogue we'll never know for sure.

(PANEL) 3: Exactly the same shot, but the beetles have moved around a little. We can see that two of the beetles are getting a divorce while arguing over custody of the children, and another beetle standing to one side considering whether to become a Jehovah's Witness or not.

(PANEL) 4: Exactly the same shot.. except that almost unnoticeably, the corpse has started to lift it's right arm... over in the corners of the coffin the beetles are all worrying about the recession.

(PANEL) 5: Exactly the same shot. The corpse has now lifted it's right arm... I don't care what the beetles are doing. They haven't lived up to their original promise as supporting characters and I've grown weary of them."

•

I could regale you with memories of our few times together, but this isn't the time or place for that, either.

I have many fond memories of Alan's first visit to America: our first face-to-face as Dave Gibbons (delivering the first stunning batch of WATCHMEN pages) was shunted around by DC from a comfortable mid-Manhattan hotel to a 42nd street dive (where his room was broken into), while DC put up Alan and his then-wife Phyllis in palatial comfort, unmindful of the division of 'royalty' this created, while Alan and Dave and our editor Karen Berger made the best of the situation with aplomb; sitting with Alan and Phyllis outside of the doors of Marvel waiting for Archie Goodwin to join us for lunch, as Alan refused to enter the building ("I wouldn't piss on Marvel if they were on fire"); wandering the Vermont woods with John, Alan, and my wee daughter Maia, her blonde hair tossing in the breeze as she happily babbled while holding Alan's and my own hand, occasionally lifting her legs to swing from our arms, as we grown-ups soberly worked out the speculative logistics of water-breeding vampires and menstruating werewolves.

I have equally precious recall of my few trips to the UK: Alan's daughters Leah and Amber waking my wife and I up with their giggles and bouncing of balloons on our sleepy heads; wandering the nooks and crannies of Alan's hometown of Northampton, drinking in the arcane histories and anecdotes as Alan spun ancient shit-tragedies into gold; entering a musky magic shop en route to another destination, ostensibly to satisfy my need for a rare book on Matthew Hopkins, the Witchfinder General, as Alan browsed for more useful arcana (the first intimation of his shaman life to come); being smoked under the table by Alan's monster-choad-sized spliffs, frightening concoctions of tobacco and other substances that left me dazed while they only seemed to sharpen Alan's already razor-edged clarity; malingering in the London Dungeon while DC pissed away an entire day filming a promotional 'Alan Moore' video amid wax effigies of torture and plague victims with tape-loop soundtracks of their agonies, eventually being graced with a glimpse of a forbidden tableau removed from public exhibition, the notorious Gilles De Rais, the fifteenth-century sadist and child-killer, sodomizing one of his young victims. I recall Alan unfolding a massive chart, too large for even his living room floor, that diagramed the intricate narrative and conceptual permutations of the ambitious (but sadly ne'er completed) THE MANDELBROT SET, eventually released abortively as BIG NUMBERS; Alan reducing Melinda Gebbie and I to tears laughing at his observations on the periodic 'cursing' timetable of Melinda's neighbor ranting outside the window of her flat, who looked and acted for all the world like the 'Gumbies' of Monty Python, complete with a hankerchief 'hat' knotted at all four corners and his mounting bellowing and fist-shaking at the sky and possibly God Himself; tossing an ashtray at Alan's head as he interrupted my first-ever, fan-struck phone conversation with Ray Harryhausen (my hero!) with the shout, "Steve, come back to bed and have another popper!" I couldn't stop laughing, though I wanted to kill the sonuvabitch.

Thereafter, the long letters of the mid-1980s long behind us and any further personal contact compromised by my lack of money and Alan's decision to never fly to the US again, our talks were relegated to the telephone, chatting about our thoughts, dreams, work, and the occasional personal advice. In the worst of times, he was still a pal, tentatively suggesting, having gone through the personal hell of separation from his spouse before me, that I ease my agony over that very evening's final separation from my own first wife by watching Steve Martin in THE LONELY GUY (not one of his most sensitive suggestions, but what the hell: these are MY reveries). As they were: Another time, another place.

•

What's important here is that you understand a bit of what it was like to work with Alan, and what he brought to each and every collaborative dance.

One of Alan's greatest strengths as a writer has always been his invitation to his collaborators, his generous nature, and uncanny ability to (a) incorporate the artists' own ideas and concepts on characters, stories, etc.; (b) write to the specific strengths of his collaborative artists, and (c) nurture, via his dense, multi-layered, perfectly-tailored scripts the absolute best work from his collaborators.

These are indeed characteristics of many of the medium's finest collaborative writers — from Will Eisner to Bob Kanigher, Archie Goodwin to Neil Gaiman, etc. — which I can, in at least four of the names cited above (Kanigher, Goodwin, Moore, and Gaiman), boast some personal experience with as an artist. Truly rare individuals like Archie Goodwin also brought such insight and skills to their editing work, which both I and Rick Veitch can vouch for from personal experience (Rick's being much, much more extensive than my own, though I'll never forget how Archie once 'doctored' a story I cowrote and illustrated by putting his finger on PRECISELY the page and panel where a simple revision would elevate the whole to a new plateau).

As both the man who was lucky enough to work with Alan (and John Totleben) as artist on SAGA OF THE SWAMP THING, and as a publisher/editor with Alan and Eddie Campbell (for the first half of FROM HELL's maiden publication in TABOO 2-7) and subsequently with Alan and Melinda Gebbie (on LOST GIRL's debut chapters, again in TABOO), personal interaction demonstrated time and time again how truly collaborative Alan's creative life could be. In the case of ST, he welcomed extensive input, story ideas, characters, and concepts from John T, Rick V, and me that the prior writer had patently rejected (and indeed bristled at). Out of that incredible fertile generosity and collaborative chemistry came stories and characters that would not have otherwise existed, including the entire Demon/Monkey King story arc (a concept John and I had pitched to the prior ST writer, and again to Alan in my first letter to him, proposing the use of real childrens' drawings as a visual device and the quote from James Agee's screen adaptation of Davis Grubb's "Night of the Hunter" as a possible touchstone — both devices Alan indeed incorporated into the three-issue arc), Nukeface (completely John T.'s original concept, as were the hallucinogenic tubers), the "Rites of Spring" issue and lycanthrope tales (both springboarded from my own story suggestions), and even John Constantine (the catalyst being John T. and I letting Alan know — from my very first letter to Alan in May 1983! — we were intent upon "design[ing] a character with [Sting's] face and features in mind, or you might find us interpreting one of your creations in like manner...").

Below and the following three pages: ***Swamp Thing Annual #2,*** *"Down Amongst the Dead Men," script by Alan Moore, pencils by Stephen Bissette. Swamp Thing goes to hell; The Phantom Stranger, The Demon Etrigan, The Spectre, Arcane. Swamp Thing and all supporting cast ©2003 DC Comics.*

I hasten to add that I am in no way trying to diminish Alan's work, merely emphasize that the result of those collaborations were indeed the results of three and four creators working hand in hand in a manner precious few writers in this field would ever invite, nurture, and bring to such rich fruition.

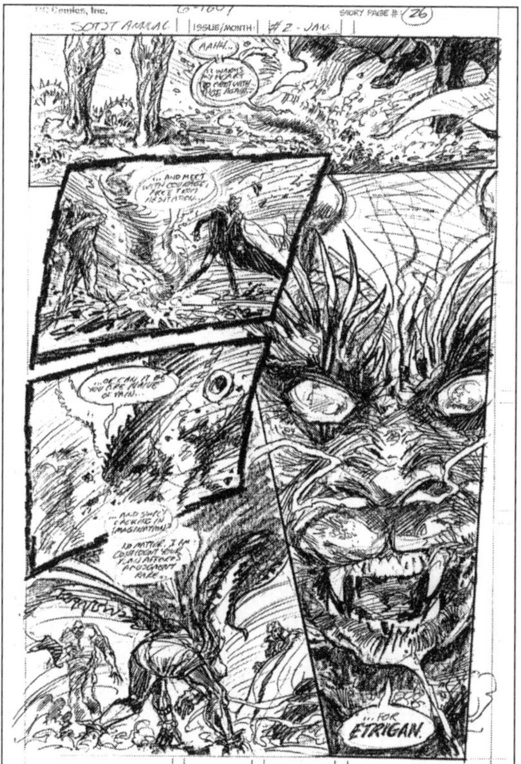

ISSUE/MONTH
AAHH..
...FOR ETRIGAN.

These were heady, playful, intensively collaborative efforts. It seemed to me that WATCHMEN was the result of an even more intensive, matured creative relationship with dapper Dave Gibbons; and I later saw, first hand (as editor and go-between at first), how Eddie Campbell's collaborative effort with Alan on FROM HELL was even more dissective and extensive. Don't ever forget, though, that with his first phone call to me in 1989 offering FROM HELL to TABOO for publication, Alan had mapped out the ENTIRETY of the serialized novel, complete with chapter names for all 16 chapters, including the prologues, epilogues, and companion feature coda. It was ALL in his fucking head from the outset — and that, my friends, still astounds me to no end.

I would later recall the mind-boggling enormity of that conversation while sitting in Alan's own living room a year or three later, as he tenderly unfolded the monstrous narrative chart for THE MANDELBROT SET, aka BIG NUMBERS. That this conceptual map was too big for Alan's own home was an omen of sorts, as BIG NUMBERS soon proved too big for its first artist (Bill Sienkiewicz) and its second (the sadly maligned Al Columbia; none of you have any idea what really went down). It was too big for its first publisher (Alan's own short-lived publishing venture Mad Love) and second (the disastrously-monikered Tundra); too big, it seemed, for the miserly vehicle of the entire comics industry circa the early 1990s. That which Alan conceived, it seemed, could NOT fit on mere pages after all, though he had the blueprint in head and in hand from the outset.

All too appropriately named, BIG NUMBERS was a little Waterloo in the end, a terrible blow to all those involved, most of all Alan's fledgling self-publishing imprint the project put paid to. Despite the terrible personal toll (professionally, financially, and emotionally), Alan recovered from the sorrowful implosion with startling grace. The resulting vacuum (not to mention the protracted death-throes the project suffered) would have destroyed a lesser creator.

There were other speed bumps, detours, and disappointments along the way.

I have here next to me the fantastic treatment for Alan's planned DC crossover epic

TWILIGHT, which would definitely have been the pinnacle achievement of its bastard breed. Alongside it on my desk is a faded photocopy of the script for the first episode of LUX BREVIS, a dystopian series Alan and John T. planned to launch for a never-to-be-publish anthology Tim Truman and John Ostrander pitched to First Comics; alas, it was never to be. I could quote chapter and verse on both, but again: no time, no space.

There's more, more than I can tell: the TABOO story Alan dictated over the phone to me one night, and promptly forgot two weeks later, suggesting I write and draw it myself if it was so damned good, though anything I might have been arrogant enough to reconstruct would have fallen far short of the tale he'd crafted; the Alan Moore script that a certain artist probably still has ferreted away, happily accepting prepayments from foolish American publishers (like me) only to not draw it again and chuckle all the way to the bank; more unpublished Moore than you can imagine,

Pencils by Stephen Bissette.
Swamp Thing ©2003 DC Comics.

locked away in publishers' and artists' files cabinets, papering the bottoms of budgie cages, blanketing the corners — no, acres! — of 'idea space' like ground moss.

Alan, ever fecund, always took such events in stride, spun his mind in fresh directions, following through the many works-in-progress still cluttering his desk, following them to their conclusions when business affairs permitted such conclusions. And all the while, he sired broods, litters, busloads of new offspring.

The magic flowed, only momentarily diverted from its path.

Just to reinforce my personal reveries a bit, while unpacking last year I came across my set of Eclipse MIRACLEMAN (the name applied to MARVELMAN stateside, due to you-know-who) reprints of those seminal WARRIOR chapters. In the second issue of the comics reprint series, Alan has a text piece ("M*****man: Full Story and Pics", 2 pages) on the origins of the character. After detailing the character's historical roots, Alan traces his own involvement, beginning with his link with the character as a young reader and fan, the catalysts for his revisionist take, and the 1981 phone call from WARRIOR publisher Dez Skinn inviting him to write a revival of the Marvelman character. And I quote:

"Garry Leach was finally decided upon being the best artist for the kind of Marvelman that we wanted to attempt, and the two of us began working towards a redefining of the character which was finally to appear in March, 1982 in WARRIOR's premiere issue. Determining an approach to the art and writing that was a realistic as we could make it at the time, we tried to establish Marvelman as very much a character for the 1980s... [Note: ellipses from original text] a superhero far removed from the derivative Captain Marvel clone of the fifties and, hopefully, a more extreme and radical approach to the superhero concept than had been attempted at any time since. This, at least, was our intention, remaining undiminished when Alan Davis took over the job of artist from Garry with WARRIOR No. 8."

Note the emphasis Alan himself placed upon the collaborative development as well as execution of the character. This was true throughout the SWAMP THING run for John and me (and, later, Rick), as I experienced and/or saw first-hand; it's also absolutely consistent with the subsequent development stages of new characters and series I've been involved in (e.g., the '1963' N-Man and The Fury: the former was visualized by Alan only as "he should look good coming through a wall," the latter as a scrawny teenager in a customized football helmet sporting a pitchfork and faux pointed devil's tale; only The Hypernaut emerged full-blown from Alan's mind and hand — I indeed penciled the character from a sketch Alan had done himself, and the man sure can draw).

Alan has typically, in text pieces and interviews, been absolutely up-front about this necessarily collaborative chemistry he nurtures, and I can also relate that Alan invites "revisionist" approaches to his work when artists changed midway through a character or series run. That is, the expansive Moore-Totleben MIRACLEMAN was

Pencils by Stephen Bissette. Swamp Thing ©2003 DC Comics.

very much a collaboration, worlds away from the prior Garry Leach and Alan Davis arcs, reflecting John Totleben's fertile thoughts, concepts, and desires as much as they did Alan's. It was ever the same with SWAMP THING: it was hardly a whimsical shift in tone that once Rick Veitch came on board as regular penciler, the series quickly moved from horror to science fiction-fantasy as its orientation, which was in keeping with Rick's personal tastes and interests.

In other cases, the collaborative artists have pushed Alan for his best work. I still vividly recall the initial phone conversations with Eddie Campbell as he weighed the options on taking on FROM HELL for serialization in TABOO; one of his desires was to "keep Alan from losing wind" before the final chapter. Eddie accurately perceived that many (too many, in Eddie's mind) of Alan's multi-part tales up to that point relied upon a final twist of the villain being unveiled as a whining bully in the end: consider Kid Marvelman, Arcane, the Monkey King in our Demon ST story arc, etc. "He's not going to wimp out on THIS one," Eddie insisted, and I suspect the strength of the personal as well as the professional bond between the two men led to FROM HELL indeed transcending much of what Alan had done before... with Eddie pushing throughout for Alan to meet and exceed the high standards they'd set for themselves from the outset.

Rich, dense, and masterfully-woven as Alan's scripts are (whether fully-scripted or, as we worked with the '1963' series, scripted via the "Marvel method," which was great fun, too), his collaborations are just that: collaborations. That they push the envelope on that chemistry to the degree that they do is one of Alan's greatest strengths, in my mind... and, thus, any claim that one party or another of the truly collaborative projects in Alan's ouevre represent anything other than a commensurate investment from ALL creative parties are quite simply false.

•

That said, the incredible consistency of quality from Alan (even in his 'lesser' works, to be defined at the discretion and via the perspective of the respective readers) speaks volumes. It's telling, isn't it, how few of his artist collaborators have even approached maintaining the high standards achieved with their work with Alan? Eddie Campbell, Rick Veitch, and a handful of others lucky enough to have worked with Alan over the years have set their own standards and created their own distinctive bodies of work, but many (and I would count myself among those who have never lived up to the 'potential' demonstrated in their collaborative work with Alan) have hardly come close.

That now said, I must note briefly that it was Alan who taught me how to write. I'd struggled as a writer all through high school and college, and managed to cobble together some fair stories once I'd entered comics professionally (usually in synch with Rick Veitch: see "Cell Food," "Monkey See," and the notorious "The Tell-Tale Fart," which so offended Eclipse publisher/editor Cat Yronwode — excuse me, cat yronwode; she chose to never capitalize her name — that she... oh, never mind). But my efforts always fell short, and the scripts I'd worked from (the best of were Bob Kanigher's staccato, to-the-point muzzle-bursts, models of authorial precision and efficiency) and short stories I'd adapted (Ron Goulart's "Into the Shop," etc.) up to that point in my career adhered to narrative conventions I found confining. I couldn't burst through into the kind of comics Rick, John, Tim Truman, and our compatriots dreamed and talked about: comics that pushed the parameters of the known templates. I wanted to do in comics what, say, Nicolas Roeg and Donald Cammell had done to my notions of cinema when I saw PERFORMANCE as a teenager, what the underground comix maestros (Crumb, S. Clay Wilson, Spain, Trina, Tom Veitch and Greg Irons, etc.) had done: blown the blinder off, kicked the doors wide open. There were new ways of telling stories, I knew, that would still fly in the mainstream markets: Alan taught me that was all possible.

Pencils by Stephen Bissette.
Swamp Thing ©2003 DC Comics.

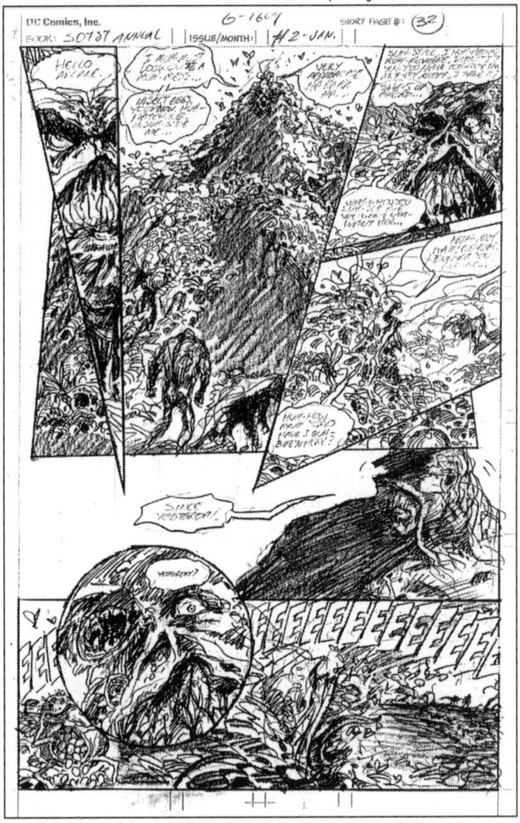
DC Comics, Inc.
STORY PAGE #:
32
ISSUE/MONTH:
#2-JAN.
HELLO
VERY

Working from his scripts, knowing the man for too-fleeting a decade, bouncing ideas and hammering out fresh approaches to tales tried-and-true or wild-and-woolly, Alan taught me the power of words, the beauty of nurturing a story idea like a crystal growing from its element, letting it take and define its own shape with an almost alchemical fidelity to the organic process of letting it grow as needed.

Alan would selflessly lend his acute vision and voice to the most mundane of concepts, treating all as fresh soil in which to plant and live for a time: minutes, if that's all he were permitted; lifetimes, if he were so invited. A late-night conversation in his kitchen in Northampton about my planned but still inchoate comics series TYRANT led to Alan musing over the voice the comic might build upon; he paced back and forth, pausing only to savor a smoke, and then turned to me with a look of gob-smacked gestalt, and whispered:

"Meat. Not meat."

He paced again, and began to repeat it as a mantra, until we were giddy with it, and so TYRANT's core was defined: of course, in the life of a carnivore, it all came down to that, didn't it?

Alan showed me the way; another lesson learned, and one I never forgot or could thank him enough for.

Even when there is a clearly defined starting point from which to work — most apparent in his springboards from existing commercial entities — MARVELMAN, CAPTAIN BRITAIN, SWAMP THING, SUPERMAN (will there ever be a truer eulogy to the silver age Superman than "The Man of Tomorrow"?), etc. — and consciously derivative works: SUPREME, '1963,' THE LEAGUE OF EXTRAORDINARY GENTLEMEN, PROMETHEA (will Wonder Woman ever seem exotic again?) — Alan gleefully assembles the tools, characters and settings that are not of his own devising, and plays. With loving fidelity to their respective wellsprings, Alan literally and figuratively explores and exhausts all previously established parameters, ferrets out their primal life source, and begins building them anew.

In doing so, he makes them his own (and that of his collaborators), in some cases shattering the moulds, in others recapturing some lost essence previous dabblers had manage to sully. It's part and parcel of why it was sooooo much fun and so rewarding to work with him for so many years, and why I still read every scrap of his work I can lay hands upon.

•

In the end — and it did end, for me at least — we drifted apart as the collaborative work became more business-driven and less creative. After I stepped aside to let Tundra assume the reins of publishing FROM HELL, per Alan and Eddie's wishes, we spoke less and less; for almost a year, we barely spoke at all, though there had been no falling out (as yet). I worked hard at a couple of points to find paying venues for Alan when times were lean; prestigious though FROM HELL was, it barely paid the rent, much less funded Alan's duties and obligations to an expansive family and communal web.

Thus was born FROM HELL: THE COMPLEAT SCRIPTS, a co-publishing venture between Borderlands Press and my own SpiderBaby Grafix that was cut off at the ankles when movie options loomed. The current FROM HELL publisher of note, Kitchen Sink Press, flew into a tizzy when they discovered Alan and Eddie had contracted with us to do the book series a year before, and those agreements had been forgotten in the movie deal negotiations. In short order, legal threats were made by Kitchen Sink's legal counsel. Borderlands and I could have fought, but it would have been Alan and Eddie who suffered. I talked all involved on this side of the ocean to just walk away (had I known how this would later impact upon me personally, would I still have done the same thing? In a heartbeat; FROM HELL was, and is, Alan's and Eddie's alone).

Thus was born '1963,' the project that pulled Alan back into the genre he had sworn off after WATCHMEN. '1963' emerged from an invitation extended by then-red-hot Image publishing, via a call from Larry Marder and Jim Valentino, extended to and through me; it took some persuasion to convince Alan to again swim in the superhero pool. Mind you, though Todd McFarlane leapt into the breach as soon as there was a crack to wedge his foot into (rushing Alan's first scripted SPAWN issue and series into stores before '1963' BOOK ONE: MYSTERY INCORPORATED saw print), it was '1963' — and the long, healing, solicitous conversations between Alan, Rick Veitch, and myself — that convinced Alan perhaps some good could be done after all in the battered and bloody superhero trenches. Alan decided that the damage he perceived done to the genre in the wake of WATCHMEN (and Frank Miller's THE DARK KNIGHT RETURNS) might be redressed — or at least upended — by a more playful approach to the genre, evoking the morals and spirit of the comics we ourselves had grown up with in the early 1960s.

For a heady four or five months, the creation of '1963' was a rush. Juggling a part-time day job with days in a shared studio with Rick, I was once again working with Alan — away from the stressful roles of 'employee/employer' publishing had foisted upon us, altering our relationship for the worst — and I tasted that delicious heaven one more time.

For a time.

It was a time of change.

My marriage was falling apart; Image, our publisher of note on '1963', was in constant upheaval; and even our beloved lark in the park with the '63 series was complicated by the involvement of Jim Lee assuming proprietary reins on the planned finale 'Giant Annual,' which Alan had conceived from the outset as an old-fashioned 60-page issue that would thrust our retro-1963-characters into collision with Image's hyper-modern 1993 creator-owned characters.

Amid all this, a phone call from Alan:
"Steve, I'm going to become a shaman. I've got however many years I've got left on this planet, and I'm going to spend them doing this." He went on to explain the first goal was to become invisible: invisible to the world at large, for only behind such invisibility could he pursue his new path. I remembered the magic shop he'd taken me to visit in England, and strained to recall what was upon its shelves.

I dreamed one night of Alan presenting a marvelous stage show, a spectacle that had something to do with FROM HELL, but that was more than that: it wasn't an adaptation, or a movie version, or a reenactment, it was a performance piece designed to alter the theatrical space. It was magic. In the dream, I found myself out in the lobby, unable to watch the performance, though I could hear it from behind the now-locked lobby doors. Alan staggered out briefly, grabbed me, and shook me. There seemed to be blood on his clothes, but no wounds anywhere; I assumed it was stage blood, but Alan was so wild-eyed and frantic that I couldn't be sure. Someone popped out of the doors, and pulled him back inside: the next act was about to begin. I awoke, seized with the necessity of relating this dream to Alan. I called, and quickly described all I could recall.
"Ah, Steve, I forgot what a disruptive presence you can be," he chuckled.

In the end, Jim Lee would disappear, orphaning the monstrous undertaking the '63 Annual represented.
We would never complete the Annual. I was outraged at Lee's unexplained abandonment, frustrated with Rick's and my own inability to solicit responses from any of the key players involved with the Annual (including, I'm sorry to say, Alan). Dealing with the ongoing collapse of my own home-life around my ears with two children to place utmost in these events, I drafted a formal announcement to Rick and Alan that I would not be able to see through the editorial chores on the Annual, which was so badly off schedule and derailed. I assured them that I would definitely hold up my end creatively, penciling my characters as planned.
(Years later, I would find myself being held responsible for dismantling the project, ostensibly due to this letter; I would also be told Alan had endured a rough stretch in his own personal life at this time, one I had not known about then, and only learned of over five years later — though I was still held responsible, as if I should have known. Thankfully, that has since been amicably settled, though the void the unpublished Annual leaves behind will forever haunt us.)

My marriage ended that summer, even as '1963' earned me more money than I'd ever earned before or since; it was absurd, earning so much for the single most frivolous undertaking of my career. I had, at least, done one last good turn for Alan and Rick (and our creative partners): '1963' and the association with Image pulled us all out of poverty, at least for a time. Building upon that fresh direction, Alan's fortunes have only seemed to increase since then, justifiably so.
As for me, I channeled every ounce of my being into seeing through the life changes, keeping my daughter Maia and my son Daniel first and foremost.

And there was another child to tend to: a baby dinosaur named TYRANT.

Meat.

Not meat.

As a parent, as a man, as an artist and writer, it was that simple, really.

Above: Saga of the Swamp Thing #24, page 23: Swamp Thing triumphant, at one with his enviroment, as was his creative team at this point in time; script by Alan Moore, pencils by Stephen Bissette, inks by John Totleben. Swamp Thing ©2003 DC Comics.

As I have found to my surprise from time to time, everyone in the comics industry seems to harbor the belief that they know what happened between Alan and me in the end, though to be honest, I don't really know myself.

Complete strangers, professionals and fans, vent heated opinions and dance around slander and character assassination in airing their views, only to insist "I don't want to have this conversation" when I step into the room (or onto the discussion board).

If they really do know what happened, I'd love to have the cataracts lifted from my eyes and see the truth of it.

Perhaps that first letter from Alan back in the spring of '83 had been a premonition: Alan's "first collaboration with a colonial" indeed ended up being "traumatic." It was a trying enough dynamic to provoke Alan to say goodbye without explanation, and refuse me the privilege of bidding farewell.

Tired of the same questions repeated over and over, of my singing the same threnody at comics conventions around the world about what had happened to Tundra and the collected FROM HELL: THE COMPLEAT SCRIPTS series and the ill-fated '1963' Annual, I voiced my perspective on these events candidly in my second interview with THE COMICS JOURNAL in 1994. It was important to me to be truthful, to analyze the issues at hand, and I was harder on myself than anyone.

Concerned that I not offend any of my friends and associates, or allow anything they considered damaging slip into print, I negotiated with interviewer (and Fantagraphics honcho) Kim Thompson a grace period between my receiving the full transcript of the interview and the publication of same. During that interim, I sent complete transcripts of the interview to almost all of the key people involved in my personal and professional life, particularly those I had mentioned.

I promised to revise or cut ANY passage anyone found offensive or incorrect, from the details of my marriage falling apart to the shared trials and tribulations of my rocky career.

Among those friends and associates was Alan.

I never heard a word.

Weeks later, mere days before Kim Thompson and the current JOURNAL editor put the typeset interview to bed, Neil Gaiman called me upon his return from visiting the UK. He told me Alan was very upset over the interview. I immediately rang Alan up.

A sentence or two from Alan — "Right, Steve, I'll keep this short. Don't ever call me, don't ever write; as far as I'm concerned, it's over. Goodbye." — a click, and it was indeed over. I was not permitted to respond, or speak.

Perhaps as Alan had scribed in his first letter to me, "being British and thus anxious to avoid causing a fuss," Alan brought it all to a neat conclusion, and that was that. Just as the spoken word transformed Marvelman from mortal skin to divine being, by refusing to hear another word from me, Alan elegantly inverted the process: I

231

became less than mortal. Exiled, I was willed out of his world.

Another lesson from Alan in the power of the word: denied a voice, one ceases to matter. I was invisible. I was no longer just a disruptive presence: I had hurt him so profoundly that I was to be banished. As I had seen in similar events with others, Alan's will was clear, and final.

With Kim Thompson's indulgence, I scoured the interview for any passages that might have offended, and struggled to ensure nothing that might have offended Alan saw print, second-guessing every step of the way. The revisions were minor; I still stand by the interview, though I am sorry it caused Alan any grief.

Personally, I grieved. In the weeks, months, years that followed, I made a couple — only a couple — attempts to mend fences; invisible men may speak, but not be heard. I accepted the shroud of exile as gracefully as possible, and got on with my life.

A few years later, I put the last of my shared life with Alan behind me. After five years of patience, I insisted upon a legal division of our last collaborative effort that remained a shared legal property — the forever unfinished '1963' series. The process tore a rift through another precious friendship, but we weathered it, and the matter was settled.

Divorce, upon divorce, upon divorce:

That very month, I retired from the industry of comics.

•

I now experience Alan's work as most of you do: as a reader.

And that's fine. His work, old and new, is everywhere.

I also see his wake everywhere; shaman Alan may be, he is hardly invisible.

I stumble upon interviews with the fellow in books with titles evoking the tenacity of verminous insects; in ENTERTAINMENT WEEKLY; in Eddie Campbell's final self-published venture to date. I see (and occasionally read) comics that are still struggling to reflect a fraction of the explosive glow Alan bathed us all in two decades ago, and every year since.

I go to the theater to see UNBREAKABLE, and find a rather dim, inchoate echo of Alan's first episodes of "Marvelman," which said much the same thing with more coherence, cohesion, and impact. I see FROM HELL on the big screen, and again later on my home screen, and find an even dimmer, danker echo of the graphic novel I was lucky enough to midwife. The previews I have seen for the movie version of THE LEAGUE OF EXTRAORDINARY GENTLEMEN seem to be all sizzle, no steak. They don't get it.

No one can capture or wield Alan's voice, save Alan.

So I read his new work, and occasionally listen (thanks to the clutch of CDs, preserving performances I will never see, save in the chambers of my skull). I don't need the latter, marvelous as the CDs may be; whenever I read Alan's work, I hear him, clearly.

I can still hear his voice as my eyes drink in the words, occasionally catch a glimmer of his eyes piercing that dark split waterfall of hair, and I am thankful that voice is still in me head, in the world, to be shared.

The man is lost to me, but he shares with us all.

Perhaps I've lost nothing, really, as much as it still hurts at times.

The magic is everywhere.

• **Stephen R. Bissette**

Notes:

A few of paragraphs of this text were originally posted on the comicon.com discussion board thread, "Alan Moore quitting his ABC books,"on 10-05-2002 to 10-07-2002. See http://www.comicon.com/cgi-bin/ ultimatebb.cgi?ubb=get_topic&f=1&t=006786&p=2

And my thanks to those who participated in that discussion on-line, prompting me to share a few of these insights and memories, leading to this essay.

Special thanks to Gary Spencer Millidge, G. Michael Dobbs, Rick Veitch, John Rovnak; and most of all to Daniel, Maia, and Marjery: the most magical of all.

OTTO GABOS

Right: Otto Gabos is a well-known Italian comics writer and illustrator who has worked for Italy's most important comics publishers. At the moment he is contributing work to the comics magazine **Mondo Naif** . Strip ©2003 Otto Gabos. The League of Extraordinary Gentlemen ©2003 Alan Moore and Kevin O'Neill.

The League of Extraordinary Gentleman: "When an Empire Falls" - Episode XXVI

WHAT HAS HAPPENED BEFORE: Mr. Griffin and Dr. Jekyll are in Pimentel, the capital of the Alverman Empire, for an uncercover mission ordered personally by Her Majesty The Queen. They must bring back the Earl of Westchester, who has mysteriously disappeared. Trouble began when Dr. Jekyll turned into the abominable Mr. Hyde, sparking off a big brawl which, skillfully handled by the Sons of Mani (a self-styled revolutionary army), degenerated into a massive riot. The rescue team is required urgently...

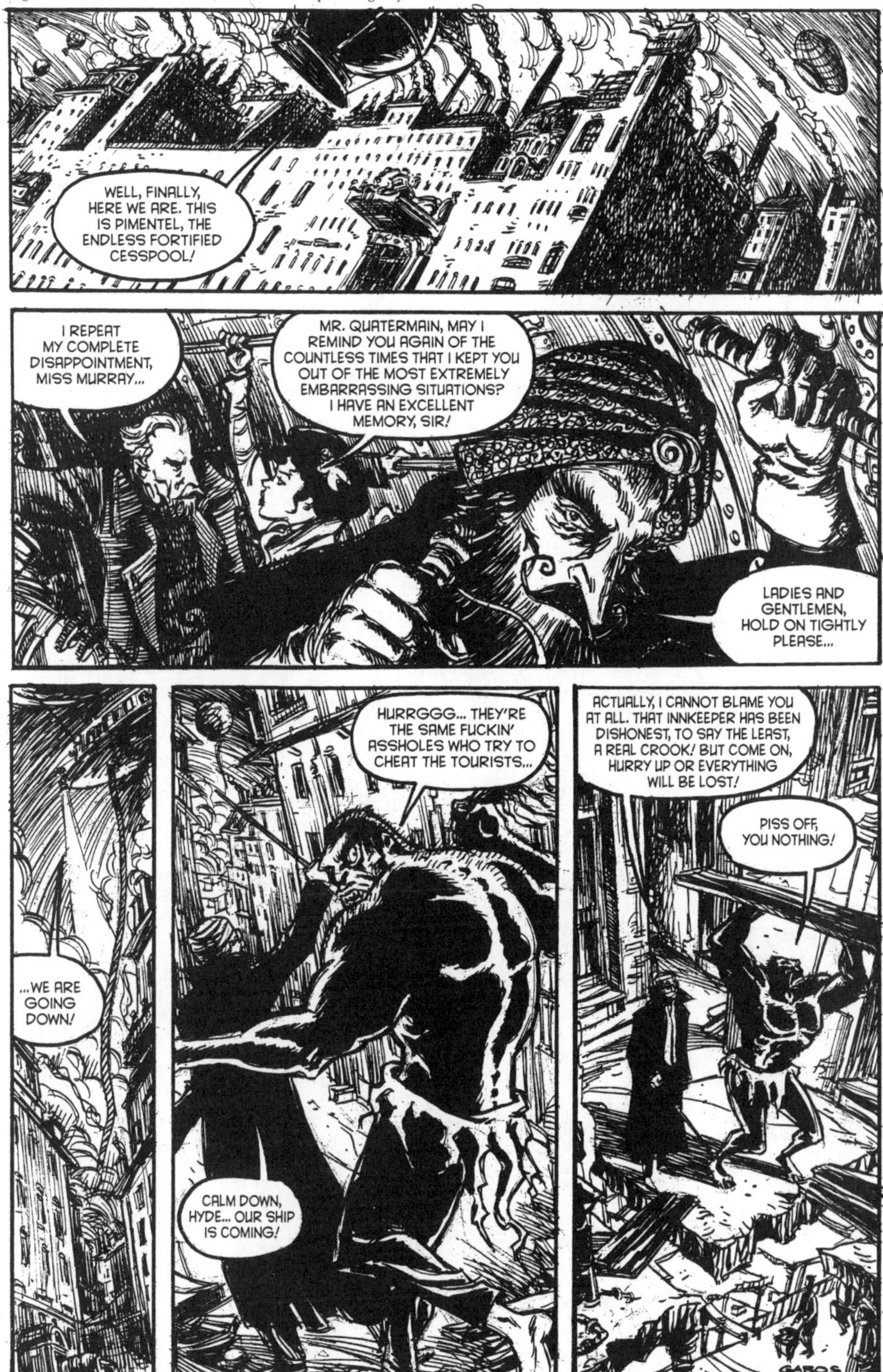
WELL, FINALLY, HERE WE ARE. THIS IS PIMENTEL, THE ENDLESS FORTIFIED CESSPOOL!
I REPEAT MY COMPLETE DISAPPOINTMENT, MISS MURRAY...
MR. QUATERMAIN, MAY I REMIND YOU AGAIN OF THE COUNTLESS TIMES THAT I KEPT YOU OUT OF THE MOST EXTREMELY EMBARRASSING SITUATIONS? I HAVE AN EXCELLENT MEMORY, SIR!
LADIES AND GENTLEMEN, HOLD ON TIGHTLY PLEASE...
...WE ARE GOING DOWN!
HURRGGG... THEY'RE THE SAME FUCKIN' ASSHOLES WHO TRY TO CHEAT THE TOURISTS...
CALM DOWN, HYDE... OUR SHIP IS COMING!
ACTUALLY, I CANNOT BLAME YOU AT ALL. THAT INNKEEPER HAS BEEN DISHONEST, TO SAY THE LEAST, A REAL CROOK! BUT COME ON, HURRY UP OR EVERYTHING WILL BE LOST!
PISS OFF, YOU NOTHING!
GABOS

TO BE CONTINUED

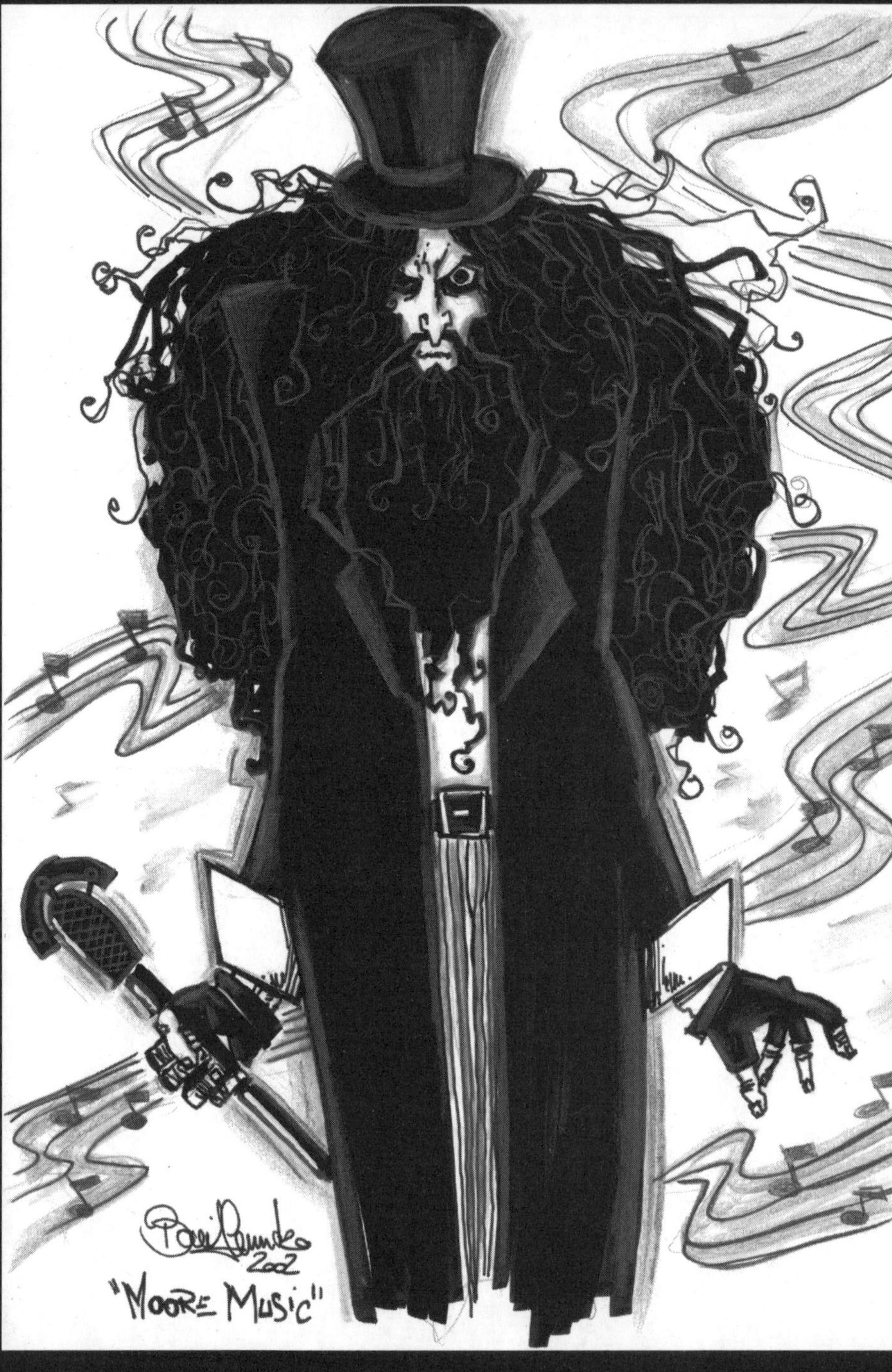
2002
"MOORE MUSIC"

MOORE MUSIC MAGIC

TIM PERKINS

Tim Perkins has been Alan Moore's musical collaborator for many years. He was in both incarnations of The Emperors of Ice Cream and has provided musical accompaniment for all of Moore's recent performance work and CDs including The Highbury Working, Angel Passage and Snakes and Ladders.
Text ©2003 Tim Perkins.

Having collaborated musically with Alan for the past 10 yeas now, I'd like to take this opportunity to comment on Al's involvement in that particular facet of the Arts, and the wider implications thereof.

I still have fond memories of Al kicking the ass out of some flimsy Tannoy speakers with an impassioned rendition of "Willy the Pimp" by Frank Zappa. One microphone and two jack leads were casualties in this onslaught of song (Al never wore slippers in my cellar), and Captain Beefheart grew another dimension to his already finely cultivated beard.

Alan's singing days seem to be pretty much over now, but my good God! What a fine voice he possessed, combining the grittiness of Tom Waits, the mystique of Leonard Cohen and the dentistry of Shane Pogue, all neatly hemmed in by Northamptonian regional synthesis.

Our first sonic expedition together (along with David J) was the "Moon and Serpent Grand Egyptian Theatre of Marvels" in 1996. The work is bookended by two songs with contrasting vocal styles ranging from cosmic carousel barker ("Hair of the Snake That Bit Me") to ethereal Blakeian charm ("A Town of Lights"). Since then, each successive album has posed different challenges and dimensions of thought. Certain methods have been strongly favoured however, and crop up throughout.

'Air sculpture' and 'psycho-geography' when applied to the studio, were two of many ways we could approach music and spoken- word, by treating sounds in terms of physical shape and design, of mood and colour. Off-the-wall concepts to get your fat arse down the brain-gym.

We loved to play with time, the bonding of past and future into one glorious present... there is only one moment... which is why Samuel Coleridge and Joe Meek are presently sharing an opium laced Knickerbocker Glory at the Gunners' gig down at PO-NA-NA's. Woooaaah!

'Multiple sensory overload' is another lunar-serpentine trait, the epitome of which was achieved, I think, at the 'Tygers of Wrath' event at the Purcell Room, Feb. 2001. Our piece, "Angel Passage" ended with a climactic fusion of music, dialogue, film and live pyrotechnics.

Creaming aside, I have admit this ain't exactly a new trick. The Russian composer Alexander Scriabin held a similar ethos for the performance of his works. Scriabin used visual backdrops and perfumed auditoriums and sought joy through the senses... (or the Yellow Pages if it happened to be more convenient at the time).

We are merely applying it in our own way and according to experience which is relevant to us. Sure, the old masters did it all before, but then they didn't have Line 6 digital amp systems or Leffe Blonde, so... fuck 'em (Rule no. 1).

If psychedelia is 'soul revealment,' then Mr. Moore is in the thick of it, clawing ever deep into a customised sensory deprivation tank of his own choosing.

Take it to the bridge.

Sweet Soul Music.

• **Tim Perkins**

JASON HALL

Pages 236-237 following: Jason Hall is the co-creator of Pistolwhip and has just written the newest graphic novel in the series, The Yellow Menace for Top Shelf. He has also written for Star Wars Tales, Batman: Gotham Adventures and is presently writing Beware The Creeper for DC/Vertigo.
Text/photographs ©2003 Jason Hall.

ALESSANDRO BONI

Left: Alessandro Boni is the author of Heart of Chastity, a well received Italian indie miniseries which mixes horror with eroticism.
Illustration ©2003 Alessandro Boni.

THE ALAN MOORE
APPRECIATION SOCIETY

Name: Jason Hall
Member Number: 424494-B
Height: 6'
Weight: 140 lbs.
Age: 30
Favorite Alan Moore books:
*From Hell, The Killing Joke, Top 10,
League of Extraordinary Gentlemen,
Miracleman, Superman: Whatever
Happened to the Man of Tomorrow,
Watchmen, V for Vendetta*

AMAS Member #424494-B
Wearing the *Official Alan Moore Writer's Costume*™
(*Sacrificial Virgin Included!)

Influence: To attempt to discuss how Alan Moore has influenced comics is quite a daunt-ing task ~ and one that will most likely be done with more eloquence and intelligence than I could possibly muster in these meager few words ~ which is why I took a picture of myself in a goofy wig and terribly fake beard instead... But I do have an interesting (okay, humor me...) example of how we perceive the esteemed Mr. Moore's influence on comics. In an issue of *Gotham Adventures* I recently wrote, I had a scene transition between two panels ~ the first showing a close-up of a lipstick mark on Mr. Freeze's glass helmet, the second showing a close-up of a lipstick advertisement billboard with a large pair of neon lips in the same exact position as those in the first panel. One of my best friends remarked that he thought it was very cool, but very "Alan Moore - Watchmen". I thought about that (taking it as a compliment) and pointed out to him that Alan Moore certainly wasn't the first person to do this type of visual scene transition in comics ~ plus they've been doing that sort of thing in movies forever. But his comment did make me realize something... While there certainly are numerous storytelling techniques that Alan Moore has invented, there are also those that we just think he's invented. And the reason for that is simple - it's because he does them so well. He improves upon them. He makes them his own. And he continues to show us that the comics medium has no limitations.

Anecdote: I unfortunately don't have any personal Alan Moore anecdotes to share, so I'll have to use one from a friend of mine (actually, the same person that I was talking about earlier), which I think successfully demonstrates the effect Alan Moore has on his readers

Could this be a possible Alan Moore sighting? You decide!

and just how much his work means to them. My friend became politely obsessed with Alan Moore when Moore took over writing Swamp Thing ~ and he had that epiphany you have when you realize you've just discovered your FAVORITE writer (or musician, or film-maker, etc.). He was so impressed and moved by the stories that he began buying extra copies of the book each month in the store and giving them to people he didn't even know, telling them that they just "had to read this". He was spreading the word. From there it was Marvelman and V For Vendetta and then everything Moore wrote that he could get his hands on. He read somewhere that Alan Moore enjoyed the work of musician (and performance artist) Laurie Anderson ~ and also that Moore was going to be at the San Diego Comicon that year ('85 or '86), which would be my friend's first comic convention. So he decided to buy Alan Moore the then new four-LP Laurie Anderson Live record set as a way of saying thanks for all the meaningful entertainment Mr. Moore had provided him. My friend presented him with the gift and whenever Alan Moore was at the DC booth, he spent all his time talking his ear off about upcoming projects or things he'd read about Moore in interviews. My friend is quick to point out that it *was* his first convention, so he didn't know about giving creators "space" ~ and he did let other people talk to Moore as well. And it's not like he followed him around when he wasn't at the DC booth. He wasn't *that* fanatical. But my friend does wonder if he falls into Alan Moore's category of fans he's scared of. Could *he* be the reason Alan Moore doesn't attend conventions anymore? Perhaps! And that is why his identity must remain safely anonymous...

Now I don't have a four-LP record set to offer Alan Moore, but I do want to thank him for all the years of innovative, enlightening, and moving stories he's provided us all ~ and for being such a huge inspiration in my own work.

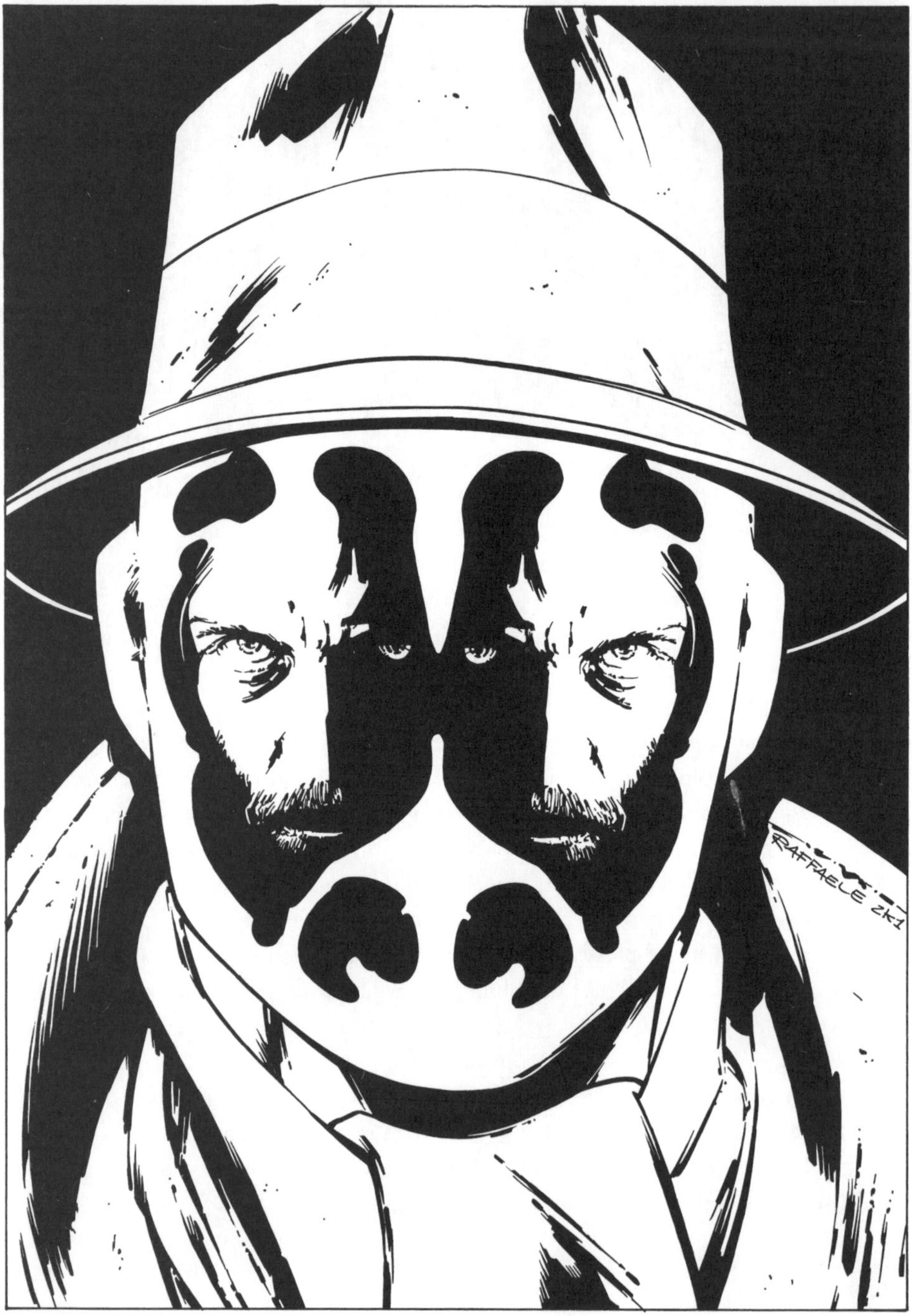
RAFFAELE 2K1

A SECRET LIFE

ARTURO VILLARRUBIA

Born in Madrid in 1963, Arturo Villarrubia is a regular reviewer for a number of Spanish magazines. He has translated several authors into Spanish, including the definitive versions of 25 stories by Clark Aston Smith. He has also written several short stories, the latest of which will be published on the Universidad Complutense website.
Text ©2003 Arturo Villarrubia.

Consider the HERO as he steps forward into the future. Eyes bright, head held high, biceps bulging, he mutters - trough clenched jaw – "A man's gotta what a man's gotta do". Pallas-like, two question spring at once in the mind of any perceptive person watching such a spectacle: Why does "he", have to do "it"? And, more to the point, "what" is he is really doing?

There are of course short answers available: the HERO is upholding stabilised social order, by seeking justice o maybe revenge. Like Francis Bacon taught us, justice and revenge are sides of the same coin. But there are also longer answers and in the course of a long a fruitful career Alan Moore has provided us with some of the most entertaining, moving and innovative ones. He is justly famous for deconstructing that icon of the twentieth century, the superhero, just before it took over the silver screen in the nineteen eighties. In works such as *"Watchmen"*, Moore did an admirable job in showing us not so much that the Emperor is really naked, but that he is cold, embarrassed and wants to go home. But lets have a look at a different figure in Mr. Moore ´s carpet. Maybe it is also a representation of a hero but this one is spelled in lower case. And what he, or she, is looking for, is not justice or revenge, it is self-knowledge.

Faithful readers will recognize them. They range from the doomed housewife who becomes a werewolf under the full moon in the *"Saga of the Swamp Thing"*, to young Sophie Bangs who travels in the world of the Cabala in *"Promethea"*. Sometimes self-discovery is imposed from outside, like the little boy who follows the main character in *" A Small Killing"*. Sometimes, like in *"Big Numbers"*, it comes from inside as the little girl that Christine encounters in a taxi.

Notes:

[1] From "Big Numbers" #12. Alan Moore is that utter rarity: an accomplished prose writer who writes good poetry.

[2] From "Supreme"#6

[3] From " The Birth Caul"

These two stories echo *"The Jolly Corner"* by Henry James, in which a man is haunted by the ghost of what he could have become. Like in James', in Moore's work the real enemy is not the nominal bad guy but the barriers that society imposes on individual growth. You are given a role and you are supposed to behave within its boundaries. These are the maps *" that we have mistaken for the world"* [1]. Why do we follow them? Maybe because we are made of ideas. *" The ideas we have, the ideas other people have about us, the ideas we have about ourselves... what else is personality?"* [2] But to follow them up in an unquestioning way can lead you to a hollow day when, staring at the stranger in the bathroom mirror, you realize that *" we have wandered too far from some vital totem"* [3]

STEFANO RAFFAELE

Left: *Stefano Raffaele has had comics published by Valiant, Marvel and Marvel Italy. He is the artist of the upcoming Dark Horse miniseries* **The Blackburne Covenant** *and Les Humanoids'* **Fragile.**
Illustration ©2003 Stefano Raffaele. All characters are ©2003 their respective copyright holders.

What is this totem? In *"In the Day the Dam Broke"*, James Thurber, pictures an epidemic of running in Broad Street. Someone starts running and in ten minutes everybody is also running. Somebody says that the dam has broken and people run in fear of an incoming surge that exists only in their minds. Most people are running because everybody else is doing it. Thurber asks what is happening to a woman who passes by and she says: *" Don't ask me, ask God"*. Moore has chosen to follow the same advice also present in the works of Alistair Crowley, a.k.a. Frater Perdurabo. Crowley believed that every man and woman is a star. The light that shines from us is none other that " *the holy splendour of imagination*" which Promethea embodies and Moore work's celebrates. This is surely the vital totem from which we stray in our daily routine.

It would be tempting to say that Moore's evolution as a writer has been from furnishing some kind of believable psychology to cartoon characters, such as ubermen and monsters, to a writer of genuine visionary power: witness Dr. Gull ´s final revelation or Sophie's meeting with the Godhead. It would be attractive but misleading because, as Peter Ackroyd wrote, the work of a good writer is all in one piece. Moore's current work contains much more than mystical explorations, including his sharpest social observations ever and successful political satire, content that most educated people would consider out of the reach of mainstream comics. Even in his earliest work, like Blake saw angels surrounding him, Moore saw, in such an unlikely place as the four-colour world of masked vigilantes, real pathos and tragedy. Thus "*Watchmen*" was if not a visionary work, the work of a real visionary, showing us how all identities are secret, asking us to look behind the masks that surround us to reach the people behind them.

And perhaps discovering that what we thought was a mask was really a mirror.

• **Arturo Villarrubia**, Madrid, 2003

SCOTT MILLS

Right: *Writer and artist Scott Mills is one of America's most prolific alternative cartoonists, his books include* **Cells, Big Clay Pot, Trenches** *and the upcoming* **The Masterplan** *from Top Shelf.*
www.bubbaandsmoot.com

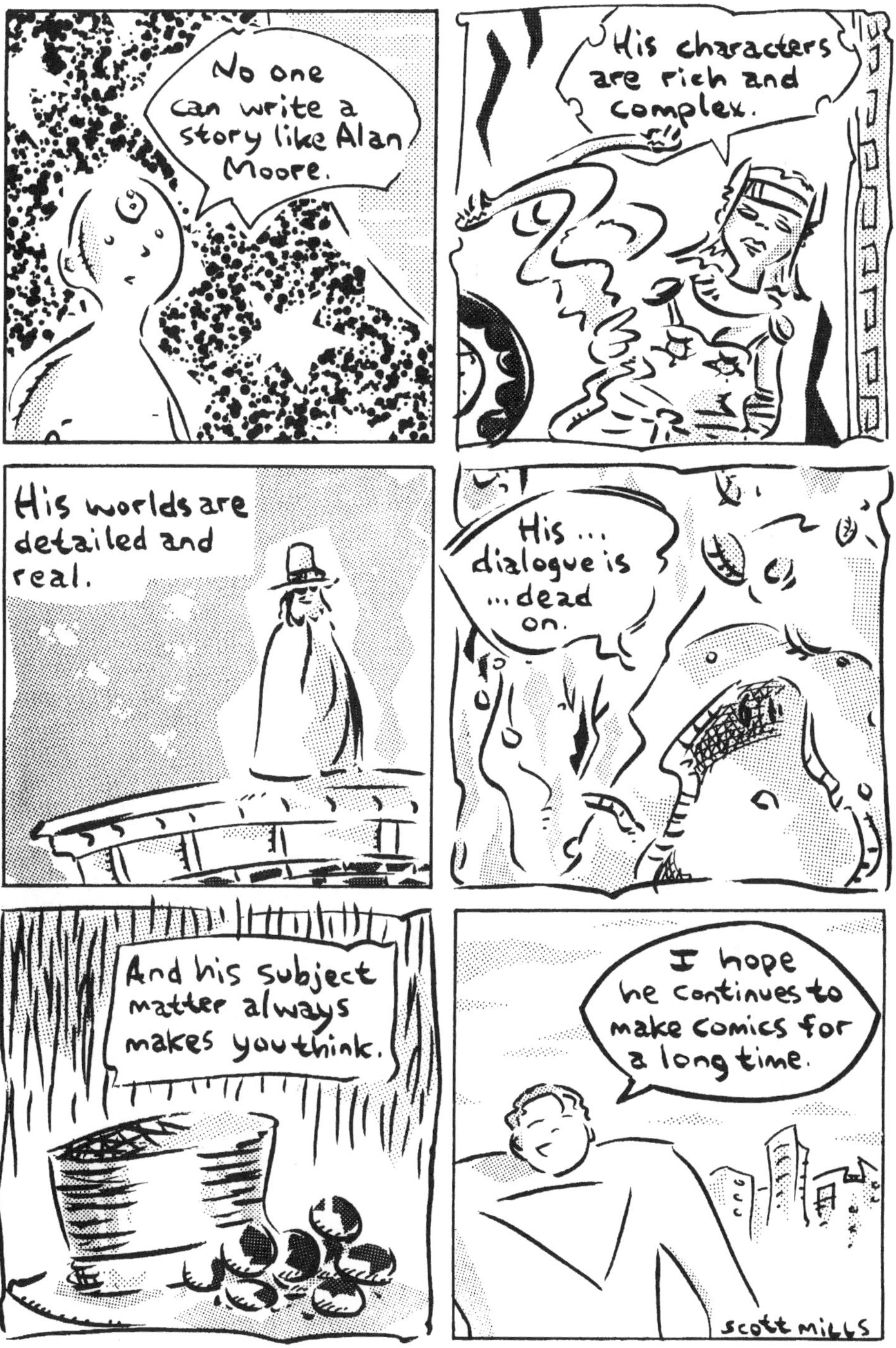
No one can write a story like Alan Moore.
His characters are rich and complex.
His worlds are detailed and real.
His ... dialogue is ...dead on.
And his subject matter always makes you think.
I hope he continues to make comics for a long time.
SCOTT MILLS

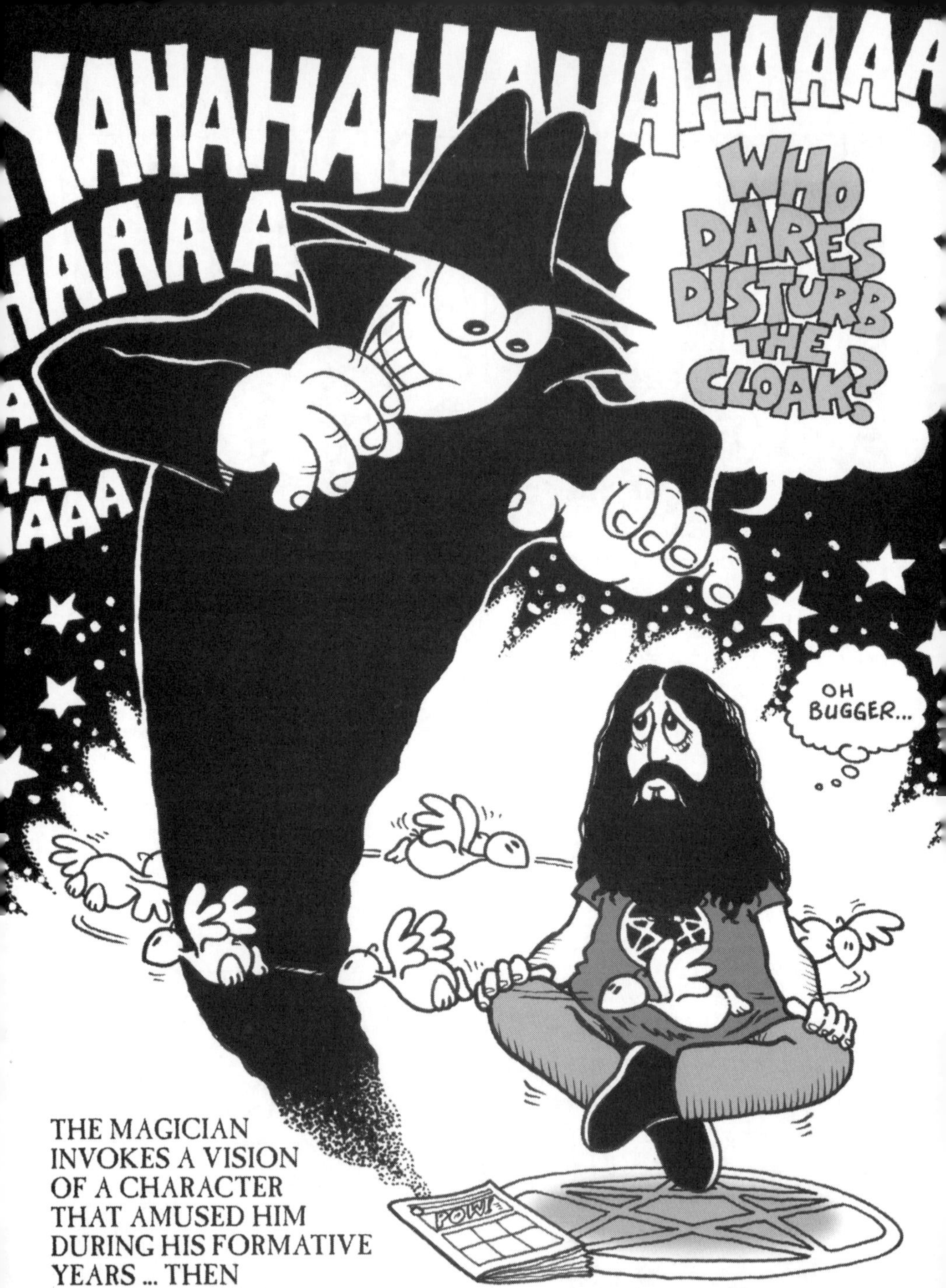
YAHAHAHAHAHAHAAAA
HAAAA A
A
HA
HAAA
WHO DARES DISTURB THE CLOAK?
OH BUGGER...
POW!
—ALAN, HAPPY 29TH ANNIVERSARY OF YOUR 21ST. BIRTHDAY!
—mike higgs

THE MAGICIAN INVOKES A VISION OF A CHARACTER THAT AMUSED HIM DURING HIS FORMATIVE YEARS ... THEN PROMPTLY WISHES THAT HE HADN'T!

MOORE MAGIC

MARCO ABATE

*Marco Abate has written stories for Italian comics series such as **Lazarus Ledd** (Star Comics) and **Martin Mystere** (Bonelli Comics). He teaches Geometry at the University of Pisa. Text ©2003 Marco Abate.*

I was fourteen, fifteen years old, at most. A winter vacation, one of the few in my life, probably the last with my parents. A Dolomiti resort, of the type with a lot of wood and a lot of nice people speaking Italian with a strong German accent. That night, I decided to take a short stroll before going to bed. I've always liked walking, and there was something in the night asking me outside. Only a short walk, nothing more, just to get a taste of the nocturnal air, just to feel the dry cold so as to enjoy more the warm of my room later (I did have a room of my own, didn't I? I don't remember. I don't remember anything else about that trip, beside this story).

A road started just outside the hotel. Well, it wasn't exactly a road; more like a wide track, possibly. Anyway, it was very easy to follow, and after a few hundred metres and a few sharp turns I lost sight of the building. The air was chilly in a pleasant way; it made you feel every breath. The snow was white, and blue, and all in between; the track was a dark line in an undulating field of blue/white shadows. No artificial lights, but there was no need for them; the full moon reflected by the snow lighted all that there was to be seen.

And then there were the mountains.

The track was cut across the side of a steep valley, and I was halfway up. Down, it was very dark, or so I suppose; to be honest, I don't remember looking down. I was looking straight in front of me, and then up, to the mountains. They were there, white and blue, all around me. Huge, aloof and majestic, almost too beautiful to behold. Sharp lines of solid rock underlined by the snow, reaching at a sky full of light.

They were alive.

I was sure of that. It wasn't a game I was playing with myself. I felt their presence deep inside me; I felt awed by them. It is difficult to express my feelings exactly, even though I remember them very clearly; they went beyond words, somehow. I was in the presence of primeval gods; scores of them, all around me. I looked in all directions; the space became so vast, the air so clear, the snow was light, the rock pure darkness. I opened to the night, and I gave myself to the mountains.

When I got back to the resort, I found my parents slightly worried. It appeared that I had been gone for almost two hours; to me, it was like only fifteen minutes had passed, twenty at most. I don't remember what I told them, probably nothing specific, at that age you don't explain much to your parents. But I knew then, and I know now, what I experienced that night.

Magic.

Now I'm forty years old. Last January, I spent some time in Zimbabwe. Two weeks in a work camp in the eastern part of the country, working in a model farm; ten days traveling on my own. I fell in love with Africa.

I met and talked to a lot of people. Around the fire in nights filled by the song of giant crickets–or, once, by the cries of hippos playing. In a train running along elephants toward a storm. Eating a mango fruit, smiling to a young mother surrounded by her frightened and yet curious children. In a car looking for a tantalizing black rhino. In several backpacker lodges, sometimes drinking, sometimes not. On the surface, Zimbabweans seemed as westernized as the rest of us; Coca-Cola was everywhere (bread might be scarce, but Coca-Cola wasn't), and pubs in Harare, the capital, were exactly like pubs in, I don't know, Atlanta, for instance. But just a bit of scratching on the surface, and you ended up in a completely different world.

I was talking to Beoula that day. She was the twenty-year-old daughter of Mr. Jura, the owner of the model farm I was working in. (Mr. Jura was a fascinating man; the principal of a high school in Harare, he left everything to teach the people in the country the best ways of farming. But that's another story.) Beoula was the daughter of her father intelligent, curious, full of opinions and ideas, a pleasure to talk to. We were in a "luxury hut" on the farm. Most of the lodgings in the work camp were in a

MIKE HIGGS

Left: *Mike Higgs has been drawing comics and cartoons since the late 60s when he created **The Cloak** for Odhams Press. His **Moonbird** newspaper strip ran for over ten years and he has produced thousands of cartoons and strips for advertising and more recently has designed and compiled many hardcover Dan Dare and Captain Marvel books. Cartoon and The Cloak are ©2003 Mike Higgs.*

dormitory (a vast, empty, one-room building, which I shared with seven local young men), but there also were a few more comfortable bungalows, mostly reserved for that commodity fast disappearing in Zimbabwe, the tourists. These huts were built in the traditional way, round white walls with a hay roof (whose only problem was that the monkeys liked to dig holes in it to see what was inside); there was no electric light, or running water, but they were very clean, and really cool even in the heat of the day–and the landscape was fantastically beautiful, and in the morning you could wash yourself under the waterfall...

Anyway, that afternoon I was in a hut talking to Beoula, of this and that and the lake. Serengeti Five, the farm (even the name had a story attached to it), was one hour walk away from Lake Rusape, a beautiful artificial lake dotted with small islands (lonely boulders in the plain, from half a metre to thirty metres high, are typical of the eastern part of Zimbabwe; and the small islands were the tips of the highest boulders, partially submerged by the lake). Well, according to the elders of the local community, Lake Rusape was inhabited.

By mermaids. Male mermaids.

Every year, usually around September or October, somebody in the community disappeared, kidnapped by the mermaids. Only one, at most two people every year, no more. It was very important that family and friends didn't grieve for the departed; otherwise the mermaids, enraged, would come back, killing somebody else or, even worse, trashing the cattle (the affluence of a family in Zimbabwe is still mostly measured by the amount of cattle possessed, even in the cities). The kidnapped people weren't really dead; they just went to live with the mermaids, in the lake. It was even possible to call them back, there was a special rite for that. But the rite was so difficult that nobody had ever been able to complete it successfully.

Looking at Beoula telling this story was fascinating. It was clear that she couldn't *not* believe it. The mermaids were part of her life exactly as the rainbow lizards running around the farm. Being an intelligent and outspoken girl (definitely an exception in Zimbabwe, where the polite way for a girl to talk to a man is not looking at him, which makes for an eerie experience), she had asked the elders the natural question: Where were the mermaids coming from? I mean, the lake was only ten years old or so, and they couldn't possibly have been there before... They came from other lakes, was the answer. Now, *all* the lakes in Zimbabwe are artificial, and most of them pretty recent too. But, on the other hand, local state boundaries are completely artificial as well, and there are lakes in Mozambique, and who knows how (and how far) mermaids travel... Nothing in Beoula's life was definitely against the existence of mermaids. And being there, listening to her, listening to her father explaining why it was impossible for him to accept Christian beliefs (and he tried, for love of a woman, but that's yet another story), listening to the camp leader telling how his aunt communicated with dead relatives to get suggestions on solving family crises... it was easy to believe in mermaids, in Zimbabwe.

Magic.

In my everyday life, I'm a professional mathematician (even though I spend part of my everynight life writing comics, which is the reason you are reading this now). Years ago, Martin Gardner used to write a wonderful monthly column in *Scientific American*, called "Mathematical Games". When Douglas Hofstadter replaced him, he renamed the column "Metamagical Themas", which is a perfect anagram. And a very apt one.

My work consists of the study of very abstract objects, often obtained by a process of generalization starting from situations which already are very abstract and (apparently) very far away from the physical world. These objects might be just figments of my imagination; but they feel very concrete to me. They are just there, incredibly beautiful and enticing, waiting for us to discover them, to describe them, to explain them–and we cannot modify or change them. They are not ours to dispose of as we please. As soon as they are discovered, they exist on their own. We cannot see them with our eyes, or taste them with our tongue; but we have other senses, a whole apparatus of logic senses, to explore them. It is mostly a matter of exercising the mind in thinking in the right way. And the understanding we get as a reward is apparently essential for understanding how the physical world works. The unreasonable effectiveness of mathematics.

Magic.

You are probably starting to wonder what all of this has to do with Alan Moore. Or maybe you don't. He *is* a magician, after all, in at least two ways. He is able to conjure stories out of thin air, and to build castles full of beautiful and fearful symmetries trapping the readers inside, forever. The mathematical side of myself is just awed by the perfect structure of most of his stories, while the writing side of myself is amazed by the perfect construction of most of his sentences (okay, he has also written some lame tales and awkward sentences, sure, but there is something to be learned even from them. And I still have to find a single weakness in *Watchmen*). I'm not very original in saying that the weaving of stories is a sort of magic, transporting the reader in new worlds he couldn't have visited by him/herself, but this is particularly true in Alan's case. For instance, every chapter in *Voice of the fire* (a wonderful book, in my opinion) really brings the reader inside the mind of a different person, in a different (pre)historical period. It allows us to perceive reality through the eyes and the mind of that person, in that time. It feels true. It works like...

Magic.

But Alan claims to be a magician in a much less metaphorical way. He claims to be an actual magician. I must admit that the first time I read this I was troubled. Here there was a man that I'd always admired, whose opinions I found intelligent, well thought out and well researched, whose writings had been a continuous source of inspiration and learning for me, claiming to be a *magician?* You know, hocus-pocus and the like? Aleister Crowley and theosophy? Come on, he must be joking... But evidently he wasn't, and even if it was not clear to me what he was actually doing then, I started to think. Well, here is a man that I've always admired, whose opinions I find intelligent, well thought out and well researched, whose writings have been a continuous source of inspiration and learning for me, claiming to be a magician... there *must* be something there. I don't know exactly what, clearly not the fortune-teller sort of magic, but I cannot exclude that thinking in a different way, exercising the mind in a novel way, one could reach a state where it could be possible to experience something different, something magic. Is it real? Is the equilibrium measure of a 27-dimensional holomorphic dynamical system real? Do these questions make any sense? I don't know; but, on a closer inspection, Alan's descriptions of his frame of mind when encountering ethereal beings bear too many similarities with my own way of dealing with mathematical objects to let me dismiss them as patently unfounded. I still don't know, but there *might* be...

Magic.

So when I was offered to write a piece for this well-deserved tribute to Alan, I decided to write about (some of) my own encounters with magic. One of the best praises I know is completely true in his case: he made me think, and in several ways. I cannot say whether my magic and his magic are one and the same thing; possibly not, but it is not relevant. Thanks to you too, there is magic in the air, Alan, I do agree.

• **Marco Abate**

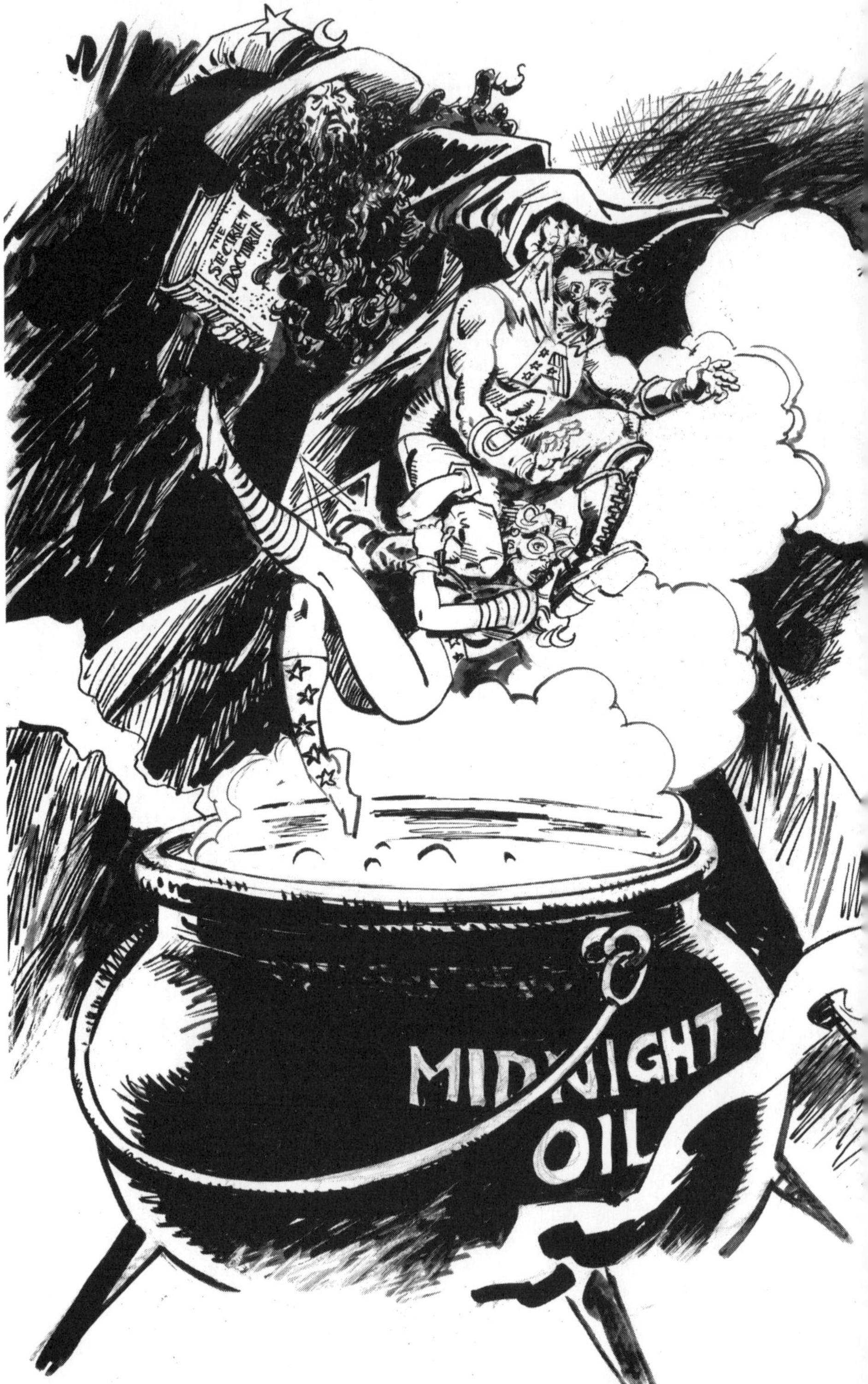
THE SECRET DOCTRINE
MIDNIGHT OIL

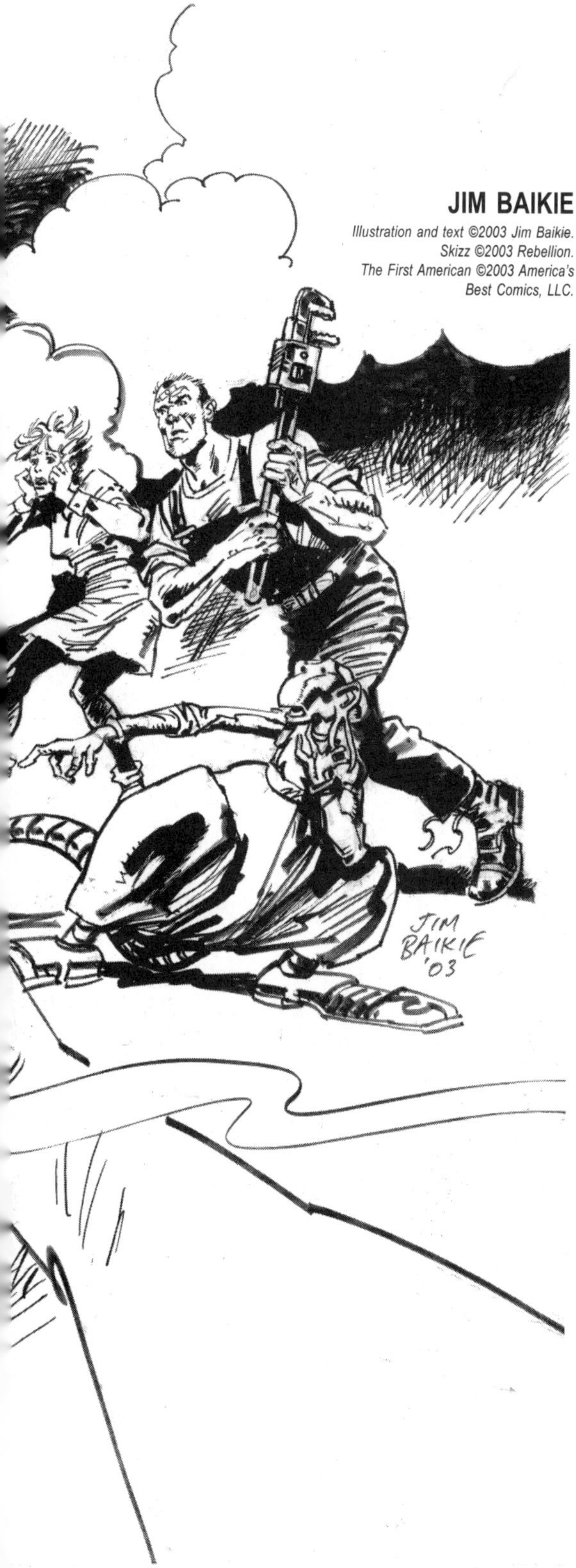
JIM
BAIKIE
'03

TOMORROW MEETS YESTERDAY

JIM BAIKIE

Jim Baikie was born in the Orkney Islands on 28th February, 1940. At the age of 14 he sold a cartoon to Vargo Statten's 'British Science Fiction Magazine,' and decided there and then to become an illustrator. While working at a London publisher's studio in the early sixties he began to pick up comics work from Fleetway in Farringdon Street, and by 1966 was receiving so many commissions he gave up the 'day job' and became a full time freelance artist. At Fleetway he met Steve Moore who introduced him to a small group of comics enthusiasts (including Steve Parkhouse and Barry Smith, virtually the first Brits to crack the American Comics market), who had an interest in the artform that went beyond mere comic collecting. At one of these gatherings sometime in the early seventies, Steve Moore introduced Jim to Alan Moore (no relation), and after a stimulating conversation about the virtues of C.C. Beck's 'Captain Marvel' and the massed talents of 'Mad', Alan and Jim agreed to collaborate on something in 'the future'.

Ten years went by. Then in late 1982, Jim got a call from Steve MacManus at 2000AD inviting him to illustrate what would be a long running weekly serial, 'Skizz.' The writer was Alan Moore. 'The future' was here!

After 'Skizz' Alan and Jim did a two book 'Vigilante' series for D.C. Comics. Then their paths diverged, with Alan taking up an invitation to write 'Swamp Thing', while Jim went to work with Marv Wolfman on 'Teen Titans,' and with Doug Moench on the 18-book 'Electric Warrior' series. Moore and Baikie collaborated only briefly after that, with 'Deathblow' for Image, and 'Supreme' for Awesome, until they got together (bigtime) to create 'First American and U.S. Angel' for ABC's Tomorrow Stories.

Jim Baikie says: "I've worked with some of the comics industry's finest writers, and I have good things to say about all of them, but the sheer amount of extra effort Alan puts into communicating with the artist makes his scripts a joy; each one reads like a fraternal letter rather than workaday instruction for stage-dressing. Alan is writing one more instalment of 'First American,' and I know I'll be laughing like a hyena as soon as the first closely typed page emerges upside down from my fax machine."

• Jim Baikie

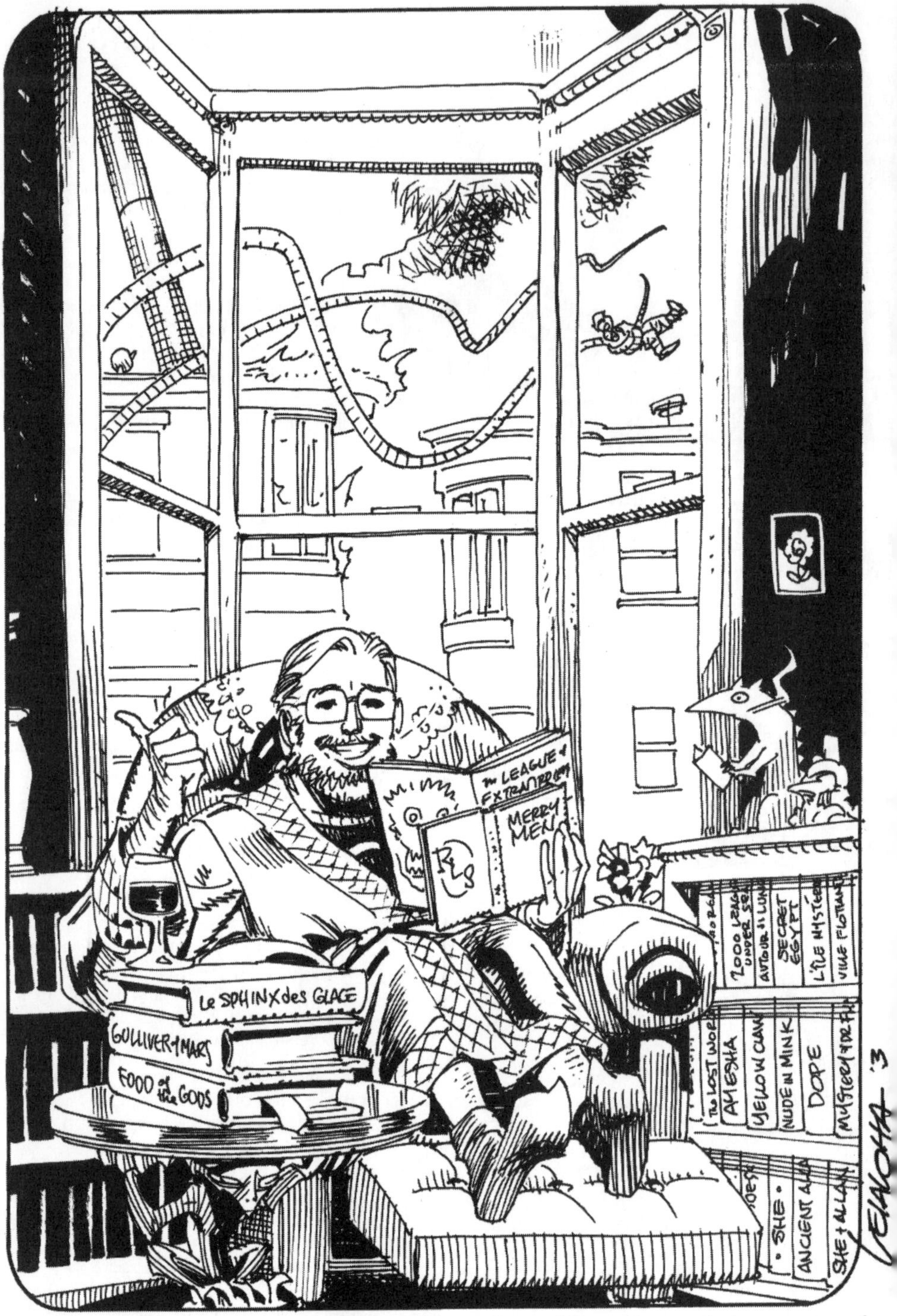

Le SPHINX des GLACE
FOOD of the GODS
MERRY MEN
YELLOW CLAW
NUDE IN MINK
DOPE
SHE
SHE + ALLAN

CLASSICS ILLUSTRATED for CLASSICS UNWRITTEN

ALAN MOORE: POST-MODERNIST

LINK YACO

Link Yaco has a Masters' degree in Telecommunications and works as a web page editor for blue chip firms. He has written comic books for several publishers and scripted the graphic story album, **SpaceChicks & Businessmen** *for Fantagraphics. He wrote the recent Marvel-authorized* **Science of the X-Men** *and has also contributed articles to* **Comic Book Marketplace** *and* **The Jack Kirby Collector.***
Text ©2003 Link Yaco.

The Oxford English Dictionary defines Post-Modernism as "...a reaction against Modernism, esp. by self-conscious use of earlier styles and conventions." This broad definition is interpreted in a multitude of ways, but the earliest definition on record is perhaps the most cogent. PoMo (Post-Modernism) was first defined in a 1942 issue of the Architectural Digest as a mixture of Classical Realism and Abstract Modernism, with many of the features of parody, but is intended more as a tribute than a critique.

PoMo appeared in popular culture as early as the 1940s. Warner Bros. cartoons utilized a grand mixture of realistically painted backdrops and abstract cartoon characters, as well as mixed media, and abstract effects. Daffy Duck and Bugs Bunny cartoons are a library of art styles. Advertising of the era similarly used both abstraction and realism, side-by-side. Films began to combine the realism of photography with abstract effects—most famously in Citizen Kane. Comic books of the time took their cue from film as they always had.

Will Eisner's Spirit stories mixed doses of reality into the surreal world of comic books. Eisner illustrated a masked crime-fighter in a film noir style with carefully staged lighting, reminiscent of the work of cinemaphotographer Greg Tolland (Grapes of Wrath, Citizen Kane) and wrote the tales in the manner of the films and adult short fiction of the era. He combined the realism of film with the abstraction of comic books and latticed the results with abstract devices such as using the windows of a house as the panels of a comic page, with a story the proceeded from room to room.

Alan Moore's Greyshirt pays tribute to Eisner and uses similar devices. These devices are abstractions. As Cubism breaks form into geometric shapes and Impressionism into small brush strokes, Eisner's devices abstract comic panels and story continuity into other forms such as windows, in houses or subway cars, or playing cards, file folders, book pages, and so on.

Eisner used the conventions of the comic genres to suspend disbelief, to then comment on the process. In this regard, he could be considered a Deconstructionist.

Deconstructionism is a school of PoMo, and it is similarly difficult to define. However, a rough working explanation is that Deconstructionism is about revealing the inner workings of an art—revealing the clockwork gears that make a piece of art tick. Most people are familiar with the building at the Louvre with the plumbing on the outside. Jacque Derida is a major proponent of Deconstructionism, although he refuses to be pinned down as such.

STEVE LEIALOHA

Left: *Steve Leialoha is a veteran of the American comics industry, his inks and pencils have graced the pages of many, many comic books including* **Howard The Duck, Spider-Man, Action Comics** *and* **Sandman.** *He has also drawn an episode of* **Shadowhawk** *and inked a panel of* **Tom Strong** *when no one was looking.*
Illustration ©2003 Steve Leialoha.

Moore's Greyshirt character is done as homage to Eisner's Spirit, and the Greyshirt stories carry on the tradition of PoMo. Moore utilizes Eisner's tricky panel construction, mocked-up newspapers, and other cinematic and multi-media approaches. But Moore advances from Eisner's groundwork. Eisner tended to use only mid-shots, and seldom used close-ups or long shots. Eisner's stories tended to be stand-alone one shots, though sometimes he had narrative arcs that connected several stories, and he had recurring characters. However, Moore working with co-scripter Rick Veitch, has developed a long story arc that connects all the Greyshirt stories. It is an origin story, a background to the character. In Rashamon-like fashion, the origin of the character seems to be completed, but then a retelling by another character casts the whole tale in a different light as new details are added.

Harvey Kurtzman also worked in a PoMo vein as early as the '50s. His work on Mad in particular exhibits the usage of a wide range of styles that range through the history of Realism and Abstract Modernism. As with Eisner, Kurtzman's influence on Moore is very apparent. In Tomorrow Stories, Moore's characters First American and Johnny Quick are so Kurtmanesque that he even uses some of Kurtzman's taglines, such as the sound effect "SMEKKITY-SMEK."

Alan Moore has absorbed the lessons of the history of the comics medium and builds upon them. Yet the result is hardly traditional, but vastly innovative. Many of his contemporaries seem to seek to achieve innovation by rebelling against tradition and discard the techniques that have been built up by the craftsmen of the trade. Moore achieves innovation by using the building blocks of the talents that have gone before him to create something new. The manner in which he juxtaposes traditional techniques and concepts is neither classic nor abstract but both—which is the definition of Post-Modernism. He applies this principle by mixing the cartoony comics style of early comics with the realistic illustration of later comics. The result is to place outrageous and surreal comic characters in realistic settings. His juxtaposition of the exaggerated comic characters, which are abstract versions of real humans, with realistic settings and situations fits the definition of Post-Modernism. He also uses the abstract modernist effects of the 1960s comics (pioneered by Ditko and Kirby and developed by Steranko and Adams) and combines those with realistic styles. Again, this is an example of Post-Modern technique.

Moore is not a Classical Realist. He is not interesting in painting a realistic portrait of some facet of our culture. Nor is he an Abstract Modernist—he does not simply exaggerate reality to reveal some aspect of it. But both Realism and Abstraction are tools of his trade, and he freely utilizes both, in a playful manner.

A typical Moore comic book character will be utterly unbelievable in conventional terms—as most traditional comics are—but Moore will do everything he can to rationalize his outlandish characters in attempt to make them believable. Much as Stan Lee did in the Kennedy-era, Moore will develop the personality as fully as possible, and attempt plausible scientific explanations for his character's backgrounds. As Stan Lee used nuclear radiation to explain the Hulk's strength, Moore uses quantum physics to explain N-Man in his "1963 Comics". But when rationalization fails, as it must with something as patently absurd as a comic book superhero, Moore falls back on something approaching parody, where he winks at the reader and acknowledges the compact we readers have entered into with him— the willing suspension of disbelief. Sometimes the parody is blatant, as with First American and Johnny Quick. Other work is on the cusp of parody, as with his early work on Marvel's Captain Britain, and his more mature work on the Watchmen for DC. Despite the degrees of parody, Moore tries hard to make us believe something that only an 8-year old would accept—that comics are real. In part, it is because he is trying to recreate the reading experience and sense of wonder we had as children, but he does that not out of a nostalgic urge, but for the same reason every author works to evoke credulity—because without that, the author cannot do his work. The first step a fiction author must take is to work in collusion with the reader to create a near hypnotic state of mind. It is only after that the writer can begin to accomplish his aims. Those aims are as varied as human individuals. Moore's aims are complex.

He is not a simple moralist. He wants to do more than convey a summary of cultural codes. He wants to examine the mechanism of fiction. To do this he turns it inside out and back again. He displays its falsehoods and then convinces us it's real again. Like a series of Chinese puzzle boxes, the secrets lie within truth within lie. In short, he PLAYS with the form. But a sense of play is not childish—it is the basis for any serious intellectual endeavor. And, in point of fact, the purpose of play behavior is

JOHN HEEBINK

Right: Heebink drew and colored *The Bod* for Image Comics, illustrates magazine covers (**Fox Kids** and **Food Quality**) and occasionally draws the **Elvira** and **Soulsearchers & Company** comic books for Claypool. He's also been artist on issues of **Nick Fury**, **Quasar** and the **Power Rangers**. His latest work is a graphic novel **Doll and Creature** . www.Heebink.com
Illustration ©2003 John Heebink. N-Man ©2003 Alan Moore, Rich Veitch & Steve Bissette.

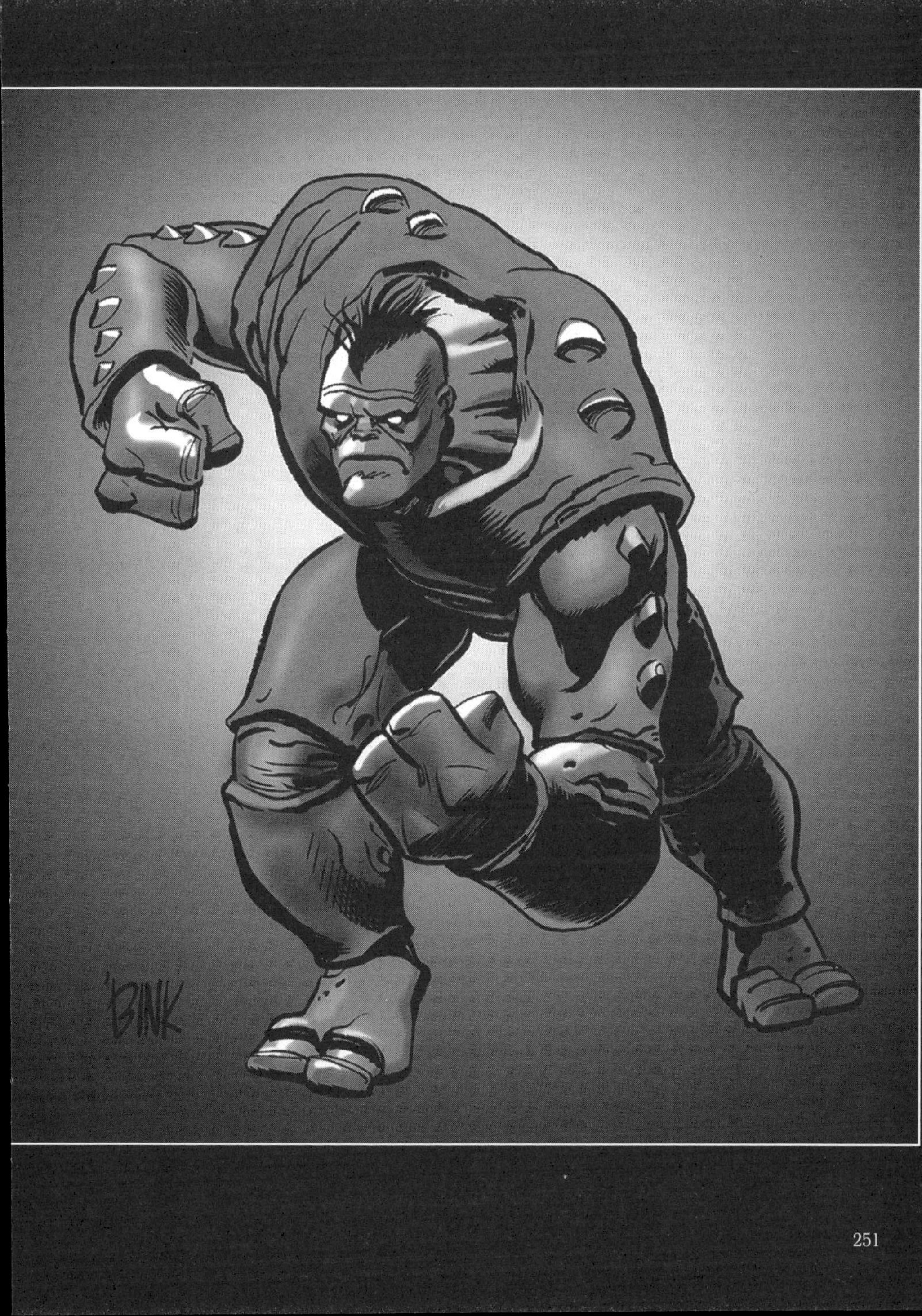
BINK

not aimless activity, but exploration of an environment. That is how we learn. That is what Moore and his readers are doing—learning. Which is why his work is so much more rewarding than that of lesser lights. Moore succeeds in his aims more than many who have attempted it because he manages to make the experience enjoyable. As author Umberto Ecco, he utilizes conventions of genre writing to open up the reading experience.

As a Post-Modernist, Moore could be described as a Deconstructionist, but he fits even better into another major school of PoMo—Metafiction. Borges is the grandfather of this school. It is similar to Deconstructionism in that it takes apart a piece of fiction, but rather than simply pull apart the work, it creates a work within a work—a series of nested loops (as computer programmers say), an infinite regression much like a hall of mirrors. The narrative voice of the fiction comments upon the work and upon its comments...and upon its comments on its comments. It is much like the Cabala, a theological writing where the comments of theologians are inserted into the text and then comments on the comments are inserted as well...and so on. "Meta" is a Greek prefix meaning "above," "next to," "beside," or "transcending." Metafiction transcends normal fiction.

A more familiar example of Metafiction is John Fowles "The French Lieutenant's Woman", which was made into a motion picture featuring Meryl Streep. James Joyce's "Finnegan's Wake" is arguably the ultimate Metafiction, but then it is arguably the ultimate fiction in any category, unreadable as it is. One of the curious features of PoMo in general and Metafiction specifically is that it has many of the features of parody but has affection for its subject matter, not disdain. In that regard, the early EC Mad comic book was more Metafiction than pure parody, for it warped its subjects almost out of recognition, put them in contexts that made them seem absurd, but always did it with a sense of play, not malice.

This is what Moore does with his characters. He has said that he regrets that his seminal work "Watchmen" so influenced comics that the original spirit was permanently degraded. There is nothing left to parody. Moore's current work explores his original source material (e.g. Charlton comics in "Watchmen," Marvel comics in "1963 Comics," and reaches much farther back with the Victorian adventurers in "The League of Extraordinary Gentlemen") with great fondness. Although there is an ever-present sense of commentary—a feeling that the narrator is metaphorically winking at the camera—Moore endeavors to reconstruct the source material, to restore its original narrative power, and EXPLAIN why it works and the nature of its virtues. He seeks to rationalize a world populated by superheroes, which he takes to an extreme in his Top Ten, where he posits a city populated by nothing BUT superheroes—and makes it more believable than DC's Metropolis or Marvel's New York City.

The reason Moore's rationalizations work so well for many of us is that we get to enjoy the somewhat guilty pleasure of reading comic books, for an intelligent adult viewpoint has been overlaid on the visceral thrills of the material. We have the best of both worlds—a youthful sense of wonder and a mature reflection upon it.

Moore has so affected the comics field that his two-level approach has become common place. His approach still has its appeal, but—as with any aesthetic approach—it depends on the skill of the author to make it effective. When others attempt it, the result seems myopic, juvenile, coy, superficial, smug and self-indulgent. Only Moore and a bare handful of others can make it work. It is Moore's specialty—his niche in the world of comics—and he is the master of the form. When Moore applies his metafictional technique, he opens up the form, rather than closes it down. His work is accessible to anyone who reads it, whether or not they are

GIUSEPPE CAMUNCOLI
Right (pencils):
Giuseppe Camuncoli has worked as penciler on **Swamp Thing, Hellblazer** (DC/Vertigo) and **Spider-Man: Tangled Web** (Marvel). His latest work is the **Vertigo Pop!: Bangkok** miniseries for DC.

JIMMY PALMIOTTI
Right (inks):
Jimmy Palmiotti has been called a Renaissance man of comics, for his great productivity and versatility. He has been active in comics since the late 1980s, co-creating **Ash, Painkiller Jane, Kid Death and Fluffy** and **The Resistance**. Especially known for his inking work, he also single-handedly created the mini-series **Beautiful Killer**.
Illustration ©2003 Giuseppe Camuncoli & Jimmy Palmiotti
Hellblazer ©2003 DC Comics.

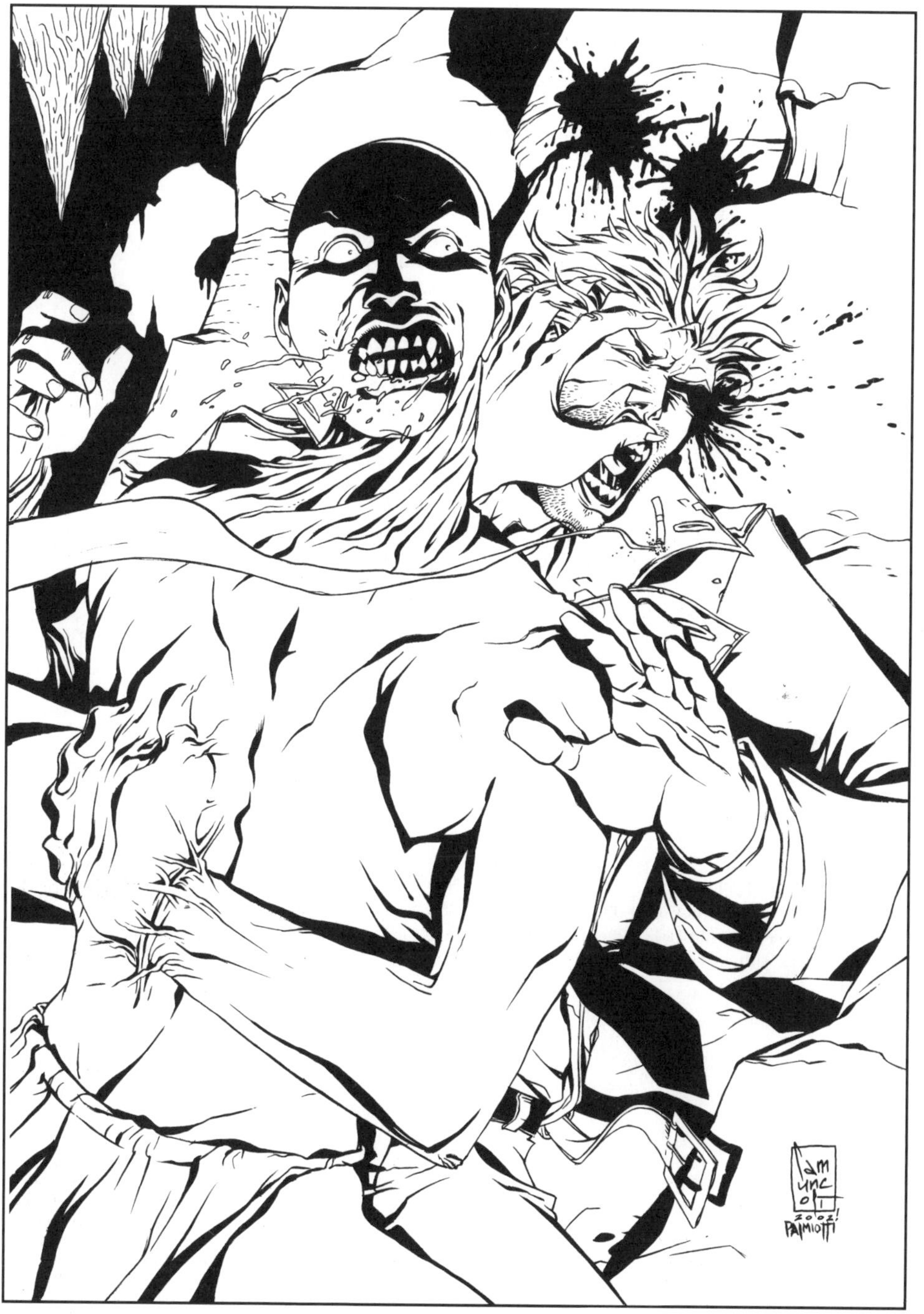

hardcore comics buffs. One doesn't have to be steeped in the history of his source material to understand what he is doing with it because he reinvents it from the ground up and, to a great degree, makes it his own. Each generation of artists absorbs its influences and synthesizes them into a new whole that is greater than the sum of its parts. Or that is what SHOULD happen. That has NOT happened in the degenerating world of comics in the past 30 years.

While contemporary comics have turned into endlessly serialized nightmares of continuity, Moore is the last of the comic book writers to work in the short form. While most comics struggle to develop a storyline over dozens of issues, Moore continues to turn out well-made single-issue and eight-page stories. In his current ABC comics, he structures most of his stories such that they stand alone, but contribute to the overall continuity of the book. This is another example of how Moore has taken the best conventions of the traditional comic, and expanded on it, whereas his contemporaries have tended to discard as much as they can of tradition. Where they stand opposed to tradition, in vain hope to move to a higher level, Moore builds upon the past. Similarly, Modernism was a reaction to Classical Realism (and thus became an artistic dead-end), but Post-modernism takes from both forms and builds upon them.

Only a very few creators, such as Moore, have stood out in an overcrowded field. Curiously, he is a writer, not an artist, who alone stands out as a unique visionary. This has not happened since the early 1960s, when Stan Lee revolutionized the field, and a decade before when EC comics' Al Feldstein, Bill Gaines, and Harvey Kurtzman brought a—until now—never surpassed level of quality to American comics. As well, we might possibly include the most successful of the crime comics creators, Charles Biro. We might include the legendary Will Eisner who, though an illustrator as well, repeatedly won acclaim on the merits of his work as literature. His career, amazingly, spans the entire history of comics, from the very beginning to the present, and he continues to write works. Most obscurely, in the past few years he has translated many of his works to his first language, YIDDISH, and managed to get them published in Holland.

Moore ranks with all these greats. As the oddball genre of comics keens its death knell, Moore's is a perfectly appropriate approach. His is the last bloom of greatness in a dying field.

It is an ongoing disappointment that the illustrators of Moore's work seldom match the pictures his words paint (with some notable exceptions). But since the greater part of comics history is filled with illustrators who overwhelmed the flimsy scripts they had to work with, it is only just that the balance is tipped for its final couple of decades.

• **Link Yaco**

SCOTT MORSE

Right: *Scott Morse is the Eisner and Ignatz Award nominated creator of* **Soulwind, Visitations, Volcanic Revolver, Magic Pickle,** *and* **Ancient Joe.** *He resides in California with his wife, dog, cat, and incessant deadlines.*
Strip ©2003 Scott Morse.

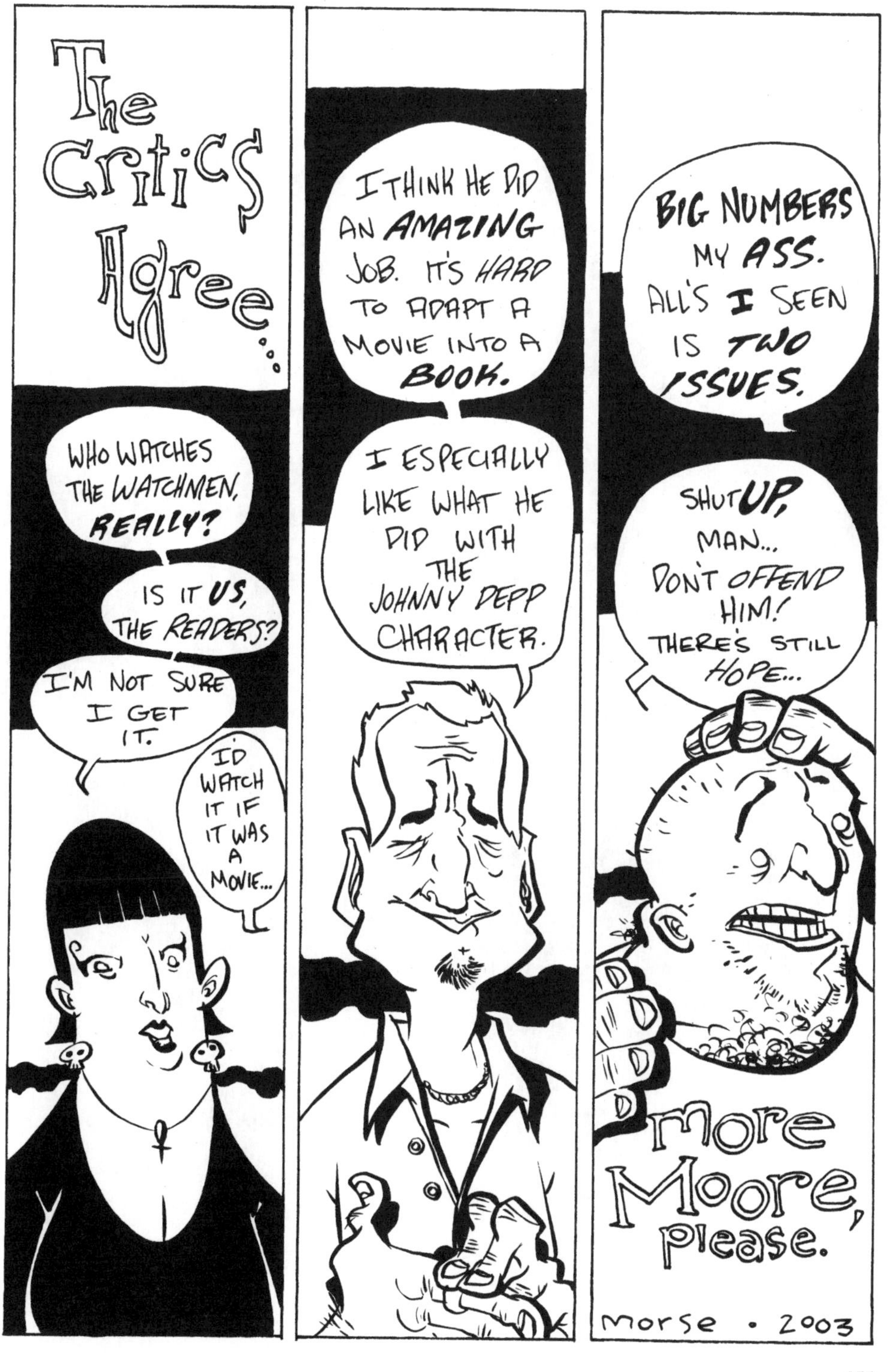

The Critics Agree...
WHO WATCHES THE WATCHMEN, REALLY?
IS IT US, THE READERS?
I'M NOT SURE I GET IT.
I'D WATCH IT IF IT WAS A MOVIE...
I THINK HE DID AN AMAZING JOB. IT'S HARD TO ADAPT A MOVIE INTO A BOOK.
I ESPECIALLY LIKE WHAT HE DID WITH THE JOHNNY DEPP CHARACTER.
BIG NUMBERS MY ASS. ALL'S I SEEN IS TWO ISSUES.
SHUT UP, MAN... DON'T OFFEND HIM! THERE'S STILL HOPE...
more Moore, please.
morse • 2003

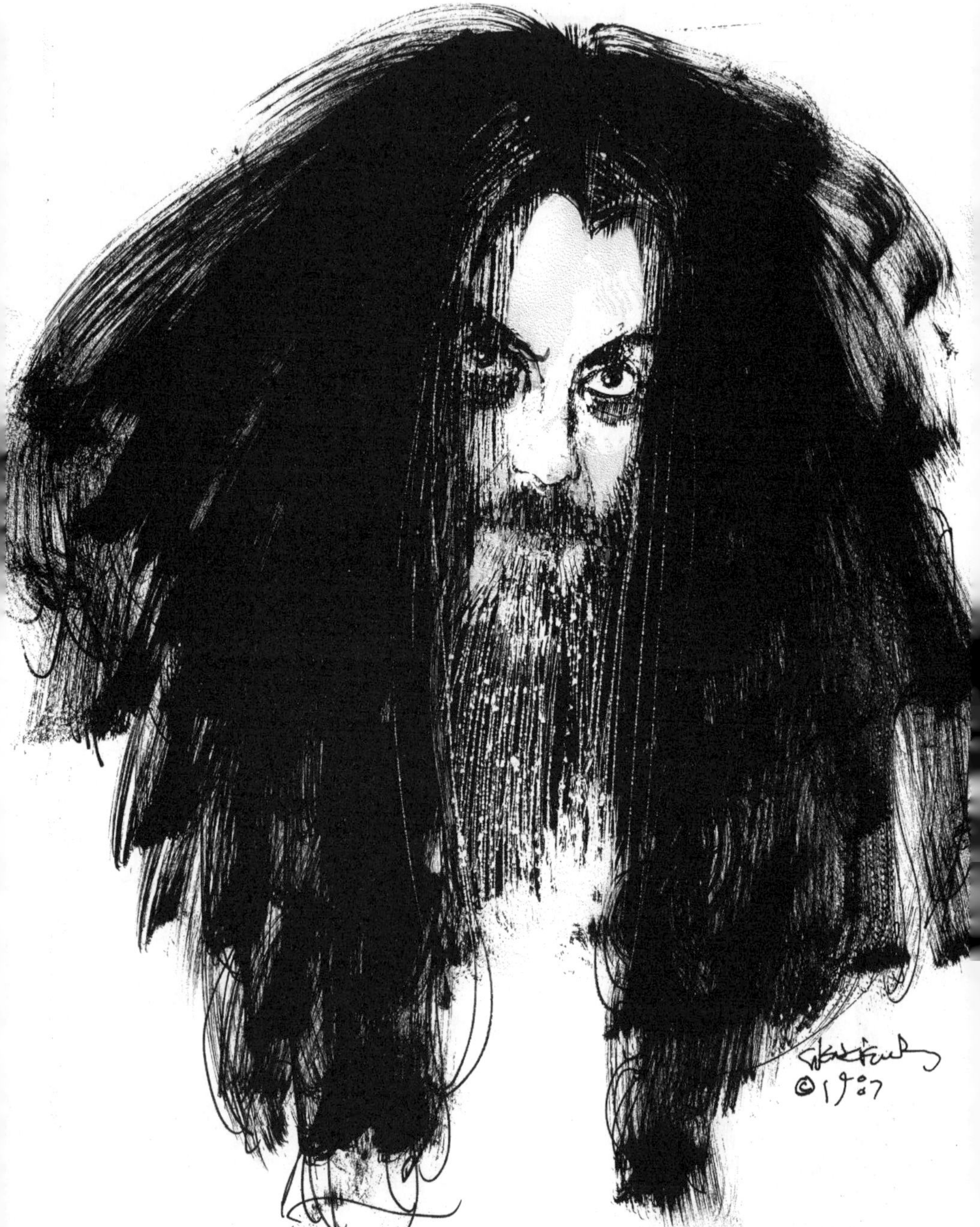

WATCHMAKER... MY WAY

MATTEO CASALI

Matteo Casali is the Italian writer and co-creator of the graphic novel **Bonerest** *(with artist Giuseppe Camuncoli), also published in Germany. A sequel is planned and he is also working on a miniseries for DC/Vertigo.*

Text ©2003 Matteo Casali.

When the chance to contribute to this amazing collection arose, I started wondering how I could do it. I thought about giving it a try by writing some Moore-inspired fiction, or maybe an article about V for Vendetta and how it made me almost cry with anger, or about that masterpiece called Watchmen... but then I would have left out all the Extraordinary Gentlemen and Swamp Things and From Hells. I had to come up with an idea that could be somewhat original (I wanted it to be!) and interesting enough to read for people who know squat about me.

That's why I decided to go the opposite way.

I pulled out of my "drawer" the lyrics of a song I wrote in late 1996 for the band I was (and somehow still am) part of. The band, an industrial-thrashy super violent bunch of maniacs called Torquemada, had been doing gigs in Italy since 1993. By the time, Mr. Alan Moore turned forty, I put together this band, acting as vocalist and writing the lyrics of all the songs. In 1997, when Mr. Alan Moore was forty-four, we went ahead and recorded our first (and so far only) CD, "Sevenfold", that did fairly well and had us tour the country — but I never knew how it did, cause the small label that released it folded after the two owners argued. (guess how it went with the money they owed us...?)

At that time, I had already made my professional debut as a comics scriptwriter (in Italy) and comics were therefore a huge influence on the way I told stories through my lyrics. All this babbling leads to the song I mentioned a few lines ago. It was called "Watchmaker", was the first track on our CD and was obviously inspired by the Watchmen's chapter that goes by the same name. The song was so fierce and disturbing that we used it to open all our live acts. Now, as we are rehearsing our new songs (the band is now called TRQ), I sometime miss the rush this track used to give me when I started growling the Moore-inspired lyrics on the mike.

I remembered the shivers I had when I first read about Dr. Manhattan's origins and motivations and how, for a guy so powerful-looking, he was in truth forever stuck in a sort of non-time pocket ('scuse the startrekkian...) from where he could watch and re-live everything over and over again, but never really be the one that makes the difference. Just like a huge cog that is vital for the mechanics of the watch he's part of. I'm sure even the beautiful words that wrap up that wonderful story, with Dr. Big Apple manifesting his will to change things, are nothing but a part of the fascinating mechanics, built by a nameless watchmaker, that keep tick-tacking their way through time. It's all in those lyrics, I tell you.

BILL SIENKIEWICZ

Left: *Bill Sienkiewicz came to prominence with his art on* **Moon Knight** *and* **New Mutants** *for Marvel Comics. He later collaborated with Alan Moore on* **Brought To Light** *and* **Big Numbers** *and wrote and illustrated* **Stray Toasters** *and* **Elektra: Assassin** *for Epic. He also provided artwork for the Jimi Hendrix biography* **Voodoo Child,** *published by Viking Penguin.*

Illustration ©2003 Bill Sienkiewicz.

Right, enough of my two cents. You probably already read (a lot) about Watchmen, so for once you'll get a chance to read something you might care ABSOLUTELY nothing about. Call it a change.

Hope it's a nice gulp of fresh air.

Torquemada - Watchmaker (1997)

It's 1945 cogs lined on black velvet
Rain on the street from my father's hands
I'm there now watching them falling
A sudden sensation of deja-vu haunts me

I am late, always will be

Ten seconds from now I drop the picture
Two hours ago it lies at my feet
The age-old light that grazes my skin
Comes from a star that died eons ago

It's too late, always has been

I can't prevent what the future will bring
You see, to me it's already happening
A voice in my past says I've arrived
But I feel as I've been here all the time

Face of the watch is now cracked forever
Hands frozen lie about a god dead for me
My hands, instead, slip through the ages
Touching reality, unable to feel it

I stand still, frozen in time

I see them all choices made and denied
But do we really choose or is our fate set?
Sand in the hourglass seems to be free
It slides back and forth and forever trapped

It's too late, always will be

Is it my father's fault I became who I am?
Cogs are still falling, am I to blame then?
This world is not made, is, has been, always will be
Shaped by no one, a clock without craftsman

So why me, who makes the world?

The answer to this final question should be pretty obvious to anyone who contributed to and/or bought this book...

Well, maybe by the time Mr. Alan Moore turns sixty, I will have another record out. And I promise I will torture you with some more rambling about a song that will surely have the "V" in its title.

• **Matteo Casali**
Reggio Emilia, 2003

KEVIN O'NEILL

Right: With writer Pat Mills, O'Neill co-created Ro-Busters, ABC Warriors and Nemesis the Warlock for 2000AD and then Marshal Law for the USA. Worked on several short strips with Alan Moore for DC, but their planned Bizarro series never materialised. He is currently completing art on the second series of The League of Extraordinary Gentlemen.

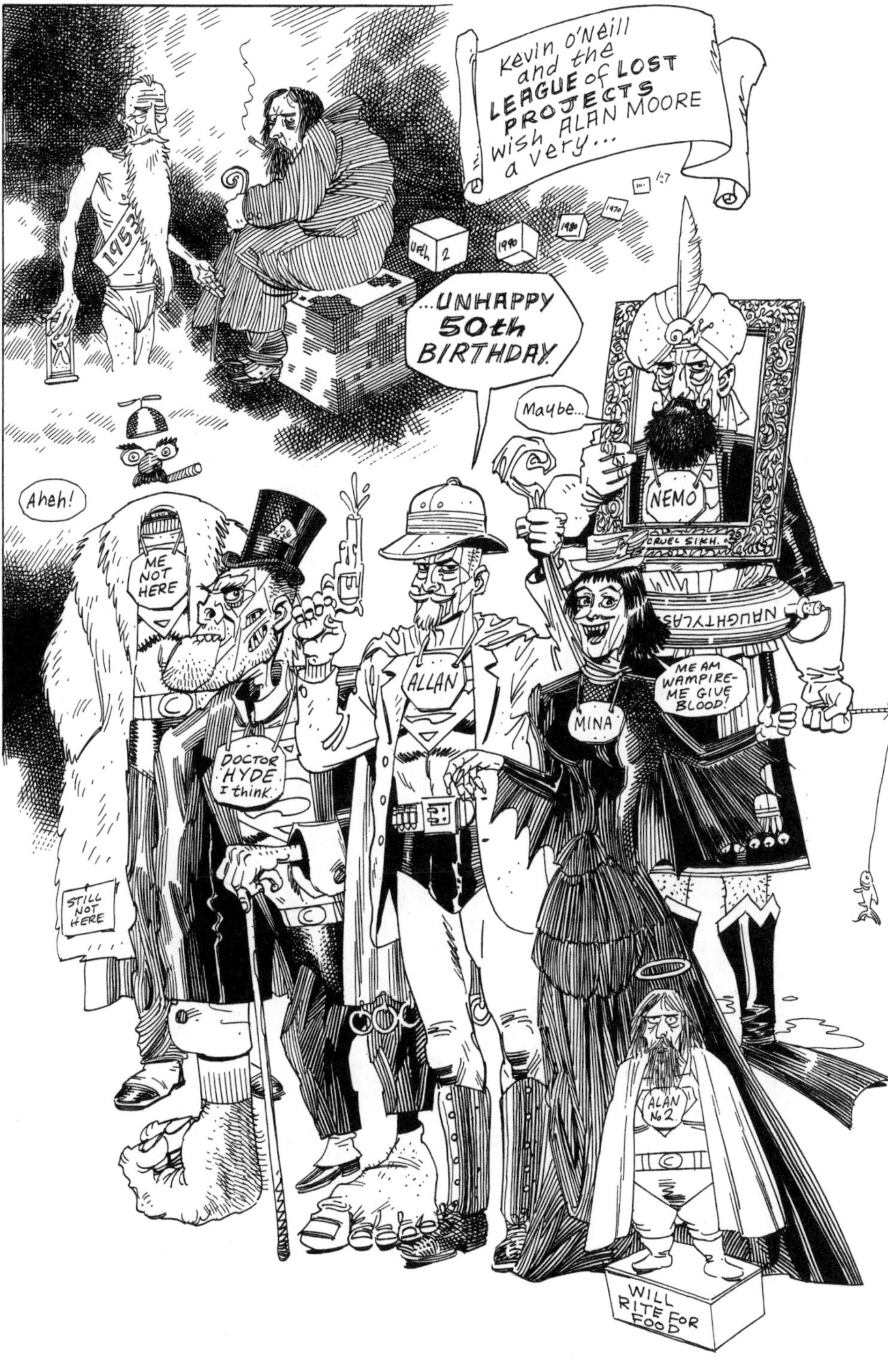
Kevin O'Neill and the LEAGUE of LOST PROJECTS wish ALAN MOORE a very...
1953
Vol 2
1990
1980
1970
...UNHAPPY 50th BIRTHDAY.
Maybe...
Aheh!
ME NOT HERE
NEMO
CRUEL SIKH.
NAUGHTYLAS
ALLAN
ME AM WAMPIRE-ME GIVE BLOOD!
MINA
DOCTOR HYDE I think.
STILL NOT HERE
ALAN No 2
WILL RITE FOR FOOD

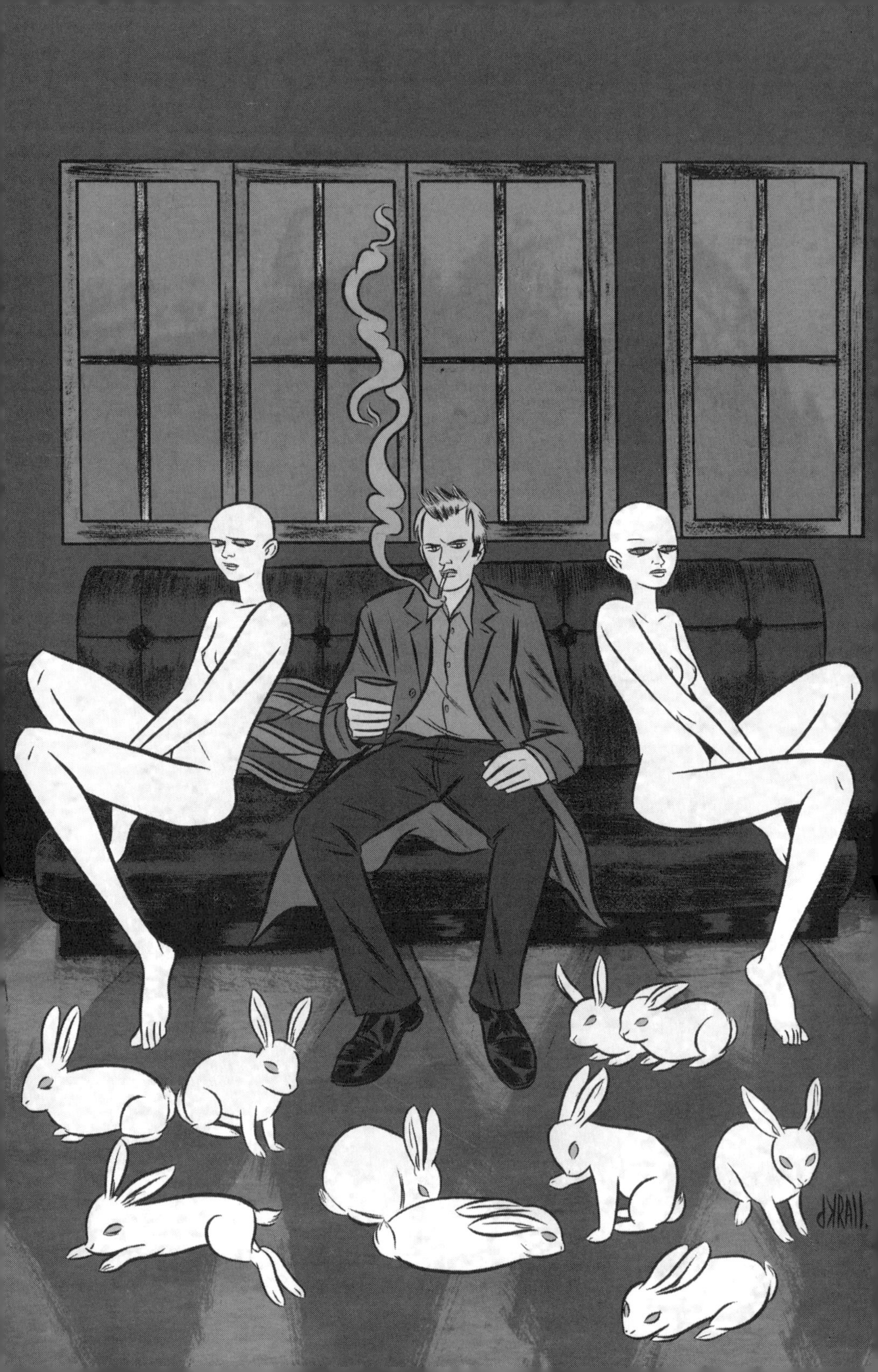
dKRALL.

MOORE'S ECLECTIC EMPORIUM

"PURVEYORS OF QUALITY MERCHANDISE, NOVELTIES, HOME FURNISHINGS AND OCCULT PARAPHERNALIA"

2003-2063

LEAH MOORE

AMBER MOORE

Leah and Amber are Alan Moore's two daughters. Leah is already making her mark in the comics business as scripter on stories in the America's Best Comics title **Tom Strong.** *Story ©2003 Leah Moore & Amber Moore.*

The young reporter's palms are slick as he knocks on the door. The glass pane is milky with cobwebs, revealing nothing of what lurks beyond. Thuds, clatters and a rasping cough filter from inside, wheezing and muffled swearing grow louder as someone, or something approaches... "Hang on, hang on, I'm coming.... bloody reporters. Thought they knew we don't open 'til noon. Yeah come on, pull up a...heap. You want a drink? Lemmesee...we got Mango and Lychee... urggh, I think that's off. We got bio-yogurts, tea, peppermint cordial... or Absinthe. No? Suit yourself. I was just sayin', we don't usually open this early... company policy. No it's no problem, just keep it quick. No he's not here, his Royal Grand Egyptian wossname is at home, or in town or something. Probably anointing his sacred orbs.

Yeah, we pretty much have the place to ourselves these days, keep it ticking over. We are *'purveyors of quality merchandise, novelties, home furnishings and occult paraphernalia'*. Humph. Not that there's much call for it. I said to him when he retired he might need something to fall back on in his old age... didn't bank on this though. First we were just sellin' the stuff he couldn't shift through normal distributors... CDs, t-shirts, action figures. We had all his spare copies of stuff he did years back. He thought it'd be great, just sign a few dusty copies of *Superlative* #6 and we'd be sorted. Amazing how people don't want to buy stuff if it's covered in tea rings and fag burns isn't it? The action figures sold at first, but when they did that *'Imaginary ideas from outside inner idea space'* range, we couldn't give 'em away. How collectable can abstract concepts be anyway? Even if they do have twenty-seven points of articulation, and detachable accessories...people didn't really see the point. Then there was the fiasco about the novel... re-issued it with pictures... lovely pictures mind... but then the publishers decided to drop the text, and just put out the drawings. They're still selling... colouring books, stuffed toys, the whole lot. Hear there's a cartoon series planned. We don't mention it to him of course... not to his good ear.

The Magick line seemed like a safe bet, you know... flog a few incense sticks to the arty student types, few tie-dye throws... but no. His Holiness the Archduke of Spook said that that wasn't good enough; he wanted us to sell the real thing. So a couple of phone calls later and we were the only retailer stocking the patented *'Magick Al's Occult Odds and Ends'* series. Need a thurible in a hurry? Chalk circles keep smudging? You get the idea. Needless to say, the denizens of Towcester aren't really big on wands, so we're still tripping over it all. Ever stubbed your toe on a grimoire? No? Didn't think so.

Yep, times are tough that's for sure. But it's not like we're complaining... we have a pretty good life, the two of us. Bloody pair of

DANIEL KRALL

Left: *Daniel Krall currently lives in Baltimore, Maryland. He's drawn* **One Plus One** *for Oni Press and works as a magazine illustrator. Illustration ©2003 Daniel Krall. Hellblazer is ©2003 DC Comics.*

spinsters. All we need is matching rocking chairs. What? Boyfriends? Pah! Not for sixty years now. Not since we opened this place. Any potential husbands were either scared off by the Grand Vizier of Grump, or just couldn't handle the idea of running this place for eternity. Bitter? No we're not bitter. And anyway, there's always pay-per-view. No, we got it pretty good here, there's three rooms upstairs, although one of them is also the storeroom, so it's pretty cozy bedding down between the boxes. We've got his old bath here as well. The bathroom was too small to put any other fittings in, but if you're used to it, the bath can pretty much be used for everything. Well, nearly everything.

We did have a little shed out back, but he wanted that turned into a grannexe for his beloved life partner when he's gone. So we'll have to run this place and bed bath the queen of perv in-between times. "Could you sharpen my pencil dear? Not that one, the Jonquil one...NO! THAT'S CHARTREUSE!" I can see it now. We sell some of her stuff in here too, you know. Yeah, it's the only thing that's still selling. What does she call 'em? 'Tijuana Bibles' I think. 'Sjust a silly name for filth as far as I can see. We sell 'em under the counter, mind. Don't want that stuff in the window; it'd get us raided for sure. We're apparently under surveillance by no less than six major government organizations, and that's not including the American ones. F.B.I., C.I.A., S.W.A.L.E.C., it's like bloody scrabble! He says they've been after him for years... like he's public enemy number one. He reckons they've been hiding over the road from him since that thing he did for the Christic Institute. Yeah right... and who says herbal tobacco doesn't make you paranoid? Anyway, he's got his place covered in so many protective spells and charms and amulets, it's amazing that the gasman can even get in. We don't have to worry here though, anyone tries to get in and we'll beat them to death with enochian tea strainers. What's that? You've got enough now? Are you sure? We've got plenty of stories yet...like the one about that time when he set fire to his hair on the gas ring, or when he bounced my head off the porch roof when I was a baby...no? Well at least take this as a gift... it's a cold cast porcelain statuette of the ninth dimension... it'd look lovely on the mantelpiece. Maybe one of our... Hey! Come back! You forgot your coat!"

The cobwebs flap and writhe around him as he claws his way out into the afternoon drizzle, gasping in deep lungfuls of blessedly pure air. His heart races, pumping blood to his trembling limbs, feeding them the adrenaline he needs to escape. As he races away from the leering shop front, he can almost hear voices, cracked and bubbling from behind the cobwebbed door.

A hunched figure watches him run, barely human beneath it's mop of multicolored tangles. Wheezing in between puffs on a foul brown roll-up, it totters over to a low chair and sweeps it free of papers and dust with one flail of its palsied arm. There is a creaking and snapping as it lowers itself into the grimy chair. From up the twisting vertiginous stair comes a rumbling. Dust is shaken from the ceiling and overburdened shelves and forms another layer on the tiny gnarled figure perched beneath. The syrupy light, which falls sluggishly from the landing above, is suddenly blotted out by the shadow of someone descending the stairs. Eventually, a towering figure emerges, its knee length black hair grayed with layers of dust and spiders nests. The eyes which glint from beneath this veil of filth are red rimmed, and dreadful in their purpose. The ragged breathing which accompanies its descent causes great clouds of dust to swirl and eddy in its wake. The hunched gnome looks up at this terrifying form, its eyes like glittering currants in a gray ball of dough. "Amber! We nearly had one! A real live man!"

"Forgeddit sis, they never stay long... you know the only eligible guy that hangs around here is Azmodeus; nice enough, but I wish he'd clean up his webs when he leaves. Yes, ever since we ran out of those Watchmen re-runs we haven't had a hope of getting out of here. Might as well accept our lot and try that two for one promotion on Kabalistic fridge magnets. Never thought the Idea Space boom would crash like it did, perhaps the whole thing of everywhere being as close as the inside of your head got a little old when peoples' mother-in-laws kept popping in from across the ether. We could have lived without the 'Instant Space-Time' memos direct from dad, and that was when we still had 'personal' lives! All that enochian chanting in-between gave me migraines.

I remember the days, the shop was new and it's not like we had a choice about working here... all those cherubim fluttering round the office, gnawing through the fax lines; no wonder I got fired really. I did think he went a little far with that 'Glyco-Gram' to your studio. Giant snakes nesting would be enough to give anyone writers block. Always gets his way.

Not that it was all bad, it was fun for a while; combing the goat hair on the book spines, air dusting the jars of teeth. It used to have such a mysterious air to it, I thought we'd end up with some of those tall dark and handsome Men In Black guys... never the way though. Here we are, older than should be allowed and sharing a storeroom with more entities than you can shake a wand at. Remember? We tried...

Maybe he'd let us retire if we could convince those creatures he summons to do a little work before they scuttle off? Of course *that* would be self-serving and an abuse of power... he didn't think that when he started balding though; he was off chanting at anyone who'd listen before the first tuft hit the floor.

I thought the move from comics to magic would do him good at first... you know? He'd worked so hard building up his own little comics empire from nothing; I thought it was time for him to rest on his laurels and reap the rewards. Never thought he'd have the idea that material gain from non-magical work would pollute his 'Ain Soph' whatsit, if only we could've had him sectioned before he transferred the royalties to the retirement fund for archaic deities. Damn those ungrateful entities... sitting around drinking the amber nectar while I make myself Amber-knackered selling signed coffee mugs with their tentacles all over! You'd think they'd have at least let us off with middle-aged spread or something, some perk in exchange for giving up our inheritance."

In the corner of the room, between stacks of faded boxes, a pinprick of light appears. Glimmering and growing into a cloud of sparkles. The papers that litter every surface flap and flutter in a chill wind which gusts from the glittering portal. A shape is forming in the centre of the swirling vortex, the muscular coils of a serpent. Atop these coils sits a hirsute head. Its heavy lidded eyes peer from between the silvery fronds of hair, which drips like Spanish moss on either side. The skin sparkles with jeweled scales, carven into deep furrows by the passage of time. A forked tongue flickers from beneath a long moustache, and the beard which sprouts from its slender serpentine chin reaches nearly to the floor. It makes a noise, what could be a greeting, were it not so drenched in sibilants. And turns to bathe the wretched pair of hags in its bloodshot and baleful glare. "Oh hullo dad..."

"I'll put the kettle on then..."

• **Leah & Amber Moore 2003.**

A FAN FOR LIFE

It's funny, I never read comics as a kid. I "discovered" them in my late twenties in the Spring of 1990, stumbling onto a comic book shop while waiting for my wife to get off work. And it was there that I happened to find Alan Moore's graphic novel, *V for Vendetta*. The impact of that one book was responsible for getting me into the business. Alan made me realize the potential of comics, and also inspired me to make my most dreaded and obsessive internal statement: "I could do this!" — and thus, a new obsession was born.

It's hard to believe that ten years later I'm actually working with Alan — comics' all-time greatest creator! — by publishing *Lost Girls*, *Voice of the Fire*, and *The Mirror of Love*; representing him and Eddie Campbell on *From Hell*, *The Birth Caul*, and *Snakes & Ladders*; and also helping to distribute his performance CDs on the RE: record label.

CHRIS STAROS

Chris Staros is the co-publisher of Top Shelf Productions and a member of Board of Directors of the Comic Book Legal Defense Fund. If you love comics as much as Chris does, take the time to visit Top Shelf at www.topshelfcomix.com. They may just point you to something new. Text ©2003 Chris Staros.

I first met Alan on April 20th, 2000, visiting him and Melinda Gebbie at his home in Northampton, England to finalize the deal on *Lost Girls*. I had always hoped that one day I'd have his autograph, but I never imagined that it would be on a contract to actually publish one of his most groundbreaking graphic novels. We spent the entire day together, with both he and Melinda treating me like a long lost friend. It was any fan's "dream day" for sure. I've been fortunate enough to visit him every year since, dropping by on my annual pilgrimage to the comic book convention in Bristol, and it's no effort at all to say that there's nothing like a cup of tea with this industry's most extraordinary gentlemen.

Above: *Chris with Alan Moore and Melinda Gebbie, Northampton 2000. Photograph by Gary Spencer Millidge*

Alan Moore turned the comics world on its ear with *Watchmen*, *Swamp Thing*, *Miracleman*, *Big Numbers*, *The League of Extraordinary Gentlemen*, and all the comics mentioned above. I for one can't wait to see what he's got up his sleeve next.

I'm truly a fan for life.

• **Chris Staros,** Publisher
Top Shelf Productions

PETER KUPER

Right: *Peter Kuper's illustrations and comics appear regularly in* **Time, The New York Times** *and* **MAD Magazine** *where he draws SPY vs. SPY every month. He is co-founder of the political comix magazine* **World War 3 Illustrated** *and has recently completed an adaptation of* **Franz Kafka's The Metamorphosis** *which will be published by Crown in 2003. www.peterkuper.com Illustration ©2003 Peter Kuper V for Vendetta ©2003 DC Comics*

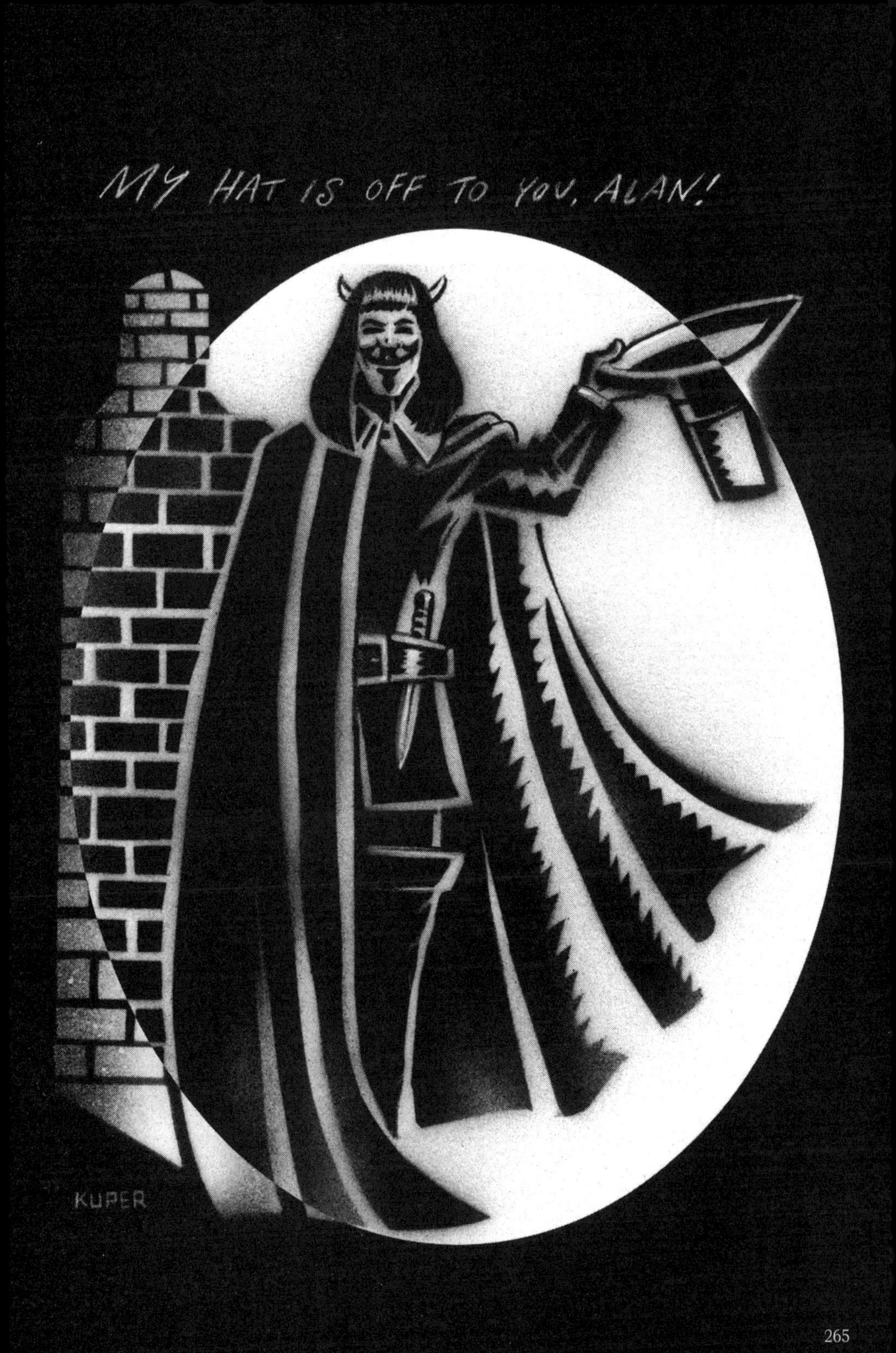
MY HAT IS OFF TO YOU, ALAN!
KUPER

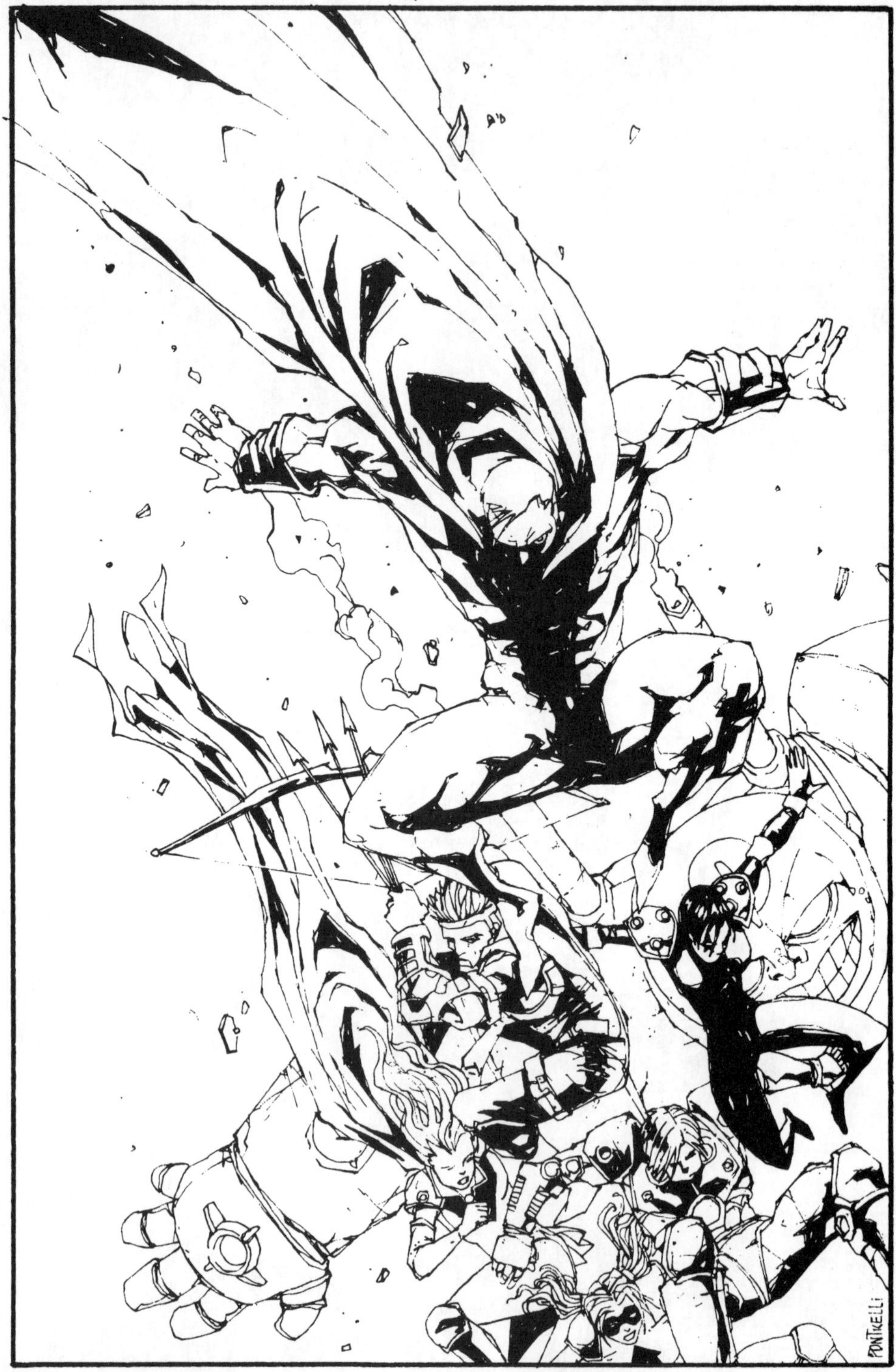
PONTICELLI

"*Après moi, le déluge* (I think he was quoting)": Alan Moore's *WildC.A.T.s*

PAOLO A. LIVORATI

Paolo A. Livorati was born in Cuneo, Italy, and is a freelance translator. As Line Editor and Translation Supervisor, from 1994 to 1998 he gave the best years (so to speak) of his professional life to comics in general and to Italian publisher Star Comics in particular. Text ©2003 Paolo A. Livorati

Between 1996 and 1997, I had the good fortune and the honor of supervising the Italian edition of the fourteen episodes of *WildC.A.T.s* written by Alan Moore. A year earlier, though, when those same episodes had come out in the US, I was not yet involved with them. I used to read the serial, sure, but virtually only to spot continuity elements that could have affected the other Image serials of whose Italian edition I was in charge. With Moore as its new writer, of course, I started reading it more attentively and realized right away that a crucial time had come for that superhero group. There was no trace left of the way previous writers took themselves so seriously. The characters would exchange scathing remarks, make fools of themselves (for a whole page, Savant shamelessly brown-nosed various heroes from other serials to convince them to join the 'C.A.T.s) and be spotted in the background, during their first fight, reading a book entitled *101 Reasons Why Comics Ruined My Life*. In the second episode, the sending-up became subtler, but none the less scathing for that; a TV cartoon called *MadD.O.G.S.* (!) first distorted the characters' names to underline their inherent silliness, then even discussed the logical gaps in the previous storyline. Just when readers thought it would all simply end in a series of amusing mockery, though, the true aim of Moore's run started to become clear – it was as if Jim Lee and Brandon Choi had given somebody permission to plot nothing less than the destruction of the 'C.A.T.s the two had created.

It was a destruction carried out with methodical precision, dismantling piece by piece everything that until then had been taken for granted. The war two alien civilizations had been fighting on Earth and elsewhere had been over for three hundred years and the winners had not even bothered to tell their soldiers on such a backwater planet; Khera, the homeworld of the "hero" Kherubim, was revealed to be founded on a loathsome and ruthless caste system; the civilian refugees among the "villain" Deamonites were living in filthy ghettoes, constantly humiliated by their vanquishers; Lord Emp and Zealot, the "nobler" among the 'C.A.T.s, belonging to Khera's two upper castes, had ended up looking down on, if not disowning, those who had been their loyal brothers in arms until just a few days earlier. Not that the characters who had remained on Earth were any better off, caught in a war waged on them by mobsters and supervillains, torn apart by internal tensions and unknowingly manipulated by a traitor in their midst. It was truly a full-scale crisis. And when, roughly in the middle of the storyline, Spartan the cyborg said to himself: "I want to know what it is [...] that is tearing the WildC.A.T.s to pieces where Defile and Helspont failed," the answer was already clear. Two cheesy and banal enemies were never able to demolish a supergroup which was often equally banal, but a great writer in a deconstructionist mood had proven too much for them.

ALBERTO PONTICELLI

Left: *Italian artist Alberto Ponticelli has worked on* **Lobo** *for DC Comics,* **Sam & Twitch** *for Image and* **Marvel Knights** *for Marvel. Illustration ©2003 Alberto Ponticelli. All characters are ©2003 their respective copyright holders.*

At the end of that long adventure, there was virtually nothing left of the original WildC.A.T.s. Not so much because the characters' certainties had been shattered, as because the same narrative essence on which the serial was based right from its start had been undermined from within. The story ended on the traitor's funeral and with Majestic replying to Savant's invitation to dance, saying: "Of course. It was we two who put the new WildC.A.T.s together... now let us dance it to its rest." Reinforced by the image of the two dancing – literally – on a grave, those words proved prophetic: with the next writers, the serial would drag itself through another sixteen feeble episodes, only to be canceled and relaunched twice. Today, *Wildcats Version 3.0* looks promising, but the original concept underlying the 'C.A.T.s effectively did not survive the Moore treatment. Who knows whether Jim Lee and Brandon Choi were aware, when they entrusted their creations to one of the masters in contemporary comicdom, that the price for their best storyline ever would be the annihilation of everything those characters had represented until then.

Six years after they were first published in Italy, I can safely say that Alan Moore's 'C.A.T.s were the highest point among all the serials I edited for Star Comics, their Italian publisher (no offense meant to those other talented writers who penned stories for Wildstorm Productions). Those fourteen episodes were a virtually perfect mix of storytelling technique, humor, plot twists, wit and sarcasm. Travis Charest's and Troy Hubbs' art also greatly contributed to that mix, along with a few characters who were introduced then and immediately gained a cult following, like the unfathomable Tao or the psychotic but sensitive Ladytron. Working on superhero comics arriving from the US in the mid-to-late Nineties was not always rewarding, but offering such a storyline to Italian readers certainly compensated for the dozens of mediocre stories which had appeared in other titles. We thank you also for that, Mr. Moore.

• **Paolo A. Livorati**

ILYA

Pages 269-272 following:
*This is the first comic strip Ilya has done in some time, and he says, the first one in YEARS that was fun to do. He is probably best remembered for his **End of The Century Club** series. Ilya's work has been published both in France, and in Italy by Alta Fedelta. Ilya also says he would like to do more comic strips one day. Strip ©2003 Ilya. All characters ©2003 their respective copyright holders.*

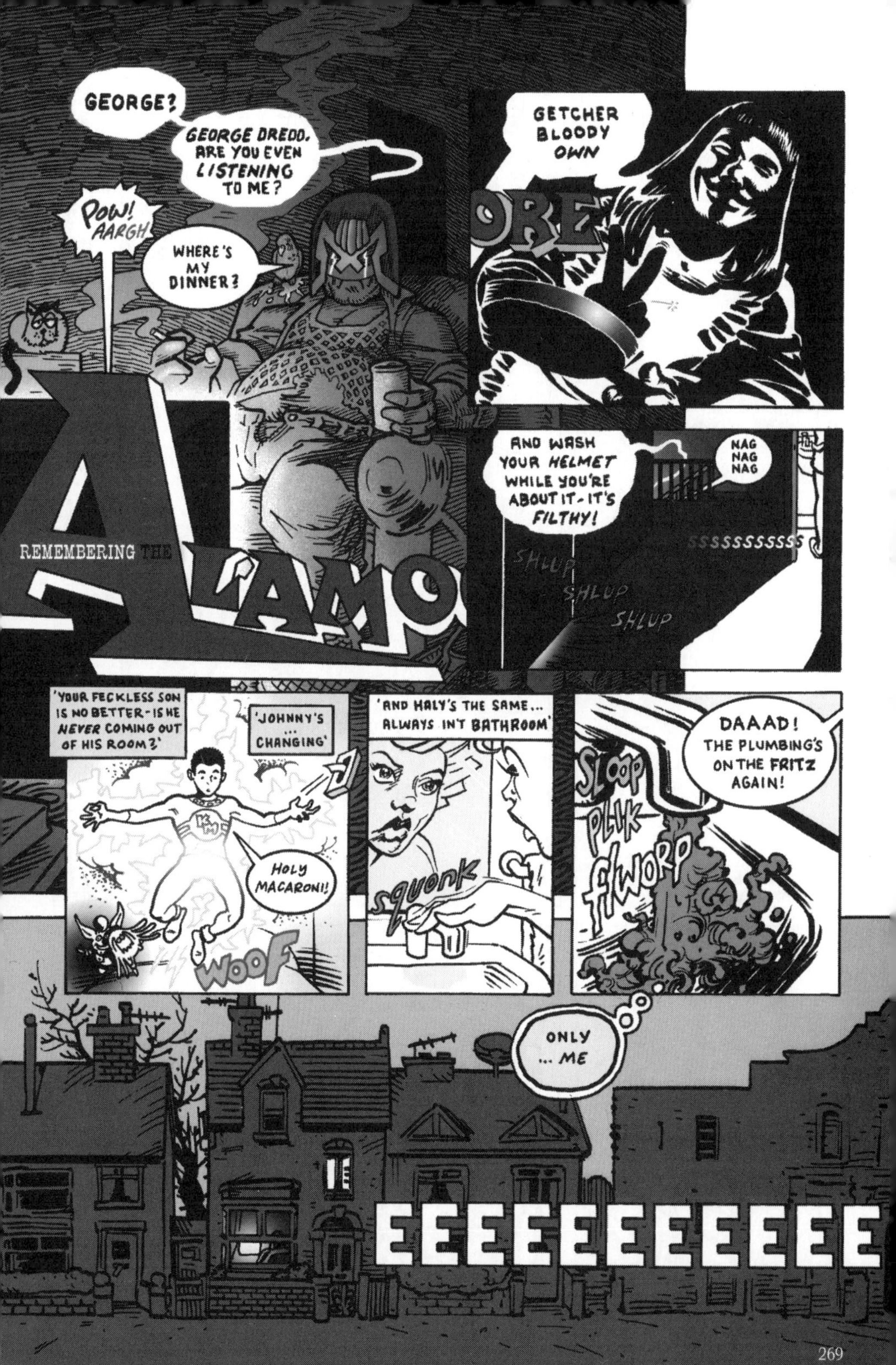
GEORGE?
GEORGE DREDD. ARE YOU EVEN LISTENING TO ME?
POW! AARGH
WHERE'S MY DINNER?
GETCHER BLOODY OWN
REMEMBERING THE
AND WASH YOUR HELMET WHILE YOU'RE ABOUT IT - IT'S FILTHY!
NAG NAG NAG
SSSSSSSSSSS
SHLUP SHLUP SHLUP
'YOUR FECKLESS SON IS NO BETTER - IS HE NEVER COMING OUT OF HIS ROOM?'
'JOHNNY'S ... CHANGING'
HOLY MACARONI!
WOOF
'AND HALY'S THE SAME... ALWAYS IN'T BATHROOM'
squonk
DAAAD! THE PLUMBING'S ON THE FRITZ AGAIN!
SLOOP
PLIK
FLWORP
ONLY ... ME
EEEEEEEEEEEE

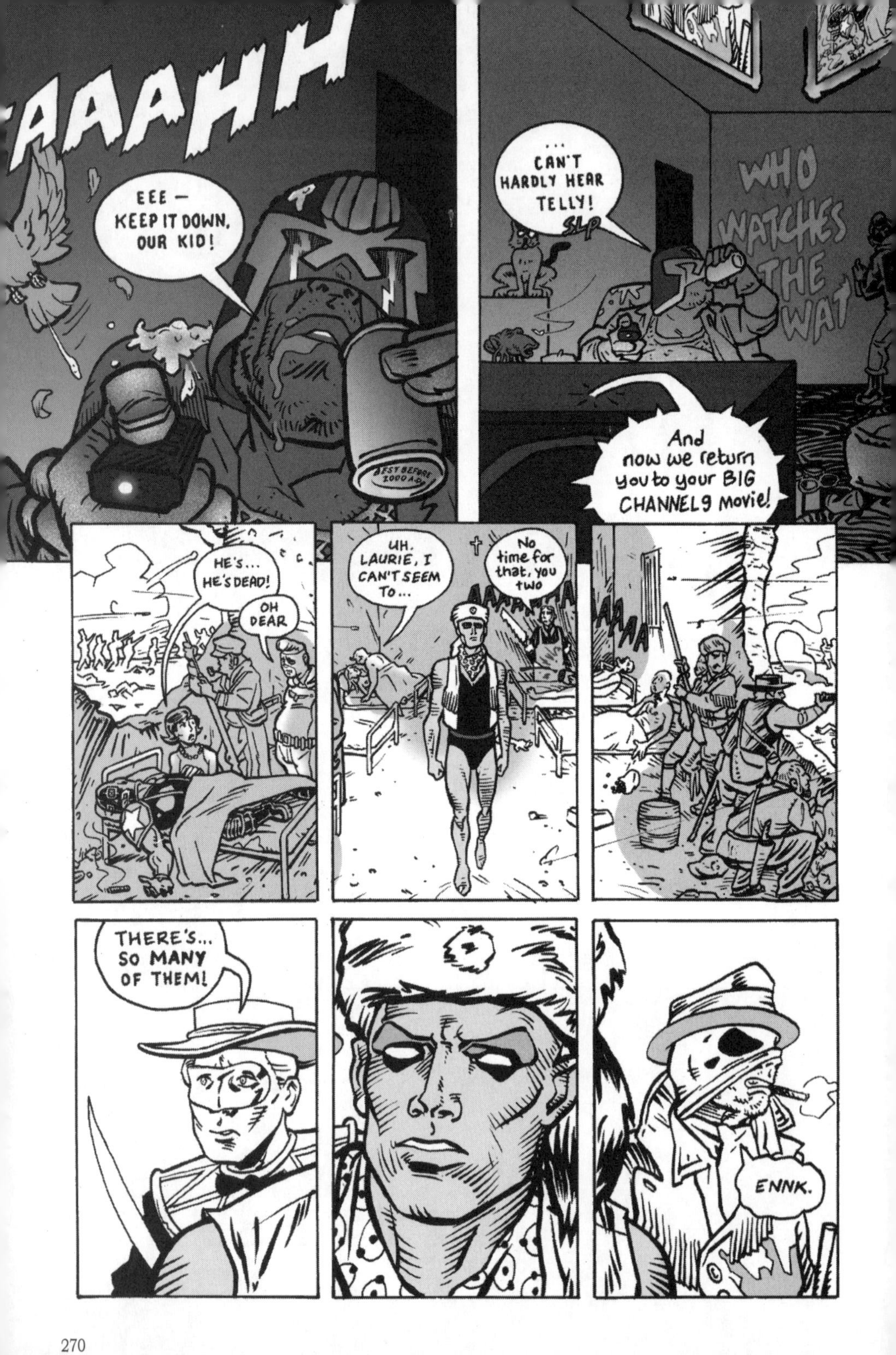
AAAHH
EEE — KEEP IT DOWN, OUR KID!
BEST BEFORE 2000 A.D.
... CAN'T HARDLY HEAR TELLY!
SLP
WHO WATCHES THE WAT
And now we return you to your BIG CHANNEL 9 movie!
HE'S... HE'S DEAD!
OH DEAR
UH. LAURIE, I CAN'T SEEM TO...
No time for that, you two
AAAAAAAAA
THERE'S... SO MANY OF THEM!
ENNK.

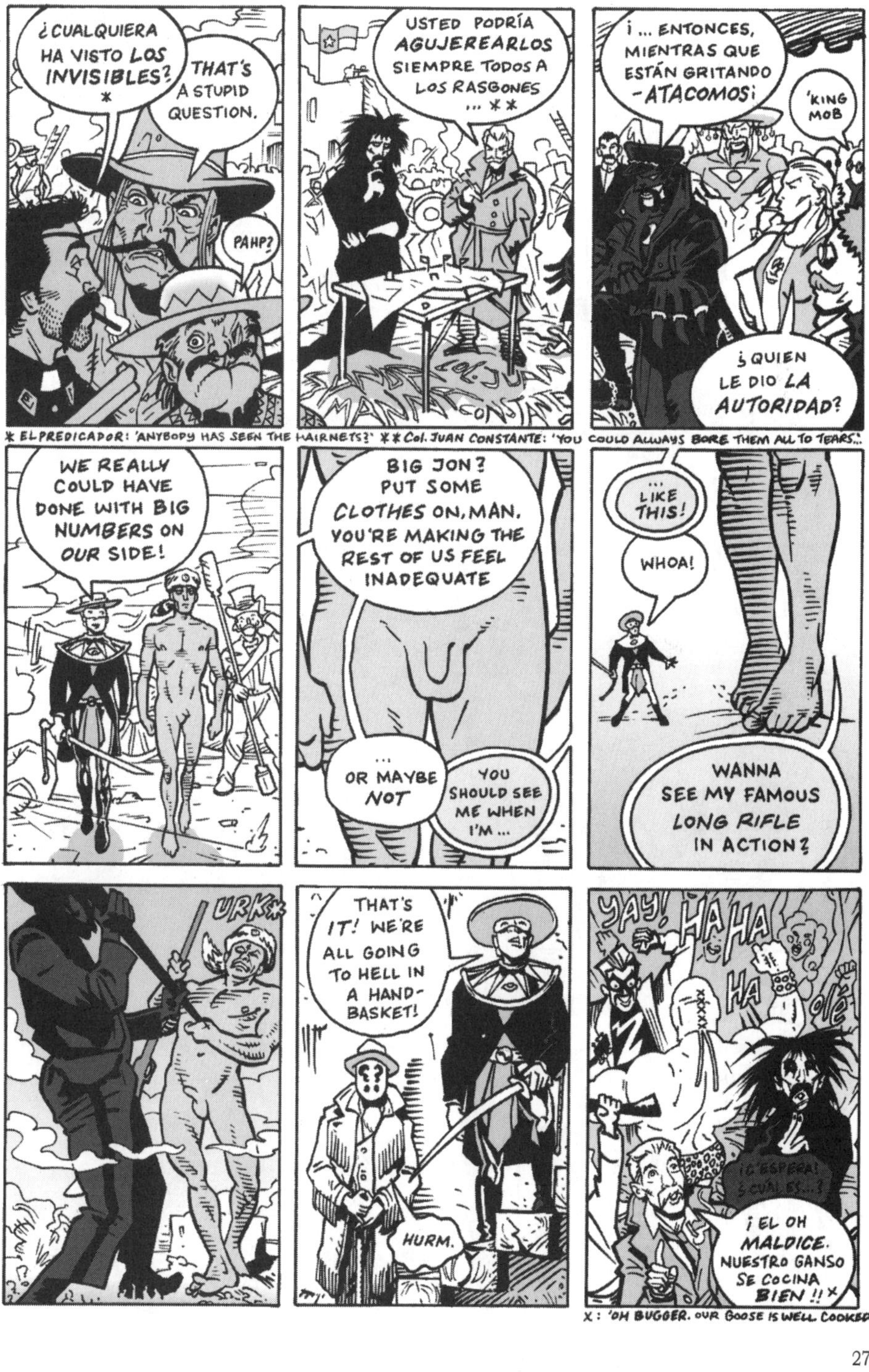

¿CUALQUIERA HA VISTO LOS INVISIBLES? *
THAT'S A STUPID QUESTION.
PAHP?
USTED PODRÍA AGUJEREARLOS SIEMPRE TODOS A LOS RASGONES ... **
COL. JUAN
MANANA
CONSTANTE
¡... ENTONCES, MIENTRAS QUE ESTÁN GRITANDO -ATACOMOS¡
'KING MOB
¿QUIEN LE DIO LA AUTORIDAD?
* ELPREDICADOR: 'ANYBODY HAS SEEN THE HAIRNETS?' ** Col. JUAN CONSTANTE: 'YOU COULD ALWAYS BORE THEM ALL TO TEARS.'
WE REALLY COULD HAVE DONE WITH BIG NUMBERS ON OUR SIDE!
BIG JON? PUT SOME CLOTHES ON, MAN. YOU'RE MAKING THE REST OF US FEEL INADEQUATE
... OR MAYBE NOT
YOU SHOULD SEE ME WHEN I'M ...
... LIKE THIS!
WHOA!
WANNA SEE MY FAMOUS LONG RIFLE IN ACTION?
URK*
THAT'S IT! WE'RE ALL GOING TO HELL IN A HAND-BASKET!
HURM.
YAY! HA HA HA
OLÉ
¡¿ESPERA! ¿CUÁLES ...?
¡EL OH MALDICE. NUESTRO GANSO SE COCINA BIEN!! x
X: 'OH BUGGER. OUR GOOSE IS WELL COOKED'

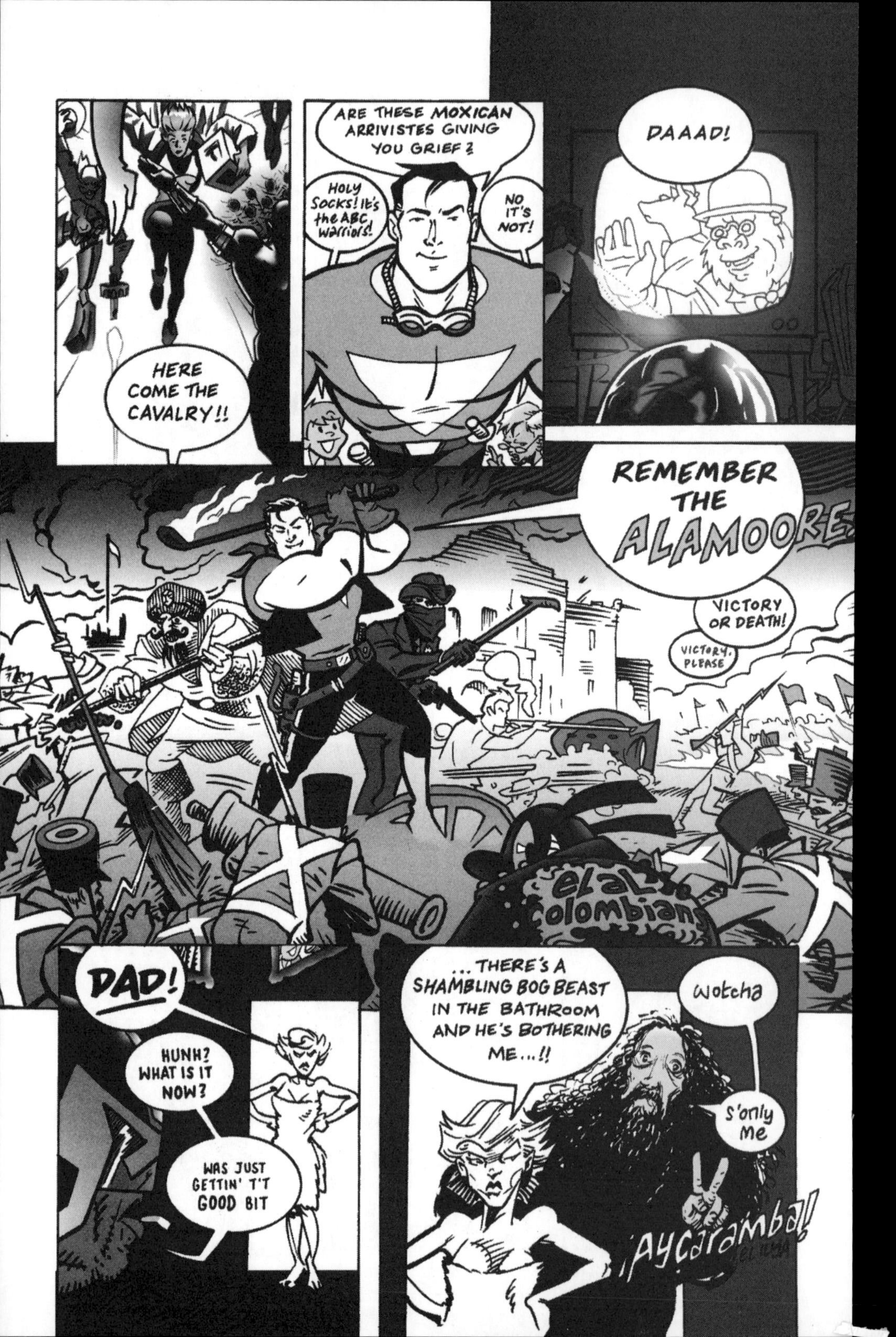
HERE COME THE CAVALRY!!
ARE THESE MOXICAN ARRIVISTES GIVING YOU GRIEF?
Holy Socks! It's the ABC warriors!
NO IT'S NOT!
DAAAD!
REMEMBER THE ALAMOORE!
VICTORY OR DEATH!
VICTORY, PLEASE
el al colombians
DAD!
HUNH? WHAT IS IT NOW?
WAS JUST GETTIN' T'T GOOD BIT
... THERE'S A SHAMBLING BOG BEAST IN THE BATHROOM AND HE'S BOTHERING ME...!!
wotcha
s'only me
¡Aycaramba!

SPEAKING THE 'TRUTH' OF SEX:
Moore & Gebbie's *Lost Girls*

JOSÉ ALANIZ

José Alaniz writes on Russian comics, disabilty in superhero comics and Alan Moore. His work has appeared in the International Journal of Comic Art.

Text ©2003 José Alaniz

Notes:

1. In the troubled publishing history of Lost Girls, only the first two issues have made it to bookstores. In 2003 Top Shelf Press is slated to release the complete collected work in a new hardcover edition. This essay thus necessarily addresses only the first two volumes.

2. Mirrors, windows, reflections, transparent surfaces, the eye-like designs of the headboard, chair and lamp – we cannot of course discount Moore's penchant for visual puns. This opening six-panel page invites the reader to associate the mirror and other objects with the comics page itself, which also functions as both window (providing access to the visual pleasures of the text) and as mirror (reflecting/"incarnating" our own imagined desires). The replication of panel-like grids (both dividing and – because transparent – uniting public and private spaces) is one of Lost Girls' chief visual motifs.

3. Tellingly, the novel opens with the seduction of a child, reflecting an ages-old (we might even call it "in-built") controversy of children's literature: the vexed question of children's sexuality, especially vis-à-vis adults. This is the theme of Rose's book on Peter Pan:

The demand for better and more cohesive writing in children's fiction ... carries with it a plea that certain psychic barriers should go undisturbed, the most important of which is the barrier between adult and child. When children's fiction touches on that barrier, it becomes not experiment (the formal play of a modern adult novel which runs the gamut of characters' points of view) but molestation. Thus the writer for children must keep his or her narrative hands clean and stay in his or her proper place. (70, emphasis the author's)

Lady Fairchild, right from Lost Girls' opening panel, is of course violating that cardinal rule. Thus as further described below, Moore & Gebbie's work seeks not to pervert a genre, but to "unveil" its true motives.

Your fantasies. You were gonna tell me. Mine started with, y'know, sex? Sex was this whole different world. I made up sorta dreams about it."

"So did I. Desire's a strange land one discovers as a child, where nothing makes the slightest sense." – Dottie and Lady Fairchild, Lost Girls

Lost Girls by Alan Moore & Melinda Gebbie, a meta-fictive pornographic series[1] based on, of all things, children's fiction, begins with the words: "Tell me a story." Panel one: we gaze into a mirror[2] – we learn later this is literally Alice's looking glass – that catches the reflection of an elegant bedroom, in which an older woman, Lady Fairchild, is evidently trying to seduce a pre-pubescent girl (we see only a flash of leg, a nude silhouette):

"Your little white breasts, they're so lovely. They'll never be as beautiful once you've grown. Will you touch them for me? ... Well, at least let me see you properly. Open your legs just a little and I'll do the same." The anonymous girl demands her story first, but Lady Fairchild is just as adamant about reading the girl's "story," namely her sex. Thus *Lost Girls*, in its opening gambit, makes the linkage between storytelling, desire and the polymorphous sex act itself a central theme.[3]

"Among its many emblems," writes Michel Foucault in *The History of Sexuality, Volume I*, "our society wears that of the talking sex. The sex which one catches unawares and questions, and which, restrained and loquacious at the same time, endlessly replies."(77) But the compulsion to speak sex, rather than a badge of liberation, says Foucault, in fact represents the efficacy of institutions of power to shape the very sensual lives of their subjects.

One way they accomplished this was through the establishment of the confession in medieval monasteries after the Council of Trent; as part of the rigorous self-examination involved in penance, there emerged a general incitement to name the sins of flesh "down to [their] slenderest ramifications," to quantify every detail, and transform sex in even its most minor and ancillary manifestations into discourse – "tell everything."(21) This injunction to yield up the "truths" of sex, by the 17th century, had spread from the monastery to Western society at large, losing its character of penance but retaining its obsessive attention to detail in a *scientia sexualis* that overlay disparate modes of discourse: medical, psychological, legal, pornographic.

By the end of the 18th century the Marquis de Sade's literary *modus operandi* seems an extension of old monastic inducements, though with a different aim: "Your narrations must be decorated with the most numerous and searching details ... the least circumstance is apt to have an immense influence upon the procuring of that kind of sensory irritation that we expect from your stories."(21) Or as Foucault himself writes:

It is no longer a question of saying what was done – the sexual act – and how it was done; but of reconstructing, in and around the act, the thoughts that recapitulated it, the obsessions that accompanied it, the images, desires, modulations, and quality of the pleasure that animated it. For the first time, no doubt, a society has taken upon itself to solicit and hear the imparting of individual pleasures.(63)

As so often with Foucault, the ultimate effect of the telling of sex is a transfer of knowledge *qua* power *qua* pleasure, with discourses speaking, shaping and determining subjects and their bodily delights, and fixing once-scattered sexualities into new, rigidified norms. Forms of discourse combining word and image, meanwhile, have historically proved among the most efficacious in this process. As the literary discursive mode of sexual revelation par excellence, pornography (one of the "body genres," in Linda Williams' phrase) contains at least as much talk as action; a steady accumulation of detail, anticipation, linguistic adornment and narratival teasing serves to heighten the bald truths of the customary sex act rendered in all its explicitness.

Furthermore, narrative (whether pornographic or not) is itself profoundly erotic, as Peter Brooks writes in *Reading for the Plot:*

Narratives tell of desire – typically present some story of desire – and arouse and make use of desire as dynamic of signification ... Desire is always there at the start of the narrative, often in a state of initial arousal, often having reached a state of intensity such that movement must be created, action undertaken, change begun. (37/38)[4]

Narrative therefore goes from delivering De Sade's "sensory irritation" through the obsessive cataloguing of details, to *becoming* the "sensory irritation" itself. In *Lost Girls,* Moore & Gebbie playfully deploy Foucault's incitements to "speak" the truth of sex and Brooks' urgent, desire-driven "thrust" of narrative to rewrite the familiar "discovery and wonder" master plot of much children's literature. They manage this through two visual/linguistic strategies – the "tracking shot" panel sequence and the confessional mode – to capitalize on the unique juxtapositional properties of the comics medium and enhance porn's visceral effects on the reader's body, yielding more sexually discursive bang for the buck.

In 1913, in a decadent art-nouveau hotel called the Himmelgarten (Heavenly Garden) on the Austrian border, three very different women with oddly similar backgrounds meet: the aristocratic 60-ish Brit Lady Fairchild, the much younger midwestern American Dottie and the repressed 30-ish married woman, Wendy. Like Macbeth's Three Witches, the women convene before the hurly-burly of World War I to tell their stories. In the case of the perverse Lady Fairchild and the nymphomaniac Dottie, the stories invariably involve sex, which they talk about and engage in at every opportunity – often combining the two activities. As for Wendy, an irritating cold-fish husband and her own restrained personality consign erotic thoughts to dreams, shades, furtive glances and obliteration via hot showers.

With its comic[5] take on graphic sex, faux period setting, double takes and sly visual puns, *Lost Girls* refashions everything, including its title, into a double entendre – a staple of pornographic and metafictional literature.[6] Gebbie's colorful palate yields lush, delicately sensuous art that nonetheless seems a parody in spots of crude Tijuana Bibles. Furthermore, a passion for narrative infects the characters almost as much as their lust for more common pleasures: Lady Fairchild writes porn novels, the hotel owner keeps a vast library of erotica, even Wendy's bore of a husband Harold secretly consumes over-the-top pornography, illustrated by an "Aubrey Beardsley." (These humorous texts appear in interludes.) At the Himmelgarten, everyone, even the prude, craves stories. Thus the series' most porno/erotic aspect is its narrative strategies.

Chapter II, "Silver Shoes," opens with a "tracking shot" panel progression which keeps Dottie's eponymous footwear framed in the foreground center of the composition, while the background "passes by"; Dottie is walking into the Hotel Himmelgarten, and catches the eye of her soon-to-be-lover, Captain Bauer – who, it turns out, is a shoe fetishist. This "dollying" approach dominates the chapter, as the narratival "camera" leads the eye across panels which divide up the hotel's verandas, corridors, garden paths, and – as Dottie and Bauer tryst – the lovers' bodies.

This "dollying" (Dottie-ing?) approach to narrative attains its "climax" along with our heroine's cunnilingus-induced orgasm on page 15, which Moore/Gebbie break up into a 6-panel grid overlaying a "master" splash page. Urged on by the relentless boustrophedon winding of the panel sequence, the "forward drive" of narrative desire, the eye positively slides all over Dottie's reveling figure, which in this splash seems split up into topographic segments. The design encourages the reader to pause at each individual body part for particular delectation: porn's specialty, a scopophilic knowledge-pleasure (a variation of what porn scholars

4. *Brooks takes his inspiration in part from Roland Barthes' description of narrative as a "striptease" in* The Pleasure of the Text. *But this desire, by its nature, is polymorphous, spilling over into objects, things. As Brooks writes in* Body Work:

The desire to reach the end [the "climax," in both literary and sexual terms] is the desire to see "truth" unveiled. The body of the object of desire is the focal point of fascinated attention. Yet this attention, the very gaze of literary representation, tends to become arrested and transfixed by articles of clothing, accessories, bodily details, almost in the matter of the fetishist. (19)

Thus the many "props" and accessories of erotic literature; Lost Girls *is translating Foucault's incitement to many-layered and endlessly detailed discourse into visual terms (the lush settings of the Hotel Himmelgarten, the many delectable and "touchable" items of Lady Fairchild's boudoir, the delicate hues of Gebbie's flesh tones). It comes as no surprise, therefore, that the stud Capt. Bauer, the "stand-in" for the presumed male reader during Dottie's tryst, is a fetishist – as, in a sense, is any reader/viewer of pornography.*

5. *Moore, like pornographers before him, betrays a desire to "redeem" the genre from its denigrated, marginalized status:*

Pornography is generally so grim and dismal, so grismal, that it tends to emphasize feelings of loneliness, depression and run-amok self-loathing rather than alleviate them. While I wouldn't claim for a moment that **Lost Girls** will do anything to change the existing state of pornography, I feel that it will at very least be a significant step in the right direction. (Moore, 2002)

6. *One bravura example of the double entendre occurs in chapter 3, "Missing Shadows," in which Wendy Potter mends her husband's pants while he irritatingly declaims his usual banalities. The "innocent" dialogue and domestic action take on an entirely different meaning in the guise of the couple's shadows, which couple shamelessly and hilariously before the viewer but unbeknownst to the characters. These shades, of course, represent their unconscious, suppressed desires, not necessarily for each other, but for the sexual pleasures and freedoms which the hotel's other guests indulge in with gusto. Wendy, the repressed "good girl" thus embarks on a journey not only of sexual liberation, but of a liberation to speak, to confess, to tell her story through more than mere innuendo.*

calls the "meat shot").[7]

Moreover, this roller-coaster for the eye suggests the movement comics of course cannot literally deliver: her lips curling, her breasts heaving, her fingers fondling her own nipple, his darting tongue, her quivering flesh, her silver-shoed foot a flash of motion, his masturbation and pounding buttocks. All driven on, on, on by comics' compulsive aspect-to-aspect logic of the left-to-right panel "thrust." Dottie's constant prattle, meanwhile, serves to add a touch of humor and to smooth the panel-to-panel progression.[8]

At the end of *Lost Girls,* Chapter II, Bauer delivers his "money shot," ejaculating in the direction opposite the "forward drive" of the "camera's" momentum (16), signaling, as in so much male-oriented pornography, the coupling's conclusion. The lower panels continue the forward motion, but in a more lethargic, post-coital vein, as the figures shrink away into a literal afterglow.

The second visual/linguistic mode which Moore & Gebbie deploy to tease out their narrative's native dynamic of desire bears less commentary, insofar as it presents Foucault's injunction to speak sex in its most familiar form: the confession/erotic autobiography of initiation. In her story before the group (chapter 7, "The Twister"), Dottie recounts a familiar-sounding tale of a tornado in Kansas that whisks a house away, over the rainbow. But the story itself has a twist: Dottie's own elemental powers of self-pleasuring:

And there it was. I mean, I was near on turned sixteen, so I'd seen twisters afore, but they was just little ones. Little ones, long ways off.

... It was like God shouted all the windows in, an' I knew right there, I was gonna die. All I could think was how it weren't fair, me only fifteen, never been with a man or gone nowheres, an' here I was dead. Caught myself holding my dress down, so's I didn't die unladylike, an' it all seemed so dumb. Strangest thing was lyin' there in that awful wind, I started feelin', y'know ... sorta hot.

Oh, now you're lookin' at me an' I'm gettin' all embarrassed, I know it sounds funny, but ... See, if I was dyin', I could do what the heck I liked! Didn't have to think 'No, I daren't' or 'No, I mustn't' or nothin'. It was scarey, but kinda excitin', just like the wind. I let go my skirt, and my hand just sorta settled down there. I shouldn't say this, but lord ... I was wetter'n June in Seattle ... (1996, pg. 27)

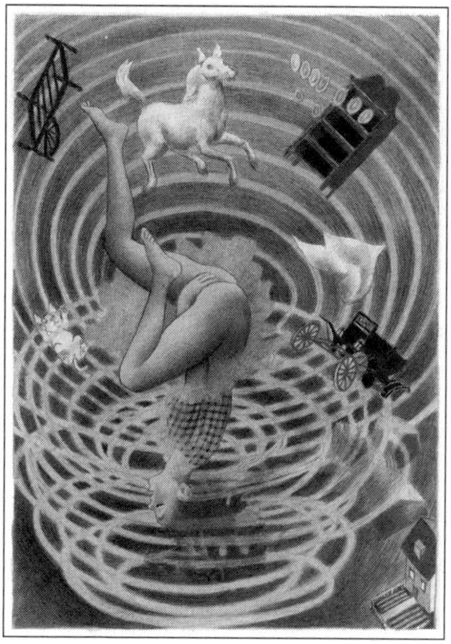

Dottie – Dorothy's – story is of course Foucault's sex-into-discourse paradigm with a vengeance; the desire in the narrative is obvious enough. Comics adds its own elements of illustration and word/image juxtaposition: humorous visual puns, such as an unwinding spool of thread, shattered glass, flowing curtains, "Shure Fire" matches, spilled ink, an opened book, a floating glove, a "No Trespassing" sign that snaps apart into an "Oz" sign, and the final, ecstatic splash in which Dorothy's orgasm expands to encompass the tornado, Kansas, possibly the universe. The earth moves. (30) (Unlike Dottie's climax with Capt. Bauer, this orgasm

7. The cinematic use of the tracking shot as a manifestation of narratival desire appears prominently in Stanley Kubrick's 1999 film Eyes Wide Shut. *A Kubrick trademark, the dolly shot both follows and precedes the protagonist as he explores a secret mansion of absurd erotic excess, pushing the viewer's gaze ecstatically ever onward to drink in body after body. Like Peter Greenaway, Kubrick uses obsessive, relentless dolly shots to build anticipation, to visually pair the forward or lateral drive of the camera with the impulsive desire to know, to see, to grasp the confessed truths of the object, to devour all optic knowledge-pleasures that slide into view. It is no coincidence that this literal penetration into forbidden erotic mysteries, for all its weirdness, much resembles a stroll through a museum, in which our distracted attention passes object after object; as with all display practices of modernity, from arcade shopping to the museum to the zoo to train travel to the freak show to cinema and finally to pornography, the potentiation of visual knowledge-pleasures, what Linda Williams (after Jean-Louis Comolli) terms the "frenzy of the visible," comes pre-packaged, commodified and served up for our always insatiable consumption. For more on the relationship of desire to these visual/display practices of modernity, see Friedberg.*

8. An alternative reading of the panel-segmented splash in which Dottie cums de-emphasizes the panel-to-panel progression, and takes the entire image in at once, much as we take in the figure (presumably Lady Fairchild) staring from the window in panel 2 "all at once," since we wouldn't read the various window segments as panels. The page's panels and Dottie's dialogue, in fact, could be read in any order, not just the usual boustrophedon left-to-right sequence I've been describing. The simultaneity or "breakdown" of narratival time thus heightens the effect of the boundary-shattering portrayal of orgasm (this mirrors the "mythic" portrayal of time I argue for in my essay on chapter 10 of Moore/Campbell's From Hell*). A tip of the hat to my colleagues at the 2002 International Comic Arts Festival, who helped me appreciate this alternate/concurrent reading.*

Right: From Lost Girls #2
© 2003 Alan Moore & Melinda Gebbie

splash page has no overlaying grid – a nod perhaps to the superior boundary-shattering powers of feminine autoeroticism?)

The perversion of Dorothy's twister experience is in the end merely an unveiling, an unstripping of the sexual subtext behind so much children's literature. As in the Gothic novels of Anne Radcliffe or Emily Bronte, the child (-like) heroine's journey is driven by her desire to know, to see, to yield up the truth about her mysterious but alluring circumstances, her desired object, and, ultimately, of her own body. Children's literature, from *The Wizard of Oz* to *Peter Pan* to *Alice in Wonderland,* is merely the house-of-mirrors estrangement of a burgeoning, frightening sexuality. In *Lost Girls,* the child heroines of those stories are all grown up – and eager to tell their tales, except for Wendy. And Wendy's beginning to waver. (As in so much porn literature, the narrative thrust involves breaking down the prudish resistance of the "good girl," so as to volcanically release her accumulated erotic potential.)

Moore & Gebbie's project figures not so much as a perversion of innocent stories which children have blithely enjoyed for generations, but a mission to unmask the veiled product of an institutionalized incitement to discourse on sex masquerading as literature for kids (written by grown men). The authors of *Lost Girls* take on the task, so long the purview of critics, to reveal the children's stories as the true perversions, thereby stripping away their symbol and metaphorical evasions, to shed light on the unabashed sexual substructure of these texts. In that sense, *Lost Girls* merely sets the record "straight."

"I ... I didn't know," says Wendy after hearing Dottie's story. "I didn't know that other people felt that way. Oh, but ... you're so brave. I don't know how you can summon up the courage to just talk about it like that."(1996, pg. 32)

Foucault would reply that courage is irrelevant; rather, it's a matter of institutionalized power structures acting on the subject, compelling it to speak, co-opting even its sensual bodily joys. Wendy, until then immune to those incitements, seems poised to join in with the general prattle on sex, to impart her own individual pleasures, to transform her amorphous, shade-like desires into the rigid, predetermined but communicable fantasies prescribed by the discursive realities of her era.

And one-handed readers everywhere, just as pre-programmed for the "sensory irritation" of narrative as anyone else, will wait with bated breath for the first words, the first truths, to cross Wendy's lips.

• **José Alaniz**

Works cited and consulted:
Brooks, Peter. Body Work: Objects of Desire in Modern Narrative, *Harvard University Press, 1993.*
————————. Reading for the Plot: Desire and Intention in Narrative, *New York: Alfred A. Knopf, 1984.*
Eyes Wide Shut, d. Stanley Kubrick, USA, 1999.
Foucault, Michel. The History of Sexuality: An Introduction, Volume I, *New York: Vintage, 1978.*
Friedberg, Anne. Windowshopping: Cinema and the Postmodern, *Berkeley: University of California Press, 1994.*
Carroll, Lewis. Alice's Adventures in Wonderland & Through the Looking Glass, *New York: Bantam, 1988 [1865].*
Moore, Alan . "Interviewed by Eddie Campbell" in Egomania, vol. 1, no. 2 (December, 2002), pgs. 1-32.
Moore, Alan & Gebbie, Melinda. Lost Girls, vol. 1, no. 1 (November, 1995), Northampton: Kitchen Sink Press.
————————. Lost Girls, vol. 1, no. 2 (February, 1996), Northampton: Kitchen Sink Press.
Perkins, Michael. The Secret Record: Modern Erotic Literature, *New York: Masquerade, 1992, portions available at <http://www.eroticauthorsassociation.com>.*
Rose, Jacqueline. The Case of Peter Pan, or The Impossibility of Children's Fiction, *University of Pennsylvania Press, 1984.*
Williams, Linda. Hardcore: Power, Pleasure and the Frenzy of the Visible, *Berkeley: University of California Press, 1989.*

ANDREA ACCARDI

Right: *Andrea Accardi is a well known Italian comics artist. His works appear regularly in the pages of the comics magazine* **Mondo Naif** *.*
Illustration ©2003 Andrea Accardi
Lost Girls is ©2003 Alan Moore & Melinda Gebbie.

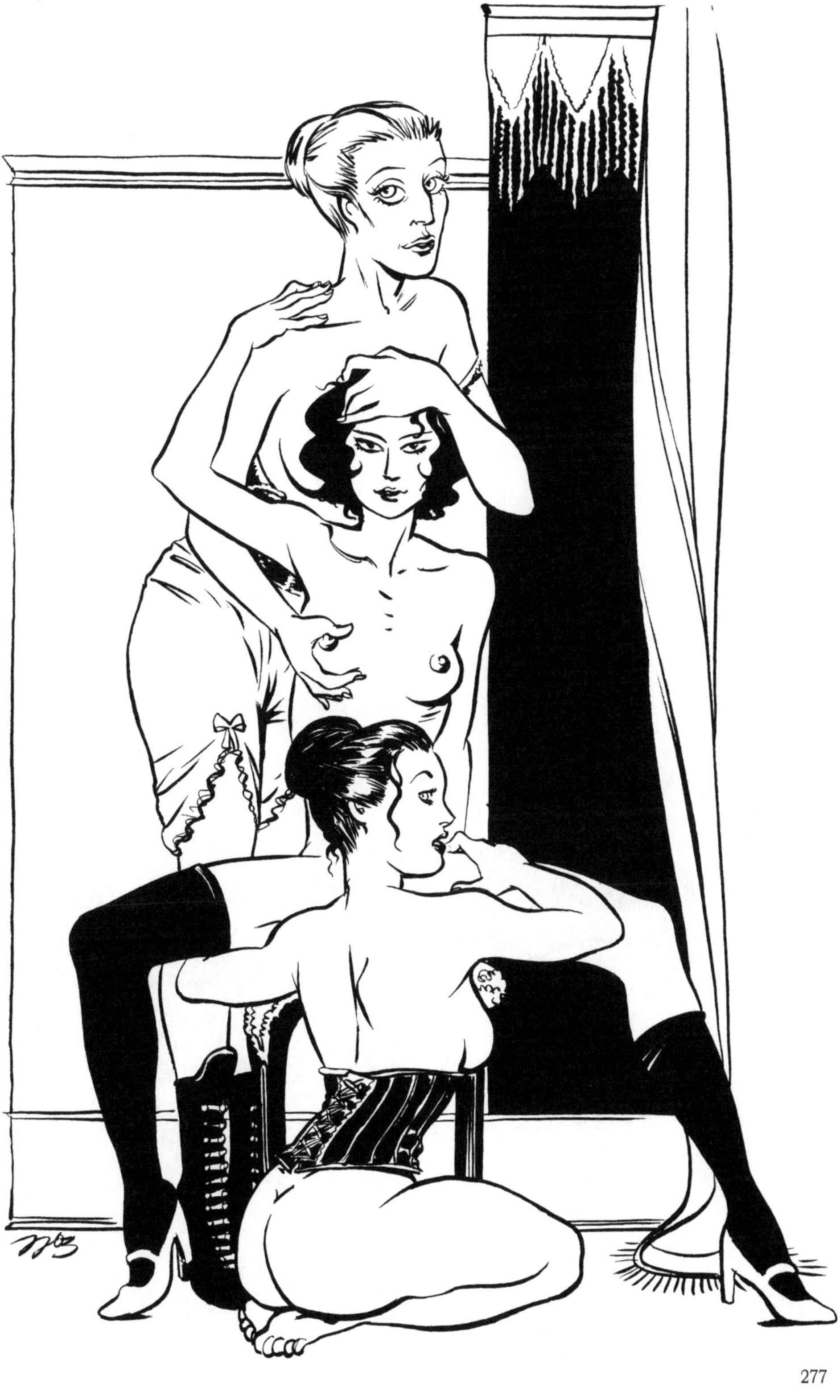

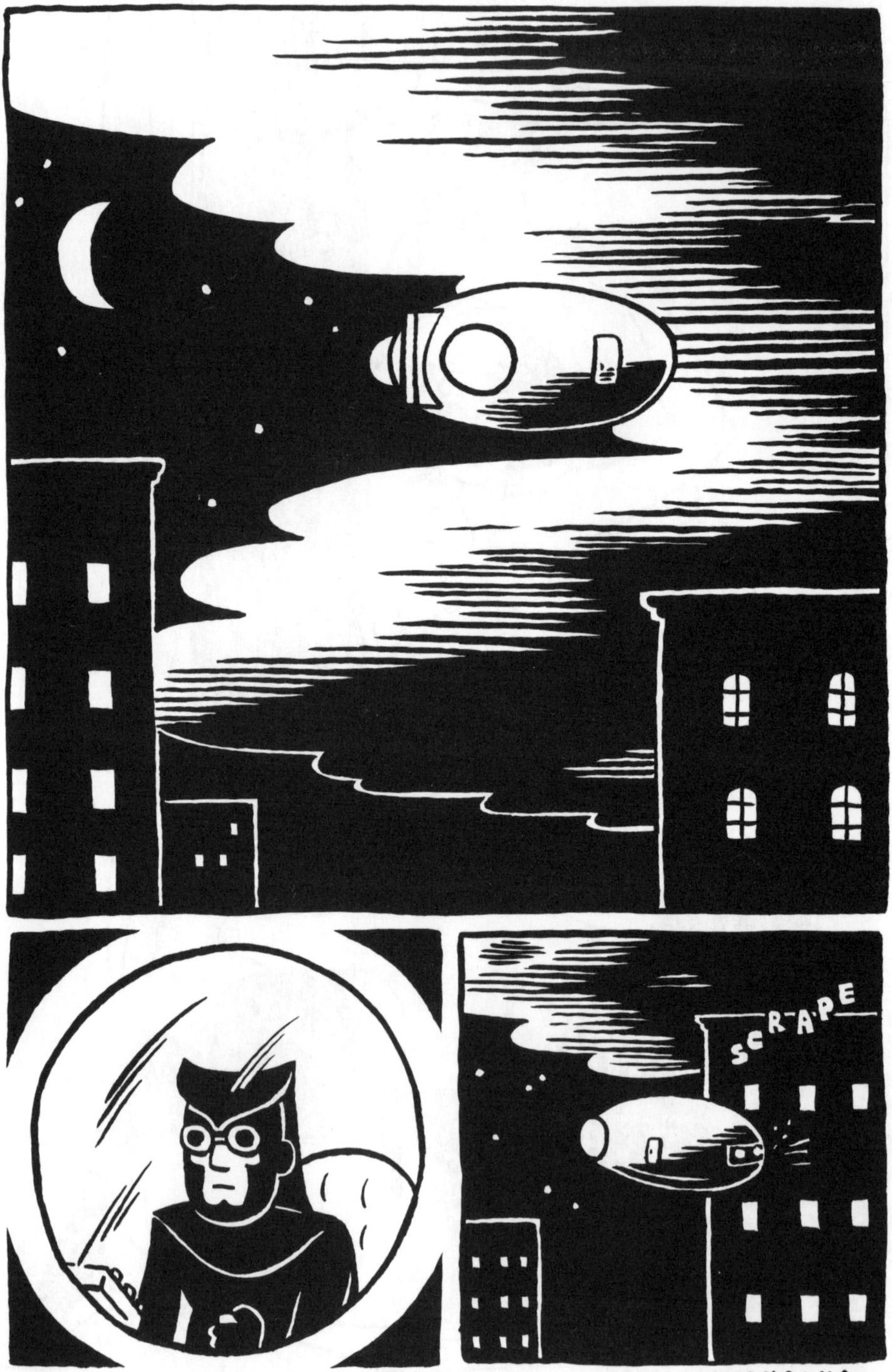
SCRAPE
KOCHALKA

REGIME CHANGE IN WHITECHAPEL

IAIN SINCLAIR

Iain Sinclair is a writer and filmmaker. His novels include **White Chappell, Scarlet Tracings, Downriver** *and* **Landon's Tower.** *His most recent book,* **London Orbital** *describes a walk around the M25 motorway. He works in Hackney. And escapes to Hastings.*

Text ©2003 Iain Sinclair

Back in the dog days of the last century, before the restaurants in Brick Lane featured celebrity snaps of Prince Charles and a few dejected English cricketers on the piss and somebody in suit and tie who used to read the news (Falklands, Gulf War), a bunch of cultural subversives were gathered to enact, in their own ways, the last rites. The skeletal book-burner John Latham with his mad eyes and posthumous (slow, deadly) voice. Derek Raymond, jaunty, spry, fruity, smart, remembering what it had been like to be Robin Cook - and writing a cod-Bond novel that went so far off the rails that it froze time, a period in the Sixties, and entered all the dictionaries of slang. Poet and performance artist Brian Catling, shaven-headed, cigar-chomping, berobed, returning to scenes of vision and poverty, labours in the ullage cellar of Truman's Brewery. Alexander Baron, solid but tentative, white raincoat like the negative of a lost life; post-war wanderings through a blasted landscape. And fellow Jewish memory-man, Emanuel Litvinoff, who once discussed alchemical epics with Elias Canetti. A few villains were also present: Tony Lambrianou, chauffeur to the rug-wrapped corpse of Jack the Hat, and the now vanished biblio-maniac Driffield. Then there was Alan Moore. The excuse was a film for Channel 4, *The Cardinal and the Corpse* - which suffered from too many cardinals and not enough corpses (the dead wouldn't lie down). Of all the faces who had to hang around, in Cheshire Street market, in the house with the peeling pink door in Princelet Street (now a regular feature in Dickens heritage romps), in the infamous Carpenters Arms (with its lost apostrophe), only one registered with the citizens, ordinary dishonest folk going about their business. 'Are you,' they challenged, not daring to believe it, 'Alan Moore?'

Alan doesn't quite believe it himself: that he is on set, grounded in the future of a definitively erased past, space-time anomalies he will activate in his serial composition, *From Hell.* This grimoire, with its fearsome apparatus of actual and fantastic scholarship, is the ultimate book on the Whitechapel Murders. The endstop. Many, many others, hacks, snoops, chancers, will follow - but they won't register. Game over. Patricia Cornwell, the latest, richest, and most absurd, brings the weight (humourless, pan-global paranoia) of the CIA, forensic SWAT teams, art dealers, foot-in-the-door men to bear on a series of terrible Victorian crimes. She is the wrong book, straddled across the razor-wire of the genre fence. It's like Miss Marple hitting Los Angeles to solve a slasher crime, the slaying of James Ellroy's mother. Wrong game, wrong century.

Not content with world domination, America wants to invade the only thing we have left: the past. They devoured *From Hell.* They liked it and they bought the company. And made it into a 'ghetto story.' With punch, panache, zizz: the stuff they do so well. And

JAMES KOCHALKA

Left: *Musician and cartoonist James Kochalka is the creator of many graphic novels including* **Monkey vs. Robot, Kissers** *and* **Tiny Bubbles.** *He lives in Burlington, VT (in the USA) with his wife Amy and his cat Spandy, all of whom appear in his daily diary comic strip, which can be read online at AmericanElf.com or in printed editions from Top Shelf.*
Strip ©2003 James Kochalka.
Nite Owl is ©2003 DC Comics.

with a brutal disregard for history, so that the pain (which burns through those stones still) of the butchering of Marie Jeanette Kelly is demeaned - by a narrative twist, wrong girl, and a happy John Ford ending in a whitewashed cottage in the west of Ireland. Alan Moore knows that these sentiments can be floated as recalled potentialities, a single flash-frame in a dying consciousness, before the darkness sets in. One bead of bright light before an eternity of stygian black.

Loping down Princelet Street, with a kind of nautical roll, non-metropolitan - backlit Durer hair - Alan stands out; not belonging to these alleys and rat runs, he is visible in ways the other writers are not. The space between what he writes and what he is dissolves. He acts. The rest of them are what they do, talk, words - or quiet moments, caught at a window, of wounded reverie. There is a thing that won't leave them alone, a vulture on the shoulder. 'The general contract,' Derek Raymond called it. Mortality.

Mortality imprints these streets like a miasma. Alan Moore, playing at the 'discovery' of a magical primer, plays at being trapped forever in this house, this place. And so it is. The Vessels of Wrath sail through the sky, clouds pierced by the steeple of Nicholas Hawksmoor's Christ Church. The extraordinary, hallucinogenic structure that has haunted artists and writers (from Leon Kossoff to Peter Ackroyd) catches Alan's eye: a stone needle in a pane of dirty glass. The church, with its balanced weight and mass, marries disparate elements: Greek, Roman, Gothic. As Moore will balance the unwieldy mass of dark history, lies, forgeries, echoes of other writers, Blakean epiphany, Crowley ritual.

There are no accidents here. Moore, on the steps of the church, is passing through, gathering what he needs. The rough walkers, the vagrants, the invisibles who challenge him, are there for the duration; no parole. Shifting facades, fresh scams; nothing changes.

• **Iain Sinclair**

JIM LEE

Right: *Although Jim Lee graduated from Princeton University with a degree in medicine, he decided to try his hand at comic book art. His first publication was* **Alpha Flight,** *in 1986. Jim Lee's first issue of* **X-Men** *sold over a million copies. His publishing house Wildstorm Productions, has launched many successful titles, such as* **Wild C.A.T.S., Stormwatch,** *and* **GEN13** *and is the home of Alan Moore's* **America's Best Comics** *line. Illustration ©2003 Jim Lee*

or them. All the visions. I made them tr

You have to remember h__ __ young and frail...

oung and   afl

How could I admit
I'd invented everythi

I was seven, the first time   __ been missing

nd I said I'd   STR

ETURNED to us.   course. Bu

ade of me...How? Ho   d invente

keep up the prete   I did, the

tricate myself.

Be a g   A

he att

ow cou

d inve

very

A

__le__e

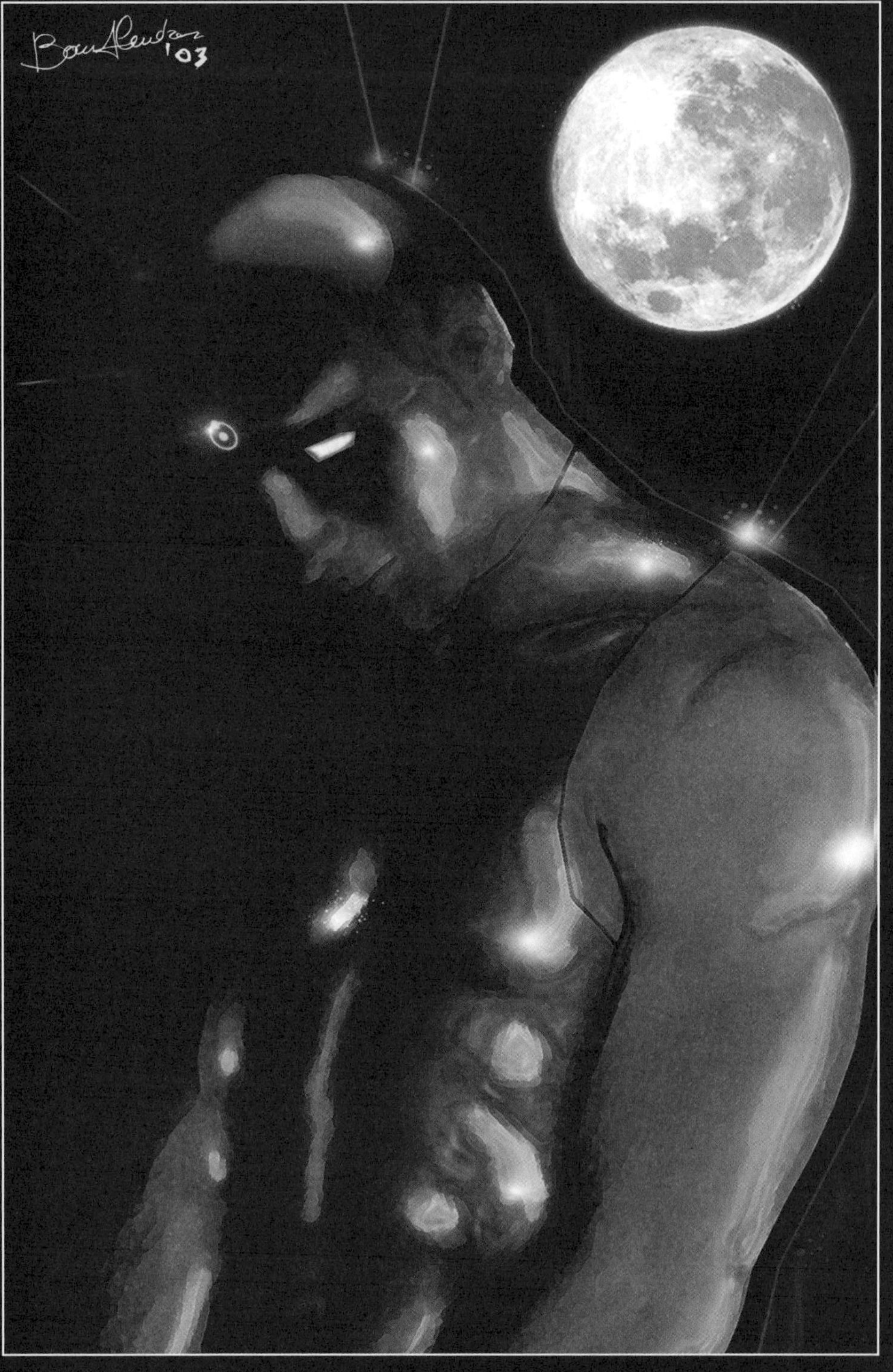

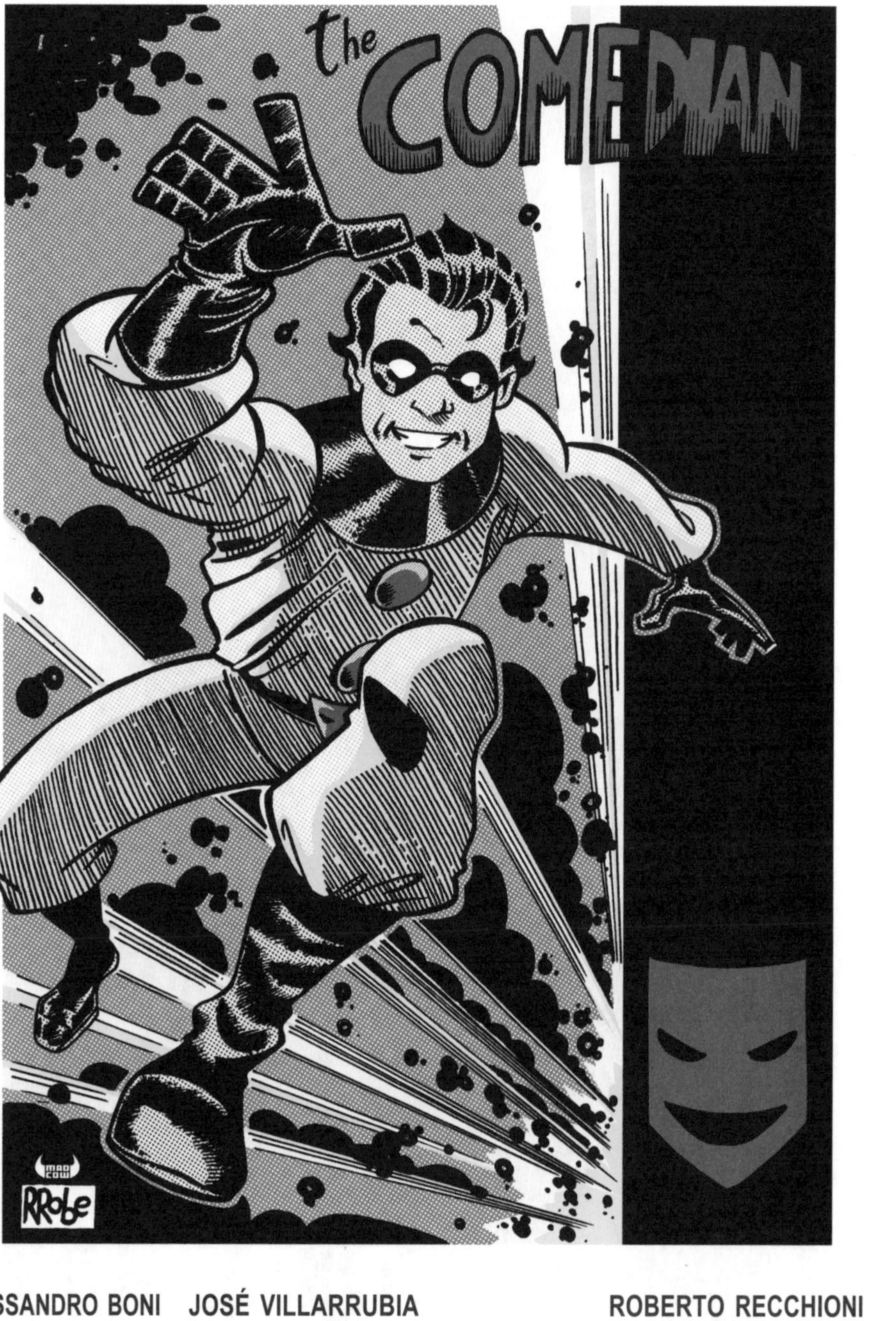
the COMEDIAN
RRobe

ALESSANDRO BONI

Left: *Alessandro Boni is the author of* **Heart of Chastity,** *a well received Italian indie miniseries which mixes horror with eroticism.*
Illustration ©2003 Alessandro Boni
Dr. Manhattan ©2003 DC Comics.

JOSÉ VILLARRUBIA

Pages 284-285 following: *Spanish born José Villarrubia is the award winning digital artist of the book* **Veils** *and has coloured many comic books for Marvel, DC and Image. He is currently producing images for Top Shelf's new editions of Moore's* **Voice of the Fire** *and* **The Mirror of Love.**
Photograph and text ©2003 José Villarrubia.

ROBERTO RECCHIONI

Above: *Roberto Recchioni is an Italian comics writer, penciler and editor. He is working on* **Napoli Ground Zero** *and the upcoming* **John Doe,** *both published by Eura Editoriale.*
Illustration ©2003 Roberto Recchioni
The Comedian ©2003 DC Comics.

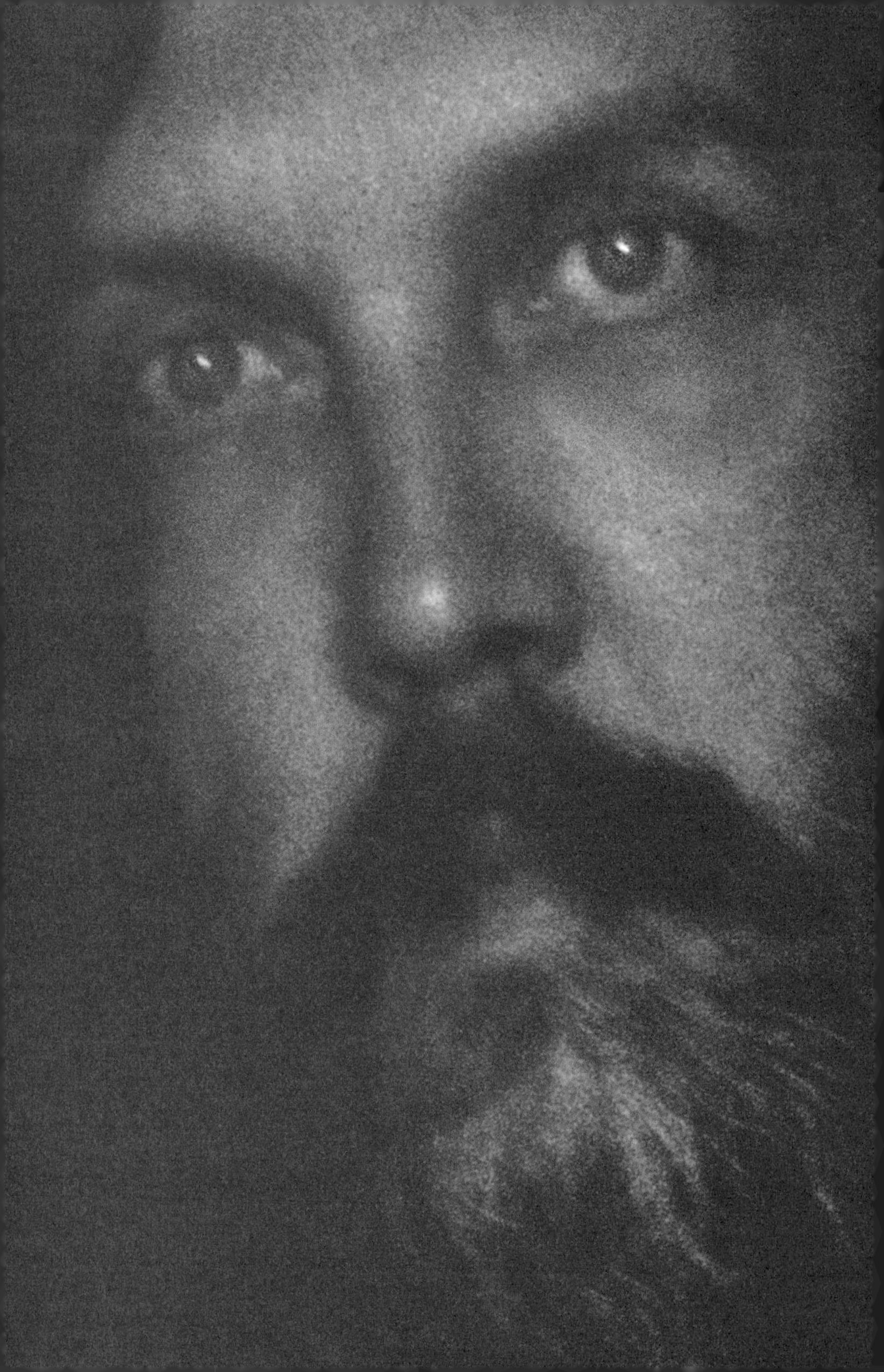

Maybe it was "The Curse". Or perhaps "Rite of Spring" or "Bogeymen". To be honest, it was eighteen years ago (how time flies!) and I don't remember any more. I don't know which was the first story written by Alan Moore that I read. I do know that it was during his American comics debut tenure in "Swamp Thing", a monster comic book that was great when Len Wein and Bernie Wrightson created it, but lost its course with consecutive writers and by then seemed beyond redemption. And yet Alan turned it into something special. Not only he made it scary for the first time, but he also made it relevant. His Swamp Thing stories dealt with classic monsters like vampires, zombies and ghouls, but also featured scarier modern horrors: social prejudice in its many forms, the destruction of the environment, and other themes that had been only treated very coyly in American mainstream comics. And Alan made them fit into a horror context and challenged the readers while scaring the pants out of them. Little did I, or anyone, suspect that shortly after this obviously gifted horror writer would create a series that changed superhero comics forever. "Watchmen" was, and is, an incredible accomplishment, well deserving of the status of masterpiece of the medium. But it did not end there. Alan followed this definite story with several other tours de force: "V for Vendetta", "Marvelman", "The Mirror of Love", "Pictopia", "A Small Killing", "Brought to Light", the sadly aborted "BIG NUMBERS", "From Hell", "Lost Girls" … These stories evolved the comics medium. Alan brought a level of writing of a literary quality unheard of until then, and never surpassed after. Last Summer, my friend the writer Robert Rodi told me that he thinks like Shakespeare, Alan is capable of undertaking a any genre successfully, an unusual feat for any writer working in any medium. His comedic books are funny, his superhero sagas epic, his horror stories frightening and his magical texts mesmerizing. Alan writes these and other types of narratives seemingly effortlessly. But it is not his versatility, amazing, as it is, that made me follow his work so closely all these years. It is the fact that he was the first writer in comics that made me cry. The turning point in "V for Vendetta", the chapter titled "Valerie", broke my heart and lifted me by reminding me of what really matters. It taught me a tough lesson that I will never forget. And this is something unique in Alan: whether he is writing monsters or superheroes or ordinary people, he manages to imbue his stories with true feeling, with real emotion. He is not afraid to take you where it may be uncomfortable, because he knows that the ends can sometimes justify the means. At the heart of the stories you just may find a true of the human experience. Alan is not just an incredible craftsman, gifted with enormous talents for spinning stories beautifully, but a great artist that can touch our souls and is not afraid to do so. For this I will forever be thankful to him.

Jose Villarrubia

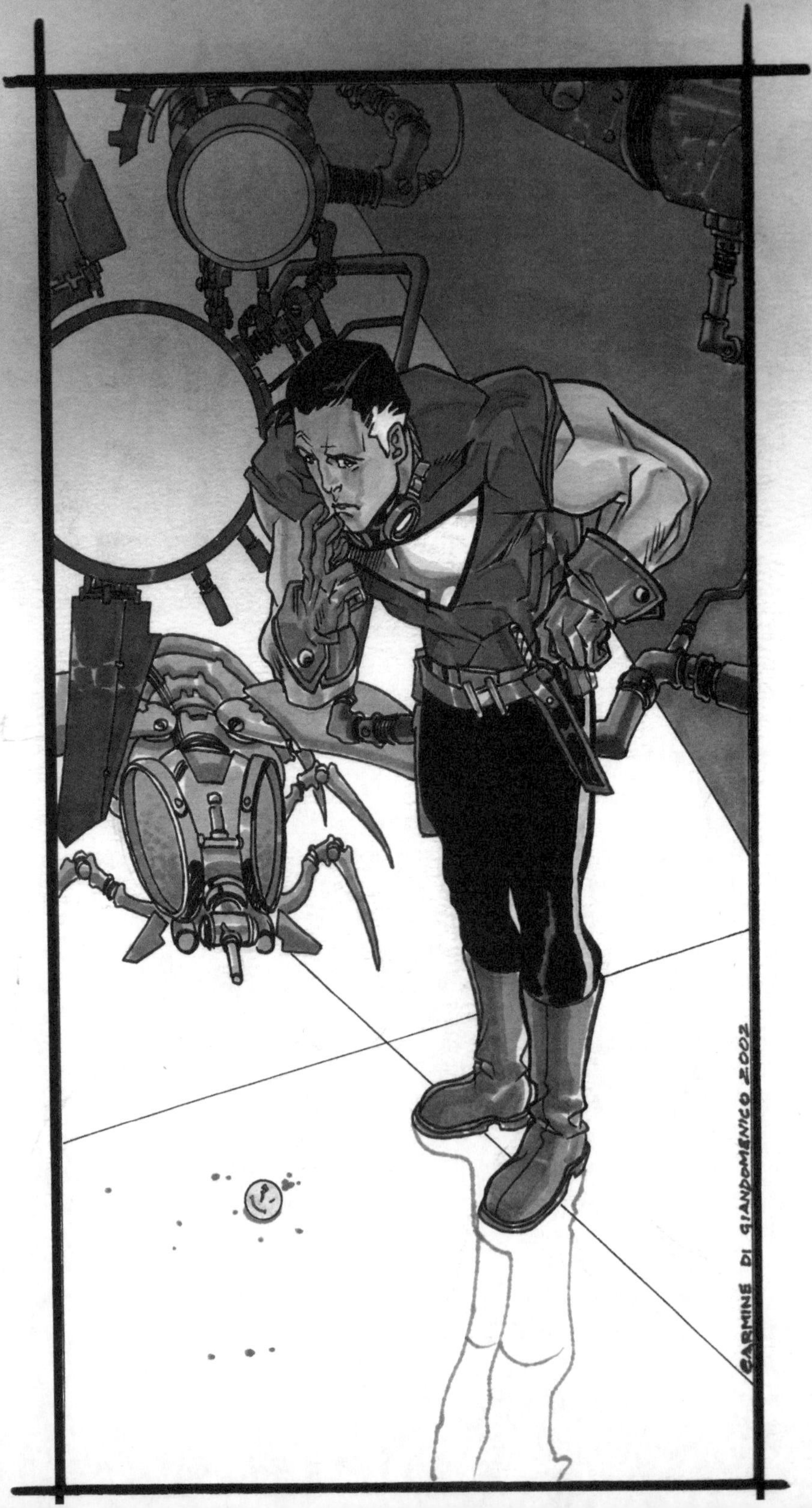
CARMINE DI GIANDOMENICO 2002

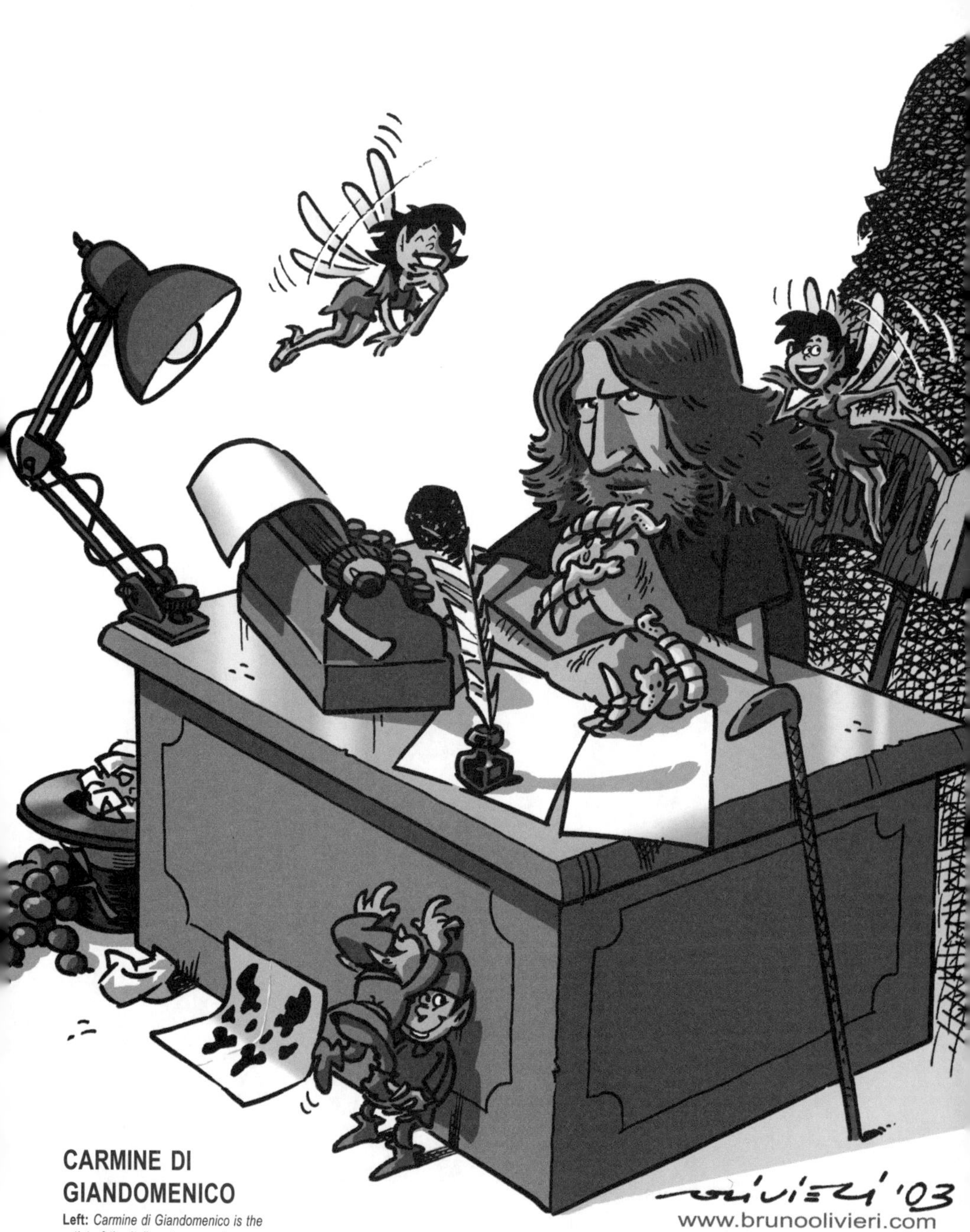

Olivieri '03
www.brunoolivieri.com

CARMINE DI GIANDOMENICO

Left: *Carmine di Giandomenico is the artist of the Italian steam-punk miniseries* **Le avventure di Giulio Maraviglia** *and the dystopian graphic-novel* **La Dottrina.** *He also drew storyboards for Tsui Hark's* **Double Team** *and Martin Scorsese's* **Gangs of New York.**
Illustration ©2003 Carmine Di Giandomenico. Tom Strong ©2003 America's Best Comics, LLC.

BRUNO OLIVIERI

Above: *Bruno Olivieri is an Italian freelance cartoonist. He frequently collaborates as inker and colorist with Disney Italy artist Silvio Camboni. www.brunoolivieri.com. Illustration ©2003 Bruno Olivieri.*

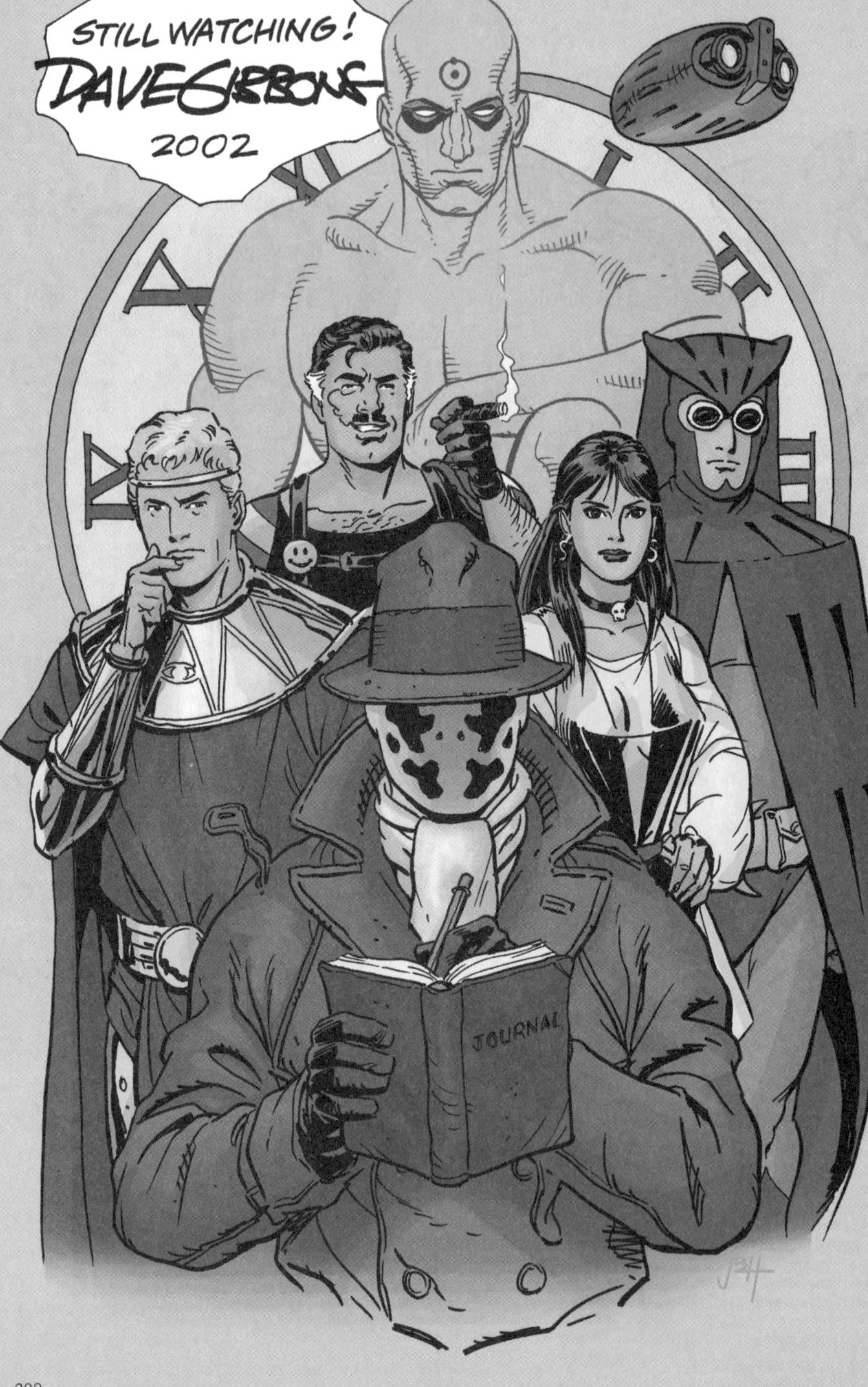
STILL WATCHING!
DAVE GIBBONS
2002
JOURNAL

HOW TO WRITE SUPERHEROES

DARKO MACAN

*Darko Macan was born in Zagreb, Croatia, where he still lives. He drew and wrote many comics, mostly in Croatian, until he started working for Dark Horse Comics in US. He's worked on **Grendel Tales, Star Wars** and **Tarzan** and has also worked for Disney comics.*

Text ©2003 Darko Macan.

1

The biggest lie Alan Moore ever told me was that superheroes were worth reading. A parenthesis is, perhaps, somewhat necessary here: in the heart of the Balkans where I come from, superheroes are not the dominant paradigm in comics. For a few post-war decades they were actively proscribed along with the rest of the "capitalist black-market narcotics". But even when the Party discipline relaxed in the Sixties and the newspaper strips like *Rip Kirby* became widely read, there was no place for superheroes. After spending weeks in the archives I found but one Kirby's *Fantastic Four* page - printed in the leading comics magazine as an illustration of how bad the comics could get. A decade later the situation was even more lax. At least one magazine - a rather slapdash one - was publishing the supers semi-regularly, but it was still very much possible to be a well-informed fan of that art form with only a cursory awareness of the genre.

And then, *Watchmen*.

For the life of me, I cannot remember how I first learned of Alan Moore or *Watchmen*. Those were the times before the Internet, kids, and even the more assertive media like music and movies lagged behind their western releases six to eighteen months here. But I remember that I circled the book's weird cover on a Titan Books flyer sometime in 1988 and entrusted the flyer, along with some savings, to a friend going to UK to visit his au pair sister. The friend - another Alan, by the way, who is now working with the European space program - found the book, read it during his UK stay and brought it to me commenting that it was "very good." For all I know, he might have been the first Croatian to read the book and I endeavoured to become the second. It took me five days (two chapters, two chapters, two chapters, then three and three), my English failed me many times but in the end I could confirm that it was... Well, you've read it. You know how good it is.

A few years later, we, the Balkanites, entered our favourite periodic pastime of wholesale slaughter and there was not a well-informed comic fan to be found anywhere. Yet, occasionally I would meet a friend or an acquaintance weary of the wartime sameness, who would ask me if I were still into comics (yes, I was) and if I had anything good to recommend. Invariably, I thrust *Watchmen* in their hands. Invariably, they came back with a comment that it was very good and asked whether I had something similar. Invariably, I drew a blank.

No, I did not, not really. I had *Maus* and *Love & Rockets* at hand, even Moore's own *Halo Jones*, so I fed them these, similar by virtue of being different, and my friends devoured them happily. But what would have happened if I had tried to give them some other superheroes after they had already absorbed *Watchmen*? You do not follow the prime cut with McFood without leaving a certain hunger unsatisfied. Once you have read *Watchmen* there is not much to follow. Only a Moore can satisfy your hunger for more. And it has been so for the last fifteen years.

Why?

2

From time to time, Moore's originality is questioned. Just last week, for example, I read a review of *Top Ten* whose writer was extremely vexed by the teleport accident scene, claiming that Moore lifted it word-for-word from a *Homicide* episode which had a guy crushed under a subway train. Somebody else, for this was online, quickly countered that there was a long tradition of such scenes in entertainment and proceeded to give a list with which I will not bother you, although I may add an equally useless piece of trivia that Moore himself used a cart-crushed guy in his *Hypothetical Lizard* novella. Before that, there were claims that Moore had borrowed the highly memorable entrance of Jason Blood in *Swamp Thing* from Bulgakov's *Master and Margarita* (and, yes, the similarity is strong) or that he had outright stolen the opening episode of *D.R. & Quinch* from a *National Lampoon* feature which I have never read.

DAVE GIBBONS

Left: *British born Gibbons began his career in 1973, contributing art to* Rogue Trooper *for* **2000 AD.** *In the US, he drew* **Green Lantern** *for DC and collaborated with Alan Moore on the highly acclaimed* **Watchmen.** *He also worked with Frank Miller on his* **Martha Washington** *series. As a writer, Gibbons has also worked on* **Batman Versus Predator and World's Finest.** *He's currently completing his semi-autobiographical graphic novel,* **The Originals** *for DC.*

colour by John Higgins

Illustration ©2003 Dave Gibbons.
Watchmen ©2003 DC Comics.

The accusers usually voice their condemnations with a hurt surprise and a feeling of betrayal and I always find myself torn between two immediate impulses: the wish to defend Moore and the urge to join the lynch mob to crucify the thief. In the end, I do neither.

I do nothing because both impulses are knee-jerk and stupid. The originality is most appreciated by those who have none and most demanded by those who are unable to recognize it in its true form. For the original thought is not only the one which is virgin-birthed into the universe (those are few and far apart), but also the one which is dug out of mud and given a new polish by a caring mind. The handcuffs and hacksaw scene in *Watchmen* might have been a rather faithful copy of the *Mad Max* finale and Ozymandias' plan pilfered out of some old *Outer Limits* episode. Nevertheless, it is not because of those elements that my worn-out copy of the Moore/Gibbons collaboration is being returned by its borrowers with a pleased and appreciative nod. Every time. *Watchmen* works because the whole has all the components of a good wedding: something old and something new, something borrowed and something blue (that'd be Dr. Manhattan). *Watchmen* works because Moore wrote it the way he has written every comic of his I have ever read: with a brain, with a heart and with a wink.

It would be too easy to praise *Watchmen*, so I won't. And I need not do it to show you the workings of Moore's brain. Let us take a look at, say, *Spawn vs. WildC.A.T.s* instead, perhaps one of Moore's lesser efforts. In it, in some projected future, we find the characters speaking slang derived from the Netspeak of today. It was not done very expertly, more in a ham-handed way of someone who may be familiar with the Internet only by proxy perhaps, but it was done with two crucial characteristics of intelligence: curiosity and respect. It could have been done as a parody, mocking the silly customs of the no-good youth in the way pre-WWII cartoonists satirized the hippies, but Moore avoided that trap. To mock what we do not understand is too easy. Even a failed attempt at understanding is admirable. In *1963*, his conscious attempt at stupid comics of yesteryear, Moore failed to be stupid enough: his take on the T-Rex-on-the-loose standard makes the point out of the lizard's useless forelimbs just as well as his version of Hulk managed to combine the theory of glass as a very slow liquid, nuclear explosions, molecular physics and the sixties-type Reds-paranoia. All without losing the sense of the story for even a moment. And those were all little smarts. When Moore is firing on all cylinders, he impresses us to the point of depression - the "ocean of emotion" or similar sequences from *Promethea* come to mind; I won't even go into the revisionist Tarot-slash-anagrams-slash-anecdote issue of the same series - he displays the workings of a brain which has too much fun with itself while managing to pay attention to every loose end and each minor character, a brain whose likeness we may only hope to find behind the reality we happen to inhabit.

And yet, a brain without a heart would be a sterile conductor of thought experiments, a fannish exercise in outsmarting others for the sake of being the idlest superior cerebrum. Luckily for us, Moore has just enough heart to temper his intellect. He loves all those people he births onto the paper - his strong women and his weak males (from the beginning, from *Captain Britain* or *Miracleman* his superheroes tend to fall into two categories: the slow of mind but good-hearted and the brilliant bastards, an interesting dichotomy deserving of a separate analysis). He loves his readers enough not to ever short-change them, he has a healthy dose of love for himself, and he loves - God help him - comics and superheroes. Those endless pastiches in *Supreme* and then in *Cobweb* ... those were intellectual exercises, but they could not have been done without love. Think on it: how limited must the audience be to equally appreciate the Kirby and Kurtzman references, the reworkings of inane kiddie comics and the use of the 19th century French engravings? All the work that went into the hidden references of *The League of Extraordinary Gentlemen* cannot be explained away as a perverse wish to play hide-and-seek with the collective mind of World Wide Web indexers and archivists. They may seem a completely pointless endeavour till we remember that it was Moore himself who said, "Love has no point. Love *is* the point."

How doomed it is to love comics, the art form which will fuck you back if you say you

BILL MORRISON

Right: *Bill Morrison was recruited to draw* **The Simpsons** *in 1990, and has contributed to an enormous enclave of books, calendars, magazines, T-shirts and all things Simpson. Since 1994, Bill has served as editor and as a principal writer and artist at Bongo Comics, helping to creatively oversee the Simpson's Comics line. Bill's own creation,* **Roswell, Little Green Man,** *was the first non-Simpson's title to be published by Bongo Comics.*
www.littlegreenman.com
Illustration ©2003 Bill Morrison.
Silk Spectre ©2003 DC Comics.

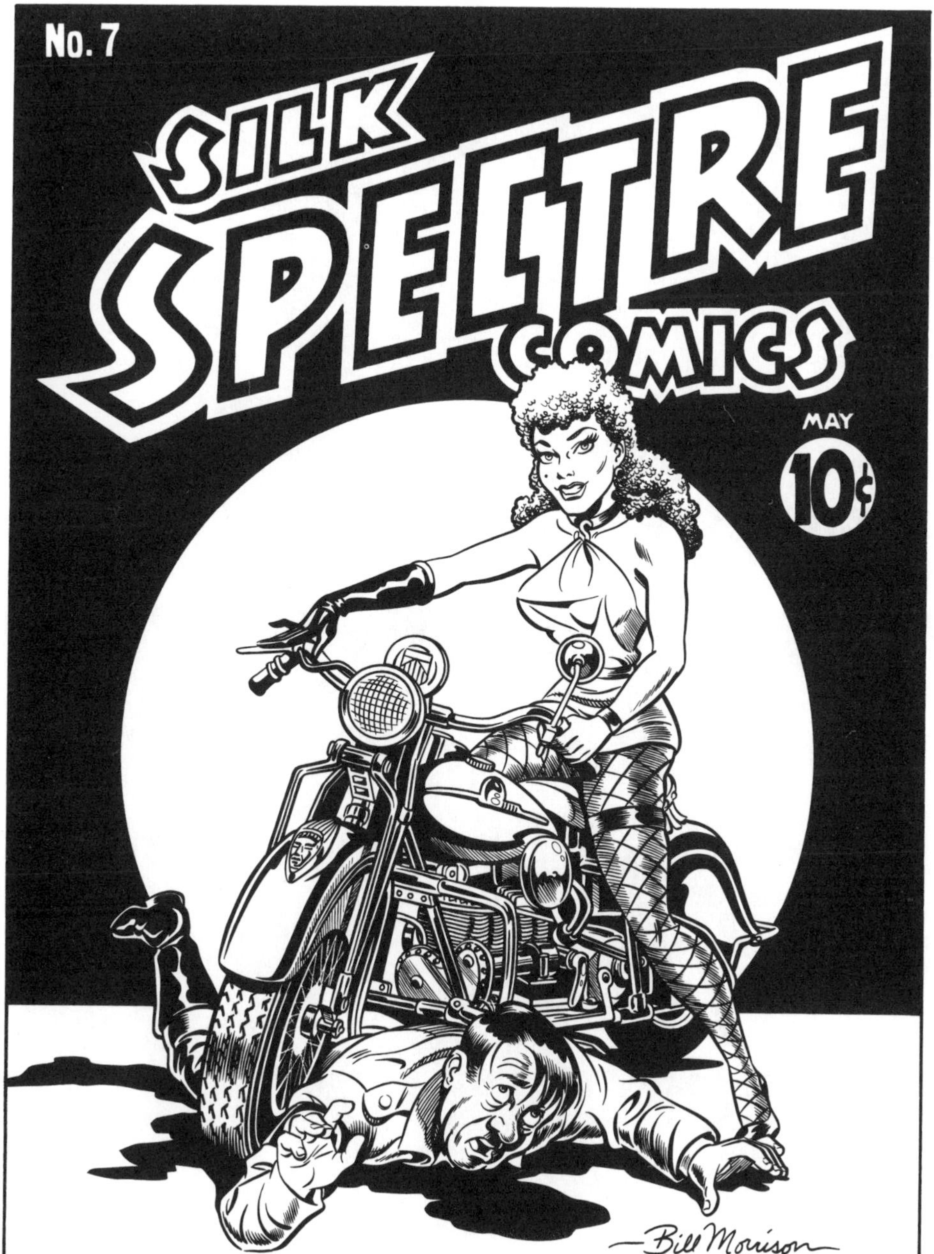
No. 7
SILK SPECTRE COMICS
MAY
10¢
—Bill Morrison—

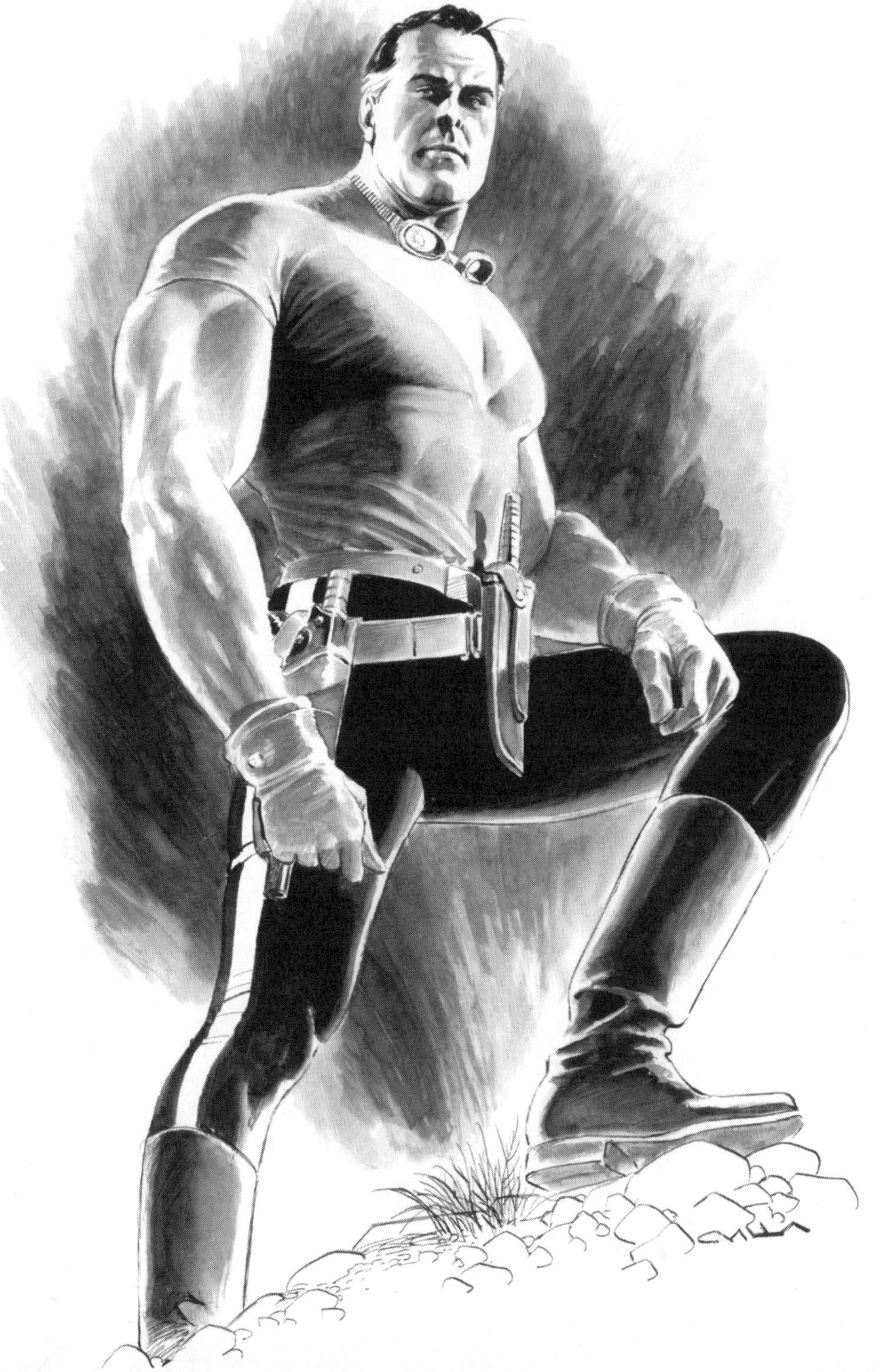

love it, because it is too young to know the difference? This is where the wink comes in. The famous wink from the close of *Whatever Happened To The Man of Tomorrow?*, the wink which is curiously absent from Moore's more ambitious work in prose and poetry, the wink which is a pact reserved for a four-colour brotherhood, a hand across the chasm of the page or understanding. We are doomed, tomorrow if not today, but we have shared a story for a moment, a thrill or two, a few laughs. We have tried and we like each other. It may not be much, it certainly is nothing important but it is plenty. Right?

A brain. A heart. A wink. A friend of mine once called himself an Alanist, affirming that he worshiped Alan Moore. I sometimes wonder whether Alan Moore exists or is he just an afterimage conceived by our minds after stealing a look at the holy trinity touched upon above.

3

I have never read *Watchmen* for a second time. I have opened it now and then, read a few pages, flipped through a chapter. I have never read it again in its entirety because I did not have to. It is already burned upon my brain.

I have read good comics later on, even brilliant ones. I have read fine superhero comics, fuelled by hate or love for the genre. I have read each and every issue of every superhero comic Moore has written upon his return to the genre and I happen to agree that *Tom Strong* is a better template for a durable serial superhuman entertainment than *Watchmen* could ever be (one more issue of *Watchmen* and we would enter soap opera territory). Yet, I do not think *Watchmen* could ever be surpassed. And I do not believe I think so only because that book came at the right time for me.

By all accounts, *Watchmen* avoided being a piece of the Charlton fan fiction by a fluke of editorial vacillation. Given freedom, Moore and Gibbons managed to produce a very, very good comic which at the same time was a summation of the comic book past, an accurate novelistic picture of the times of its conception and the portent of the times to come. Moore has done better books (*V for Vendetta* is often cited as a example), warmer comics (*Halo Jones* is my favourite) and more personal works (those CDs where his Northampton accent completely baffles my Balkan ear; oh well, they look nice on the shelf and impress the pagans), but none more important or having a greater impact. *Watchmen* helped the comics industry up on its feet, without noticing it was aiding a paraplegic.

There have been many attempts at replicating the *Watchmen* "formula", but none have succeeded. The tortured epithet-laden phrases substituted poorly for the elegance of Moore's wit, the epigone bastards failed to be brilliant and the heroes were neither lovably dumb, nor good at heart. But most of all, the wink was absent, there was no understanding of the rules in the comics game. These wannabe-Moores wanted the *Watchmen* money and the *Watchmen* fame, demanded them loudly and lewdly, but forgot to woo us with convincing lies, to put their everything into their words.

And this is something Moore never forgets. He has produced weak scripts but never, one feels, for the lack of trying (for the trying in the wrong direction, perhaps). I, for one, have never felt cheated after reading an Alan Moore's comic book. No, not even after *Blood Feud*.

Which is why *Watchmen* remains where it is, eighteen years on.

Which is why it is a brilliant book to hook your friends with, but a damned tough act to follow.

Which is why Alan Moore is such a terrific liar that he could convince me - like so few before him and even fewer since - that superheroes were worth reading. And I think I may have even figured out how he wrote superheroes so true.

You see, you have to be one yourself first...

Cheers!

• **Darko Macan,**
Zagreb, twelve days past the very last deadline

MATT KINDT

Pages 294-295 following:
Matt Kindt is the co-creator and artist of the **Pistolwhip** *series from Top Shelf and is currently at work on a 300 page WWII spy graphic novel* **2 Sisters** *about...two sisters, pirates and V-2 rockets over London. Strip ©2003 Matt Kindt. All characters are ©2003 their respective copyright holders.*

CLAUDIO VILLA

Left: *Claudio Villa is one of the most famous and acclaimed Italian artists. He is the regular cover artist of Italy's best selling comic and national icon* **Tex,** *published by Bonelli Comics since 1948.
Illustration ©2003 Claudio Villa
Tom Strong ©2003 DC Comics*

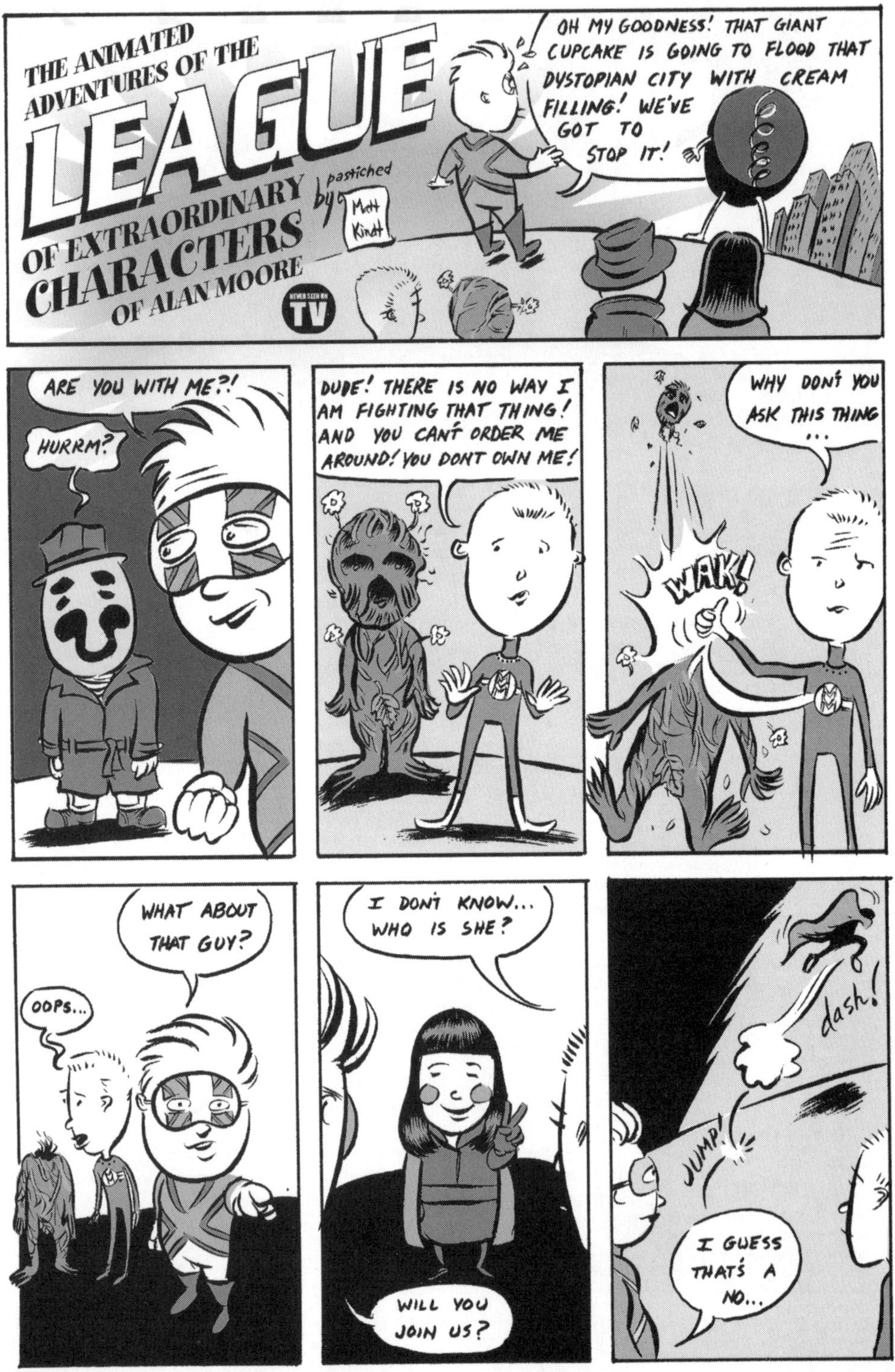
THE ANIMATED ADVENTURES OF THE
LEAGUE
OF EXTRAORDINARY CHARACTERS
OF ALAN MOORE
pastiched by Matt Kindt
NEVER SEEN ON TV
OH MY GOODNESS! THAT GIANT CUPCAKE IS GOING TO FLOOD THAT DYSTOPIAN CITY WITH CREAM FILLING! WE'VE GOT TO STOP IT!
ARE YOU WITH ME?!
HURRM?
DUDE! THERE IS NO WAY I AM FIGHTING THAT THING! AND YOU CAN'T ORDER ME AROUND! YOU DONT OWN ME!
WHY DON'T YOU ASK THIS THING ...
WAK!
WHAT ABOUT THAT GUY?
OOPS...
I DON'T KNOW... WHO IS SHE?
WILL YOU JOIN US?
dash!
JUMP!
I GUESS THAT'S A NO...

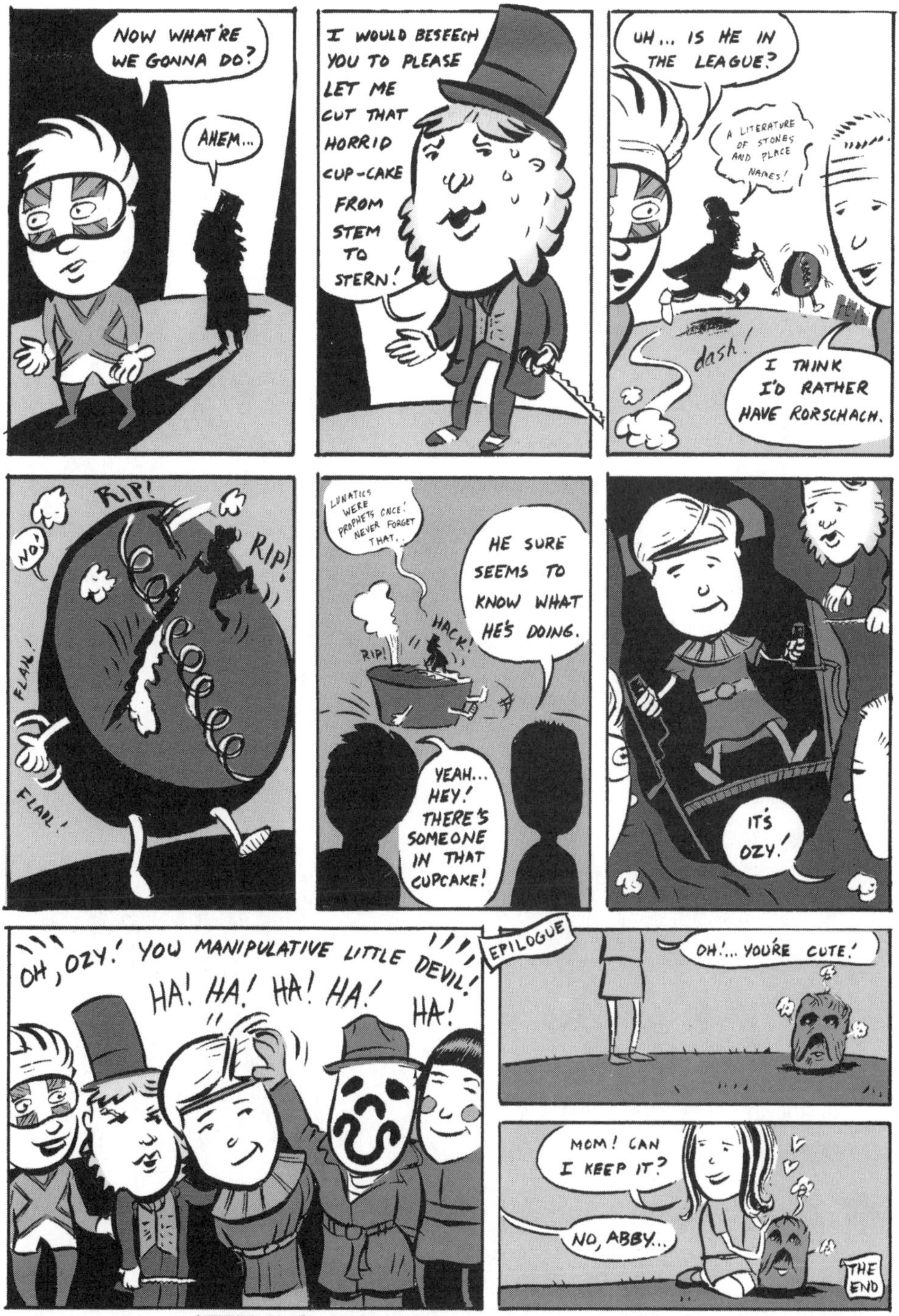
NOW WHAT'RE WE GONNA DO?
AHEM...
I WOULD BESEECH YOU TO PLEASE LET ME CUT THAT HORRID CUP-CAKE FROM STEM TO STERN!
UH... IS HE IN THE LEAGUE?
A LITERATURE OF STONES AND PLACE NAMES!
dash!
I THINK I'D RATHER HAVE RORSCHACH.
RIP!
RIP!
NO!
FLAIL!
FLAIL!
LUNATICS WERE PROPHETS ONCE! NEVER FORGET THAT...
HE SURE SEEMS TO KNOW WHAT HE'S DOING.
HACK!
RIP!
YEAH... HEY! THERE'S SOMEONE IN THAT CUPCAKE!
IT'S OZY!
OH, OZY! YOU MANIPULATIVE LITTLE DEVIL!
HA! HA! HA! HA! HA!
EPILOGUE
OH!... YOU'RE CUTE!
MOM! CAN I KEEP IT?
NO, ABBY...
THE END

HEY KIDS! IT'S AN APPENDIX: PAGE 1, PANEL 1: Homage of Dr. Manhattan in Vietnam. PAGE 1, PANEL 2: From Watchmen issue #5, page 6, panel 1. PAGE 2, PANEL 3: From Hell Chapter 2, page 29. PAGE 2, PANEL 5: From Hell Chapter 2, page 30. PAGE 2, PANEL 6: Watchmen issue #11, page 27. PAGE 2, PANEL 8,9: Swamp Thing: Love & Death Trade, page 197.

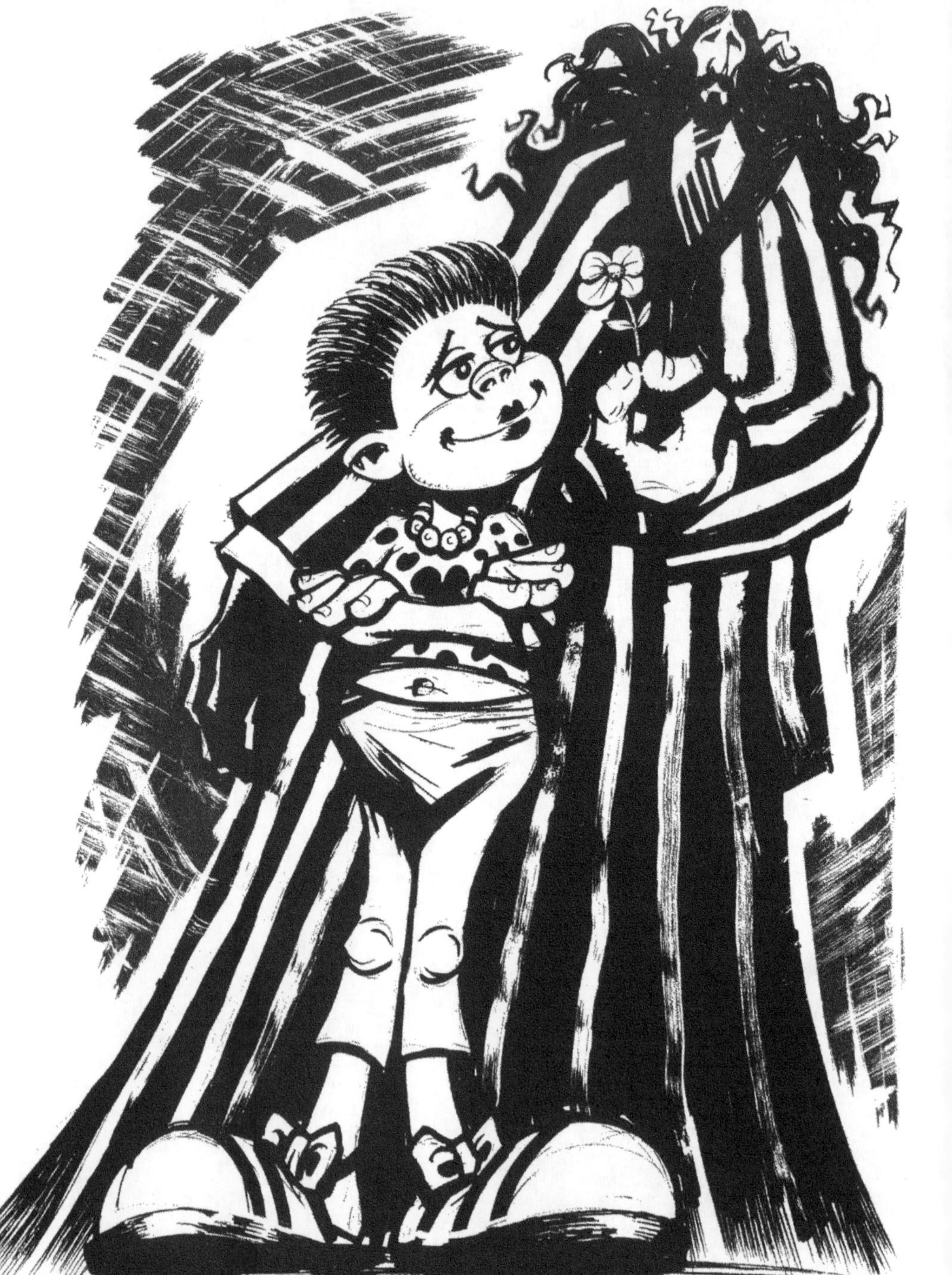

BLUE MAN BLUES

JOHN HIGGINS

John Higgins started working as artist at **2000AD** *around the same time as Alan Moore and drew some of his Future Shocks strips, as well as Judge Dredd. He was also the colourist on* **Watchmen** *and The* **Killing Joke** *and painted a year's worth of covers for* **Swamp Thing** *Text ©2003 John Higgins.*

Alan Moore a comic Genius.

Not impressed.

Alan Moore changed the face of modern comics.

Still not impressed.

Alan Moore at a comic convention in London in the mid-1980's at the start of the WATCHMEN phenomenon, dressed (in his usual understated style) in a candy-striped suit. He is the star attraction of the convention, and the centre of attention for hundreds of comics fans and fellow professionals a like.

Everyone wants a bit of his time, but Alan had decided the most important person there was a bored six-year-old girl at her first comics convention. She doesn't know or care who the hell this hirsute and interestingly garbed giant is, but is enthralled as he proceeds to entertain her with stories, conversation and magic tricks and made her the centre of all his attention.

Now I'm impressed!

I can think of very few other people who would have or even could have done the same thing in his position.

To work with Alan has been a creative joy, and to read Alan's work has given me many hours of entertainment. If that was all to say about him, that would still be more than enough to sing his praises here. But that six year-old girl was, and is one of the most important people in my life—my daughter, Jenna. And for me, that long ago incident underlines what it is that makes Alan Moore special and why he is such a creative powerhouse. He really does care about the little things!

I was one small part of the WATCHMEN team, and right from the beginning Alan (and Dave) made me feel fully part of that team, how ever minor my input was. Though there is one totally and original first I can claim in relationship to the WATCHMEN.

WRITER WITHOUT HEAD

Pages 298-301 following:
Writer Without Head is the pseudonym for a secret collective of comic, theatre and novel writers from Spain.

AILANTD

Ailantd is a Spanish comics artist and designer of 3D virtual landscapes. Some of his comics work has been collected in **MMM Histories** *and he has also contributed to* **Alan Moore's Magic Words,** *adapting Moore's lyrics into comic strip form. Strip ©2003 Writer Without Head & Ailantd.*

I told the very first WATCHMEN joke.

One of the earliest WATCHMEN plotting sessions between Alan and Dave took place in a London pub beer garden. It was early March, and it was too damned chilly to be sitting outside drinking cold beer. They were postulating theories on how Dr Manhattan could materialise, "Would there be an electrical charge before he arrived or after he left?" "Would the displacement of oxygen atoms be violent enough to make a noise?" "Would he create a vacuum when he left an environment?" This was their job, my job was the colour, and all I knew about Dr Manhattan was, he was blue. "Dave, Alan, I feel a little bit like Dr Manhattan just now!" They both gave me a look of polite interest. "I think my dick has turned blue in the cold."

OK it might not have been a very funny WATCHMEN joke, but it was definitely the first!

What can one say about Alan Moore that has not been said before? I have no idea!

JOHN HIGGINS

Left: *Higgins painted* **The Thing From Another World** *for Dark Horse and has also worked on* **Pride and Joy** *and* **Hellblazer** *with Garth Ennis before self-publishing* **Razorjack.** *www.turmoilcolour.com Illustration ©2003 John Higgins.*

Just believe it all and know he is a one off.

• **John Higgins**
February 2003

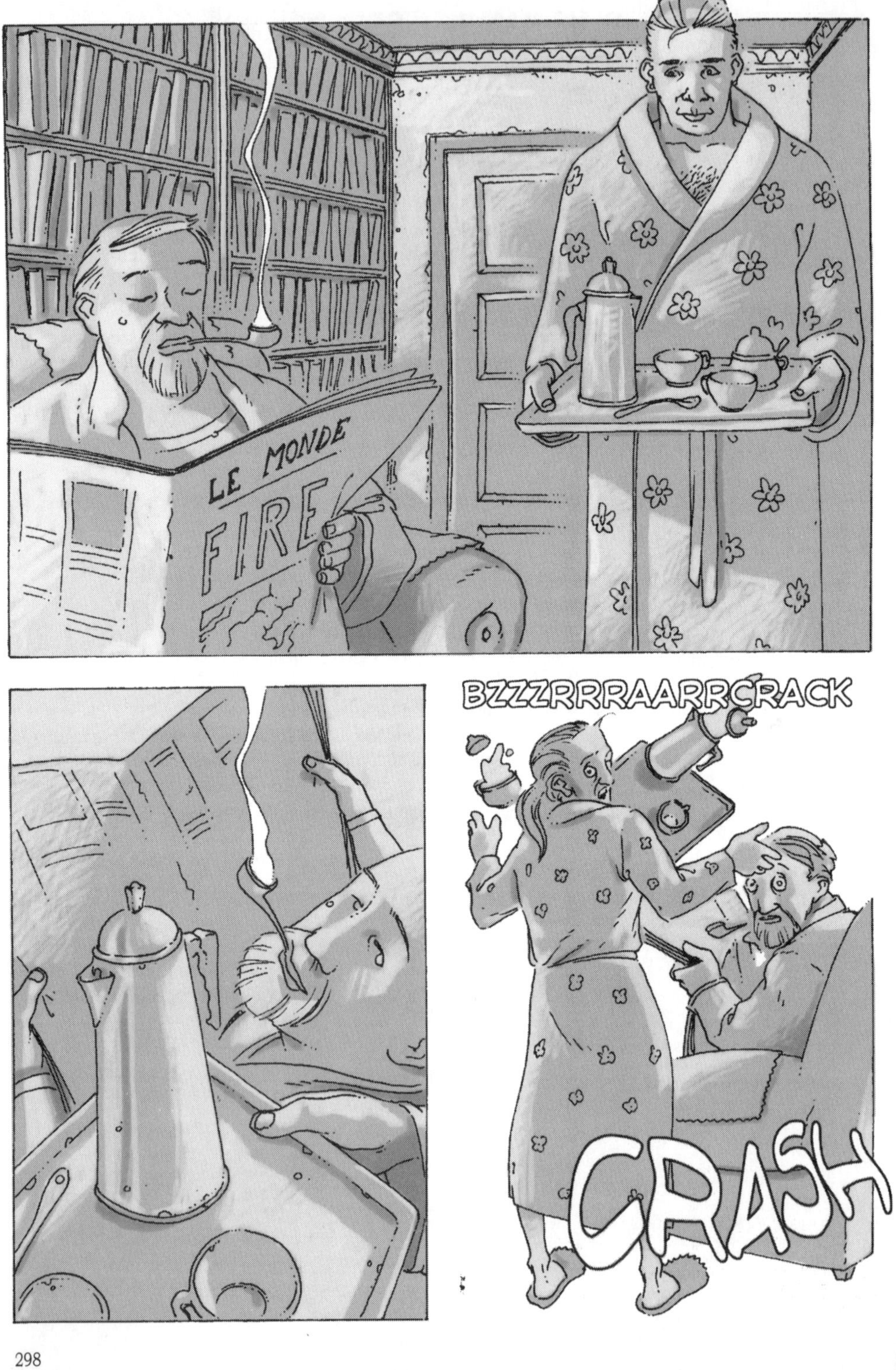
LE MONDE
FIRE
BZZZRRRAARRCRACK
CRASH

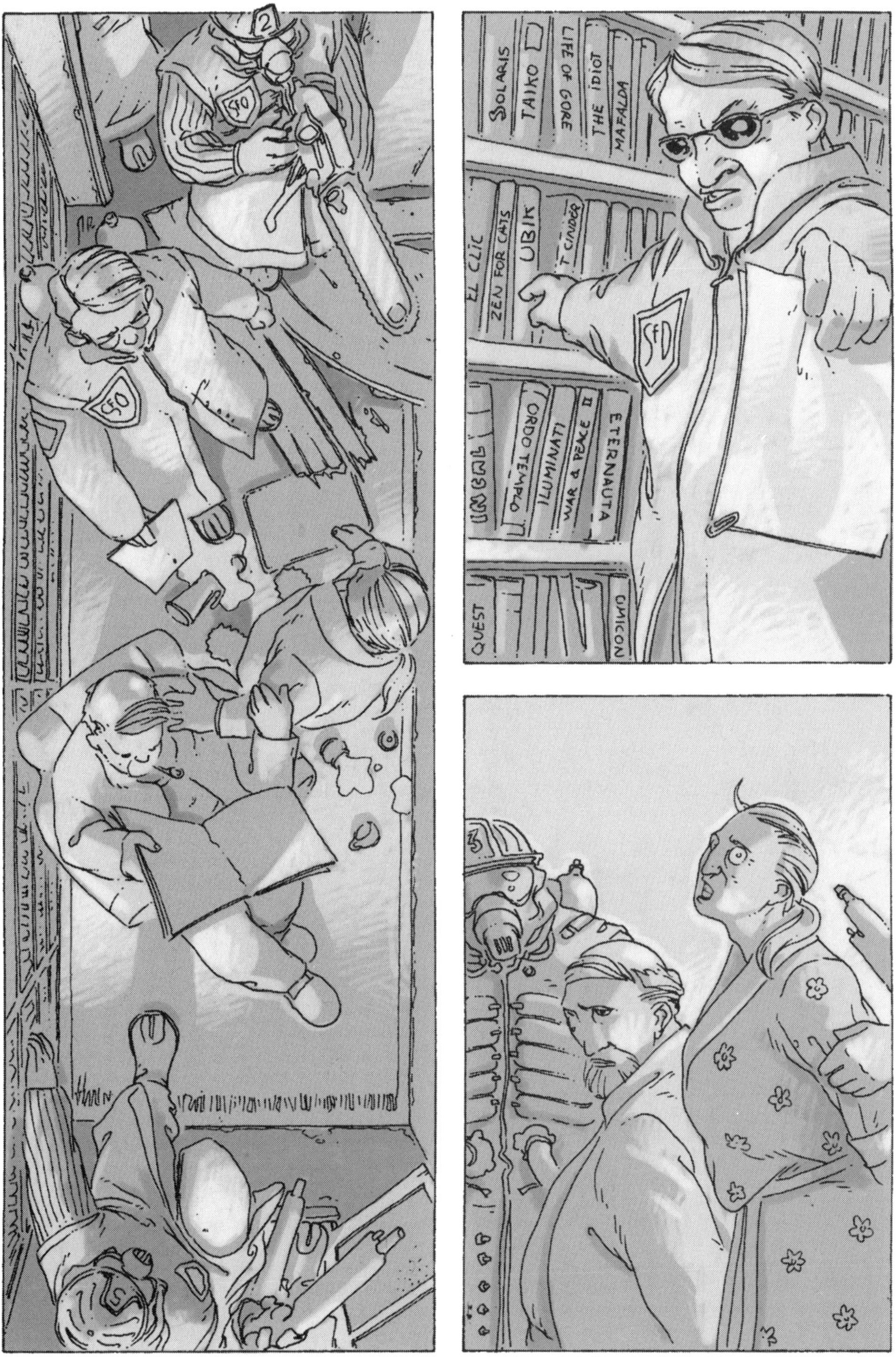
SOLARIS
TAIKO
LIFE OF GORE
THE IDIOT
MAFALDA
ZEN FOR CATS
UBIK
T CINDER
ORDO TEMPLO
ILUMINATI
WAR & PEACE II
ETERNAUTA
QUEST

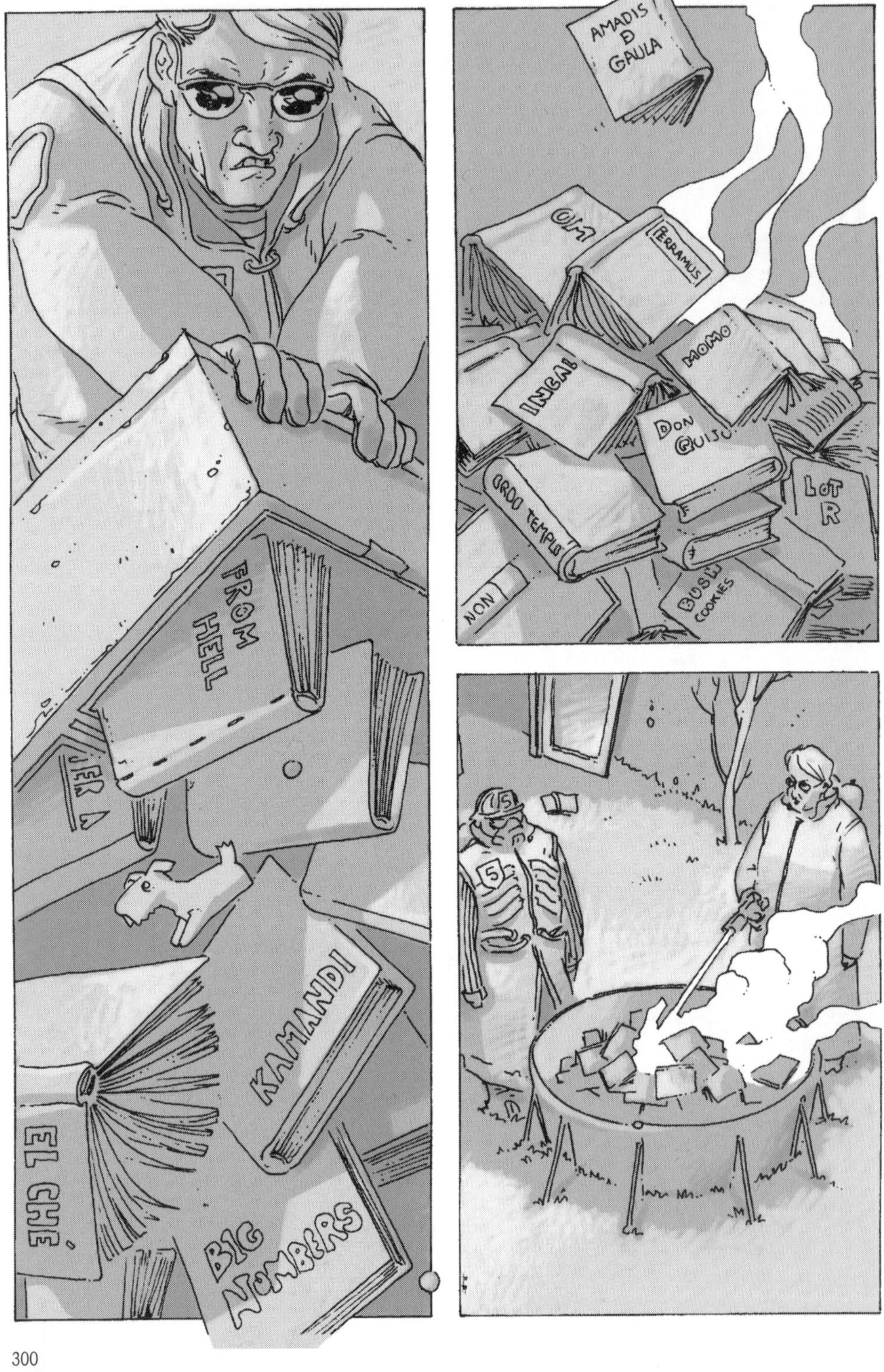
FROM HELL
KAMANDI
EL CHE
BIG NUMBERS
AMADIS D GAULA
PERRAMUS
MOMO
DON QUIJO
LOT R
NON
COOKIES

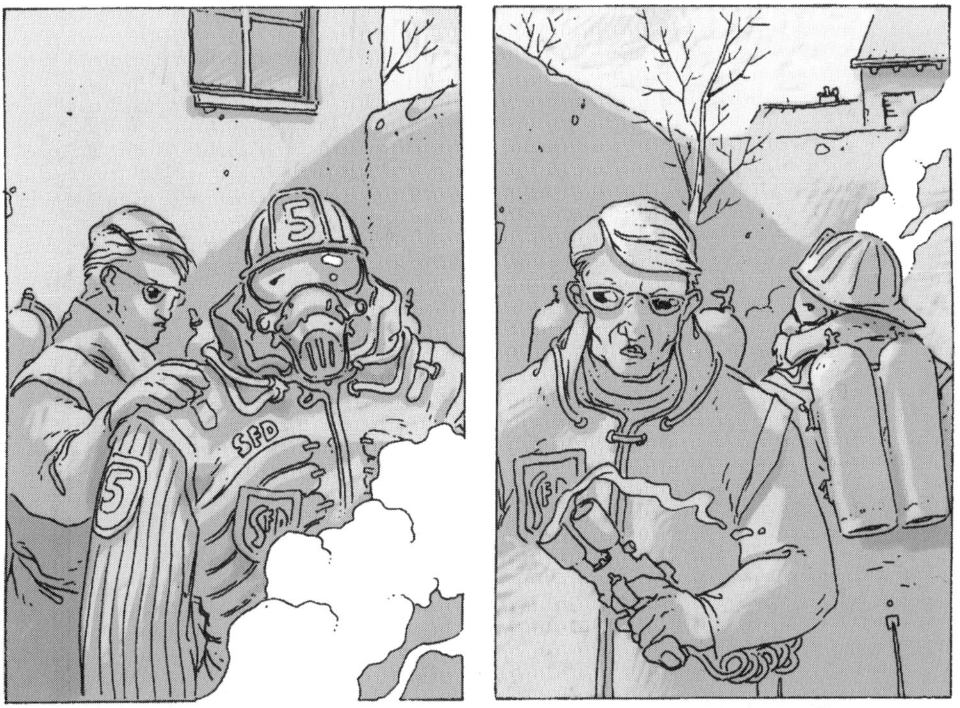
5
SFD

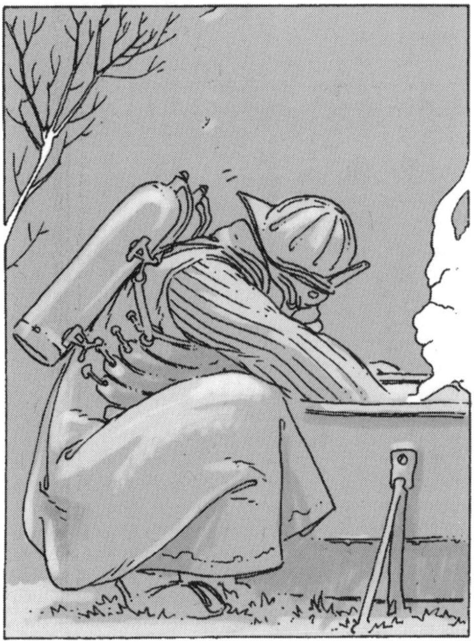

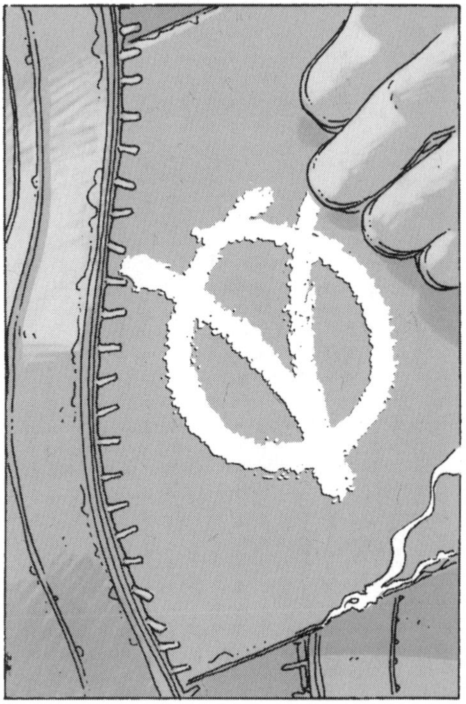

BY **WRITER WITHOUT HEAD**
ART BY **AILANTD**

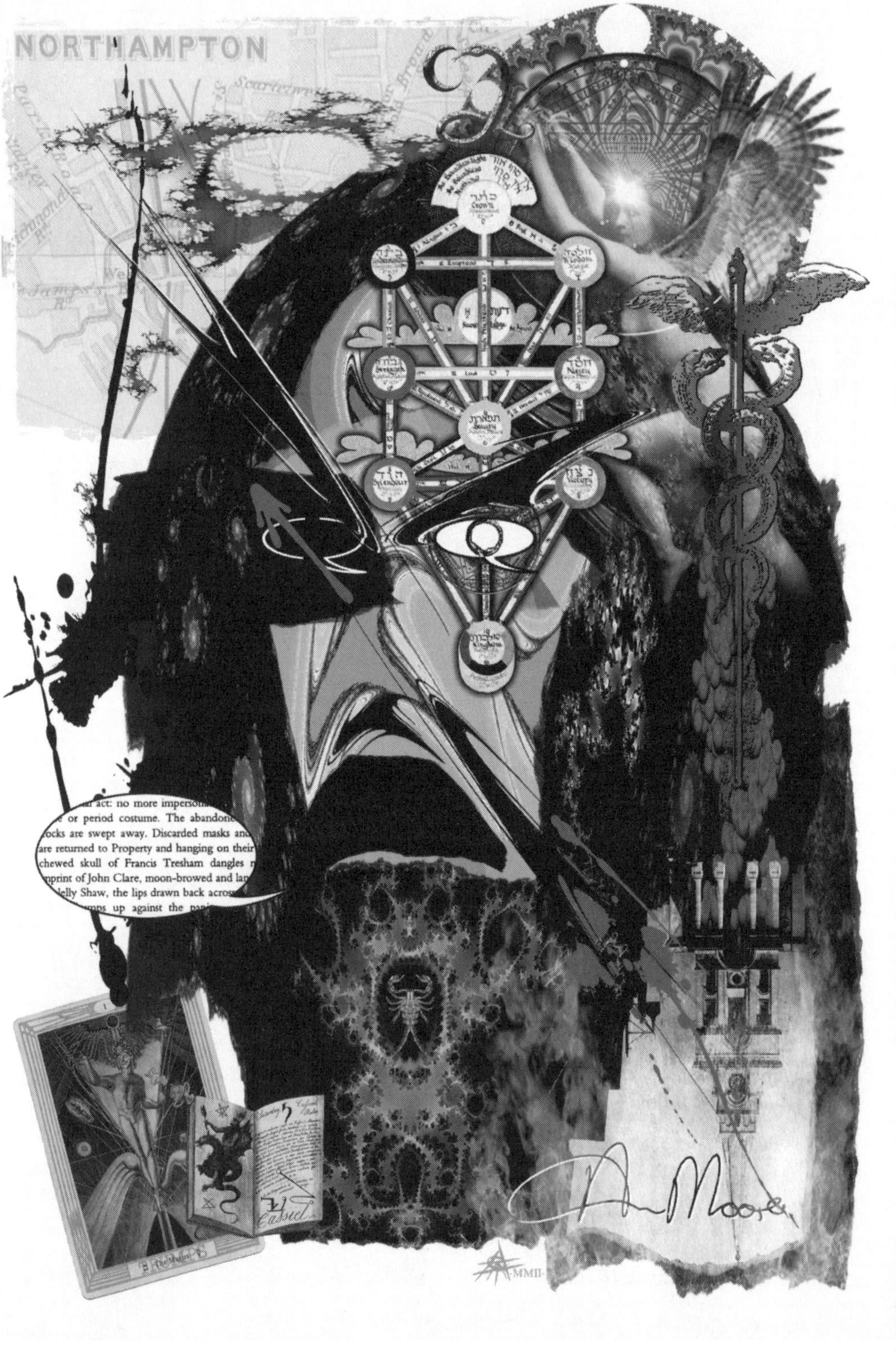
NORTHAMPTON
act: no more imperso
or period costume. The abandone
ocks are swept away. Discarded masks an
are returned to Property and hanging on their
chewed skull of Francis Tresham dangles
nprint of John Clare, moon-browed and la
lelly Shaw, the lips drawn back acros
up against the
MMII

CORRESPONDENCE: FROM HELL
Introduction: Dealing With Pagans

DAVE SIM

Dave Sim, who lives in Ontario, Canada, has spent the last 25 years writing, drawing and publishing a 300-issue monthly comic book series about an aarvark called **Cerebus**. He's considered by many to be the godfather of comics self-publishing.
Text ©2003 Dave Sim.

Dealing with pagans (as I infrequently do) is an interesting business. When Gary Spencer Millidge contacted me about contributing to this publication, he mentioned in his fax that Cerebus is the first comic book that he reads when he receives his fortnightly shipment (Cerebus is the comic book that I write and co-draw—if you are a feminist forget that you ever heard the name and you can continue to exist in your happy little mythological world). Since it is, by now, common knowledge in the comic-book field that I am not a feminist and that I am vehemently opposed to feminism, for anyone in the comic-book field to acknowledge that they read Cerebus is a most exceptional circumstance. Owing to the implicitly...expulsive?...quality of feminism, Cerebus has not been mentioned in polite society—pagan or otherwise—for some years now. Nor have I. So Gary's observation, for me, begged the question which it immediately raised: is this true? Does Gary read Cerebus (leave aside the question of whether he gives it any amount of priority)? Or is there some manner of pagan chicanery afoot? Is he (let's be completely indelicate here) in Alan Moore's thrall? I ask this because Gary's communication had been preceded by another from a fellow in New Jersey, inquiring if I had in my possession an Alan Moore script which had been sent to Gerhard (Gerhard does the backgrounds on Cerebus and we jointly run the company) (I would say we're partners, but that, unfortunately, bespeaks a different connotation these days) and myself some years ago when Alan and Neil were talking about doing a joint anthology title and which he wished to publish in a volume celebrating Alan Moore's 50th birthday (this same volume? Or are we about to be inundated with books celebrating Alan's 50th as we were with "Princess Diana Tribute" books five years ago?). Neil Gaiman had, evidently, mentioned to this fellow in New Jersey that Alan and Neil had jointly concluded that the copy of the script which we had been sent was the only copy of said script in existence. Neil didn't have a copy. Alan didn't have a copy.

Now, I ask you, exactly how likely is that?

Pagan stories always..."sound" funny...in exactly this way. Like a Neil Gaiman fairy tale. (lilting musical voice) "And there was only one copy of the story in all the lands and all the worlds and by the strangest of chances it came about that the story had fallen into the possession of a Deluded Acolyte of the False and Wicked Judaic, Christian and Islamic God Who Doesn't Believe that Abortion is a Virtue."

You see what I mean? Wait, it gets better.

Coincidentally, there had arrived in the same day's mail as the envelope from the fellow in New Jersey another envelope containing an ad slick for (I swear I'm not making this up) a collection of stories which had won an "L. Ron Hubbard Writing Competition" —said ad slick containing a nice, big quote from Neil Gaiman about what a jolly good show it is that a science-fiction writer who founded his own religion—er—"religion"—had indirectly produced such a volume of great writing. And which also contained a very nice cover letter from someone in California saying what a jolly good show it would be if I ran the ad in Cerebus. To which I could only reply (albeit only mentally—I see no need to get stuck, however cosmetically, in the tar baby that is the spiritual residue of whatever L. Ron Hubbard has left behind in this vale of tears) that it would be an equally jolly good show if the earth's core were to turn to permafrost. Alas, life does hold its little disappointments for us all, doesn't it?

The fellow in New Jersey had interviewed me some years ago on behalf of another (I am coming to suspect) pagan publication and mentioned in his letter that he found himself "having to" contact me again. In a letter from someone representing Alan Moore (however indirectly) the phrase "having to" does tend to jump out at you, having the "whiff" about it of someone being compelled to discharge a completely unpleasant but unavoidable duty. That part, at least, rang true. In pagan society I can well

JOHN COULTHART

Left: John Coulthart lives in Manchester, England and divides his time as an illustrator, comic artist and CD and book designer. His most recent work was the illustration and design for the Moore/Perkins CD, **Snakes and Ladders.**
Illustration ©2003 John Coulthart.

imagine that having any manner of contact (however fleeting) with Dave Sim would be considered an unpleasant duty which would be undertaken only if it was completely unavoidable. Or perhaps the fellow is merely a feminist and has picked up his aversion to Dave Sim by that brand of osmosis which is peculiar to the politically correct and which is the only discernible means by which they arrive at their political opinions. Like sheep with scrapie: if one of them has the opinion, they all have that opinion.

Anyway, I found the script right where I had left it in my "don't under any circumstances for one second lose track of where this is" drawer next to my drawing board. Swiftly, I put it in an envelope and mailed it off to New Jersey within minutes of receiving the letter. Didn't want Neil's fairy story to have an unhappy ending. "And the Deluded Acolyte of the Wicked God Who Doesn't Believe Abortion is a Virtue returned the story to the Brave and Noble Necromancer and he and all the children celebrated by spending the night raising the spirits of the dead from out of the earth including Princess Diana because her grave was just over the road a ways from the Necromancer's house and because all the children, of course, loved Princess Diana. The. End."

I mean, it was Alan's script. He wants it back, he can have it back. What am I going to? Pour holy water and sacramental wine on it?

Anyway, it was a couple of days later that I got the fax from Gary. Not enough time for the script to actually have made it to New Jersey, but that really has nothing to do with how, you know, pagan stuff works. "Space and time are mere uni-dimensional extrapolations of the earth-bound three-dimensional limits possessed of the blahdy-blah-blah-blah, etc." I mailed it and, presumably (in doing so) had passed some pagan test or other. "...for on the third day, there came unto the Deluded Acolyte a fax. And the fax sayeth unto him..."

So, okay. I have a bit of a problem. I would like to contribute something to Alan's birthday celebration but pagans are like homosexuals and feminists and socialists (most of them are homosexuals and/or feminists and/or socialists, but let's leave that discussion for another time). You support the idea that they shouldn't be hunted down and shot or burned at the stake or drawn and quartered or made a public laughing-stock by contrasting their viewpoints with reason and common sense (broke that last one myself which is how I've ended up on the outside of the comic-book field looking in), and the next thing you know, they're running around telling everyone that you're a closet homosexual or a closet feminist or a closet socialist or a closet pagan— "HE'S ONE OF US! HE'S ONE OF US! I KNEW IT! I KNEW IT! HAHAHAHAHAHAHAHAHAHA!" As with most of my dealings with people these days, it's a lose-lose proposition. Reinforce their viewpoint that everyone and everything is interchangeable—that Dave Sim is secretly one of them but is just going through a...phase...or some Freudian or Jungian closet homosexual/closet feminist/closet socialist/closet pagan... trauma... or other—or decline to participate and be accused of being, well, I don't know "The Antialan" or something.

Well, where angels fear to tread:

So, anyway, this is a dialogue/correspondence which Alan and I conducted by fax (at my instigation) and which I published in the back of Cerebus *(issues 217-220) a number of years ago after the last installment of* From Hell *had been published (to very little— which is to say no—fanfare. A fact which irritated me since at the time— as I do today—I thought that* From Hell *was a high water mark for the comic-book medium, a graphic novel in every sense of the word, mature, majestic, sweeping, beautifully conceived, beautifully realized and, consequently, of virtually no interest to the comic book industry. I thought that devoting vast amounts of space to a discussion of it in the back of* Cerebus *in four consecutive issues was the least that it deserved. And which, unfortunately, was about all that it got.)*

In retrospect, to me, the most memorable part of our exchange came when I asked Alan a question about morality—that is, right and wrong—and he answered the question by talking about talking backwards and how everything is the same backwards as it is forwards. Which, of course, isn't true. Right is always right and wrong is always wrong even when we are unable to perceive the distinctions between them accurately.

You know, it occurs to me that it would be really nice if, as a 50th birthday present, I could just type "IN THE NAME OF ALMIGHTY GOD COME OUT OF ALAN, THOU VILE AND ACCURSED." And have it work. Just like that when Alan read it. But, alas, I don't think demonic possession—at least of the sort that Alan seems to have involved himself with—works that way. As the Synoptic Jesus found out (I suspect) very much to his own chagrin as he went about casting unclean spirits out of people. You can cast them out, sure, but... "When the vncleane spirit is gone out of a man, he walketh through drie places, seeking rest: and finding none, he sayth, I will returne vnto my house, whence I came out. And when hee commeth, hee findeth it swept and garnished. Then goeth he, and taketh to him seuen other spirits more wicked then himselfe, and they enter in, and dwell there, and the last state of that man is worse then the first." It's interesting to note that even though this verity of Jesus' (Luke 11:24-26) was about a man, he seemed to have struck a...feminist?...nerve: "And it came to passe as hee spake these things, a certaine woman of the company lift vp her voice, and said vnto him, Blessed is the wombe that bare thee, and the pappes which thou hast sucked." I suspect this "certaine woman" was Mary Magdalene out of whom Jesus was said to have cast seven devils. You know what I mean? Early prototype of the mouthy feminist? "And hee said, Yea, rather blessed are they that heare the word of God and keepe it." Yes, exactly. And so much more eloquent than "You are SO busted, Mary."

Oh, sorry. Forgot where I was. Anyway all of Alan's words are in a non-italic typeface. So, if you're a pagan simply read all of the non-italic blocks of type and skip over all of the italic blocks of type. My apologies to Gary Spencer Millidge for "outing" him as a Cerebus reader (note: he never said he liked Cerebus—no one would be so foolish as to say that, publicly, in our Feminist Age—he just said that he read Cerebus) and...

Happy birthday, Alan.

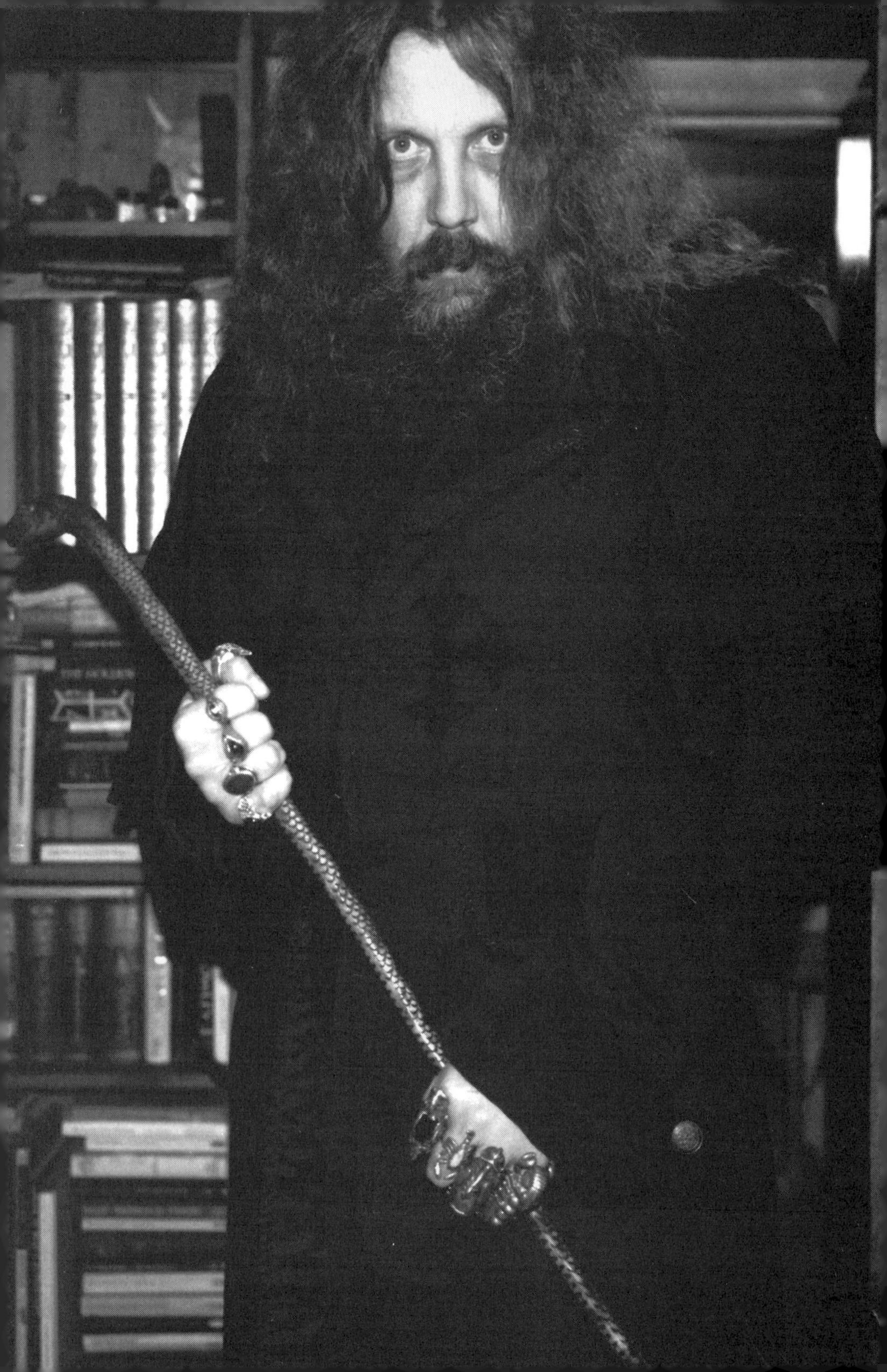

CORRESPONDENCE: FROM HELL
Part 1

*This correspondence between Canadian writer and artist **Dave Sim** and **Alan Moore** was originally published in the letters pages of the Cerebus monthly comic book, issues #217 to 220 and is collected here for the first time. Text ©2003 Alan Moore/Dave Sim.*

One of the reasons I wanted to do this "chat" with you is — I know you don't read The Comics Journal faithfully anymore and I can't say as I blame you (I often find myself wondering why I still read it) — there's this Robert Cwiklik fellow who went on a bit of a strange rant in the Journal about why the comic-book medium is unsuited to do large, complex works. Just as I was preparing myself to devour From Hell in its entirety he was on the Journal's letters page saying that Cerebus is a "serious work, but it isn't realistic." Well, that's water off a duck's back, but as I was reading From Hell — particularly that marvel-filled final volume — the thought came to me, "You know, I'd bet that Cwiklik fellow wouldn't think this is realistic, either." Interesting that what is water off a duck's back to Dave Sim author was a knife in the ribs to Dave Sim Fanboy. I was quite indignant on your behalf. And I realised as I analysed the difference in viewpoints that the crux of the thing was; "What is and isn't reality?" Personally, I find that work which functions on the level of mere "this is what happened, this is what they said, this is what it looked like" to be unsatisfying — or, at least, less satisfying. So, I thought maybe an informal dialogue between two thoughtful chaps who tend to perceive reality in terms of "wheels-within-larger-wheels-within-still-larger-wheels-within-wheels-so-large-you-could-vomit-contemplating-them" might serve as a counterpoint — an invigorating tonic — to alleviate the symptoms produced by the Journal's cold-porridge diet of "a wheel is a circular frame of hard material, solid or spoked, that is capable of turning on an axis" (Gary Groth presumed to be the axis, of course). Or maybe we can just dispense with the opposing viewpoint in this initial exchange and get right into the interesting and really interesting things you and Eddie accomplished in From Hell.

Well, first off, I suppose I should briefly preface this by pointing out that my reasons for not following the *Journal* very closely of late are probably different to your own and aren't necessarily born of any disenchantment with the magazine itself, per se. Despite its occasional forays into pointless sniping, manufactured slanging matches, and all the rest, it probably remains the most incisive magazine related to the comics field that is currently available. The lapse in my reading of the *Journal* and indeed all other publications in the same area comes entirely from my own current sense of distance from the comics industry. Despite my abiding love of the medium, it is not my *only* interest or indeed even my *major r* interest at the moment. Consequently, at a time when there are very few comics that I actually see or read, comics commentary tends to disappear from my reading list altogether. No criticism of anyone other than myself should be inferred from this.

Given the above, it probably comes as no surprise that I haven't seen the article you speak of, but if your summary of its viewpoint is accurate, I don't imagine I'd have had many thoughts about it one way or the other. I'm sure that these are someone's genuine opinions, but opinion is surely a devalued currency at this juncture of the twentieth century, simply by virtue of the vast amount of it there is flooding the market. To assert that comics as a medium doesn't lend itself to longer works seems pretty meaningless, even if we ignore *Our Cancer Year, Maus, Stuck Rubber Baby,* and all the rest and assume that it's true: that comics as a medium does not readily allow works of any great length. Even if this *were* true, the proper response could only be "So what?" The commercial practicalities of the movie industry more or less guarantee that films above two hours long will be comparatively rare. This doesn't seem to have proven a great restriction to the field of cinema. In painting, the simple laws of physics and human architecture more or less determine that a canvas, even at its largest, will be not bigger than the average domestic wall. Really, it isn't so much length as what you do with it. I've been telling myself this since puberty and have come to see that it contains great wisdom.

PIET CORR

Left: *Piet Corr a.k.a.* **pietdesnapp** *is a freelance photographer and lecturer, born in Northampton. His work has been exhibited in galleries and libraries all over England. Photograph ©2003 Piet Corr.*

As regards the increasingly quaint notion of "Realism," a concept dependent upon the broader notion of "Reality," then I'm afraid that I'm equally at a loss. Traditional notions of realism in art, which are anyway in constant revision, would seem to be left floundering in the wake of Einstein and the quantum physicists that followed after him. The physicist Niels Bohr, while conducting particle experiments using the vats at the Carlsberg brewery in Copenhagen, famously remarked to the effect that all of our observations of the cosmos or the quanta can only be seen, in the last analysis, as observations of ourselves, of the processes of our own consciousness. This became known as "The Copenhagen Interpretation," and while I might quibble over the man's choice of beers, I'm not inclined to argue with his basic theory.

The simple fact of things is that we can never directly perceive any such phenomenon as this putative "reality": all we can ever perceive is *our own perceptions*, with these perceptions assembled into a constantly updated mosaic of apprehensions (or misapprehensions) that we call reality. If, for example, we take a dramatic human event such as a murder, then what is the reality of the situation? Is it the forensic evidence and nothing more? Well, yeah, maybe. If we're meat and nothing more, then I guess you could argue that forensics are the only reality in such a situation. If, on the other hand, there is more to us than meat and ballistics, then other considerations must surely be taken into account. What were the thoughts and feelings of the victim? Of the murderer? Of those who witnessed or were connected to the crime? Aren't these a part...perhaps the major part...of the reality of the event, even though they are subjective impressions? What of abstracts such as the murder's sociological implications? What of its mythic or poetic meaning in the broader scheme of things?

These are all surely equally valid facets of reality. I suggest that if reality were genuinely a simple matter of forensics, ballistics, and gross physical mechanics, we'd all have things a fucking sight easier. The distressing or glorious truth is rather that our fantasies are real things. They exist, albeit in an immaterial realm beyond the reach of science or empirical investigation. They influence our behaviour and thus influence the material world, for better or worse. In effect, fantasy is a massive *component* of reality and cannot really be discussed as a separate entity in itself.

Mervyn Peake's sublime *Gormenghast* trilogy, sniffily excluded from the accepted canon of worthwhile English literature for reasons probably not dissimilar to those that you attribute to the *Journal* piece, is a portrait of the ritual-bound emotional dream life of England in the forties and fifties, a haunting and meaningful snapshot that could not have been formulated as anything *but* fantasy. If we are to exclude anything beyond the chain-link fence of traditional realism from that which we accept as serious and worthwhile art, then in one sublime stroke we shall have utterly gutted the entirety of world culture. Good-bye Swift, Rabelais, and all art or literature based upon a classical or mythological theme. Good-bye Pynchon, Burroughs, Blake. Wilde has to go, or at least *Dorian Gray*. Hawthorne for *The Marble Faun*. Henry James for *The Turn of the Screw*. As for M.R. James, W.H. Hodgson, Wells, Verne, Eddie Poe, and other similar genre-bound losers, they haven't a hope. While we're setting fire to the curtains, let's not forget the utter lack of human, emotional, or conversational realism in most eighteenth-century literature, and torch that as well. Then we can presumably all wander up the same irrefutable real and gritty cul-de-sac as Hemingway and fellate our father's Webley with as much verisimilitude as we can muster.

The idea that Art should only ever be a mirror to reality has always seemed ass-backwards to me, given that Art is always and everywhere well-groomed and impeccably turned out, whereas Reality wears a pair of two-year-old Adidas trainers and a *Toy Story* T-shirt. As far as I'm concerned, it's rather the job of *reality* to try and reflect Art. The purpose of Art is not to mirror reality, but to shape it by the imprints and aspirations that it leaves in the human mind.

Anyway, enough about Art and Reality. Let's talk about me.

Well said. I had a couple of occasions to watch you interacting with your wife of the time — now ex-wife — and I was struck by the fact...oh, sod it. Let's talk about your writing and leave you out of it, shall we?

As I told you on the phone, I don't really want to follow a tedious question-and-answer format with this. When I visited that Scots bastard Eddie Campbell (it really does take one to know one), we were both into our cups one afternoon and he started in on your scripts. You know, he would just get Anne to go through them and underline what had to be in the panel and bollocks to all your windy exposition. Having read a number of your scripts, I pointed out that you were always very good about letting the artist know that a lot of the description was for your benefit and could be used or not used as it suited him or her (hi, Melinda). Well, Eddie was having none of it and goes into his studio and roots out one of your scripts and begins a dramatic reading of one of your lengthier descriptions. Or undramatic reading, rather, by way of emphasising his own point. So, Eddie's sitting in the kitchen droning your description, and I'm sitting on the postage-stamp-sized back porch (Campbell Enterprises being a smoke-free environment) facing into the kitchen. Now, having just read a hundred or so pages of From Hell in photocopy form, I am as immersed in 1888 London as I'm ever likely to be, anyway, and I start disappearing mentally and psychically into your description. With Eddie droning and droning it begins to envelop me like an incantation, and I begin rocking back and forth on the white plastic kitchen chair I'm sitting on, thoroughly inside of your word-rhythms and invocations, simultaneously resentful of the sneer on the old Campbell mug and anticipating the good-natured or not-so-good-natured (both of us being Scots bastards) row that is imminent as a result of our divergent reactions. Something had to give, and it turned out to be the chair I was sitting on. One leg snaps off, pitching me over backwards and hurling one of Eddie's prized, limited-edition Guinness glass steins out of my hand — the stein bounces neatly down a half-dozen stairs before smashing into a million fragments. Of course, I'm apologising all over the place, and Eddie is crestfallen. They don't make the glass steins anymore, do I have any idea how many Guinness he had to drink to get each one of them (as if THAT was some torturous ordeal for him), etc., etc. He had had six of them (six being the number of the Lovers in the tarot — and what else, metaphorically speaking, is the even-handed balance of a writer and artist than a literary/artistic love affair?), and now he had five (the number of the Hierophant, interpreter of arcane wisdom, which in its negative aspect is epitomised by the imposition of said interpretation without the accompanying wisdom). Served him right, I actually thought. Served him bloody well right.

I imagine you must've had some hard moments writing some of those descriptions, weaving a word-invocation around yourself to draw yourself into the proceedings. I'm thinking particularly of Volume Seven, which depicts the most grisly and ritualistic of the murders.

Well, I can't in all honesty claim to be surprised by the incessant complaints of this embittered transportee. This kind of craven back-stabbing is, of course, only to be expected of a clan that sided with the English during the Highland clearances and slaughtered the McGregors in their beds. Do you know, there's a hotel situated at the top of Glencoe where to this day they have a sign on the lounge door that reads "No dogs or Campbells"? And this isn't just me saying bad things about Eddie: this is the deep and resonant bass voice of History itself saying bad things about Eddie.

On the matter of what has been viewed in some quarters as an untoward wordiness in my panel descriptions, might I draw your attention to the final volume of *From Hell*, specifically to page two, panel five of our epilogue, *The Old Men On The Shore*. In the script description for this panel I unfortunately allowed myself a moment of laxity and omitted the words "INSPECTOR ABBERLINE'S HEAD IS STILL ON HIS SHOULDERS DURING THIS PANEL. IT HAS NOT RETREATED TORTOISE-LIKE INTO HIS NECK, NOR HAS IT IN SOME FASHION MANAGED TO REFRACT LIGHT AROUND IT LIKE A KLINGON SPACESHIP SO THAT THE INSPECTOR RESEMBLES SOMETHING OUT OF MAGRITTE WITH HIS BOWLER FLOATING THERE SUSPENDED ABOVE THE EMPTY COLLAR OF HIS COAT." Last time I'll make that mistake, obviously.

For the unsuspecting reader, let me step in and say that I freely admit to having provoked you, Mr. Moore, into an uncharacteristically mean-spirited jibe at your collaborator and our mutual friend. "Let's you and him fight" being something of a Scottish national motto common to all members of our sour-dispositioned geographical accident, as it were. I am ashamed of myself and will attempt to be better than my genetic nature for the rest of this discussion. Besides, I've gotten the cart very much before the horse in skipping forward to Volume Seven, haven't I? Let's begin at the beginning. Gerhard has just read the story in its entirety and read it the same way I did — the story first and then the meticulous appendices, referring back to the pages and panels in question. I'm sure it wasn't false modesty that led you to be so self-deprecating in these afterwords, but rather a genuine modesty, being as you were the first to so extensively research an historical work in the comics form and to share the extent of that research with your readers. "Is this going to look pretentious or vainglorious" must have occurred to you on more than one occasion — comic-book creators feeling compelled to hide most traces of their "light" under the ponderous "bushel basket" of the lowest common denominator. One thing did strike me in reading these notes — that the entirety of the story seemed to be "in place" from the get-go. When you tell us that this point or that point would be developed more fully in future volumes, by God, they were.

So. At the very beginning, were you reading about Jack the Ripper to any great extent and then began to evolve the theory of interconnected mayhem across two centuries that is the real centrepiece of From Hell? *Did your interest in the suppression of matriarchal societies come first? Freemasonry? I'm asking you to go back almost a decade, I realise, but I am interested in which chickens came before which eggs and vice versa, to the best of your recollection (as they say at Senate inquiries).*

Well, I suppose I'd have to preface my answer by saying that all of my serious work has to some extent always been intended as a kind of study and exploration of a given dynamic process. *V For Vendetta* set out to explore the dynamics of fascism and anarchy in the form of a fantasy/adventure narrative. *Watchmen* set out to explore, amongst other things, the dynamics of power in a post-Hiroshima world. With *Lost Girls* it's the dynamic interaction of war and eroticism that is under scrutiny. Please understand that I'm not claiming any of these dynamic explorations as massive philosophical successes: I'm simply trying to give a name to the process involved.

With *From Hell*, the seed idea was simply that of murder, any murder. It had occurred to me that Murder is a human event at the absolute extreme of the human experience. It struck me that an in-depth exploration of the dynamics of a murder might therefore yield a more extreme and unprecedented kind of information. All that needed to be decided upon was which murder. Perhaps predictably, I never even considered the Whitechapel murders initially, simply because I figured they were worn out, drained of any real vitality or meaning by the century of investigation and publicity attached to them. I started out by trawling for more obscure and unusual homicides, like the case of Dr. Buck Ruxton, for example (a kind of 1930s Lord Lucan figure who killed his wife and nanny but never managed to pull off the necessary subsequent disappearance).

It was only towards the end of 1988, with so much Ripper material surrounding me in the media on account of it being the centenary of the murders, that I began to understand that, firstly, there were still ways to approach the Whitechapel murders that might expose previously unexplored seams of meaning, and secondly that the Ripper story had all the elements that I was looking for. Set during fascinating and explosive times in a city rich with legend, history, and association, the case touched peripherally upon so many interesting people and institutions that it provided the precise kind of narrative landscape that I required. You see, to some extent the peripheries of murder...the myth, rumour, and folklore attached to a given case...had always seemed more potentially fruitful and rewarding than a redundant study of the hard forensic facts at a murder's hub. This traditional approach to murder might tell us Whodunit (which is admittedly the most immediate of practical considerations), but it does not tell us what happened on any more than the most obvious and mechanical level. To find out anything truly significant, we must take the plunge into myth and meaning, and to me a case with the rich mythopoeic backwaters of the Whitechapel murders suddenly seemed like the perfect spot to go fishing.

Having defined the purpose and the territory to my satisfaction, I then undertook my preliminary reading of the ground site. By this I mean that I visited and explored the territory of the murders personally, and also that I explored the landscape of the murders in terms of the literature surrounding the event. By this, I mean that I made a very broad reading and mapping, as if from a considerable altitude, a considerable distance from the event itself.

For example, I have some notes culled from a very old issue of *The Fortean Times* which deal with a group of alleged psychics being given photographs of cattle mutilations and asked to "read" them Psychically. Phrases like "ears cut off...genitals mutilated...888...lines of force in the ground..." seemed resonant to me, as did an article in another issue of *Fortean Times* in which one of their writers, possibly Matt Hoffman in his column of American arcana, drew parallels between a plotted graph of inexplicable cattle mutilations and a plotted graph of violent crimes against women during a similar period. Obviously, these snippets never found their way into the finished *From Hell*, but they formed a part of my high-altitude mental impression of the Whitechapel events: a kind of fuzzy, low definition map, as seen through cloud where nevertheless certain prominent features of the symbolic landscape could still be seen. Rivers of theory. High points of conjecture and ley-lines of association.

This initial mapping gave me a glimpse of the whole territory in its entirety, if not in detail. I could see what features of the narrative landscape seemed the most significant and promising, even if I couldn't provide a precise soil analysis at that point to say exactly *why* they seemed promising. The mathematical theories of C. Howard Hinton, son of Gull's friend James Hinton, seemed promising. The Iain Sinclair-inspired reading of London as a mythic and historical constellation seemed promising. The Masonic theories of the late Stephen Knight, whether true or not, seemed to open up fascinating territories of lore and tradition. The Masonic notion of the Universe, of space-time, as a rough and solid block hewn out by the Great Architect, with the the job of finishing the work left to the Great Architect's mortal servants, the Dionysiac Artificers and the Freemasons, well, that seemed to fit in with everything else. Hitler's conception in 1888 seemed highly resonant. The matricentral/patriarchal notions of myth and history came from an intuitive reading of the "London Pentacle" as described in chapter four, filtered through the intuitions of Robert Graves.

Basically, what I'm saying is that, yes, I did have the broad shape of the whole thing in my head, with many of the details already there, before I started. By chapter two, for example, I already had the Monster-Ripper-Halifax Slasher-Moors Murderers-Peter Sutcliffe arc of murder that we see in the last chapter firmly in my head. I did not, however, find out about Ian Brady's childhood vision of the floating head until later. I knew that I'd later be alluding to Brady when I had Gull ponder aloud upon the familiarity of the name "Brady Street" during the first murder, but I was not then aware that Brady's partner Myra Hindley would have her own name commemorated by the sacking manufacturer's premises outside which the third murder occurred. I knew that the last line of the whole book would be Robert Lee's " I think there's going to be another war," but I didn't decide to use the Von Stuck painting of the Wild Hunt, painted with Adolf Hitler's adult face superimposed upon that of the god Odin in 1889, the year of Hitler's birth, until about a month before the last issue went to press. I knew that Netley would be dying before the book concluded and that obelisks were somehow important to the symbology of the book, but I hadn't at this point found all that marvellous shit about Netley's coach colliding with an obelisk and spilling his brains on the cobbles.

The thing is, if that first high-altitude mapping is perceptive and accurate enough, whatever tiny surface details are unearthed upon closer inspection are bound to fit right into it somewhere. That's how I work, anyway.

As regards my self-deprecating tone during the appendices, it wasn't any kind of modesty so much as gruff attempt at apology for having done such a fucking sloppy and unprofessional job. I mean, "I think I read this is some book somewhere but I can't for the life of me remember which one and I can't be bothered to look for it" is hardly the high standard of investigative reportage that *From Hell* is often touted as being, is it? And the fact that something hasn't been done in comics before is really no excuse for doing a sloppy job. There's nothing at all wrong with bushels. Sometimes one needs something to hide under.

Then again, you're probably right and I'm probably being too hard on myself. At least I didn't forget to draw the main character's head.

Considering our mutual predisposition (and the larger reasons for this chat) — that it is often an evasion to say someone is "reading too much" into a given occurrence — I was amused to note when I dug out the offending panel that Abberline's dialogue is, "All the things you never get around to. All the things that never get sorted out." Doubtless the much-maligned Mr. Campbell (and we really MUST stop it) was offering his own artistic reinforcement to the two-tiered observation. Doubtless, as well, we can look forward to a safe retirement having squirreled away our rare "missing Abberline head" first printings of Volume Ten. My personal favourite in the "reading too much into it" category is in chapter four, page 8, where Gull informs Netley that "Women had power once: Back in the caves, life hinged on..." etc. Eddie has clearly lettered "Back as Balk" — balking at the expressed sentiment (the sexist swine) and adding a pen-stroke to turn the "L" into a "C."

"To find out anything truly significant, we must take the plunge into myth and meaning." I agree. Millions don't. When I

visited you back in 1988 at the time when you were first gathering the From Hell *raw materials, I remember thinking how...generous you were with your thinking, considering there were two writers in the room (the other being Jamie Delano). By contrast, I was completely miserly with my own thinking. I was in the end bit of* Jaka's Story's *first book and mentally assembling what would eventually become* Reads. *My own "high-altitude mapping" (good way of putting it, by the way) consisting of taking what was the best current thinking on the nature of the Big Bang, the factual Stephen Hawkings dry-as-dust material, and constructing a creationist myth to suit the available facts. As you're aware, I made liberal use of your "all stories are true" insights, and I was gratified indeed when you said that the creationist myth part struck you as the nearest thing to a mystical experience in print form. At one level of perception, all of us inclined towards "high-altitude mapping" are really just talking to each other, anyway, aren't we? These interests that we have, lovingly sculpted and finely burnished and then fitted into place so as not to violate the pleasure and enjoyment of our more...literal-minded readers,* The Comics Journal, *etc., etc. Neil did a lot of it in* Sandman, *I try to do it in* Cerebus, *you do it in your own work. You know what I mean? I'll be chortling to myself, "Wait'll Neil sees this one," or "Alan, you're going to love this."*

The gestation period for Reads *mirrors what you're talking about with your* From Hell *experience. Every little tidbit I would run across (most of them, anyway) just seemed to find its place in the finished work.*

I remember asking you — since you were the only person I ever met who thought about things the way I tend to (and Reads *was very much on my mind when I asked): Do you ever worry that we're doing these things in service to something that we would be rather horrified we were in service to if we found out? You know, what is widely and derogatorily known as Dylan's "Christian kick" when he sang, "It might be the Devil or it might be the Lord, but you're going to have to serve somebody" seems to echo that same kind of...unease, shall we say?*

Your answer at the time (as I recall) was: "I have considered it, and I've decided as long as it makes a good story, that's all that's really important." I decided if it was good enough for Alan Moore, it was good enough for me. For this, you might well have to smoke an extra turd in the infernal depths and I might well have to get it lit for you. Before I get into the specifics of From Hell, *I was wondering if you've ever reconsidered your position since then and if there were ever any worrying synchronicities of small events attached to the writing of* From Hell *that gave you pause along these lines.*

Well, Dave, that's a hell of a question to ask a man who worships a snake.

I suppose I'd have to say that for anyone who has had or believes themselves to have had an extra-normal experience, a reaction of pants-shitting holy terror is only to be expected, as are all sorts of confused and meaningless spiritual anxiety dredged up from whatever vestigial religious upbringing we went through or whatever hysterical Dennis Wheatley occult novels we happened to read during our formative years. So, yes, there have been moments, back at the outset when I got into this kind of work, when I found myself gripped by a terrified Faustian penitence: "Adders and serpents, let me breathe...I will burn my books!" Like I say, that was back at the outset.

The further I explore these ideas, however, the more it seems to become apparent that concepts like "good" or "evil" mean absolutely nothing above a certain fundamental human level. A bit higher up still, and even things like individual consciousness have no meaning. Go further and there is nothing at all that is recognisable within a human framework.

If I had to explain my basic feelings on the subject with a crude physical model, I'd have to say that at the core of things there is a blissful, hermaphrodite, endlessly creative white singularity that you might as well call absolute God. This is the light source in the canvas of existence. The light then polarises into two different frequencies, one which might be called "God considered as Female" (or black, or negative...these terms don't mean anything like what we hold them to mean upon a material level; they have nothing to do with gender or colour or value differences) and the other one which might be called "God considered as Male."

After that, the light hits something which you might metaphorically refer to as a prism. Students of the Qabala might prefer to call it the Abyss. In terms of modern physics, you might imagine it as the curved perimeter of space/time. When the white light hits this prism, it breaks up into a full spectrum of entities: Gods plural, Demons, chimera, angels, fairies, grey aliens...a plurality of spiritual colours and forces to which we have appended names, images, and identities. As this reaction spreads further from its source it seems to slow down or curdle or thicken in some way until, at the far extremities, you have physical matter. Everything in this entire continuum is a refraction of the original singular light source. The entities which we traditionally think of as "other" are in a sense nothing but ourselves unfolded — or at a higher frequency. Evil and Good don't really come into this equation. In my scheme of the Universe, there really can be nothing that is not ultimately God. Or, in the case of the Devil, God when he's drunk, as a great man famously remarked.

Anyway, if that's cleared up the entire structure of Existence for you, I'd like to return to what you said about all of us really only writing for each other. This is true on one level...which is to say a technical level...in that if we've pulled off something clever in terms of comic-book narrative, we know that there are only a few people sufficiently perceptive regarding the intricacies of comic-book narrative to completely appreciate how bloody cute we've been.

On the other hand, I must admit that I've been having those "Wait until Neil or Dave or whoever sees this" feelings much less frequently of late. More and more, the person I'm writing for is that famous imaginary friend of the fledgling writer, the conjectured reader. I feel a need to try and hone or evolve my work towards a deeper level of intimacy with the reader, by which I don't necessarily mean friendliness. Intimacy isn't always comfortable. I suppose what I mean is that I simply want to extend the reach and potency of my work. By "extending the reach" I don't mean that I want more people to read it or for it to sell more copies, but simply that I want the people who are exposing themselves to the work to feel it reach further into them than similar work has managed to reach before.

This possibly vain attempt seems to me to require a step beyond mere technique into something that is much more intuitive or feeling-based (sorry, Dave) than it is based on rationality, logic, and ability. Of course, every ounce of that precious rationality and technique will be needed to anchor the intuitions in a legible material form, but in order to get to the kind of deep-rooted human areas that I want to reach, the rational needs to be transcended in some way. What I'm trying to say in this confused meander is that, these days, I am attempting to reach through what dramatists call the fourth wall...the one between the audience and the story...and establish an eerie one-to-one relationship with the reader, or listener in the case of the two performance CDs. These days, I would almost prefer it if nobody noticed my technical flourishes, since if they're recognized as technical flourishes, to some degree they have failed to do their job of affecting the reader subtly and unnoticeably at a distance.

As for my endless, compulsive, and liberal mouthing-off about whatever I happen to be working on at the moment, I can't say it's a big source of worry to me. If people hear that I'm planning a 400-page-plus, eight-year-long examination of the Whitechapel murders with full appendices and involving exhaustive research and then decide that they are going to beat me to it and do the very same thing, then frankly whatever they've got wrong with them is much more serious than whatever I've got wrong with me. I take my hat off to them and wish them the very best of luck, the poor, wretched, doomed bastards.

Well, we're really into the meat of it now, aren't we? My personal construction of things — and this interested me when I read your answer — resembles your own in many significant ways, with different shadings of emphasis. As you said in our phone conversation setting this whole thing up: "These things are all very subjective, aren't they?" Indeed they are. In my view, the success of the Jewish He Who Cannot Be Named God and His Christian modification/corruption (depending on your subjective view) can be attributed to the notion of a Great Unity, a notion which cut through the complexity of beliefs in the ancient world. Everything was all One at one time. Call it a DNA-level insight into the Big Bang at a time when it was still perplexing the best minds that planets just wandered about the heavens like slow-motion pinballs. This might be the entire sum and substance of what was accomplished, but its centuries of endurance might be attributable to the fact that it was enough — despite whatever mythologies and cautionary fables were grafted onto it. The Latin motto of the United States, to me, reflects this: E pluribus unum. From many, one — or in the larger sense: From many, One. There was One who became many (all aspects of the Godhead which manifested themselves in various cultures and religions,) and there is something inherently good, productive, worthwhile, satisfying in mentally rewinding the tape through the process of fragmentation and making that original Unity a central consideration in all endeavours. I would agree with the observation that the light — or Light — polarises into two frequencies, one male in its aspect and one female. What I was driving at was that the end of Church & State, distilled to sound byte level, comes down to "HE did it." The ending on Reads comes down to "SHE did it." I'm not sure that this really has anything to do with The Light — after all, what we know to be the known universe is pretty much an out-of-the-way cul-de-sac in an unimportant suburb of the cosmos. For the last while, anyway, I've been rather comfortably ensconced in the notion that God, the Light, is indeed Male — that reproduction in and of itself represents a kind of consolation prize once that encroachment, act of bad faith, really big misunderstanding, original sin takes place (the bad news is that we're getting further away from Enlightenment; the good news is that there are a lot more of us than there used to be). I was "holding back" on all this back in '88 when I visited you, thinking (much to my regret), "Well, this is it, once Reads comes out Alan is going to be the first one in line advocating that I be ostracized from the community of all right-thinking hermaphroditic God-and-Goddess United devotees," I find it immensely gratifying that we are able to discuss how things seem to each of us respectively without...feeling?...threatened. Even though you're wrong, I mean.

Just kidding.

I was also interested in your observation on appealing to the intended reader —and I understand the sense in which you intend it (I think). A kind of guerrilla incursion into the psyche, the senses, and the emotions. I thought with From Hell you were particularly adept at this. Gull's line to Netley:"You realise that I only share these private thoughts in recognition of your lack of cognisance?" Netley: "Why, thank you, sir...I can't say what that means to me." Gull: "Ha Ha Ha. Why, of course you can't. That is precisely why I trust you." On the one hand, it's very much a literary device. You have to stuff volume two full of all of the thinking you've done about the pentagram configuration, as much of the research as you've done, and graft it onto Gull AND come up with a good reason for him to say it out loud (this last part being the most difficult to manage). It really ends up being analogous to the mystical experience — the vertigo of finding oneself Inside the mystery. It still allows the literal-minded reader to say, "This Gull fellow is off his nut. That's what Alan's saying," which casts him or her into a situation of empathy with Netley (while allowing him or her to maintain a feeling of superiority to Netley). By the time you get us to St. Paul's — and it really must be said that Mr. Campbell outdid himself on this London tour section — all of the dialogue has had a preordained quality, an echo-resonance that mirrors the Inside-the-mystery experience. Even the most literal-minded reader had to be wanting to get "outside" by the time Netley sees it as an imperative.

I've certainly come to share your view that there is no harm in talking openly in front of other writers. The thievish-natured usually make such a mess of it that it isn't worth troubling about and the genuinely creative usually turn it into something so new and different after they've filtered it through their own awareness that it becomes worthwhile "cross-pollinating," as it were, for that very reason.

Which brings us back to the actual murders documented in From Hell. *I remember talking to you on the phone and asking how the book was coming along, and you said that the parts concerned with the actual murders were telescoping on you. Because there was so much information to be gone through and fitted into place, it wasn't as clear how long each section was going to be to get the business covered. I mean, you didn't seem to be tearing your hair out or anything, just remarking on it like a mountain-climber who has come upon an unanticipated outcropping. How difficult a problem did you face with this? Were there any hair-pulling moments and/or central guiding intentions that pulled you through them? Is there any way to make your answer interesting, considering how vague and pedestrian the questions are?*

I suppose the short answer is "no": I'm sure everyone will be relieved to hear that my hair is the same rich, luxuriant cascade of tumbling auburn that it ever was, with no ugly bald patches. On the other hand, that isn't to say that the tendency of the data to expand in one's hands didn't become a problem.

With hindsight, I imagine it's a problem that will be familiar to anyone working in a research-based or semi-documentary field, and it further strikes me that the nature of the phenomenon is probably mathematical. There's a form that's frequently used to exemplify fractal mathematics known as the Koch Snowflake. What this is, basically, is an equilateral triangle. An iterative computer program is applied to this and told to append a smaller equilateral triangle, exactly half the size of the original, to each of the three exposed sides. This gives a sort of Star-of-David shape, which now has twelve exposed sides. The computer will then add half-sized equilateral triangles to each of the three exposed sides. The computer will then add half-sized equilateral triangles to each of these twelve new facets, making the basic star shape more prickly and giving it lots of new exposed facets to which the computer will continue to add half-sized equilateral triangles ad infinitum. As you can imagine, the perimeter line of the shape becomes crinklier and pricklier with each new iteration of the program. The interesting thing is that since the original equilateral triangle can be drawn within a circle of a given diameter and area, the *area* of the resultant snowflake-like shape can never exceed the area of the original circle. The perimeter of the snowflake, on the other hand, can become infinite.

Another way to look at this would be to ask, "What is the length of the perimeter of Great Britain?" Now, basically speaking, there is no answer to that question that is not relative to the length of the ruler that you happen to be using. If, for example, you have a mile-long ruler and you go around Britain placing it from point to point and total up the result, you will get a figure that is accurate, but only for someone using a mile-long ruler. Obviously, using a yardstick or a foot rule would enable you to include the perimeter of all the little inlets in your measurements that a mile-long measure would exclude. This would give you a much bigger figure for the length of your perimeter. If you throw away the foot rule and use a micrometer, then the figure will become greater still. Eventually, if measured with progressively finer instrumentation, the perimeter of the country could be said to be infinite in length, although the basic *area* of the country has not changed even slightly.

As so, too, *From Hell*: the Whitechapel murders took place over a finite period of time and claimed a finite number of victims. Looked at in terms of the area of information covered, this appears at first glance to be a containable task with clearly defined limits. The problem is all in the surface detail. As more detail becomes apparent with closer and closer examination, so too does the "surface" of the narrative become more crinkly, prickly, and fractal. The perimeter of the story starts to extend towards infinity. The space and time needed for each episode expands.

Like I say, this caused unanticipated problems, but I imagine they were much worse for Eddie than for me. Writing twenty extra pages isn't anywhere near as much of a physical and mental burden as drawing them.

Speaking of Eddie, I'd have to only partly agree with your assessment of Gull and Netley's coach jaunt in chapter four. It's a staggering piece of work, and if you'd asked me at the time, I'd have rated it along with the very best things he'd ever done, if only because of the tremendous narrative power required to sustain visual interest in a protracted tour around a bunch of relatively dull-looking city buildings. However, I think that since that episode, Eddie's work has continued to get stronger and stronger. In my opinion, chapter ten, the Marie Kelly chapter, surpassed anything that came before it. I've not made up my mind yet, but I think that the final chapter may even have topped that one.

Eddie's development as an artist over the course of the strip has been phenomenal, especially given how bloody good he was to start with. For me, it's more often the tiny details that take my breath away than the obvious set pieces: the natural grace and solidity of a character's hands in the foreground. The composition of the wall tiles when Abberline's throwing up in the toilets of Scotland Yard. Horse breath. Smeared and miasmal lights in Oxford Street. Without the anchoring strength and involving sense of human reality in Eddie's drawings, I doubt that I could have even attempted some of the more metaphysical flights of fancy that provided, for me, the high points of the narrative. I think really that any way you look at it, it's an overwhelming visual achievement.

And then he goes and ruins it all eight pages from the end of the bloody epilogue.

I'm moved to speculate that the entirety of From Hell *was a kind of incantation, hinging on the fact that "X" number of Abberline heads had to appear in their proper sequence for the kingdoms and riches of this world to be laid at your feet. "Campbell?" (Netley to your Gull, perhaps?) "Yessir, Mr. Moore?" "Bring me something to hit you with."*

I wrote at some length about Eddie in previewing Bacchus, *so I'm loath to add any further niceties. I have to say, however, that I find Eddie's drawing style one of the most — if not THE most — compelling in our environment. His use of spidery-thin lines and bold slashes of black — Krigstein seems the only obvious stylistic precursor — gets my drawing hand twitching just to look at it. I remember showing Bissette photocopies of my Alec and Bacchus send-up on one of my visits to the other Northampton. "Too pretty," was his amiable assessment. Quite right he was, too. A pretty style wouldn't have suited From Hell. In fact it's impossible to picture anyone else drawing the book, as I'm sure you'd agree. All I have to do is picture Eddie's cover for the yet-to-be-realised* Dance of the Gull-Catchers *and I start snickering. Not bad for a yet-to-be-realised cover. Right, that's enough. The bastard did cut my nuts off in his bloody comic book.*

Okay, the next question I'm going to take in stages (to avoid me prattling on for five pages getting the entirety of the question said all in one go). In our 1988 conversation, you had a number of really amazing observations about the energy (for the more literal-minded reader, make that "energy") released in the act of murder. Amazing and disturbing — and I say that as a person who prides himself on not being easily disturbed (and quite enjoys it when he is). The carnival atmosphere at the scene where the first body was found — building from the one cop standing guard — into the ghoulish bedlam of the next day. This is definitely one of the implications of that release of energy, isn't it? An obvious initial "ripple in the pond" after the fact — obvious in any kind of "high-altitude mapping." I'll let you take it from there.

The kind of ripple effect you're talking about is just about the first sort of pattern that one is able to make out with the initial high-altitude mapping. In fact, thinking about it, I'd say it's less like a ripple effect, with hindsight, than it is like a blast distribution pattern: you have the central area of utter devastation in the relatively small confines of Whitechapel during a relatively small period of time, the autumn of 1888. Spread out from this, there are a distribution of points that seem on first glance to have a relationship to the central point of impact: to the point where some event or personage of considerable size collided explosively with the landscape of history. These points are seemingly randomly and evenly distributed to either side of the impact zone, which is to say in the past that precedes the event and in the future that comes after it. The event is seen as a strange sort of four-dimensional shape or entity, with points of coincidence or significant incident marking the being's extremities and the limits and extents of its time-spanning form.

The immediate noticeable effect of this meta-shape as it impinges upon normal three-dimensional human historical linear consciousness could be described, I suppose, as a kind of *glamour*. I mean that both in the conventional sense of "the glamour that surrounds murder and murderers;" their sensational appeal in the eyes of the "public," and also in the medieval/magical sense of "a glamour; a charm; a spell or enchantment." Frankly, I don't think there's really any appreciable difference between the two definitions, in that they both have exactly the same effect of placing a certain dark or dazzling obsession in the minds of whoever they happen to affect.

The earliest effects (if one ignores for a moment premonitions like *Jekyll and Hyde* or Billy Blake's *Ghost of a Flea*) are those manifested in the streets of London and Whitechapel during the period of the murders. To some extent, these manifestations are closer to the source of the blast, as it were, and the reaction is more "pure" and extreme than later reactions mediated by distance or the passage of time. Maybe it's possible to glean more information from these initial reactions than it is from later, more considered ones.

For example, it seems like *everyone* got a little bit crazy around the time of the Ripper panic. The annals of the Whitechapel killings are full of unlikely characters acting as amateur detectives, running round Whitechapel in blackface make-up or turning up half-mad in public houses with blood on their clothes and muttering about stabbing women. The men of London, or at least a small but significant percentage of them, seemed to polarise between writing into the papers with wild and heroic schemes for catching the killer, or writing into the papers with sick, masturbatory fantasies in which they pretended to *be* the murderer. If it were only the men that were affected by the murders, then we would have a fairly neat and contemporary moral of the "men are not damn good" variety to tie up our observation with, but this is not the case.

The women of the East End, according to reports of the period, were gripped in part by a kind of appalled fascination with the murders. Many would talk, almost longingly according to accounts, of the likelihood of their being the next victim. Some commentators have remarked that it almost seemed as if they were actively fantasizing about this eventuality. Now, this is disturbing. It certainly deserves scrutiny, although it would probably be unwise to leap to any hasty conclusions. One woman of the period, when asked, said that she'd thought how nice it would be to be one of the victims, simply because people had said *such nice things* about all the women murdered to date. The implication is that it would be worth going through evisceration to be lionized thus. Bear in mind that life for these women would in all likelihood not extend that much longer anyway, just speaking statistically, and that dying of malnutrition, or in childbirth, or from a "ginny" kidney is probably not instantly preferable to sudden death at the hands of a murderer. Also, to be killed by such a celebrated figure would somehow be to link yourself to him with the act of death...a reverse of the Mark Chapman syndrome, maybe...and, of course, people would say such nice things.

I myself see this phenomenon, both the male and female components of it, as a kind of echo in the "mind-space" of the period. Richard Dawkins might call it a "meme," the information equivalent of a gene, a kind of replicating virus-like idea permeating society and influencing how we think and act. Rupert Sheldrake, much less respectable than Dawkins, might talk in terms of a morphogenetic resonance, a thought-form reproducing itself in what Sheldrake terms a "morphogenetic field." For my part, being much less respectable than either of the two above gentlemen, I would talk in terms of the murders being events not only in the "real" material world, but also in the terrain that I term "Idea Space," a kind of medium or field or space or dimension in which thoughts occur. I believe this space to be at least in part mutual, rather than discrctc, which is to say that I believe that this "space " impinges to some degree upon all consciousness and that it is co-accessible. Sometimes, certain ideas or notions seem to be or are said to be "in the air." What do we mean by that? When James Watt invented the steam engine, it turned out that several other inventors had come up with the idea independently during roughly the same period. Charles Fort remarked on this to the effect that he guessed it was just "steam-engine time." I'm sure that you get the general idea: that consciousness, including at a group level, is a kind of medium in which ideas or thought-forms are the equivalent of solid objects or land masses, and in which the awareness and "self" of the individual can be seen as a moving point in the fabric.

In terms of the Ripper crimes, I suggest that maybe the idea forms of Leather-Apron and his victims became almost like the compelling and archetypal figures in some Nohplay of the human soul, with at least part of the "audience" responding and identifying unconsciously with the central players, even to the point of miming or mimicking their behaviour. This kind of conjecture becomes especially interesting, to my mind, when you apply it to a case like that of the "Halifax Slasher," as alluded to in the notes for chapter fourteen. Here, there was no real material figure at the centre of the case. There was *only* the echo in the mind of the onlookers, a reverberation without a signal.

The further we move away in time from the epicentre of the event, the more rarefied the effects become, and yet they are still noticeable. Most serial murderers, it seems, are aware of Jack the Ripper as a kind of benchmark in their field — almost a patron saint. Albert de Salvo, as just one example, in his confession to the cops said that when they knew the details of his case, it would outdo Jack the Ripper.

Then of course we have the echoes in our media, in our slasher films, and in the minds of those singular obsessives, the Ripperologists. Add to these the lines of chance and coincidence ravelling out from the case itself and leading into both the ancient past and the present day and we have a pretty good preliminary picture of the ripple or blast-pattern that *is* the case, just as much as the initial murders can be said to *be* the case. We have the basic grid on which to map the murder.

Yes. Extraordinary in every sense of the word. I remember sitting spellbound back in '88 as you went through the litany of personalities and celebrities interconnected with the murders. Of course the only Victorian personality of whom I had any great awareness was Wilde — I was in the midst of researching him for book two of Jaka's Story and what would become Melmoth. Although his own debacle wouldn't come until the mid-'90s, the seeds were definitely sown by 1888. You quote from "Lord Arthur Savile's Crime" — one of my favourite Oscar Wilde short stories — and, of course, most of his published wit centres on the "double life" which was his own undoing. Number thirteen Little College Street, where he got involved with male prostitutes and "renters" (blackmailers) isn't far from Whitechapel, if I'm not mistaken. When he had his hair permed, he took great delight in the fact that he was said to resemble a bust of Nero in the British Museum. When he started going in for "rough trade," he used to tell intimates that he was "feasting with panthers." I used to think that was hyperbole until you consider what a starving thug would resemble when presented with a champagne supper in a private room at one of the better restaurants. The From Hell chapter showing the contrast between Gull starting his day in his pampered and elegant home and the prostitutes starting their day expressed this very eloquently. It seems an implication of Empire, doesn't it? England's global empire with London at its heart and Whitechapel in the heart of London. Oscar Wilde was probably only the most public incarnation of a spreading awareness: "We are Rome! Everything is ours for the taking!" How many double lives were being led? It beggars the imagination, when so many human souls were there for the taking, for mere pennies. I'd like to get back to Gull himself — or whoever Jack the Ripper was — but that being "ground zero," as it were, I thought I'd see if you had anything to add to what I've said here about the "outward bound" ripple effect specifically, before I switch that particular gear?

Regarding Oscar Wilde and his double life, it's probably worth mentioning a piece on *Jekyll and Hyde* that I saw which made a convincing case for saying that the whole central metaphor of Stevenson's nightmare story related to a current of suppressed homosexuality in male Victorian society and also, possibly, in the author himself. It referred specifically to the scene in which Edward Hyde is approached in a dark street by a refined, elderly gentleman who whispers something to Hyde that precipitates an outbreak of animal violence. This, and the reaction of Stevenson's wife to the book...she thought it hideous and did not approve of its publication...add weight to the suggestion that possibly it was thought to be too revealing of this Uranian socio-sexual undercurrent. To some degree, even if we do not focus on homosexuality as the central issue, the plight of Henry Jekyll is resonant as a metaphor for the whole of a Victorian society where virtue was never lauded so loudly in public nor vice practised so excessively in private. You can almost see in that novel the exact point where the mass Victorian mind became uneasily aware of its own shadow: Hyde as Jekyll's shadow; Jack as Gull's; Wilde's panther-snacks as the shadow of society's own corseted sitting-room asexuality.

Jumping the rails completely and moving on to your invitation for any final words on the "ripple effect," I should probably muddy the waters further by throwing in another possible metaphorical way of looking at the phenomenon. This is a kind of game invented by physicists and mathematicians in order to model and study the behaviour of the early universe. I believe it's called "The Game of Life."

What happens is, you take a checkerboard of potentially infinite size (or do it on a computer, which would be a lot easier) and then randomly scatter a number of black checkers into the board, letting them fall where they will. This done, you apply a couple of very simple and fundamental rules. Maybe one rule is that for any two pieces with a diagonal space empty between them, a piece will be added to fill that space. Maybe another rule says that for any three pieces in a connected line laterally, the central piece will be removed. These aren't the actual rules of the game, which I'm afraid I don't remember, but the point is that the actual rules are that few and that simple.

If these very simple rules are applied to the randomly scattered checkers on the board and then applied again to the new configurations that result and so on, what happens is that you very quickly get complex, orderly and beautiful radiating patterns arising out of the completely incoherent initial chaos. This suggests that from simple and random start conditions, complex order can radiate, given the application of a minimal number of simple rules.

Applying this to the Whitechapel crimes and to the development of the field of Ripper theory since then, it's possible to see how the initial event might very well have been something utterly random and chaotic. (I think of Eddie's persuasive theory that I read somewhere a while back, which was that Jack the Ripper was, in all likelihood, simply the lunatic nearest the asylum door when it was left open, and he happened to be holding the bread knife at the time. This, on reflection, has a great deal to recommend it.) Taking the initial meaningless chaos of this supposed event, we next apply a couple of very simple rules. For rule one, maybe, we could say, "Speculation on the crimes will only extend insofar as it is profitable for it to extend." Rule two might be: "Published speculations on the Whitechapel murders will be profitable in direct proportion to their degree of novelty."

Apply these very simple and practical rules to the incoherent and chaotic sprawl of bloodstains, alibis, and random events surrounding the Whitechapel crimes, and it seems very possible to me that you would quickly find spectacular orderly blossoms of idea and theory radiating out from the murders, in breathtaking arrays of increasing complexity and symmetry. Perhaps this is our ripple pattern, or, at least, another useful way of understanding it — another useful model.

This is probably stuff I'll be covering in *Dance of the Gull Catchers*, but it strikes me that the interesting thing is the point where this radiating and increasingly complex matrix of theory and idea starts to become *self-aware*, which is to say aware of itself as a process, as a developing body of myth. You can see some signs of "Ripperology" starting to include itself as an entity within its own field of study, with critical appraisals of the evolving field of Whitechapel literature appearing in *Begg, Fido*, and Skinner's *Jack the Ripper A-Z* alongside information on the crimes themselves, and you can certainly see it at work in *From Hell*. I suppose what I'm saying is that the initial ripple effect reaches a point where you get all sorts of rich interference patterns and overlappings and feedback loops, so that the simplest of initial splashes or ripples can quickly become a complex and shimmering moiré effect straight out of one of Jim Steranko's good days. Anyway, those are my only current musings on the subject, so back to you.

End of Part One

PIET CORR

Right: *Piet Corr a.k.a.* **pietdesnapp**
*is a freelance photographer and
lecturer, born in Northampton. His
work has been exhibited in galleries
and libraries all over England.
Photograph ©2003 Piet Corr.*

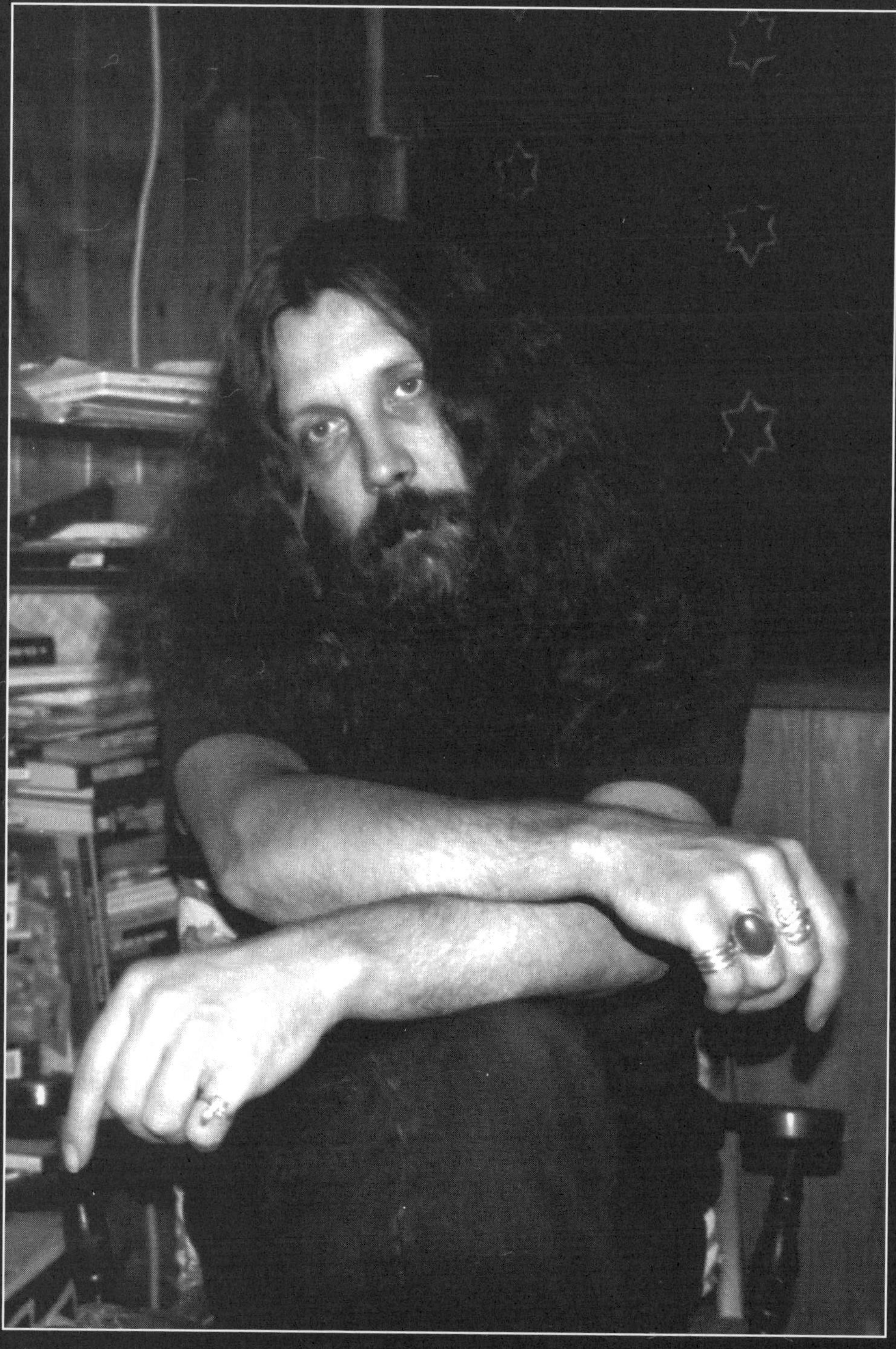

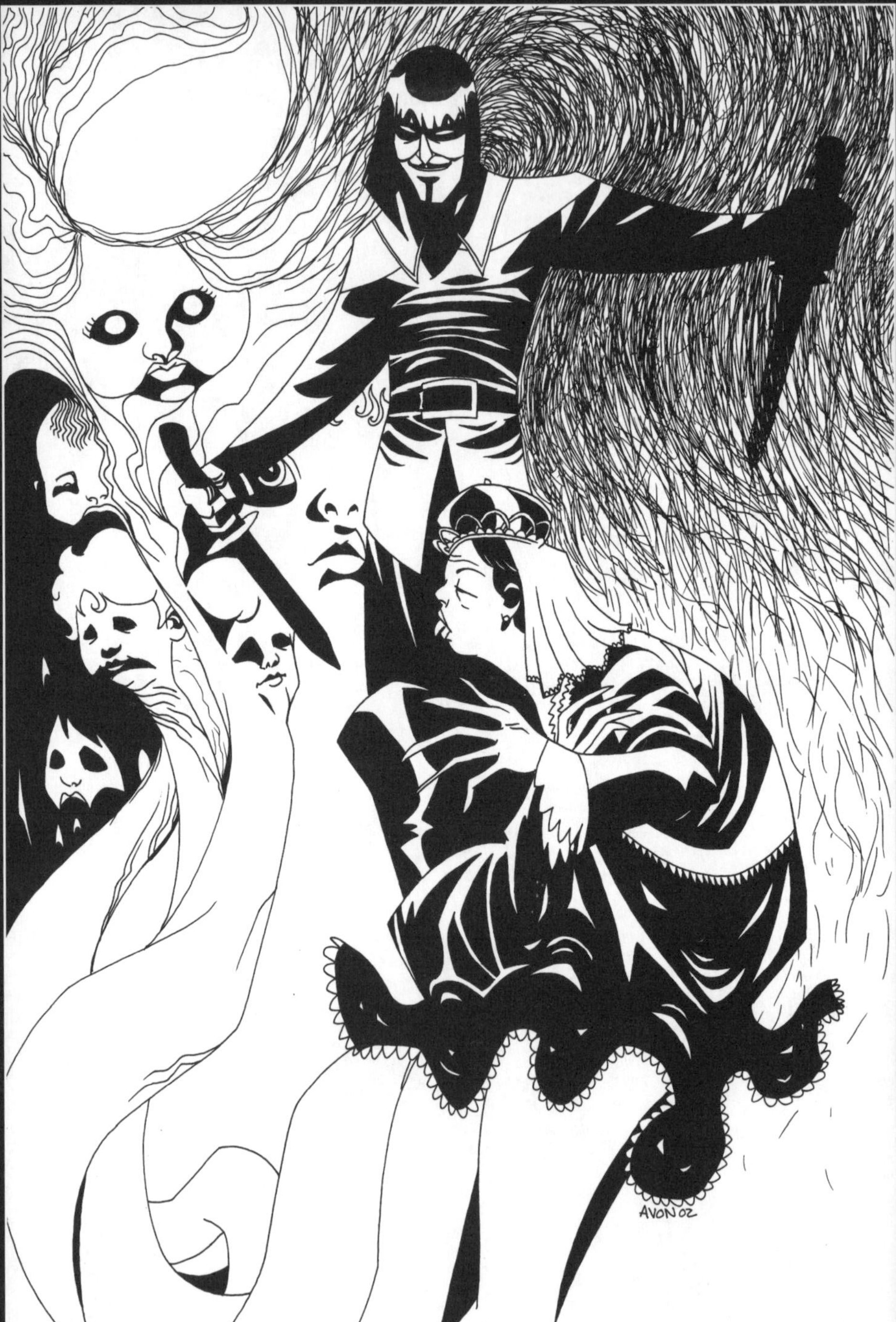
AVON 02

CORRESPONDENCE: FROM HELL
Part 2

Yes, the impact of relentlessly suppressing the sin of the cities of the plain in the first global Christian Empire while illicitly partaking of the "love that dare not speak its name" shouldn't be underestimated as a large — perhaps largest — dynamic. Although it is easy to do so, given our late-twentieth-century vantage point. And on your most recent thinking — are these events important because they attract so much attention or do they attract so much attention because they're important? A simultaneous "yes" would seem to be both our answers (or...er...all four of our answers).

Let's edge our way back to Dr. Gull. I remember thinking, when I hit the first sequence with Queen Victoria, "Well, there goes Alan's knighthood." Bit of a long shot in any case, I suppose, and more's the pity. I've thought Her Royal Majesty (the current one, that is) would be well served by a Rasputin-like figure in proximity, and you could probably make it from Northampton to Buckingham Palace in a couple of hours (if the traffic was good) as required.

I think you might have been of admirable service through the whole Fergie and Di fiasco. Then again, perhaps not.

Anyway, you twice alluded to a dispute with the much-maligned (at least by us) Mr. Campbell in your appendices regarding Victoria Regina. Muckraker that I am, I'd like a blow-by-blow account and — while you're dishing up the dirt — any other points of friction in the creative end of the collaboration.

In all seriousness, you both strike me as very strong-willed and focused in your creativity, and while you were the writer on this project and Eddie the artist, you are also quite an illustrator and Eddie (I'm sure you'll agree) is quite a writer. It would be unnatural if you didn't "lock horns" on one point or another.

I'm afraid this is going to come as a bitter disappointment, but I don't remember any real serious disagreement passing between my ancestrally challenged artist and myself during the entire eight years of the work's duration. I mean, the thing with Queen Victoria wasn't really an issue, and Eddie didn't make half as much fuss about it as implied in my appendix notes. It's just that I don't like to let an opportunity to slander and misrepresent him go by. I don't know why. He's never done anything to me. He just sort of brings it out in me, do you know what I mean?

Basically, he said he felt that I was being, historically speaking, a little unfair and unnecessarily harsh in my portrayal of Queen Victoria and that reality flew out of the window whenever Fat Vicky made an appearance. For my part I was surprised, since I thought reality had flown out of the window with the giant three-headed goat-god in chapter two. Anyway, as far as I remember, I said that he was probably right, but that I didn't much care because I thought that the Hanoverians could pretty much look after themselves and that having one's descendants own roughly a third of all property in the British Isles might go some small way to providing solace for being portrayed as a miserable old cow in *From Hell*. Also, I promised that I wouldn't be having any more appearances from Victoria, so Eddie needn't worry himself, and then threw in a couple more scenes with her anyway, just for the sheer heck of it. So, yeah, that's both our OBEs down the shitter really. Ah well.

Other than that, I don't think there's been a single disagreement between us. That's not to say Eddie hasn't occasionally picked me up, quite correctly, on more important historical details, like the occasion where I had Netley driving Gull over a then-uncompleted Tower Bridge and received a stinging and sarcastic doctored photograph of the half-completed bridge with a little tiny coach and horses plunging over the unfinished edge of the structure and into the Thames below, complete with a little "Yaaaagh!" word balloon. He thinks he's clever and funny, but he isn't. It's not big to make fun of people's genuine and inadvertent mistakes like that; it's just childish.

I suppose that you would expect more quarrels, really. I mean, you're right when you point out that Eddie and I are both strong-willed and stubborn people, but then, on the other

MICHAEL AVON OEMING

Left: *Oeming started his career at the age of 14 inking for Innovation Comics. He's the artist on* **Bastard Samurai,** *Image Comics' hit series* **Powers** *and is currently working on* **Parliament of Justice.**
www.mike-oeming.com
Illustration ©2003 Michael Avon Oeming.
V for Vendetta ©2003 DC Comics.

hand, he puts away three bottles of a particularly mischievous little Chianti before brunch, and I am generally medicated to the point where I can only signal with my eye movements. This means that while we have probably had strong, even violent disagreements, neither of us could remember the thread of his argument for long enough to convey it to the other one, or even why we'd called in the first place. If there is not actual solidarity amongst the deliberately dysfunctional, neither is there any coherent disagreement. That's a working partnership right there.

You should both be able to get a substantial grant from the Betty Ford Clinic for a Guide to Successful Comic-Book Collaboration. If need arises for either corroboration or a ringing endorsement, please don't hesitate to call upon Gerhard and myself.

Now, then. Dr. William Gull.

I'm going to start by paraphrasing certain of your observations from 1988, particularly as regarding ritualistic murder. In those societies which practised the sacrificing of animals and humans to appease their gods, it was as much for the release of mystical energy involved as for anything else. This is something we've "lost track of" in our technological and scientific age, viewing — as an example — the emperors and priests of Rome sacrificing animals and then reading auguries in their entrails as a particularly gruesome and brainless enterprise. And yet it was really just the most extreme aspect of another way of life where natural phenomena of all sorts could be read as another language. A crow landing on a soldier's shield or an owl showing itself in the daytime had the clearest possible meaning to those living their lives in that context. Evidence would seem to indicate that auspices of this kind had at least as good a success rate as medical diagnosis and a sight better success rate than, say, weather forecasting in our own time. The ritualistic shedding of blood unleashes energy within the perpetrator analogous to the wave of energy — in the external world — that we have already discussed and which is common in considering any murder scene from Dealey Plaza to Nicole Brown Simpson's condominium walkway.

In your research into the psychology of serial killers, I saw a lot in common with my approach to Church & State *and* Mothers & Daughters *— taking a series of scientific "givens" and applying "high-altitude mapping" to the implications that present themselves as story-point touchstones. You don't invent any facts; you just read them differently. In light of your theorising, the ritual and aura phases in the mental cycles of the serial killer take on a whole new dimension and perspective.*

I'm going to give you a chance, now, to clarify some of this — particularly as it applies to your fictional extrapolation of Dr. William Gull — before I get to my specific questions about that breathtaking volume seven.

At the risk of driving this "high-altitude mapping" metaphor completely into the turf, I suppose that as you close in upon or descend towards the narrative from your initial high point of observation, the perspective and parallax adjust themselves around you as you free-fall through the field of information. The picture beneath you doesn't change, but the resolution improves so that what were previously flat features on a two dimensional landscape resolve themselves into a more definite topography. On a flat map, a high mountain might appear identical at first glance to a deep valley. Only when you start to close in on the territory itself does the physical difference become apparent.

Concerning my early notions about the idea of human sacrifice as related to the above, I'd have to say that my perspective modified itself radically during the course of the work. This is not to say that I think my earlier notions are wrong, so much as to say that I now feel I have a broader picture. I still believe that, in some instances, the violation of taboo involved in taking a human life might involve such a ritually powerful psychological shock in the mind of the high priest (or serial murderer) that it propels him over the edge into some desired higher or at least altered state. You could support this with the testimonial of Joseph Kellerman, the serial-murdering "Shoemaker" from Flora Rhetta Schreiber's book of the same name. Kellerman's "aura" phase, during which he suffered from visual and auditory hallucinations, continued right up to and during the actual murders themselves. What's interesting is Kellerman's comment during the book ...and I'm paraphrasing from memory now...that while at first he would have hallucinations, feel weird, hear voices, and then go and kill somebody, as his killing career progressed there came a point where he was committing the murders in *order* to see hallucinations, feel weird, and hear voices. The murders, in other words, became his way of accessing an alien universe — an altered reality.

Like I say, this was my basic prognosis at the opening of *From Hell*, and I think it still holds water. What I hadn't considered, however, was the obverse of the coin: what is the *victim's* relationship to the killing?

Two books led me to what I feel is an improved understanding of this issue. The first was *The Random House Dictionary of the English Language*...definitely the most powerful *Grimoire* of magical spells in my extensive collection...which translates the Latin root of the word "sacrifice" as "to make holy." The second book was Patrick Tierney's *The Highest Altar* (Viking Books, 1989), in which the author recounts his travels and studies in Peru as part of a deeper investigation of the nature and meaning of the phenomenon of human sacrifice.

According to Tierney, the object of human sacrifice, at least in the fairly broad region that he studied, was to translate the supposed "victim" into a god, who would then hopefully intervene on behalf of the mortal tribe in the court of the immortals. The best families would compete for the honour of having their son or daughter be the chosen one, after which one child or youth would be selected. This incipient deity would then spend perhaps a year on a grand tour of the country, born aloft on waves of adulation that would make Elvis and Michael Jackson weep with envy. Every step they took would be on rose petals. At the end of the year, they would be made holy. This was often done by taking the child up to the top of some Andean peak, seating them in a beautifully decorated shrine full of offerings, administering an anaesthetic drug, and then leaving them to die of exposure. This is actually one of the best ways to die, by all accounts, since the body and mind simply sink into a warm, coma-like torpor and sleep from which they never wake up. With this shucking of the gross material body, the essence of the child would be free to make its way into the tribe's visionary afterlife landscape and take its place amongst the gods, remembered and petitioned by its people forever.

Now, while it might seem a considerable leap from some mountain-top bower of incense and tropical flowers to what Iain Sinclair referred to as the meat decor of Miller's Court, I think that some intriguing observations are made possible when the Whitechapel murders are considered in this rarefied context. For example, the statements made by Whitechapel women of the period, that I was discussing earlier, to the effect that they wouldn't mind being a victim themselves if it made people say nice things about them. These superficially tragic and desolate sentiments take on a different and more resonant cast if considered in the light of Peruvian families competing for *their* child to be chosen as the one made holy. It's as if those women had the idea that a lifetime of regret and mean, impoverished living could be wiped clean with one sudden movement of the right knife, in the right hands. Literally at a stroke they would be transformed into a local saint, as Polly Nicholls had been, as Mary Kelly had been.

My own ideas about the nature of the magical experience revolve around the concept of an "Idea Space," in which some of the more complex of these entities might actually be considered to be "alive" in some special sense. Within this framework, the idea of sacrifice takes on a slightly different colouring. I myself have made sacrifices in a ritual context, but since I'm in the unfortunate position of being a diabolist *and* vegetarian, I'm afraid living sacrifices were out of the question. My own solution is to consider the mechanics of the act of sacrifice in the following light: if you wish to make a supplication to a supposed entity that is composed entirely of ideas and lives in a realm composed entirely of ideas, then it should be clear that something physical would be of no use whatsoever to such a hypothetical being. Such a being would not traffic in actual *things* so much as in the *ideas* of actual things.

Now, let us accept for the moment that any entity or object that we can perceive in the material universe is composed of two basic components. Firstly, there is the reality of its actual physical being: its material presence in space or time. Then, there is the *idea* of the object or entity, an immaterial presence unbounded by the same considerations of space and time. As a ready example, I could cite the death of a loved one: the physical presence is gone, broken down to its constituent chemicals, its constituent atoms. That person does not exist physically anymore as a discrete physical entity. The Idea-Presence of that person cannot die, however. It hangs around and wakes you up crying at four in the morning. Five years later it taps you on the shoulder while you're doing the washing up and it makes you smile.

In my own ritual sacrifices, I have burned objects of meaning and significance to me, including the original to one of the magical drawings I sent you a while back. The idea is to sacrifice, in the conventional sense of "giving up," something which is of value to me. It is also to remove the physical component of the object, leaving only the memory or Idea Space presence of the object intact. In my terms, this removal of the physical component makes the object "sacred," i.e., existing only on a level above the tangible and material world.

Richard Dawkins, author of the excellent *The Blind Watchmaker* and a staunch materialist who would have no truck at all with any of my vague metaphysical notions, would maybe describe this "Idea Presence" as the sum of a person's *memes*, a sort of idea-space equivalent of genes, an ideological genetic code that will endure after the death of the individual and continue to interact with the material world. Dawkins cites the fact that while there are no measurable genetic traces of the philosopher Socrates to be found anywhere in the world, there are *memetic* traces to be found on every hand: Socrates' ideas are still current and still have their effect upon the world of human thinking. My own ideas are perhaps a tad more mystical than Dawkins', but he provides a useful model.

In terms of the Whitechapel crimes, we cannot establish a real material physical identity for the being we call Jack the Ripper. Not Gull, not Druitt, not Stephen, and certainly not poor old bloody James Maybrick. Jack the Ripper, in a very real sense, never actually had a physical existence. He was a collage-creature, made from crank letters, hoaxes, and sensational headlines. He exists wholly in Idea Space, looming forward from our books of theory and our fictions, from our slasher films and our contemporary mythology of serial murder, from the pages and appendices of *From Hell*. He is unencumbered by a physical body or human identity. He has transcended human reality to become, like it or not, one of our immortals.

In a sense, it might also be said that in choosing his victims, he elected them to the same extra-human estate that he himself was destined for. Five anonymous Whitechapel women now live in the realm of legend forever, are translated from weak and ailing flesh into symbols, martyrs, saints of a kind. Look at the grave marker to Marie Jeanette Kelly, "the primadonna of Spitalfields," erected in Leytonstone churchyard by besotted ripperologist John Morrison. If the realm of concept and consciousness is, as I believe it to be, truly the realm of the sacred, then in the crucible of the Whitechapel murders, both killer and victims were in a sense "made holy."

I'm reading the Old Testament right now and — as pertains to our discussion here — the sacrifices made to the God of Israel by his chosen people have given me much food for thought. In David's Psalms he makes reference (I'm paraphrasing obviously) that the ritual sacrifice of seven bulls, seven sheep, etc., which had been a centrepiece of worship to that point, were not really...necessary?

Required? Appreciated? History has certainly shown that the Bible has as many interpretations as there are readers, but it seemed to me that God was grudging in his tolerance of the Priesthood, the Tabernacle, Solomon's Temple, ritual sacrifice. A kind of: well, fine, if that's what you want, by all means — just don't forget the Ten Commandments. Which the Tribes of Israel always did. I found myself wondering if the sacrifice wasn't tolerated by God because it had a kind of energising, focusing effect that was useful in keeping the easily distracted and tempted mass of the congregation within the fold. Rather like the unleavened bread as a metaphor for racial purity. Certainly God seems to save his greatest wrath for those who "pass their children through the fire" — human sacrifice — as well as those stiff-necked women with their groves and graven images and baking cakes for the Queen of Heaven (!), which seems to be an implication of tolerating sacrifice of any kind. Let them burn the flesh of a few bulls and sheep, and before you know it they're burning incense and sugar cane and their kids to Baal and his (or her) mates.

Now, meanwhile back at old Gull, I'm not sure if you intended his dismembering of Mary Kelly — that is, the way you portrayed it — to draw an interesting parallel between medical science and magic ritual, but I found that part genuinely engaging (in a terrifying sort of way). Hinton appears to him only after the initial bloodletting and as he begins to bank the fire into an inferno. Then...then!...the nearly poetical description of his autopsy, his demeanour calm, his voice even and measured, being a kind of intonation or invocation clearly heightening his awareness as he subsides into a hypnogogic trance state.

Harking back to our conversation in '88, I was prepared for the sudden, larger insight which takes hold of him (or he of it) on page 19 of Chapter 10.

If it isn't "giving away the game," I was wondering if you might fill in the blanks represented by panel 6 on that page and the last panel on page 19 and the first panel on page 20. If it were any other writer, I'd pass them off as window-dressing and gobbledygook. In your case, I'd be willing to bet that these panels constitute — at the very least — either a "Eureka! That's it" insight you yourself achieved at some point in researching From Hell *(and you can certainly be forgiven for not sharing it with me and my readers if it came at some personal cost to you) or an intimation of a finished puzzle whose pieces you're rearranging from time to time but which haven't coalesced into anything coherent beyond the state at which they arrived in your own awareness.*

Or am I way off base here?

The scene in question was something that evolved from my own experiences and ruminations concerning the non-ordinary consciousness; the magical state; the process of going mental; call it what you will. Obviously, I'd had some of the conceptual groundwork for the scene floating around for years, and all of the gross physical mechanics of the situation were as set down in the doctor's report of a century earlier. What I didn't have until comparatively recently was any clue as to how the occurrence in Miller's Court might actually feel to the perpetrator, beyond, that is, the statistical analyses of serial murder compiled by Robert K. Ressler and the F.B.I's VIVAP program. Those lucid behavioural profiles were too sharp, too clinical: a virtual and digitised reconstruction of the murder scene that was mathematically accurate but necessarily bloodless. I needed something at once less distinct and more authentic. More blurred and less objective. Something that made more sense, by making less.

In my own experiences of an influx of apparently "magical" consciousness, notably in the more intense instances, the actual condition could be described as very much like what is known in psychiatric terms as a "fugue state." As the name implies, this is a state of consciousness very much like a musical fugue, though not always as harmonic or uplifting. As with a musical fugue, several different strands of information, the mind's music, are being played at once. As with a musical fugue, an attempt to focus on one particular strand of the arrangement will render you unable to hear the unified whole, and vice versa: in order to enjoy the piece as a whole work, you must forgo briefly the pleasure of listening to the progression of the individual and separate musical structures that it is composed from. In terms of listening to music, this is a harmonious experience. In terms of human consciousness, it is much more likely to be disorienting, overwhelming, even terrifying.

During the fugue state, the mind is like a twenty-four-track mixing disk with separate strands of complex information on each separate track. The engineer responsible for the final mix that is one's consciousness, unfortunately, is a baboon. Tracks (of thought) suddenly blast in out of nowhere or just as suddenly drop out of existence. Melody swells up, is gone, its presence only registered moments later. Both speakers cut out, and when they cut back in there are six of them. One is playing what sounds like Inuit opera, another broadcasts a debate on superstring theory conducted entirely in a Maori dialect. At some point during all this, the rational everyday self that is frantically trying to weave all this alien sensory input into something that at least nods to conventional reality, very sensibly takes the coward's way out. It gives up, shouts "Danger, Will Robinson" a couple of times, then shoots out blue sparks, and falls onto its side. It dies. This forces the self that exists *behind* our "front identity" to take over the wheel of the moving vehicle. After that, it gets rather difficult to describe, firstly because what is going on isn't remotely human, and secondly because one's self isn't actually present while all this is occurring. Whoever is in control of the vertical and horizontal, as it were, isn't you. Recollection of the experience is necessarily non-linear, fragmentary. Time, mind, identity, cause and effect...all of these have been behaving in unusual ways. A certain confusion is forgivable.

As regards Chapter Ten, what I wanted to convey was a sense of this, of Gull's mounting fugue state as he tunes into voices from times past, visions of the inner body, different levels of perception, and different perceptions of his own identity. The brief, endless instant of being obsessed, possessed, ridden, or taken over by one of the archetypes, the god forms. The shattering and sudden knowledge that you are not you, have never been you, are only a fragile and temporary mask for...I don't know. Shit, I write comics, okay? I don't know...for essential Platonic entities/events, for the Great Old Ones, for Cthulhu. For things that are more like language, or embedded codes, than they are like life, although they live. Things that are no more than an eternally reiterated acting-out of their own primal legends, things that *are* their own stories. Which stories our own apparently individual thoughts, identities, and actions can only reiterate and repeat. Deities, or sections of the fundamental text whereby are our lives scripted, all of them. The reason that all stories are true is that there is only one story.

William Gull's progressive alteration of the text that is Mary Kelly's physical body shades into William Burroughs, maybe with Brian Gysin as Netley. Cut-up technique, they call it. The scalpel interrupts the   normal linear continuity of things, allows new possibilities. Sometimes, intimations of the future leak through, luminous dribbles of the eternal. The consciousness of the artist, of the writer, or of the beef-sculptor, is changed along with the deliberate disruption of the work in question, of his successful and much-visited Dorset Street installation. Gull drifts in and out of different times, different texts, different identities. The mutilation he is carrying out unfolds in his mind, through escalating levels of metaphor, becomes all mutilations, all murder. The Babylonian Goddess Tiamat, described by Robert Graves as the primal Mother-Deity in her earliest incarnation, is supplanted by the male god Marduk. Their legend reflects this, with Tiamat reinvented as a malignant and evil serpent-monster, a dragon that is slain and dismembered by the solar Marduk during the creation as described in the *Enuma Elish*. Gull, momentarily and forever, becomes Marduk, just as his victim is translated, transliterated into Tiamat. For a moment the flash of becoming is too brief, too instantaneous to register on the doctor's mind. A second or two passes, and the comprehension of what has just happened to him starts to filter through. Enervated, palpitating from the rigors of the experience, he tries to assemble a jigsaw awareness from these burning fragments, but before he can do so the next voice in the fugue enters, the next wave of alien consciousness crashes in, carrying him away.

I can't say much more than the above, Dave, and I apologise for stating the above so obscurely and in such an overwrought manner. There are language difficulties that are attendant to describing these conditions, as I'm sure you appreciate. It's not that I have any reservations about discussing these matters clearly and lucidly; it's just that I can't. There's some sort of quantum uncertainty law in operation that means that if a thought is pinned down too hard, if a thing is defined too exactly, then the essence and life of that experience is not properly conveyed. Like the problem of knowing *either* the velocity *or* the location of a particle, if that makes sense. The problem is in finding a balance where extra-rational phenomena and perceptions can be discussed in a rational way without diminishing them, which is something I'm clearly still working on. Back to you.

I've only experienced it once myself — back in 1979. And, as you say, the human experience is to try to relate it to others, and you do find yourself stuck between the rock of diminishing the experience by trying to express it lucidly and the hard place of expressing it accurately and coming across as ...well, "overwrought" hardly does it justice. It took me about a week to come down far enough to even perceive how I was coming across in conversation: something of a cross between a Travelling Salvation Show preacher and Cthulhu himself. Deni and my mother decided that I needed psychiatric help — not surprisingly and, in retrospect, I can't fault them individually or jointly for their conclusion. I finally got a handle on it...and this is going to sound odd, I know...by learning to portray myself as normal. You know, "What would a normal person say in this situation?" In my day-to-day life, I became an actor portraying Dave Sim— or at least as accurate a portrayal as I could muster from what I remembered of once being that Dave Sim. My interior life, on the other hand, consisted of sorting through the metaphorical filing cabinet which had exploded in my brain over the course of ten or fifteen seconds. There was so much to go through and so much to assess. I remember thinking, "I really should write a book." And then laughing, right? "Idiot, you are writing a book." And thus was born the concept of the 300-issue maxi-series.

When Gerhard read our last exchange he couldn't remember the sequence I was asking about — which isn't surprising and, as I told him, the thing that I found really charming and (yes, Alan, thank you for my new word) glamorous about it. Everyone remembers the sudden intrusion of the 20th-century office on the following page, just as everyone will remember (or I hope some of them will) the 300-issue maxi-series. The trigger is of far more interest to me, and I thank you for filling in the missing piece in my particular jigsaw puzzle. I'd talk about the trigger for the 300-issue maxi-series, but fortunately this is your interview, not mine.

Gull finds what he's looking for, doesn't he? Even though he doesn't really know what it is that he's looking for. Inside that eternal moment he achieves the highest possible altitude — his own high-altitude mapping, as it were — but he's a flawed vessel. He's a killer of nearly unimaginable proportions, but he is still only human, flesh and blood. I thought it was a nice touch to have him step up on a desk to deliver (what is to him) a god-like harangue that seems (to us) an almost touchingly pathetic demonstration of his own severely limited, severely human limitations. And afterwards, he knows it's over. Any insights you'd care to share about what your fictional Gull might've thought about as he reflected on his moment, at the apex? Or am I asking you to write another book? I am. I'm asking you to write another book, but since you're doing it for free, I don't mind if it's a short one.

It seems to me that this is really two questions in one envelope. You want me to write two books. Okay

Given the candour of your own comments above, and in light of the fact that some of the more mystical elements of *From Hell* are derived from personal experience and insight, it seems necessary to draw a line between me and my fictional William Gull ("Sidney Greenstreet after a crash course at the Abby of Thelema," as Iain Sinclair recently, with heartless accuracy, described him). My own responses to the extremities of consciousness outlined above and what happened afterwards were a good deal less dramatic than your own experiences, probably because I'd at least had a few months to get prepared for the event before it happened. I went through the necessary ritual embarrassment of declaring myself to be a magician in the November of 1993, almost like vaccinating yourself with a mild and controlled form of mental breakdown so that you'll hopefully have sufficient antibodies to fend off the greater madness when it comes.

The lightning bolt proper didn't hit me until the early January of 1994. More importantly, it hit me in the middle of a deliberate (although relatively minor and casual) magical working, and most importantly of all, it didn't hit me when I was alone. I was with another magician, and it hit him too. Thus, to some extent the subsequent tumult of extra-normal experience was what we had asked for and expected (except of course we didn't, not really), and furthermore we each had the other's confirmation and validation for some of the more peculiar moments.

The couple of months of preparation, were, I think, vital. Your filing cabinet analogy is an excellent one, in that it seems our ability to cope with experience, any experience, depends upon our ability to instantly sort experience into the extensive perceptual filing system that facilitates our view of reality. Crossing a street, quite unconsciously, we are sorting the world around us into different categories in our perceptual filing system: motionless car — no threat. Moving car — slow, not threat — safe to cross the street ahead of it. Moving car — fast, threat — wait at the curb until it's gone past. Woman with perambulator — no threat. Three drunk guys shouting and waving a bottle — threat, avoid.

I'm not saying that we break the whole of reality down into threat/no threat...the process is much more complex, with hundreds of different vectors in our sorting system. While ordering in a restaurant we subject the menu to a filing system organised around "like/don't like." While creating a piece of writing or art we make our creative discriminations along the lines of "good idea/ bad idea." The thing is that in all these different instances, in order to make decisions about any of these things, we first have to be able to recognise and identify each phenomenon. We have to know what a slow-moving car is, what a well-done steak is, what a bad artistic idea is. These things have to exist already or have a place in our filing system before we know how to respond to them.

With the magical experience, what happens is that you suddenly get a whole mess of stuff in the in-tray that you don't have the first fucking clue how to classify. This is not a woman with a perambulator, or a well-done steak. This is something that may be a rose, a century, the Platonic essence of the colour green, or all of these at once. This thing over here is a Sqmrlpstgyzlt: it eats a by-product of human jealousy and it shits previously undiscovered prime numbers. The only sane thing to do in the face of sensory input like this is to go mad. The filing cabinet will not cope, its systems of taxonomy exhausted. It spills over in a big flood of disorganised data across the office floor.

By becoming a magician two or three months prior to the catalytic event, in effect I was ordering a bigger filing cabinet ahead of time. When the event happened, I had at least some rudimentary means to classify it within a system and make sense of it. I've heard it said that all of our human perceptions might be seen as our individual windows on the Universe. The magician is consciously attempting to alter his or her window's width or its angle, so as to get a different view of the landscape outside. The schizophrenic, on the other hand, has had his or her window kicked in by some great big astral skinhead in eighteen-hole Doctor Martens boots. Both of them are experiencing the same flood of phenomena and probably many of the same perceptions. The magician, however, has a means of processing this information. The magician has something to bail with. The schizophrenic can only sink beneath the flood. As Aleister Crowley once succinctly put it (and I'm not paraphrasing here), "The only difference between a schizophrenic and myself is that *I'm* not mad."

Anyway, what happened after my own Pentecostal excursion was that I told my friends and family about the experience in the same relatively calm and orderly way I would tell them about any other event. I told them that I was completely aware that my experiences may be delusional, but that as an unusual mental phenomenon I found them interesting in their own right and so worth pursuing. After a few weeks of wandering round in a kind of productive and very creative daze where I produced a number of illustrations and co-composed and recorded a couple of the best songs I've ever written ("Hair of the Snake that Bit Me" and "Town of Lights," if anyone's remotely interested), I switched to a more analytical mode and began to formulate my Idea Space model, as alluded to above and elsewhere. By this time, my family and associates had become reassured that I was certainly no *less* rational, functional, and creative than I had been before, so they either shrugged and let me get on with it or else actively encouraged me to discourse upon the subject because they found it interesting too.

Basically, I didn't have to "act normal" or to publicly deny that such a thing had seemingly happened to me. I'm personally glad about this, because it allows a continuity of identity, with less potential schism or confusion between the external or internal world as a result.

In addition to this, it strikes me that maybe people sort of expect guys with haircuts and beards like mine to rave and prophesy every once in a while, and so don't pay it much attention. You've probably just got the wrong hairstylist, Dave. Maybe I could set myself up as an image consultant and spin doctor to the discriminating necromancer.

Okay, so the above is the story as far as I'm concerned. My fictional Gull, although he too goes through a dreamy and drifting spaced-out period after his non-ordinary event, is running on a very different program. What happens with Gull, the sense of almost post-coital flatness that descends upon him, is more influenced by the classic personality profile of the serial murderer than it is by my own experiences.

Your classic, textbook serial murderers will often seem to reach a point where whatever complex and iterative emotional equation they were working through has evidently been resolved. At this point, sometimes perhaps they kill themselves. More often, they will either give themselves to the police (like Ed Kemper did) or make deliberately shoddy mistakes in their work that they know will lead the police straight to them (like Henry Lee Lucas did). Kemper, who would rape, kill, and decapitate his victims, sometimes even in that order, finally murdered his mother, whom it might be argued he had been trying to get up the nerve to murder all along, his other victims being only surrogates — rehearsals. After this climactic and cathartic homicide, Kemper gave himself up to the police. When they asked him why he hadn't just carried on killing, he seemed puzzled by the question and replied, "There wouldn't have been any point." The program had run its course. The final calculation had been made. There wouldn't have been any point.

This is what happens to Gull: he reaches his pinnacle. He plants his ensanguined flag. The expedition, the ascent, is concluded. There is nowhere to go but down, into aftermath. The fuel rod of purpose is spent. Rather than asking, "What doth the Lord require of me?" Gull realises that, his task concluded, he is no longer required for anything, or at least not by the Lord. The long climb down, the decline towards his death amongst the straws of an Islington asylum, begins. As for what exactly is going through his mind, I really couldn't tell you. I suppose you'd have had to be there.

Actually, I made the conscious decision some time ago — perhaps seven or eight years — to make myself look normal. Part and parcel of the decision to portray a normal person. No good. Doesn't matter how short my hair is or how clean-shaven I am, people still look at me as if I just landed from Mars. But the point about yourself is well taken — speaking as an outside observer and listener, the hair and the beard aren't a patch on the eyes and the voice. Also, it turns out that my inward self ended up just having to go on a little fifteen-year (minus a week) stroll through...what's the phrase from Lennon's "Mind Games"? Through "Absolute Elsewhere." At that point my portrayal and my actual self remerged into a mostly blissful union, and (God willing) I look forward to them...us...ME living happily ever after. ("Heehee — 'Them,' he says." "All right, all right, that's enough.")

Now, there was a bit of a lapse between my last fax and your reply, and I had almost considered sending you a supplementary one. By asking, "What was your fictional Gull thinking about?" it would be easy to infer that you hadn't covered that. Which you had, and it was one of the most satisfying parts of the story to me. So, I felt (yes, Alan — FELT) bad in retrospect. Through the immediate aftermath of my own "lightning bolt" hitting, I can remember being on the cusp of really expressing something — really getting a handle on it — and someone asking me a really basic question which not only blew my train of thought to smithereens but really sapped me of that weird strength and super clarity that I was experiencing. "Dr. Gull? Are you fit to continue?" In the context of the hearing / trial it's a very basic question, but in Gull's own context, the residue of the "like unto a god" state he has achieved in the abattoir of Miller's Court, it would definitely echo and re-echo through the macrocosm and microcosm of his magnified awareness. "Hold on, I was just getting to...getting to..." and he really was. His perception of himself as the fulfilment of what the Masons are/always were/always wanted to be, the embodiment made flesh, as it were, facing the embodiment of the most ancient structure, the living edifice of the Masons. "Dr. Gull? Are you fit to continue?" It forces him to try himSELF in the upper reaches of what he has connected with. I read into it his own awarenesses shutting down like the lights going out on a skyscraper on each floor from the top down, the momentum carrying them past the lighted floor of even cursory consciousness, taking him from the indictment of those he saw as being as insects before him to being unable even to discern whether this was the trial part of his Eternal Moment or if he was still in Miller's Court. "No, I'm not fit to continue — either as a would-be god OR as Dr. Gull." And so he doesn't. And so he doesn't.

It strikes me that the danger of these "lightning bolts" is in mistakenly interpreting them — or mucking in your own ego and personality with the actual...intention of them? If they can be said to have an intention. "The necessary ritual embarrassment of declaring myself to be a magician..." There is a lot of embarrassment involved, isn't there? On one hand, you KNOW what you experienced. You're really forced to describe them as "unusual mental phenomen(a)" when you know how inaccurate that is. Having just finished a biography of William Blake, I understand he suffered terribly from this. In many ways, he was the original self-publisher. I mean, I really want to do a good multilayered story with Cerebus, and I have a compulsion to say a lot of — probably too many — things in the six thousand pages. But, man, at least I don't have a sense of being put here on Earth to put everything right. To me, Blake clearly thought he was Moses or Jacob or the heir to their legacy, anyway. Chosen by God to tell the world what really happened, get everyone to agree that every Renaissance painter he didn't like was a fraud and everyone he did like was a prophet or a beacon on the hill, everyone he liked was an angel from his personal God until he didn't like those people anymore, at which time they were one of the Legions of Hell sent to torment him. People like that I find very worrisome. Because it's difficult to discount him out of hand. Certainly the endurance of his work would tell us that he wasn't just a great design guy with a lousy finish, as he was popularly perceived at the time. But how much further "up" from there am I willing to go? And where does his crusty, envious-of-success, self-righteous human ego stop and the "enlightenment" begin?

It's why I've always liked Robert Crumb's "Meatball" strip. "Meatball" bonks people on the head and has this variety of effects. Sometimes it's a whole city, and sometimes it's Kim Novak on the Tonight Show (that one really cracks me up). It's completely unpredictable, and it has as much in common with a pie-in-the-face as it does with Celestial Choirs.

Any thoughts on this before we retreat from Gull and discuss the aftermath chapters?

Regarding Gull's glimpse of his trial and how a chance remark from "the future" reveals different meanings when taken in the context of his "present," your summary is pretty well spot on.

As for the dangers of the visionary experience. I think that you're absolutely right to point out the problems of how our own desires, ego, and run-amok imaginations can easily lead us into delusion when interpreting such an experience. For my part, I regard my observations concerning magic and vision as part of an ongoing dialogue. Working on the basis that it's better to travel hopefully than to arrive, I try to avoid conclusions, no matter how juicy and tempting they may be. I'm afraid that I side with those boring and anti-poetical language revisionists on this one, the people who insist that the language should be revised so that the word "is" is removed and the phrase "seems to me to be" is substituted. (Robert Anton Wilson also usefully suggests the substitution of "sombunall," a contraction of "some but not all," for the word "all," but that's a different issue.)

By avoiding a definite conclusion (especially, say, a conclusion like "I am the Messiah"), what you tend to encourage instead is a kind of constantly self-modifying and unfixed model of how things are that doesn't get mired down in bottomless abstract concepts like "truth." It acknowledges that its view of the world was slightly different yesterday and may be utterly different in a year's time while still enabling one to work with and process the information at hand. The best way to explain what I mean is to court the embarrassment you mention by citing a personal example.

After my initial apparent experience with non-ordinary states in the early January of 1994, I went through a superficially similar but subjectively very different-seeming experience about a month later, in the February of that year. I'll leave out the details, but the upshot was that I found myself seemingly in conversation with an entity that at first identified itself as "One of the Nine Dukes," and then upon closer interrogation as "Asmoday." Its "body," when I asked it to show me what it looked like, consisted of a shifting and shimmering latticework of repeated spider motifs, all identical but at different scales. These, while keeping their colouring consistent, appeared to be constantly turning themselves inside out through a spatial dimension that was foreign to me, becoming on the reverse a similar shifting lattice, this time with a reiterated lizard motif. This would turn itself inside out and become the mesh of spiders again, and so on. As a constant background to this effect, there was a beautiful pattern composed of peacock's-tail eyes. The entire thing was like a 360-degree sphere or field of presence that surrounded my head, moving and speaking lucidly to me (and with great politeness and charm, it must be said).

As with my first experience, other magicians were with me at the time (although not the same people). I remarked to one of them at the time when I was apparently speaking to the supposed entity that it seemed to me that the creature's body was actually a sort of display, since a physical body would clearly have been completely redundant. I wondered if the "bodies" of such creatures aren't more in the nature of the "icons" that people use to represent themselves when surfing the net? Perhaps the perceived forms were more like compound symbols, characters in an unknown language that were meant to impart a kind of non-verbal information to us. At that moment, it struck me that the entity I appeared to be seeing was conveying to me several things by its apparent form: Firstly, it was highly skilled in mathematics and in the visual arts that pertained to mathematics. Secondly, it had at least one more spatial dimension to play with than I did, and it seemed to take an almost smug delight in pointing this fact out to me. There was a quality of likeable vanity that seemed to imply that the emotional range of the entity was not vastly different from that of a human being. (This has not been the case with some of the other "species" of imaginary creature that I like to imagine I've encountered, and thus seemed worth noting.)

Days later, after the experience, I did some research to see what I could find relating to the demon Asmoday, or Asmodeus as he is more often known. It seemed that Asmodeus is considered to be the patron demon of mathematics and handicraft, which fit in with my general perception of the creature but proved nothing one way or the other. There was also some fascinating material on this particular demon's ability to grant an "Asmodeus Flight," wherein the magician will be plucked up into the air by the demon and allowed to fly over his town. On looking down, the demon-borne conjuror would see all the houses below as if their roofs had been removed, so that the occupants inside could be seen going about their lives. This was a fascinating and compelling medieval image, but again didn't seem to signify for much.

Last year, my esteemed colleague Dave Gibbons called me with reference to something he'd come across in a cutting edge science/higher mathematics book called *Fourfield* by Tom Robbin. Mr. Robbin's fascinating book, a dissection of the theory and application of fourth-dimensional maths, takes time off at one point to wonder creatively about what a hypothetical four-dimensional life form, if such a thing existed, might look like to us. Basically, the author's best and most well-informed guess is that such creatures would most probably resemble a shimmering latticework of multiple copies of themselves, all at different scales. This made my ears perk up, and when I was later in receipt of a computer program allowing me to run models of some basic fourth-dimensional forms, I was intrigued to note that some of the other hyperspatial solids on display resembled the visible forms of other non-physical entities that I believed myself to have encountered.

Working from the hypothesis of entities existing at higher levels of space, the "Asmodeus Flight" fable suddenly seemed to have a lot of new possibilities: a three-dimensional human mind, plucked up into the higher reaches of the fourth-dimension by a higher-dimensional entity, and allowed to look down at the three-dimensional landscape below from a fourth-dimensional perspective. The houses, their interiors now visible in the same way the insides of a two-dimensional square are visible to us from up above in our third dimension, seem to the medieval eye to have had their roofs removed. Could it be that the sorcerer in question was actually seeing *around* the roofs and walls via the perception of a fourth dimension beyond the three our world is apparently bounded by?

Now, the upshot of this long-winded digression is that, in light of the above, do I believe that I have actually spoken to a trans-physical four thousand-year-old entity first mentioned in *The Book of Tobit*? No. Do I therefore believe that I have *not* truly conversed with the aforesaid entity? No. I see no particular imperative for me to believe or conclude anything. Meeting the demon Asmodeus was an apparent experience I had. Getting out of bed this morning and having breakfast was another apparent experience. I do not choose to grant either the status of "reality." What I'm *most* tempted by is this whole fourth-dimensional hypothesis, which I find very exciting and which has the ring of "truth" about it, at least in my ears. Do I therefore believe it to be the Truth that gods, angels, demons, and Grey aliens are all actually higher-dimensional creatures, communicating with us through the veil of fourspace? No. It's a good story, though, and I'm very happy to play with it until I find a better or more satisfying one. This, to me, seems a very solid and practical survival strategy. It is admittedly difficult to practice it while in conversation with something that has four hundred eyes and scares the shit out of you, but I believe that such an approach is as close as I'm ever likely to get to sanity.

Moving on, this is not to say I disapprove of Billy Blake's approach to the territory. He walked in his visionary landscape of the mind and talked to his long- dead visionary peers nowhere save inside his skull (he freely admitted as much on some occasions), and yet had the will to insist upon his vision of the world — to insist that was the world in which he roamed and resided, a golden fourfold city of the imagination rather than the dung-jewelled gutters of Oxford Street. If he occasionally seems to have an inflated opinion of himself, it would seem to me only a natural counter-reaction to his seeming wretchedness and failure in all save the eyes of a few close friends (and, of course, posterity). You're right in naming him the first self-publisher, near as damn it, and I think that you might find more in common with him than there seems to be at first glance: a man who had a vision and decided that the best way to convey it was by devoting his life's work to an extended fantasy narrative, a symbolic world where invented characters would play out the drama of the creator's divine insight. Further to this, the work must be created entirely by the self: Blake did almost everything save build his printing press by hand or cut down the trees himself to make the paper. Maybe part of what puts people off about Blake is that he expressed so much of his vision in the language and symbols of the conventional Christian religion of his day, terms which have worn thin in contemporary ears. This is not to discount your own view of Blake of course, simply to suggest that my own is maybe a bit more forgiving and more prepared to overlook the occasional bout of hubris. Lord knows, Dave, we're not above the occasional bout of hubris ourselves, are we? And we haven't even written *London* or painted *Glad Day* yet.

Which biography are you reading, incidentally? Gilchrist's is still probably the most basic and the best, but I very much liked Peter Ackroyd's recent contribution. You've probably got the Albert Goldman "Blake: Saint or Shit-heel?" biography where Blake mainlines a quart jug of Laudanum, exposes himself to neighbourhood children through the privet hedge of his back garden, and refers to the Angel Raphael as a "fucking dress-wearing kike bastard" in private correspondence to the artist Fuseli, whom Blake addresses as "Gloria."

Not so exalted as Gilchrist but not as degraded as Goldman, I'm forced to admit. I mean, I knew when I picked it up that a two-hundred-page Blake biography (the author's name is James King) could constitute little more than a children's Big Golden Book of Billy Blake and His Friends. What few illustrations there are are in muddy black and white, so to say I had no high expectations in the realm of the definitive is to understate the case dramatically. Actually, I was taking a break between reading the Old Testament and plunging into the Apocrypha (since the Bible in question is a reproduction of the 1611 King James Translation, I was amused when I took notice of the biographer's name). Since I came to the Bible by way of Malcolm Muggeridge's A Third Testament (talk about man's reach exceeding his grasp!) and his autobiography, and Muggeridge's pantheon is pretty firmly established around Blake, Pascal, St. Augustine, and a handful of others, I thought I owed it to the old reprobate to at least skim a "Life of..." before looking at the actual work in one of those lavish coffee-table editions which are our present age's most visible testimony to that which endures — or, at least, that which has endured thus far. Since Muggeridge, by his own admission, spent most of his creative energies in the sewer environs of newspaper and television "journalism" basically lying to others (and himself) for money, I think a lot of Blake's appeal to Muggeridge is his "seeming wretchedness and failure." That is, Blake stayed true to himself and his own sense of what is right and what is wrong, and to a Muggeridge that's a lofty plateau to which to aspire, indeed. Blake's chosen road — to Muggeridge — must've seemed separated from that of Our Lord and Saviour Himself only by a degree. You know? Jesus cleared the bar at sixteen feet, Blake managed eight feet, and dear Old Muggs was hard-pressed to get his ass over it at four feet — and in his own heart attributed this to his inability to forsake all riches and the kingdoms of this world and go forth naked before the etc., etc., etc. That is, I think Muggeridge saw Blake as a Job-like figure, tested and tormented at every turn, whose faith endured and who, consequently, at the Pearly Gates got a straight-A report card with a B-minus for deportment. My vantage point, structurally, being a little closer to Blake — keeping Cerebus away from movies, television, lunch boxes, etc. — I tended not to see the Christ-like heroism in Blake that Muggeridge did. What I saw was a fellow who was unable to see the truth in how he was assessed by his peers: great design, lousy finish, and who was forever losing himself in hubris — to me at a wide remove from the "occasional bouts of hubris" to which any human being is prone. Although he was a prayerful man, I pictured him to be always praying to have the world rearranged so it was a little more sensible — you know, with, like, William Blake on top dispensing the Word of God to the great unwashed. It never seemed to occur to him (I mean, literally) that he might be better served by taking a bath himself. Muggeridge, of course, is an entirely different figure in England than he is elsewhere. He didn't declare himself a Christian until well into his twilight years, and — not surprisingly — this was greeted with a great deal of derision, i.e., you've only decided to forego the pleasures of the flesh because you can't get it up anymore and it galls you that others can. I saw a great deal in common with Blake in this — that much of his excessive zeal came from wanting to externalise the torments that his penis getting hard caused him. Once Blake subsides and stops throwing everyone out of his life and trying to pass off his personal prejudices and preferences in art and wisdom as divine in origin, he gets a nice little circle of acolytes to hang on his every word, kneel at his feet, and kiss his door-knocker on the way in for a visit. Which to me looked like just another submission to his own hubris and was probably more attributable to God rewarding his wife Catherine for putting up with the curmudgeon-from-birth than any kind of reward for Blake himself. But perhaps not. I think there's a persuasive argument to be made that creativity of any kind is an allegory or microcosm of whatever is taking place inside the eternal moment in our lifetimes. And maybe it was standing room only in the vaults of the heavens when Blake sat down to write and illustrate a poem, and you couldn't give away complimentary passes to whatever Napoleon was scribbling in his notebook that night.

Do you know what I mean?

Uh...actually, I'm not entirely sure I do. The end of the first page of your fax was cut off, so that for several uncomfortable instants I thought you were suggesting some sort of relationship between Catherine Blake and Malcolm Muggeridge, which really would have been going too far.

I'd agree any creative work acts as a microcosm...if a blurred and inexact one...for the entirety of what I'd call conceptual space and what Blake would call Heaven. I wouldn't even qualify it as conceptual space as it is "during our lifetimes." since to me the essential nature of conceptual space is that it is instantaneous, a hyper-moment filling the entirety of the continuum, in which all other moments are subsumed like specks in amber. In Heaven, in Olympus, in Asgard, in Satori, in Restau, in Dreamtime there is a large, radiant and complex event that is constantly in the process of occurring. Osiris wasn't dismembered in the past. Isis didn't reassemble him and impregnate herself upon him in some remote historical or prehistoric time, nor is the subsequent birth of Horus on a recorded date so that we can send the guy a greetings card. It could be said just as accurately of these dreamtime events that they will occur in the far future or that they are occurring right this moment now. The "once upon a time" parenthesis with which we bracket our fondest myth-events is careful not to say *which* time. Angels, as Immanuel Swedenborg insisted, know nothing of time.

Anyway, I'm probably misconstruing your point entirely here. Are you suggesting that there might be a case that William Blake, despite his many undisputed personality problems, may have had more access to "Heaven" than an entirely different sort of intellect and visionary like, say, Napoleon? If that *is* what you were asking, then I suppose I'd have to say that without wishing to make pointless comparisons between two such dissimilar men, it might be possible that they both travelled in the same territory but visited vastly different resorts. Some systems, like for example the Qabalah of the Western Mystery tradition, divide what I'd call Idea Space and Blake would call Heaven into a number of distinct zones. To vastly oversimplify, Napoleon's specific form of Sephiroth, known as Geburah: the red, martial sphere of stern judgement. Blake's work and published thoughts would seem to me to place him in the region of the sixth, solar sphere, known as Tiphareth.

Actually, looked at according to a model like this, a different reading of Blake's hubris is possible; each of the spheres in the system has various attributes and associations, as if each sphere were like a drawer in the overall filing cabinet of the whole array. (This is one model of the "bigger filing cabinet" I mentioned earlier.) The solar sphere of Tiphareth is associated with risen solar redeemer figures such as Jesus, Bacchus, Apollo, Horus, and so on. Each sphere has its own particular "virtue" and its own "vice." In the earthly sphere of Malkuth, for example, the specific vice could be said to be "inertia" and the virtue "discrimination." In Tiphareth, the virtue is "Dedication to the Great Work," which would take too long to explain, and the vice is "pride."

My probably imperfect understanding of what is meant by pride in this context came during a magical exploration of the sixth sphere, undertaken as usual with one of my similarly minded associates, in this instance a musician. At one point during the event, I got carried away with a self-serving monologue on how special and wonderful creative people were, completely opiated by my own marvellousness. At this point, my glazed and trancing companion spoke for the first time in twenty minutes, making a single, gnomic utterance: "A gold pig."

As soon as he'd said it he looked puzzled, told me that the phrase had just popped into his head, and advised me to ignore it as meaningless, which of course I was unable to do. It struck me, at the time, as a perfect image of the pride of artists: a gold pig. Flashy, brilliant, and valuable, but also vaguely squalid, absurd, and tasteless. It seemed to me that creators should not confuse themselves with whatever light comes through them. At best, they can take comfort in the clarity and lucidity of the window that their work lets the light into the world by. They can try not to block the light with their own shadow, they can try to widen their window or aperture, and they can take satisfaction in their success at this. But they are not the light. I suppose that sometimes a window might look down at the wonderful long rectangle of late-afternoon gold that it's casting across the floorboards, at the Brownian gavotte of the dust particles in its falling shafts, and believe itself to be the Sun. I'm not saying that I personally believe this to be the case with William Blake, just that it might support your different view of the man.

Anyway, this has almost certainly nothing to do with whatever you were asking. Let's get back to this Cath Blake/ Malcolm Muggeridge thing. What have you heard?

From what I'm given to understand, in the Great By and By, Old Muggs (having been summarily dismissed as an overenthusiastic fanboy and edged out of Blake's chat circle) has latched onto Catherine and is boring her senseless with a recitation of his conversations with Mother Teresa. "You really MUST meet her when she gets here. I — heheh — I really MUST tell you about this SPLENDID letter that she sent me after the SECOND interview I did with her — did I mention that I interviewed her TWICE...well, anyway..." I picture Catherine — with glacial smile — endeavouring to catch her husband's eye. Mr. Blake (she always called him that, didn't she?), who IS this creature?

On the contrary, I think you provide a very adequate working model for what I was talking about. I intentionally used the phrase "the vault of the heavens" as opposed to "Heaven" for that very reason. I was being something of "a gold pig" myself in passing judgement on Blake based on an — at best — cursory examination of his life. Who am I to pretend to speculate authoritatively about Blake's prayers and their character (or lack thereof)? I mean, there's nothing wrong with speculation but it is important to differentiate between authoritative speculation, and rumination. There is a persuasive argument to be made — or at least food for thought — that by pursuing the life of a prophet, as Blake seemed to do, using his engravings of Dante's work (just as an example) to "correct" Dante, puts him outside the parameters of my own meager jurisdiction. Whether he was misapprehended in doing this, overstepping his bounds in a profound sense, he did seem to make the choice to enter the Big Arena in doing so and any criticism or deprecation of him in which I indulge myself has much in common with a fat-ass couch potato holding forth on how the wide receiver SHOULD have run that last play.

One of my more enduring ruminations has been that reality is a succession of hierarchies. That we are observed by those on the next level up and those on the next level up from them and so on. 99.9% of what we do, say, write, and in all ways concern ourselves with has much in common with — say — a Gilligan's Island marathon of many centuries' duration. I think we are as excruciating as that to them. But just as there are diamonds in a coal field, every once in a great while there comes along someone whose works are worth watching — and every once in a greater while, someone who engages the attentions of a handful of presences on the second or third level up. Ergo — the Big Arena I've alluded to. Given Blake's own devout belief in his God and his own belief in retribution for a sin committed, the fact that he endured and was not cut off before his time and achieved a measure of peace in his last years would indicate the Large Possibility that he was Onto Something. That, although his meticulously assembled lifelong creative work looks (for the most part) like fevered gibberish to me, the case could be made that in the "next circle up" he had untied some Gordian knot or solved a long-standing riddle or presented some new Gordian knot or long-standing riddle for consideration in the course of his work. Perhaps the untying and solving could be attributed to the Heavenly, and the creation of knots and riddles could be attributed to the Infernal — but, to me, this sort of territory moves into the Dangerously Ruminative — which might be the instrument of my own destruction I inadvertently created by engineering a vehicle for near-total creative freedom.

But, finishing the previous thought, if there is any veracity in my rumination, it is not hard to picture how Blake COULD be one of the elect. As someone who sees himself (as it were) watching the Big Arena on a snow-grizzled television screen, I did want to allow of the possibility — while still allowing the possibility of my previous rumination.

"A gold pig" on a smaller scale, served the same purpose that "Are you fit to continue, Dr. Gull" served in From Hell, didn't it? It seems to me that the wisest ambition of the creative-type type is to develop the facility to recognise the significance of these...resonant admonishments?...where they occur and try to reduce the frequency of their occurrences.

I would agree with you (ruminatively) that there is an existence composed of Pure Light at the upper reaches of these hierarchies that I picture — mirroring itself in our own world in those individuals who choose to go through life praying and/or meditating, eating little, and having few or no possessions. Perhaps the spheres that you've described constitute spheres of containment for those who just can't "let go" of hierarchies, judgement, dedication, etc. Like Gull at the end of From Hell (finally! A reference to what we're supposed to be talking about), rising and falling, but clearly trapped within the confines of what-he-has-made-himself-into. He has always been Gull, he has always been Tom, he has always been Jack the Ripper, he has always been Blake's "Ghost of a Flea." There are a lot of different ways to read your ending to the book. Everything is pre-destined, whatever Alan Moore is and is a part of and everything that you do or say and everything that happens to you has always happened to you. Or is this what you're saying? Is there such a thing as free will or if — as an example — you choose to move to Hollywood tomorrow, you have always chosen to move to Hollywood? I use this as an example because I can think of few things more unlikely than Alan Moore moving to Hollywood. Any ruminations — or authoritative speculations — on this one?

i.e. Do you see any merit in doing something you yourself would perceive as being at the outer thresholds of likelihood (knowing yourself and what is likely and unlikely for that "self" as you perceive that "self")?

What a great cliff-hanger, eh? Continued in part three.

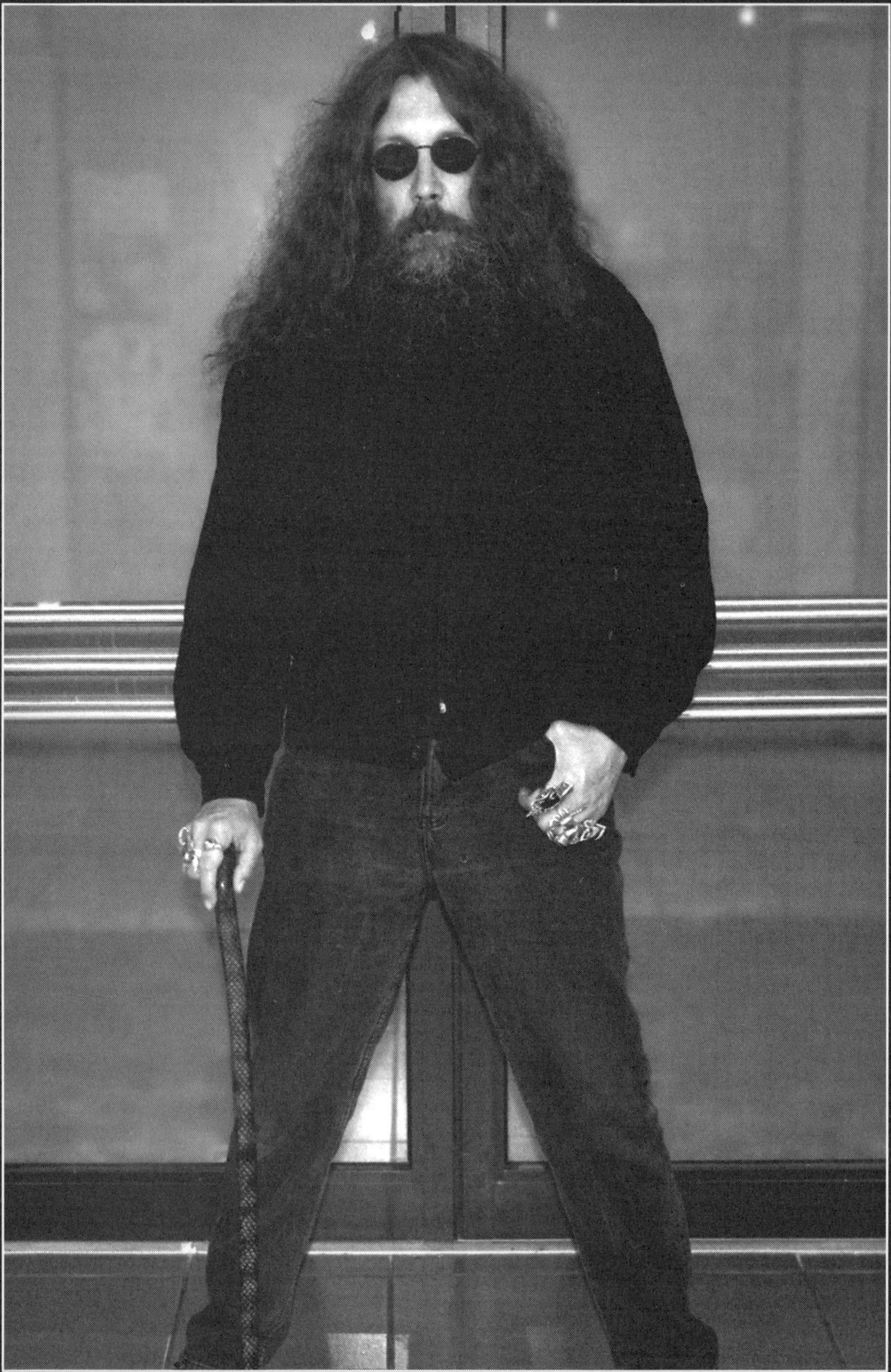

CORRESPONDENCE: FROM HELL
Part 3

On the subject of a hierarchical structure to existence, the Qabalah is again an interesting model because of its sophisticated structure, which allows for many different interpretations of its own nature. On one level, many practising magicians would choose to see the structure of the ten Sephira — or spheres that make up the array known as the *Otz Chiim* or Tree of Life — as a hierarchical one, with sephiroth number one, Kether, as the absolute godhead at the top of the tree and sephiroth number ten, the earthly sphere of Malkuth, down at the bottom. The Golden Dawn based their own highly hierarchical order upon which sphere on the tree one had attained to, working up from the bottom. As a neophyte, one's task is to come to terms with the concept of Malkuth before progressing on up the tree towards the higher levels, eventually assuming the ultimate and possibly chimerical grade of Ipissimus (this is the same as being God, only better, as people tend to respect you more if you're self-made).

Qabalah seems to work fine when operating under these assumptions, but for my own part I tend to interpret the system differently: rather than viewing it hierarchically as a structure with a top and bottom, I see it as a map or circuit-diagram that connects two remote points (Ultimate God and the world of Matter) by the shortest possible route. The energy can flow either way, and the structure itself has no preference. Generally, we tend to think of the moon as being above the earth and the sun as being above that (or, in Qabalah, of Yesod being above Malkuth, with Tiphareth above them both), but, in actuality, there is no "up" or "down" in space, nor, I believe, in the structure of the *Otz Chiim*. If Kether is seen as special for being the ultimate source and godhead of the process that is the Universe, then Malkuth at the opposite end is also seen as special for being the ultimate manifestation of that initial divine explosion. Neither is higher or more important than the other.

Another thing worth remembering is that the Tree of Life arrangement is seen both as a conceptual map of the entire existence and as a map of the individual human soul, the latter being a microcosm of the former. In that sense, every individual has the entirety of the Tree within themselves and the potential to experience it, even though the vast majority may never stir themselves to do so (Inertia being the vice of Malkuth). This is an important point and one which seems to match with some of my own more extreme impressions during these episodes: the most peculiar entities that I believe myself to have encountered, including presences which appeared to be genuine Gods, have seemed to me to be at once utterly alien or Other, and at the same time have seemed to be a part of myself. Now, the rationalist view of all magical encounters is probably that all apparent entities are in fact externalised projections of parts of the self. I have no big argument with that, except that I'd hold the converse to be true as well: *we* are at the same time externalised projections of *them*. In one sense, the simplest viewpoint might be to accept that all manifestations, ourselves included, are simply different stages of the unfolding of one multi-dimensional being into form.

One important magical ritual, known as the Abramelin ritual, demands of the practitioner that he or she remove themselves from society for a given period and work towards contacting the Holy Guardian Angels. At the moment this is finally achieved, the successful Magus must next plunge directly in Hell and subdue the demons there to his or her will. Now, this ritual is very definitely talking about *real* angels and *real* demons, but at the same time it's talking about getting in touch with your highest consciousness or nature and using power drawn from this to bring your lower levels of consciousness, your demons, into line, so that the whole multi-level entity is working in unison and harmony.

I suppose all of this is a long-winded way of saying that I don't necessarily think that we are held in disdain or contempt by whatever forms of consciousness may exist on the "higher" levels. I really don't think that "they," for the want of a better term, see things how we probably would do in their situation. In fact, in my experience, human frames of reference tend to fall away completely if one even ventures a short distance up the structure. Form itself doesn't exist above the eighth sphere, and individual consciousness doesn't exist above the

PIET CORR

Left: *Piet Corr a.k.a.* **pietdesnapp** *is a freelance photographer and lecturer, born in Northampton. His work has been exhibited in galleries and libraries all over England. Photograph ©2003 Piet Corr.*

seventh. The sixth is as high as I've ventured as yet, and people who know a lot more about it than I do have advised me that there is less and less to actually experience the higher you get, while the dangers get more and more severe. Kether, the "highest" allegedly attainable point, is in one sense nothing more than the initial concept of existence itself. To go higher than Kether is to venture into a state higher than God that is called the *Ain*. This translates as absolute nothingness, the purest possible state of being. There may be magicians who have gone there, but if so, they never came back.

Now, moving on to what you actually asked about, which was where I stood on the Free Will vs. Determinism issue: if Stephen Hawking is correct when he suggests that Space-Time itself is a fourth-dimensional solid probably shaped a bit like an egg or an American football, with the Big Bang at one end, the Big Crunch at the other, and all other moments suspended forever somewhere between, then I don't see how Free Will can possibly exist. Time, while it is not actually the fourth-dimension in the sense that H.G. Wells popularised it as being (after the theories of C. Howard Hinton, funnily enough), is, as I understand it, more properly conceived as the *shadow* of a fourth spatial dimension perceived by human consciousness.

What this means is that our view of our own three-dimensional body is limited: if you had fourth-dimensional vision and were standing at a point outside our continuum, you would perceive your human semblance as a form of horrifically long millipede that would wind back and forth over every landscape you have ever or ever will cross during the course of your life. The millipede tapers slightly at both ends. At one end is genetic slime and at the other extreme is dust or ash. Now imagine that each section of the millipede is one instant of your life from birth to death, all fused together. The way our perception of time works in this analogy is like a peristaltic ripple of awareness that starts at one end and passes through every segment in the chain of the millipede's body in sequence. As each individual segment is lit up by awareness, it only has awareness of what it is, i.e., a segment located at certain co-ordinates. When the awareness moves on to the next segment in the body, it is aware of itself as a nearly identical segment at a new co-ordinate, and it makes the reasonable assumption that it is the *same* segment and that the segment has moved. In fact, the segment is unwittingly part of a larger organism, and the only movement is the movement of that organism's awareness through that organism's convoluted form.

To quote C. Howard Hinton's own somewhat different way of expressing the notion. "Were such a thought adopted, we should have to imagine some stupendous whole, wherein all that has ever come into being or will come coexists, which, passing slowly on, will leave in this flickering consciousness of ours, limited to a narrow space and a single moment, a tumultuous record of changes and vicissitudes that are *but to us*." (Italics mine.) Unless I'm missing something, this seems to rule out the conventional notion of Free Will. However, to put a bright complexion on things, was Free Will ever that much use in the first place? I have no doubt that against all odds, I *could* move to Hollywood tomorrow, but what would that prove? From a determinist standpoint, it would only demonstrate that I was meant to be in Hollywood tomorrow, in a sense already *was* in Hollywood tomorrow.

Quite aside from that, to some degree the notion of Free Will resides in the mathematics of the situation. As an example, if I take one individual and try to predict whether he or she will marry, divorce, contract cancer, win the lottery, or convert to Catholicism, I'm on a hiding to nothing and I can't win. That individual has free will, and I cannot predict what he or she is going to do, or what will happen to him or her.

If I look at a hundred individuals and try to predict how many of them will contract cancer, how many will marry, how many will win the lottery, and so on, then my chances for making an accurate prediction go up considerably. If I look at a billion individuals, I can make chillingly accurate predictions about what will happen, statistically, to the group. The perception of Free Will is here seen as something that is relative to the degree of mathematical resolution. You individually may seem to have free will, but at higher levels of magnification, you will not be able to avoid doing exactly your bit and no more to see that those statistical figures turn out correctly. There is no Free Will. What happened...happened. What will happen...will happen. This is in certain light a scary and highly claustrophobic thought. Reality becomes a tightly constrained tunnel which we are being forced to walk down, with no way to turn back or take a different route. Sometimes the urge to break out must be overwhelming...which brings me to a very personal anecdote that seems relevant both to the above notions and to the broader subject matter of *From Hell*.

I'm a little uncomfortable talking about this, because firstly it is frankly terrifying, and secondly it is very difficult to explain without giving entirely the wrong impression of what I'm saying. I'll try anyway.

When I was six years old, I was sitting in our living room, in a straight-backed wooden chair, beside the dining table. My Mother, whom I loved dearly, was kneeling at my feet fastening my shoes for me, which I was either too incompetent or too lazy to do myself. On the table there was a carving knife. I remember looking at the knife and realising in a vague and dreamy way that it would, technically speaking, be physically possible for me to pick up the carving knife and stab my mother through the back of the neck. Now, please bear in mind that I did not want to do this, indeed had not the slightest intention of doing it. It was just that the idea had entered my head, out of nowhere.

Upon closer examination, at the kernel of the idea was this: I knew that I was not going to kill my own mother. The idea was unthinkable. I knew that this was definitely not going to happen, in the same way that you and I both know that I am not going to move to Hollywood tomorrow. These things, while theoretically possible, are *not in the script*. Therefore...and this is the nearest my adult mind can get to paraphrasing what was going on in my six-year-old mind...if I *did* stab and kill my own mother, right there and then, then I would have gone outside the script. Done something that wasn't destined to happen. Ad-libbed. I'd have broken through the fake scenery. I'd force the director to come out and give me a talking to. I'd wake from the dream, bust my way out of the relentless single corridor of predetermination into...whatever.

Of course, while given to unusual thoughts, I am not actually insane. Consequently, I didn't stab my mother; I just felt creepy and horrible for ever having had the thought at all. After a while, the incident was put to the back of my mind as just one of the many mental aberrations that mark our childhoods.

What brought it to mind was a quote during my serial killer research that was attributed to Ed Kemper. Now, Ed came to decapitation and actual serial murder later in life, after first serving a sentence as a juvenile for the killing of his own grandparents. For no apparent reason whatsoever, the thirteen-year-old Kemper shot his grandmother through the back of the head. He then waited for his grandfather to get home and shot him too, though this seems more of an afterthought. When asked why he'd killed his grandmother, Kemper said that the gun had been to hand and he'd thought something along the lines of: "I wonder what would happen if I killed grandma?"

I don't know. Maybe I'm interpreting Kemper's comment in light of my own experience, but this seems to me to hint at a similar sort of urge: if we commit the unthinkable taboo of murder, something that is outside the script, then in some way we will transcend the relentlessly ordered continuum of time and reality. We will have done something that was not meant to happen. Of course, as with the Alan Goes To Hollywood scenario...good name for a band, that, incidentally...then we would of course do no such thing. We would not break free of predestination, we would simply find out that our destiny included the pointless murder of our mothers or an equally pointless visit to Hollywood, and always had done. All the same, I can't help wondering whether some variation upon this perverse urge to escape identity, time, and reality might have fuelled some of our more demented killers now and again. A harmless speculation and nothing more. Make of it what you will.

Yes. It's not hard to imagine the claustrophobic awareness of being trapped inside the script as being a source of all manner of mischiefs. Hitler, for example, or people fitting that personality profile wanting to extrapolate that sense of exit-through-breaking-of-taboo into bigger broken taboo = bigger exit. As I consider it, one of the great satisfactions of doing a single story for twenty-six years is the sense of submitting to that deterministic inevitability. The 300 issues exist and have always existed (leaving aside the possibility of my premature demise) in a specific form. The story has always ended the same way. That becomes a kind of life line much easier to hold onto than "I have eighty-two issues and fifteen and 1/4 pages left to fill — what if I do it wrong?" Very reassuring to know that — in one sense — the story is already done.

Taking your millipede illustration (marvellous, by the way), I would see the role of Free Will reflected in the fact that while it is possible to chart the geographic location of the millipede — beginning with birth and ending with death — the millipede is also aware. Which would seem to indicate (I'm really getting out of my depth here) that the Big Football is actually a nearly unimaginable, nearly infinite number of Big Footballs consisting of ...I need a term here...Awareness Possibilities? I.e., you didn't stab your mother with a knife (good boy, by the way), but the fact of the awareness of the potential act drew you from a state where the possibility of the act did not occur to you, to a state where it did. I'm reminded of Jesus' Sermon on the Mount where, in reference to "Thou Shalt Not Commit Adultery," he brings forward the new insight that lusting after a woman in your heart isn't good either. He stops short (or I think he, or He, does) of making them equivalent transgressions, but does seem to be pointing in the direction of ...awareness proximities...and the need for self-discipline out of proportion to what was generally accepted as necessary up to the point where he, or He, introduced it.

This ties in with Norman Mailer's insight — relatively early in his career — of the possible nature of God as an Embattled Being. The outcome is not clear. God wrestles with the Devil in a cosmological sense as He wrestles with the Devil in each of us. We have the possibility to fulfil His Plan, but each conscious decision and each act either drains a little of His Essence or contributes to it. If you add in another layer of "imagination" wherein each imagined decision and each imagined act likewise drains a little of His Essence or contributes to it — a layer in which you did kill your mother just because you pictured it so vividly — Free Will becomes an enormous thing to contemplate.

The late Diana Trilling, just as an aside, said that when Mailer's conversation got this..."rarefied," I believe was the term she used...she used to ask him if he liked chop suey (or something of an equivalent "grounding" nature). The beleaguered Cerebus reader can be forgiven for asking, "Where is Diana Trilling when we need her?"

If we presuppose the existence of an omniscient or near-omniscient or omnipotent or near-omnipotent Being, who is to say that that Being is incapable of arresting the seeming inevitability that the Big Football can only have that shape? Clearly a Stephen Hawking is working with a model that does not presuppose such a Being capable of affecting outcome. As a scientist it would be impossible for him to do so. Perhaps that's the message that science overlooks. Perhaps God's Plan is intended to be a flower, which starts out looking very much like a football in the bud state and then opens out. If He doesn't exist, it is a given that we are a given number of millipedes winding about the bit of ground we have wound about before we return to dust and the Big Football is just that, is only that, and can never be anything more than that.

A great deal could hinge on whether we are just before the bulge in the Big Football or just after it. The fact that (from what I understand) we are currently in a narrow window (cosmologically speaking) where the sun and the moon appear to be approximately the same size when seen from the Earth might have something in common with this. A sign of our "outward boundness" reaching the end of our potential state and the beginning of our kinetic state..

Individual self-discipline to not only resist committing acts of "bad faith," but to resist contemplating them could, in the context of such a speculation, be just enough to "snap open the 'chute" or cause the Big Flower to blossom at the crucial instant when we reach the apogee of the Big Bulge — where presumably a kind of psychic weightless state will obtain before psychic gravitation reasserts itself.

In such a scenario, Stephen Hawking becomes humankind's Ghost of Christmas Yet-to-Be — pointing to our unhappy and possibly inevitable (possibly not) fate. He also becomes a "byword among men" for his folly in presupposing a universe made up solely of matter and energy, his debilitating infirmities a manifestation — a physical Sign from On High. "Physicist, heal thyself." In my view, such a presupposition — it's all just one big football, so let's just grab our millipede happiness where we can get it — is an inevitable "stumbling block" in the path of the arrogant "now-we-know-everything" late-twentieth-century humanist, scientific, if-the-evidence-isn't-capable-of-being-duplicated-in-a-lab-it-isn't-evidence corruption we have — collectively — become. A failure of will and self-discipline to clean up our individual "contemplating acts of bad faith sphere," which would thus clean up our individual "acts of bad faith sphere," and which would thus clean up our collective "acts of bad faith sphere" — said failure of will and self-discipline having humanism and the core belief that nothing exists except matter and energy as its primary source of sustenance.

Talk about rarefied. I need oxygen.

Do you think awareness — individual awareness — harnessed effectively, is capable of affecting things on such a scale, given your own experiences with it (he asked, limping off in the direction of the medicine cabinet for a couple of Tylenol)?

Tylenol-induced afterthought: I suppose any speculation along the lines of the above would hinge, to a great extent, on whether one conceives God to be inside or outside the Big Football. I would tend towards speculating "outside" — although I wouldn't hazard to guess whether any part of your speculative construction would fall "outside" as well. It does seem to me that a construction with two dichotomous, polar-extreme absolute realities (which you allude to) might get chalked up on Norman Mailer's Embattled God scoreboard as a "win" for the Devil, given that you perceive them as having equal importance — or at least that neither has greater importance.

Well, the idea of sin has always seemed a bit iffy to me in the first place, so the idea that even *contemplating* sin might have any negative value attached to it doesn't really appeal to me. If Space-Time is a coexistent solid with past, present, and future already written, then, as I've suggested above, that pretty well deep-sixes the traditional notion of Free Will. (Wasn't that a film about a whale, anyway?) If there's no such thing as Free Will, then I can't for the life of me see how there can be sin, evil, or the Dark Side of the Force. I've always suspected that the only reason Christian theologians kept the Free Will idea around so long was that the central concept of Sin pretty well falls to bits without it.

Of course, this football of coexisting Space-Time has some other interesting properties when considered morally. For example, if there is truly no linear time as we understand it, then the events that make up the vast hyper-solid of existence can be read with as much validity from back to front as from front to back. The physics, as I understand it, would work just as well whichever way you wrote the equations. Due to the orientation of our perceptions, we read the Universe as following the course of time's arrow, and we believe that the arrow points only one way. This reading of the Universe is, however, not more essentially "true" than its opposite. Hawking's equations for what is happening at the event horizon of a singularity turned out to be *an exact time-reverse* of his equations for what is happening during the Big Bang. The Big Bang is the Big Crunch talking backwards. Whoo-oo-ooh. Spooky.

Even stranger is what happens if you bring that premise down from the cosmological to a human moral level: that our lives are as "true" if we view the film in reverse. In this reading of the world our inert bodies are dug up from the ground or magically reassembled in the inferno of a crematorium oven. After a brief period, the brain and heart miraculously start working and we are born as old people. We maybe meet our spouse at the divorce hearing...the relationship feels bad at first but gets better over the years until it reaches one night of absolute magic in our teens or whenever, after which we never see them again. Daily we draw heat and energy from the air with our reversed actions. We invest that energy into the faecal matter that we ingest through one of the two symmetrical time-reverse mouths that terminate our alimentary canal. We regurgitate a healthy amount of food daily. Our teeth sculpt the pulp back into, say, half a potato. Our cutlery will attach the other half to it. Stick it in a pan of unboiling water for a while to take the heat and softness out, then put its skin back on. When you've got a bag full, take it back to the supermarket and they'll give you some money for it. (The money will come in useful when you have to pay the distributors, who need to pay the retailers so that the retailers can give them lots of copies of *Cerebus* back to you for disassembly.) The store will unbuy it back to the farmer (at mark-down, obviously), and the farmer will bury the thing so that it can break down into it component chemicals; turn its chlorophyll back into photons to be hovered up by sunbeams and sucked into the immense fission-reaction that is the sun.

In a construction like this, we enter a charmed and often charming world where the laws of moral cause and effect become strangely altered; serial murderers become midwives. Thieves become benefactors. Artists and writers siphon pictures and stories from the minds of their readers, maybe convert them into perceptions and experiences and events for the childhood that still lies ahead of them. The image of a rose in our mind floods down the neural channels to the retina, where it is encoded in photons. The light pours from our eyes to make the vision of the flower — the cosmos. Tyrants become liberators and vice versa. Sin is a one-way thing that doesn't really seem to hold up in this palindromic world view.

As to whether God is inside or outside the system, I maybe ought to clarify some of the Qabalistic notions I was flashing around earlier: If I understand the system correctly, then God is neither/both inside nor/and outside the system, since God is the system. The godhead sephiroth, Kether, is seen as entity at the moment of its creation out of nothing, usually symbolised by a point within a circle. That energy then passes through several modifying stages, these being the various sephira that make up the arrangement of the tree. Having come into existence as a single point of pure being at Kether, it is next given a reference point and expressed outwards by the second sephiroth, Chokmah; is imprinted with the possibility of eventual form at Binah; is nurtured at Chesed; is purged of unworthy elements at Geburah; and so on "down" the tree until it is finally manifested in physical form at Malkuth, the sphere of the physical universe.

The energy is all God. God is existence. When gods are applied to the Tree of Life arrangement, it's customary to put them in whichever drawer of the filing cabinet they seem appropriate: Apollo at Tiphareth; Thoth and Hermes at Hod; Venus and Nike at Netzach; and so on. The god associated with Kether is usually the One Almighty God, the Creator of the Bible and the Koran. Aleister Crowley, however, made the valid suggestion that Pan might represent Kether as well as any of them: Pan, it will be remembered, is the Greek word meaning "All." God is All. The physical Universe, including our bodies, is the physical body of God. All feeling is the feeling of God. All Self is the Self of God. The only game that can be played between God and the Devil, Norman Mailer to one side, is solitaire. And that, as the Carpenters have wisely remarked, is the only game in town.

Can the thoughts or deeds of one person affect the continuum? Well, yes, but the situation is actually far worse than that: the thoughts, deeds, and minute antennae movements of an *ant* can affect the whole continuum. The continuum is a monstrous fractal tapestry of events, all of which are intimately connected, all of which are ultimately the corpus of one organism (see above). God/Existence is, in one sense, an example of the ultimate fugue.

Speaking of ants and fugues, I'm reminded of M. C. Escher's *Ant Fugue*, and a brilliant written piece based upon it by Douglas R. Hofstadter. This appears in Hofstadter's excellent anthology of consciousness-related writings, *The Mind's I*, and in it Hofstadter considers the anthill as a model of fugue consciousness: the individual ants are chemical robots with nothing that we would recognise as awareness, responding only to pheromone signals. This bottom level of an anthill's consciousness has a more sophisticated level of signal-consciousness that rules it and guides it. This consciousness cannot be said to exist in the mind of any one individual ant, and yet somehow it exists in the complex interaction of all of them. Up above the signal level of consciousness is a level of symbol-consciousness that guides and mediates the signal level beneath it. This level, the unfathomable symbol-level of anthill consciousness, could be said to be the living awareness of the anthill considered as an individual entity.

The players in Hofstadter's story (Achilles, a tortoise, and an anteater, if I remember correctly) admit that they cannot possibly imagine what the symbol-level of anthill consciousness would be like to experience. This is likened to the experience of listening to a fugue: if you concentrate on the individual components, you cannot be so conscious of the elaborate overall pattern of the fugue. If you listen to that overall pattern, you lose awareness of the individual voices from which it is composed. If we substitute "God/Existence" for "anthill" in the story, then the central point remains true. God's consciousness is the whole of the fugue. Most of the time, we can only follow our own individual voice. Occasionally, our consciousness might expand to the point where we get more of a sense of the overall structure of the fugue. The danger of this is that in doing so, we risk losing our own individual voice. In Qabalistic terms, those who achieve the level of Kether could be said to experience the full fugue. By the same terms, very few Qabalists in their right mind would aspire to Kether without intense and serious preparation, since the principal risk is that one will be annihilated — absorbed into that ultimate whiteness, into the full pattern of the music, never to emerge. The individual voice is lost.

On a final note regarding Free Will, it seems to me that the suffocating claustrophobia of the determinist scenario is considerably alleviated by the fact that even if all events happen to a fixed schedule and in a fixed order, we are still at considerable liberty in how we perceive, read, and interpret those events. The divine ghost of Consciousness, which bestows meaning as part of its purpose, can pass back and forth unhindered through the writhing ball of centipedes that is our human world, and it can paint whatever picture it likes of its journeys.

To return, startlingly at this juncture, I'm sure, to *From Hell* for a moment, what we have in the Whitechapel murders is a real cluster of events that really happened in our real human world. The events are fixed and immutable; they cannot be changed any more than the words in the Bible could be changed. However, just as with the Bible, those events can be read in an almost infinite variety of ways. Leonard Matters reads it one way, with a doctor maddened by bereavement inflicting vengeance on whores for a son of his, dead of syphilis. Tom Cullen reads it another way, with Montague Druitt sexually insane and murdering five women before throwing himself into the Thames. Michael Harrison reads it with the syphilitic Duke of Clarence in the title role. Stephen Knight reads it and swaps Prince Eddy for his doctor, Sir William Gull. Harlan Ellison reads it and gets his excellent "The Prowler in the City at the Edge of the World." I read it and overprint it with a bunch of psycho-geographical and mythico-historical notions, and we get *From Hell*. When each event has such a multitude of facets...like James Joyce's day in Dublin...then our "imprisonment" within the straitjacket of a predetermined Universe suddenly starts to look more like a trip to Disneyland. Or even to somewhere actually nice.

    Well, I'm not sure I'm talking about sin or evil or Evil, per se. If the deeds and minute antennae movements of an ant can affect the whole continuum (and I would tend to agree with that), then I think the individual choice between "0" and "1" has significance out of what we would perceive as conventional proportions. Just a speculation — or a rumination (have to keep track of my own language, don't I?) — but I would tend to see a moral and ethical choice as a moral and ethical choice whether it is viewed on "play," "fast forward," or "quick reverse." I think it's easy to mistake complexity or a larger inventory of facts for knowledge, insight, and/or truth. Better telescopes and spectrographic analysis of data do not — to me — refute the notion that God created the stars. We have an infinitely more complex picture of the largest imaginable...Venue...for want of a better term, in the Scientific end of things, and (judging from my headache) once you put all of the arcane philosophies and magiks and alchemies into some semblance of a structure, as you have (clearly) spent a great deal of energy and time doing, you end up with an equally complex picture of the largest imaginable Venue on the Mystical end of things. Even assuming that both models become even larger over the next — say — twenty years (and what reason would I have for doubting it?), the question would still come down to: is God, per se, the accumulation, the sum total of all these structures, or did He create all these structures? To me there's a large distinction between saying, "we are part of God's pancreas" and "we might possibly be housed in the pancreas of a nearly unimaginably large being created by God." Likewise the notion that God is an accumulation of all perceptions of Him. I would agree with your anthill analogy (I loved what Rick Veitch did with the beehive in Maximortal along the same lines) — there is a being that is created of the sum of humankind, all plant life, the beasts of the field, the fowls of the air, the fish that swim, etc., etc., an accumulated Awareness Totality composed of Archetypes and fractal complexities far beyond the capacities of the individual awareness to CONceive, let alone PERceive. There are just too many microcosms of that structure in all of the perceptions I have or know about for me to be even remotely inclined to disbelieve its veracity. But, to me, that's not God. Call him Bang-Bulge-Crunch (last seen in Strange Tales, issue 77 — I'm sure you remember the classic Kirby cover: "There's no escaping the terror of: Bang-Bulge-Crunch") if you want a name for him, but it or he is still a closed system and not infinite. God is infinite, ergo Bang-Bulge-Crunch is not, by definition, God.

    Picking up on your optimistic last paragraph, I whole-mindedly and (steady, now) wholeheartedly agree. There is a persuasive argument to be made that we are on the cusp of a genuinely more Mature Age where the "no-two-snowflakes-alike" quality of individual awareness and expression is going to be seen as an unanticipated bonus of humanity having not done too bad a job of getting to 1997 more or less in one piece. If we haven't achieved the complete eradication of War and Poverty and Disease and Famine, at least we have learned a few lessons — it would be hard to imagine anyone coming forward at this juncture and presenting themselves as the Next Nixon or an Improved Stalin or the 21st Century's Answer to Joe McCarthy. If we can keep progressing on our present course to a place where divergent philosophies and opinions are seen to be just that — and not grounds for incarceration, oppression, or wholesale purging (or even full retail purging) — I think most of us will be pretty astonished at the general improvement that would result.

    I don't want you to think I'm edging away from what we're talking about (although I think we may have clarified the differences between us to whatever extent that is possible — unless you're interested in me bringing out my perception of Mailer's Embattled God for another three-minute round. It is your interview), but I understand you've written a wonderful graphic novel called From Hell. *What's it all about, then? I'm sure my readers would be fascinated to...*

    Just kidding.

    I often find — long after I'm done with one of the Cerebus books — that I was telling myself something in the course of telling the story. I mean, quite apart from what I was consciously putting into it (and I find that that sometimes makes me smile when I run across one I've forgotten), my unconscious mind was either warning me about what was up ahead or giving me a more accurate perception of what I'd just gone through that my conscious mind (at the time) was still wrestling with.

    Anything in From Hell *that surprises Alan Moore when he looks back on it?*

I'm sorry, Dave, but your theology is all to fuck: you've clearly forgotten that issue of *Amazing Adventures* during the mid-seventies where Roy Thomas conclusively proved that Bang-Bulge-Crunch was only a part of either Eternity or Ego the Living Planet, I forget which. And, anyway, they were all Kang the Conqueror moving backwards through time. I guess this fundamental religious schism pretty well puts paid to the "Church of AlandDaveology" that we privately discussed, and in fact I've already taken the precautionary move of having you declared an Anti-Pope and Enemy of Mankind. No hard feelings.

    Regarding the retroactive surprises that the unconscious can spring on you during the course of a work, although I'm very familiar with the phenomenon itself, I've had a hard time remembering any actual examples of the process with regard to *From Hell*. I suppose the main surprise didn't so much hinge upon one particular sequence or episode as upon the whole of the work: despite my faith in the "high-altitude mapping" approach described earlier, I still found myself slightly unnerved by the way in which subsequently unearthed fragments of information would fit so seamlessly into the parameters of my first scribbled schematic. One example out of dozens would be the details of John Netley's death, his horse colliding with an obelisk. While writing chapter four, with all its emphasis on obelisks and Netley's growing unease with these symbols, I was not even completely sure that any coachman named John Netley had ever existed, much less died in such a thoroughly appropriate manner.

The thing is, if *From Hell* had not been labelled as a fiction and a melodrama from the outset, if *From Hell* had, like nearly all the other Ripper fictions, chosen to describe itself as fact, then I would no doubt have been greatly cheered to find these validations of my vision of "the truth." All Ripperologists spin gorgeous insubstantial cloths of fantasy upon the hard forensic loom of the established "evidence." The problem is that many of them do not choose to perceive the resultant work as fiction. What I would describe as "the plot of my fiction," they would more likely describe as their theory of the truth. In such a mindset, familiar to all conspiracy theorists and *X-Files* fans, any fragment of fact, rumour, or urban myth that can be made to fit with the evolving pattern is seen as strong confirmatory evidence of that theory's reality. Best of all, a *lack* of any evidence can also be interpreted as proof of the theory's validity: Why didn't the police unearth more evidence about Jack the Ripper at the time? Because they were part of the cover-up. Why hasn't any verifiable evidence from the flying saucer crash at Roswell turned up? Because "they" are keeping it from us.

During the course of writing *From Hell*, I met an author whose books are, I believe, popular in the New Age-Occult market, these being books on something called "psychic questing." The premise behind this, as far as I can see, is that you decide to go on a quest with a couple of mates of yours who happen to be psychic. Maybe you're looking for the Holy Grail or the Spear of Destiny or, I dunno, your car keys or something. Your psychic mates will lead you to a bunch of stone circles, ancient churches, and similar significant sites, picking up lots of clues on the way (many of them psychically. It's just, you know, this *vibe*. You wouldn't understand). Quite possibly, along the way things will go wrong. This is usually a sign that you're under psychic attack, and a quick check with your psychic mates will almost certainly confirm this. Looking in the newspaper, you may find that the 5:15 train from Liverpool to London has crashed that day, which you will sensibly conclude was probably caused by the malevolent psychic energy aimed by your astral adversary, rebounding from your force-screen of white astral light to reap havoc amongst innocent commuters. At the end, you write a book about your true-life adventures. I'm being hideously unfair here, I'm sure, but you get the gist.

Anyway, during my brief conversation with this author, he told me that he himself had been investigating the astral residue of Whitechapel, along with a couple of paranormal pals, and that his findings suggested that my "theory" in *From Hell* was pretty much the way it *actually happened*. I felt as if I was being cruel when I politely pointed out that *From Hell* was, in fact, a made-up comic-book story, with probably about as much bearing upon historical "reality" as Disney's *Pocahontas*. Nothing against the guy personally, you understand, and I'm sure his approach to psycho-geography is every bit as valid as my own, but I really did not want to put so much as a toe into the inviting pool of "The Truth." Truth is a well-documented pathological liar. It invariably turns out to be Fiction wearing a fancy frock. Self-proclaimed Fiction, on the other hand, is entirely honest. You can tell this, because it comes right out and says, "I'm a Liar," right there on the dust jacket. Were I to read the biography of Prime Minister-in-waiting Tony Blair (saw him on a walkabout through town centre a few weeks back. Looked like a fucking Thunderbird puppet), then at the end of it I would still not know where I stood with Tony Blair. I do, however, know where I stand with Hannibal Lecter and the Wizard of Oz.

To get back to the point of this meander, while I was working upon *From Hell* I was constantly unnerved and amazed by the amount of confirming "evidence" that turned up to support my "theory," precisely because I knew that it *wasn't* a theory: it was a fiction. This is a much more strange and wonderful phenomenon than simply being able to say, "I was right all along! William Gull *was* Jack the Ripper!" When the Universe seems to confirm our fictions as opposed to our supposed theories, then this suggests a strange relationship between fiction, mind, perception, and cosmos that is far more gripping than simply solving a whodunit.

I once heard an anecdote about a contemporary magician who decided to put this principle to the test by adopting a belief so strange that nobody could possibly mistake it for reality and then seeing what happened. The belief he decided to go with was that Noddy, the little toy-car driving and belled-hat wearing protagonist of Enid Blyton's children's books, was in fact the absolute creator of the Universe and the God of all Gods. Within a couple of weeks he abandoned the experiment in alarm, finding himself upon the brink of conclusively proving that Noddy was the Supreme Being. He'd come across magazine articles showing freshly discovered cave-drawings of an obviously sacred figure wearing what appeared to be a tall pointed hat with a little bell on the top. He'd read an interview with Enid Blyton herself in which she described a strange vision that had come to her while under the influence of gas at the dentist, in which she had been whisked across the Universe at the speed of light to meet God himself, although he couldn't describe the details of their conversation. This, along with a whole mess of other stuff and previously hidden meanings in Bible passages (Cain is banished to the Land of Nod in Genesis, for example), seemed to indicate that Nod was God and Enid Blyton His prophetess.

With *From Hell*, and in light of the above, I suppose I'd have to say that if there was one line that struck an eerily resonant unconscious chord with what later developed in the book, it would be a line from the prologue, spoken by Robert Lees and included for no real reason other than that it sounded good and seemed appropriate: "I made it all up, and it all came true anyway. That's the funny part."

Me? An anti-pope? Why, if you think your strategic alliance with the Extreme One will serve your nefarious purposes now that he has been cast out by the Five-Fold Asses of the Graven Image...

    I really mustn't joke about such things. Having resigned as "leader" of the self-publishers when I was called the "godfather" of self-publishing on CBC Radio, I now have a letter on my coffee table from a new self-publisher calling me the "patron saint" of self-publishing (without the quotation marks). In all seriousness, I find this troubling — the fact that there seems to be neither appreciation nor awareness of anything Larger than that which is in front of the late-20th-century collective nose.

    I can't help but think that your last reply is of great value in that area. We are liars — most charitably we could be described as fabricators or inventors. We take a snatch of conversation, a bit of a book we once read (and have misremembered most times), a fragment of a recollection from our own past, and create a lie that we make as interesting as we can. The value I see in your last reply is that it is somewhat incumbent on us (or, at least, I think it is) to relay to would-be writers — would-be professional liars — a cautionary note about what is in store if they really immerse themselves in it. Call it karma or hubris or a "snare for the unwary" (in the biblical sense of the phrase) that if you go around earning your livelihood by lying, those lies are quite likely to come back to you in — as you put it — "unnerving" ways. Yours seems the most sensible course and the one I've adopted as well. "Isn't that interesting?" and then get back to what you were doing. It might well be a "sign"; it probably isn't a sign, and you're on the slippery slope to L.-Ron-Hubbard-Land if you take it as a Sign. "Isn't that interesting? Oh, almost forgot —I'm out of toothpaste. I must go and buy some toothpaste." I think of Oscar Wilde writing "The Picture of Dorian Gray" before he met Alfred Douglas. Talk about a "snare for the unwary." Jaka has turned up in my life on three or four occasions, but always at a distance or in such a way that it was easy enough to avoid her. Which I do. Having drawn her umpty-ump times, I know the difference between an approximation and the genuine article. Stare at her for a few seconds. "Isn't that interesting? Right, that's enough staring," and back to whatever I was doing.

    We traffic in allegories and metaphors and symbols. I don't know about you, but almost every conversation I have with someone takes place on at least two levels: the enjoyable human level and the writerly mind busily dissecting each tidbit and putting it into its little allegory, metaphor, and symbol compartments. I've found I'm much better off paying more attention to the former than the latter. When the situation was reversed — the writerly mind dominating and the human side of things a distant second — being a writer was a burden. It was always in the way.

    I've just had a letter from a fan asking if you and Neil and I go out and get drunk together, like regular chaps. I've discussed this with you before, back in my drinking days — that is, heavy drinking days — and the last person I wanted to get drunk with was another writer. The first thing I wanted after coming back from a convention or signing, where I'd been tippling with other creative-type types, was to go out and have a proper piss-up where all I talked about was how the Leafs were doing, whether the coach or the general manager should be fired, and just be an all-around fool à la Guys. Virtually no one that I socialise with in Kitchener has more than the vaguest idea of what I do for a living. "So, you still doing those cartoons?" "Yeah, it keeps me off the streets for the most part." The travel interested them. Some deluded individual or other was willing to pay good money to fly me to an American city and put me up in a hotel, and people come to get my autograph. Now that I don't go to the conventions and such, the "so what's new and exciting in your life?" question goes by the board in pretty short order. "Nothing much, working hard. Always working hard."

    It seems the best of both worlds — the gratification of everything that goes into being a writer and artist, having a certain "name value" in my chosen profession, steady work, a better income than most — and just being a face in the crowd with nothing to remind me of the other part of my life when I go home at night.

    Having spent a large part of this series discussing the former reality or "reality" (in both our cases), I thought I'd give you the chance to assure everyone that you aren't ensconced in a Doctor Strange-style loft, draped in velvet raiments, with retorts and beakers bubbling, and doorways to other dimensions opening and closing around you as you're reading this.

    What's Alan Moore like when he's "down the pub"?

Oh, Dave, if only it were that simple. Alarmed and worried for my well-being, as I'm sure the average *Cerebus* reader must be by this juncture, and much as I would love to reassure them that despite those occult ramblings I do still lead an ordinary life, I'm afraid that would be bending the truth more than a little. The interior of my house looks more like something drawn by Steve Ditko every day, only maybe a little less paranoid and angular. The room I'm typing in now, which is my living room, is divided by a wooden partition that includes an arched, stained-glass window on which the design of the OTz ChIIM is picked out in stars. Periwinkle/violet ceiling, also covered in gold stars. Arched and architectured wooden bookcases built in everywhere, and hardly anything but magic books: big, marvellous looking things. A couple of 1776 bibles. Barrett's *The Magus*. Signed first edition of Austin Spare's *Golden Hind*. A beautiful facsimile edition of *A True and Faithful Relation Of What Passed For Many Years Between Dr. John Dee and Some Spirits*. Three different *Necronomicons*.

Up on the top shelf, the two-hundred-year old skull of a Tibetan monk, inlaid and decorated with silver, the skull cap removable as a drinking bowl. Framed letter from Leah Hirsig, written in Switzerland in 1927 and signed for Crowley. Next to the stained-glass OTz ChIIM, a framed one-panel "Road Bit" from Veitch featuring a dream of me and my mother that he had the same week she fell ill with cancer and which was published the same week she was diagnosed terminal...a lovely, uplifting little cartoon that shows us both filling a gorge with plastic flowers. Chalices. Ouija Board. Sword. Mask. Wand. Jars of incense. Pictures of Gods and Demons and other imaginary things. The robe is in the wardrobe upstairs. I only wear it on special occasions, since it's far too beautiful to just knock around the house in. Orange silk with a periwinkle silk collar and belt. Much classier than that second-hand Oxfam-shop shit that Dr. Strange was always hanging about in.

I suppose the point I'm making is that when I "came out" as a Magician, I came all the way out like a full, screeching drag queen. I openly talked about my experiences and ideas with anybody from cab drivers to members of my family. The mysterious and wonderful thing is that it hasn't made the slightest bit of difference to anything. Everybody accepted it as if, on reflection, it was the most normal thing in the world. I insisted on treating demons, angels, and giant talking God-Snakes as if they were a part of my normal everyday existence...and thus by extension a part of general everyday existence. Nobody argued, and, indeed, a large percentage would timidly venture some bizarre experience of their own, as if relieved to finally have somebody to breathe it to. I insist that Magic is Real Life. I behave as if it is, and everybody just sort of, you know. Goes along.

Maybe my relationship with Northampton is different to your relationship with Kitchener, I don't know. I've always lived here and was relatively well known even before I became involved professionally with comics. If you look distinctive and live in a fairly small place all your life, you end up becoming a part of the landscape that is, if not unchanging and everlasting, a great deal more stable and enduring than most of the buildings that make up the town centre these days. Probably because of the television and magazine exposure back in the 'eighties and the odd bits and pieces since, a lot of people seem to be aware of what I do and who I am. That said, they also tend to leave me alone for the most part, which is why I live here. I do get somebody every couple of weeks who'll come up to me in the pub or the street and say something nice about my work, but then I'll get just as many people who'll remember me from when I worked at the pipe-laying company or who remember me as Chick Moore's nephew. Or even Mad Ginger Vernon's great-grandson. Or Leah and Amber's dad who does the comics and got on that *Pop Will Eat Itself* record.

There's a continuity here that I am much more a part of than I am of the comics industry's continuity. One of the things about that continuity...and I'm mailing you a copy of *Voice of the Fire* so that you'll at least have an idea of what I'm talking about...is that it is very old and scarred and knowledgeable, and that it finds very few things surprising any more. When I told my family (who are all very traditional, no-nonsense members of the traditional working class) about becoming a Magician, nobody batted an eyelid. My mother went into a state of child-like marvel at the Snake God picture and wanted a copy immediately, as did my devoutly Christian auntie. Conversely, neither of them wanted the Asmodeus picture anywhere in the house. Older people who've listened to *The Moon and Serpent Grand Egyptian Theatre of Marvels* C.D. often seem more receptive and less spooked by it than many of the younger types who've heard it. I almost got a sense, during those early weeks, that at least as far as my family went, the idea of somebody deciding to become a magician was just one of those things that *happened* every couple of hundred years. Interesting, but nothing to get excited about, and we've still got to pay the bills, after all. No big deal, but worthy of respect. Probably more worthy of respect than writing comics, which is much less Universal.

Also, to me, Magic is not a strange and alien planet that we visit, so much as a new set of eyes to look at *this* planet through, a new language by which our ordinary lives can be expressed more luminously. For a Magician, walking down the street to buy a pack of cigarettes at the corner shop is a Magical experience. Anything from the licence plates of cars to the candy wrappers in the gutter to the casual remarks of passers-by is a potential source of information or inspiration. The Magician is reading things according to the rules of a different grammar, but he or she is reading the same book as everyone else. There really isn't any need for the Occultist to become distanced from the world by his or her behaviour, although a great many seem to do so. A laudable exception is Austin Osman Spare, the only Magician this century to offer any serious competition to Crowley. Spare rejected his promising art career in the West End, turned his back on that entire world, and lived in the slums of Brixton or the East End, exhibiting in the back rooms of pubs rather than the galleries that he was offered. He associated almost exclusively with the chronic urban poor, not out of any warped middle-class notion of charity but simply because they were the people he most liked to be with. They also probably accepted him for what he was: good at drawing, good laugh to have a drink with, looked after his mates, and could make it rain by drawing a squiggle on a piece of scrap paper. Smashing geezer.

I suppose what I'm saying is: "What you see is what you get." These days, after a great deal of hard work, I have refined the Hydra down to one head. I'm Alan Moore when I'm talking to my daughters, or to my eighty-nine-year-old aunt, or to the police, or to my readers, or to myself. I'm Alan Moore when I'm writing *Supreme* or *From Hell* or my part of this discussion. I'm the same person I am when I take out the bin-bags on a Thursday night. This is not easy, but it is at least possible, and, I believe, desirable.

Okay, I guess I'm all through. Looking down to the bottom of the screen here, I see I'm on page 38 of the document I've christened "SIM 1." Might I take this opportunity to personally apologise to your readers, who have certainly never harmed me, for an experience that was probably not dissimilar to being trapped in a stalled elevator with David Koresh and Charles Manson. Of course, on the other hand, they've never gone out of their way to be nice to me, either, so fuck 'em. They ought to be grateful that they're not personally involved in this conversation, so it's not their Tylenol headache. They ought to be doubly grateful that I'm not sitting in the same room as them, talking to them and making eye contact with them, in which case you can stop thinking Tylenol headache and start thinking temporal lobe seizure. I'm not joking, At least not these days.

Dave, this has been a very enjoyable conversation. Thank you for giving an old man the opportunity to talk about himself at such extraordinary length and in such a prestigious forum. Of course, I realise that if you *really* liked me then I'd have got a cameo in *Guys* like my slipshod, head-omitting collaborator, but I guess I'll learn to live with it. *Cerebus*, as if I need to say so, is still to comic books what Hydrogen is to the Periodic Table, and is one of the only comics that I still read and enjoy regularly every month. Alright, so this is only in the hope of finding myself face down in a pool of my own vomit in some minor panel of *Guys*, but you must learn to take compliments graciously.

Incidentally, I had this dream of the last issue of *Cerebus*...the last page of so, in fact. He was ascending towards some sort of minimalist special effect, and it was in *colour*. I remember there was quite a bit of azure blue. That's all I can tell you.

My very best to you and Gerhard. Get over here again soon, and we can continue this conversation over cold beers and hot temporal lobe seizures.

Take care,

Alan

Well, I'll certainly be taking you up on that particular offer. Perhaps this November or the next I think would be appropriate, given that the late fall is the season of each of the chapters of Voice of the Fire *(ISBN 0-575-05249-X, Victor Gollancz imprint, the Cassell Group, Wellington House, 125 Strand, London WC2R OBB. £10 plus postage). Just as an aside, I read the book on a recent vacation with the girlfriend and — having left it behind when we were switching hotels — it provoked the nearest we come these days to a serious argument when I insisted we had to go back for it...NOW. RIGHT now. Priding myself on my singular immersion in my Judeo-Christian heritage (of very recent vintage), I fancied the ectoplasmic Alan Moore snickering into his orange silk cuff at the devotee of the Lamb of God barrelling down a Florida highway, ardent to reconnect with the Magician's Booke.*

With as much grace as I can muster, thank you for your compliments on Cerebus. Of course all of the cameo appearances in Guys *were self-publishers and self-published characters (I had to substitute* Hilly Rose *for* Katchoo *at the last minute when* Terry Moore *went "over the side" — such a changeable landscape), but there are three novels remaining in the* Cerebus *saga and my competitive nature won't allow your incarnation in your ancestrally challenged collaborator's* Bacchus *series stand as the definitive Alan Moore character (which it is — at the moment) in comic-book land.*

My relationship with Kitchener is very different from yours with Northampton, which is probably to be expected, having as much to do with the distinction between the relative newness of this city and the "old and scarred and knowledgeable" quality of your own stomping ground. As I'm fond of saying, most places in the United Kingdom have pubs that are hundreds of years older than Canada itself. Voice of the Fire *is marvellous in conveying exactly that sense of very, very deep roots that permeates the North American awareness (mine, anyway) when travelling around your quaint little island (I'll nod, Alan, but I shan't kneel, you know).*

It's been an exhilarating experience, our little exchange of views (little, he says, as the Dave Sim/Alan Moore fax file enters its second trimester on top of the office filing cabinet). And if our respective belief systems remain intact — mine, that Alan has fallen prey to the implied limitations of Bang-Bulge-Crunch and his Legions of the Fallen and We Won't Get Up and You Can't Make Us, and yours (correct me if I'm wrong) that Dave has been gulled (oblique From Hell *reference) by that peculiar Solar Redeemer cult that got Way out of hand and has closed himself off from all this Really Cool stuff that is only a pentagram and a ritual away...*

Well, at least we have avoided dredging up the really old business. Like Nero immolating our crucified lads when he found himself short of patio lanterns for one of his little garden parties, or all of the magnificent pagan temples and statues that fell to the wrecking ball. "Old and scarred and knowledgeable," indeed. If there is more than enough recrimination to go around, I would hope that we have at least arrived at a place in history where, with insight born of overview, it is possible to attribute the largest blame for past atrocities on the imposition of systems of belief by force...and to recognise that it is the imposition — and not the beliefs — that needs to be eliminated.

Let me also express in answer to your observation that you are far, far more a part of Northamptonshire's continuity than that of the comic-book industry that I can't...nor would I want to...take issue with that. But I would draw the distinction between the industry and the medium...very, very sharply. With the progress of your contributions to the medium: from Swamp Thing *to* Watchmen *and* V for Vendetta, Brought to Light, *and* A Small Killing, *and with your (to this point) summit achievement with* From Hell, *it is very sad to consider that future opportunities for a comic-book writer of your stature would be limited to* Spawn *and* Supreme, *entertaining as they are — and, believe me, I find them very entertaining.*

I don't see it as your failure, but rather a failure of the medium and the current configuration in which it finds itself. It seems to me that the medium has always been (and never more so than today) an amorphous being composed of the sum of the awarenesses and actions of the loose community of individuals who are its most active participants and practitioners. A persuasive argument could be made that there just aren't enough crazy people with too much money around anymore, as was the case when I let Bissette off his leash to put together his dream horror anthology and twenty thousand dollars or so later kicked him out of the nest, whereupon he spent thousands of his own money (which he didn't have) to keep it going until he got swept up in Kevin Eastman's singular and selfless Tundra madness, which eventually merged with Denis Kitchen — who was crazy years before any of us were. Crazy and selfless. The madness and the money went west and adhered to super-heroes and Hollywood, twin banes for those of us who are always attempting to fry larger fish.

Perhaps no small part was played by that peculiar British instinct to hastily raise up an icon and then just as hastily put it out to pasture (a skill honed to perfection with rock 'n' roll's British invasion). I think you and Neil both had about fifteen minutes to enjoy the laurel crown before would-be British successors and fans began demoting you from the pantheon to the metaphorical British Elba. A most quaint...and peculiar...little island.

I had a chance to spend some time with Neil and Scott McCloud at Will Eisner's 80th birthday party (there's a name-dropping sentence if ever there was one). Through good luck, I've been able to just do Cerebus *for nearly twenty years now. What little interest I have in other forms of art, entertainment, and communication is insufficient to tempt me away from the comic-book field (and I don't see that changing after 2004, frankly). I do recognise that others are not that way. If Neil is drawn to writing a television series or a novel or an illustrated book like* Stardust, *if Scott finds himself lost in cyberspace (I think I've fallen, but it's hard to tell because there is no "Up"), and if you are going to devote your energies to another novel or a CD, well...*

At least the medium...the medium, not the industry...got Sandman *and Mr.* Punch *and* Zot *and* Understanding Comics *and* From Hell *out of you before you left. And maybe you're just on holiday and you'll be back when the madness and the money reconfigure themselves. Maybe not.*

Anyway, thanks — sincere thanks — from those of us who aren't going on any holidays anytime soon, for giving us — for giving the medium — such a high watermark of an achievement.

Next: Alan Moore's *Conclusion*

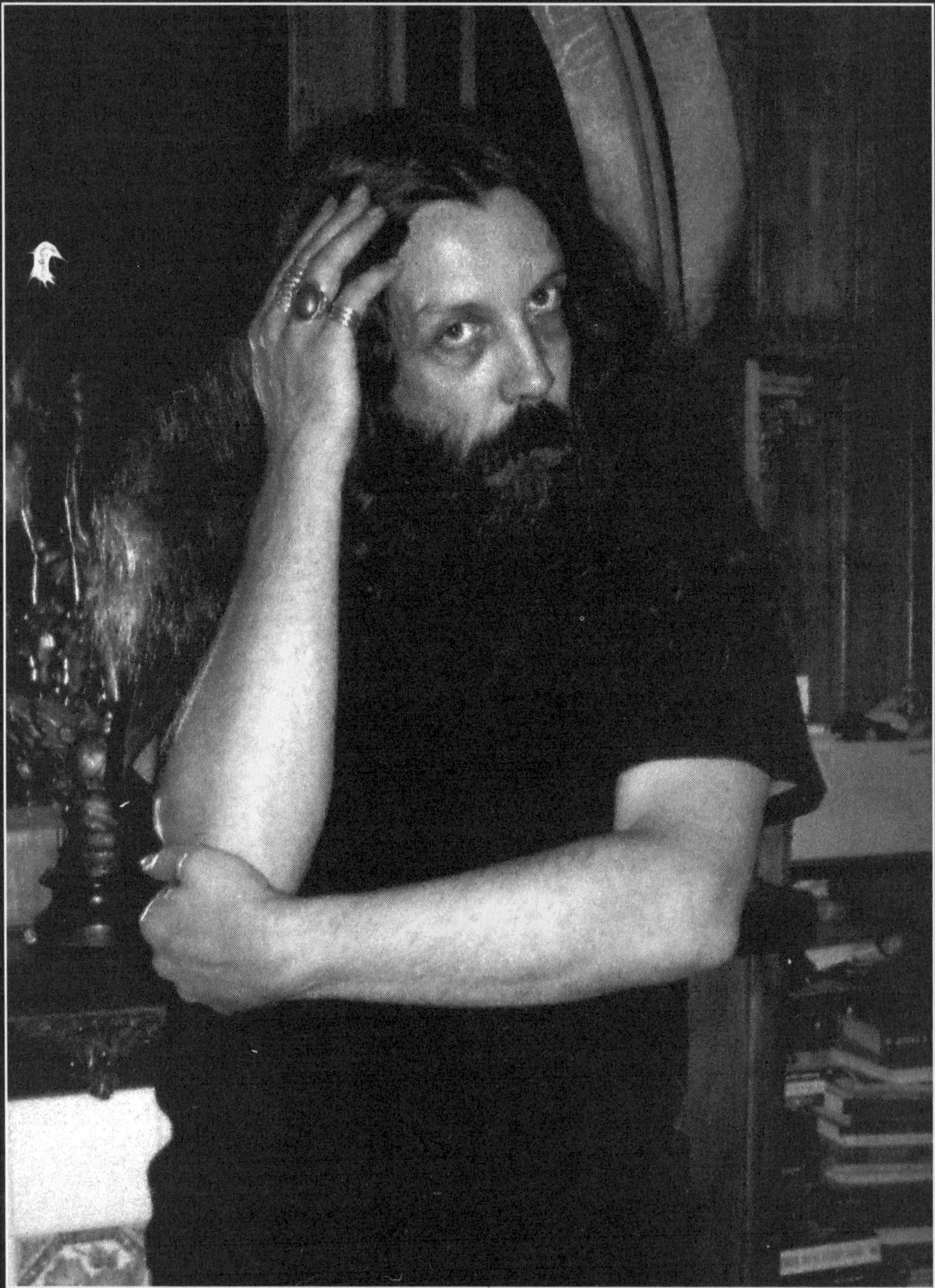

CORRESPONDENCE: FROM HELL
Conclusion

Well, since you invite me to correct you on your assumptions regarding how I see you, it would be rude of me not to. Whatever Dr. Gull's notions of an eternal war between the rational male solar force and the irrational female lunar force might lead one to suppose, this is not my own point of view. I tend to see both forces as elements in a far wider dynamic balance and tend to shy away from polarised positions such as Sun vs. Moon, Man vs. Woman, Christianity vs. Diabolism, Lobo vs. Wolverine, and so on.

Admittedly, I do have several bones...whole war fields full of bones, in fact...to pick with organised religion of whatever stripe. This should be seen as a critique of purely temporal agencies who have, to my mind, erected more obstacles between humanity and whatever notion of spirituality or Godhead one subscribes to than they have opened doors. To me, the difference between Godhead and the Church is the difference between Elvis and Colonel Parker...although that conjures images of God dying on the toilet, which is not what I meant at all.

What I'm saying is that, to me, organised religion seems to be an accumulation of dead ritual, lifeless dogma, and largely fear-driven belief that has built up around some original kernel of genuine spiritual experience. From what I understand of the original Essenes, for example, they were Gnostics. That is to say, their spirituality was based not upon faith or belief but upon personal apprehension and knowledge, or *gnosis*, of the powers at work in the Universe. They didn't *believe*. They *knew*. If there ever was such a historical personage as Jesus Christ, and if this person did have a group of Apostles around him, they were not acting from belief either. Saul/Paul had the heavenly searchlight turned upon him during his day trip to Damascus. Pentecostal Fire danced on their tongues. Thomas...a pure-bred I'm-From-Missouri Gnostic if ever I heard of one...even put his hand in the wound of the resurrected messiah. Gnosis...personal knowledge and experience of the spiritual...I have no problem with.

What I do have a problem with is the middle management who have manoeuvred themselves between the wellspring and those who thirst in the field of spirituality just as efficiently as they've done it in every other field of human endeavour. It seems to me that when the blueprint for the modern Christian faith was first sketched out by the Emperor Constantine and his marketing department, it was constructed largely to solve a couple of immediate Earthly problems that Rome was faced with at the time. They had a city divided by different theological factions, the largest and noisiest probably being the early
Christian zealots. Then there was the cult of Mithras, which was smaller but which included the bulk of the Roman Military. Finally there was the cult of Sol Invictus, the undefeated Sun, which was relatively small but very popular amongst the merchant class.

Constantine's posse came up with a composite religion to unite Rome: Christianity would incorporate large chunks of Mithraism, including the stuff about being born in a cave surrounded by shepherds and animals on the 25th of December, and would make concessions to the cult of Sol Invictus, the Undefeated Sun, by sticking a big Sun-symbol behind the messiah's head in all the publicity handouts. This is politics.

The effect in spiritual terms is to move the emphasis away from any genuine personal spiritual experience. Whereas for the original Gnostics such a personal knowledge of and direct communication with the Godhead was the cornerstone of their spiritual life, after the priesthood moved in the basic proposition was vastly different: "You don't need to have had a transforming experience yourselves, and in fact neither do the priesthood need to have had a transforming experience. The important thing is that we have this book, about people who lived a long time ago, and *they* had transforming experiences, and if you come along on Sunday we'll read to you about them, and *that* will be your transforming experience." This sounds to me like a co-opting of the divine impulse — a channelling of the individual's spiritual aspirations into a mechanism for social regulation.

So, no, I'm not a big fan of organised religion of any kind.

On the other hand, I have nothing but respect for your recent involvement with

PIET CORR

Left, and page 352:
Piet Corr a.k.a. **pietdesnapp** is a freelance photographer and lecturer, born in Northampton. His work has been exhibited in galleries and libraries all over England.
Photograph ©2003 Piet Corr.

Christianity*, although it was news to me. Stripped of the dogma and the strictures of organised religion that have grown up about it, I have a great deal of sympathy for the story at the core of Christianity. Judaeo-Christian symbology and concepts make up a significant part of magical thought, and my own workings have touched upon some of these areas with a fierce intensity. I won't bore you or your readers with the rambling details, but one of my investigations into the Qabalah involved a vision of the Mysteries of the Crucifixion, and it goes without saying that something like that certainly leaves an impression. I would imagine that my personal notion of Jesus is possibly a great deal more immediate and real than that of a great many people who would profess to be practising Christians.

I suppose this is how I would define the relative definitions between our positions in terms of language and linguistics. As I see things, the underlying spiritual landscape of all the world's religions and belief systems is the same territory, just as a canine quadruped is essentially the same animal the world over, whether we choose to label it *chien* or *hund* or *dog*. As with dogs, so too with gods. All religions and beliefs are in a sense language systems, a range of symbols and icons with which we attempt to give form to the infinite and formless. Just as with language, most belief systems have their own unique beauty, their own advantages and drawbacks. In its purest form, Christianity is a very moving and powerful holy language indeed, and I sometimes like to speak it, to frame the Universe in those terms. I don't see magic as being something that is in opposition to Christianity, Islam, or even secular Humanism. I see all of these forms as being languages, while I see magic as being more akin to linguistics, the science of languages. Note that I don't imply that magic is necessarily a superior form of study because of this, any more than I'd look down on you for learning Russian while I was taking a linguistics course.

Also, once you move aside the symbols and look behind them, we'd probably find that our viewpoints had more in common than one might suppose. The serpent deity that I have a particular affinity for is understood to be the serpent entwining the tree in Eden. According to the numerological system of Gematria, the serpent in Eden and Jesus Christ have an equivalent value; they are in a sense understood to be the same thing. This was the basis for the belief of the early Gnostic Ophite Christians, who believed that Jesus was a form of divine, illuminating energy called the Christos and that this energy was identical to the divine, illuminating serpent energy known as Kundalini. You might not find the idea very palatable, but when my mind is focused upon my snake deity/imaginary friend, then it is at least in part focused upon that aspect of the serpent that is Jesus. In a sense, the snake is Jesus in another language: the redeeming solar force that brings light and knowledge, that rises again from its own sloughed-off skin. Thus, I imagine that most of the differences between our outlook may be similarly differences of language. At any rate, we can certainly agree to coexist peacefully. If you don't burn me at the stake, I won't sour your milk or give your offspring a clubfoot.

As for my relationship with the comics industry and comics medium...which are, as you observe, two different things...then I'd have to say that while I obviously still have a strong relationship with comics in all their aspects, that relationship has changed and modified itself over the years. Given that the comics field itself had changed so radically during the same period, this isn't really surprising. Something has happened, and I don't think that any of us have quite taken it in yet. Parameters have changed and paradigms have shifted. My view on things, while probably egocentric and worthlessly subjective, is probably as follows:

I think something happened in the middle eighties. Basically, all of our dreams came true and turned out to have been small dreams after all. I've been involved with comics one way or another since my days on the peripheries of the British comics fan scene in the late sixties, and the dream was always pretty much the same, with minor seasonal variations. The idea was that we all recognised that comics were as noble and valid a form of art as anything else, that they didn't have to be aimed solely at kids, and that if we were only given a chance, then everybody else would see this too. Comics would be given the serious public and critical attention that they deserved, and then...well, and then everybody would live happily ever after, I guess. Something like that. Mostly, our fantasies didn't get that far. Virgins fantasising about first coitus, we only took our dream to the point of orgasm. We didn't waste time on thinking about avoiding the wet spot afterwards or what we were going to say to each other in the morning. And now it's morning.

The middle eighties was when comic books finally got laid. Media attention. Frank Miller in *Rolling Stone*, MTV. *Maus* cops the Pulitzer. *Watchmen* on University reading lists. The style and music press raving about *Love & Rockets*. Fuck, man, we had the "Cerebus-the-Aardvark Party" running in British elections in '88. Reason tottered on its throne. Everybody was on Top of the Pops. We got everything we ever asked for, just as one often finds in real life or the better fairy stories, and just like in real life or the better fairy stories it turned out to be shit. For a few years there, everything we touched turned to gold, and now what the fuck are we going to do with all this gold? All this shit? With honest and sincere effort, we made comics what we wanted them to be: as popular as any other 20th-century medium. As respected as any other 20th-century medium. What on earth were we *thinking*?

The comics medium, its pure and platonic essence, remains unchanged by the above. It is only our relationship to it that has changed. Much of what provided the drive and motivation for that Darwinian struggle up from the gore-rich mud of the fifties to the evolutionary pinnacle of the eighties turns out to have been delusion. The beautiful room, to borrow a phrase from author Edmund White, is empty. Our Darwinian view of a steady but sure upwards progress and development has been superseded by catastrophe theory. Put crudely, catastrophe theory states that it really doesn't matter how bloody evolved or fit for survival you are if you happen to be under a big enough mudslide, a falling comet, or a long enough ice age. With a big enough wipe-out, God or the DNA simply has no choice but to slowly rebuild by diversifying whatever few fragments of life managed to survive the destruction.

Our vision was limited. Our reason for doing comic books...to elevate the medium to its proper cultural position...has disintegrated upon accomplishment under the weight of realising that the culture we were trying to find our place in is no culture at all. We need a new reason to carry on doing this stuff, a reason that is unconnected with fad, fashion, and the myopic short-term concerns of the industry. We need to create good comics with no social agenda, no goal that is based upon contemporary notions of success. In the course of a twenty-five-year (?) monsterpiece like *Cerebus*, you yourself have seen the comics industry shift and fluctuate more than most, and yet *Cerebus* has a constancy that suggests that the work itself is the most important thing, rather than the work viewed in relation to the comics field. In fifty years, I doubt that anybody will be much interested in, say, the relationship of Dave Sim's *Cerebus* to the late-eighties comic-book self-publishing phenomenon. What they'll be interested in is *Cerebus* itself, the fact that it was created, was brought to fruition over such an astounding period of time. They will be interested, in short, in the timeless elements of art that are undoubtedly in the work, rather than the work's relationship to the comics field of its day.

The work itself is the only thing. *From Hell* was created with no thought to how the comics industry might receive it, or of any effect it might have on the medium. It had no agenda and simply was itself. *Cerebus* is the same, as are a number of the other fine titles that currently grace the medium. It seems to me that our only course of action can be to let the comic-book medium be its own motivation, so that our motivation is simply to produce good and enduring comic books of whatever stripe with no aspirations for the medium beyond that. The work will speak for itself, and if what it says has any profundity then it will endure. We should not concern ourselves with anything further.

As for where this leaves me, I find myself currently close to the end of one major personal cycle that includes the eight or nine years of *From Hell*, the five years spent on *Voice of the Fire, Lost Girls* (which approaches completion), a couple of years on *A Small Killing, Big Numbers* (which may achieve completion as a television series sometime soon), and various other things. The work for Image and Extreme has been very enjoyable, lucrative enough to finance the less commercial projects (see above), and hopefully of some small use in the struggle to reinstall proper story values into mainstream comics. I imagine that I'll be involved with more of this stuff for at least the immediate future, and it's something I'm looking forward to. Something with a little more finesse but still very much in the fun/adventure ballpark is this *League of Extraordinary Gentlemen* project that Kevin O'Neill and I are putting together.

As far as strictly serious comic-book work goes, I'm probably going to coast for a few months before committing myself to another major work. I have an idea for a lengthy and utterly non-commercial history of the development of magic, in step with the development of language, consciousness, art, and culture. It would be nine volumes long, and I'd be working on it with fellow occultist Steve Moore (no relation). Maybe nine different artists working on it. Nothing decided as yet. Beyond that, Neil Gaiman and I have been talking at long intervals about a kind of anthology-magazine-type thing. I have no doubt that it will happen eventually, but as yet it's still only very nebulous as far as any practical considerations go. These are my only plans for strictly serious comics work following the end of *Lost Girls*, but they're both pretty ambitious. On top of this, I'll be working on a CD-ROM with Dave Gibbons, finishing my third CD recording (a double album of techno dance music, if anyone's even remotely interested), and working on the follow-up to *Voice of the Fire*, which currently has *A Grammar* as its working title. By the time I've finished with all of the above, I'll probably be pushing fifty. *Cerebus* will be finished. It'll be the twenty-first century, and we'll all be living on the moon and wearing anti-gravity shoes. We'll see how everything stands (or floats) then.

I hope that answers your questions, and sorry that it's taken me so long to reply to this last part. Again, it's been a great virtual conversation, and I can think of no nobler forum than your extraordinary comic book for it to appear in. Incidentally, I only just noticed that the spooky photograph of me that you stuck in the issue preceding the start of our chat is taken from the inner sleeve of *The Moon & Serpent*. Did you finally find a copy, or what?

Anyway, my love, as ever, to you and Ger. *Cerebus* goes from strength to strength, to the point where even running this conversation in issue after issue probably won't completely destroy its reader base. Take care of yourselves, and I'll talk to you soon, although probably not in public.

Peace.

• **Alan Moore**

* Dave's footnote: I don't consider myself really "involved" with Christianity. In part three, I should've drawn a sharper distinction between my high regard for the "Lamb of God" Jesus of John's Gospel, as distinct from the "Son of Man" Jesus of Matthew, Mark, and Luke — and likewise clarified the fact that I consider the former incarnation to be a less heretical one than the three latter incarnations; but that I consider all four to be timely, inevitable, but nonetheless regrettable Judaic corruptions. I agree with Alan's views on theological "middle management."

• **Dave Sim**

THE ALAN MOORE BOOKSHELF

The vast majority of Alan Moore's work has been reprinted in a variety of different formats and much of it is still in print in convenient trade paperback form. What follows is not an attempt at a complete bibliography (there are far more comprehensive lists included in the "further reading" books below) but most of the following (with some notable exceptions) are readily available from bookstores, comic stores and the Internet.

As an aid for the Moore neophyte, the editorial team and our affiliates have assigned a comparative indication to some of the books, "Essential," "Highly Recommended" and "Recommended" although everything featured on this list should be regarded as a high quality comic book on its own terms and will not disappoint.

Compiled by
GARY SPENCER MILLIDGE
and **OMAR MARTINI**
with kind assistance from
smoky man, Chris Staros *and*
Dave Whitwell.

THE BALLAD OF HALO JONES

From the British weekly 2000AD, originally collected into several volumes from Titan Books in 1986, the whole story is now available as The Complete Ballad of Halo Jones (2001), which includes all of Moore & Ian Gibson's strips in one neat package.
Currently available in the UK from Titan Books and on import in the US.
www.titanbooks.co.uk
RECOMMENDED

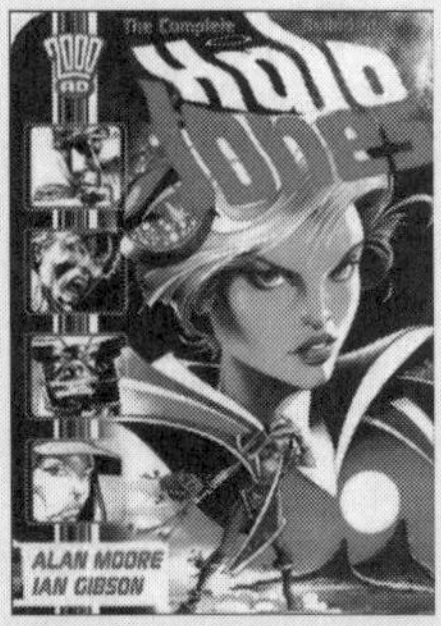

ALAN MOORE
IAN GIBSON

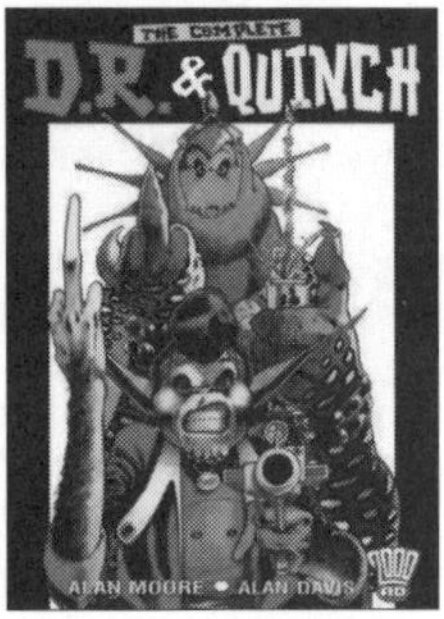

THE COMPLETE
D.R. & QUINCH
ALAN MOORE • ALAN DAVIS

D.R. & QUINCH

Collecting all the strips from the weekly 2000AD comic, first collected in 1986, The Complete D.R. & Quinch (2001), includes all the strips by Moore and artist Alan Davis, published byTitan Books in the UK available on import in the US.

SKIZZ

A new collection of the entire Skizz storyline by Moore and Jim Baikie from the pages of 2000AD (originally published 1989) has been published byTitan Books in the UK available on import in the US. www.titanbooks.co.uk

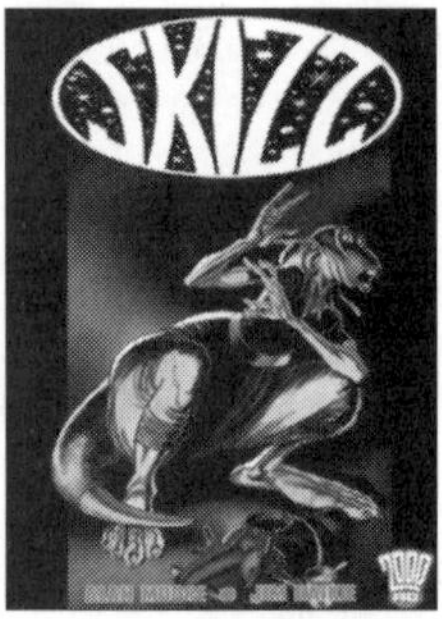

SKIZZ

EARLY WORKS

Maxwell the Magic Cat
Moore's long running newspaper strip from the Northants Post was collected into four slim volumes in 1986 and 1987 by Acme Press but are now long out of print and difficult to find.

Alan Moore's Shocking Futures *and* **Alan Moore's Twisted Times**
were both compilations of the best of Moore's two or three-page shorts from 2000AD weekly, published by Titan Books in 1986 and 1987 respectively, although both volumes are now very scarce.

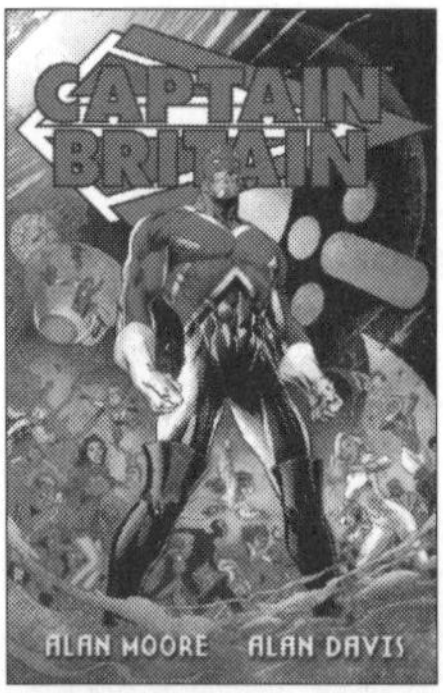

CAPTAIN BRITAIN
ALAN MOORE ALAN DAVIS

CAPTAIN BRITAIN

Moore's stint as writer on the British Marvel superhero character (with art throughout by Alan Davis) culled from assorted Marvel black and white weeklies (including Marvel Superheroes, Mighty World of Marvel and The Daredevils) is collected in its entirety in this single trade paperback volume.
After assorted legal difficulties and false starts, Marvel finally published a new collected edition in 2002, freshly coloured and with a new introduction by Moore.
www.marvel.com

MIRACLEMAN

aka Marvelman, the Moore run on the legally disputed hero from the pages of Warrior was originally collected into three volumes by Eclipse Comics (with additional books scripted by Neil Gaiman):
A dream of Flying vol. 1 (1988)
Red King Syndrome vol. 2 (1990)
Olympus vol. 3 (1990)
With art by Alan Davis, Garry Leach, Rick Veitch et al, all volumes are highly sought after and difficult to find. It's hoped that once the legal wrangles are resolved that the books will be put back into print.
HIGHLY RECOMMENDED

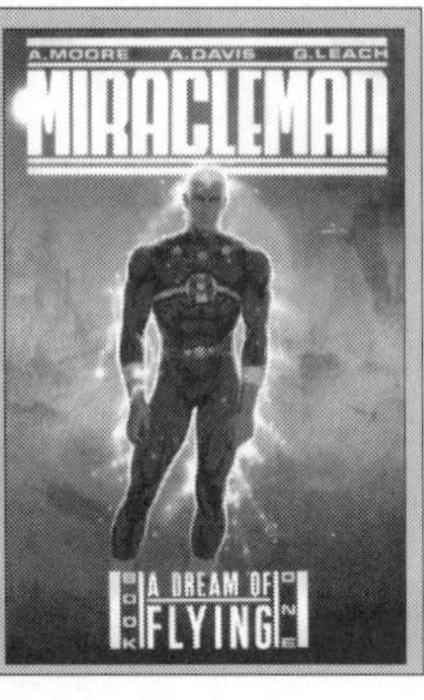

A. MOORE A. DAVIS G. LEACH
MIRACLEMAN
BOOK ONE
A DREAM OF FLYING

THE BOJEFFRIES SAGA

Moore's often overlooked third Warrior series, drawn by Steve Parhouse. additional strips were serialsed in A1 Magazine and some were specifically created for The Kitchen Sink/Tundra 1992 full-colour compilation, which is now sadly out of print.
RECOMMENDED

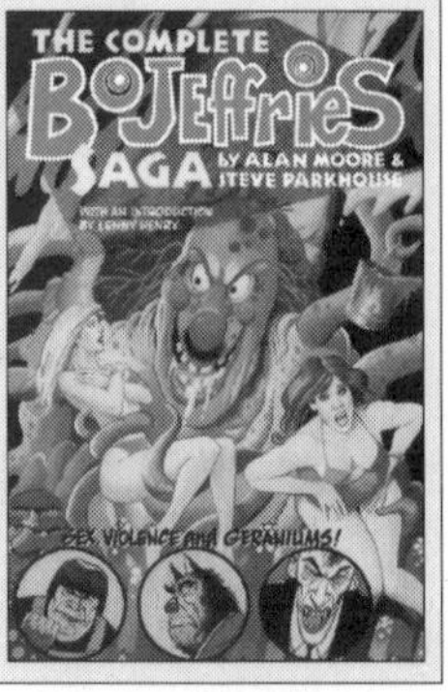

THE COMPLETE
BOJEFFRIES
SAGA BY ALAN MOORE & STEVE PARKHOUSE
SEX, VIOLENCE AND GERANIUMS!

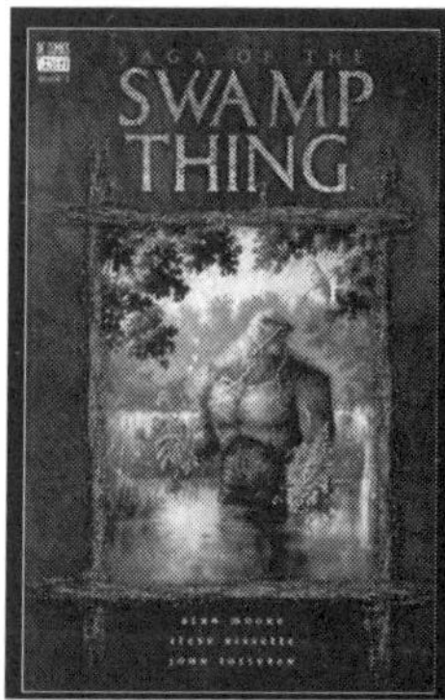
SAGA OF THE
SWAMP
THING
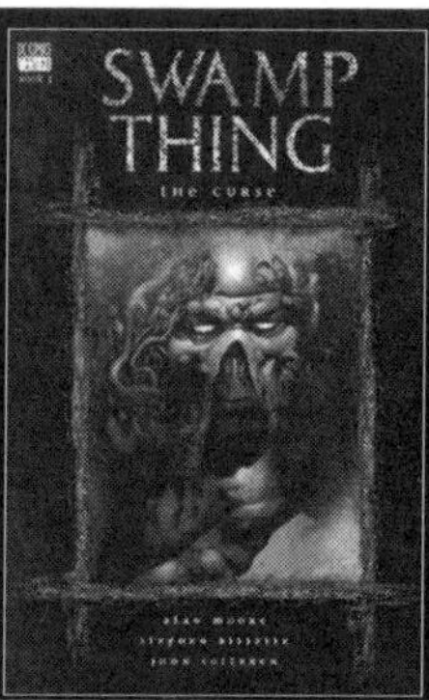
SWAMP
THING
the curse
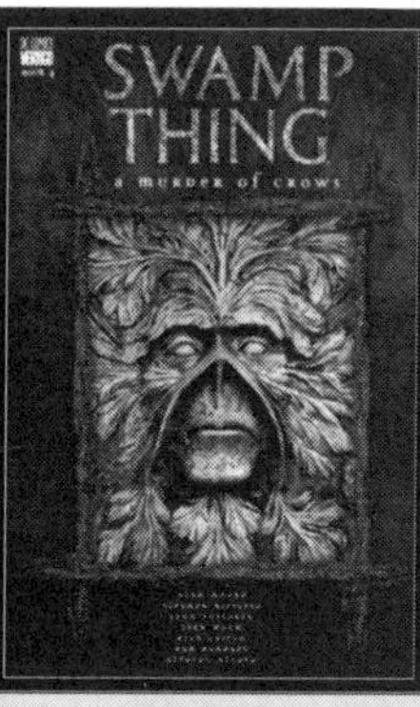
SWAMP
THING
A MURDER OF CROWS

SWAMP THING

Moore's first major work in the US and still an immense classic. Five trade paperbacks collect Moore's entire four-year run on the title with artists Steve Bissette, John Totleben and others. The first volume was originally collected in 1987.
Saga Of The Swamp Thing vol. 1
Love and Death vol. 2
The Curse vol. 3
A Murder of Crows vol. 4
Earth to Earth vol. 5
All currently in print from DC /Vertigo in the US and Titan Books in the UK.
ESSENTIAL

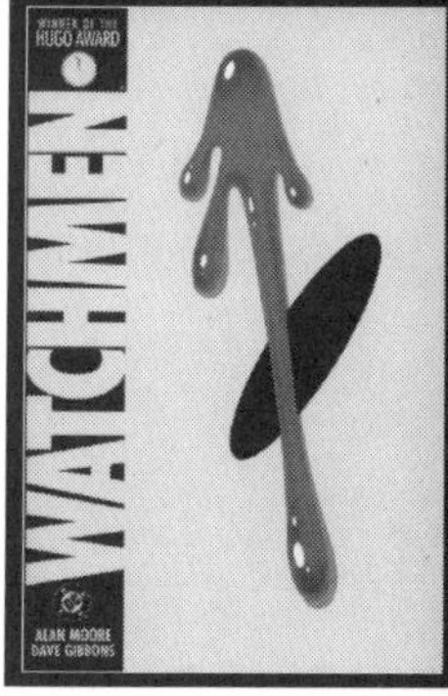
WINNER OF THE HUGO AWARD
WATCHMEN
ALAN MOORE
DAVE GIBBONS

WATCHMEN

The groundbreaking deconstruction of the superhero. The perennial best-selling trade paperback collects the whole 12-part series by Moore and Dave Gibbons, first published in book form in 1987.
Always in print from DC Comics in the US and Titan Books in the UK.
www.dccomics.com
ESSENTIAL

BATMAN: THE KILLING JOKE

A fan-favourite collaboration with Brian Bolland, this full colour 48-page graphic novel from 1988 represents Moore's only major Batman piece.
Always in print from DC Comics in the US and Titan Books in the UK.
www.dccomics.com
RECOMMENDED

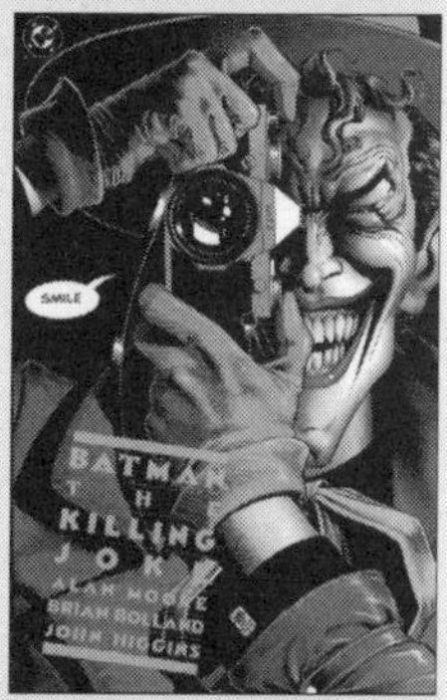
SMILE
BATMAN
THE
KILLING
JOKE
ALAN MOORE
BRIAN BOLLAND
JOHN HIGGINS

OTHER DC WORKS

Moore's two-part Superman tale, with art by Curt Swan and George Perez, has been collected and kept in print by DC Comics in a single volume; **Whatever Happened to the Man of Tomorrow? (1996)**
DC will also be publishing a collection of all Moore's other minor DC work in summer 2003; **Across The Universe,** *featuring stories from Vigilante, Omega Men, Tales of the Green Lantern Corps, Batman Annual and the classic Superman "For the Man Who Has Everything."*
www.dccomics.com

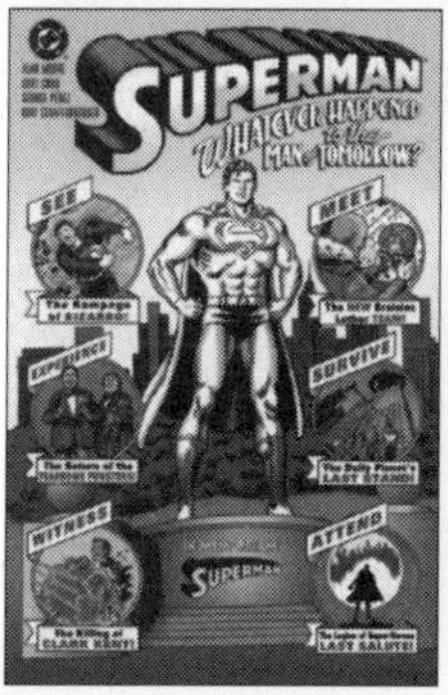
SUPERMAN
Whatever Happened to the Man of Tomorrow?
SEE
MEET
SURVIVE
WITNESS
ATTEND

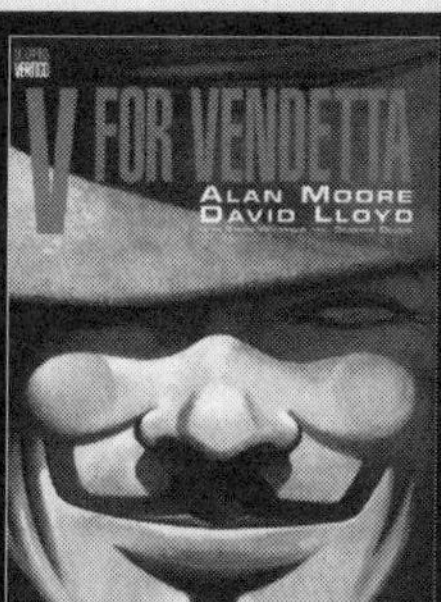
V FOR VENDETTA
ALAN MOORE
DAVID LLOYD

V FOR VENDETTA

Serialised in black and white in Warrior Magazine and later completed and coloured in a ten-part series from Vertigo, this trade paperback collects the entire stunning saga by Moore and David Lloyd, first collected in 1990.
Always in print from DC /Vertigo in the US and Titan Books in the UK.
www.dccomics.com
ESSENTIAL

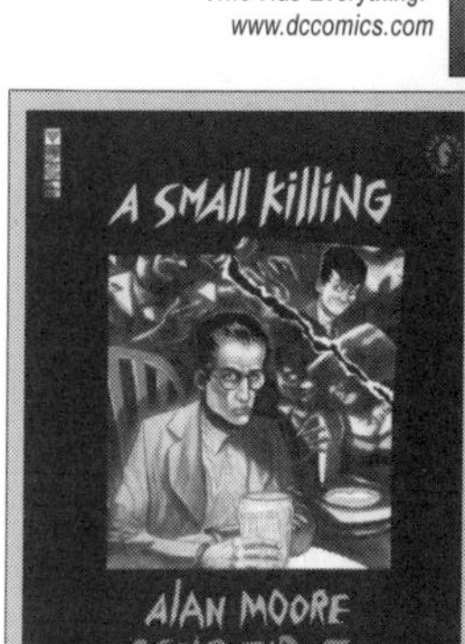
A SMALL KILLING
ALAN MOORE
OSCAR ZARATE

A SMALL KILLING

Moore's first standalone graphic novel from 1991, aimed at the book market, published by Gollancz with full-colour painted art by Oscar Zarate and declared by Moore to be his most underrated work. Dark Horse published the first American edition in 1993 and a brand new edition in both hardcover and softcover is due for publication in spring 2003 by Avatar.
www.avatarpress.com
HIGHLY RECOMMENDED

BROUGHT TO LIGHT

A "flip-book" commissioned by the Christic Institute, with one half written (30 pages) by Moore and illustrated by Bill Sienkiewicz, "Shadowplay: the Secret Team," originally published in 1989, it is now long out of print.

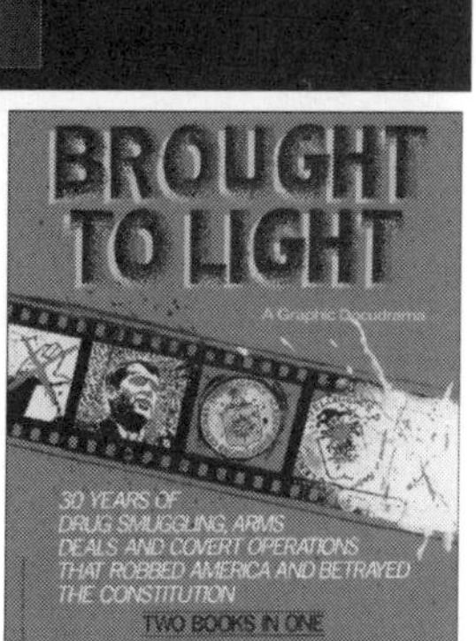
BROUGHT
TO LIGHT
A Graphic Docudrama
30 YEARS OF
DRUG SMUGGLING, ARMS
DEALS AND COVERT OPERATIONS
THAT ROBBED AMERICA AND BETRAYED
THE CONSTITUTION
TWO BOOKS IN ONE
This side: Shadowplay - The Secret Team
THE CHRISTIC INSTITUTE

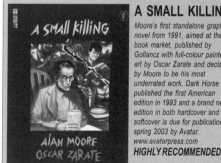

FROM HELL
alan moore • eddie campbell

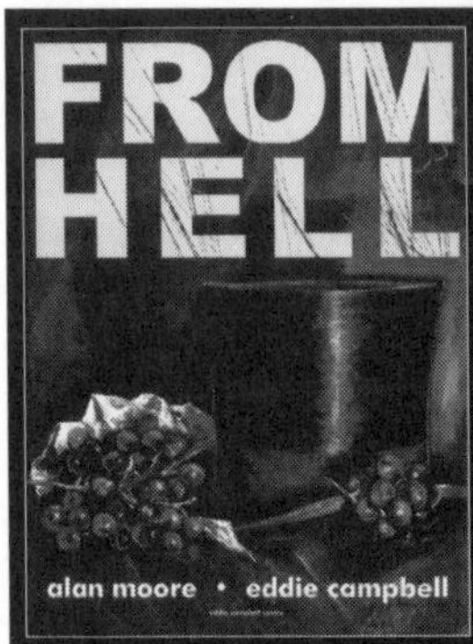

FROM HELL

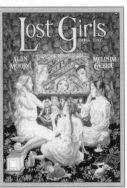

Originally serialised in the Taboo anthology in 1989, then released in chapter-long segments by Tundra, and later Kitchen Sink, the entire 600-page story has finally been collected in a single volume by artist Eddie Campbell's own publishing imprint (in 1999) and made into a Hollywood movie starring Johnny Depp.
In print and available from Top Shelf Productions.
www.topshelfcomix.com
ESSENTIAL

LOST GIRLS

The other serial from Steve Bissette's Taboo, two issues were also published by Kitchen Sink in 1995 before they went bust, leaving the strip in limbo.
Moore's erotic fantasy, delicately illustrated by Melinda Gebbie is finally due to see completion in a 240-page hardcover edition to be published by Top Shelf in 2004.
www.topshelfcomix.com
HIGHLY RECOMMENDED

Lost Girls
Alan Moore
Melinda Gebbie

THE BIRTH CAUL

Eddie Campbell's fabulous visual adaptation of Moore's performance CD, complete in one volume and self-published by Campbell in 1999. Still in print and available from Top Shelf.
www.topshelfcomix.com
HIGHLY RECOMMENDED

alan moore & eddie campbell
theBirthCaul

Alan Moore
& Eddie Campbell
Snakes & Ladders

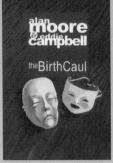

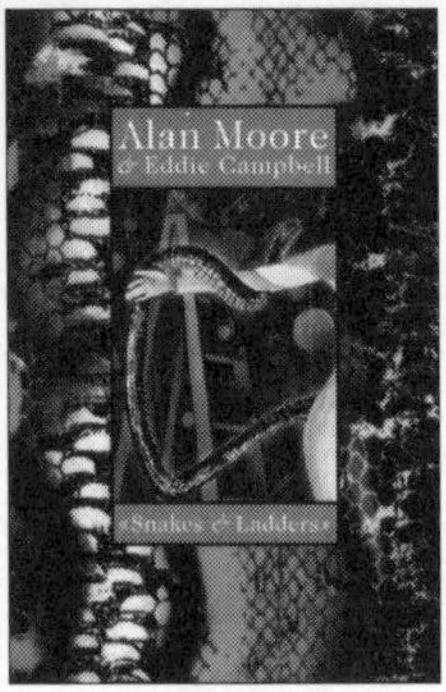

SNAKES & LADDERS

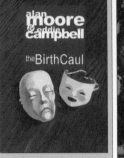

Eddie Campbell's second adaptation of a Moore performance CD, once again complete in one volume and self-published by Campbell in 2001. Still in print and available from Top Shelf.
www.topshelfcomix.com

BIG NUMBERS

Alan Moore's one remaining unfinished masterpiece, only two issues out of a planned twelve issue series were ever published by Moore's own Mad Love imprint (in 1990). Illustrated by Bill Sienkiewicz, long out-of-print and hard to find, if the series was ever to be completed, it would almost certainly deserve an "essential" rating. Well worth hunting around for.
HIGHLY RECOMMENDED

Big numbers
1
ALAN MOORE
BILL SIENKIEWICZ

SUPREME
THE STORY OF THE YEAR

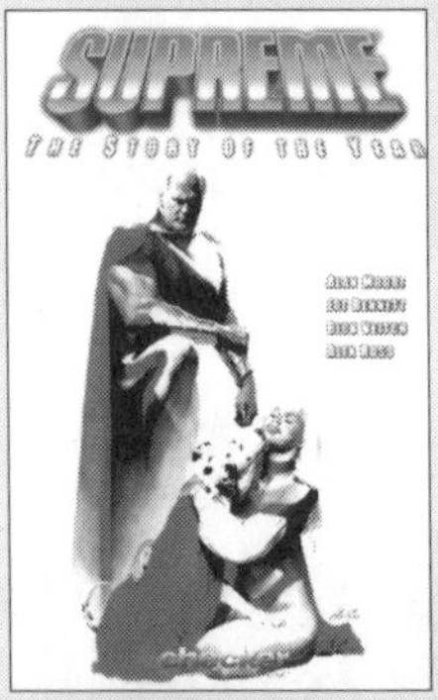

SUPREME

Checker Books are currently reprinting Moore's run on the title in two volumes complete.
The Story of The Year vol. 1 (2002)
The Return vol. 2 (2003)
www.checkerbpg.com
RECOMMENDED

WILDC.A.T.S.

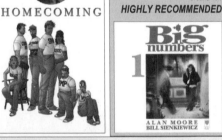

Moore's year long stint and mini-series spin-off collected in three volumes by Wildstorm/DC Comics
Homecoming vol. 1 (1998)
Gang War vol. 2 (1999)
Voodoo:Dancing in the Dark (1999)

HOMECOMING

THE LEAGUE OF EXTRAORDINARY GENTLEMEN

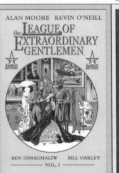

Flagship ABC title which has just been adapted into a Hollywood movie starring Sean Connery. First six issues by Moore and Kevin O'Neill collected into limited hardcover and mass-market softcover versions (first published in 2000)with a second six-issue series almost complete
www.wildstorm.com
HIGHLY RECOMMENDED

ALAN MOORE KEVIN O'NEILL
the LEAGUE OF EXTRAORDINARY GENTLEMEN
BEN DIMAGMALIW BILL OAKLEY
VOL. 1

ALAN MOORE
TOP 10
ILLUSTRATED BY
GENE HA
ZANDER CANNON

TOP 10

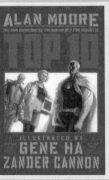

America's Best Comics title by Moore, Gene Ha and Zander Cannon now available from Wildstorm/DC Comics collected into two volumes, both available in limited hardcover or in mass-market softcover (2000).
www.wildstorm.com
RECOMMENDED

PROMETHEA

Moore's most impressive America's Best Comics title, with art by J. H. Williams III and Mick Gray, planned to run 30-odd issues and culminating with the end of the world. The entire series is being collected into both limited edition hardcover editions and softcover versions in six-issue chunks, the first volume published in 2001.
www.wildstorm.com
HIGHLY RECOMMENDED

ALAN MOORE
TOMORROW STORIES
KEVIN NOWLAN
RICK VEITCH
JIM BAIKIE
MELINDA GEBBIE
HILARY BARTA

TOMORROW STORIES

ABC's anthology series features a number of rotating strips pairing Moore with various artists and like all ABC titles, the title is being collected into both limited hardcover editions and softcover versions (2002).
www.wildstorm.com

TOM STRONG

Moore's heroic ABC title with art by Chris Sprouse and Al Gordon, two volumes already available in both limited hardcover and softcover versions (2001).
www.wildstorm.com

ALAN MOORE
TOM STRONG
CHRIS SPROUSE
ALAN GORDON
ARTHUR ADAMS
GARY FRANK
DAVE GIBBONS
JERRY ORDWAY

ALAN MOORE
The New Collection by the Author of WATCHMEN
PROMETHEA
J.H. WILLIAMS III
MICK GRAY

VOICE OF THE FIRE

Moore's first, and so far, only novel. Despite the notorious first chapter, it is clearly an immense work. The original Gollancz publication from 1996 is now out of print (cover shown on right), although Top shelf will be publishing the first American edition in hardcover in August 2003 with thirteen photographic plates by José Villarrubia.
www.topshelfcomix.com
HIGHLY RECOMMENDED

VOICE OF THE FIRE
ALAN MOORE
A DARK MIDWINTER TALE FROM THE HEART OF ENGLAND

OTHER TITLES

The Mirror of Love
José Villarrubia's photographic interpretation of Moore's 40-stanza poem (which originally appeared in Moore's AARGH! benefit book) with 40 new colour plates in a hardcover volume due for publication in Sept 2003 from Top Shelf.
www.topshelfcomix.com

The Mirror of Love
by Alan Moore & José Villarrubia

The Alan Moore Songbook
Originally compiled by Caliber Comics (1998) from short comics adaptations of Moore's songs which appeared in Negative Burn. The volume is now out of print.
Avatar are publishing a number of adaptations of Moore's lyrics in **Alan Moore's Magic Words** *(2002) and* **A Suburban Romance** *(2003) adapts one of Moore's early plays.*
www.avatarpress.com

POCKET ESSENTIALS COMICS
Lance Parkin
ALAN MOORE...

FURTHER READING

Pocket Essentials:Alan Moore
by Lance Parkin, published in the UK by Pocket Essentials in 2001. A fine biography and highly detailed comprehensive bibliography.
www.pocketessentials.com

The Extraordinary Works of Alan Moore *by George Khoury scheduled for publication in summer 2003 by TwoMorrows. Promises to contain the most extensive interview ever undertaken with Moore.*
www.twomorrows.com

The Extraordinary Works Of ALAN MOORE
by George Khoury

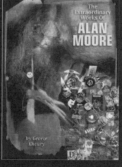

MUSIC & PERFORMANCE CDs

The three CDs on the right are currently available on Steve Severin's RE: label (available in the US from Top Shelf).
Two earlier CDs, The Birth Caul *and* The Moon and Serpent Grand Egyptian Theatre of Marvels *are now unavailable although there are tentative plans to re-issue them on the RE: label. Moore's* Brought to Light *CD (with Gary Lloyd) is also currently out of print.*
www.stevenseverin.com
www.topshelfcomix.com

THE HIGHBURY WORKING

Alan Moore & Tim Perkins, performed upstairs@ the garage, Highbury, November 30th 1997
RE: PCD03

ANGEL PASSAGE

Alan Moore & Tim Perkins, performed at the Purcell Room, London, February 2nd 2001
RE: PCD04

SNAKES & LADDERS

Alan Moore & Tim Perkins, performed Conway Hall, Red Lion Square, London on April 10th 1999
RE: PCD05

CONTRIBUTOR INDEX

Contributors are listed alphabetically by first name in bold, followed by title of their piece in italics, the contribution type and finally, page number in bold.

Adam Hughes *League of Extraordinary Gentleman* illustration **138**

Ade Capone *A Reader's View* text **171**

Ailantd *Fire* strip (artist) **298**

Al Davidson *Voice of the Fire* illustration **143**

Alabarcez Mendonça *Alan Has Red Hair* poetry **136**

Alan Moore *Mr. Monster* illustration **25**

Alan Moore *Hungry Is the Heart* strip (writer) **158**

Alberto Ponticelli *Supreme/Youngblood* illustration **266**

Alessandro Bilotta *A Small Sense of Not Belonging* story **185**

Alessandro Boni *Dr. Manhattan* illustration **282**

Alessandro Boni *Moore Music* illustration **234**

Alex Horley *Swamp Thing/Rorschach/Tom Strong* illustration **72**

Amber Moore *Moore's Eclectic Emporium* story **261**

Andre Carrilho *Alan On the Other Side of the Mirror* illustration **35**

Andrea Accardi *Lost Girls* illustration **277**

Andy Smith *Tom Strong* illustration **142**

Angus McKie *The Omnipotents* strip **47**

Antony Johnston *Pick Up the Phone* text **119**

Antonio Solinas *Wearing Alan Moore* text **64**

Art Brooks *Who Writes the Writer* strip (writer) **197**

Arturo Villarrubia *A Secret Life* text **239**

Ashley Wood *Words* strip **140**

Batton Lash *Where Does He Get His Ideas?* strip **152**

Ben Templesmith *Mr Griffin* illustration **214**

Bill Koeb *The Hair of the Snake* illustration **32**

Bill Morrison *Silk Spectre Comics* illustration **291**

Bill Sienkiewicz *Portrait* illustration **256**

Brad Meltzer *The Tenth Justice* greeting **31**

Bruno Olivieri *Portrait* cartoon **287**

Bryan Talbot *Portrait* illustration **124**

Carla Speed McNeill *Call and Response* strip **80**

Carmine di Giandomenico *Marvelman* illustration **139**

Carmine di Giandomenico *Tom Strong* illustration **286**

Charlie Adlard *League of Extraordinary Gentleman* illustration **187**

Chris McLoughlin *Portrait* illustration **58**

Chris Staros *A Fan for Life* text **264**

Claudio Villa *Tom Strong* illustration **292**

Dame Darcy *Hungry Is the Heart* strip (artist) **158**

Daniel Acuña *Who Writes the Writer* strip (artist) **197**

Daniel Krall *John Constantine* illustration **260**

Darko Macan *How To Write Superheroes* text **289**

Darren Shan *Saga of the Vile Thing* story **95**

Dave Gibbons *Watchmen* illustration **288**

Dave Sim *Dealing With Pagans* text **303**

Dave Sim *Correspondence: From Hell* Interview **307**

David Lloyd *Out of his Head* illustration **184**

Davide Barzi *SandokAlan* strip (writer) **38**

Donna Barr *Less Is Moore* illustration **4**

Duncan Fegredo *The Moore the Better!* illustration **118**

Dylan Horrocks *The Other Swamp Thing* text **59**

Dylan Horrocks *Moore Morality* text **75**

Dylan Horrocks *Tom Strong* cartoon **76**

Eduardo Risso *Portrait* illustration **137**

Emiliano Mammuccari *From Hell* illustration **144**

Eric Shanower *Little Margie* illustration **29**

Gabriele Dell'Otto *Swamp Thing* illustration **216**

Gary Phillips *1986: The Mother of All Years* text **157**

Gary Spencer Millidge *Preface to the English Language Edition* text **5**

Gary Spencer Millidge *An Extraordinary Gentleman* strip biography **11**

Gianluca Costantini *portrait* illustration **40**

Gil Formosa *Marvelman* illustration **26**

Gil Formosa *An Unearthly Gentleman* strip (artist) **89**

Gil Formosa *Moore, not Nemo* cartoon **77**

Giorgio Cavazzano *Rorschach* illustration **178**

Giuseppe Camuncoli *John Constantine* illustration (pencils) **253**

Giuseppe Pili *Alan Moore and the Mystery of Transubstantiation* text **33**

Howard Chaykin text **77**

Howard Cruse *Comic Strip Writing Tips* cartoon **123**

Iain Sinclair *Regime Change In Whitechapel* text **279**

Igort *Time* text **179**

Ilya *Remembering the Alamo...* strip **269**

J H Williams III *Moon And Serpent Metaphysical Portrait* text/illustration **104**

James Kochalka *Nite Owl* strip **278**

James Owen *The Tipping Point* text **193**

James Owen *Promethea* illustration **195**

Jason Hall *The Alan Moore Appreciation Society* text **236**

Jean-Marc Lofficier *Quantum Strings* text **88**

Jean-Marc Lofficier *An Unearthly Gentleman* strip (writer) **89**

Jeff Smith *Who's Boneville's Favourite Comics Writer?* cartoon **55**

Jim Baikie *Tomorrow Meets Yesterday* illustration **246**

Jim Baikie *Tomorrow Meets Yesterday* text **247**

Jim Lee *Portrait* illustration **281**

Jimmy Palmiotti *John Constantine* illustration (inks) **253**

Joel Meadows *Italian With Alan* text **154**

John Coulthart *32 Short Lucubrations Concerning Alan Moore* strip **209**

John Coulthart *Portrait* illustration **302**

John Heebink *N-Man* illustration **251**

John Higgins *The Little Things* illustration **296**

John Higgins *Blue Man Blues* text **297**

José Alaniz *Rutting In Free-fall* essay **129**

José Alaniz *Into Her dead Body* essay **145**
José Alaniz *Speaking the 'Truth' of sex* essay **273**
José Villarrubia *Turning Point* photograph **284**
José Villarrubia *Turning Point* text **285**
Ken Meyer, Jr *Happy 50th* illustration **8**
Ken Meyer, Jr *portrait* illustration **56**
Kevin O'Neill *The League of Lost Projects* illustration **259**
Leah Moore *Moore's Eclectic Emporium* story **261**
Len Wein *Random Thoughts* text **37**
Leo Ortolani *R For Revenge* cartoon **170**
Lew Stringer *Affable Alan Moore* strip **192**
Link Yaco *Alan Moore: Post Modernist* text **249**
Luca Enoch *V* illustration **188**
Luigi Siniscalchi *Watchmen* illustration **156**
Marc Singer *Unwrapping the Birth Caul* essay **41**
Marcello Albano *The Magician* text **125**
Marco Abate *Moore Magic* text **243**
Mark Buckingham *Portrait* illustration **87**
Mark Millar *How I Learned to Love the Alan* text **205**
Massimo Giacon *1963* illustration **94**
Massimo Semerano *From Hell* illustration **71**
Matt Kindt *The Animated Adventures of the League of Extraordinary Characters* strip **294**
Matteo Casali *Watchmaker... My Way* text **257**
Metaphrog *Louis: Lost on the Moore* strip **65**
Michael Avon Oeming *V for Victoria* illustration **318**
Michael Moorcock *Homage to Cornucopia* text **51**
Michael T. Gilbert *Mea Culpa, Alan Moore* text **23**
Michele Medda *The Alanmoory Lesson* text **208**
Michele Petrucci *V* illustration **78**
Mike Collins *I Met a Traveller from an Antique Land...* illustration **102**
Mike Collins *Alan Moore: I Knew Him When* text **103**
Mike Higgs *Who Dares Disturb the Cloak?* cartoon **242**
Nabiel Kanan *portrait* illustration **53**
Neil Gaiman *The Scorpio Boys in the City of Lux Sing Their Strange Songs* poetry **57**
Omar Martini *The Dark Side of The Moore* interview **107**
Oscar Zarate *Memories and Quarrels* strip **181**
Oskar *SandokAlan* strip (artist) **38**
Otto Gabos *When an Empire Falls - Episode XXVI* strip **233**
Paolo Livorati *Apres moi, le deluge (I think he was quoting)* text **267**
Pasquale Frisenda *Master of Reality* strip (artist) **100**
Pat Mills *Poisoned Chalice* text **79**
Pedro Mota *Alan On the Other Side of the Mirror* text **34**
Peter Kuper *My Hat is Off to You, Alan!* illustration **265**
Piet Corr photographs **36, 106, 306, 317, 330, 342, 352**
Randy Lofficier *An Unearthly Gentleman* strip (writer) **89**
Rich Johnston *Smoke Circles* cartoon **74**
Rich Koslowski *Gil Lenderthol Speaks* strip **126**
Rick Veitch *Rare Bit Fiends* strip **135**
Rob Williams *Allow Me to Introduce You to The Fury* text **151**

Roberto Recchioni *The Comedian* illustration **283**
Robin Smith *Script Droid Alan* illustration **121**
Sam Kieth *portrait* illustration **215**
Scott Mills *A Few Kind Words* strip **241**
Scott Morse *The Critics Agree* strip **255**
Sean Phillips *Constantine* illustration **155**
Sergio Toppi *portrait* illustration **70**
Shannon Wheeler *Alan Moore* strip **191**
smoky man *Editor's Foreword* text **7**
Stefano Raffaele *portrait* illustration **172**
Stefano Raffaele *Rorschach* illustration **238**
Stephen Bissette *Mr. Moore and Me* essay **217**
Steve Leialoha *Classics Illustrated for Classics Unwritten* illustration **248**
Steve Niles *Why I Hate Alan Moore* text **73**
Steve Parkhouse *Sex, Vampires and Christmas Shopping* text **83**
Steve Parkhouse *Gardening With the Bojeffries* cartoon **84**
Steven de Rie *Urbanus Gets: Much Moore Than He Bargained For* strip **60**
Terry Gilliam *Introduction* text **9**
Tim Perkins *Moore Music Magic* text **235**
Tito Faraci *Master of Reality* strip (writer) **100**
Trevor Hairsine *The Fury* illustration **150**
Trina Robbins *Alan Moore's Closet* paper doll **207**
Walt Simonson *Rorschach's True Identity* cartoon **93**
Will Eisner *Birthdays Are Good* illustration **6**
Willy Linthout *Urbanus Gets: Much Moore Than He Bargained For* strip **60**
Woodrow Phoenix *The Wonderful Wardrobe of Alan Moore* story **174**
Writer Without Head *Fire* strip (writer) **298**

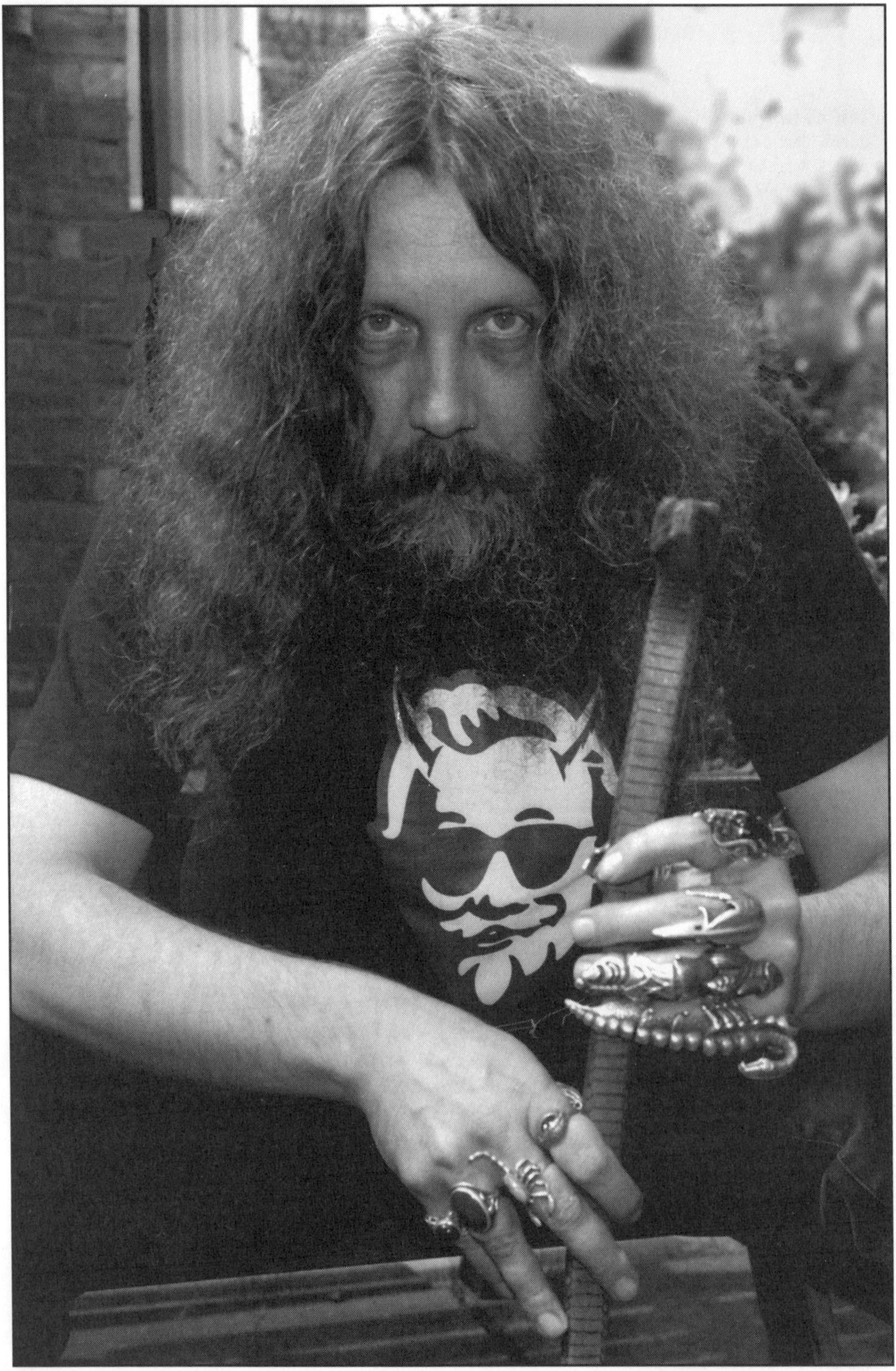